PRESIDENT JAMES BUCHANAN
A BIOGRAPHY

President
James Buchanan

A Biography

By

PHILIP S. KLEIN

Published by American Political Biography Press

Newtown, CT

All publications of
AMERICAN POLITICAL BIOGRAPHY PRESS
Are dedicated to my wife
Ellen and our two children
Katherine and William II

This particular book is
Dedicated to:

BHYC Fleet Captains

John Butler
Robert Carter
Samuel Emerson
William (B.G.) Hardt

Professor Klein dedicated his work to:
My Father
H.M.J. Klein

CONTENTS

PREFACE

The man who elects to play the role of peacemaker may, if he succeeds, be soon buried in historical oblivion, for it is the perverse tendency of mankind to glorify war but to forget those who surmount crises by thought rather than by threat. A peacemaker who fails, on the other hand, is likely to receive for his efforts only resounding curses from both the warring camps. Such was the fate of James Buchanan.

His presidential career was dedicated to peace, but his administration culminated in a frenzy of secession which was immediately followed by a civil war of unprecedented fury. These events challenge our interest and curiosity. Why was Buchanan's peace policy unproductive? To what degree was its failure attributable to the chief executive, or to the people who chose him as their representative, or to the existing method of government?

James Buchanan, fifteenth president of the United States, remains one of the least known statesmen of the American nation. To date the only useful biography of him is the two-volume documentary work by George Ticknor Curtis which was published in 1883 and financed by Buchanan's heirs. Many people remember Buchanan only as the bachelor in the White House who either caused the Civil War or who ought, somehow, to have prevented it. It is time, a century after the end of his presidential term, to re-create the life of James Buchanan and to reconsider his place in the American heritage.

A good many years ago, Professor Frederick L. Schuman, then at the University of Chicago, put me to work on Buchanan's diplomatic career. Later, at the University of Pennsylvania, Professors St. George Leakin Sioussat and Roy F. Nichols guided me in the study of Buchanan's early activities in politics and encouraged me to project a biography of him. The present volume, which grew slowly and was completed only after many interruptions, is the fruit of their suggestion.

After preparing what would have been a more extensive work, I concluded that it would serve a better purpose to present not an exhaustive but a concise account of Buchanan's career, with the primary emphasis on balance. Thus, while I have tried to treat at least briefly all the episodes which Buchanan thought important, I could not in a book of this size give the details of all the activities of a man who served almost continuously in public office from 1813 to 1861. I have sought, however, to deal with the subject in a constructively critical spirit; that is, to consider Buchanan's problems with understanding, but without any desire either to exalt or to degrade him for the decisions he made. The reader may decide the wisdom or the error of his ways.

The Buchanan described by his own contemporaries in the years before 1861 is a person very different from the Buchanan portrayed by many writers of post-Civil War reminiscences. This biography seeks to present the former. Buchanan's associates up to the outbreak of the war judged him by values and standards then prevalent; but the war changed many of these patterns. Jeremiah S. Black in 1879 complained that the story of Buchanan's life had "never been honestly told." "Abolition lies," he wrote, "will take the place of history, 'and none shall see the day when the cloud will pass away.'" The existence of sharply conflicting opinions about Buchanan means that the modern biographer must bear a heavy responsibility to prove his interpretation. Hence, this work will be documented in detail, mostly by reference to manuscripts and newspapers of the pre-Civil War era.

The presentation is chronological, and material has been selected for emphasis chiefly according to Buchanan's own concept of what was important or trivial. However, I have sketched only the main lines of Buchanan's extensive participation in foreign affairs; the details may be found in numerous specialized studies. Also, I have purposely condensed the treatment of the presidential years because these have been described very fully by many scholars, notably by Roy F. Nichols in his *Disruption of American Democracy*.

But very little is generally known about the first forty years of Buchanan's public service. Before he became president, he had already engaged in as long and energetic a political career as that of Webster, Clay, Calhoun, or Benton. This era of his life, his schooling for the highest office, has not hitherto been adequately explored. I have tried to explain his role in party politics, especially Pennsylvania politics, before he came to occupy the White House. Judgments of Buchanan as president ought to be based upon knowledge of the man prior to that time. He was, after all, nearly sixty-seven years old when he was inaugurated.

I have been concerned with his work as a lawyer and with the influence of his legal experience upon his political thinking. Also, I have sought to expose the many ramifications of his personal life, his relationship with his friends, his management of the complicated family problems which engaged much of his attention, and the conduct of his private business affairs.

I have used, in several parts of this book, some of my writing published earlier under the titles: *The Story of Wheatland* (Lancaster, 1936), *Pennsylvania Politics, 1817-1832, a Game without Rules* (Philadelphia, 1940), "James Buchanan and Ann Coleman," *Pennsylvania History*, XXI (Jan., 1954), 1-20; "The Inauguration of James Buchanan," Lancaster County Historical Society *Journal*, LXI (1957), 145-171; and "James Buchanan at Dickinson," in *John and Mary's College* (Carlisle, Pa., 1956), pp. 157-180.

Many people have helped me gather material. The staffs of libraries, historical societies, and archives have given me friendly guidance and greatly aided me in my search. I am especially indebted to the Hamilton Library and Historical Society of Cumberland County, the Lancaster County Historical Society, the Crawford County Historical Society, the Historical Society of Berks County, the Northumberland County Historical Society, the Wyoming Historical and Geological Society, the Historical Society of York County, the Historical Society of Western Pennsylvania, the Historical Society of Pennsylvania, the Historical Society of Massachusetts, the Essex Institute, the Boston Public Library, the Pennsylvania Historical and Museum Commission, the Library of Congress, the National Archives, the State Library of Pennsylvania, the Library Company of Philadelphia, and the Libraries of the University of Pennsylvania, the University of Georgia, Franklin and Marshall College, Dickinson College, and The Pennsylvania State University.

Those persons who kindly sent me copies of privately owned Buchanan manuscripts or permitted me to study their collections have been named in the bibliography. I wish here to express my appreciation to them. I am grateful to Lancaster Newspapers, Inc., for providing me with facilities for a protracted search of their files of early Lancaster newspapers, to the late E. E. Bausman for permission to use the papers that Buchanan deposited with his executors, and to Louis S. May, Esq., for making his office available for work on these. I would like also to express my thanks to Horace Montgomery, Malcolm Freiberg, Sylvester K. Stevens, Sanford W. Higginbotham, Whitfield Bell, Jr., the late John Lowry Ruth, Talbot T. Speer, William A. Russ, Jr., Asa E. Martin, George D. Harmon, the late C. H. Martin, H. Hanford Hoskins, Maurice G. Buchanan, Annie Gilchrist, Henry J. Young, Charles Coleman Sellers, the Reverend E. J. Turner, Herbert B. Anstaett, John B. Rengier, and J. Bennett Nolan for many and varied kinds of assistance. In concluding this list, I want to mention especially the friendly help and encouragement given me by the late Philip Gerald Auchampaugh, the most assiduous student of Buchanan in this generation.

It is a further pleasure to acknowledge the useful work of some former students whose research illuminated many obscure points: Dorothy Airhart, Leon Davidheiser, Richard F. Fralick, Robert E. Franz, Robert F. Himmelberg, Dirck Parkin, Margaret Strobel, Gerald L. Wagner, Guy J. Way, and Dale G. Wheelwright.

Dean Roy F. Nichols of the University of Pennsylvania, Professor Norman A. Graebner of the University of Illinois, and Professor-Emeritus Burke M. Hermann of The Pennsylvania State University read the entire manuscript and greatly aided me in shortening it and in eliminating errors. Professors Holman Hamilton of the University of Kentucky and Edward J. Nichols of The Pennsylvania State University also gave me valuable constructive criticism. I thank these gentlemen for their interest, their time, and their help. For those mistakes of fact and judgment which may be found in a book of this scope, I take entire responsibility.

The Council on Research of The Pennsylvania State University gave financial support to this study over a number of years, and the Social Science Research Center of the University aided me by the purchase of microfilms. For these marks of confidence I thank them. Finally, true to tradition, my wife, Dorothy Orr Klein, typed the manuscript in its entirety through several drafts and participated in all the essential chores from beginning to end. I acknowledge my greatest debt of gratitude to her.

P. S. K.

Union Mills, Md.
August, 1961

PROLOGUE

Worry and anxiety marked the faces of the people fleeing eastward along the Marietta Pike toward Lancaster, Pennsylvania. Constantly they looked back from their carts piled with boxes and furniture at the faint red glow in the darkening sky beyond Chestnut Hill. Occasionally small squads of horsemen came galloping out from town and headed for the Susquehanna River ten miles to the west. Most of the riders seemed intent on their own business; but where the pike ran past the spacious grounds of Wheatland, home of former President Buchanan, some would shout, "You damned rebel!" or "I hope they burn you out like they did Thad Stevens."

It was Sunday night, June 28, 1863. The latest reports warned of 35,000 Confederate troops at York, a southern army closing in on Harrisburg, and a skirmish in progress between the rebel advance guard and local militia at Wrightsville. The river bridge between Columbia and Wrightsville was said to be aflame, and the glow in the sky seemed to confirm that, but could Lee's army storm across the shallow Susquehanna somewhere else?

James Buchanan had walked down from his house to the spring on the lower lawn which bordered the pike, his favorite spot in the evening. He liked to look over the low stone parapet into the clear water and watch the moss and white sand swirling gently in the undercurrent. Nowhere else in the world had he ever found the sunsets more relaxing or the world more serene than here, under the willow by his Wheatland spring. But not so this night. Would Wheatland be standing tomorrow, or in ashes? Would he be alive, or dead, or some kind of ridiculous trophy of this senseless, unthinkable war? He did not know, nor did he really care very much.

With the first news of Lee's advance into Pennsylvania, he had packed Harriet off to Philadelphia and shipped away his most important papers. He had tried to make Miss Hetty leave, but she said firmly that she would stay if he did. He had told friends who urged him to get out of the invasion area that he would remain at Wheatland if it should be surrounded by a hundred thousand rebels. He and Miss Hetty would see it through together.

As he walked through the oak grove and back to the house, Buchanan felt the crushing certainty that his whole life had been a failure. Such a thought he rarely admitted to his consciousness, but tonight he could not banish it. The Columbia Bridge seemed the symbol of the two great tragedies of his career. Nearly half a century before, while trying to save that bridge in a law court, he had lost Ann Coleman. Through all his later years, eschewing domesticity for politics, he had labored to keep strong the bridge of understanding and mutual regard between people of the North and the South. The bridge was burning now, ruined as completely as his own life's work.

Exactly fifty years ago, he remembered with nostalgia, he had for the first time accepted a public office. Since then he had served continuously in nearly every public capacity, from the lowest to the highest in steady progression. He had worked unceasingly to strengthen and to develop the best political society that man ever invented; but now the South had broken off half of it, and Lincoln's party seemed intent upon making the other half into a form of government that would have horrified the Fathers of the Constitution. Buchanan had once dared to hope that his presidency might rank in history with that of George Washington; now the very name Buchanan was one for people to curse and spit at, north and south.

His father had warned him. Buchanan, with the vivid memory of early days peculiar to old people, recalled distinctly a letter his father had written to him at a time of youthful crisis. "Often when people have the greatest prospect of temporal honor and aggrandisement," the old gentleman had said, "they are all blasted in a moment by a fatality connected with men and things, and no doubt the designs of Providence may be seen very conspicuously in our disappointments."

Buchanan suddenly felt a twinge of chagrin that his father never lived to see him rise to fame. In what other society, he wondered, could the child of a poor, orphaned immigrant be able to work his way up to the first chair of state? Some eighty years before, his father had come to America. He had trained his son for eminence. "I am not disposed to censure you for being ambitious," he used to tell young James, and he had set a good example. When he had arrived from Ireland, he had little but ambition to help him. James wished that his father had told him more about the family background and the early years in Ireland; but he had not.

After entering the house, Buchanan went directly to the study and began to write. If the rebels came, they would find him at work— preparing his story of "Mr. Buchanan's Administration on the Eve of Rebellion."

PRESIDENT JAMES BUCHANAN
A BIOGRAPHY

1

PENNSYLVANIA PIONEER • 1783 - 1809

WAGONS IN THE WILDERNESS

James Buchanan paused often in his chores around the Irish farmstead during the early spring of 1783. For several years he had been thinking about migrating to America after the Revolutionary War. Now that the United States had won independence the young man faced the moment of decision. He had deep roots in the land of his birth. As he looked out over the fields toward the nearby waters of Lough Swilly, he worried about leaving a green and settled land where the name he bore signified kinship with a considerable part of the local population. The Clan Buchanan had been proliferating in Scotland and northern Ireland for seven centuries.

As a baby, he had been brought to the forty-acre farm in County Donegal called the "Big Airds," the home of his mother's brother, Samuel Russell. Samuel's daughter, Molly, remembered the cold, rainy day when her father came riding in with little James bundled up snugly under his greatcoat. What happened to the parents of James Buchanan remains a mystery. His father, John Buchanan, had married Jane Russell in 1750, and the couple had several children before James was born in 1761. There is some evidence that the mother died about that time and that the father then disappeared. After 1764, no trace of the parents can be found.[1]

The Russells had given a good home and a good education to their adopted nephew. He was twenty-two now, he had a little money of his own, his uncle had done all that could be expected, and America in the spring of 1783 seemed fabulously inviting. Uncle Samuel had a brother, Joshua Russell, a tavern owner near Gettysburg, Pennsylvania, who had written that he could meet the boy in Philadelphia and provide for his immediate care.[2]

On July 4, 1783, young Buchanan went aboard the brig *Providence* as a paying passenger. We can imagine some of his thoughts and dreams as he stood at the rail while the lines were cast off and the creaking ship slowly eased her way out of the channel from Londonderry, but even his wildest flights of fancy would scarcely have approached the reality of the future.

Joshua Russell met Buchanan in Philadelphia and returned with him to the Russell Tavern on the Hunterstown road. During the leisurely trip on horseback, James acquainted himself with the new country and with his uncle Joshua. They passed through Valley Forge. Here, explained Joshua, he had served as wagonmaster during the grim winter of 1777-1778, carrying flour from York to the starving Continental army. In Lancaster the street names sounded more European than American—King, Queen, Duke, Prince, and Earl; and the names of the nearby townships reminded him of home—Drumore, Antrim, East Earl, Donegal, Letterkenny, Manor, and Coleraine.

The broad Susquehanna, which they crossed by flatboat at Wright's Ferry, sparkled in the late summer sunlight, its clear blue shallows studded with projecting rocks and framed with low wooded hills. West of the river the settlements grew sparse and the road, rough. Joshua Russell, having travelled it many times, had at last decided to use his experience on the pike as the means of an easier livelihood. He had bought a 200-acre tract in what was then Cumberland Township, York County, and had built a large stone tavern along the main road west.

James had nearly forgotten Ireland by the time the two came in sight of Russell's Tavern. His uncle, he found, had become a man of consequence in this country; he was known by sight all along the road. His estate comprised not only the inn but outbuildings, quarters for eight Negro slaves, and fenced fields for scores of cattle. Joshua's wife Jane greeted him with all the warmth he might have expected from one bearing his mother's name.[3]

Uncle Joshua's nearest neighbor was James Speer, a widower with five children, who farmed a 270-acre tract just up the road. The youngest of the Speers, Elizabeth, soon stopped at the tavern to meet the new nephew from Ireland. She was sixteen and she was pretty. James took her walking, trading his Irish charm for information about herself, her family, and Pennsylvania. Elizabeth had been raised in southern Lancaster County, but her father, a strict Presbyterian, had moved west because of a theological disagreement with his pastor. Her mother, Mary Patterson Speer, had died and Elizabeth now kept house for her father and four older brothers.[4]

Buchanan soon learned from the passing wagoners of an opportunity for work at John Tom's little trading post called "the stony batter," 40 miles west of the Russell Tavern. Here, in Cove Gap, freight wagons from the East met pack trains from Bedford and John Tom handled the exchange. The modern pilgrim to this spot, a wild and gloomy gorge hemmed in on all but the eastern side by towering hills and now far removed

2

from any center of commercial activity, properly asks what induced an ambitious young man to go there to seek his fortune.

But Cove Gap was important in 1783. Three parallel ranges of the Allegheny Mountains barred the way to the West except at this point where a double gap pierced the two most easterly ridges, leaving Tuscarora Mountain the only remaining barrier. Travellers from Philadelphia and Baltimore headed for Cove Gap on their way to Pittsburgh. At Stony Batter, inside the Gap, roads ended, goods piled up, and John Tom ran his backwoods store. At times as many as a hundred horses jammed a corral there, but goods came in by wagon so much faster than they could be shipped out by pack train that John Tom had to run a warehouse as well as a trading post.[5]

After a few years as Tom's helper, Buchanan got the chance to buy the Stony Batter property. Legend has long had it that this transaction involved some sharp practice, but the court records show only that on December 15, 1786, John Tom offered to sell his property to Buchanan for 200 pounds, Pennsylvania currency, promising in the contract that the land was "free of all Taxes, Debts, dues or demands." A few days after Buchanan had recorded these terms of sale, however, John Ferguson of Chambersburg sued Tom for over 500 pounds owing to him and guaranteed by the property. The December County Court confirmed this judgment against Tom, and the February Court ordered a sheriff's sale of Stony Batter, the proceeds to go to Ferguson. Buchanan bought the 100-acre tract for 142 pounds at the public sale on June 23, 1787.[6]

After buying Stony Batter, Buchanan rode off to the foot of South Mountain to claim Elizabeth Speer as his bride. She was just twenty-one, and he twenty-seven when they married on April 16, 1788. The young couple moved into Tom's log cabin which, though crude and rustic by later standards, was quite comfortable for their day. Their property included several log cabins, some barns and stables, a storehouse and store building, cleared fields, and an orchard.

The Buchanans' first child, christened Mary, was born in 1789. On April 23, 1791, Elizabeth presented her husband with a son whom they named after his father. Tragedy marred what should otherwise have been a very happy year: little Mary died. The Presbyterian philosophy of pre-destination combined with the melancholy prevalence of infant mortality doubtless softened the blow, but it would have been an unnatural mother who after this experience did not lavish more than the usual care upon her surviving child. James Buchanan, from the very first year of his life, occupied a position of special importance in the household. His status might appear to have been threatened by the birth of more children, but the reverse seems closer to the fact. The next five additions to the family were girls: Jane in 1793, Maria in 1795, Sarah in 1798, Elizabeth in 1800

3

(who died within a year), and Harriet in 1802. The second boy of the family, born in 1804, died the same year. Not until the birth of William Speer Buchanan in 1805 was there another boy in the Buchanan home, and by that time James was almost ready to leave for college. Two more boys were born after he left home in 1807.

Thus, for the first fourteen years of his life, James Buchanan, as the eldest child and only boy, retained the place of favoritism into which he had been born. He lived in a woman's world at home, and until the family moved to Mercersburg he had no playmates except his sisters, over whom he exercised an acknowledged authority. While he commanded more than the usual child's prerogative to be waited upon, he also had more than the usual childhood responsibility, and he soon developed a good opinion of himself that was daily strengthened by the deference of the younger children. When he reached his early teens, he must have been obnoxiously conceited and self-assured.

MERCERSBURG

Stony Batter proved a poor place to raise a family. The clearing resounded with the turmoil of stamping horses, drunken drovers, and cursing wagoners. Elizabeth Buchanan disliked this raw and uncouth society and lived in constant fear for the safety of her small children who wandered through the ceaseless confusion of horses, wagons, and scattered produce. The business prospered enough that the father, in 1794, was able to buy the "Dunwoodie Farm," a splended 300-acre tract of rich limestone land and timber located about five miles east of the Gap along the West Conococheague Creek, near the village of Mercersburg.[7]

The new farm, pleasant as a retreat, still did not get the family out of the Gap except at the sacrifice of the store business. Therefore in 1796, Buchanan bought a large lot in the center of Mercersburg and built on it a two-story brick house to serve both as a home and place of business. Putting his brother-in-law, John Speer, temporarily in charge of Stony Batter, he moved the family to Mercersburg. Here life proved much more genteel and orderly. The community of several dozen houses was almost entirely Scotch. To the Presbyterian Church, one of the oldest in the State, came the Campbells, Wilsons, McClellands, McDowells, Barrs, Findlays, Welshes and Smiths. Buchanan gradually transferred his business into town and soon established himself as one of the leading citizens. For a time he served as local justice of the peace.[8]

When the family moved to town, James was six; Jane, three; and Maria, one. Until now Elizabeth Buchanan had been their only teacher. In spite of her lack of schooling, she had accumulated extensive knowledge

4

of literature and could quote verbatim and at length from Milton or Pope or Cowper. She read a good deal of theology, probably more as a kind of good work than as a matter of philosophical inquiry, but she had sincere piety which she unconsciously passed on to her children. She was a good storyteller and loved particularly to dwell on the career of George Washington, whom she painted in glowing colors which the children never forgot. She named her tenth child after their hero and George became her favorite in the latter years of her life. The Buchanans in all probability met President Washington when he stayed at the Russell Tavern during the excitement of the Whiskey Rebellion in the winter of 1794-95.[9]

James attended the Old Stone Academy at Mercersburg where he studied Greek and Latin, first under the Reverend James R. Sharon, later with Mr. McConnell, and finally under Dr. Jesse Magaw who had just completed his studies at Dickinson College and who later married Buchanan's sister, Maria.

The events of that magic decade in life between the ages of five and fifteen impress a permanent mark on men. Any biographer would like to have all the information possible on those creative years; yet seldom is much to be found.[10] Here the tangible evidence is almost always fragmentary.

There were some lasting influences, however, which can be seen without reference to pen and ink records. The little village of Mercersburg was one of them. It was a homogeneous community where the tempo of life was leisurely and sedate. Even the scenery conduced to a sense of peace and calm. The rich farmscape, studded with oak groves and framed by the beautiful Tuscarora in the West, brought from at least one traveller of that day the involuntary exclamation: "What a Paradise!" James Buchanan lived in Mercersburg only ten years, but for the remainder of his life he tried when he could to duplicate those surroundings. His sympathies were always rural. His summers on Dunwoodie Farm gave him a personal attachment to that manner of life which he never lost; at his Wheatland plantation near Lancaster he re-created, in a sense, the scenes of his boyhood. Manufacturers and their problems he never understood; cities and their ways made him miserable. He was at heart an agrarian and never adjusted his thinking to the requirements of a growing industrial society.

His father's store was also a significant influence. Here he heard, not entirely understanding but taking it all in nevertheless, many a political argument. Even as a lad of eight he had no difficulty in knowing that his father was an uncompromising Washington Federalist; by the time he was fourteen he had absorbed a good many of the reasons why.

The store also introduced the boy to the problem of keeping things accounted for and in their proper places. It gave him a daily object

5

lesson in the practical utility of legible handwriting and of reckoning figures with absolute accuracy. And it illustrated the way in which money could grow from an exchange of property. Anyone who has taken the trouble to look at Buchanan's mathematics notebooks will recognize that he had a passion for neatness and for figures. Practically every penny that he gave or received throughout his life he methodically recorded in his account books. While American Minister to Great Britain, with an estate already in excess of $200,000, he kept a careful day-by-day record of the petty disbursements of his valet, down to the last ha'penny for pins or tuppence for suspender buttons. He once refused to accept a check for over $15,000 from his friend Jeremiah S. Black, because there was an error of ten cents in it. When as president he paid three cents too little for an order of fine food for the White House and the merchant receipted the bill as paid in full, he discovered the error and forwarded the three cents, explaining that he wished not to pay too little or too much but precisely what was due.

His parents influenced him strongly. Buchanan, by the time James was ten, had become one of the leading businessmen of the Mercersburg region. His heavy features, his bluff and hearty countenance, and his watery blue eyes suggested more of canniness than of kindness, and conveyed a hint of animal force guided by wariness and suspicion of his fellows. "The more you know of mankind," he would say, "the more you will distrust them." Though middle age and success were softening him somewhat, he still worked like a man of restless and unsatisfied ambition. The community considered him a "hard man." If honest, he was also unyielding. He gave credit but not extensions of credit, and he never loaned money except on excessive guarantee. He idolized James, who he long thought would be his only son, but made him firmly toe the mark in practicing the idea that hard work and scrupulous attention to business make wealth. John Tom had practiced neither and had lost his property; Buchanan practiced both and had supplanted his erstwhile employer.

James both loved and feared his father. The squire assigned chores to the boy beyond the competence of his years, carefully scrutinized his performance, and was always more ready with criticism than with praise. James learned fast and outstripped those his own age in handling assigned work, but he rarely experienced the joyous sense of a task well done; it was never done well enough for the squire. The boy hungered for commendation, but he seldom got it. There was little friendly informality and playtime between father and son; it was a man to man relationship between man and boy, full of mutual reliance and respect, but without humor or comradeship.

Elizabeth Buchanan, much more easygoing and humane than her husband, became the center of the finer feelings of the household. Modest

6

and self-effacing as the father was proud and arrogant, she tried actively to live the Christian life. Her philosophy was that of the Ten Commandments and the Sermon on the Mount, applied to every little act within her view. Her ambition was to get to Heaven; her life a quiet acceptance of every event as the particular manifestation of God's will directed to her family. Young James could never quite accept such blind faith or such utter resignation, yet it impressed him deeply and embedded itself in his inquisitive mind. It was odd: his father was never satisfied, and his mother was always satisfied; but anyone looking at the daily course of their lives without knowing their minds might guess exactly the opposite.

Doctor John King, pastor of the Presbyterian Church at Mercersburg and a trustee of Dickinson College at Carlisle, also exerted a strong influence. Some men have that rare combination of qualities which, unknown to themselves, inspires admiration and imitation in others. Doctor King had such qualities. He was a fine scholar but so unpretentious, witty, and human that no one talking with him casually would have sensed a formidable mind. He had strong convictions of Christian living which he practiced, without apparent purpose or effort, as a simple matter of course. He had dignity and poise which he seemed to communicate to others, rather than making them unhappily conscious of their own deficiencies in manner or address. When he preached, people stayed awake from sheer personal respect for the man. James Buchanan later wrote that he had "never known any human being for whom I felt greater reverence than for Dr. King," and he took with him into maturity a vivid memory of the conduct and the kindly spirit of his Mercersburg pastor.[11]

DICKINSON COLLEGE

When Buchanan became sixteen, King urged his father to send him to college. He saw in the boy a dual prospect: the development of a keen young mind and the addition of a cash customer to the sorely depleted student rolls of Dickinson College. Though the elder Buchanan really needed his son in business and around the farm, he knew from his own limited experience the advantages of education. He worried about the future security of his growing family. In addition to James he now had four small daughters and a baby boy, and another child was on the way. If he should die or suffer a setback in his business, his own children might find themselves in the same unhappy situation in which he had been reared; they might have to be distributed around among those who could provide for them.

Mrs. Buchanan would have been happy to see her son enter the ministry, but her husband knew better what pursuit would fit the requirements. Money could be made in buying and selling property, but one needed a lawyer to protect it. He wanted his son to prepare for the study of law. The decision was soon made, arrangements were completed to enroll James in the junior class of college, and in September, 1807, the young man and his father saddled their horses for the trip to Carlisle.[12]

Dickinson College, when Buchanan went there, was slowly rallying from a series of misfortunes. After twenty years of effort, the trustees had finally been able to provide the college with "a new and elegant building." Scarcely six weeks after the dedication, someone carelessly left a scuttleful of hot ashes in the cellar and burned it to the ground. Then Dr. Charles Nisbet, who had been headmaster of the college since its inception, died, and good relations between the students, the faculty, and the trustees rapidly deteriorated. But the town of Carlisle posed the main problem. Jeremiah Atwater, the new president, reported that the pleasures "of high life, of parade, of the table & ball chamber" appeared to be the main object of life. "Drunkenness, swearing, lewdness & duelling seemed to court the day." The students were "indulging in the dissipation of the town, none of them living in the college." It was folly, he concluded, "to expect that a college could flourish without a different state of things in the town;" and in a final burst of outrage he exclaimed, "I hope that as God has visited other states, he will *yet visit Pennsylvania.*"[13]

These were the circumstances to which James Buchanan referred when he wrote of Dickinson, many years later, that the college was "in wretched condition" while he was a student there. When Buchanan arrived in Carlisle a new college building designed by Benjamin Latrobe had been almost completed and classes were being held in it, though no student rooms were ready for occupancy.[14]

Left on his own for the first time in his life, Jimmie Buchanan began to canvass his prospects in this enticing environment. Of the forty-two students enrolled, eight were seniors, nineteen were his mates in the junior class—all of them Pennsylvanians but two—and the remaining fifteen were freshmen or assigned to the Latin School. The college course did not yet include the sophomore year.

His courses would include Latin, Greek, mathematics, geography, logic, history, literature, and philosophy. President Davidson would be his teacher in history, geography and philosophy; Professor John Hayes would be in charge of languages; and Professor McCormick, of mathematics. These three comprised the entire teaching staff.

Teachers often stamp upon the student mind a more vivid and lasting impression of their own personality than they do of their subject matter. Dr. Davidson was a teacher whom the students remembered with discomfort during their college days but with sentimental attachment thereafter. He had written a geography text in very poor verse, required the students to buy it, and demanded that they memorize and recite from it verbatim. A pedagogue in school and out, formal, solemn and precise, Dr. Davidson was, nevertheless, a kind and gentle man. He never liked to take a strong stand, much less to translate it into action, and in dealing with administrative problems he always tried to avoid solutions by the exercise of authority. Whenever possible he took the line of least resistance, seeking to solve problems by a peaceful and pleasant meeting of minds. In town and on the campus he was known by the appropriate nickname of "Blessed Peacemaker." Such was the man who, within the year, was to burn an impression on James Buchanan's callow mind as with a red-hot poker.[15]

Buchanan especially liked Professor James McCormick who for years had lodged and boarded half a dozen students at his home. One boy recalled that "Mr. McCormick and his wife were as kind to us as if they had been our parents. He was unwearied in his attentions to us in our studies, full of patience and good nature, and sometimes seemed quite distressed when, upon examining a pupil, he found him not quite as learned as he was himself."[16]

Buchanan at first took his work as a student very seriously, spending most of his time in preparation and trying his best to make a good impression in the classroom. But it did not take him long to find that the life of a "grind" was no passport to comradeship among his classmates. To the contrary, he wrote that "to be a sober, plodding, industrious youth was to incur the ridicule of the mass of the students." Discovering that he had little difficulty in keeping up his class assignments, he began to participate more freely in the extra-curricular activities of the day. "Without much natural tendency to become dissipated," he said, "and chiefly from the example of others, and in order to be considered a clever and spirited youth, I engaged in every sort of extravagance and mischief."[17]

From knowledge of his later activities, we may reasonably assume that he got into drinking bouts sufficiently rowdy to come to the attention of the faculty; that he smoked cigars contrary to the regulations of the college; and that he manifested in and out of the classroom a conceit which proved at first irritating and at length intolerable to his professors. On the Fourth of July, 1808, which the Dickinson boys celebrated with a huge dinner at the Glebe Farm, he downed sixteen regular toasts before starting on the volunteers.[18]

Despite all the distractions, Buchanan kept up with his class work, passed his public examinations in August, and concluded the college year with an excellent academic record. He returned to Mercersburg in the autumn of 1808, quite satisfied with himself and ready to go back to school in a few weeks as a senior. On a lovely Sunday morning of September he was lounging at ease in the sitting room of his home, enjoying those

9

deliciously languorous sensations of well-being that the gods confer only upon college students on vacation. His reverie was interrupted by a knock at the door. His father answered it and returned shortly with a letter which he tore open with curious interest. As he began to read, his expression changed to one of pain and anger. Whatever this was, it was uncommonly bad news. Buchanan senior abruptly thrust the paper at his son, turned, and left the room without a word.

James looked down at the cause of this sudden shattering of his thoughts. The letter, in Dr. Davidson's writing, said that Dickinson College had expelled Buchanan for disorderly conduct. He read it again to get it all. Dr. Davidson wrote the elder Buchanan that his son would have been dismissed earlier except for the respect which the faculty entertained for the father. They had tolerated young James to the very limit of endurance and would not have him back under any circumstances.

James was thunderstruck. Knowing that it would be useless to take up the matter with his irate father, he turned for advice to his friend Doctor King, who had just become President of the Board of Trustees of Dickinson. "He gave me a gentle lecture," said Buchanan of the interview. "He then proposed to me, that if I would pledge on my honor to him to behave better at college than I had done, he felt such confidence in me that he would pledge himself to Dr. Davidson on my behalf, and he did not doubt that I would be permitted to return."[19]

While the board minutes disclose no discussion of Buchanan's case, it is impossible to believe that King did not know in advance that his neighbor and protégé from Mercersburg was getting into serious trouble. It is more than likely that Dr. Davidson's action had been approved in advance by the board, or may have originated there, as a means of bracing up the lad by a sound scare which would both tame his spirit and exert a sobering influence upon the rest of the students.[20]

Chastened and with the resolution to be more circumspect in his conduct, Buchanan returned to Dickinson for the winter term. Unfortunately, his strenuous application to work had the result of further inflating his intellectual vanity—the trait which had been the root of his difficulty in the first place. Take, for example, the problem in navigation which he prepared for Professor McCormick, requiring the construction of an imaginary ship's journal in which the exact latitude and longitude of the point of destination were to be determined from the daily sailing data. Buchanan chose for his journal a trip from Boston to Madeira—an island which he had frequently visited in fancy while quaffing its amber produce in the taverns of Carlisle. After some thirty pages of careful notations of traverse tables, estimates of drift, and calculations of magnetic variation and deviation, he found that his final figures on the location of the western tip of Madeira varied by only one mile from the values given on the printed

10

geographical charts. The concluding sentence in this problem illustrates perfectly the mental attitude of the boy. "I therefore conclude," he wrote, "that my journal was nearly exact, and that the latitude and longitude of that part of Madeira were well laid down."[21]

All too soon the year was over. On September 25, 1809, the faculty presented to the Board of Trustees the names of fifteen young gentlemen whom they certified "as prepared to receive their Bachelor's degree, they having gone through the usual courses, and been publicly examined in the Languages and Sciences." Buchanan's name was on the list.

In the meantime, however, trouble had been brewing over the award of senior honors. Two literary societies, the Belles-Lettres and the Union Philosophical, met weekly in rooms at opposite ends of the fourth floor of the college building. All the student competition of the day centered in these societies. Each society chose one candidate for the award of first honors of the college; the faculty chose the winner, and the other man automatically received the second honor. The award of first honors was not only a society victory but also gave to the successful student the distinction of having first place on the program of senior orations at the commencement exercises.

The Union Philosophical Society unanimously chose Buchanan as their candidate for the first honor. But this did not satisfy James. He thought the Union Philosophical Society so much superior to its rival that it should, this year, have both the first and the second honor. He therefore put through a motion that the Union P. should present two candidates, himself for first place and Robert Laverty for the second.

This was too much for the faculty. They had observed some improvement in Buchanan's outward conduct but none in his conceit, and they determined on this occasion to deflate it. They gave the first honor to the candidate of the Belles-Lettres Society, second honor to Laverty, and rejected Buchanan entirely on the ground that it would have a bad effect on the morale of the college to honor a student who had been so troublesome and had shown so little respect for the professors.

This announcement completely outraged the young man. He wrote an agitated letter to his father, complaining bitterly of the injustice and prejudice of the faculty. The first honor should go to the best scholar; he was the best scholar, as everyone knew and the record showed. He refused to believe the decision was final and kept his oration ready.

His father replied with a masterful letter of condolence, full of sly innuendo. He had received his son's letter, he wrote, "though without date" (inexcusable carelessness!), and was mortified that James would receive no honors, especially as this "was done by the professors who are acknowledged by the world to be the best judges of the students under their care." He hoped that his son had fortitude enough to take the decision like a man.[22] James read this over carefully several times, smarting with embarrassment, but his temper subsided, and he turned to another polishing of his oration, very appropriately entitled "The Utility of Philosophy."

In the meantime the Union Philosophical Society was in an uproar. Laverty withdrew as second honor man and offered the place to Buchanan. When he refused to consider this, the seniors of the society proposed that they all refuse to speak at commencement, but Buchanan also opposed this proposal because he did not wish others to become involved on his account. At length the faculty itself resolved the impasse by writing a kind letter to James, stating that he would be expected to present his oration, though not in the first place on the program.[23] By Commencement Day, September 19, 1809, the air had cleared. Alfred Foster of Carlisle would deliver the salutatory oration in Latin on "The Excellence of Knowledge," Buchanan would follow him on the program, and Laverty would deliver the valedictory.[24]

Buchanan wrote in his autobiography that he left college "feeling but little attachment towards the Alma Mater." Regardless of this sentiment he could scarcely have denied that his two years at Dickinson left a lasting imprint upon his life. He learned respect for the law there. Time was to come when President Buchanan would assert to extremists, both northern and southern, in a land torn by passion: "I acknowledge no master but the law." He also learned respect for property, which he translated into a veritable obsession for precision in all his later business dealings. He developed a respectful attitude toward religion, which he considered a matter of individual belief rather than a formal creed to be unquestioningly accepted. Finally, one can see in his later life the shadow of his Dickinson teachers. Buchanan the student played ringleader in making fun of old Dr. Davidson, but Buchanan the man came to resemble him. The description of Davidson could be applied almost without change to Buchanan in maturity: vain, formal, solemn and precise; yet withal kindly and gentle, always eager to settle disputes without force and solve problems by a friendly and pleasant meeting of minds. The Blessed Peacemaker.

James Buchanan as a Congressman.
Portrait by Jacob Eicholtz. Smithsonian
Institution.

Above: Ann Caroline Coleman, Buchanan's fiancée, who died mysteriously in 1819. Buchanan Foundation. *Below:* Buchanan's birthplace at Stony Batter. Part of this log cabin has been preserved at Mercersburg Academy, Mercersburg, Pennsylvania. Herbert Beardsley.

Above: East King Street, Lancaster, looking toward the square. Buchanan's law office occupied the second floor of the building in the center of the picture. Lancaster County Historical Society. *Below:* A sketch of Wheatland published during the campaign of 1856. Author's Collection.

Top: Buchanan's penmanship and signature. Of Harrisburg he writes, "It is not a place to visit, if your talking apparatus is out of order." Pattee Library, The Pennsylvania State University. *Bottom left:* President Martin Van Buren. Author's Collection. *Bottom right:* John Wien Forney, Buchanan's energetic and devoted political manager for twenty years. Library of Congress.

A Whig cartoon of 1840 exploits the "Ten Cent Jimmy" lie. Buchanan is made to tell Van Buren to reduce the price of labor while unemployment reigns and children starve. Lancaster County Historical Society.

Cartoon of the election of 1856. Buchanan, holding four aces, declares he will make every state eat "Union Soup." Fillmore is "going blind." Frémont has tripped over the "Rock of Disunion." Buchanan Foundation.

A SERVICEABLE GARMENT —
OR REVERIE OF A BACHELOR.

Two anti-Buchanan cartoons of 1856. *Above:* The bachelor candidate surveys his old "Federal coat" with its "Democratic patches" and decides that if he wins he can afford a new outfit. Buchanan Foundation. *Below:* The Fire-eaters and slavery ride on the Democratic platform (Buchanan), uncertainly supported by Benton, Pierce, and John Van Buren. Library of Congress.

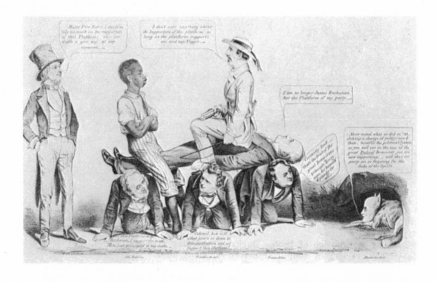

He was elected President by fraud and trickery! under his administration the Treasury was robbed! duplicity and cowardice marked his career! finally, he sold his country to a band of Southern conspirators, and now lives to be pointed at with the finger of scorn, by all true men! and will go down to his grave unlamented.

JAMES BUCHANAN.

JUDAS.

Top: One of the many forms of abuse of Buchanan during the Civil War—a northern envelope charging him with selling the country to "a band of conspirators." Smithsonian Institution (Ralph E. Becker Collection). *Bottom:* Simon Cameron, a political maverick who became a powerful enemy of Buchanan after 1848. National Archives (Brady Collection).

Top: Pierre Soulé of Louisiana. Library of Congress. *Center:* Stephen A. Douglas of Illinois. National Archives (Brady Collection). *Bottom:* William H. Seward of New York. National Archives (Brady Collection).

Two contemporary drawings by newspaper artists. *Top:* East Portico of the Capitol during Buchanan's inaugural address. *Bottom:* The inaugural parade, with the model warship in the foreground. Library of Congress.

Above: Miniatures on ivory of Buchanan and Harriet Lane by J. Henry Brown. Smithsonian Institution. *Below:* Buchanan greets a guest at a White House reception. Library of Congress.

Top: Washington, 1853, after the new wings had been added to the Capitol. Between Pennsylvania Avenue, center, and Maryland Avenue, left, appear the Smithsonian Institution and the projected Washington Monument. Library of Congress. *Bottom:* The East Front of the Capitol, 1857, with the new dome under construction. National Archives.

Chamber of the United States House of Representatives (*top*) and of the Senate (*bottom*) as they appeared before being remodelled in the 1850's. Library of Congress.

Buchanan's Cabinet in mid-1859. *Seated left to right:* Jacob Thompson, Interior; John B. Floyd, War; Isaac Toucey, Navy; Jeremiah S. Black, Attorney General. *Standing left to right:* Lewis Cass, State; President Buchanan; Howell Cobb, Treasury; Joseph Holt, Postmaster General. Library of Congress (Brady-Hand Collection).

Top: Black who replaced Cass in December, 1860. National Archives (Brady Collection). *Center:* Vice-President John C. Breckinridge, Lincoln's opponent in 1860. Library of Congress. *Bottom left:* Lewis Cass who also served in Jackson's Cabinet. National Archives (Brady Collection). *Bottom right:* Aaron V. Brown, Postmaster General, who died in office. National Archives (Brady Collection).

Left: Secretary of War Floyd, a friend who caused the president much anguish. Library of Congress. *Right:* Treasurer Cobb, at one time Buchanan's choice for his successor. Library of Congress. *Bottom:* Major Robert Anderson, the "key" of the Charleston forts. National Archives (Brady Collection).

President Buchanan at the time of the Kansas
crisis, 1858. National Archives (Brady Collection).

2

PREFACE TO POLITICS • 1809 - 1819

COUNTRY LAWYER

The most immediate question in James Buchanan's mind when he graduated from Dickinson College was where to find a good legal preceptor. His father already had the answer. He had observed James Hopkins of Lancaster as he tried a case in the Cumberland Valley and had been so impressed by the performance that he urged James to study with him. Hopkins was a leader of the Lancaster bar and an attorney of state-wide reputation. James welcomed the prospect of working at the State Capital, applied to Hopkins for a preceptorship, and was accepted.[1]

Lancaster, when Buchanan came there in December, 1809, to begin his legal career, had for generations claimed the distinction of being the largest inland town in the United States, though its resident population scarcely exceeded 6000. It lay ten miles north of Mason and Dixon's line, ten miles east of the Susquehanna River, and sixty-two miles west of Philadelphia. The Conestoga Creek which bordered the town had given its name to the famous freight wagons which plied the broad turnpike to Philadelphia, the finest road in all America. Lancaster's business rested on factors of long-range dependability—thrifty, industrious people, fine farms, a thriving iron industry, and excellent travel facilities. The working population was mostly German, but Lancaster boasted an English aristocracy which rivalled Philadelphia society. Politically the town had been dominated for years by the Federalists.

The courthouse, a small two-story building modelled roughly on Independence Hall, occupied the square at the intersection of the two main streets. It was terribly crowded, serving simultaneously as the State Capitol building and as headquarters for county business. King and Queen Streets, running off at right angles from the square, were lined by close-set brick houses, most of them inns. Newly arrived legislators or strangers like young Buchanan were greeted, when they got off the stage, by a complete outdoor gallery of tavern signs depicting the crowned heads of

13

all Europe, Indian chiefs, and national heroes; the animal kingdom with its lions, leopards, stags, bulls, bears, horses, swans and eagles; and symbols of the crafts, such as the plough, the wheat sheaf, the grape, the cross keys, the compass and square, or the hickory tree.[2]

Buchanan found quarters at the Widow Duchman's inn on East King Street, just a block and one half from the courthouse and nearly across the street from Hopkins's imposing mansion at the corner of East King and Duke Streets. Within a city block of Buchanan's rooms lived not only his college chum, Jasper Slaymaker, but also the Governor of Pennsylvania, the Judge of the District Court, and iron baron Robert Coleman reputed to be the richest man in Pennsylvania. James Buchanan felt that although he stood on the bottom rung of the ladder, it was the right ladder.

After a month he wrote home enthusiastically about his work under Hopkins whom he described as courteous, instructive and interested in his pupils. His father advised him to cultivate his preceptor's good opinion and told him to tend strictly to business and "not be carried off by the many amusements & temptations that are prevalent in that place." "Go on with your studies," he said, "and endeavor to be Eminent in your profession."[3]

The pressure which the father put on his son to make good proceeded not entirely from paternal pride. He really wanted James to prepare himself so that he might better help support his brothers and sisters, in case of necessity. Four more sons had arrived in the household within the past seven years, three of whom survived.[4] The Mercersburg family now consisted of four girls and three boys, the latter between the ages of one and six. "Your company and assistance in this family are wanted very much, and desired," he wrote to James when Edward Young was born, "but I am willing to forego all these advantages in order that you may have an opportunity of . . . preparing yourself . . . in the profession you have chosen." A little later he remarked, "I hope the privation I have suffered & will suffer in giving you a good education will be compensated by the station in society you will occupy."[5]

James worked hard. "I determined," he said, "that if severe application would make me a good lawyer, I should not fail in this particular. . . . I studied law, and nothing but law." Day and night he read and struggled to extract the full meaning from pages of print and to incorporate it accurately in his mind. For relaxation he got into the habit of strolling out to the edge of town in the evening where, while watching the sun descend below the gentle slope of Chestnut Hill, he tried to put into spoken words the material he had studied during the day.

At length, in 1812, the term of his preceptorship drew near its end and he had to consider what to do next. Lancaster seemed a logical place to "hang out his shingle," but there were some drawbacks. The

State Capitol was being shifted to Harrisburg, leaving Lancaster crowded with expert lawyers facing reduced opportunities. There would be stiff competition.

About this time the name Kentucky began to exercise a magnetic charm on Buchanan. The West had recently come into the news. The first Mississippi River steamboat had just opened a new two-way trade between Pittsburgh and New Orleans; Harrison had defeated Tecumseh at Tippecanoe; Henry Clay, Felix Grundy and other western "War Hawks" in Congress clamored for war against England. But beyond the promise of adventure, Buchanan saw a practical opportunity in the West. His father was part owner of a tract of some 3600 acres of Kentucky land. Its title had been recently challenged. James wanted to go to the site and handle the case before the court at Elizabethtown.

The father, not eager to hazard his property to the efforts of his inexperienced son, tried for two months to discourage the venture. A new country would be a poor place for a lawyer, he wrote to James. "He may obtain land, but that is all. Were I commencing the practice of law & knew I had talents & attention, I would open an office in a county where both suits and money were plenty & although I might have many difficulties in establishing myself there, yet I would have no fears of not coming in for a share of the business finally. Lancaster is such a place as I describe, & when you first went to the place, that was one of my objects, that you might have an opportunity of settling there."[6] When James replied that he wanted to take the trip for his health, as a vacation, the elder Buchanan warned him that it would be nonsense to expect such a trip to benefit the health. It would be more likely to ruin it. " I speak from experience," he said.[7]

Nevertheless, James Buchanan bought a horse and started for Kentucky. He stopped on the way to see the family, made the acquaintance of his new brother, Edward, and learned with delight that his favorite sister, Jane, now nineteen, had become engaged to Elliot Tole Lane of Mercersburg, and that sister Maria was in love with his old school teacher, Jesse Magaw. He got the details of the land litigation, the permission of his father to act as his attorney, and resumed his journey. As he jogged along, his pack trunk scuffing gently at the back of his saddle, he dreamed of the impact he would make in the shirt-sleeve courts of that wild new country.

Buchanan spent the summer in Kentucky, most of it at Elizabethtown, but he made side trips to Bowling Green and Russellville. He very probably encountered Thomas Lincoln who lived near Elizabethtown and was on the court docket for some land-title cases at this time. His son, Abraham Lincoln, was three years old. The Buchanan case, which had been in litigation since 1803, had become so entangled that any hope of a quick solution soon faded. Buchanan reported of a trip to court: "I went

15

there full of the big impression I was to make—and whom do you suppose I met? There was Henry Clay! John Pope, John Allan, John Rowan, Felix Grundy—why, sir, they were *giants*, and I was only a pigmy. Next day I packed my trunk and came back to Lancaster—that was big enough for me. Kentucky was too big." Kentucky's Ben Hardin reported that Buchanan told him that he had expected to be a great man there, but that "every lawyer I met at the bar was my equal, and more than half of them my superiors, so I gave it up."[8]

These reminiscences, though not quite accurate, emphasized the main reason for Buchanan's decision. He left Kentucky convinced that if the professional competition there would be as keen as in Lancaster, there was a great deal more wealth in Lancaster, and he might best put his wits to work where the fees were highest. After turning the land case over to Ben Hardin, he set out for home.

James was back in Lancaster by November 17, 1812, in time to be admitted to the bar along with Jasper Slaymaker and two other young lawyers. Wishing to remain there, but uncertain whether he would be able to maintain an office, he appealed to Hopkins for advice. His preceptor suggested that he apply to Attorney General Jared Ingersoll for the post of deputy prosecutor (now district attorney) in newly created Lebanon County. "I am a young man just about selecting a place of future settlement," he wrote to Ingersoll, "and your determination will have a considerable influence on my choice."[9] On February 20, 1813, Buchanan started his practice in Lancaster, inserting a notice in the papers that he would maintain his office on East King Street "two doors above Mr. Duchman's Inn, and nearly opposite to the Farmer's Bank."[10] A month later Buchanan learned that he had been appointed prosecutor for Lebanon County.[11] That, at least, would take care of the office rent. His father was pleased, but tempered his congratulations with the hope that James would act "with compassion & humanity for the poor creatures against whom you may be engaged."[12]

Buchanan's first two years of practice barely kept him going; he made $938 during 1813 and $1,096 the following year.[13] The odds and ends of practice which were the usual lot of a young attorney came his way and he gratefully took whatever business the older lawyers referred to him and handled it promptly.[14] As he approached his twenty-third birthday he bought, in partnership with the town's jovial 400-pound prothonotary, John Passmore, the small tavern on East King Street which the two of them already used for offices and living quarters. Buchanan's father must have assisted him in this deal, or else he had a good local credit rating, for he paid $4000 in cash on the property in 1814 and promised to pay another $1000 within a year. He visited his old home occasionally during this period. While there he talked politics with his father. Loyal Federalists

16

both, they deplored the attacks of the Democratic Legislature on Federalist judges, and condemned the government for its mismanagement of the war with England.[15] In 1813 Jane Buchanan married Elliot Lane, and James was probably in Mercersburg for the wedding ceremony.

STATE ASSEMBLYMAN

On August 24, 1814, the British army routed the Americans at Bladensburg, marched on Washington, and burned the public buildings almost before their occupants had time to flee. That same day the Lancaster Federalists met to nominate their slate for the fall elections. In due course delegate Peter Diller arose to nominate James Buchanan as the district's choice for State Assemblyman.

At that time he was serving as president of the local Washington Association—a young Federalist organization. He had aroused enthusiasm in the party by his recent speech at the Fourth of July barbecue in which he had roundly lambasted Madison for bungling the war effort and called on Federalists to pitch into the fighting to force an honorable peace as quickly as possible.[16] The Federal party, though it had controlled Lancaster since 1789, had long been the minority party of the state and was growing steadily weaker. Its older leaders welcomed the addition to their ranks of a popular and forceful young man. Buchanan, on his part, wanted to enter politics and hoped that campaign publicity and service in Harrisburg would improve his law business. There was no chance of his losing the election; in Lancaster, the Federalist candidate always won. His father, still never willing to admit that his son had done just the right thing, told him he had made a mistake and would do better to become a leader of the bar than to be "partly a politician and partly a lawyer."[17]

At the very moment that Buchanan committed himself to politics, his first political duty bore down swiftly and unexpectedly upon him. When news of the burning of Washington reached Lancaster the morning after his nomination, he knew he would have to go to war if he expected to get any votes. The local Federalist party deplored the war, but its members would defend their country.

At a general mobilization in Lancaster on August 25, Buchanan made a speech and was among the first to register his name as a volunteer. Two days later a company of young men of the borough, led by Henry Shippen, Esq., "mounted their horses, armed with sword, pistols &c., and marched to Baltimore, without waiting for formal orders, to aid in defending that place."[18]

Shippen's Company, composed of about two dozen of the "most respectable young gentlemen of Lancaster," had no official status as part either of the militia or the regular army; it was simply a group of private

17

volunteers. After arriving at Baltimore, the "Lancaster County Dragoons," as the troop called itself, offered their services to Major Charles Sterret Ridgely of the Third Cavalry Regiment. Major Ridgely called for ten volunteers to go on a secret mission; Buchanan joined this squad and all proceeded four miles beyond the city, full of excitement in the belief they were on a dangerous mission—until they opened their sealed orders at the designated point.

They were to go to Ellicott's Mills and seize about sixty good horses from the residents of the vicinity, "always preferring to take them from Quakers." It was an assignment not particularly gratifying to the "young gentlemen of Lancaster," all of whom had their own mounts and had never until now seriously considered horse-stealing. A steady deluge of rain added to their discomfort. That night Buchanan had the ill-luck to draw a bunk space next to the tent wall and got thoroughly soaked. They encountered no Redcoats, but by the time they had accomplished their mission the Marylanders of the locality had become nearly as serious an enemy as the British. Nonetheless, they seized the horses, rejecting "several pairs for ladies who were sick and required them" and paraded down Market Street past Gadsby's Hotel in Baltimore where the rest of the Lancaster volunteers gave them a burlesque salute amid guffawing laughter. In a few days the British withdrew from the city and Major Ridgely discharged Captain Shippen's Dragoons.[19] James wrote to his parents that night to relieve the anxiety he knew they must feel after reading the newspaper accounts of the British assault on Baltimore.[20]

Only a month remained until election day. The Pennsylvania Federalists now began for the first time in years to have some hopes of regaining their power. Pennsylvania's Democratic governor, Simon Snyder, although still popular with his party, had been losing strength because of the defection of disappointed office seekers. Furthermore, the public linked his name with the failures of the national government to wage effective war.

Snyder was re-elected, but the Federalists cut his majority to half of what it had been in 1811. All through the state there was increasing support for Federalist tickets. Buchanan was elected by a poll which delighted him, for he led the ticket in the borough and ran third highest among sixteen Federalist candidates in the full county vote.[21]

In the midst of his jubilation, James received a sobering note from his father, full of doubts, cautions, and admonitions. "Perhaps your going to the Legislature may be to your advantage & it may be otherwise," wrote his parent. "I hope you will make the best of the thing now . . . . I am fearful of this taking you from the bar at a time when perhaps you may feel it most."[22]

The stage rode smoothly from Lancaster to Middletown, but in the last ten miles of the trip to Harrisburg it jolted fearfully over an ancient path which no repair crew had ever touched. Most travellers passed this short distance on horseback rather than risk an upset. Buchanan thought that Harrisburg looked a little less like a sleepy country village since the Legislature had moved there in October, 1812. Front Street, shaded by a row of stately poplars regularly spaced, opened on the Susquehanna River to the west and was bordered by a wide paved footwalk to the east, a favorite promenade in summer but now swept with early December snow. The river bank, about twenty feet above the water level, afforded a fine view of the upriver rapids and the long r.˙ˡge of the Blue Mountains to the northwest. The ferry landing which ha.˙ ʰ. ɔn the town's origin was right next to the great stone mansion of founder John Harris, and a little below it construction work progressed on a line of stone piers stretching toward the opposite shore. Theodore Burr, the famous bridge architect, had begun his stupendous project of a two-span covered wooden bridge over half a mile long. If he succeeded, Harrisburg would boom.

With a flourish, the stage drew up in front of the Golden Eagle Inn on Market Square. The driver, as he unloaded the baggage, growled that they would have to travel lighter—there was a fourteen-pound limit per passenger. The courthouse, then serving as State Capitol, stood at the head of the square about three blocks from the river and overlooking it down the row of brick homes and business houses which faced the covered market stall in the center. The temporary capitol building was a brick structure, two stories high. It had two small wings and a semirotunda in front, the whole surmounted by a circular wooden cupola containing a bell. On its small roof was mounted a vane of copper gilt, representing an Indian chief as large as life, with a bow in his left hand and a tomahawk in his right. The Dauphin County courtroom on the first floor which served as the chamber of the Assembly was scarcely large enough to accommodate the hundred legislators. The thirty Senators were more comfortably housed in a second-floor room nearly the same size.

The functions of a Pennsylvania Assemblyman, Buchanan discovered, were pettier than he had first imagined. Everyone had half a dozen local petitions and a few paltry private bills on the clerk's file. The court dockets were so jammed, judicial procedure so slow, and decisions so partisan (for Federalists monopolized the bench and bar) that many Democrats appealed directly to their friends in the Assembly for private legislative relief rather than depend upon judicial process. Buchanan had little such business to present, but he did press for the incorporation of new textile manufacturing plants in Lancaster, offered petitions to place the property of drunkards in trusteeship, recommended a reduction of the tax on whiskey, and urged the creation of new judicial districts.[23] Through

19

Hopkins's influence he was immediately made a member of the six-man Judiciary Committee of the House. After hearing a few speeches he made up his mind to avoid impromptu expressions on the floor and to speak only after thorough preparation.[24]

His first formal speech grew out of the national crisis on military man power. Although Congress had rejected a conscription bill, the Pennsylvania Senate had adopted such a measure because Philadelphia feared a British attack and the Federal Government seemed helpless to defend the port. The Pennsylvania bill divided all draftees into groups of twenty-two, from each of which one man should be called to service. The other twenty-one then had to make up a $200 bounty purse for the conscript. The legislators who opposed this scheme proposed simply to raise six more regiments of volunteers at state expense.

On February 1, 1815 Buchanan spoke at length against the conscription plan and in favor of a volunteer bill which had been introduced in the House. This maiden speech proved more significant than Buchanan realized at the time. He attacked special privilege in the city of Philadelphia, championed the interests of the West against the East, defended the poor against abuse by the rich, and balanced the wishes of the State against the different interest of a minority from Philadelphia. His speech was good debate, but it was not good politics. So far from Federalist doctrine did it stray that William Beale, Democratic Senator from Mifflin County, urged Buchanan to change his party at once and join the Democrats, asserting that he would have no need to change his principles.[25] Buchanan encountered such political repercussions from his maiden effort that when the volunteer bill came up for final vote in the House, he was "necessarily absent." Fortunately for him, the whole issue terminated when, on February 17, Governor Snyder announced the news of peace with England.

For the remainder of his term, James Buchanan kept quiet. His speech had warned him of the danger of proclaiming private opinions from a political rostrum and had provoked such resentment that he doubted the wisdom of trying for renomination. His father advised him to go ahead; to put a law student in his office and get enough legislative experience to be ready, later, for Congress. As to opposition, he would have to expect that to develop in the same ratio that his fortunes improved; he had better depend upon Providence to shield him "from the shafts of malicious enemies."[26]

Thus admonished and encouraged, James decided to run again in 1815. In order to re-establish himself in the confidence of his party he planned to demonstrate the soundness of his Federalism on the Fourth of July in an oration at the big rally of Lancaster's Washington Association. He would make it a real political speech, a partisan harangue, a "rouser" that would clear up any doubt whether he was a Democrat or a Federalist.

20

Early in the afternoon the crowd began to assemble in the front of the courthouse to hear young Jimmie. He was already a familiar figure about town, but a newcomer to the hustings. Lawyers' Row knew him as a conscientious, tireless plugger who was not more intelligent, but usually more painstaking and better prepared, than his colleagues. The tavern fraternity found him, in regular attendance at meetings, affable, easygoing, always equipped with a black cigar and ready for another glass of Madeira. Parlor society had discovered him, and the local Masons had their eye on him.

His distinguished appearance, emphasized by a peculiar mannerism, singled him out for attention in any group. A tall, broad-shouldered young man with wavy blond hair, blue eyes, and fine features, he had developed an odd posture. He had a defect in one eye. In order to compensate for it he tilted his head slightly forward and sideways in a perpetual attitude of courteous deference and attentive interest. The mere appearance conveyed so definite an impression of assent and approbation that many people, on early acquaintance, sincerely believed that they had completely captivated James Buchanan and reciprocated by attentions to him which he attributed to traits more complimentary to him than a wry neck. Partly because of this physical peculiarity, Buchanan made a good "first impression" on almost everybody he met. Difficulties often arose when those who thought they were close to him realized that they had been reading his looks rather than his mind, and such persons would break off with a sense of personal injury.

As he stood on the courthouse steps facing his friends, Assemblyman James Buchanan looked the part of distinction, and he knew it. With sonorous voice he now set out to prove his Federalism. This, he said, was a celebration of men who had "burst asunder the chains that bound them to Great Britain" and had "presented to the world a spectacle of wisdom and firmness which has never been excelled." On this foundation was built the glorious Constitution of the United States. But there was a powerful faction in the nation which had bitterly opposed the Constitution. "The individuals of which it was composed were called anti-Federalists, and were the founders of the Democratic party." Having failed to destroy the Constitution, these men transferred their hatred of it to the glorious Administration of General Washington, reviling and cursing both the man and his measures. Who were these dark and malignant characters? "Demagogues," said James Buchanan, "Factionaries," "friends of the French," men of the "blackest ingratitude" who were obsessed by "diabolic passions." Such were the leaders of Democracy.

And how did the factionists use the power they had won by foul means in 1800? They began with the destruction of the navy. Then they

21

declared war on commerce; not satisfied with depriving it of naval protection, they proceeded to annihilate it by embargo. Having wrecked business until "the stillness of death pervaded every street," they proceeded systematically to wreck credit by destroying the Bank of the United States and by stopping national taxation.

Then, having totally prostrated the national economy, they declared war. Why? There was no invasion. There was no longer a serious question of rights on the high seas; few ships were out, the merchants made no protest, and England was already offering to adjust this issue. What then was the cause? It was, said Buchanan, "the over-weaning partiality of the Democratic party for France." Napoleon Bonaparte dictated Democratic party policy, and James Madison, in following this direction, "preferred his private interest to the public good."

And what were the results? The country was wholly unprepared for war. Without any remaining basis for taxation, and now afraid to try new taxes, the government borrowed at ruinous rates until it was on the verge of bankruptcy. Instead of conquering, the nation had itself been invaded. "The very capital of the United States, the lofty temple of liberty, which was reared and consecrated by Washington, has been abandoned to its fate by his degenerate successor, who ought to have shed his last drop of blood in its defence."[27]

The throng in the square was getting excited; young Jimmie was giving them more than they had bargained for. "Thanks to Heaven," Buchanan went on, "that we have obtained a peace, bad and disgraceful as it is; otherwise, the beautiful structure of the federal government, supported by the same feeble hands, might have sunk, like the capitol into ruins." The true policy of the future would be to abandon forever the wild projects of that "philosophic visionary," Thomas Jefferson, and to "turn out of power those weak and wicked men, who have abandoned the political path marked out for this country by Washington."[28]

The speech was a political success. The Washington Association ordered a large number of copies to be printed for state distribution, and the local Federalists within a month had named Buchanan to lead again their ticket of Assemblymen. But the attack provoked a hatred of Buchanan among the Jeffersonian Democrats of Lancaster County which was destined to endure from that moment to the day of his death. Even James's rabidly pro-Federalist father thought his attack was too severe and would hurt the feelings of his friends of the opposite party.[29]

Buchanan's speech on the theme "turn the rascals out" put him in tune with the national political movement to rejuvenate the Federalist party by alliance with disgruntled conservative Democrats. This combination would soon promote DeWitt Clinton for the presidency and a little later would take control of Pennsylvania.[30]

COUNSEL FOR THE DEFENSE

On his return to Harrisburg in December, 1815, Buchanan again sat with the Judiciary Committee and was named also to the Committee on Banks.[31] Most of the session was devoted to banking problems which had grown out of the chartering, the year before, of 41 new state banks, few of which could now redeem their note issues. A majority of the Committee on Banks recommended that the state, by law, should require banks to redeem their notes in specie by a given date or forfeit their charters. Buchanan prepared a minority report urging the legislature to stay out of the matter until the banks had been given more time to solve their own problems. With the same *laissez-faire* point of view, Buchanan opposed the recharter of the United States Bank which was then under hot discussion in Washington.

Although the Assembly took no action on the Bank proposals, the discussions bothered Buchanan and made him reconsider his political ideas. The impetuous, unstable and mob-produced actions of the radical Democracy he found revolting, sometimes frightening. Control of business and politics by a closed corporation of the wealthy he could not accept as just. He had respect for the will of the majority, but he had an equal respect for individual rights in property. He believed that the greatest glory of the American Constitution was that it embodied this dual concept; that it drew a careful balance between the demands of persons and of property. But no existing political party accepted both of these doctrines. With his ideas, Buchanan was not sure in which party he belonged.

Nor was he certain, at the end of the session, what to do next. The Lancaster Federalists believed in passing around the loaves and fishes; one term in the Assembly was usual, two the maximum tolerated by local tradition. His friend Jasper Slaymaker was next in line for the job. He was not even sure that he wanted to return to Lancaster, for it had been less cordial to him since he had entered politics. He had angered some leading Federalists by his militia bill speech and infuriated practically all of the Democrats by his Fourth of July oration. For a time he dallied with the thought of going to Philadelphia to practice, but his father counselled him against making rash and hasty changes.[32] After struggling with the decision until he got an attack of bilious fever, which generally accompanied his emotional crises, he determined to go back to Lancaster and try to improve his practice. He was still making only $2000 a year and had notes to meet.[33]

During the next four years, therefore, Buchanan plunged into "unremitting application to the practice of the law." His cases covered the whole range of a country lawyer's practice. He engaged in criminal and civil suits, tried cases, consulted, settled estates, served notices, arranged property transfers, drew up articles of incorporation, unsnarled tax controversies, and, in short, took up any litigation or question of legal opinion which came his way. Although most of his business was transacted in the Lancaster courts, he frequently appeared before the bench in York, Dauphin, Lebanon, and Cumberland Counties.[34]

Slowly, by dint of sheer mental labor and the application of time to his business, Buchanan built up a reputation for thoroughness and competence which brought more and more property work to his desk. His arguments before court and addresses to juries were anything but brilliant or spell-binding, but they achieved their object by sheer mass of data tightly knit by logic. Some called him a hair-splitter. He did not, however, emphasize detail at the expense of the main point. He carried argument into areas so minute they were boring, but he never lost connection with the basic issue. This habit was to affect his political speeches, from which it is extremely difficult to extract any sentence without materially damaging a train of thought. He was long-winded, but in planned papers never repetitive. A Lancaster judge wrote of him: "he was cut out by nature for a great lawyer, and I think was spoiled by fortune when she made him a statesman."[35]

Buchanan was at this time called to a case which tremendously enhanced his legal reputation. The Democrats in the Pennsylvania Legislature for years had been warring upon the Federalist judges of the state by bringing indiscriminate charges against them. The root of the problem was political, stemming from the efforts of the Jefferson Administration in the early 1800's to get rid of Federalists in the courts. Judges, both state and federal, held life tenure in those days, subject to "good behavior," but were removable for cause by impeachment. The Pennsylvania Democrats had been gunning for Judge Walter Franklin for years; now they thought they had him.

After the Pennsylvania militia had been mustered into Federal service in July, 1814, a Lancastrian named Houston refused to serve. A state militia court-martial convicted and fined him. Houston appealed the case through the courts, and Judge Franklin gave him a favorable verdict, on the ground that state authority ended when the militia entered the national army. The Supreme Court of the United States reversed this decision, and the Democratic legislature impeached Franklin for rendering a faulty opinion.[36]

Franklin selected Buchanan to handle his defense for many reasons. He had been outspoken against the judge-hunting activities of the Legislature, he was a personal friend and neighbor of Franklin, he had had recent experience in the Assembly, and he would certainly spare no effort in preparing his argument. It was nonetheless remarkable that the sole responsibility was handed to a twenty-five-year-old attorney.

Buchanan argued that if a legislature destroyed a judge merely because it objected to the legal opinion he expressed in a trial, without any hint of crime or misdemeanor, it equally destroyed the constitution which established the legislature and judiciary as independent and co-ordinate branches of government. A witness in the Senate wrote that the argument "was conducted with great ingenuity, eloquence, and address. It made a deep impression."[37] The impeachment managers were nonplussed and adjourned the trial for several weeks until they could prepare their reply. It was not convincing, and the Senate acquitted Franklin.

But this decision did not end the matter. On February 24, 1817, a committee of the House drew up another set of impeachment articles against Franklin and his lay associates, this time on the grounds that Franklin had refused to force two Lancaster attorneys, W. C. Frazer and Patton Ross, to turn over a $300 judgment they had collected for a plaintiff, having kept the sum as a part of legal fees due them. The House entered a two-to-one vote for impeachment. Buchanan again conducted the defense, but this time he requested the assistance of his preceptor. They achieved an acquittal before the Senate by a vote of 21 to 9.[38]

As if this were not enough, still another set of articles of impeachment against Franklin was adopted by the Legislature in March, 1818. Franklin wrote Buchanan to collect half a dozen witnesses he would need from Lancaster and come to Harrisburg on March 5th or 6th. Buchanan tried to secure the help of Hopkins and Parker Campbell of Philadelphia, but neither was able to be at Harrisburg at the required time. "Of course," wrote Campbell, "you will have to proceed in the case of the Judges *per se*. . . You will have to 'cry aloud and spare not.' If some of the principal actors in this disgraceful scene are unmasked, it may prevent a recurrence of their sinister projects."[39]

This trial terminated in a fight between the House and the Senate which threw the impeachment into the background. The Senate originally agreed to sit as a court in the House chamber, with the House in attendance in Committee of the Whole; but after a few days the Senators decided to meet in their own chamber, inviting the House to sit with them there. This the House chose to consider an intentional insult, perpetrated in defiance of parliamentary rules. The House held an indignation meeting in its own hall and when sufficiently inflamed by oratory, tumultuously invaded the Senate, bursting through the door, climbing through the windows, jamming the gallery, and packing the aisle. Everyone began shouting at once. Eventually the leaders of both groups exchanged apologies, and the trial reconvened, but by that time the Legislature was so much absorbed in its own contest over rules of order that the impeachment seemed a perfunctory interruption.[40] Franklin was again acquitted.

Buchanan's success at these trials greatly extended his reputation and expanded his practice. Probably not many people read his arguments,

but everyone knew that a lawyer who had three times in three years successfully defended the President Judge before whom he tried most of his cases
would be a good man to have as counsel. Buchanan's income rose from
$2000 in 1815 to $8000 in 1818. He now began to experience, as his father
had predicted, the kind of whispering campaign which commonly centers on
a young man who progresses fast.

3

BIRTH OF A BACHELOR • 1819-1820

ANN COLEMAN

Buchanan's associations in Lancaster rapidly broadened as he settled down to practice. His first close friend in town, except for Jasper Slaymaker, was Amos Ellmaker, a Yale graduate who had later studied law under Judge Reeve at the Litchfield School in Connecticut and finished his training in James Hopkins's office while Buchanan was a student there. Through Ellmaker, Buchanan met Molton C. Rogers, son of the Governor of Delaware, who had also studied at Litchfield and was admitted to the Lancaster bar in 1811. Buchanan dined at the same bachelor mess as Rogers and in 1816, when these two formed a loose partnership, Rogers moved into Buchanan's law offices on East King Street. Many local Dickinson alumni expanded the circle of Buchanan's acquaintances, some of them men of influence like Judge Alexander Hayes and William Norris and others, young men of prominent families such as Henry Shippen, George Ross Hopkins, and William A. Boyd. James saw much of Gerardus Clarkson, son of the Episcopal Rector, and of John Reynolds, both officers of the Farmers Bank. He associated in many law cases with William Jenkins, a Hopkins student of 1801 who had grown rich in the iron business.

By October, 1816, Buchanan had progressed along the road to acceptance in Lancaster far enough to be named as one of the managers for the annual society ball. In November he petitioned for admittance to the Masonic Lodge and was sponsored by Rogers and Reynolds. After his initiation on December 11, 1816, he rose rapidly to Junior Warden, Worshipful Master and after a few years to Deputy Grand Master of the First District. As his responsibilities in the community grew, he spent less and less time with the footloose young men who nightly frequented the back rooms of the local taverns. He had enjoyed their company as an escape from work and loneliness, but he had no talent for stories, hated gambling, and had too often made a fool of himself by getting drunk and winding up dancing on a table top. He now received more invitations to

27

dinner and often spent evenings at fashionable homes. He did have a talent for making himself agreeable to families of standing in the town and for raising the hopes of their unmarried daughters. As the years passed and his reputation as a promising young lawyer continued to grow, he became Lancaster's most eligible bachelor. He relished the role.[1]

Sometime in 1818, Molton Rogers began courting Eliza Jacobs, daughter of Cyrus Jacobs who had amassed great wealth as an ironmaster and now lived at Pool Forge, east of Lancaster. Eliza's brother was studying law under Buchanan at the time. Before long Rogers proposed that Buchanan should join him some evening as an escort for Eliza's cousin, Ann Caroline Coleman. He was delighted with the suggestion.

Ann Coleman was the belle of the town and the daughter of one of the richest men in the country. A willowy, black-haired girl with dark, lustrous eyes, she was by turns proud and self-willed, tender and affectionate, quiet and introspective, or giddy and wild. That she remained unmarried at twenty-two may have been because she was emotionally unstable, but more likely it was due to the stubborn insistence of her parents that she make an advantageous marriage.

Her father, Robert Coleman, had been born near Castle Finn, in County Donegal, Ireland, not far from the ancestral home of Buchanan. Migrating to America in 1764 as a youth of sixteen, he had worked first as a laborer and then as a clerk for ironmaster James Old of Reading, Pennsylvania, and later married his daughter. By 1800, he had come into possession of half a dozen fine iron properties and ranked as one of the nation's first millionaires. A strong-willed, hot-tempered and vindictive man, he had an inordinate pride in his wealth and was continually suspicious that others had designs on it. He was sensitive about social prestige, possibly because he had once had none, and enjoyed public deference. He had served as a lay judge of the Lancaster County court, was a trustee of Dickinson College, and a warden in the local Episcopal Church.[2]

Coleman moved to Lancaster in 1809 and established his family of five sons and four daughters in a town house on East King Street, half a block from the square.[3] The eldest daughter, Margaret, married Judge Joseph Hemphill of Philadelphia, commonly known as "Single-Speech Hemphill" because his maiden speech in the 7th Congress proved also to be his last. For years Ann Coleman had watched Jimmy Buchanan, the handsome six-footer from Mercersburg, walking between his office and the Courthouse past her front window. They undoubtedly met before 1818 at one or another of the annual balls in the great room of the White Swan Inn, but there is no indication that they saw much of each other until then.

Now Ann and Buchanan began a serious courtship, and things moved rapidly. The winter of 1818-1819 must have been a revelation to him. Once he had penetrated the mysterious circle of the iron families, a

28

whole new world opened. Robert Coleman seemed to have as many mansions as kings had castles. Buchanan could visit with Ann at the Elizabeth Furnace Mansion, or at Cornwall, or at Speedwell Forge, or Hopewell Furnace, or Colebrookdale, or Martic Forge and always be within the family. Or they might go on a sleigh-ride with Rogers and Eliza Jacobs to Pool Forge and stop by on the way home at the Jenkins' estate, Windsor Forge. Everywhere there was food, wine, brandy, gaiety and an invitation to stay a few days. Buchanan sometimes wondered whether he was not aspiring too far above his station, for he could not return such hospitality.

James and Ann became engaged during the summer of 1819. About the same time, Molton Rogers gave his heart to Eliza Jacobs. Lancaster ladies whipped up a whirlwind of excited speculation and gossip about the possibility of a double wedding, with two of the community's richest fathers footing the bill for what would surely be a festive occasion unmatched in the past. But not everyone viewed the prospect with pleasure. Mrs. Coleman did not approve of her daughter's choice and her father, now 71 years old, also had his doubts. It is very likely that as a trustee of Dickinson, he wondered whether Ann ought to marry a man who had been once dismissed and twice under faculty discipline there. As a careful businessman he probably disapproved of the wager on the 1816 election by which Buchanan lost three tracts of Warren County land to Rogers.[4] He may also have been dismayed by the antics of some of Buchanan's associates, such as Jasper Slaymaker and John Reynolds, who had gained notoriety a few years before by a practical joke which cost them $6700. These two, while riding past a public sale in a carriage, had shouted out a bid, then whipped up the horse and driven off. They were recognized, and the auctioneer knocked down to them as high bidders a hotel and ferryboat line in Columbia.[5] According to Robert Coleman's lights, these were not the ways to protect or develop a fortune.

In the latter part of the summer, Buchanan drove to Mercersburg to tell his parents about his bride-to-be and then set out for Bedford Springs for a brief rest. He had gone there for the past two summers and had been delighted with the sparkling waters, the beautiful serpentine walks up Constitution Hill and Federal Hill, the quiet artificial lake, and the magnificent hotel with its broad verandas. He thought he would try the new Pennsylvania turnpike and got as far as Sideling Hill when he encountered a short unfinished stretch of the road which proved impassable. As he was about to turn back, a young Irishman from a group of nearby workmen came up and offered to have his crew carry the gig over the rocks and get him on his way again. In fifteen minutes they had done the job. "My name is John Hughes," said the genial foreman.[6] Many years hence Buchanan would have occasion to remember that name.

29

On his return to Lancaster, Buchanan found his office in pandemonium. The autumn of 1819 had developed into a nightmare for men of property and the lawyers who handled it. The delirium of the financial panic had reached its peak, land was selling so fast and cheap that even the sheriff's fees could not be realized, and Buchanan was frantically busy. One complex case proved a particularly heavy drain on his time—a suit upon which depended the continued existence of the Columbia Bridge Company, an enterprise in which many of his local friends had a financial interest. William Jenkins and the Farmers Bank were deeply involved, and the case had ramifications which required Buchanan to go to Philadelphia several times.[7]

As if this were not enough, the political scene was in turmoil. The local Federalist party was falling apart and had turned to its young men for help. Furthermore, the Missouri Compromise question was at this moment alarming the country "like a fire bell in the night." During the week of November 23, Buchanan attended public meetings and served on a committee with James Hopkins and William Jenkins to prepare official resolutions instructing the District Congressman to oppose the extension of slavery to Missouri.[8]

With these preoccupations, he did not spend very much time courting during October and November. Always conscientious and willing to serve, he applied himself to business without pausing to recognize the implications of his activity. The town did otherwise. Since his engagement to Ann Coleman, he had become a major subject of conversation and his every act or omission was subjected to special scrutiny. The teacup set soon agreed that Buchanan was in love not with Ann but with the Coleman fortune.

Sometime in November, Ann began to worry about this gossip, which inevitably found its way into the Coleman household. When her parents further poisoned her mind on the subject, she gradually began to believe "that Mr. Buchanan did not treat her with that affection that she expected from the man she would marry, and in consequence of his coolness she wrote him a note telling him that she thought it was not regard for her that was his object, but her riches."[9]

Ann's letter put Buchanan in a difficult dilemma, and her reflection upon his integrity hit him where he was most sensitive; it hurt his pride and self-respect. He must have felt that, in the light of Ann's suspicions, any marked quickening of his interest thereafter would only be construed by her as additional proof of her charge. Hurt and frustrated he answered Ann's note politely but in a tone of injured innocence and made no apology or explanation. There was as yet, however, no formal breach, and matters might have been happily resolved had not another incident occurred.

This event is best explained in the words of a niece of the lady who unwittingly precipitated the crisis. "Some time after the engagement had been announced," she wrote, "Mr. Buchanan was obliged to go out of town on a business trip. He returned in a few days and casually dropped in to see . . . Mrs. William Jenkins, with whose husband he was on terms of intimate friendship. With her was staying her sister, Miss Grace Hubley, . . . a pretty and charming young lady. From this innocent call the whole trouble arose. A young lady told Miss Coleman of it and thereby excited her jealousy. She was indignant that he should visit anyone before coming to her. On the spur of the moment she penned an angry note and released him from his engagement. The note was handed to him while he was in the courthouse. Persons who saw him receive it remarked afterward that they noticed him turn pale when he read it. Mr. Buchanan was a proud man. The large fortune of his lady was to him only another barrier to his trying to persuade her to reconsider her rejection of himself."[10]

For several days thereafter Ann was so distressed and low-spirited that her mother persuaded her to go to Philadelphia hoping that a change of scene would improve her mental state. Her vitality was already low, and she caught cold on the way to the city. She left Lancaster on Saturday, December 4, in company with her younger sister, Sarah, to visit with sister Margaret, apparently intending to see the series of plays and operas currently being offered at the Philadelphia Theatre.

After Ann's departure, Buchanan immersed himself in business. On Monday, December 6, he succeeded in getting a settlement out of court of the Columbia Bridge Company case. He was at the prothonotary's office for a considerable part of the day, entering the decisions of the arbitrators, getting signatures of the principal parties to the agreement, and winding up the details.[11] It was a great triumph for him.

Early Thursday morning, December 9, the thunderbolt struck. A special messenger from Philadelphia brought the shocking news that Ann Coleman had died suddenly at her sister's home shortly after midnight. Judge Thomas Kittera of Philadelphia, who knew the Colemans, recorded in his diary the events of that fatal day which changed the course of James Buchanan's life and with it possibly the course of American history.

"At noon yesterday," wrote Kittera, "I met this young lady on the street, in the vigour of health, and but a few hours after [,] her friends were mourning her death. She had been engaged to be married, and some unpleasant misunderstanding occurring, the match was broken off. This circumstance was preying on her mind. In the afternoon she was laboring under a fit of hysterics; in the evening she was so little indisposed that her sister visited the theatre. After night she was attacked with strong hysterical convulsions, which induced the family to send for physicians, who thought this would soon go off, as it did; but her pulse gradually weakened

31

until midnight, when she died. Dr. Chapman, . . . says it is the first instance he ever knew of hysteria producing death. To affectionate parents sixty miles off what dreadful intelligence—to a younger sister whose evening was spent in mirth and folly, what a lesson of wisdom does it teach. Beloved and admired by all who knew her, in the prime of life, with all the advantages of education, beauty, and wealth, in a moment she has been cut off."[12]

Judge Kittera might well have added, what crushing intelligence to her ex-fiancé. The news swept through Lancaster like a soul-chilling wind. One gentleman wrote of it as "the most affecting circumstance that has ever taken place here since I have been an inhabitant."[13] There immediately arose the hint of suicide, though no one could produce any valid evidence of it. The hideous part was that nobody apparently did know exactly what had happened, and it is entirely probable that James Buchanan lived out his whole life haunted by doubts and self-accusations. But people thought and talked even if they did not have the facts. One Lancaster lady wrote of the public reaction against Buchanan: "I believe that her friends now look upon him as her Murderer."[14] The Colemans seemed to feel that way about it.

Buchanan immediately wrote an anguished letter to Ann's father requesting permission to see the corpse and to walk as a mourner. The letter, despatched to the Coleman home by messenger, was refused at the door and returned unopened. In this note, Buchanan had written: "It is now no time for explanation, but the time will come when you will discover that she, as well as I, have been much abused. God forgive the authors of it . . . I may sustain the shock of her death, but I feel that happiness has fled from me forever."[15]

As he came face to face with the bitter hatred of the Colemans and the insidious suicide rumors, Buchanan slowly began to recognize the full horror of his situation. Unable to endure solitude, and even less able to confront people on the street, he fled to the rooms of Judge Walter Franklin, who was then living next door to the Coleman home. Here he tried to compose a fitting last tribute to Ann for publication in the *Lancaster Journal*. A printer's devil from editor Dickson's office, who was sent for the copy, recalled finding Buchanan "so disturbed by grief that he was unable to write the notice." Judge Franklin finally composed it himself.[16]

The Hemphills brought Ann Coleman's body to Lancaster on Saturday, December 11, and on the Sabbath she was buried in the St. James Episcopal churchyard in a ceremony witnessed by a vast number of people. Buchanan tried unsuccessfully to get a grip on himself and go back to work. A Lancaster girl's report suggests what he had to face. "After Mr. Buchanan was denied his requests," she wrote, "he secluded himself for a few days and then sallied forth as bold as ever. It is now thought that this affair will

32

lessen his Consequence in Lancaster as he is the whole conversation of the town."[17]

A few days after the funeral, James Buchanan stepped from the rear door of his quarters into the gloomy morning darkness of December, made his way carefully across the cobblestone courtyard back of the Leopard Tavern, passed under the stone archway which led out to Duke Street, and there climbed aboard the early stage for the West. Huddled in his greatcoat, he made no effort to lean forward when the coach passed by the St. James churchyard.

In later years he could not have reconstructed if he had wished that agonizing, endless ride from Lancaster to Mercersburg. His mind was numb;. his spirit, in utter confusion. What now? He could not stay in Lancaster, nor could he leave without tremendous sacrifice. And in the background of his thought there dinned one half-formed yet persistent conclusion: that this tragedy marked the end of James Buchanan. What he would be hereafter would have to be, somehow, different from what he had been before. Buchanan shivered from more than the cold, and let his thoughts merge with the bleak greyness of the winter dawn.

The family impressed itself upon him this Christmas in a way he had not before appreciated. In it he found warmth and sympathy, trust and admiration, expectation of great achievement from the eldest son and brother as well as the assumption that he, very soon, might be their guardian and provider. The realization of his increasing importance within the family and of the responsibility that he bore for others gave to James a renewed sense of purpose in life. It appealed to his already strong concept of personal duty and pleasantly nourished his ambition for eminence, giving to both a gratifying quality of unselfishness. While the Coleman marriage would probably have eased the path and quickened his pace to achievement, position, and wealth, he did not doubt after the first shock of the tragedy had passed that with determination and application he could attain these objects without outside help. In fact, the gossip attending Ann's death made it almost a mandate that he prove himself, in order to maintain his self-respect.

But even such rationalization could not quite overcome James's reluctance to face again what he knew must await him when he returned. His pride and vanity were wounded to a degree that he had to have some armor to protect him. His mother supplied the material for it. She had that kind of faith which assumed that whatever happened was an act of the Deity intended especially for her instruction and benefit. On one occasion when a fire destroyed the homes of several neighbors and her own was saved by a sudden shift in the wind, she had written: "Our situation was indeed deplorable, but that Omnipotent being who governs all nature graciously interposed in our behalf."[18]

On this solid rock of faith, James Buchanan built his protective wall. His armor would be an unquestioning acceptance of what is, as the manifestation of divine order. There now began to appear in Buchanan's correspondence those sentences which, over the years, he was to repeat incessantly: "Sufficient unto the day is the evil thereof." "It is better to bear the ills we have than to fly to others we know not of." He used them as a statement of resignation, as a balm for personal disappointments, and as a convenient means of side-tracking the necessity of seeking original courses of action. Today he would do the routine work for today; God would take care of tomorrow. This attitude brought peace of mind but stifled imagination; it lowered emotional tension but destroyed zest for any cause; it counselled patience but obscured the importance of right timing in human affairs; it eased adjustment but eliminated experiment.

It was fortunate that his desk was piled high with unfinished business when he got back to his office in January, 1820. He plunged into preparations for the February session of court and found that attention to the troubles of others distracted him from his own. He spent some time developing his "casebook," a bound volume in which, with meticulous neatness, he transcribed the main facts of cases he had tried, noting at the end the judgment of the bench and the general principles of law which applied. He indexed this volume in another notebook in such a manner that he could continue into the future, making the references cumulative.[19]

Before long it became fairly apparent that his recent notoriety would improve his law business. His tragedy had resulted, in part, from his neglect of private affairs in order to attend to the interests of his clients. This was good advertising. He also found cases coming to him from those who had no love for the Colemans and from persons who sympathized with his plight at the same time that they trusted his legal ability.

Several trials, unimportant in themselves, contributed to his expanding reputation. A man charged with threatening the life of another retained Buchanan to defend him. When the plaintiff took the stand Buchanan asked him:

"Well, sir, suppose you were a man of more nerve, a man not easily frightened by threat—put yourself in the position of a courageous man—would you have cared for the threat of my client?"

"I am a man," replied the plaintiff, "of as much courage as anybody, sir."

"Then you were not frightened when my client threatened you?"

"No, sir."

"You are not afraid of him?"

"No, I am not."

"Well, then, what did you bring this charge for? I move its dismissal."

34

The court dismissed the case.[20]

In another case, tried in Harrisburg, Buchanan was retained by the plaintiff in an action of ejectment. After examining the deeds to the property, James told his client that he had no case—that a link in the title was missing. The client insisted, however, that Buchanan go ahead with the case. At the trial the attorneys for the defendant overlooked the weak point in the title. When, after the conclusion of testimony, they saw and tried to remedy their error, Buchanan held that under the rules then in force they could not introduce further evidence. The court so charged the jury, and Buchanan's client won. The Supreme Court of Pennsylvania later upheld the verdict of the lower court.[21]

An observer in the courtroom during the famous property trial of Bowman v. Königmacher in 1820 wrote: "I never heard better pleading in the Court House of Lancaster before: Hopkins & Jenkins for Königmacher & Buchanan for Bowman,—who argued very ably."[22] Judge Alexander L. Hayes of the County Court stated that "he never listened to an advocate who was equal to Mr. Buchanan, whether in clear & logical arguments to the Court, or in convincing appeals to the reason and sympathies of the jury."[23] This developing reputation brought to Buchanan not only personal gratification and more business but led to an increasing number of applications by young law students to take their preceptorship under him. James was particularly pleased when ironmaster Cyrus Jacobs engaged him as his legal advisor in June, 1820.[24]

FLIGHT TO POLITICS

In the meantime, Pennsylvania politics built up to a high pitch of excitement. Many persons, it is true, referred to the election of 1820 as an "era of good feeling," but this expression had a very special meaning and was limited to the presidential canvass. There was little "good feeling" among political rivals for state and local office.

The Pennsylvania contest for the governorship in 1820 developed into a bitter, violent fight which the Federalists confidently hoped to win because of a split among the Democrats. William Findlay, a neighbor of the Buchanans in Mercersburg, had served one term as Democratic governor and was standing for re-election. The Federalists now coalesced with a disgruntled portion of the Democrats to form a party called the Independent Republicans, who nominated Joseph Hiester, a Revolutionary veteran and an old Federalist.[25]

The Federalists of Lancaster, casting about for a Congressional candidate to head their ticket for the district comprising Dauphin, Lebanon and Lancaster Counties, settled on Buchanan. The election contest hinged almost wholly upon the office of governor and by midsummer had become acrimonious and bitter, as campaigns always do when a large party splits and a portion of it allies itself with the traditional enemy. Buchanan's opponents not only dragged out the Coleman affair but also brought his father prominently into the mud-slinging.

One long effusion of July, in the form of a public "Letter to James Buchanan, Esquire" made cruel reference to his recent tragedy and blamed him for a vile attack on Findlay for ownership of a Negro slave, Hannah, alleging that Hannah had formerly been the property of Buchanan's father. As a final touch, the letter was signed "Colebrook," to suggest authorship by one of the Colemans.

If Buchanan was angry at the crude references to Ann, he was furious that his father and old Hannah should be dragged into a political smear. Until the Findlays took her, Hannah had been his childhood nurse, ignorant, innocent and devoted. His father had become responsible for her as executor of an estate, and had eventually fixed her with the neighboring Findlay family who provided a home for her. Buchanan had an affection for the old lady and never left Mercersburg without visiting her and taking her some little remembrance.[26] The newspaper charge that he had assailed Governor Findlay for enslaving old Hannah made him see red.[27] His father cautioned him, "That piece is well calculated to irritate & hurt your feelings. . . . Let not your passions get the better of your sober judgment. If you are the author, meet the dispute with firmness and truth, & if you are not the author, let them expose themselves a little further that they may be taken in their own snare. I will be anxious to hear from you on this subject."[28] Buchanan categorically denied that he had anything to do with the "Hannah" stories, but the episode abated some of his youthful idealism about politics.[29]

On the evening of August 25, the Lancaster "Federal-Republican" delegates got together to select formally the slate agreed upon privately long before. They named Buchanan for Congress and Edward Coleman, Ann's brother, for the State Senate. The whole ticket was pledged to work for the election of Joseph Hiester to the governorship. A few weeks later the conference committee of the three counties comprising the district nominated Buchanan and John Phillips of Dauphin County for Congress as "friends of reform." The terminology was significant. Locally Buchanan's supporters were "Republican Federalists" signifying the coalition back of Hiester; but for national office his supporters were "friends of reform," a designation which openly recognized the current uselessness of party labels in Washington. On September 1, the supporters of Findlay held meetings and reported a "Democratic ticket" including Jacob Hibshman of Lancaster for Congress, and Molton C. Rogers for State Senator.[30]

Buchanan stayed aloof from the rough and tumble political fight. He made only a few formal speeches and sent no contributions to the

36

newspapers, letting the editors write on his behalf. His political métier was not the hustings and the editorial column; it was the private letter and the personal conference. He liked to discuss strategy but left it to others to execute the tactical maneuvers. The Findlay men tried hard to draw Buchanan into an open skirmish, but he always parried by a purposeful disdain to join in a newspaper brawl. His editor friends, explaining his refusal to stump the district, wrote: "Those acquainted with the gentleman, know that his time is more usefully as well as more profitably employed." For a conservative constituency this was psychologically sound. In the fall election Buchanan and Phillips carried their district by a comfortable majority, and Federalist Joseph Hiester became governor.

Buchanan would not go to Washington for more than a year; the session of Congress to which he had been elected would convene in December, 1821. In the meantime he faced a heavy schedule of cases at court, and had to familiarize himself with his approaching duties as Congressman. December court awarded him a decision in the long drawn out case of Bowman v. Königmacher. In January he defended a group of men charged with manslaughter,[31] and in May scored one of his greatest courtroom triumphs by successfully defending William Hamilton against a charge of the murder of Ann Piersol.[32]

On June 11, 1821, Buchanan's father died. The old gentleman was just entering the driveway of his Mercersburg home in a rig he had driven from Dunwoodie Farm when the horse bolted, throwing Mr. Buchanan out of the carriage. His head struck the iron tire, and he died soon thereafter. James went to Mercersburg immediately to take charge and found, to his chagrin, that his father had failed to leave a will. James spent the rest of the summer working out details of the settlement of the complicated estate in a manner that would enable his mother to get along with as little worry as possible, finance the education of the three boys, William, George and Edward, and care for the unmarried girls, Sarah and Harriet.

THE SEVENTEENTH CONGRESS

Late in November, James left by stage for the national capital, entrusting his King Street rooms to a housekeeper. Rogers would stop in occasionally, he told her, to pick up some wine and jugs of apple brandy. He wanted the rooms kept clean but otherwise undisturbed, as he would be back in Lancaster from time to time to attend to his practice.

In Washington he found quarters at the establishment of a Mrs. Peyton in company with Representatives Andrew R. Govan of South Carolina, Henry D. Dwight of Massachusetts, and George Blake, a Bostonian friend of Daniel Webster.[33] The capital city itself was a disappointment he had been forewarned to expect. The national Capitol stood unfinished since its destruction by the British in 1814. From Capitol Hill stretched Pennsylvania Avenue, lined with poplars and conveying a hint of dignity when viewed at a distance, but it presented only a morass of mudholes to those who had to travel it on their way to the president's house at the other end. The White House had been rebuilt and repainted, and at each of the corners of the square it occupied stood one of the department buildings. Between here and the Potomac stood a small group of shabby houses near the Navy Yard and another along the river's edge farther north. A few fine edifices, mostly private homes or foreign embassies, dotted the terrain north of Pennsylvania Avenue, but most of the buildings were small and shoddy—even the hotels.

On December 3, Buchanan and a number of other new members, including John Tod of Pennsylvania and George McDuffie and Joel Poinsett of South Carolina, were introduced to the House. The chamber itself was poorly designed for its purpose. The gallery was simply "a platform raised a foot or two above the floor, which gave the honorable members an excellent opportunity of attending to the ladies who had come to listen to them."[34] Huge pillars so blocked the view that no one could see the whole assembly and many legislators could not see the Chair.

Buchanan found a few familiar faces—John Findlay from Franklin County, Joseph Hemphill of Philadelphia, Ben Hardin of Kentucky and John Sergeant with whom Buchanan had associated in legal work in Philadelphia. Sergeant, Chairman of the Judiciary Committee, briefed him on the various members. "I well remember Mr. Sergeant putting me on guard against Mr. Randolph's friendship,"[35] he wrote. John Randolph of Roanoke, brilliant, eccentric and vitriolic, was the showman of Congress, a man who could always electrify the gallery but he was not considered a "business member" of the House.

Philip P. Barbour of Virginia occupied the Speaker's chair, and Henry Baldwin of Pennsylvania had been named chairman of the powerful Ways and Means Committee. Buchanan quickly got acquainted with Ninian Edwards of Illinois, an old Dickinson alumnus. But William Lowndes of South Carolina commanded his chief interest. He had learned of Lowndes through Langdon Cheves, former President of the Second Bank of the United States, a South Carolinian who had for several years been living in Lancaster. The news that the South Carolina Legislature had just unanimously nominated Lowndes for the presidency in 1824 gave special interest to his presence in the House.

Buchanan made Lowndes his ideal, for he displayed those qualities which James admired and tried to cultivate in himself—sincerity of purpose, full command of information, gentleness of address, an aversion to giving offense to an opponent, and utter fairness in debate. Randolph

38

once remarked after hearing Lowndes present the argument of an adversary prior to demolishing it, "He will never be able to answer himself."[36]

Buchanan quickly showed that he planned to be a "business member" of Congress. He was appointed to the Committee on Agriculture two days after the House organized, and he made his first speech ten days after his arrival. Within three weeks he had taken the floor formally on three occasions. Writing to Judge Franklin of his early impressions, he confided that after hearing various members speak, he was "forcibly struck with the idea that the reputation of many of them, stands higher than it deserves." His own speeches, he reported, had received a "tolerable share of attention, which in a very great degree I attributed to the curiosity of the Members," though he himself had felt much embarrassed. Most important, he could make himself distinctly heard, a rare achievement because of the poor acoustics of the hall.[37]

Just before Congress adjourned for Christmas, Buchanan received news from Harrisburg that gave him something to think about during the brief recess. The State Legislature had just elected William Findlay to the United States Senate by an overwhelming majority. That meant that Buchanan's party was defunct in Pennsylvania. The confused Washington scene would doubtless provide new issues and bases of allegiance, but these would have to be worked out. At the moment he was literally a man without a party.

A few days before Congress reconvened, several gentlemen called on Buchanan with a proposition. They wanted him to accept the notes collected by Lowndes on the War Department Deficiency Bill, construct them into a speech, and deliver it. Lowndes was ill and unable to do this job himself. He wished to save John C. Calhoun, Secretary of War, from his present embarrassment. Would Mr. Buchanan take over? He would, indeed! With the most exquisite pleasure.[38]

There was in the House at this time a group calling itself the Radical party whose object was to limit the activities of the federal government to the narrowest possible range. One means to this end was retrenchment, a rigorous cutting down of the expenses of government. William Harris Crawford of Georgia led this party, which was particularly hostile to John C. Calhoun. The root of their antagonism was doubtless their conflicting ambition for the presidency, but the immediate source of trouble was Calhoun's alleged extravagance in administering the War Department. Congress had appropriated $100,000 for Indian Administration for the year 1821—only half the usual amount provided for this purpose. The Secretary of War had spent $170,000 which was less than usual but $70,000 more than Congress had provided. The Deficiency Bill on which Lowndes had planned to speak would enable Calhoun to pay the debts incurred by the Indian Bureau of his Department.

39

To be asked to do a favor for both Lowndes and Calhoun during his first month in Congress indicated fast progress. It gave Buchanan the opportunity he wanted to stake out some political lines in Washington. Rumors that Buchanan would speak for Lowndes leaked out, and the House listened with careful attention to his remarks.

This speech revealed Buchanan's debating technique and identified his particular talents in the forum. He entered the problem tentatively, without convictions, admitted the plausibility of the opposition view, and asserted his personal opinion with modesty and calculated understatement. This introductory statement had the ring of sincerity and created a sympathetic attitude in the audience—a lawyer's bid for the jury.

He then stated the general principle from which the rest of the reasoning would flow. "It ought to be a maxim in politics, as well as in law, that an officer of your Government, high in the confidence of the people, shall be presumed to have done his duty, until the reverse of the proposition is proved."

From this platform Buchanan launched into the details of his problem, examining every possible meaning and ramification, and tracing all to the stage of *reductio ad absurdum* except the one he supported, which at length stood out like a beacon of sanity and good judgment by contrast. Had Calhoun violated the Constitution? No. Was he to pay the bills of his Department out of his own pocket? No. Was he intended to be a seer, able to predict precisely the expenses of the army for years in advance? No. Would the nation be safe if every executive officer ceased to function when the previously voted funds ran out? Should the president admit the invader because Congress had failed to budget for an invasion? Was it reasonable to expect that the Indian Bureau, after a generation of activity, could suddenly cut its program in half? If that were done, would not the Secretary of War then be compelled to legislate in deciding what portions of his functions, defined by statute, should be performed? Would this decision not destroy the function of Congress in defining the scope of executive action? Did Congress intend to force the executive to alter the laws of the land? If as a result, the border settlements were exposed to Indian massacre, would Congress approve? Or did Congress expect the executive to be endowed with the power to perform miracles—to do the accustomed work without funds? Even if the Department of War had erred, did Congress plan to repudiate contracts honestly entered into by individuals with responsible agents of the United States Government, punishing the innocent instead of the guilty? "Why, then, considering this question in every point of view in which it can be presented, is there any objection against voting $70,000 to supply the deficiency in the appropriation of last year?"[39]

This speech serves as a fair sample of Buchanan's platform manner. Reason, supported by quantities of illustrative and supporting data, embellished by pathos ("the shrieks of helpless women and children under the scalping knife!"), converged upon an inevitable answer. In a reasoned debate, Buchanan could so exhaust a subject that any reply was bound to be a reiteration. Against wit or ridicule he was helpless, but in serious debate he was formidable.

Many complimented him on his defense of the Deficiency Bill which quickly passed by a large majority, despite a sarcastic sally by John Randolph. Buchanan then settled down to work on the two main objectives of his current tenure: to achieve re-election and to keep in touch with presidential politics.

He obtained free public documents for the home constituency. When these were unavailable for distribution, he laboriously copied some in longhand for particular friends. He worked, through the War Department, for the appointment of some Lancaster boys to West Point. He demanded an inquiry to determine who had pocketed Pennsylvania's militia fines and got himself appointed chairman of a select committee to conduct the probe.[40] He introduced a group of resolutions to extend the post-road system throughout his Congressional district; and he busied himself in other ways to keep his name in the newspapers and show that he was an active public servant.[41] Returning home at the end of the session, Buchanan learned that he was to be the guest of honor at the Federalist celebration of the Fourth of July at Swenk's Spring, along the wooded Conestoga. At the party enthusiastic supporters assured him that his services were duly appreciated and would be "long remembered by his constituents."[42] The toasts, written in advance by the arrangements committee, were indications of renomination. In fact the Federalists, meeting at the end of August, did renominate him. It was quite a distinction to be run for Congress a second time, for the local Federalist practice had always been to pass this job around among deserving workers. Buchanan felt certain that in this case it was his industry that had broken the precedent.

James kept his ears open for rumors on the presidential race. William Lowndes soon drifted out of the picture because of a serious illness which forced him to leave Congress early in 1822. "Whose chance from present appearances is best for the office of President?" Buchanan wrote in March. "In my opinion should the election take place tomorrow the contest would be chiefly between Calhoun and Crawford. I consider Adams out of the question . . . his disposition is as perverse and mulish as that of his father."[43] Among the members of Congress Buchanan found not the slightest trace of distinction between Federalist and Democrat; the names persisted, but they no longer signified anything. Many Democrats held

41

Federalist ideas, while as many nominal Federalists were Democratic in principle. He thought that Monroe's administration, though Democratic in name, generally pursued the Federalist policy.[44]

Two events during this first session of the 17th Congress showed new trends in Buchanan's political thought. The Bankrupt Bill raised the question whether the federal government should admit to bankruptcy proceedings all classes of citizens—farmers, laborers, artisans and others— or whether bankruptcy procedures should be restricted to the mercantile class, as had been customary. Federalist John Sergeant sponsored the bill and during the Christmas recess of 1821 persuaded Buchanan to support it; but as debate proceeded, James wavered and in March made a long speech in opposition which contributed to the defeat of the measure. As Buchanan had a strong personal attachment to Sergeant, his action must have been based on some serious political soul-searching. What had he discovered? A simple but, to him, a basic assumption: that in an organized society property rights had to take precedence over human rights. He did not develop this idea in its full implications, but he had the main point. To extend the bankruptcy privilege would destroy property because of the impossibility of controlling abuse of the privilege if it were extended to all classes. To destroy property would be to destroy government and society. He began dimly to see that human rights might conceivably be developed together with property rights, but that without the security of property every man would be doomed to the law of cannibalism in which no right of any kind could be guaranteed.

This speech has usually been cited as the beginning of Buchanan's adherence to the doctrine of States' rights. It is true that in his comprehensive argument he warned that to give the federal courts jurisdiction over bankrupts from the entire population would lead to federal consolidation. But this was a subsidiary argument. His main theme was that the bill would increase the perpetration of fraud because man was basically criminal and would give way to temptation. "Rest assured," he concluded, "that our population require the curb more than the rein." This was Hamiltonian, not Jeffersonian.

A second Congressional event that also aroused Buchanan to some original thinking was President Monroe's veto message of a bill to finance repairs on the Cumberland Road by permitting the federal government to collect tolls. Buchanan had supported several proposals to improve the Cumberland Road because he thought the road would strengthen the Union and benefit Pennsylvania, but Monroe's veto pointed out the Constitutional difficulties involved in a federal effort to collect a local tax. Buchanan was so impressed by his own failure to see what a Pandora's box of federal intervention this would open that he tried repeatedly thereafter to have the whole Cumberland Road retroceded to the individual states.

In this instance, he did lean to the States' rights view, defending the domain of state jurisdiction from invasion by federal authority.

What political complexion did Buchanan hold in 1822? Was he Federalist or Democratic in principles? It seemed that he was both. Fortunately for him, so were many of his constituents.

4.

THE KING MAKER • 1821 - 1827

THE CALHOUN BAND WAGON

Since 1800 New York and Virginia had divided the honors of control of the national government, Virginia taking the presidency and New York the lion's share of the federal patronage. This "dynastic alliance" always controlled presidential nominations by the old scheme of the Congressional caucus and planned again to exercise its power by selecting William Harris Crawford as the presidential nominee in 1824. As there would be no Federalist candidate, the Democratic nomination would be equivalent to election; it would be, at least, unless someone contested the nomination. Pennsylvania's younger politicians readied themselves for just such a contest.

To overcome the New York-Virginia alliance they thought it necessary to establish a counteralliance and to manage a nomination by some means other than the traditional method. Pennsylvania had no favorite son ready for the presidency in 1821, but she had a unique and original system of making nominations which, together with her 28 votes in the electoral college, might very well upset Crawford and elect someone of her choice. The Pennsylvanians proposed to use the method of nomination by a state convention of delegates chosen for the purpose, the same procedure by which they had picked their gubernatorial candidates in 1817 and 1820.

Buchanan found the prospects fascinating. "I have long thought that the general government have rested so secure in the support of Pennsylvania that they have thought it unnecessary to do her common justice," he wrote in 1821.[1] Along with others, he welcomed the plan of a combination of Ohio, South Carolina, and Pennsylvania to take the measure of New York and Virginia. John C. Calhoun, Secretary of War, would be the logical leader of such a coalition. He was a striking man with piercing eyes and thick black hair, brushed back defiantly, a man of experience and leadership; a nationalist, a friend of internal improvements, of a national

44

bank, and of a protective tariff; a man of honor who would not slight his friends. If he were to become president, Pennsylvania's turn could not be far behind, and some cabinet offices would be scattered along the road to the White House.

Calhoun visited Pennsylvania's Bedford Springs in 1821 and made a tour of observation until mid-September. He returned to Washington full of rosy hopes for the future, for in the course of his expedition he had signed up the leading representatives of the Family party of the state, an organization which was destined to guide Pennsylvania politics and to plague James Buchanan for many years to come.

George Mifflin Dallas of Philadelphia, patrician son of Alexander J. Dallas, created the Family party which got its name from the fact that nearly all the lieutenants were kin to their captain. Favored with reputation, money, brains, and political ties strengthened by blood and marriage, Dallas nourished the hope of outstripping in distinction his famous father. Samuel D. Ingham of New Hope along the Delaware, William Wilkins of Pittsburgh, Richard Bache, Thomas Sergeant, and John Norvall of Philadelphia, Thomas J. Rogers of Easton, and a few others formed the backbone of the Family party's leadership.

During Buchanan's first weeks in Congress in December 1821, the Family Congressmen from Pennsylvania called on Calhoun in a body to invite him formally to stand as a candidate for president. After his grateful acceptance, the Family spread pro-Calhoun literature all over Pennsylvania and systematically attacked John Quincy Adams. Plans to secure a nomination of Calhoun by the State Legislature proved premature in 1822, but Dallas and Ingham indoctrinated their followers with the idea that support of Calhoun would be one of the main issues of the 1823 contest for the governorship.[2] By January 1823, George McDuffie thought that Pennsylvania would "unquestionably support Calhoun" and nominate him at a state convention.[3]

Buchanan became interested in Calhoun's prospects, partly because so many of his Pennsylvania colleagues were talking about the subject and partly because he happened to live with George McDuffie. It was probably no accident that Buchanan's first real speech was a ringing defense of Calhoun's administration of the War Department, and the rather unusual attention accorded to this effort, which mystified the orator, may have proceeded from genuine curiosity whether Calhoun had carried Pennsylvania's Federalists into camp. Buchanan refused to commit himself to Calhoun, but kept a position from which he could at any time go along with the movement without apparent inconsistency or embarrassment.

Early in 1823, Buchanan's friend Stephen Pleasanton dropped a hint that a change in Monroe's Cabinet was imminent. "Poor Penna.," he wrote, "has not a man in the dominant party . . . fit to be placed in the

45

Cabinet. All the large states can have a man in the Cabinet but her. If she had a prominent man she would clearly be entitled to the Appt. of Secretary of Navy. . . . Can you name one?"[4]

It was extremely odd that such a letter should have been addressed to Buchanan. He assumed that Calhoun was back of it and used it in the way in which Pleasanton presumably intended. He consulted with his Democratic law partner, Molton Rogers, in framing a reply which was prepared for Calhoun's eye. Calhoun, he wrote, could gain the presidency by pressing Pennsylvania's claim for recognition in the Cabinet, or destroy his chances if he disregarded the Keystone State. This exchange brought Buchanan almost within the ranks of pro-Calhoun Democrats.[5] As it developed, the incumbent Navy Secretary, S. L. Southard, surprised everyone by keeping his Cabinet place in preference to the offer of a seat on the Supreme Court. Calhoun promised, however, that Buchanan could count him "among the friends of the state here" whenever the occasion demanded.[6]

George McDuffie wrote Buchanan a flattering letter at this same time, commenting that "though you are called a federalist & myself a republican, we agree upon almost every question of importance . . . not excepting the interesting question of who shall be the next president." McDuffie then proceeded to instruct Buchanan on the "safest course" for those who were backing Calhoun's prospects. He wanted to obtain a strong public expression from Pennsylvania; that would bring Ohio along immediately.[7]

Buchanan at this point would probably have come out openly for Calhoun except for complications created by the state election of 1823. The Federalists would have to run a candidate for governor; they could not at the same time back a presidential candidate already appropriated by the opposition.

The pro-Calhoun Democrats selected John A. Shulze as the Democratic candidate for governor. Although Shulze said nothing on the subject of the presidency, his backers spread the word that a vote for Shulze in 1823 meant a vote for Calhoun in 1824. Except for the fact that Shulze's chief competitor for the Democratic nomination, George Bryan of Lancaster, had been double-crossed at the convention, there probably would have been no Federalist nomination and no contest, but Bryan's friends were so outraged that it seemed sure that they could be induced to bolt. The Federalists, therefore, placed a candidate in the running and succeeded in influencing the angry Bryanites to join them.[8]

These activities put Buchanan in a quandary. He tried to keep the presidential question out of the state election and also to keep himself clear of it. Before the Federalist nominating convention, he strongly dissuaded John Sergeant from standing as a candidate for governor because he

46

knew that if his friend Sergeant ran, he would be compelled to campaign actively.[9] After Sergeant declined and Andrew Gregg accepted the Federalist nomination, Buchanan gave only perfunctory attention to his party's canvass.[10] His colleagues censured him for his conduct. "It is bruited about that you have rather held back in this business which rumor is I presume no secret to you, nor the cause of it. . . . The presidential question is assigned as the cause of this backwardness."[11]

It was certainly a frustrating summer for everybody. Although the presidential issue was officially taboo and not to be mentioned formally, everyone privately talked of nothing else. The frequent appearance of Jackson's name during the summer came as a surprise to the politically informed, for his candidacy seemed to spring out of thin air. No one of standing sponsored him, but on the only occasion when his name was publicly brought forward—at the state convention which nominated Shulze for governor—the chairman had to smother the wild demonstration which greeted the pro-Jackson resolution by calling loudly for a vote on a different subject.[12]

Buchanan had hoped to escape part of this awkward political campaign by going to Boston in June with Mrs. George Blake, one of his dining companions for the past two years at Mrs. Peyton's. Mrs. Blake teased him about his apparent aversion to the fair sex, persuaded him to escort her to public functions in Washington, and conducted a vigorous campaign to find a wife for him. But he had to forego the Boston trip at that time because the Pennsylvania Supreme Court had scheduled an adjourned session for the first three weeks of July, and he was concerned in nearly every case on the docket. He wrote Mrs. Blake in midsummer that Lancaster was as dull as could be and that, like the children of Israel in the wilderness, he longed after the fleshpots of Egypt.

He had been having a good time in Washington where, among the ladies, the knowledge of the Ann Coleman affair had given him a kind of romantic appeal. He had not forgotten Ann, nor had he lived the life of a recluse. Washington was full of lovely maids and matrons, but personable young bachelors were few. Buchanan knew the Van Ness girls, Cora Livingston and Catherine Van Rensselaer of New York, the Crowninshield misses from Vermont, Priscilla Cooper, who became the wife of his friend Robert Tyler, the Caton sisters from Baltimore, and many others, including a sprightly Julia and a giddy Matilda about whom he wrote glowing encomiums. He spent August with the Blakes in Boston; but despite the best efforts of his kind hostess, he returned home no closer to matrimony than he had been before.[13]

In Lancaster he learned that the Federalist campaign for governor had fallen apart. In October Shulze won the governorship by the largest majority in the history of Pennsylvania.

THREE CHEERS FOR OLD HICKORY

The first few months of the new Congressional session, from December 1823 to March 1824, were filled with the excitement of president-making. Calhoun thought that his election was certain if only Pennsylvania would nominate him; but Ingham, Dallas, and his other friends in the Family party hesitated, for they had not been able to bring Governor Shulze into their plans. Meanwhile the cry for Jackson spread wildly.

In February, 1824 the Congressional caucus in Washington nominated Crawford according to plan. A rump affair, boycotted by all but two or three Pennsylvania representatives, it would not be an important factor in Pennsylvania. On the other hand the caucus made it startlingly clear that there would have to be either a knockdown fight between the friends of Jackson and the friends of Calhoun or some kind of jointure between them, for supporters of these two seemed to be divided fairly evenly. The Family party, however, considered it safe to push a plan for a State nominating convention in Harrisburg on March 4 at which they intended to introduce Calhoun's name as presidential candidate, with Jackson as his running mate.

After carefully sounding out public opinion, Buchanan now abandoned his earlier preference for Calhoun. Some of the Federalists had taken hold of the sprouting Jackson movement and stood a good chance of appropriating the management of it. This was too good an opportunity to ignore, particularly since many western Democrats had become enthusiastic Jacksonians but lacked leadership. Even Judge John Bannister Gibson, a Democratic party regular, wrote to Buchanan in January: "Heaven knows what will be the upshot . . . but it seems to me that Jackson is carrying it away from all the rest. Next to J. C. Calhoun he is my man."[14] During this time of uncertainty, Buchanan kept his own counsel.

In February, four days after the Crawford nomination, Calhoun's friends in Pennsylvania held a meeting in Philadelphia to select delegates to the Harrisburg convention. Their courage broke at this point and George Dallas himself urged the meeting to select delegates favorable to Jackson, with Calhoun as their second choice.[15] This was a bombshell to Calhoun, and made Jackson the choice of all parties in Pennsylvania. From here on it would be a scramble to see who could gain control of the whole Jackson movement and thus control the Pennsylvania patronage. Three groups of Pennsylvania politicians accepted the fact of Jackson's popularity, and each of these became a Jacksonian faction determined to dominate the whole.

The first to propose Jackson's candidacy were a number of small-fry editors and country politicians who were the real "original Jacksonians" of the Commonwealth. The second group of Jacksonians had been the supporters of Governor Hiester in 1820; they were men of both Federalist and Democratic parties who called themselves the Independent Republicans and were soon to adopt the name "Amalgamators." These men, after the Jacksonian movement had gotten fairly well started in the West, assumed for themselves the title of "original Jacksonians." Among the Democrats were Henry Baldwin of Pittsburgh, Molton C. Rogers of Lancaster, Isaac D. Barnard of West Chester, Robert Patterson of Harrisburg, and others opposed to the Family or Dallas faction of their party. Among the prominent Jacksonian Federalists were Andrew Gregg and James Buchanan.

Finally leaders of the Family party, belatedly observing which way the wind was blowing, pledged themselves to Jackson and claimed the privilege of dictating to all the others. They became known as the "Eleventh Hour Men." Everyone assumed that their object was to put Jackson into the White House for one term only, as a necessary preliminary to the election of their favorite, Calhoun.[16]

The Federalists renominated Buchanan for a third Congressional term in the fall of 1824. The nomination was a tribute to his work in Washington, for the Lancaster party had never before endorsed anyone for a third successive term. But another influence was also at work. Many Federalists admitted that, sooner or later, they would have to make a clean break with the past, either by starting a new party or by joining some faction of the traditional enemy. Buchanan endorsed the latter plan and ran on a ticket labelled "Federal-Republican." Some of the old-guard Federalists resisted by throwing away their votes in the election, but Buchanan won his race with the support of "amalgamators" of both parties. The varied preferences for president which the rival candidates for Congress held played no part in this campaign. The local elections continued to be fought on the traditional local issues.

In the presidential election, held three weeks later, the popular vote surprised even the winners in Pennsylvania. Jackson's poll was 35,929; Adams's, 5,436; Crawford's, 4,182; and Clay's, 1,705.[17] But the Electoral College vote showed no such landslide. There Jackson received 99 votes; Adams, 83; Crawford, 41; and Clay, 37. Since no candidate had a majority, the choice devolved upon the House of Representatives which had to make a selection from the three strongest candidates. Clay was free to throw his influence where he wished.

THE DISPUTED ELECTION OF 1824

Exactly what happened in Washington in the interim between the meeting of the Electoral College and the vote by the House of Representatives will probably never be known. Politicians from all over the Union swarmed into the national capital to add their voices to the Congressional hubbub, and those from Pennsylvania were perhaps more involved in it than any. James Buchanan, George Kremer, Samuel Ingham, Philip Markley, Molton Rogers, Walter Lowrie, William Findlay, and even Albert Gallatin, had a finger in the presidential pie.

James Buchanan was one of the most willing "fixers" of the Pennsylvania delegation. Two rumors current about the capital in December gave him the impetus to action. One was that Henry Clay would use his influence to elect Adams if Adams would promise to appoint him as Secretary of State. The other was that Jackson, if elected, would continue John Quincy Adams in the State Department. Buchanan felt that these rumors placed Jackson at a disadvantage in his contest with Adams, and put Clay in an awkward situation. The premiership in the Cabinet had become a stepping stone to the presidency, and Buchanan thought that if Clay's friends could be informed that Jackson had not determined to appoint Adams (implying that Jackson might appoint Clay), a good many Clay men would support Old Hickory. Only this backing could elect him.

Buchanan disliked Adams and, like most Pennsylvania politicians, had to support Jackson whether he liked him or not. It was natural, therefore, that he should have been anxious to prevent an Adams-Jackson alliance. In the fall of 1824 Buchanan was supporting Jackson with Clay as his second choice.[18]

Congressman Philip S. Markley, an ardent Pennsylvania supporter of Clay, urged Buchanan to get a statement from Jackson that he had not promised to appoint Adams. "The friends of Jackson," he wrote, "or rather the people of Pennsylvania feel a more than ordinary interest in the election of Genl. Jackson by Congress. I have heard many of the most influential and prominent republicans of the State . . . express their sincere desire that the friends of Mr. Clay cooperate with the friends of Jackson in his election—as Mr. Clay is at present decidedly the second choice of Penna. They hope that his friends on the present occasion will not take a course which will mar his future prospects in this State."[19] Molton C. Rogers, now Secretary of the Commonwealth and Chairman of the Jackson State Committee assured Buchanan that "it would give great pleasure to a number of the friends of Mr. Clay in this State, if he should use his influence in favor of Jackson. In that event he might hope for the vote of Pennsylvania on some future occasion."[20] Buchanan later denied under fire that he had ever been a political agent of Mr. Clay, but it was no secret in Washington in the winter of 1824-1825 that Buchanan's particular wish was the election of Jackson by the aid of Henry Clay, and it was a natural assumption that, should this occur, Buchanan would later welcome Clay's elevation.

By the last week in December Buchanan decided the time for action had come. In the hope of getting the support of Clay's friends for Jackson and in the hope also of preventing Clay from consummating what he felt would be a fatal move (alliance with Adams) Buchanan determined to learn from General Jackson's own lips whether or not he had ever said that Adams would head his Cabinet.[21] Not wishing to act entirely upon his own responsibility, however, he wrote to Rogers at Harrisburg, inquiring whether to ask the proposed question. "I can perceive no impropriety in Gen. Jackson making the declaration you mention," Rogers replied, "if it will contribute to his election. Although I have the highest opinion of Mr. Adams' qualifications for Secretary of State, yet, I would not endanger Gen. Jackson on that account."[22]

Thus reinforced, Buchanan approached Jackson's friend, Major John Henry Eaton, with his question; but receiving no satisfactory answer, he prepared to interview General Jackson himself. On December 30, 1824, Buchanan called on Jackson. After the company which was present had left the apartment, Jackson asked Buchanan to take a walk with him. The General could scarcely have been unprepared for the propounding of some proposition of more than ordinary importance; even if Eaton had not forewarned him he must have noticed that Buchanan was purposely waiting out the other guests. Jackson's practiced eye must surely have seen the tension under which the young man was laboring.

The Hero of New Orleans, now Senator from Tennessee, was something of an enigma in Washington. Albert Gallatin described him as "a tall, lank, uncouth looking personage, with long locks of hair hanging over his face, and a cue down his back tied in an eel skin; his dress singular, his manners and deportment that of a backwoodsman."[23] Josiah Quincy called him "a knightly personage," and "vigorously a gentleman," but not a man with whom to differ because he thought that "Heaven would not suffer his opinions to be other than *right*."[24] James Parton characterized the Old Hero as "honest, yet capable of dissimulation; often angry, but most prudent when most furious; . . . among dependents, all tenderness . . .; to opponents, violent, ungenerous, prone to believe the very worst of them." Some thought Jackson a boor, a villain and a murderer, others a paragon of the virtues of an honest freeman, but all agreed that he had a mysterious *presence*, that he looked the part of a leader of men, and that he possessed a dangerously unpredictable temper. He was no one to trifle with. Buchanan, when he went directly to Old Hickory with the delicate question that the whole capital had been covertly asking, took up a task which wiser men had been unwilling to risk.

After some desultory conversation, Buchanan spoke of the presidential situation and of the rumors current in Washington. These had already done some harm, he said, and would do more. He repeated what Markley had said: that many of Clay's friends would like to vote for Jackson, but they were distressed by the rumor, which had never been contradicted, that the General had made up his mind to put Adams into the State Department. Then Buchanan "popped" the question. Had General Jackson "ever declared that in case he should be elected President he would appoint Mr. Adams Secretary of State?" Without hesitation Old Hickory rejoined that he had never said whether he would or whether he would not make such an appointment, "that these were secrets he would keep to himself—he would conceal them from the very hairs of his head." Buchanan asked if he were at liberty to repeat this answer and, after being assured that he was, terminated the interview. "I need scarcely remark," he said later, "that I afterward availed myself of the privilege."[25]

A few days later Buchanan called on Congressman George Kremer of Pennsylvania and repeated to him the gist of Markley's conversations and the outcome of his talk with Jackson. Buchanan's object was apparently to get the Jacksonians to refine on the statement already made; that is, to change the negative declaration that Jackson had not decided to appoint Adams into a positive one: he had decided not to appoint him. Buchanan certainly hinted to Clay that Adams would not be the appointee. On one occasion and in Clay's very lodgings, Buchanan "introduced the subject of the approaching Presidential election, and spoke of the uncertainty of the election of his favorite (Jackson), adding that 'he would form the most splendid cabinet that the country ever had.'" When one of the group present asked how it would be possible to have one more distinguished than that of Mr. Jefferson, Buchanan replied, looking at Mr. Clay, that he "would not have to go out of this room for a Secretary of State." Buchanan was worried. On January 2 he wrote to Thomas Elder: "If I were to inform you that I consider [Jackson's] . . . election certain, it would not be what I believe myself." But he had done all he could and more than he should. He now sat back to await developments.[26]

James was pleased with his little excursion into the turbulent waters of presidential politics. He had been prudent and remained on terms of friendship with the three chief prospects of the future: Calhoun, Jackson, and Clay. He had helped each and hurt none. Whatever happened, he had laid his groundwork well.

But Buchanan had embarked on deeper waters than he knew. Had he been aware of the full extent of the bargaining, intrigue, and bribery, he would have felt more apprehension at being involved in the business at all. If anyone got caught, everyone associated with him would be in for a hard time trying to prove his innocence. Ingham was busy with Cook of Illinois, whose vote would control that state, guaranteeing him a territorial governorship for his support of Jackson. Some of Buchanan's friends spent their time peddling the idea that a Jackson victory now would mean sure success for Clay the next time. The Jackson promoters, of course, had one basic advantage over the others. They alone could legitimately claim that they wanted to honor the mandate of a majority of the nation's voters.

If adherents of minority candidates intrigued, it could be set down as corruption, but for the Jackson men to do it would seem merely an effort to execute the will of the people.

On January 24, three weeks after Buchanan's interview with Jackson, the Clay-controlled Kentucky and Ohio delegations publicly announced their decision to support Adams. It was a bold decision in the face of threats that the election of Adams would bring violence. Lafayette, who was on a triumphal tour of the United States at the time, probably thought he was going to see action on the old stamping grounds again, for his chronicler reported that "the Pennsylvania militiamen talked of laying seige to Washington if Jackson were not chosen."[27]

On January 28, the *Columbian Observer* of Philadelphia published a letter from Congressman George Kremer—an Ingham satellite—baldly charging that Clay had offered to vote for whoever would give him the State Department; that Jackson had turned him down; that Adams had signed the bargain; and that Clay would be announced as Secretary of State shortly. Clay called Kremer a liar and challenged him to a duel but backed down after Kremer started the rumor that he would duel with squirrel rifles.

In due course, the House elected Adams, and he appointed Clay to the State Department. The Jacksonians did not revolt, but some of them vented their fury by burning Clay and Adams in effigy. Two Pittsburghers who sent a barrel of whiskey to treat the fellows were indicted for inciting a riot—"That is to say for holding out inducements to other persons, to roast in effigy a Kentucky Gambler over a burning tar barrell," but the County Commissioners quickly disposed of the case by announcing they would pay no witness fees.[28] The Jacksonian editors in Pennsylvania bannered their papers with the huge, black headline: "Shameful."

James Buchanan was prudent. He said nothing.

BUCHANAN'S AMALGAMATION PARTY

If ever a man needed the talent of compromise, that man was James Buchanan in the years of the presidency of John Quincy Adams. During those years, he tried to weld into a single political organization as motley a political assortment as anyone ever attempted to control. It would be a personal party, a Buchanan party; one based on his reputation for personal integrity, his concrete achievements for his constituents, and his promises for the future. Jackson would be the cement of this miscellany, but when it took form it would stand solidly as a monument to Buchanan.

The challenge fascinated him, demanding techniques well suited to his personality. In the first place, party-making was a bookkeeping matter. Each county leader, in this confused state of politics, had his own following. Buchanan knew the votes each commanded as well as the strength of his local opposition. He kept accounts; determined where he needed strength and how much; figured the percentage of increase from particular appointments; pondered what approach would influence local groups.

The man who had the patience and the sharpness of eye could assemble into a meaningful picture this mathematical jigsaw puzzle. Untroubled by the distractions of poverty or parenthood, Buchanan had the time to devote to such a task. He followed up careful calculation by careful action: a complimentary letter here, a mild disengagement there, a letter of recommendation to this man, an appearance at one strategic meeting, and meaningful absence from another, a loan to a newspaper editor, a hint that so and so would be good material for a vacant judgeship, a batch of public documents to one, a bundle of *National Intelligencers* to another, some whiskey to a third—these were the things that absorbed James Buchanan in the years of the Adams Administration.

They were busy, tantalizing, frustrating, exhilarating years, full of political promise. His planning was as arduous, devious and logical as that of a chess game, and as devoid of the appearance of emotion. Like a chess player, Buchanan worked single-handedly. He had associates, colleagues, partisans, and friends, but he took none of these as a partner in his political activities. Not even his brother George, though his trusted agent, was his confidant. He had the added advantage of private means and thus could follow a political career without depending on it for a living. Since his father's death he had been making money fast by purchasing property around Lancaster at sheriff's sales. Values had been rising at a fantastic rate. Pennsylvania land that had gone for 62 cents an acre in 1814 now brought $400 an acre. Just recently he had bought several buildings on the southwest corner of the square in Lancaster, because he felt that they would be a sound investment. He would use some of his cash to play politics instead of playing politics to make money.

In the Pennsylvania elections of 1826, the Federalists left the state scene, as ten years before they had withdrawn from national politics. Shulze was unanimously nominated on March 4, 1826, by the Democratic convention in Harrisburg and the Federalists ran no candidate. Shulze's 72,000 votes indicated that he had the Democrats plus the support of all the rest. Buchanan's aid to Shulze was his personal statement that, while not yet a Democrat, he certainly was no longer a Federalist.

At the level of the Congressional District and the county, however, the old party names stuck. Buchanan was nominated and elected to Congress again on a Federalist ticket of the 4th District, along with his friend Charles Miner of West Chester, now an ardent Adams man. The Democratic Congressional candidates, who were Jacksonians, lost. Their defeat was almost incredible in a region where, on the presidential question, the people would have voted a twenty-to-one majority for Jackson.

After the 1826 elections Buchanan planned to cut loose from the old party names and to begin his fight for control of the Pennsylvania Jacksonians. Using the pressure of the approaching presidential campaign, he proposed to amalgamate into a voting bloc the Federalist German farmers of the East and the Scotch-Irish frontier Democrats of the West. Though formerly political antagonists, these two groups now both enthusiastically acclaimed Jackson and both resented the Philadelphia-centered control of the Family party. They could do one of three things: endorse Adams, follow Ingham and Dallas who worked mainly for Calhoun and kept all the offices to themselves, or join Buchanan's Amalgamation party which stood solidly for Jackson and promised to share its power with the yeomanry of the State.

Buchanan's associates in the Amalgamation movement were men to be reckoned with. Henry Baldwin of Pittsburgh could stand eye to eye with William Wilkins, the Family's only strong representative there. Molton C. Rogers of Lancaster had just finished a term as Secretary of the Commonwealth. General Isaac D. Barnard who had served brilliantly during the War of 1812 before settling down to the practice of law in West Chester, had been among the first prominent Pennsylvanians to come out for Jackson and had demonstrated his power by frightening Dallas out of his plan to nominate Calhoun at Harrisburg in March, 1824. In 1826, Governor Shulze gave him Rogers's place as Secretary of the Commonwealth and in 1827 the Legislature selected him as United States Senator. Barnard's connection with the Amalgamation group gave the Family something to worry about. George B. Porter, a young Lancaster lawyer of great influence among the lower classes, a militia general, a man of explosive, picturesque language, and of political ambition, abandoned the Family party to join Buchanan.

Many others prominent in Pennsylvania came to the support of Amalgamation and through it became, for the time, co-workers of Buchanan: Calvin Blythe of Mifflin County, Secretary of the Commonwealth after Barnard's election to the national Senate; George G. Leiper, veteran Congressman from Delaware County; Daniel Sturgeon of Fayette County; John Wurts and Thomas Kittera, Federalist Congressmen from Philadelphia; John B. Sterigere of Montgomery County; Joshua Evans, Congressman from Chester County; and of special importance, Henry A. Muhlenberg of Berks County.

These men defined the nature of the Amalgamation organization. It included those high in the state administration, many of the Federalist Congressmen, a number of old-line Democrats who were disgusted with or excluded from the Ingham group, and key representatives in every portion of the Commonwealth. They were all for Jackson, all for the creation of a new party, and nearly all for the future elevation of Henry Clay to the White House, though this phase of Amalgamation was purposely left vague.

One of the leaders of the Family party, observing these developments, wrote that the rapidly growing Amalgamation scheme was "fairly attributable to Mr. Buchanan, who has for some years past been fond of being considered a Democrat in the liberality of his principles, whilst he desired the support of the federalists as their Magnus Apollo." The day would come, he feared, when "Mr. Buchanan would have 'bestridden our narrow world like a Colossus' with the patronage and power of Pennsylvania at his feet."[29]

BARGAIN AND SALE

Buchanan was congratulating himself during the week before the state election of 1826 upon how nicely the Amalgamation plans were progressing. He began to see the whole prospect unfolding before him in logical, inevitable steps that must shortly sink the Family claims to control in confusion and bring him to the forefront as one of the top managers of a triumphant Jackson organization in Pennsylvania. Then he got that letter.

It was from Duff Green, Calhoun's campaign manager, dated October 12, 1826.

> You will discover from the Journal & Telegraph that Mr. Clay & myself are at issue. The part taken by you on the occasion referred to, is known to me; and a due regard to your feelings has heretofore restrained me from using your name before the public. The time, however, is now approaching when it will become the duty of every man to do all in his power to expose the bargain which placed the Coalition in power. Will you, upon the receipt of this, write to me and explain the causes which induced you to see Genl. Jackson upon the subject of the vote of Mr. Clay & his friends a few days before it was known that they had conclusively determined to vote for Mr. Adams; also advise me of the manner in which you would prefer that subject to be brought before the people.[30]

He read it and his vision collapsed. If that "bargain and sale" business was ever opened up again in a formal way, he was done for, not because he had done anything wrong but because all the appearances would be against him. He had done it again—had tried to act in good faith, but he had proceeded in a manner that laid him wide open to misinterpretation and every kind of malicious gossip.

Who was responsible for disinterring this dead cat and tying it to his coattails, he wondered. Green and Calhoun probably wished a rehashing of the political deal for the purpose of guaranteeing to Jackson his single term and of blasting forever Adams and Clay in order that Calhoun might be the only presidential candidate with unsinged reputation in 1832. Ingham, too, was certainly in it. He knew that no public discussion of president-making in the first two weeks of 1825 could go very far without embarrassing his rival, Buchanan. Ingham would find this move especially serviceable: not only would the candidates opposed to Calhoun be ruined, but Buchanan and his Amalgamators, sympathetic to the future prospects of Clay, would be completely upset in Pennsylvania.

Buchanan worked for four days phrasing a reply that would suit the requirements: one which would assert his innocence and at the same time threaten unpleasant consequences, should the issue be forced. "The facts are before the world," he wrote, "that Mr. Clay & his particular friends made Mr. Adams President, & that Mr. Adams immediately thereafter made Mr. Clay Secretary of State. The people will draw their own inferences from such conduct & from the circumstances connected with it. They will judge the cause from the effects. I am clearly of opinion that whoever shall attempt to prove by direct evidence any corrupt bargain between Mr. C. and Mr. A. will fail; for if it existed the parties to it will forever conceal it."[31]

With this the matter simmered for a while, but the following summer Jackson himself came out against Clay alleging, in a public letter to Carter Beverly of Virginia, that a Congressman had sought to make a corrupt bargain with him on Clay's behalf. Clay then demanded to know who was this Congressman. Now Ingham began a correspondence with Buchanan to force him into as unfavorable a position as possible.

"It is useless now to regret," he wrote, after everything had been made public but Buchanan's name. "Shd Clay demand of Genl Jackson his author he will have no alternative, nor could he have had from the first. . . : You will therefore be joined into the battle under a fire,—but I see no difficulty in the case if you take your ground well and maintain it boldly."[32]

If Ingham saw no difficulty, Buchanan saw a great deal. He now had the hard choice of publicly confessing agency in a dirty bargain attempt, or of openly calling Andrew Jackson a liar. After a month of agonizing, he brought the "bargain and sale" controversy to its climax by a long letter to the public, in which he denied the truth of Jackson's charge: "I called upon General Jackson . . . solely as his friend, upon my individual responsibility," he wrote, "and not as the agent of Mr. Clay or any other person."[33]

Everyone interpreted the affair according to his own lights. "It places Jackson in a most awkward predicament," wrote a friend of Adams.

"I am surprised at his indiscretion. . . . It turns out exactly as I suspected . . . that the author of the communication would prove to be a warm partisan of the opposition. . . . But what surprises me more than anything else is the situation in which the General places *his friend.* From this statement he not only carried the proposal but advised him to accede to it; and yet *he is still worthy of esteem.* Buchanan is ruined if anything can ruin a man who is a partisan in party times."[34] Another gentleman of the same party wrote: "Buchanan . . . is in a pitiable predicament. Nothing short of a miracle can save him. His advice [to Jackson] is perfectly understood by the public. I wish that *rascal* Ingham was in his place. I doubt if in fact he is not more steeped in guilt than any of them."[35]

Henry Clay declared that while Buchanan labored to "spare and cover General Jackson" he failed in every essential point to sustain him. "Indeed," he continued, "I could not desire a stronger statement from Mr. Buchanan."[36] R. P. Letcher held the same tone, writing that he was truly delighted that Buchanan had extricated himself from the dilemma in which Jackson had placed him and had "come forth victoriously."[37] William Rawle of Philadelphia confided to his diary on the night Buchanan's public reply was received: "The question must now turn upon the veracity of Mr. Buchanan or of Gen. Jackson. If we believe the former, General J. must have quite misapprehended—or wilfully misrepresented the connection. If the latter, the Gen. had reasonable grounds for believing that Mr. Clay's friends collectively authorized Buck—to make the overture. . . . Jackson appears to great disadvantage unless we discard all that is asserted by Buchanan."[38]

John C. Calhoun felt that the Buchanan letter would "produce a reaction" against Jackson, but that it would not be so serious as to jeopardize his election. "Mr. B. it is clear feels the awkwardness of his situation," he said, "which has throughout modified his conception of the state of the case. Hence we see throughout the statement an effort to get clear of all conception of agency on his part, and to give a character of innocency to the whole affair."[39]

By and large the Jackson press agreed to say that Buchanan's letter did support General Jackson in all his charges against Clay.[40] Not so, however, the Jacksonians of the Amalgamation branch in Pennsylvania who were wild with rage. Molton Rogers told Buchanan: "My own opinion is that Jackson's prospects for the presidency are much lessened, if not totally destroyed by his impolitic if not unkind conduct in relation to you in this affair. There is as far as I have been able to learn, but one opinion. The Governor is indignant at his conduct, & there would be no difficulty in bringing him out decidedly on the occasion, together with all the officers of the Government. . . You owe it to your own character to defend yourself, and I would suggest a meeting in Lancaster to express this opinion on the subject. . . It will be impossible for you to support Genl. Jackson. He has left you and your friends no alternative."[41] The situation had changed. Temporarily, at least, it appeared as if Buchanan held the pivotal position. The Adams men threw open their arms in the hope that Buchanan would rush into their embrace, and there were many who, when asked what side they would take if the matter were made a sheer issue of veracity, replied in the words of James Stevenson of Pittsburgh, "Why, by God, I will believe Buchanan in preference to Gen. Jackson."[42]

To Ingham, Buchanan wrote: "If General Jackson and our editors should act with discretion the storm may blow over without injury. Should they on the contrary force me to the wall and make it absolutely necessary for the preservation of my own character to defend myself, I know not what may be the consequence. . . . It is in your power to do much to give this matter a proper direction. . . . My friends here are very indignant but I believe I can keep them right."[43] To Duff Green, who had thought it prudent two weeks before to apologize for making so much trouble, Buchanan wrote stiffly that although he would never join the Adams party, he could not be responsible for damage to the Jackson cause that might result from a further attempt to pin the bargain on him.[44]

The controversy did not destroy Buchanan, but it did earn for him the life-long distrust of General Jackson, and it cooled noticeably the ardor of his friends for Old Hickory. Buchanan wrote of Jackson's statement that it was "a most extraordinary production so far as I am concerned;"[45] Jackson, on his part, confided to Amos Kendall that Buchanan's address was "such a production as surely I had not a right to expect from him."[46] Jackson, too, may justly have felt some irritation with the Calhoun leaders who for a year had known the ground on which Buchanan stood, although they had never troubled to point out the wide difference in their views. Van Buren assured Jackson that "Although our friend Buchanan was evidently frightened and therefore softened and obscured the matter, still the fact of your entire aversion to all and any intrigue or arrangement is clearly established."[47] The widespread publicity given the affair probably strengthened the belief of the average voter on each side that the opposition was crooked and added bitterness to an already violent campaign. As a result Buchanan became more secretive and cautious than ever in his subsequent political maneuvers.

5

FAREWELL TO FEDERALISM • 1828-1832

THE BUCHANAN-JACKSON PARTY

Buchanan now staked his political future on an outright change of party. He would, after having been four times elected to Congress as a Federalist, run as a Democratic candidate for the same office. "It will require the greatest excitement of party feelings, to induce many of the Jackson Democrats to vote for a Jackson Federalist," wrote one of his friends.[1]

He opened his personal campaign in 1828 by a speech to Congress on February 4 in which he broke his usual habit of keeping election politics out of policy speeches and joined the Adams-baiting pack in the House. As the attack on the Administration progressed, Buchanan at length jumped into the fight and made a truculent speech against the President. While moderate in comparison to the efforts of many of his Jacksonian colleagues, it still was a deliberate political onslaught. Buchanan brought to bear against Adams not epithets and slander, but a lawyer's marshalled evidence which proved the more damning for its restraint of phraseology and the evidences of scholarship it suggested. It was not a rant; it was the presentation of proof, wrought into argument, that the Administration had been despotic, unconstitutional, dishonest, immoral, corrupt, and would imperil the nation if continued in office. It set Buchanan before the country as a powerful champion of Jackson and initiated the Amalgamation campaign in his own election district.[2]

During the last week of May, 1828, Federalists and Democrats favorable to Jackson met at the Lancaster Courthouse. Their resolutions announced Buchanan's new organization which had, until now, been only a prospect:

> Resolved: That at the county meeting to be held on the 27th day of August next, the Delegates be requested to nominate and settle such ticket, as will give as general satisfaction as possible to the friends of Andrew Jackson throughout the county &

district, without reference to the political distinctions which have heretofore divided us.[3]

There it was, out in the light of day, over the signatures of twoscore men who, for a generation past, had run against each other for office under the labels of Federalist or Democrat.

After the storm signal went up, it took less than a week for the hurricane to descend. Its violence was aggravated by informal agreements which could not be kept secret regarding the candidates who would be chosen in the fall. As the new Jackson party had to choose between leaders of two groups, it was inevitable that there should be twice as many claimants as there were nominations to be made. John McCamant, for example, who had been a frequent Democratic candidate for Congress, had to move aside in favor of Buchanan. McCamant was broad-minded enough to understand the necessity and to retire gracefully. He accepted (against the advice of his friends) a nomination to the State Legislature.[4]

Other plans terminated less happily. E. C. Reigart, who had long been a Congressional aspirant of the Federalist party, but who had been turned down at every nomination meeting in favor of Buchanan and at last had gone over to the Adams party, was beside himself with rage. He became obsessed with the determination to ruin Buchanan, and through the summer months poured forth in the *Marietta Pioneer* such slander as Lancaster County had never known in an election.

Benjamin Champneys, a brilliant young lawyer of Lancaster who had formerly worked closely with the Family party, had been persuaded to join the Amalgamation movement by General George B. Porter. Champneys grudgingly accepted a place on the state assembly ticket. He felt that this post was far beneath his dignity and took the assignment only as a means of keeping in the public eye.

In Chester County, Charles Miner, who had been a Federalist colleague of Buchanan for two terms, wrote to his wife that he planned not to stand for Congress again. Miner had become an Adams supporter, despite his recognition that Adams would undoubtedly lose in Chester. Why not retire now rather than wait and "risk being run out?" "Buchanan," he concluded, "is really a strong man, and much as we differ on the presidential question, I should be sorry to see him out of Congress. This to your private ear."[5] But Miner's friends would not hear of his retirement, and it was not long before he was placed in the Congressional race against Buchanan, with whom he had been accustomed to run in double harness.[6]

By July 4 the campaign reached full tide. Buchanan managed to be at three meetings that day—at Yellow Springs, later at Downingtown, and at the end of the day at a huge Jackson banquet in the woods of Langdon Cheves's residence, "Abbeville," in Lancaster.[7]

The toasts at these affairs fairly well summarized the particular points of Buchanan's political strength in his district. His backers praised him for his successful support of duties on iron, hemp, molasses, and liquor during the tariff debate of the spring; for his exertions to get the Pennsylvania militia fines of 1814 turned back to the state; for obtaining a large refund from the federal government to Pennsylvania distillers who had been overtaxed; for exposing corruption in the Adams Administration; for aiding the Irishmen of the district by moderating the naturalization laws; for asserting the rights of farmers and manufacturers; for supporting local internal improvements; for endorsing a system of public education; and most particularly for the early and loyal fight for Jackson.

Buchanan expected to face violent opposition, but the reality exceeded anything he had imagined. His old partisans portrayed him as the architect of the whole "bargain and sale" plan. They circulated a garbled account of his 1815 speech against Jefferson and Madison, misquoting him as saying on that occasion: "If I ever had a drop of Democratic blood in my veins, I would let it out." The Adams men also published handbills recalling Buchanan's former presidency of the Lancaster Washington Society, the official committee of the Federalist party.[8]

They represented his speeches on the tariff as antagonistic to protection and favorable only to the wishes of southern freetraders. They characterized his part in the inquiry into the conduct of Adams's Administration as an example of his political profligacy and eagerness to promote himself by tearing down the reputation of others. They charged him with being a friend of slavery and of the slave trade—a charge particularly effective in the Quaker and Pennsylvania German regions—and they claimed that he frequently absented himself from Congress to attend to his private law business, although he drew pay during his absence.[9]

Buchanan kept out of the mess, letting his party editors handle all rebuttal until the *Marietta Pioneer* of August 15 came out with the headlines:

> *Fathers! Husbands!! Brothers!!!*
> *Read. Pause. Reflect. And Then*
> *Vote for James Buchanan if You Can!*

The article charged that Buchanan had asserted, "within the hearing of two or more respectable witnesses, that Mrs. Adams, the wife of the Chief Magistrate, was born out of wedlock."[10]

Upon seeing this Buchanan sat down and wrote a letter to the presumed author, demanding all particulars of the charge, names of the people claiming to be witnesses, and details of the occurrence.[11] Editor Reigart replied in phraseology which quite failed to support the charge in

62

the original article. Later a number of Buchanan's friends who had been at Yellow Springs stated that they had heard Buchanan speak of the lady "in terms of the most unqualified praise."[12]

Reigart was not the only editor who helped to make this national campaign notorious for scandal-mongering and slander. Many Adams papers broadcast that Jackson's mother had been a common prostitute with the British Army, that the General was the son of a Negro, and that his wife was a bigamist. It was then that the Jackson press retaliated with the canard about Mrs. Adams.

Buchanan refuted the charge about absence from Congress so thoroughly that his enemies came back with another accusation: he had started the inquiry himself in order to have the advantage of showing his rebuttal. With characteristic precision, Buchanan had kept an account book listing every day spent in Congress. He proved that he had reported every absence to the Treasury, and had his pay for these days deducted from his salary. He had missed only one roll call of importance because of a case in court, and in that instance the fate of the bill had not depended upon his vote.[13]

The tariff question had become extremely important to citizens of Pennsylvania by 1828. In the Keystone State, protection had ceased to be an economic issue interesting only to manufacturers; as early as 1824, when the tariff problem seriously entered politics, the farmers of the state also wanted high duties. By 1827 nearly every economic class and every political party favored the protective system.

Jackson, Calhoun, Adams and Clay all posed as the ardent champions of protection in Pennsylvania, but the first two came from the South where the protective tariff now encountered heavy opposition. Adams and Clay were strongest in New England which was devoted to protection. Buchanan had to develop a position on the tariff which would coincide with Jackson's, be competitive with the view of Adams and Clay, and satisfy Pennsylvania. He had already devised the required formula. In his first speech on the tariff he laid down ideas which he never thereafter abandoned, even though he was at times under strong political pressure to do so.

Buchanan advocated a national economy based upon self-sufficiency. A tariff, he believed, should first, protect agriculture, and particularly agricultural products which were the raw material of domestic manufactures; second, protect those manufactures which used domestic raw materials or were essential for national defense; and third, guarantee some equality of protection for the products of every section of the country. Buchanan opposed prohibitive tariffs, tariffs which would tend to give any type of producer a monopoly, and rates which would give an exclusive advantage to any single region or whose impact would affect chiefly the

63

poor. All of these viewpoints he had clearly defined in speeches in 1823 and 1824.

The tariff question came to the forefront in 1827, when the Woolens Bill was introduced in Congress. This bill taxed the cheapest woolen goods at the highest rate; the most expensive were not taxed at all. It provided for duties on raw wool, but they were much lower relatively than those on imported cloth.

The proposed statute put Pennsylvania's Congressmen in a dilemma. It worked hardship on everyone who bought woolen cloth and brought relief to only a few wool raisers of western counties. It also gave a monopoly of wool manufacture to the New England States, without any *quid pro quo* for other sections. It was an Adams measure which, if opposed by Jacksonians, would give the Adams Coalition a wonderful opportunity to assert that it was for, and Jackson against, the protective principle. In Pennsylvania this idea would possibly be fatal to Jackson's popularity.

Buchanan considered the Woolens Bill so bad that he would not support it even in exchange for new duties on Pennsylvania's favorite commodities: iron, hemp and molasses. It was exclusively a New England bill. If it passed, Pennsylvania would need a tariff against New England more than against Old England. It taxed the poor of the whole Union to give New England exclusive control of the cloth market. Let his opponents call his course inconsistent: he would not sacrifice American farmers and the interests of three sections of the Union—South, Middle and West—to the greed of a few New England manufacturers. They had been at the committee hearings by the drove. But how many farmers were there to testify? How many westerners or middle state men? None. The bill was a New England fraud from start to finish.

This line of debate got a cool reception at home. Buchanan was one of only seven of Pennsylvania's 26 Congressmen to vote against the Woolens Bill. Many of those who supported it, Buchanan charged, disapproved it, but "believed their constituents to be so Tariff mad that they were afraid to vote against it."[14] Ingham, too, opposed it: the Jacksonian leaders agreed that they could not afford to permit it to pass under Administration auspices and believed they had grounds enough to justify their opposition because of the defects in the details of the proposal.

But the measure passed the House. In the Senate, Martin Van Buren, now a staunch Jackson adherent, caused a tie by refusing to vote, thus forcing Vice-President Calhoun to make the decision and incur the odium of one side or the other. Calhoun, venom in his heart against Van Buren, took the only course he could: he sided with his own section and voted down the bill. In Pennsylvania, newspaper editors let loose with the headline: *"John C. Calhoun—The Arch Traitor"* and under this printed the names of the seven Congressmen who had opposed the bill, labelled "*The seven Traitors of Pennsylvania.*" Buchanan headed the list.[15]

Pennsylvania reacted sharply to the defeat of the Woolens Bill. A state convention in favor of tariff protection which met in Harrisburg on June 27 assumed the aspect of a Clay-Adams electioneering meeting and became the basis for a second at the same place on July 30, which was advertised as a national convention of all friends of protection. Henry Clay was scheduled to be there, and all friends of the manufacturing interest were invited. The Jacksonians boycotted both meetings, stating that the program was "actuated only by a desire to seduce Pennsylvania from the cause of Jackson, under false pretences that himself & friends are opposed to the Tariff, while Mr. Adams is in its favor."[16] Buchanan's brother George wrote worriedly from Pittsburgh, "The Woolens Bill is the great handle of Mr. Adams's friends here."[17]

During the summer, as the tide against Jackson continued to rise, Buchanan began to receive letters of this tenor: "I now prefer Mr. Adams . . . from a conviction that the interests of Pennsylvania are more likely to be promoted by the ascendency of northern men & northern measures than of southern men and southern measures."[18]

In order to meet the charge of "southern men and southern measures" Buchanan seized upon the only real stand Jackson had ever taken in regard to the tariff, his Coleman letter of 1824, and made as much of it as he dared.

In a letter to the *Lancaster Weekly Journal,* he wrote:

> Although the mass of the population of the Southern states may be hostile to the tariff policy, yet some distinguished individuals have risen above the prejudice by which they are surrounded. Among them I take pleasure in mentioning . . . General Jackson . . . . I do know and I wish to be understood as speaking from personal knowledge, that General Jackson not only voted for the Tariff [of 1824], but that he was its decided and efficient friend. He did more to reconcile many of the Southern members of Congress to it than any other man in the country did or could have done.[19]

True, but Jackson supported this bill because he thought it necessary to the national defense; he did not support it because he believed in the protective principle, and he urged his southern colleagues to support it for the same reason.

Buchanan had to show, somehow, that the New England States and the Adams Administration were opposed to a tariff. Early in July 1827, while on a brief electioneering trip to western Pennsylvania, he dropped a remark which foreshadowed the plan. A communication to the *Franklin*

Repository signed "Agricola" quoted him as saying: "We [meaning Jackson's friends] will next session bring before Congress a tariff bill so *larded* with other than protection to wool growers and manufacturers of wool, and involving principles which we know the East will not agree to, [that] we will . . . throw the odium of its rejection off the South on . . . the East."[20]

The story of the Tariff of Abominations is well known. But as soon as the trick bill was proposed Pennsylvania took it up with an enthusiasm which had not been anticipated. All the Pennsylvania Jacksonians worked hard for it, and the Adams men supported it. The bill, once passed, was received with joyful acclaim in Pennsylvania. By midsummer of 1828, reports were widespread that the cause of Jackson was "rising rather than declining."

The result was a good deal of an impasse. Neither side could claim a clear victory on the tariff issue, but the important thing for the Jacksonians was that a tariff bill of their making had passed. In the North this was used as *prima facie* evidence of Jackson's soundness on the question. But the individual Congressmen who had voted against the 1827 Woolens Bill had not been forgiven. Every one of them faced a hard struggle to retain his place in Congress, and none more so than James Buchanan.

James wrote that "the persecution against me in this county has exceeded all reasonable bounds. Some of the leaders of the Adams party have transferred all their abuse from Genl. Jackson to me. The purest & most disinterested acts of my life have been misconstrued, & out of them charges have been raised to destroy my reputation."

In view of the state of public feeling, the tactics of the campaign were of great importance. Anything might happen in such an emotionally charged atmosphere, and the letters Buchanan got from his lieutenants in various parts of the state showed no assurance that Jackson would carry the state, or that Buchanan was safe in the district.[21]

In the local election early in October, however, Buchanan demonstrated the strength of his hold on the voters of Lancaster by polling 1371 votes in the city against 309 for his opponent; and 5203 in the District against 3904. These results, which carried through the entire local ticket, showed that the Amalgamation plan of uniting Jackson Federalists and Jackson Democrats had been a resounding success.[22] In the presidential election of November Jackson defeated Adams in the Lancaster County District by a majority of 1467 out of a total of 8905 votes.[23]

THE FIGHT FOR THE SPOILS

Sitting in the quiet of his study on East King Street, Buchanan reviewed the course of recent events and tried to sketch out in his mind the immediate future. He could not stand many more contests like this one. What had been accomplished? The most remarkable thing was his own election as a Democrat after having been elected to Congress four times as a Federalist. That was a gratifying testimony to his personal reputation and had been worth the violence of the campaign. The battle had left a good many wounded veterans, but the important thing was that it had been won and the victory proclaimed the existence of a strong new party in Pennsylvania of which James Buchanan was the leader.

Pennsylvania cast so impressive a vote for Andrew Jackson that everyone took it for granted that the Keystone State would have a distinguished place in the new Cabinet, but to find a man combining personal capacity and political availability proved a thorny task for the new Administration. Old Hickory would "have his own trouble with Pennsylvania," wrote one of Buchanan's editors from Harrisburg; there were "more quarters than one" in which "something like a vice-royalty will be expected."[24] As the original Jackson men cut no figure in state politics, it was certain that the main struggle for influence would develop between Buchanan's Amalgamators and the Family party, neither of whom appealed particularly to General Jackson. The Amalgamators were tainted by their partiality for Henry Clay, the support of the Federalists, and Buchanan's part in the "bargain and sale" scandal. The Family party suffered from the deserved stigma of its nickname, "Eleventh Hour men." It represented the city and business element of politics, which the western frontier voters hated, and openly proclaimed its intention to put Calhoun in the White House as soon as possible.

Buchanan had worked out a comprehensive plan for his party: get Henry Baldwin into the Cabinet; promote Senator Isaac Barnard for governor in 1829; after his election, let him use his influence to persuade the Legislature to send Buchanan to the Senate as the replacement; and run George B. Porter for Congress in Buchanan's place to assume direction of the Amalgamation men in the House. The scheme showed clearly that Buchanan had advanced from the county and district level, and had broadened his view to encompass the state and the nation. The new program appealed to the rural and poorer class of Pennsylvanians against the urban and richer class. The voting strength of the western frontiersmen led by Baldwin, the latent power of the German farmers, organized by Buchanan and Henry A. Muhlenberg, and the class consciousness of the newly aroused workingmen of Philadelphia would be combined to challenge the political and financial monopoly which Philadelphia and Pittsburgh, now controlled by the Family party, had long imposed on the Commonwealth.

Buchanan went to Washington shortly after the presidential election to superintend the details. He had been rooming with Senator Barnard for a year, but the two of them now moved to Mrs. Cottinger's where they could be joined by Congressmen James S. Stevenson of Pittsburgh and John B. Sterigere of Chester County.[25] Buchanan was in poor shape for the job which had to be done; he had been violently ill for several months during the latter part of the election campaign with bilious fever. These attacks, which seized him whenever he faced a hard fight, gave him nausea, violent headache, and diarrhea and kept him near the slop bucket into which he vomited bile until he was empty and then painfully retched air. He was scarcely well when he returned to Congress in December, and by the beginning of the new year suffered a recurrence of the fever which lasted throughout February.[26]

Rumor had early picked Samuel D. Ingham and Henry Baldwin as the two Pennsylvanians most likely to be honored by a Cabinet post and until February, 1829, it was a question who would succeed. Buchanan had no hopes for himself, but he did expect that Jackson would select Baldwin for the Treasury Department.[27] He had defended Jackson in 1819 when he had been under attack for his Florida expedition, had been the first Pennsylvanian to ask him formally to be a presidential candidate, and had worked ardently for the cause ever since. Baldwin's son had recently bought a plantation next to the Hermitage in Tennessee and had been on terms of intimacy with Jackson throughout the summer of 1828.

The prospects seemed so good that the Amalgamators failed to exert themselves as hard as circumstances demanded. When Buchanan had discussed with Baldwin the possibility of nominating him for governor in the spring of 1829, he had positively declined under an assurance from Jackson that he would be placed at the head of the Treasury, and when the president-elect invited Baldwin to come to Washington for a conference in February, it was assumed that the appointment would now be offered to him.[28]

On the other hand, Ingham appeared to have little chance. Just a year before he had been defeated in the contest for United States Senator by a vote of 11 to 108 in favor of Barnard. Furthermore, Ingham was now so ill at his home in New Hope that his friends feared for his life.

But Buchanan and his partisans did not know that the Eleventh Hour Men had sowed all manner of doubts about Baldwin among Jackson's advisors, and that a few of them had called upon Jackson, representing themselves as spokesmen for the whole Pennsylvania delegation, and had demanded the highest place for Ingham. Calhoun's friends joined in the effort.[29] Their strongest argument was that the appointment of Ingham would ensure the nomination of a strong pro-Jackson governor of Pennsylvania. The Amalgamators, warned the Calhoun men, hoped to see Clay in the White House, and if they got control of the state administration they might succeed.

Late in February Jackson announced the appointment of Ingham as Secretary of the Treasury. The loss of this key appointment to the enemy was bad enough, but for Buchanan it was only half of the disaster. Baldwin, cut to the core by the ridicule heaped upon him by the Family press, considered himself entirely crushed and announced his "complete withdrawal from political contests."[30] To lose the services of Baldwin in the western region would nearly cripple the Amalgamation plan.

Buchanan could do little to help in Washington because Jackson distrusted him and he had been counting on Baldwin to be his direct channel to the White House. He tried to promote the appointment of his faction's candidates for various federal offices, but Jackson gave the appointments to the Dallas men.

By June, Buchanan's enthusiasm for Andrew Jackson had cooled perceptibly. The love and admiration which Pennsylvanians had expressed for Jackson personally had not, he wrote, "been transferred to his administration."[31] The Amalgamators had lost the fight in Washington and had to salvage what they could in Harrisburg.

On March 4, 1829, while a howling mob wrecked the White House in an effort to congratulate the newly inaugurated president, his friends in Pennsylvania congregated in Harrisburg to stage a bitter grudge fight for control of the state Jacksonian party.

Buchanan stayed away from the Harrisburg convention. He had worked out the strategy, informed everyone of the task to be done, and now left it up to the county workers to go into the fight and win. But these men were no match for some of the old and skillful politicians working for Ingham, whose convention delegation was managed by Dr. Joel B. Sutherland of Philadelphia. Barnard, after leading a field of ten candidates through thirteen ballots, finally lost the nomination for governor to the Family candidate, George Wolf, by the unexpected switch of three western delegates. The defeat was particularly galling to the Amalgamators, not so much because the final three votes which nominated Wolf had been bought by Sutherland as because Barnard's own five-man delegation from Chester County had been barred from the convention on the first day in favor of a contesting Family delegation. The Barnard men shouted "foul," called a general party conclave to condemn the Harrisburg proceedings, and planned another convention in May to place Barnard in the field. They denounced Wolf's nomination as the result of "intrigue and management in order, if possible, to secure the vote of Pennsylvania at the next presidential election for John C. Calhoun."[32] It seemed clear that the nomination of Wolf would be contested and that Barnard, or even Shulze, might be selected to run against him.

Buchanan wrote hastily to Barnard, expressing his mortification at the proceedings of the convention. There should have been an immediate protest, he thought, but now that the convention had adjourned, it was too late; they would all have to support Wolf. "There is no course left but submission. . . . Your enemies would be delighted if you should consent to be a candidate. This, however, I feel certain you will not do."[33]

By April, matters approached a crisis, for Barnard's friends seemed determined to hold another convention in May. By valiant work Buchanan at last managed to avert an open split among the Jacksonians and to prevent the meeting of the proposed convention. He saw no advantage in fighting the men supported by the Jackson Administration, especially at this time. Anti-Masonry had rapidly come to the fullness of its mushroomlike growth and, in alliance with the old Adams party, would certainly defeat a Democracy split in two.

Buchanan therefore urged the Amalgamators to abandon all formal opposition to Wolf and develop a campaign to gain some influence over him. Barnard should remain quietly in the Senate; Shulze should make all the removals he could, filling the places with supporters of Wolf so that the new governor would be placed in the predicament of being unable to give office to men of his own choice without firing political friends.[34] Buchanan's county organizations would circulate the idea that Wolf was strong for Calhoun but lukewarm for Jackson. This would give them some leverage at Harrisburg after the election.

In June 1829, the anti-Masons nominated Joseph Ritner for the governorship. He had the advantages of residence in the western part of the state, Pennsylvania-Dutch blood, and a reputation as an ardent protectionist, but the Jacksonians felt these were more than counteracted by his support of Adams in 1828, his ridiculous conduct when Speaker of the state House of Representatives, and the deplorable absence of delegates at the anti-Masonic nominating convention. The Family party did not fear Ritner; it feared the defection of the Buchanan men.

Buchanan worked throughout the summer trying to keep his partisans in line, a task very much complicated by the type of following he had purposely created. Diverse elements could be held together under the pressures and expectations of 1828, but it was a different matter to keep them united in the face of defeat and without prospects of reward.[35] Barnard made no real effort to keep the Amalgamation group intact in Chester County, letting his followers drift to the anti-Masons or the Family without protest. He occupied himself chiefly with the bottle, trying to forget his recent defeat. "For God's sake," Buchanan wrote to him, "summon up that resolution which belongs to your character & abandon the practice forever. . . . You have been but once disappointed; & disappointment is the common fate of public men. The Senate of the United States is a theatre as exalted as that to which your friends wished to elevate you. . . . Pardon my frankness & attribute it altogether to kindness."[36]

Barnard, however, never recovered. He was a dead weight on the Amalgamation party and became useless in the Senate from which, within a little more than a year, he resigned.

Buchanan took his two-week vacation at Bedford Springs as usual, but returned home in mid-August to take the stump for Wolf. He talked mostly at meetings of Barnard men, telling them that, although he had not been in favor of the nomination of Wolf, it was now the duty of all Jacksonians to support him. His speeches placed him on perfectly open ground with Wolf, but hardly quieted the apprehensions of the Family party that Barnard's friends, for revenge, would vote anti-Masonic or not vote at all.

The poll in October gave shocking evidence that Joseph Ritner had support other than that of the anti-Masons. Wolf's victory was no landslide, and explanations of why it was not were soon pouring in from every direction. Buchanan wrote,

> Anti-Masonry has overwhelmed us like a tornado in this county. Until within a few days of the election none of us had an idea of its extensive influence. . . . The majority against us will exceed 1500. It was 1300 in our favor last election. . . . In the face of our enemies, it would be miserable policy to divide ourselves into hostile, opposing factions.[37]

The Amalgamators, while they knew that they could expect no voluntary favors from the new governor, did feel that they were sufficiently strong to demand recognition and hoped to benefit from Wolf's fears if not from his gratitude. Unless he conciliated them, said they, he would not have a chance of re-election in 1832, and the only policy which could possibly save him from being run out at the end of one term was a distribution of the offices between the two factions. The alternative was anti-Masonic victory.

During November and December, Buchanan wrote letters every day or two to Governor Wolf, recommending friends for office.[38] The major struggle of the Amalgamators centered on the Attorney-Generalship, an appointment they determined to make a test of the governor's attitude toward them. Wolf displayed great political acumen when he side-stepped the factional fight by declaring that he would make residence at Harrisburg a *sine qua non* for this appointment. Thus, he summarily eliminated every candidate except the one of this choice, Samuel Douglass.[39]

The contest between the friends of Champneys and Buchanan in Lancaster touched off a fight which illustrated the state of feeling between the rival factions throughout the state. The Wolf Democrats held a victory meeting after election, whereupon Buchanan's friends resolved likewise to celebrate. They selected the courthouse as a meeting place and made preparations to gather immediately upon the adjournment of the current session of the court. Champneys, in the hope of effecting a reconciliation, agreed to appear on the platform with Buchanan and G. B. Porter, but the harder core of the Wolf party and the local sheriff determined that there would be no celebration. The minute court adjourned they rushed to the building, had the bell rung, surged into the court room, hoisted the sheriff into the chair, and enacted a scene "seldom witnessed in a civilized country." The would-be speakers, teetering atop the judges' bench, attempted to harangue the crowd but became a target for flying inkstands, pitchers, glasses, and spittoons.[40]

The opponents of Amalgamation blamed Buchanan, stating that nothing less than riot could be expected from an effort to unite red-blooded Democrats with Federalists and that Buchanan's hostility to Wolf was the reason for the outbreak. Buchanan made haste to write to the governor to "learn whether my enemies have made any impression against me on your mind" since the famous meeting at Lancaster. "I anticipated no disturbance," he said, "and . . . attended for the single purpose of uniting, not of dividing the party, as my preamble and resolutions abundantly testify. . . . I confess I think my case a very hard one. Having actively supported not only your election, but that of the whole county ticket, . . . I find myself now denounced as if I had been your cold friend if not your enemy. . . . It is my determination firmly to sustain your administration. . . . Having long since announced my determination to retire from Congress at the close of the present term, I have no interest but the good of the country & the party in desiring to save the District . . . from the grasp of anti-Masonry. This can be done, only by a thorough union & pre-concerted action of your friends, under the name of Democrats. . . . Union is absolutely necessary to our success. Nothing shall be wanting on my part to promote a reconciliation of your friends, provided I can interfere with any reasonable hope of accomplishing so desirable a purpose."[41]

This letter lacked something of candor, and Wolf knew it. In fact, there lay on the governor's desk half a dozen others from friends he trusted explaining in minute detail that "in every county where ·[the Amalgamators] had any influence," that party "played us false."[42] But when it was all said, Wolf still faced the plain fact that Buchanan's party held a balance of power which could destroy him. Reluctantly the governor asked Champneys to swallow his pride and to "act cordially with Porter and Buchanan." When Champneys resisted, an administration spokesman wrote more urgently: "My intention was with deference to intimate my own opinion that no sacrifice of personal feeling on your part which might produce a strong Union & ultimate success could possibly place you in a less enviable situation. I do not now, nor have I ever supposed that [Buchanan] will ever very cordially support us. Still I have hoped that something like the course I have suggested might give a little better aspect generally to the politics of Lancaster, and essentially strengthen the real & sound democracy at home."[43]

Buchanan succeeded better in forcing the idea of union on the governor than he did on his own partisans. Scarcely had the ink of his protestations of friendship to Wolf dried on the page when he was invited to a Chester County meeting called for the specific purpose of rejecting resolutions favorable to the state administration. Barnard remarked to him at this affair that "any attempt to identify you with the Gov. was calculated to do you mischief."[44] A little later the anti-Wolf Democrats of Philadelphia invited Buchanan to a dinner. The committee had purposely extended invitations only to persons living in the city in order that the governor would not have to be invited (a ruse intended to mock Wolf's "residence rule" for naming the Attorney General), but it informed Buchanan that "if you, Barnard, &c. should happen to be here, the Com. would at once call upon you."[45]

The situation, indeed, appeared to be hopeless. Buchanan, observing the political chaos, formally announced in the spring of 1830 that he would retire from politics; he knew he could be nominated only by his own faction, and he knew with equal certainty that this faction could not elect him. The death of Judge John Tod of the State Supreme Court led him to hope for that appointment. Many of his friends wrote to Wolf that Buchanan might be persuaded to accept the position if it were "offered to him without a recommendation being presented," but that he would not seek it.[46] This peculiar approach originated with Buchanan himself; the mere thought of rejection affected him like salt on a snail's back. Wolf eventually named John Ross of Bucks County to the judgeship, thereby giving to Ingham an unexpected and staggering blow, for Ross and Ingham for years had been at loggerheads with each other. The governor wrote later that Buchanan "wanted me to appoint him," and that the "refusal to do so has made me appear very contemptible in his eyes."[47]

In December, 1830, William Wilkins was elected to the United States Senate by a last minute coalition of the warring Democrats who, on the twenty-first ballot, got together rather than permit the imminent victory of the anti-Masonic contender. A year later, upon the resignation of Senator Barnard because of ill health, the Pennsylvania Legislature named George M. Dallas to fill the unexpired term.

Buchanan glumly reviewed the ruins—Baldwin shelved, Barnard retired and dying, himself withdrawn until the storm should blow over; the Family installed in Jackson's Cabinet, in control of the governorship, and in command of both seats in the United States Senate; the Democratic party in Pennsylvania split hopelessly and facing inevitable defeat by a political rag, tag, and bobtail united in the weird idiocy of anti-Masonry.

73

Life was a vast joke, and hope was futile. The situation was nearly as ridiculous as it was painful.

"Sufficient unto the day is the evil thereof." At least he could finish his work in Congress with some éclat and distinction. There was important work to do, and he would be called upon as a veteran to direct it. Without any certainty of the future, and without a great deal of interest in it, Buchanan settled down to his last two years as a legislator.

THE CULMINATION OF A CONGRESSIONAL CAREER

The first session of the Twenty-first Congress, which convened in December 1829, found Buchanan in an unusually dour and touchy frame of mind. He grumped about a departure from the customary mode of selecting a Clerk of the House, and let go a blast at Congressman James K. Polk, a young member from Tennessee, which was quite out of keeping with his normally placid deportment. Polk had made a speech on an important resolution, concluding with a motion to lay the matter on the table, a motion which, by rule, admitted no debate. Buchanan requested Polk to withdraw his motion and allow him to say a few words, but Polk refused. The House then voted down the motion to table, and Buchanan got the floor. He was sorry, he said, that he had to bother the House with a vote because his colleague lacked common courtesy. The gentleman from Tennessee was within his rights but very ungracious, after speaking at length himself, to conclude with a motion which, if successful, would prevent anybody else from saying anything. Polk flushed with angry embarrassment. A little incident; a little incident such as a man never forgets.[48]

One of the most conspicuous contributions which James Buchanan ever made to the government of the United States was his Minority Report opposing a proposal to abrogate the 25th Section of the Judiciary Act of 1789. The motion to repeal went to the House Committee on the Judiciary of which Buchanan was now chairman, succeeding Daniel Webster. A large majority of the Committee, representing a comparable majority in the House, favored the repeal and reported a bill for the purpose. But Buchanan showed that "though he may have quit the Federalist Party, he had not abandoned Federalist doctrine." He prepared his report, got the signatures of two of his committee members, and took his case to the House.[49]

The Constitution gave to the federal courts jurisdiction in "all cases in law and equity, arising under this Constitution, the laws of the United States, and treaties." The 25th section of the Act of 1789 further defined this general grant, assigning to the Supreme Court final judgment in three classes of cases: 1) those in which a state court should decide that a law or treaty of the United States was void; 2) those in which the validity of a state law was called in question on the ground that it violated the federal Constitution; and 3) cases involving appellate jurisdiction on construction of the Constitution, laws, and treaties of the United States when their protection had been invoked, but denied, to parties in state suits.

Buchanan rested his defense of these jurisdictions of the Supreme Court upon three propositions. First, he said, "it ought to be the chief object of all Governments to protect individual rights." Without the 25th Section, state courts could deny any or all of the rights supposed to be guaranteed to citizens by the federal Constitution, and the citizen so deprived of his rights would have no recourse.

Second, there could be no uniformity in the construction of the federal Constitution, of the laws of Congress, or of treaties, without the ultimate jurisdiction of the Supreme Court. Without the 25th Section, each state could decide for itself the meaning of a phrase in the Constitution or federal statute or treaty. Thus, a federal law or international agreement might be valid in one state and in another be held void.

Third, the only alternative to these jurisdictions of the Supreme Court was disunion. "The chief evil which existed under the old confederation, and which gave birth to the present constitution, was, that the General Government could not act directly upon the people, but only by requisition upon sovereign States. The present Constitution was intended to enable the Government of the United States to act immediately upon the people of the States, and to carry its own laws into execution by virtue of its own authority."

"We have in this country," he concluded, "an authority much higher than that of the sovereign States. It is the authority of the sovereign people of each State. In their State Conventions, they ratified the Constitution of the United States; and so far as the Constitution has deprived the States of any of the attributes of sovereignty, they are bound by it, because such was the will of the people. The Constitution thus called into existence by the will of the people of the several States, has declared *itself* ... to be 'the supreme law of the land'; and the judges in every State shall be bound thereby."[50]

Buchanan presented the case for the Minority Report with such force that the House adopted it by a vote of 138 to 51. Buchanan properly considered it "a most signal and permanent victory for national unity and federal sovereignty." Personally it was a victory of the constitutional lawyer over the party politician, but in a larger sense it preserved the national jurisdiction of the Supreme Court. Had the popular sentiment for repeal of the 25th Section prevailed, wrote a modern judge, "who can say that the eloquence of Webster or the political skill of Lincoln or the military genius of Grant would have availed to save the Union from disintegration?"[51] More likely, none of these would ever have had the chance to try his powers.

As a final flourish to his Congressional career, Buchanan acted as chief manager of the prosecution of Judge James H. Peck of Missouri, against whom the Judiciary Committee reported articles of impeachment in March, 1830. Judge Peck had imprisoned and disbarred a St. Louis attorney, Luke E. Lawless, citing him for contempt because Lawless had written newspaper articles which criticized Judge Peck's opinions. Buchanan conducted the prosecution in collaboration with Henry R. Storrs of N. Y., one of the readiest debaters in the House, George McDuffie of South Carolina, Ambrose Spencer, for twenty years a Judge of the New York Supreme Court, and Charles Wickliffe, a lawyer from Kentucky. William Wirt and Jonathan Meredith acted as attorneys for Judge Peck.

The Senate acquitted Peck by a vote of 22 to 21. John Quincy Adams confided to his diary that it was "highly probable that Jackson did not wish to see an impeachment of a Judge, commenced by Buchanan, successfully carried through."[52]

The chairmanship of the Judiciary Committee and the impeachment proved a welcome distraction to Buchanan in the dismal days after the election of Governor Wolf and the triumph of the Family, but as the Jackson Administration grew older some new rays of hope began to shine for the Amalgamators. On January 4, 1830, President Jackson appointed Henry Baldwin to a seat on the Supreme Court left vacant by the death of Judge Bushrod Washington in November, 1829. The Family had pushed hard to have John Bannister Gibson appointed, but the Buchanan men pressed for Baldwin, urging as a main reason for choosing him the fact that the Calhoun newspapers in Pennsylvania and the national capital had been denouncing Baldwin so bitterly.[53] In the Senate, Baldwin's nomination was approved by everyone except the two members from South Carolina.

Within eighteen months, events occurred which completely destroyed Calhoun's chances for the presidency as a successor of Jackson, estranged the Calhoun forces in Pennsylvania from the president, and revived the influence of Buchanan and his Amalgamators. The violent threats of South Carolina to nullify the federal tariff laws, the dramatic uncloseting of the long-hidden skeleton of Calhoun's attack on Jackson during the Florida war of 1818-1819, and the breakup of the Cabinet over the Peggy Eaton affair, which for months had been the main topic of drawing room conversation in Washington, made it clear to all that Jackson and Calhoun had come to the parting of the ways. The vice-president's break with Jackson left the Family party of Pennsylvania with little influence in the national capital. As the feud sharpened it became a certainty that Jackson would accept a second term. Much as the Family party tried to

76

prevent it, Buchanan and his associates joined with Jackson's promoter, William B. Lewis, to have Pennsylvania take the lead in calling for the renomination of "Old Andy" and got the State Legislature to issue a formal call on February 3, 1831.[54]

By the spring of 1831, at Van Buren's suggestion, the national Cabinet dissolved and all the Calhoun men in it, including Ingham, quit the Jackson Administration. This set-back to the prestige of the Family proved a life-giving tonic to the Amalgamators, who now tried to get Jackson to appoint Buchanan to the Attorney-Generalship, or possibly to the Treasury Department.[55] Van Buren astutely obtained for George Washington Buchanan, James's brother, an appointment as federal attorney for the Pittsburgh district.[56]

At the same time Buchanan's friends began to plug him for the vice-presidency, as running mate to Jackson in 1832. Newspapers in Amalgamation counties in Pennsylvania and in nearby states where Buchanan had supporters placed his name on their mastheads under Jackson's and called public meetings to endorse the plan. Buchanan had already announced his determination to retire from politics and had turned down an invitation to run for the State Legislature, but the vice-presidency was a little different. The Calhoun movement which had long dominated the Pennsylvania scene now lay prostrate; but Buchanan's party was still very much alive and he decided to let the vice-presidential business boom a little just to prove it.

6

RELUCTANT DIPLOMAT • 1831 - 1833

THE POLITICS OF THE RUSSIAN MISSION

At the very time that there was so much talk about Buchanan for a Cabinet post or Buchanan for the vice-presidency, he received a letter from John Henry Eaton. In it Eaton invited him to become the Minister to Russia. The offer of the Russian Mission was a distinct letdown, since this assignment was a sort of genteel exile for those political figures who could neither be ignored nor trusted, and it came at a most inopportune moment. Buchanan had no desire to leave the United States when the political scene was so exciting. Ingham was out of the picture; his absence had created a vacuum in Pennsylvania politics, and Buchanan stood poised to fill it. Now that Ingham was also out of the Jackson Administration, people wanted to know what place Buchanan would have in it. For the time being he could give no hint of his plans for the immediate future, because Eaton had informed him that the invitation was to be considered entirely confidential.[1]

Buchanan replied to Eaton that he ought not to accept. He did not know French; he was very busy with his law practice and could not leave for some time without grave injury to his clients.[2] Eaton responded that the president would not ask him to leave for a year, "unless something more than is now expected arises." With this foggy assurance Buchanan had to be satisfied. He accepted the mission on June 12, and asked again that he be allowed to make public the appointment. His preparations for departure and his sudden interest in the study of French would give it away anyhow. "Is there any reason why I should . . . defer these preparations?" he plaintively inquired. Jackson scrawled an impatient note to Eaton which the Major forwarded: "Say to him in reply, to go on and make his preparations and let the newspapers make any comments that they may think proper, and mind them not. It is only necessary that he should not give them any information." There would be no announcement of the appointment until the present minister, John Randolph of Roanoke, returned to America; and no one knew when that would be.[3]

Throughout the summer of 1831 hints of all kinds of appointments, including the right one, circulated widely in the press, as did stories that Buchanan had been snubbed by Jackson.[4] His vice-presidential prospects continued to boom, but they were considerably hampered by the unconfirmed rumors that he would get a mission.[5] Another manifestation of Jackson's kindness which perturbed Buchanan was the appointment of his colleague in the Amalgamation plan, George B. Porter, to the governorship of Michigan Territory in place of General Lewis Cass, who was now in charge of the War Department. With Ingham "sacked" and Porter and Buchanan about to be shipped out, Pennsylvania's Democratic party was without leadership. The whole development appeared to be no accident; the parts fitted together too well. The object was to build a Van Buren party on the wreckage of both the Family and the Amalgamation factions.

During July Buchanan had a bilious attack. He used it as an excuse to travel north under doctor's orders. In late August and early September he went "wandering about among the New Yorkers & the Yankees," centering his activities at Saratoga and Boston, while he tried to learn about American trade problems with the Baltic and the Black Sea.[6]

By the time he got back to Lancaster on September 9, he knew that his vice-presidential hopes had gone aglimmering. Pennsylvania would probably name Dallas as its candidate. Buchanan wrote to Jackson: "Now I have no wish to be a candidate for the Vice Presidency, on the contrary my nomination was got up without my consent & it is my intention to decline. . . . I think no man ought to hold that office but one of mature age who has obtained the confidence of the American people by distinguished services. . . . In short, he ought to be next in the confidence of the people to the President himself."[7] Shortly after Jackson received this, he publicly announced the appointment to Russia.

Buchanan's mother now learned for the first time of the assignment. "Would it not be practicable even now to decline its acceptance?" she asked. "Your political career has been of that description which ought to gratify your *ambition* & as to pecuniary matters, they are no object to you. If you can consistently with the character of a gentleman & a man of honor, decline, how great a gratification it will be to me. . . . P.S. At what time do you intend paying us that visit, previous to your departure from the country which gave you birth, and I expect, to me, the last visit? Do not disappoint me, but certainly come."[8] Elizabeth Speer Buchanan was sixty-six.

For the next several months, Buchanan tried to pull together all the loose ends of his many activities in preparation for a two-year absence. He visited Jackson in Washington and his mother at Mercersburg. He worked actively among Pennsylvania politicians to try to salvage something from the chaos which the previous months had brought, and answered

Jackson's effort to create a new Pennsylvania leadership by joining forces with his old rivals, Wolf and Dallas. Governor Wolf was in the worst predicament of all. Immediately upon hearing of Ingham's dismissal from the Cabinet, he had written asking Ingham to swallow his anger and refrain from attacking Jackson. Otherwise, everyone would assume "that the Administration of the State was in hostility with that of the Union—a position in which for the present I have no desire to be placed."[9]

In the Pennsylvania election for Senator on December 13, 1831, Buchanan agreed that his friend, Henry A. Muhlenberg, should throw his floor ballots to Dallas in order to prevent the election of an anti-Mason or an Adams man. Ironically, it was Barnard's seat which was to be filled. Nonetheless, anything but support of Dallas meant a complete destruction of the Jackson party, which would carry all down with it. Pennsylvania had an obligation to look out for her own interests, interests which a Van Buren control would readily sacrifice.

On January 12, 1832, Buchanan's nomination to the Russian Mission was almost unanimously confirmed by the U. S. Senate. On the 13th Van Buren's confirmation as Minister to Great Britain was defeated by the casting vote of Vice-President Calhoun—sweet revenge for Little Van's trick on the Woolens Bill vote of 1827. Within a week, Governor Wolf wrote a letter to Jackson which Benjamin Champneys showed to Buchanan prior to sending it to its destination. Wolf urged Jackson to appoint Buchanan to the English Mission, in place of Van Buren.[10]

Buchanan understood perfectly the meaning of the epistle and the mode of its delivery. Champneys had become the most unrelenting foe of Amalgamation. His visit was the olive branch, and Wolf's letter itself was a declaration to Andrew Jackson that the Democrats of Pennsylvania stood united for him, but not for Martin Van Buren.[11] As to the proposal, Buchanan sent his thanks to the governor and acknowledged that "London would to me be a pleasant exchange for St. Petersburg," but he added that he had no intention of pressing the suggestion.

In the meantime, he completed preparations for his new duties and for the supervision of his personal affairs during his absence. Edward Livingston, Secretary of State, wrote him detailed instructions for managing the Legation[12] and suggested that Buchanan, in case he did not wish to continue John Randolph Clay as Secretary of Legation, avail himself of the services of a department clerk, Dr. Robert Greenhow, who knew languages and had travelled much in Europe.[13] Buchanan selected Clay.

He gave power of attorney to two Lancaster friends, John Reynolds, editor of the *Lancaster Journal*, and Dr. Nathaniel W. Sample, instructing them to sell his library and all his personal property in Lancaster, to superintend the management of his real estate, to collect his dividends and interest, and to conduct prosecutions of all who failed to pay on time.

He authorized them to invest his income in state and federal bonds or in Lancaster real estate.[14]

On March 21, 1832, he left for Washington. He was in a dismal frame of mind, reasonably certain that he was permanently severing his connection with Lancaster and positive that he was about to embark on a pursuit "in which my heart never was: to leave the most free and happy country on earth for a despotism more severe than any which exists in Europe."[15]

In Washington he visited his friend Stephen Pleasanton of the Auditor's office and got the details of his pay straightened out. He would receive $9000 per year, an "outfit" fee of one year's salary, and also the cost of passage home. The Legation was provided with a special contingent fund for the purchase of postage, newspapers, minor gifts, and stationery.[16] He made final arrangements for John W. Barry, of the U. S. Army, a son of Postmaster General William T. Barry, to accompany him as private secretary, and acquired the services of a mulatto servant, Edward Landrick, as valet.

Returning to Lancaster he found everything in order except his arrangements with the English Presbyterian Church, where he was a regular worshipper, although as yet not a member. While attending service on April 1, his last Sunday in Lancaster, he was reminded that his rent for Pew 35 was due, and wrote a check to cover the matter.[17]

ST. PETERSBURG

At New York the following Sunday he boarded the "Silas Richards." "I suffered from seasickness during nearly the whole voyage," he confided to his diary. He was particularly impressed and respectful of Captain Henry Holdridge, who had crossed the Atlantic 88 times. "An excellent seaman," he called him, and "possessed of much more information than could have been expected from one in his profession." After a 25-day voyage, they arrived at Liverpool, where Buchanan presided at the passengers' dinner for Captain Holdridge at "The Star and Garter." A year later, however, after he had had more sailing experience, he began to refer to Holdridge as "the Yankee captain with whom I crossed the Atlantic, who would carry sail in a hurricane."[18]

Buchanan's two-week sojourn in England was a whirl of sight-seeing and social life to which he responded with a combination of the eager enthusiasm of a touring schoolmarm and the steely-eyed appraisal of an investment banker. Mr. Ogden, the consul at Liverpool, inaugurated his excursion into high life by having him invited to the estate of Mr. William Brown, the international banker. "Both its external and internal appearance," wrote Buchanan, very much impressed, "prove the wealth and the taste of its opulent and hospitable owner." Ogden warned Buchanan of the need for security in diplomatic activity and gave him a special cipher he had invented—"so that my secretary may decipher one letter and yet know nothing about any other."[19]

After five days in Liverpool, he set out for Manchester on the railroad—his first ride in this new contrivance: "a distance of thirty miles —in one hour and twenty-five minutes," and through two tunnels. On the way to London he made the basic stops—Birmingham, Kenilworth Castle, Warwick Castle, Stratford upon Avon, Blenheim, and Oxford. After several weeks in London he proceeded to Hamburg and on May 24 set sail for Lubeck and St. Petersburg, arriving at his destination on June 2.

The Russian capital, built by order of Peter the Great a century before, was at this time one of the most brilliant cities in the world: a center of literature, music, the theater and ballet. Built on the delta through which the Neva River flows into the Gulf of Finland, it served as Russia's "window looking out on Europe." Along its main avenue, the Nevsky Prospekt, stood the Winter Palace and the Mariinsky Palace, the great-domed cathedral of St. Isaac, and the Admiralty Palace crowned with delicate spires. Buchanan had learned something of St. Petersburg from the charming Mrs. George W. Campbell who had been a great favorite of the late Czar Alexander while her husband served as American Minister to Russia some years before. He had also talked with Baron Krudener, Russian Minister to Washington, and to his delicate blonde wife who, in earlier days, had been a power at Alexander's Court. He had been prepared for lavish splendor, but the reality exceeded his expectations.

By the middle of June he had rented as Legation headquarters the Ville Dame Brockhauser at Wassilioshoff on the Grand Neva #65, a site which commanded a delightful view of the river and of all the activity of the port, though it was considerably removed from the activities of the government. The villa was spacious, with a courtyard, stables for six horses, a carriage and sleigh house, and a special apartment for the servants. Buchanan took it furnished with bronzes, marbles, tables, buffets, silverware, linen, pottery, porcelains, crystal, cooking utensils, and other household appurtenances—enough equipment to provide regular settings for six and occasional parties of thirty.[20]

On June 11 he presented his letter of credence to the Emperor Nicholas I. After the usual exchange of civilities the monarch rather surprised the new envoy by coming forward, shaking hands with warmth and cordiality, and wishing him a happy stay in the city. The Empress, too, was congenial, and very talkative. She thought the Americans were wise to keep out of European troubles, because they had enough of their own at home, especially with the southern states and their resistance to the tariff. "I endeavored in a few words to explain this subject to her," said Buchanan, "but she still persisted in expressing the same opinion, and, of course, I would not argue the point."[21]

Nicholas, who had assumed the throne upon the death of his elder brother Alexander in 1825, had been trained more for war than for statecraft. Although he liked to pose as "a simple, honest officer and servant of the state," his political ingenuity scarcely extended beyond the imposition of police rule throughout his domain. Just the year before Buchanan's arrival, he had ruthlessly crushed a liberal uprising in Poland under the slogan, "orthodoxy, autocracy and national unity." In foreign policy he was especially interested in maintaining the integrity of Turkey in order that no other powers could force an entry into the Black Sea.

Buchanan soon had a long conversation with Count Nesselrode, the Russian Foreign Minister, about the objectives of his mission. He found that Nesselrode already knew a good deal about him from Prince Lieven, the Russian Minister in London, and Baron Krudener, the Minister to the United States who was happily on furlough at St. Petersburg that summer. There was little new business to introduce. John Randolph, in his short sojourn in the city, had already presented to the Foreign Office a complete file of papers covering the wish of the United States to conclude a treaty of navigation and commerce and a treaty concerning maritime rights with Russia. As the Russian Ministry had been in possession of all the documents for over a year and had given no hint whether it wished to treat on either subject, Buchanan determined for the present not to ask Count Nesselrode for any answer to the propositions made by Mr. Randolph. "I shall wait until I become better acquainted with the views and wishes of the Imperial Ministry," he said, "before I introduce the Negotiation to their attention, or do any act which can subject me to the charge of importunity."[22]

The first months were both leisurely and exciting. Buchanan had occasional conferences with Baron Krudener and with Count Nesselrode, feeling out their sentiments on the pending negotiation, but mostly he sat in the Legation studying French, reading international law, writing letters home, and wishing for mail. In fact, he had not been in St. Petersburg twenty-four hours before he wrote to Secretary of State Livingston the extraordinary fact that the American Legation had received no news from the home country for over a year, and its personnel had no idea what might be going on in the United States. He requested the immediate inauguration of a monthly courier service to London.

To his friend, John Reynolds, he gave a pretty clear picture of his state of mind and mode of life. "I would much rather for my own part occupy a seat in the Senate or in the House; I say this not from despondency, for that would be without reason; but simply from the circumstance that a man devoted to free principles cannot be happy in the midst of slavery.

"So far as it regards my own person I shall dress so as not to compromise the Republican simplicity of my country. Over my equipage I have in a manner no control. I must submit to the established customs, or forfeit many of the most essential privileges of a foreign minister. If I were to drive through the streets of Lancaster in the same style I do here, I should soon have a mob of men, women & children in my train. I must drive four horses; otherwise I could not go to court. My driver like the rest is a Russian with a long flowing black beard, dressed in the peculiar costume of his country. There is a postilion on the leader; but what is the most ridiculous of all is the Chasseur who stands behind. He is decked out in his uniform more gaudy than that of our Militia Generals with a sword by his side & a large chapeau on his head surmounted by a plume of feathers. It is this dress which constitutes the peculiar badge of a foreign minister. The soldiers at their stations present arms to the carriage, on the streets they take off their hats to it, & it is everywhere received with so much deference, that I feel ashamed of myself whenever I pass through the City. It is ridiculous flummery. . . .

"What a dunce I was not to have learned the German language! It would have been almost as useful to me here as the French. I now understand the latter tolerably well; but it will be long before I shall speak it fluently.

"When you write, do not say anything which would be offensive to the Government. They are not very delicate about opening letters here. You had better perhaps give this caution to my other friends. . . . We can send out what we please by American Captains, but everything which comes in must pass through the Post-Office."[23]

The treaty negotiation proceeded in a most peculiar and erratic manner. Buchanan, after study of the documents, discovered that Randolph's arguments all urged the benefits of the projected treaty to the people of the United States but failed to present the corresponding advantages to Russia. Buchanan proposed to convince the Imperial Ministry that the treaty would also promote the best interests of Russia.[24] Good diplomacy always emphasized the *quid pro quo*.

In an unofficial talk with Baron Krudener he learned, with some surprise, that Russia was much irritated by the American tariff of 1828 and held it accountable for a sharp decline in trade. Buchanan got late statistics to prove that Russo-American trade had greatly increased in 1831 and 1832; the sugar refining plants around St. Petersburg had received almost all of their imported raw sugar from the U. S. ships alone. He made it plain that with a treaty giving security to commercial enterprise, hundreds of American vessels would ply the rich Black Sea area, bringing in needed raw materials from all over the world and taking back hemp and bar iron. At St. Petersburg the sugar import trade would be greatly enlarged, and the wool export comparably increased. Russian internal manufacture would be greatly diversified by the import of more raw materials and Russian shipping would be stimulated by the export of her excess raw materials to America.

Krudener insisted, however, that Russia desired a relaxation of the tariff of 1828. It was with some excitement, therefore, that Buchanan received New York newspapers which contained a draft of the Tariff Bill of 1832, proposing reduction of duties on hemp, sail duck, and hammered iron. He informed Krudener of it immediately and received a call from him the next day. He said that this was pleasing news, and that Count Nesselrode was at that moment on his way to Peterhoff to bring the question of the commercial treaty to the attention of the Emperor.

For two weeks thereafter, the Russians pointedly ignored and avoided Buchanan. He was at a loss to know why until he gathered from some source that they had taken offense at some comments in the recently arrived batch of American newspapers (which the Russian government agents had perused with care before delivering them to the American Legation). Obviously, Krudener and his colleagues had known of the tariff revision before Buchanan did.

Eventually, Krudener called and stayed to dinner but appeared "studiously to avoid every allusion to the proposed negotiation." After they rose from the table, the Baron casually remarked that the Emperor had referred the American proposals to Count Cancrene, the Minister of Finance.

This news dumfounded Buchanan. Noting his confusion, Krudener asked: "Do you not consult your Secretary of the Treasury on similar occasions?"

"But you mean," replied Buchanan, "that the Treaty has been before the Emperor?"

"Yes, certainly," replied Krudener, laughing.

Buchanan promptly obtained an audience with Count Nesselrode and found Baron Krudener already in the chamber. They talked freely, and both Russians conveyed the impression that it was almost a certainty that a commercial treaty would be concluded. Buchanan now believed that if the tariff bill passed, "without any essential change in the duties proposed on Russian productions, . . . we shall obtain a Treaty without much difficulty."[25]

Baron Krudener left for the United States in the middle of August. Buchanan hurried off letters to his friends Reynolds, Reigart, and Jenkins, informing them that the Baron intended to visit Lancaster County to examine its agriculture and urging them to "treat him kindly and with special distinction. . . . He is fond of the good things of this life & certainly I have not yet seen any place where they abound more than in Lancaster."[26]

On August 19, an American ship brought news to Buchanan that the Tariff of 1832 had passed both houses of Congress and had become law without the president's signature. He promptly transmitted to Nesselrode the information that duties on iron were down from $22.40 to $18 per ton; on sail duck, from 12½ cents per square yard to 15 per cent ad valorem (a radical reduction); and on hemp, from $60 to $40 per ton. He hoped the commercial treaty would now be speedily negotiated in order that it could be acted upon by Congress soon enough to give shippers time to prepare for spring voyages.

Then a month and a half passed without a word. Rumor said that the treaty would be rejected, and Buchanan heard several times that "it was vain for any nation to attempt to conclude a Treaty of Commerce with the Russian Government, whilst Count Cancrene continued as Minister of Finance."[27] Nonetheless, the American Minister tried to use his time to advantage. He contrived an interview with Baron Stieglitz, the Court Banker, who was a good friend of both Nesselrode and Cancrene and, perhaps of more importance, financed most of the Russian trade with the United States. He maintained a New York office and had large personal interests in the Black Sea area which improved trade would stimulate. Buchanan repeated all the arguments to him, invited him to dinner several times, and was gratified to discover later that Stieglitz had carried the conversation back to Nesselrode.[28]

The time passed pleasantly. Buchanan was much entertained, and responded by giving a series of stag parties. He found Russian society to be a strange compound of barbarism and civilization. The Russians employed the best French cooks but usually ate a sour soup that would have repulsed a Delaware Indian. The Russian ladies of high caste were beautiful and educated, yet they seemed hugely entertained when Buchanan told them fairy stories to which they responded like children.[29] Perhaps their credulity was not so remarkable when one considered that part of the reverence for Russia's patron saint, Alexander Nevsky, stemmed from the tradition that he once sailed up the Neva on a grindstone.[30]

Buchanan was greatly surprised to discover that the Russian nobility drank very little and that the ladies regularly sat with the men after dinner. "They have been too quiet for me!" he wrote to Reynolds. The lower classes were more convivial and drank "a species of hot white brandy enough to kill the Devil."[31]

One morning Captain Barry rushed into Buchanan's quarters in great agitation. He had just seen one of the Legation servants, a Russian, going through the papers in the record room. Buchanan frowned and told Barry to sit down. "Let him go," he said. "It can't possibly do us any harm, and it just might do some good." He had known, before he ever got to St. Petersburg, that there was no security of information in Russia, and he had made it a point never to put in writing anything that could give offense or disclose a secret. In practically every document he wrote, official and private, he included some comments highly complimentary to the Emperor.[32]

Then, in October, Buchanan received a formal note stating that his Imperial Majesty declined to negotiate a commercial treaty. It was a blow, but it was not entirely unexpected. The note suggested several reasons for the negative decision: the *project* did not sufficiently protect Russian masters against the desertion of their seamen in American ports; reciprocity was not clearly provided in all cases; and there was an implied limitation upon the right of the Russian government to change its tariff duties at will. Buchanan drafted a reply giving his solutions to the various problems and went to bed discouraged. He was certain that the reasons offered were not the real ones. The personal opposition of Count Cancrene, Minister of Finance, and Mr. de Bloudoff, Minister of Interior, had led the Emperor to reject negotiations.

A few days later, in response to a call from Count Nesselrode, he went to the Foreign Office and engaged in a conversation so amazing that, as he told Livingston, "you will, I think, be satisfied that but few more singular occurrences have been recorded in the history of modern diplomacy."

Nesselrode reviewed the rejection of the treaty, and mentioned emphatically that Cancrene and de Bloudoff had brought the Emperor, very reluctantly, to their point of view. Then he dropped his wary diplomatic manner, became "frank and candid," and told the astonished Buchanan that if he should rewrite his modifications to the treaty, stressing certain points which the Count would mention, he would take it straight to the Emperor, with the hope that it would be accepted.

Buchanan returned to the Legation with his head swimming. Although he had too much to do to spend time speculating on this odd turn of events, he could not doubt that Nesselrode, for some reason, planned to put through the treaty against the wishes of the Cabinet, and that the Emperor was sympathetic. All day Tuesday he worked, and on Wednesday, after a short absence, found a card in the tray from the Baron de Brünnow, a Counsellor of State and confidential friend of Nesselrode. Thursday Brünnow came again and this time sat with Buchanan for half the day, carefully coaching him on the phraseology of his proposed note. Where Buchanan had written: "In pursuance of the *wish* expressed by His Excellency the Vice Chancellor," Brünnow wrote: "In pursuance of the *conversation* between his Excellency and the Vice Chancellor, &c." Brünnow must have laughed at Buchanan. To announce in the formal note that Nesselrode had engineered this plan would wreck the Count's career and destroy the possibility of further negotiations. The matter was to be kept in strictest secrecy, and the English Minister, in particular, must get no hint of what was maturing.[33]

Buchanan wrote happily to Livingston that he had "the fairest prospect of speedily concluding a Commercial Treaty," but despite the apparent rush of mid-October, nothing happened during November. He again began to wonder whether he had been hoaxed and complained to Nesselrode that Mr. Clay, his Legation Secretary, had already missed the last boat of the season while waiting to take the treaty to America. In December Buchanan had an idea. The Emperor's birthday was on the 18th of that month, an occasion celebrated with a grand fete. "I thought it might expedite the conclusion of the Treaty, . . . to manifest a wish that it might be signed on that anniversary," he said. Nesselrode was delighted, but he questioned whether copies could be prepared in time. Buchanan put extra secretaries into service to make the necessary drafts in English and in French and on December 15 learned that Nesselrode had been authorized to sign the treaty.[34]

On Tuesday morning, December 18, the whole diplomatic corps went to the Emperor's birthday levée. The corps was arranged in line to receive the Emperor and Empress, with Mr. Bligh, the newly arrived British Minister, in the lowest station. "You may judge of my astonishment," wrote Buchanan, "when the Emperor accosting me in French, in a tone of voice which could be heard all around, said, 'I signed the order yesterday that the Treaty should be executed according to your wishes,' & then immediately turning to Mr. Bligh asked him to become the interpreter of this information. . . . His astonishment and embarrassment were so striking, that I felt for him most sincerely. . . . There can be no doubt but all that occurred was designed on the part of the Emperor. . . . After the Emperor had retired, Mr. Bligh, in manifest confusion . . . asked me what kind of a Treaty we had been concluding with Russia. . . . This incident has already given rise to considerable speculation among the knowing ones of St. Petersburg." That afternoon Buchanan went to the Foreign Office and signed the treaty.[35]

The treaty opened a new era in Russian diplomacy. It was the first agreement of its kind which the Imperial Government had made with any nation, though others had long sought such a compact. It put the ships, cargoes, and crews of each country on a basis of reciprocity. The shippers of the one country were to receive the same treatment in the ports of the other that they received in their home ports. Furthermore, a "most favored nation" clause had been included. It was perfectly well known that more than a hundred American ships visited Russian ports for every Russian vessel sailing to America and that Russian discrimination against foreign shippers was much more extensive, petty, and exasperating than the American practice. Therefore, Buchanan and others could well ponder why the treaty had been made at all.

There were many aspects of high policy and domestic planning which formed a part of the decision. Europe was a powder keg, and Russia needed friends who could carry supplies to her if she became involved in war. England had just reached an agreement with France on the Belgian question, a coalition that weakened Russia's position in the balance of power. Russia desired to improve the economy of her southern regions around the Black Sea, to increase her merchant marine, and to achieve greater internal diversification. A fight for cabinet prestige between Nesselrode and Cancrene had something to do with the result. But probably most important of all was the Polish question. Only later did Buchanan begin to understand what the Emperor really expected of him.

Buchanan noted an immediate change in the attitude of the Russian nobles who now summoned him from his comparative isolation across the Neva to their balls and parties. He reported becoming "a favorite in several of their first families,"[36] and that both the Emperor and Empress had "been marked in their attentions" to him, "indeed, so much so as to excite some little observation & perhaps envy." Baron Cancrene made the *amende honorable*, praising the treaty and paying Buchanan compliments "of such a character," he wrote, "as I know I do not deserve, and therefore I shall not repeat."[37] On several occasions, the Emperor while walking along the streets of the city in plain dress, as was his custom, encountered the American Minister and made it a point to stop and chat with him, calling him "Buchanan."[38] The Empress, whom Buchanan praised as a fine dancer, often took him as a partner at court balls.[39] It was no wonder that Buchanan found his prestige miraculously mounting. For a time he took all these attentions at face value, though somewhat astonished, for he knew he possessed "but few of the requisites for being successful in St. Petersburg society."[40] Then an affair began to develop which suggested some ulterior reasons for his lionization.

Emperor Nicholas was terribly sensitive to criticism which foreigners directed against him personally for instigating the horrible atrocities of the Polish War and for the enslavement of the Polish people thereafter. The newspapers of England and France heaped abuse upon him as the brutal author of the outrages, and the British Parliament had taken up the cry. For democratic insurgents all over Europe this was the best possible ammunition and they fired it broadside with abandon.

Buchanan's remarks in all his letters and notes to the State Department had been very temperate on the Polish issue, and in several instances he had stated that the atrocities proceeded only from the age-old hostility of the peoples and had been inflicted by unruly officers at the front; he indicated that the Emperor was not the author of the system; that, given the violent, unreasoning disposition of the Poles, the Emperor had no alternative but to use force with them. If Buchanan represented the United States, or could have any influence there; if the United States took a view of the Polish struggle more temperate than that of the western Europeans, this would have an important quieting effect on the revolutionary impulse, the Emperor reasoned. America was its home; America was its spokesman. If America saw mitigating factors, it would moderate the frenzy of European revolutionaries on the subject.

Two days after the treaty had been signed, Count Nesselrode began a conversation with Buchanan on an entirely new subject and in a manner so formal and solemn that Buchanan was wholly nonplussed. In two minutes more he was completely flabbergasted. The Washington *Globe*, it appeared, had been reprinting from the French and English journals some of the worst attacks against the Emperor. That these should appear in the administration organ at the very moment that the new treaty was in transit seemed in very poor taste. Would Buchanan not write to Jackson and request him to have the editor of the *Globe* stop printing this kind of material and to direct him to publish some compliments about the Emperor? Nesselrode had a note on the subject already prepared which Buchanan could send to the president.

Buchanan saw in an instant what he was up against. He tried to explain that in the United States even the president could not tell a newspaper editor what to print; there was no government control; in fact, the Constitution forbade such control. Why, Buchanan asked, did not the Russian papers print some denials of the French and English articles and have them translated and circulated so that the American editors would have the other side of the story? He himself had tried to get at the truth of recent events in Poland but had not been able to learn anything even in St. Petersburg. He would welcome the true story, and he was sure that the American editors also would.

But Nesselrode persisted, wondered why the *Globe* was called an "official" paper if it was entirely independent of the government, and suggested "that General Jackson himself must certainly have some influence over the editor." Buchanan finally concluded the subject by telling a story about Baron Sacken who had, on one occasion, complained to Jackson of the attacks which had been made upon the Emperor in the American newspapers. In reply, the president requested him to examine the papers again, and "if they did not contain a hundred articles abusing himself to every one that attacked His Imperial Majesty, he would then agree there was cause for complaint."[41] Nesselrode laughed heartily, passed to other matters, and Buchanan thought he had disposed of the problem. He was wrong.

90

On January 9, a cart drew up before #65 Grand Neva, where the draymen removed three large boxes, struggled with their load into the Legation, and presented a bill for 1638 rubles—$330, for postage! Until this day, James Buchanan had never received a single piece of mail from the Department of State; now he got nearly half a ton of it: files of American newspapers, journals of the House and Senate, books, dispatches, and letters. "Such a mass was never sent by Mail before from Havre to St. Petersburg," he exclaimed.

By the time Buchanan had waded through the most recent of this material he learned a few things. Baron Sacken, temporarily in charge of the Russian Mission at Washington, had become involved in a squabble with Livingston and Jackson which Nesselrode presumably knew all about. The Baron had again asked for some action to put an end to the *Globe* articles. When he received no satisfaction, he wrote a note, charging Jackson with insincerity; he proclaimed friendship for Russia in his messages to Congress but encouraged the *Globe* to print articles abusive of the Emperor. This was a pretty mess to be brewing at the very time that the treaty was about to come up for discussion in the Senate!

Livingston, apparently, expected Sacken to send a letter withdrawing the charge against Jackson, but it had not yet been received. Buchanan talked to Nesselrode about this unfortunate business and learned that no disavowal was likely to be made, primarily because Sacken insisted that he had shown his letter informally to the Secretary of State before sending it, and that Livingston had read and approved it![42] Buchanan thought that there must be some misunderstanding, and he promised to get more exact information. What was the news of the treaty? asked Nesselrode. The Emperor had acted with great dispatch; he was very eager to know when the United States would ratify. Buchanan had no idea. The only late word he got from America was through "scraps contained in English newspapers kindly furnished . . . by Mr. Bligh, & an occasional remark in the letters received from the United States by Baron Steiglitz."

The last three months of the Mission were like scenes from a comic opera. Buchanan's position, as he came to learn with shock after shock, was that of the only man in the cast who did not know the plot beforehand. The cause was the combination of the assininity with which the State Department handled its communications and the assiduity with which the Russian secret police tapped them.

Not until July 31, for example, did Buchanan receive any information from Livingston. He had indeed read the Sacken letter in advance and *had not objected to it*! This took all the wind out of Buchanan's sails. It was obvious that Nesselrode had had a copy of Livingston's note for months, for the American chargé at Paris—"a jack-ass" Buchanan called him with kindness—had placed all the dispatches in the hands of the

Russian Embassy to be forwarded. The Russians copied everything, sent duplicates to their own Ministry, and delivered the originals, with all seals broken, to Buchanan four months later.

Apparently the Russians read everything before Buchanan did. Nesselrode had known about the passage of the American tariff three weeks before Buchanan had gotten word of it—and that from unofficial sources. Buchanan pleaded with the State Department never to send dispatches by mail "unless they be of such a character that they may be perused & copied not only at St. Petersburg, but in all the Governments through which they may have passed." Never once, he said, had he received a piece of mail which had not been opened. "The letters have been sent to me either almost open, or with such awkward imitation of the seals as to excite merriment. The Post Office Eagle here is a sorry bird."[43]

By the end of May Buchanan had still not heard officially that the treaty had been ratified by the Senate. The Emperor, at an audience, inquired "with a good deal of earnestness in his manner" about the ratification, and Buchanan had to answer lamely that he had no official verification, but he had heard indirectly that the treaty had been ratified some months ago.

Worst of all, the State Department failed to send any reply to Buchanan's Dispatch #8, describing the inside mechanics of the commercial treaty negotiation and requesting instructions about the treaty on maritime rights, which was still pending. Buchanan feared that a reply might have been "transmitted through the Russian Post office." Eventually the answer came, but it was too late.

The maritime treaty was intended to define the legal nature of blockades, to enumerate articles constituting contraband of war, and to establish the principle that "free ships make free goods." When Buchanan proposed that talks be instituted on the maritime treaty he soon discovered that Nesselrode was "not disposed to enter upon the subject." Buchanan's disappointment was all the more bitter, for Jackson had written, not too enthusiastically, after the conclusion of the commercial treaty—"[it] is as good a one as we could expect . . . , and if you can close the other as satisfactory, it will be a happy result."[44] But Nesselrode had shut the door, and there was no use pushing at it.

THE CONCLUSION OF THE MISSION

More happily, Jackson had given Buchanan permission to come home whenever he wished. He had feared he was in for a two-year tour of duty, but he might be able to get out of Russia that summer and be home in time for the next senatorial elections. Feeling that he had done all he could, he took advantage of the temporary lull in Legation business to travel to the interior of Russia. During June he went to Novgorod and Moscow. At the end of the month he was back at the Legation, refreshed by his vacation, and ready to make plans for his return home.[45]

Buchanan's personal world had changed with astonishing and sobering rapidity. His sister Harriet had married without even telling him in advance, and he chided her for her neglect. "I felt toward you both as a father & as a brother. . . . Do not for a moment suppose that I am offended; I am only disappointed. I confess I did not feel very anxious that you should be married. This indifference was no doubt partly selfish. I had often indulged the hope that we might spend the evening of our days together in my family."[46] His youngest brother, Edward, had joined the ministry largely to gratify the hope of his mother that one of her children should be a clergyman. He, too, had married. He did not mention the girl, though James later learned it was Ann Eliza Foster of Pittsburgh, whose brother was the young song writer, Stephen Collins Foster.[47]

His favorite brother, George, a brilliant young lawyer with whom James had hoped to share practice, had died of tuberculosis. In July, just before leaving St. Petersburg, he received the news that his mother had died two months earlier. His best drinking crony in Lancaster, George Louis Wager, was critically ill. Washington Hopkins, son of his old preceptor and a close friend, had died. To Reynolds he wrote: "How many of my friends and acquaintances shall I miss from the social circle after an absence of less than two short years. . . . Truly this is not our abiding place."[48]

Since he was to return much earlier than he had expected, Buchanan now turned his thoughts to his private business. During his absence Reynolds and Sample had managed his estate well. They had bought a house for him in Lancaster; it was the former home of Robert Coleman. "Although I do not think it was a great bargain," he wrote to Reynolds, "I feel as much indebted to you & the Doctor as if you had got it cheaper."[49]

Reynolds reported that he had banked $12,268 from Buchanan's local enterprises: about $5,000 interest from investments such as bonds, mortgages, and loans and the rest from the collection of debts. He had purchased several properties for investment and had finally sold the Sterrett Gap property for $6,500. Furthermore, he had paid for the Coleman estate and insured it. Financially, it had been a fairly good year for Buchanan.

Buchanan had his last audience at Peterhoff on Monday, August 5, 1833. Of this occasion he wrote that the Emperor "bade me adieu—and embraced and saluted me according to the Russian custom—a ceremony for which I was wholly unprepared, and which I had not anticipated. Whilst we were taking leave, he told me to tell General Jackson to send him another Minister exactly like myself. He wished for no better . . . Thus has my mission terminated."[50]

7

DAYS OF DECISION • 1833 - 1834

RETURN FROM RUSSIA

Buchanan took a tour of the Continent on his way home, travelling by steamboat from St. Petersburg to Lubeck, then to Hamburg, Amsterdam, the Hague, Brussels, Paris, London, Edinburgh, Glasgow, Belfast, Dublin, and at last to Liverpool for passage to Philadelphia. At Hamburg he visited for several days with Henry Wheaton, the international lawyer, before starting his tour of the Low Countries and the Rhine Valley. "Although not given to ecstasies," he wrote, "I felt a little romantic in descending the Rhine. . . . I never took much to the Rhenish until I got into its native country. There I became acclimated to it & now feel that the taste will accompany me through life. But I have some talent in this line."[1]

In Paris he had to resume the role of an active diplomat for he discovered that he was the only American Minister in western Europe and, with a threat of war on the horizon, he had to act as spokesman for his country. Lafayette called on him, and the French Foreign Minister, the Duke de Broglie, sought him out, as did Count Pozzo di Porgo, Russian Ambassador at Paris.[2]

De Broglie expressed his regret that there had been unpleasantness over the recent claims dispute and hoped that the French Chamber of Deputies would soon appropriate funds to meet the provisions of the American Treaty and terminate the difficulty. Count Porgo of Russia made fun of the French—"a turbulent and restless people." Buchanan should sit in on some sessions of the Chamber of Deputies—"They were like cats, all in a passion, and all making a noise, and afterwards laughing; wholly unfit for liberty." They wanted Napoleon and glory again, not liberty.[3] In case of war, the central Europeans would stick together; there was no telling what would happen with England and France except that England would try to raid neutral commerce and set up illegal blockades. He hoped the United States would not stand for such nonsense. Buchanan agreed and reminded him that this was the object of the maritime treaty he had

95

tried to negotiate. The very reason why it was refused, replied Borgo. It would have been an obvious attack by Russia on England; would have set her aflame, possibly have been a trigger for the very war all were trying to avoid.

In London, Buchanan found himself in the heart of European power politics. All the members of the London Conference to settle the fate of Belgium were still in residence. At dinner at Prince Lieven's in the Russian embassy he sat with Talleyrand of France, Esterhazy of Austria, Bülow of Prussia and Lord Palmerston of Britain. Talleyrand, in conversation later, asked him about the family of Alexander Hamilton and told him the story of the day Aaron Burr had sent up his card. "I returned the card," said Talleyrand, "with a message that I had the portrait of General Hamilton hanging up in my parlor."[4]

Buchanan conferred and dined with Palmerston and found him unusually interested in promoting friendly relations between England and the United States. Esterhazy and Bülow assured Buchanan that their governments hoped soon to open diplomatic relations with the Americans. "Our position in the world is now one of much importance," he wrote to Jackson. "Indeed, the freedom and friendship with which I have been treated everywhere are an evidence of the high character of our Country abroad."[5]

Buchanan finally journeyed to the Emerald Isle where he visited the home of his ancestors at Ramelton. "There I sinned much in the article of hot whiskey toddy which they term punch," he wrote to Reynolds. "The Irish women are delightful."[6]

The autumn passage of the North Atlantic gave Buchanan some time to reflect upon recent events and his political prospects. He had gone to St. Petersburg as a used-up politician and was returning something of a hero. Though a tyro in diplomacy he had, with a little practical common sense, knowledge, and downright honesty, met successfully on their own ground the most adroit and skillful politicians in the world. The emperors and empresses, the dukes and counts, the chancellors and ministers who wore the medals and ribbons seemed to him not much better informed than he was. For the first time in his life he began to think seriously about the presidency. Why not? He could do it.[7]

DEMORALIZED DEMOCRATS

The politics of Pennsylvania had changed during Buchanan's absence. After he had pulled out of the vice-presidential race, Senators Wilkins and Dallas had jumped into the contest and got the endorsement of the Pennsylvania convention in 1832. Van Buren, in ten ballots at Harrisburg,

96

never received more than 4 out of 132 votes.[8]   But at the national Democratic Convention at Baltimore in May, Pennsylvania's entire block of 30 votes went to Van Buren.   Simon Cameron took credit for this astonishing defiance of the instructions of the state convention.   "I had more enjoyment," he told Buchanan, "by pestering the folks at Harrisburg, until they actually swallowed the dose of Van Burenism, than I ever had in anything connected with politics."[9]   Dallas and Wilkins completed their downfall by voting in the Senate for a recharter of the Bank of the United States. After Jackson's veto of the recharter bill, and his triumphant re-election with Van Buren as vice-president, the political stock of Wilkins, Dallas and Co. fell to a record low.

Buchanan took it for granted that Van Buren would succeed Jackson in 1836, but he told Reynolds that he had "some misgivings upon this subject," and would remain uncommitted "because I cannot see clearly the course of duty."   "I shall support the candidate of the party who may be regularly nominated," he said.   "To Mr. V. B. I have no personal objection."[10]

Pennsylvania deserved a Cabinet post as reward for her steady support of Jackson, but the internal politics of the state made it more difficult than ever to find the right man.   Jackson made the Treasury post available, but he would not have Wilkins or Dallas and was dubious about Buchanan.   Buchanan, on his part, gave no chance for a rejection when he learned his name was under discussion, writing that he would not for a moment accept "a Department so thankless, so laborious & so perplexing as that of the Treas."[11]   He did not want to be the agent to destroy the Bank of the United States.   The president eventually appointed William J. Duane of Philadelphia, a friend of Van Buren, who was not deeply involved in the state power struggle.

Buchanan considered himself lucky to have been out of Congress during 1832 and 1833.   The violent controversies over nullification and the Bank had battered the fortunes of many legislators, especially those from Pennsylvania.   The folks back home, with careless illogic, wanted the Bank rechartered, and their hero, Old Andy, re-elected—an easy combination for a backwoods farmer to vote for but a devilish hard program for a Congressman to live with at Washington.   The Bank vote was a test, there; any friend of the Bank was an enemy of Jackson.

Buchanan wanted to be a Senator and therefore had to clarify his stand on the Bank and nullification.   He told Jackson that he was pleased with the Bank veto, but added that he had been "inclined to be friendly to the recharter of the Bank of the United States."   He promised to vote for no Bank bill that did not remedy the objections raised in the veto message.[12]

South Carolina's Ordinance of Nullification of November 24, 1832, declaring the tariff laws of 1828 and 1832 "null, void, and no law,"

97

threw the nation into a panic. One of Buchanan's friends wrote: "I am firmly of the opinion *rebellion* will be the order of the day, accompanied by all its horrors." Duff Green was calling for recourse to the sword, and tempers were so inflamed that it was "indeed time for the people seriously to think of a civil war." Secretary of State Louis McLane reported that there was good reason to believe that the southerners were planning to set up a separate confederacy.[13]

Buchanan considered the nullification doctrine "against both the letter & spirit of the Constitution, as well as absurd in itself." He was not so sure about the question of secession; that problem was shrouded in "shadows, clouds & darkness." He had no sympathy for South Carolina in this nullification affair, but he would stand on his principle of strict construction and would not go along with some of his friends in toasting resolutions to a consolidated government.[14] The question of secession, he feared, would "be the touchstone of the party for the next twenty years." Secession was much more reasonable than nullification; it was no half-baked measure, but it meant revolution and dissolution of the nation. For this very reason Buchanan felt the fear of it would tend to destroy sectional parties, since no party would openly stand for war on the government.[15]

In Pennsylvania, George Wolf, who had been re-elected governor in 1832, wanted to keep on good terms with the national Administration. This meant he could no longer favor Wilkins and Dallas, both of whom had discredited themselves by supporting the Bank and opposing Van Buren. Dallas's short term as senator was about to expire, and all through the spring of 1833 the State Legislature had been balloting in vain to try to choose his successor. Dallas himself had no chance. Governor Wolf supported one of his cabinet, Samuel McKean, but he could not muster a majority partly because Buchanan's friends had lambasted McKean, despite Buchanan's intimation that no senator could be elected in opposition to the Governor. Finally the Legislature adjourned without naming a senator and postponed the decision until the next session in December 1833.[16]

Buchanan's friends worked hard for him. Had he been at home during the spring, they said, he would surely have won. To such letters, Buchanan replied that he could probably not win and did not much care; his public career was finished, and he was concerned only about what to do after his return. "To recommence the practice of the law in Lancaster would not be very agreeable. If my attachments for that place as well as my native state were not so strong, I should have no difficulty in arriving at a conclusion. I would at once go either to New York or Baltimore; and even if I should ever desire to rise to political distinction, I believe I could do it sooner in the latter place than in any part of Pennsylvania. What do you think of the project?"[17] It was quite obvious what his political managers would think of it. They would think that they had better get busy and line up the votes for that senatorship, or they would lose a good meal ticket. They went to work at the Fourth of July party barbecues where they proposed toasts to Buchanan for U. S. senator, for vice-president and, as George Plitt reported, even "for the Presidency itself."[18]

The "Susquehanna" docked in Philadelphia on November 24, 1833. A crowd of friends met Buchanan at the gangplank, escorted him to his quarters, and explained the details for a homecoming celebration—a huge $5-a-plate dinner that night. Dallas and his friends had refused to attend, but nonetheless the banquet hall was jammed.[19]

The balloting for senator would be renewed on December 7. That left two weeks for work. Simon Cameron, electioneering like a demon in Harrisburg, reported that he had drummed up thirty sure votes against McKean and thought that the Legislature would concentrate, after a few ballots, on Buchanan, but Buchanan remained fairly certain that McKean would win. The results of the election caused considerable astonishment. McKean was elected on the third ballot by a majority of 74 out of 130 votes, while Buchanan polled only five votes. There was more here than met the eye. The day before, Cameron asserted he had 43 votes promised against McKean, which were presumably to go to Buchanan. It was quite clear that Buchanan himself insisted that he did not want to tangle with the Wolf Administration at this moment.[20]

Between his return from Russia and the election, Buchanan had been to Washington to talk to the president. Jackson wanted Wolf and Buchanan to work together. The party needed them both; a split between them would throw Pennsylvania to the anti-Masons. Buchanan would get his chance later, for Jackson said he planned to send William Wilkins to Russia leaving the senatorship vacant, and Buchanan would then succeed Wilkins in Washington.[21] Buchanan knew this before McKean's election. He wrote to one of his backers: "Mr. Wilkins will soon obtain an Executive appointment. . . . I must be greatly mistaken if in that event I should not be elected to the Senate without difficulty." "All's well at Harrisburg," he concluded. "The party are firm & decided in support of Gen. Jackson's administration & in opposition to the Bank."[22]

The picture was clear. The Pennsylvania Senators who had voted for the Bank would be out, the anti-Bank men in; the State Administration would be at peace with the Buchanan party, and both groups reconciled to Van Buren. What could be a happier prospect for the election of 1836? Buchanan would join McKean in the Senate and stood a good chance for the vice-presidential nomination. Much as the Pennsylvania voters had formerly resented Van Buren, a union of Wolf and Buchanan in support of him should bring his opponents into the fold.[23]

SENATOR BUCHANAN

The year 1834 proved a busy one for Buchanan. He furnished and moved into the house where he had so often visited Ann Coleman. At night he lay awake thinking about the past and imagining what might have been. Damn the whole episode, he thought. They had both acted like lunatics. He still had Ann's letters tied in a packet with silk ribbon, but he wished sometimes that he could forget about their courtship and its aftermath. Now he had to find someone to take care of his house. For a while he had part-time servants, but he anticipated a tour of duty in Washington before long and wanted a permanent and trustworthy caretaker. He often ate his meals at the old White Swan Hotel on the town square. The proprietor, had a niece, Esther Parker, who was helping around the inn that summer. She had just turned 28, was clean, neat, happy in disposition, and a fine cook and housekeeper. Buchanan mentioned that he was looking for someone to manage his establishment at 42 East King Street and was a little surprised when Parker asked if he would consider Esther, or Miss Hetty, as he called her, for the job.[24]

Buchanan talked to the girl and set up a tentative arrangement: she should stay at the White Swan but work part-time at the King Street house during the summer and fall. If he should be elected to the Senate they would then decide whether she would take a permanent position as housekeeper, in which case he would, of course, expect her to move in, for he would be away most of the time and wanted the house occupied in his absence and ready for him on quick trips home.[25]

In the course of the summer he visited Washington, Philadelphia, Harrisburg, and New York. He also went to see his sister Jane, now Mrs. Elliott T. Lane, at Mercersburg, and while there inspected the grave-stones for his mother and brother George at nearby Spring Grove Cemetery. After a stop at Bedford Springs, he made a trip to Greensburg and saw his sister Harriet who had married the Reverend Robert Henry. There Buchanan learned to his dismay that Henry's family in Sheperdstown, Virginia, owned two slaves. This was political dynamite, and he lost no time in informing his brother-in-law that he wanted to buy those slaves into freedom. Buchanan drew up a deed of transfer, known as a "deed of complete emancipation" in Virginia, and a "deed of conditional manu-mission" in Pennsylvania, providing for the sale of Daphne Cook, aged 22, and Ann Cook, aged 5, by Ann D. Henry to James Buchanan, under the provisos that they should leave Virginia, that Daphne should give service to Buchanan for seven years and then become free, as provided in Penn-sylvania law; and that Ann should be bound until the age of 28—seven years past the age of maturity. Terms of the sale were to be arranged later. Anyway, thought Buchanan, this might help to solve his house-servant

100

problem.[26]   He found sister Harriet in poor health but rejoicing in her infant son, James Buchanan Henry.

At Pittsburgh he called on his loyal political manager, David Lynch, a hard-drinking, hard-hitting son of the canal-digging Irish, who had worked his way into politics by outroaring and outfighting the opposition.   Davy was not much appreciated by Pittsburgh society, but he rounded up votes whenever they were needed.   He was postmaster now, and doing well in every respect except that of getting the mail delivered. Buchanan then visited his sister Maria and her husband, Dr. Yates, in Meadville and his brother Edward who had moved there with his new wife, Eliza Foster.

About this time Buchanan became involved in some kind of a romantic affair which, like most of his episodes with women, remains more of a mystery than a story.   It centered at 518 Walnut Street, Philadelphia, the home of his friend Thomas Kittera.   With Kittera lived his widowed mother, his sister Ann, and three young girls all of whom had lost their mothers in infancy.   Two of them were Kittera's own nieces, Mary Kittera Snyder and Elizabeth Michael Snyder, children of his dead sister and "Handsome John" Snyder, a son of former Governor Simon Snyder. Grandmother Kittera and Aunt Ann had taken charge of these children after their mother's death in 1821.   The third child living at the Kittera's was Elizabeth Huston, the daughter of Buchanan's sister Sarah, who had died in 1825.   James at that time had made arrangements for the Huston baby to be raised by his friends, among girls her own age.

Whether Buchanan became attached to Aunt Ann or to Mary Snyder remains an unsolved puzzle.   There seem to be no letters extant between Buchanan and either of them, but there are a number of letters from Buchanan to Thomas Kittera which end with such cryptic statements as "be particular in giving my love to my intended," or refer to "my portion of the world's goods," or to that part of the family "in which I feel a peculiar interest."   Even from such crumbs of evidence one can discern that the affair in progress had little mark of the divine passion.   Rather, Buchanan's life-long friendship with all of the Kitteras suggests a marriage of convenience in the making, and probably with Mary when she became a few years older.[27]

The election of United States Senator to replace William Wilkins would be held on December 6, 1834.   Buchanan, apparently, believed he had this under control for he did little open electioneering and stayed out of Harrisburg.   Cameron was on hand acting as manager, but it is probable that Governor Wolf's known approval of Buchanan was the more effective force.

The anti-Masons backed Amos Ellmaker; the Whigs put up Joseph Lawrence; the Wolf Administration supported Buchanan; and the

101

Philadelphia Dallas faction used Joel B. Sutherland as its man to block Buchanan's election. If the anti-Masons and Whigs had been able to work together they could easily have elected a senator, but they found it impossible to cooperate. Buchanan got 25 votes on the first ballot, 42 on the second, 58 on the third, and a winning majority of 66, on the fourth and final vote. The large scattering of Democrats came over to Buchanan after it was clear that none of the others could win; but Sutherland held back until the very end, true to the Eleventh Hour tradition, and then threw his votes to the last remaining Buchanan competitor within his own party. Nothing was to be gained by the move. It simply demonstrated spectacularly that the Philadelphia City group would not bend the knee to anyone, be it Jackson, Wolf, or Buchanan.

There was one problem of the senatorship about which Buchanan worried a great deal. It had placed Wilkins and Dallas in an impossible situation, and it would plague any Pennsylvania senator as long as there was serious discussion in Washington of the tariff, the Bank, and the slavery issues. How could a senator work with the national Administration and with his own State Legislature when these two took opposite views on a particular bill, especially if the vote on it was made a party test at Washington or at Harrisburg?

Buchanan told the committee of the Legislature which informed him of his election that he held the right of instruction to be sacred. "If it did not exist," he said, "the servant would be superior to his master." He would either obey instructions from the State Legislature or resign, but in giving a vote against his own judgment, he continued, "I act merely as their agent. The responsibility is theirs, not mine."[28] In rare instances, however, he might question whether the instructions of the Legislature did in fact represent the public will, and in such a case he would try to speak for the people. He wanted to make his position very clear on the instruction doctrine, for if the anti-Masons got control of the State Legislature they would certainly try to embarrass him by ordering him to vote against all the Democratic measures.

This statement, he thought, protected him all around. When he voted with the national party under instruction, he could take the credit; when he voted against it under instruction, he could pass the buck to the State Legislature; when the issue was extremely obscure, he could do what he pleased by challenging the Legislature's interpretation of the public will; and if matters were hopeless, he could resign on principle without the appearance of losing his temper. "Be wise as the serpent and harmless as the dove." He hoped this set of rules conformed to the maxim.

The following week he went to Harrisburg with Cameron and had a high time. "No man has ever left Harrisburg under more favorable auspices," wrote Cameron. Back in Lancaster Buchanan went to the

Swan Hotel and engaged Miss Hetty as housekeeper. He then began to pack and to make final arrangements for the winter's absence. He called on his brother Edward who had just moved from Meadville to a new charge, the Protestant Episcopal Church in Leacock Township, Lancaster County, stopped in Philadelphia for a short visit to his "intended" at the Kitteras' and then hastened on to Washington.

On December 15, he appeared in the Senate, a cozy, clublike body in 1834. Buchanan had served with a good many of its members when they had been colleagues in the House. The desks surrounded the speaker's rostrum in concentric half-circles, the fireplaces were spaced evenly around the back wall, the small semicircular visitors' gallery was set above the main floor like boxes in a theater, and the red velvet drapes and mural paintings created an atmosphere at once elegant and intimate.

Van Buren presided with confidence, urbanity, and good humor. Buchanan's friend, Webster and his tormentor, Clay, sat on the other side of the chamber with their Whig colleagues: Ewing of Ohio, Frelinghuysen and Southard of New Jersey, Clayton of Delaware, and many others—too many; the Whigs had a majority. Among the Democrats were Benton of Missouri, Silas Wright of New York, W. R. King of Alabama, Felix Grundy of Tennessee, John Tyler of Virginia, McKean from Pennsylvania, and Calhoun. The latter had changed in many ways. No one was sure what party he belonged to—he had made a peculiar one for himself based on that "peculiar institution," the South. He no longer looked or acted like a favored presidential aspirant.

Buchanan realized that despite his original disappointment with the Russian Mission it had been a lucky break for him, for the United States in the period of his absence had been through violent political storms. The Senate had made war on Jackson, and the Hero had carried it into their own country. Buchanan considered himself fortunate in not getting the senatorial seat in 1833, when he would have had to vote for the resolution censuring Jackson in response to the instructions of the State Legislature. That act would have finished him; it ruined Wilkins, and made McKean powerless to promote patronage. But the main fight seemed now to be over.

Buchanan analyzed the political future in these terms. A Democrat had to be a Jacksonian, and that meant also being a follower of Van Buren. He had to give up all hopes for salvage of the Bank, and fight its recharter to the death. Pennsylvanians would not like to do this, but they could risk the demise of the Bank better than the hatred of Old Andy. The opposition, while seeming to unite under a new party name, the Whigs, was still disorganized; in fact, its main unity lay simply in hatred of Jackson himself. When he left the scene, the Whig party would disintegrate, and the Democrats were bound to win unless they foolishly permitted themselves to fall apart. If they could bury some of their local grudges and work together, their party was certain to control for years to come.

Buchanan wanted a part of that control; if possible, the most important part. He analyzed his duty logically, and proceeded to business. He had to support Jackson in the Senate undeviatingly. He would have to overcome the widespread hatred of Pennsylvanians for Van Buren. That would be more difficult but not impossible, for most politicians knew how their bread was buttered. He had to bring to a conclusion the Pennsylvania feud between the Amalgamators and the other Democrats. He had made his peace with Wolf, and had seen the Ingham-Dallas-Wilkins faction lose its influence, but there was still trouble in his own back yard. Henry A. Muhlenberg, his choice as successor to Barnard as a partner in control, had been flying the track. His friends thought he should have had the senatorship but, having sacrificed that to Buchanan, they felt that he surely ought to replace Wolf as governor in 1835. This would be fatal, for the Wolf-Buchanan team had just been brought firmly into Jackson's confidence. If Muhlenberg could wait until 1838, he and Buchanan could cut the whole cake. If not, well, God knew what the result would be.

8

THE GENTLEMAN FROM PENNSYLVANIA • 1835-1837

THE WOLVES AND THE MULES

After Buchanan's election to the Senate, many of his friends urged him to consummate the destruction of the Family party and to consolidate his triumph by ousting Wolf from the governorship and installing his own man, Henry A. Muhlenberg. Muhlenberg was ready for it. Most of the Amalgamators were ready for it. But Buchanan knew that the times were not ready. Governor Wolf after two terms in office had too much strength both in Harrisburg and in Washington to give up without a struggle, and in a fight he had this advantage: control of the county officeholders. The sensible course was to permit Wolf to fill his constitutional term and then, in 1838, let Muhlenberg succeed him as head of a united Democracy. It would be foolish to try to replace him in 1835 at the cost of a split party. But to convince the Muhlenberg enthusiasts that they should adopt the long-range plan was a different matter.

Buchanan tried to reconcile the contesting factions by bringing both parties to higher ground where they could agree. To this end he wrote letter after letter to friends all over the state, urging that the key factor should be loyalty to Van Buren. He fathered the idea that a resolution should be presented to Democratic members of the State Legislature, prior to the March 4 nominating convention, pledging positive support of Van Buren for the presidency. This proposal, he hoped, would focus attention on the larger aims of the party and provide a platform on which all could stand. And if they could agree to one thing, maybe they could reach an agreement on others. The scheme might have worked if precisely the right person had introduced the Van Buren resolution, but a staunch pro-Muhlenberg partisan brought it to the floor. Wolf's friends immediately sensed an attack on the governor and for this reason defeated it, though they wrote to Buchanan afterward assuring him that they had acted only from local motives and thought highly of Van Buren.[1]

105

No further conciliatory efforts were made, due to shortage of time; and the county meetings held for the purpose of selecting convention delegates became scenes of heated controversy and factional recrimination. In many counties the "Wolves" and the "Mules," as the rival partisans were called, held separate party conclaves and sent opposing delegations to Harrisburg where, for the first three days, each group contested the other's right to be seated. At length practically everyone was admitted. As soon as the delegates were accredited, the Mules won a close decision to adjourn the meeting and to reconvene at Lewistown on May 6. They hoped, by delaying and moving the convention out of Harrisburg, to improve their chances. But the Wolf minority remained in session and renominated the governor on March 7. The Mules met as scheduled, and placed their man officially in the race. Thus the schism was hopelessly widened. Two Democrats were going to run for the governorship, each with strong backing and each protesting loyalty to Buchanan and Van Buren.

Buchanan tried again. In a letter to Jacob Kern, Speaker of the State Senate, he urged the retirement of both candidates and the call for a new convention. Instead of easing the tension, this suggestion aggravated it, and both factions now tried to win Buchanan's support. The Mules promised to back him for the vice-presidency if he would come out for them, but he refused. "Will you forsake your friends," Muhlenberg wrote him, "and go over to your enemies who are only waiting opportunity to cut your throat?"[2] Wolf, on his part, gratified Buchanan by appointing Thomas Kittera to a judgeship.[3]

After the formal nomination of Muhlenberg, Buchanan stated that he would vote for Wolf but would take no part whatever in the canvass. If Muhlenberg drew enough votes from the anti-Masons, Buchanan had weak hopes that Wolf might be elected, but his best guess was that the anti-Masonic candidate, Joseph Ritner, would win. When rumors began to circulate that Van Buren was pulling strings to help Muhlenberg, Buchanan counselled noninterference. "I have been defending little Van on this point everywhere," he wrote. "Those who know him will feel at once how ridiculous the charge is. . . . There should be a studied neutrality in Washington."[4]

Shortly after the Muhlenberg convention at Lewistown, the national nominating convention of the Democratic party met at Baltimore. Everyone knew that Jackson intended Martin Van Buren to succeed him as president. In fact he suggested that if no other way were open to accomplish this, he might resign before his term had expired, and personally put in Little Van. But Jackson's increasingly dictatorial handling of national problems had caused wholesale secession from his party, and his attempt to hand-pick his successor did nothing to quiet the anger of his former friends. Instead of the "Old Hero," he now became "King Andrew."

The Baltimore Convention was called a year early, at the president's request, in order to get Van Buren's name in front of the people before other candidates had a chance to build an organization. Pennsylvania, as expected, sent 60 delegates, 30 Mules and 30 Wolves, all of whom backed Van Buren. After adopting the two-thirds rule, in order to achieve a "more imposing effect," the convention proceeded unanimously to nominate Van Buren for president. Col. Richard M. Johnson of Kentucky received the vice-presidential nomination. Buchanan wrote to Van Buren during the Baltimore convention: "My opinion is that the division in our party will make Ritner Governor; but that will not seriously affect the Presidential election. . . . The friends of Muhlenberg in our party, are almost to a man your sincere and devoted friends. So is a very large majority of the friends of Wolf."[5]

In the election for Governor of Pennsylvania in October, 1835, Ritner received 94,023 votes; Wolf, 65,801; and Muhlenberg, 40,586. The combination of Whigs and anti-Masons elected 76 of the 100 members of the State Assembly and captured six of the eight senatorial vacancies. Although the Democrats had enough "holdovers" in the Senate to give them a small majority in that body, it was a thumping defeat all round. It was a bitter lesson, but probably the only kind that could chasten the selfishness and jealousy that pervaded both factions. They were all out of jobs now—Wolf, Muhlenberg, and all their friends and partisans; they would stay out of office until they swallowed their pride, shook hands, and began working for their party again. Buchanan resisted the temptation to say, "I told you so." He had a job, to be sure, but not for long. In December 1836, the Legislature would ballot again to fill his senatorial post for another term.

THE ELECTION OF 1836

James Buchanan always did things the slow way, the hard way, the sure way. He had no talent for the sudden devastating move, the brilliant stroke, the daring gamble, or the quick quip which by-passed a problem in a gale of laughter. He did not try to change his own position or to give new meaning and direction to the Pennsylvania Democracy. He began laboriously to rebuild his power from the bottom up, starting again in Lancaster County.

The usual Democratic state convention would be held on March 4, 1836, at Harrisburg to determine the composition of the electoral ticket for the presidential vote in the fall. For a time it looked as if the Wolves and Mules would each run separate sets of electors, for each faction persisted in holding its own county meetings, but Buchanan persuaded the Wolf meeting in Lancaster, for the sake of conciliation, to endorse the idea of placing pro-Muhlenberg electors on the ticket from the eight Congressional districts in which Muhlenberg had recently polled a majority. The Mules had their general meeting scheduled for January 8 when they intended to choose an electoral ticket. If they insisted on having none but their own men as electors and would not acquiesce in a ticket which gave them representation only in the areas where they had a voting majority, then they would have to be excluded from the Harrisburg convention entirely, with a "pray, what the Devil brought you here?" "I have told them," Buchanan explained to the Wolf managers, "that they have to yield to the majority. But I hope they will not have to be forced into submission. It is better to receive them cordially at once, & have an end of it."[6]

This left it up to the Mules, at their January meeting, to accept the olive branch and to include on their own proposed ticket the names of Wolf men in appropriate districts. It was a sane proposal, calculated to bring out the maximum Van Buren vote in every district by running as electors the men most popular locally. Buchanan pointed out another significant reason for adopting this plan. Pennsylvania reformers, after twenty years of effort, had succeeded in forcing the Legislature to call a convention to revise the state Constitution of 1790. Delegates to it would be elected a month before the presidential election of 1836. Unless the Democrats in each county got together, it was certain that the opposition would control this convention and, as Buchanan warned, "make sad work of it." A single electoral college ticket would help to maintain a united front among Democrats when they voted for delegates to the constitutional convention.

Buchanan worked effectively to reunite the Pennsylvania Democrats, but the anti-Masons, especially Governor Ritner and Assemblyman Thaddeus Stevens, helped even more. The Democracy in Pennsylvania was so flat on its back that Stevens could not resist the temptation to kick it. On December 19, 1835, he moved the appointment of a legislative committee "to investigate the evils of Free Masonry." This proved a mere pretext to bring prominent Democrats to the bar of the Legislature and make them sweat. Ex-governor Wolf, Chief Justice Gibson, George M. Dallas, Francis Shunk and others were called. Even Buchanan would probably have had a summons if he had not been in Washington. When these gentlemen refused to testify, and the crowd applauded Shunk's spirited protest against invasion of his civil rights, Stevens thundered the warning that the gallery itself would be arrested for contempt. The proceedings were so transparent, so useless, and so vindictive that they boomeranged against the committee; but even more important, the attack on the Democrats made them forget some of their own differences and unite in self-defense. The Whigs were disgusted and threatened to break off their coalition with the anti-Masons.

108

On top of this upheaval came the Bank proposal. Wolf had been for retrenchment of the huge State canal building program and had urged taxation to put the state on a firmer financial basis. Governor Ritner now proposed a repeal of taxes, great extension of the public transportation system, and the issuing of a State charter for the Bank of the United States for which the Bank was to pay the State $9,000,000 to be used for internal improvements.

When the Bank Bill passed the Assembly as expected, it was assumed that the Democratic majority in the Senate would kill it. But Nicholas Biddle's men had done their work well; the Senate passed the recharter bill on February 15, 1836, with the aid of eight of the leading Democratic members. One of them had, only a month before, presided at the Muhlenberg Democratic Convention which adopted resolutions denouncing a recharter of the institution. How the Bank agents persuaded these men or how much they paid them to turn renegade, no one knows; but the enormity of their treachery formed the basis of the presidential canvass in Pennsylvania and proved to be the incident which saved the day for Van Buren and Buchanan.

Democratic indignation over the arrogant investigation by Stevens and the recharter of the Bank under circumstances redolent of bribery paved the way for a reasonably harmonious Democratic meeting on March 4. Buchanan's project for a unified electoral ticket was approved, and the party prepared to spend the next four months taking revenge on the anti-Masons and assailing the Bank as a monster even more hideous than Jackson had painted it.

Buchanan turned down an invitation to speak to the Democratic mass meeting at Harrisburg on the 4th of July for the Senate remained in session beyond this date, but he did send along a vigorous anti-Bank speech. The approaching struggle in Pennsylvania, he concluded, "would be a struggle for life or death. The Democracy must either triumph over the Bank, or the Bank will crush the Democracy."[7]

The Bank issue grew so hot that Buchanan had to modify some of his personal arrangements to keep himself clear of attack. The transfer of treasury funds from the U. S. Bank to other selected institutions led to a scramble among bankers for a share of the money. "I have refused in every instance to interfere in obtaining public Deposits for any Bank," he wrote to an applicant. "I have been repeatedly & strongly urged upon this subject from different quarters and have always given the same answer. If as a Senator it would have been improper for me to interfere in behalf of other banks in which I had no stock—how much more so would it be in the case of the Harrisburg Bank? When the question of the distribution of the public deposits was before Congress, I sold out my stock in the Manhattan Bank—a large Depository—at a very great sacrifice."[8]

109

In the October elections the people of Pennsylvania gave a resounding rebuke to the Legislature which had rechartered the Bank; only 18 old members were returned. Of 72 Democrats elected, 63 were newcomers. But the vote on delegates to the Constitutional Convention told a different story. Of 133 delegates elected, 66 were Democrats, 66 Whig-anti-Masons, and one an independent with Whig leanings. It was a split right down the middle which carried with it a serious threat to the presidential prospects of Van Buren in the national election in November.

The Constitutional Convention, with a majority of one on the Whig side, would undoubtedly adopt an amendment abolishing offices for life. This measure would jeopardize the position of every justice of the peace in the state, and make his tenure dependent upon current politics. As this provision would undoubtedly go into effect before the end of the Ritner Administration, it would probably be used to eliminate any J. P.'s who had been leaders in Van Buren's cause. So, at least, they thought in the panic of the moment. For this reason these key leaders in the little communities, almost all of them Democrats, hung back. When the November vote was counted, Pennsylvania brought in not the 15,000 majority for Van Buren which Buchanan had predicted, but a thin 2,183 out of nearly 200,000 votes cast. Had these votes gone the other way, Pennsylvania's electoral college votes would have been lost to Van Buren, and that would have thrown the election into the House.

Now that Van Buren had won, Buchanan had his own future to worry about. In three weeks the new State Legislature would ballot to fill his place in the Senate. He wrote to Van Buren that he would have Muhlenberg as his opponent, a wholly unexpected turn of events, for Muhlenberg in October had publicly announced that he favored Buchanan. The Bank men had manipulated the change by flattering Muhlenberg and offering him their support, though their real purpose was to keep the Democrats divided.[9]

Buchanan was furious with Muhlenberg. Could he not see that there was no conceivable prospect of party victory in the future except by re-union? Wolf had been voted out, but his partisans remained active and important and would never ally with the Bank crowd. Buchanan's friends held the same view. Muhlenberg commanded one-third of a minority party in Pennsylvania, and a poor third at that. His strongest supporters were those apostate Democrats who had voted for the State recharter of the Bank, men who cared nothing about Muhlenberg except as a pawn to keep alive the fight among the Democrats. And this was the man Buchanan had picked as a partner three years ago! Well, sufficient unto the day. . . .

Muhlenberg saw another picture. Berks was the strongest Democratic county in the state. A few years before, the Democrats of Berks and Lancaster combined were polling so large a vote that a union

110

might well have commanded control of the party. Since Lancaster had gone over to anti-Masonry and the Bank, Buchanan could not even poll a majority in his own county, but nevertheless he sat in the Senate. Ex-Governor Wolf had been named Comptroller of the U. S. Treasury. Muhlenberg, who kept his county strong for the party, had received nothing but requests to stand aside, first in the contest for governor, and now in the campaign for Senator. Why should he not get his share? Why should Buchanan continue to have the glory, and others trail along with mere promises for the future, probably as hollow as those made in the past?

The legislators at Harrisburg, however, snuffed out the Muhlenberg hopes. The Whigs and anti-Masons could make no headway in promoting a coalition to elect him and failed in their effort to force a postponement of the election. Finally, they gave up. The two houses met and quickly re-elected James Buchanan to the Senate by a party vote.[10]

RELATIONS WITH VAN BUREN

Buchanan found it a pleasant relief to get back to the Senate. He now had a job for six more years and, for the first time in a decade, could make some solid plans. He sought out his friend Senator William R. King of Alabama and they arranged for lodgings together. The usual talk about the sterling character of "southern gentlemen" caused a good deal of amusement among northerners, but if anyone merited respect for his personal qualities, it was King. He would now be vice-president if the party had heeded Buchanan's advice, but because of a nonelection by the Electoral College, the Democrats would probably wind up with Col. Richard M. Johnson, a profligate from Kentucky who lived with a mulatto and gave northerners good reason to sneer at southern pretensions to gentility. King presently sat as president, pro tempore, of the Senate. Washington had begun to refer to him and Buchanan as "the Siamese twins."[11]

Shortly after his re-election, Buchanan became involved in a debate on the admission of Michigan to statehood. The dispute concerned a constitutional question as to the proper mode of calling a state convention. Senator Calhoun challenged the validity of a Michigan Constitutional Convention which had met at the suggestion of Congress and without prior sanction of the State Legislature. Calhoun asserted that the action of the convention was a nullity.

Because it was a partisan matter, the discussion of the Michigan issue ranged far and wide, bringing in eventually Pennsylvania's recharter of the U. S. Bank. What would happen, a Senator asked Buchanan, if the constitutional convention now preparing to meet in Pennsylvania should determine that the state charter recently awarded to the Bank was a nullity? Would not this be breach of contract? On this subject Senator Morris of

111

Ohio introduced a letter from George M. Dallas stating that the Pennsylvania convention should repeal the Bank charter. Morris called this advice "incendiary," "revolutionary," and "calculated to excite the people to rise up in rebellion against the laws." It attacked the United States Constitution which guaranteed the sanctity of contracts.

Had Buchanan been a mere ward heeler he would have sat back to relish this attack on his hated enemy; had he been vindictive, he could have found ways to turn the knife in the wound, but his objectives were larger than these. For years he had been trying to patch up the broken Democracy of Pennsylvania, and for years Dallas had been the primary impediment to union. Now he saw a chance, quite accidentally, to put Dallas in his debt. Jumping to the defense, he demolished the arguments of Morris.

"Mr. Dallas never did assert that the convention about to be held in Pennsylvania will possess any power to violate the constitution of the United States," he began. "Why, sir, such propositions would be rank nullification; and although I never had the pleasure of being on intimate terms with Mr. Dallas, I can venture to assert that he . . . is opposed to this political heresy. . . . No, Sir; Mr. Dallas has expressly referred to the Supreme Court of the United States as the tribunal which must finally decide whether the convention possesses the power to repeal the bank charter." But what, asked Calhoun, if the Supreme Court upheld the Bank in such a litigation? "I can tell the Senator from South Carolina," rejoined Buchanan, "that we shall never resort to nullification as the rightful remedy."[12]

Buchanan's vigorous defense of Dallas brought a prompt message from the latter expressing his "warm personal thanks" and a wish "to cultivate greater intimacy." Buchanan replied on the same day that he was "not only willing, but anxious" to let bygones be bygones and to become friends.[13] The exchange marked the point at which Buchanan, for the first time in his life, became the acknowledged leader of the state Democracy and fountainhead of federal patronage for Pennsylvania.

Unfortunately, a good many Pennsylvania Democrats now favored the Bank, higher tariff rates, extension of internal improvements and other anti-Jacksonian policies; hence the slim Van Buren majority of the previous November. To ignore these people in the patronage distribution would further damage the Democracy in Pennsylvania; to get jobs for them would be the task of a magician. Wilkins, who had the stature for an important office, had ruined his chances by running for vice-president against the winning ticket. Cameron had frankly joined the friends of the Bank. Dallas, though no longer a Calhoun partisan, had voted to recharter the Bank and still acted as one of its solicitors. To promote Wolf or Muhlenberg would only start that old feud anew. Buchanan might take

112

a Cabinet post but at the risk of angering the many Pennsylvania Democrats who thought that he already had taken more than his share of the offices. Furthermore, if he left the Senate he would invite a new scramble for his place which the anti-Masons might win.

Buchanan talked with both Jackson and Van Buren, telling them that Pennsylvania deserved and expected a place in the Cabinet, but he declined to name his man. If he supposed that he would get a Pennsylvania appointment by this course, he was destined to disappointment. "I fear from what I have heard," he wrote Van Buren in February, "that I may not have made myself understood. . . . It is my firm conviction . . . that if a Cabinet officer should not be selected from Pennsylvania, it will give great and general dissatisfaction."[14]

The president-elect undoubtedly recognized more clearly than Buchanan the hopelessness in 1837 of acquiring much grace in the Keystone State by such an appointment. More could be gained elsewhere by this means. The Pennsylvania Democrats would have to unsnarl their own mess, and it would take more than a Cabinet office to do it. Van Buren could help, however, without risking an invasion of Washington by these factionists. There was always the foreign service.

Van Buren appointed Dallas to the Russian Mission. Buchanan apparently had not been consulted on this move, though it undoubtedly gave him secret joy. In writing to the president-elect about it, he signed the letter not with the usual "Yours very respectfully" but with a rare and intimate "ever yours." Nonetheless, the party still demanded a Cabinet officer from the state. "In writing thus," said Buchanan "you know, I have no views towards myself, as I should not change my present situation for any other."[15] Just how sincere was he about this? Would he not take the State Department if it were offered? He had just been voted Chairman of the Senate Foreign Relations Committee in a two-to-one victory over Henry Clay, a triumph he keenly relished. Would it not be the cream of the jest to be Secretary of State while Dallas was at St. Petersburg? Of course, and he would take the job if it were offered, but these were matters which, as Old Hickory used to say, "he would hide from the very hairs of his head."

The Cabinet appointments were finally announced. No Pennsylvania name was on the list. Buchanan was disappointed in the extreme, particularly because John Forsyth was continued as Secretary of State. His relations with the Secretary had recently been soured when Forsyth rejected Buchanan's first report as Chairman of the Foreign Relations Committee with the tart observation that "the Committee seem to have had an imperfect knowledge of the facts in relation to our affairs with Mexico."

113

Buchanan had slaved over this report, read everything available, and spared no effort. "Imperfect knowledge of the facts!" He knew the facts, to be sure. One of the facts was that the recent Secretaries of State, McLane excluded, were either lazy or ignorant, or both. His reply was sarcastic:

> Mr. Buchanan has been honored with the opinion of Mr. Forsyth that 'the Committee on Foreign Relations of the Senate seem to have had an imperfect knowledge of the facts in relation to Mexico.' Such an opinion emanating from the Secretary of State cannot fail to produce a happy effect in promoting harmony between the different branches of the Government. The Committee will not, however, reciprocate the compliment paid them by the Secretary, lest they might do him an injustice, which would be extremely repugnant to their feelings.[16]

The exchange brought on a storm, the intervention of the president, a letter of explanation from Forsyth which included a guarded apology, and a response from Buchanan that the fracas was "happily terminated" and would be considered "a family matter."[17] However, the men despised each other from then on and welcomed every opportunity to show their feelings. Buchanan later wondered whether he might not have replaced Forsyth in March, if he had managed to muzzle his temper in February.

Buchanan was on such poor terms with Levi Woodbury of New Hampshire, the new Secretary of the Treasury, that he addressed all requests for appointments in that department directly to Van Buren. "I am discouraged from making any requests in that quarter," he told the president.[18] The Secretary of War, Joel Poinsett, was from South Carolina, which had not even voted for Van Buren. Poinsett was an able man and had strongly supported Jackson in the nullification crisis, but his appointment gave gratification only to Whigs in Pennsylvania. The Harrison paper in Pittsburgh, the *Manufacturer*, highly approved.[19] The selection of Benjamin F. Butler, a New Yorker, as Attorney General galled Pennsylvanians and heightened the rivalry between New York and Pennsylvania. Amos Kendall, the Postmaster General, had nourished Jackson's belief in Buchanan's duplicity in the old "bargain and sale" affair. He would receive no favors from Kendall, and he feared for the fate of Dave Lynch, whose scandalous ineptitude in the management of the Pittsburgh post office would not escape Kendall's efficient eye. Finally, there was Mahlon Dickerson of New Jersey in the Navy Department. Dickerson would be no problem, although he could not be expected to exert himself very much to provide a new dry dock for Philadelphia.

114

After the Cabinet appointments were made known, Buchanan changed his subscript "ever yours" to "ever your friend" on his letters to Van Buren. At the end of three weeks of job-seeking for his political creditors, he reverted to the customary "Yours very respectfully." He was not going to be a big wheel in this administration, he realized, but just another cog in the machine.

According to Buchanan's philosophy of life and of politics, the way to act in such a circumstance was to function as smoothly and as quietly as possible. He saw neither truth nor virtue in the homely maxim that the squeaky wheel gets the grease, nor in Cameron's view that the best way to progress was to fight or buy the man who might be able to gratify your wish. Patience, acquiescence, logically contrived procedure, the appearance of consistency, refusal to make irretrievable commitments, and a ready willingness to capitulate in matters of minor political advantage —these constituted Buchanan's political temperament.

Van Buren recognized these traits of character and keenly appreciated the perplexities of the Pennsylvania Democrats. New York had taught him all there was to learn about factional fights. Therefore, Buchanan was able to make more progress than he had anticipated. He secured a position in the Treasury for Henry Petriken who had led the opposition to the Bank charter in the Pennsylvania Legislature, and placed George Plitt in the Wisconsin Land Office. Simon Cameron, through Buchanan's influence, obtained a good job (which he disgraced) settling Winnebago Indian claims. Henry Muhlenberg went to the newly created Austrian Mission in which Buchanan was especially interested, since he had worked for its establishment during his sojourn in Europe. Muhlenberg's appointment so infuriated George Wolf that he immediately resigned from his Treasury post, declaring that his old rival had walked off with the honors. Buchanan persuaded Van Buren to pacify Wolf by offering him the best federal job in Pennsylvania: the collectorship of the Port of Philadelphia. One of the Dallas supporters had to be discharged in order to make way for Wolf, and they became incensed.

It was a patchwork of patronage, but at least it demonstrated that neither Van Buren nor Buchanan was playing favorites with any Democratic faction. On the contrary they were acting on the assumption that they would all have to pull together during the 1838 campaign for the governorship if they wished to rid the Commonwealth of anti-Masonry and prevent a Whig success in the national election of 1840.

115

9

THE ROOT OF ALL EVIL • 1837 - 1840

THE SECOND BANK OF THE UNITED STATES

March 4, 1837, dawned bright and clear and by midmorning when Martin Van Buren drove to the White House to join Jackson, the sun had brought warmth and gaiety to the crowds which lined the avenue from the White House to the Capitol. At the eastern portico the members of the Senate, the Cabinet and the Diplomatic Corps led the way to the rostrum. The stately Hero of New Orleans, just up from a sickbed, acknowledged a roaring ovation from the crowd, and Mr. Van Buren advanced to deliver his inaugural address. Buchanan stayed for the inauguration ball at Carusi's that evening and then headed for Harrisburg as fast as he could go.

There the Legislature was in an uproar over the Bank. The Van Buren partisans, variously known as the "radicals" or the "hard money men," had instituted an investigation of the Bank which they were using as a weapon of attack, while Whigs, "improvement men," and "paper money boys" were trying to make the inquiry serve the Bank's ends. One of the Whigs noted that the anti-Bank crowd was led on by "a gang of scoundrels . . . including Buchanan, and Jesse Miller."[1]

The Legislature vindicated the Bank, whereupon George R. Espy unexpectedly moved to repeal the Bank's charter. This motion renewed the fight at the worst possible time, for the Panic of 1837 had now descended upon the nation. Even the Bank's enemies had no wish to outlaw the institution at this particular moment, for they would be blamed for aggravating the financial distress. Fifty-two Democrats in the House had at first agreed to support the repeal motion, but when the roll was called only twenty-one of them actually voted for it.

Back in Lancaster Buchanan tried to think out some solution to the problem. It appeared to him that the Bank had first bought up the national Congress to get its charter renewed, and now it had bought up the Commonwealth of Pennsylvania. He had learned in Harrisburg that the leading Democratic members of the investigating committee, who were

116

supposed to produce proof that the institution was corrupt, had been bribed by the Bank. Two junior members, who respected the opinion of their elder colleagues, had signed the whitewash report on the assumption that it was *bona fide*. Later they learned that their senior committeemen had withheld a lot of damning evidence and, after the vindication of the Bank, had been its guests at a big dinner celebration in Philadelphia.[2] Buchanan, mortified by the result, wrote, "This bank business will divide the party for years to come."[3]

His friends agreed. "I begin to believe that [the Bank] will get the uppermost of us again," wrote one of them.[4] And why should it not? The issue cut clean through party lines in Pennsylvania; there were Bank and anti-Bank followers in each major party and in every faction.

The question presented two very different aspects. To the rank and file of Democratic voters the destruction of Biddle's "monster" symbolized the transfer of political privilege from the aristocracy to the "common man"; but to informed politicians Jackson's war on the Bank signified rather the transfer of the money center of the nation from Philadelphia to New York; from Chestnut Street to Wall Street. Whatever Jackson's reasons for the attack, there seems to be little doubt that the chief motive of his intimate advisors, Van Buren and half a dozen others, was to oust Biddle in order to seize financial control themselves.[5] Thus the struggle over the Bank proved to be an important phase of the ancient rivalry between Pennsylvania and New York. This feature of ante-bellum politics, the incessant contest for power and position between the two wealthiest and most populous states of the Union, may perhaps bear a heavier responsibility for the disruption of the Democracy and the later breakup of the Union than historians now suspect. Here parochialism played its divisive role at the center of the nation rather than at its extremities.

Trade reports of the early 1830's had already shown that New York City had supplanted Philadelphia as the leading import-export city of America, a distinction the latter had enjoyed since colonial times. The rapid rise of New York City, hastened by Van Buren's political connection with Jackson, was the underlying fact which explained why the Bank issue in the Pennsylvania Legislature always disrupted the Democrats and why the Dallas faction had to find some formula to keep the Bank, backbone of Philadelphia's financial eminence, in operation.

Buchanan had to choose between supporting the financial interests of eastern Pennsylvania and sustaining the national policy of the Democrats. As the former course would have threatened his influence nationally and placed him locally in the camp of his Philadelphia rivals, he chose the latter, fully aware of the many pitfalls which the decision opened. In order to emphasize the national aspect of his position, he raised a question in the Senate which made everyone sit up and take notice, for it

117

had apparently been overlooked before. "Suppose," he said, "General Jackson and the bank had been in alliance and not in opposition. What then might have been the consequences, had he been an enemy to the liberties of the people? Can any man say that our liberties would not have been in danger?" All the forms of the Constitution might have remained, but who could believe that any subsequent election would ever be *bona fide*; that the whole framework of public information could not be bought up and rigged; that frauds could not be excused by mercenary courts; or that a president would not always be able to name his successor?[6]

At home, Buchanan restricted his talking to a reiteration of his simple maxim, "The party must crush the bank, or the bank will crush the party." His followers, desperately worried by the schism created by the Bank issue, had no better advice to offer. One wrote, "What have we gained by opposition to the Bank? Principle—what does it mean? Patriotism—where is it? Pledges—in the pocket!! Politics—I am ready to quit."[7] Another asked, "What do you think of a *conciliation* party? I mean to organize the old fashioned Democratic party? It must come to that."[8] That, thought Buchanan, would be like trying to take the eggs out of the omelette and put them back in the shells. A third proposed to forget about the Bank and to take up "fresher, more interesting topics."[9] Buchanan's friends coincided only on one point: they thought that he could strengthen and unify the state Democracy by consenting to run for governor in 1838. "You alone can unite our divided party," ran their plea. But those who knew him best predicted that he would refuse. "He aims at higher game," they said.[10] They were right, for Buchanan announced that he would not exchange the senatorship for a three-year scramble in Harrisburg. Of all political positions, the governorship of Pennsylvania traditionally carried the least prospect for subsequent honor.

By the time the Legislature had finished its indecisive discussion of the Bank, Buchanan found himself in the midst of another series of personal attacks like those in the election of 1828. Perhaps his enemies thought there might be some truth in the idea that he alone could unite his party.

The Lancaster *Intelligencer* started the assault with a new version of the old "bargain and sale" story which, to Buchanan's utter astonishment, Francis P. Blair republished in the Washington *Globe*, the administration organ.[11] In May Buchanan went to Harrisburg where he dropped in at a session of the Constitutional Convention. Some of his friends invited him to come front and sit inside the bar. Immediately thereafter, one of the delegates, Coxe of Somerset, arose and delivered a tirade of abuse against him which Buchanan reported "had no more connexion with the subject under discussion than it had with the question that distracted the sages of Lilliput, whether eggs ought to be beaten from the larger or the

118

smaller end." Buchanan's one-time warm friend, John Sergeant, Chairman of the Convention, made no effort to call Coxe to order. The central theme of his philippic was that old chestnut: "that Buchanan had once thanked his God that he had not a drop of Democratic blood in his veins, and if he had, he would let it out."[12]

Coxe had once asked certain people of Lancaster to sign an affidavit that they had heard Buchanan make the alleged statement, but Anthony McGlinn was the only person who was willing to furnish a sworn signature. Buchanan also swore, calling Coxe "a dirty, low, malicious fellow." Did anyone believe that he had been at any period of his life "such an arrant fool?"[13] He demanded evidence and wanted the convention to give him a chance to refute. But Coxe was not after debate; he merely wanted to get the item back into circulation and he succeeded brilliantly. Picking up the cue from Coxe, others began to use the convention as their forum to attack Buchanan.

Some members of the convention at length became so accustomed to spreading poison that one of them forgot himself and gave a dose to one of his friends. Thaddeus Stevens, in a speech about apportionment of votes in Philadelphia, referred to that proud city as "a great and growing ulcer on the body politic," and then, without any apparent reason, launched into a slurring commentary on Whig leader William Morris Meredith. Meredith, not a man to sit back and listen quietly to an insult, rose and for two days poured forth a stream of personal invective against Stevens while the Democrats, now out of the picture, sat back entranced. Stevens manufactured venom so fast, said Meredith, that when he ran out of enemies, which was hard to imagine, he had to spray it on whoever stood nearby. He was a great man in little things—by far the greatest in the littlest that the country could boast. "You sneaking catamount," he shouted, "you and your vulpine Coxe." The affair temporarily broke up the Constitutional Convention, and threatened to break up the Whig-anti-Masonic alliance. "Whether this dissolves the coalition remains to be seen," wrote C. J. Ingersoll.[14]

Senator John P. King of Augusta, Georgia, had invited Buchanan to come south for a visit during the summer, but the growing political pressure and a number of private affairs discouraged the expedition. "Until the fit of fault-finding is over," he replied, he would have to stay at home.[15] His private business needed care in these days of panic,[16] and he also had to work out the estates of his mother and his brother George, both of whom had died without leaving wills.[17] But most important of all, Mary Kittera Snyder (or was it Aunt Ann?) had said "yes." Senator W. R. King had ribbed him during the early spring about neglecting his usual affairs from "the anxieties of love."[18] On June 3, Buchanan wrote to Mrs. Francis Preston Blair, "I would gladly join your party to the Hermitage next year,

. . . but long ere that time I expect to be married & have the cares of a family resting upon my shoulders."[19]

The happy prospect clouded that particular spring, for the state of feeling in Philadelphia was so violent against him for attacking the U. S. Bank that he had been mobbed by a gang of political roughnecks on one of his visits. ' Charles J. Ingersoll told him that the assaults upon him in the Constitutional Convention had still further inflamed public opinion, and that he really ought to stay out of the city until things calmed. Possibly for this reason Mary Snyder went to Baltimore where Buchanan visited her.[20]

Buchanan went to Bedford Springs in July for several weeks of pleasant recreation, walking with his old friend Judge Henry Shippen of Meadville along the wooded stream which rippled through the glades below the huge hotel. In the morning they would stop at the little white summer-house enclosing the beautiful mineral spring and "drink of the waters," according to their doctor's prescription. Until noon the guests ordinarily stayed within easy reach of the other little white houses until the volcanic effects of the "waters" had subsided. After midday all sought the rocking chairs which lined the huge porch or promenaded up and down, greeting newly arrived friends and gossiping. In the evening there was dancing in the great ballroom with schottisches, polkas, and a new step called the hop-trot dubbed by some rakes the rabbit-hop. Buchanan loved to dance and spent more evenings in society than he should have, considering the amount of work he had planned to do. But the ladies insisted and he was always a willing respondent to a roguish eye.

By the end of August he was back in Lancaster and hard at work on a series of important Senate speeches he was to give on the new Administration program to solve the currency and banking problems.

BUCHANAN AND THE SUBTREASURY BILL

Although the Panic of 1837 grew very serious during the spring and summer, President Van Buren decided not to call a special session of Congress to deal with it until September. During the summer months, Buchanan had been in constant correspondence with Jackson and Van Buren about the financial crisis. The latter had asked for suggestions to be included in the presidential message to the forthcoming special session of Congress and Buchanan, anticipating that he would be a leading spokesman for the president, proposed that Congress should establish a new bank or, as that name had come into disrepute, "an Agency" connected with the Treasury and the Mint to collect and disburse public money. The agency should neither issue notes nor discount paper; its function should be to receive bullion for deposit both from the collectors of the United States and from individuals. It could issue to individuals receipts which could then be sent to any part of the nation and be cashed back into bullion at a branch agency for a slight transmission fee. This system would facilitate domestic exchange and prevent wide variations in exchange rates in different parts of the land. More particularly, it would prevent exchange merchants from periodically squeezing businessmen who needed specie when there happened, temporarily, to be a local shortage. But Buchanan was certain that neither the government nor the nation could function on a specie basis, as Senator Benton and others believed. The notes of state banks would have to be used and the government would have to receive these notes in payment of land and of customs duties. The Treasury, however, ought to accept only the notes of specie-paying banks in the vicinity of the new agency and its branches, and "nearly all danger in dealing with such Institutions might be avoided by frequent settlements."[21]

President Van Buren, in his message, proposed a "sub-treasury" system or federal collection, deposit, and exchange agency very much like the one Buchanan had described.

Buchanan made one of the best speeches of his life in support of the subtreasury proposal on September 28, 1837, when he and Silas Wright of New York contested the issue with Webster and Clay. He divided the honors with his opponents on constitutional phases of the argument, but he had the better of them on practical finance. Both Clay and Webster, continually in need of money, had long experience as debtors to the Bank of the U. S., but Buchanan was a private banker himself. Jackson thought enough of the Bank speech to write that it "must become a lasting monument" to the talent of its author, and a "text-book" of the party for all time to come.[22]

The Subtreasury Bill passed the Senate, but it was laid on the table in the House and did not become law until 1840. Pennsylvania Democrats were amazed at the Senate line-up on the vote: Van Buren's best friends opposed him; his enemies, like Calhoun, supported him. "No wonder he is called a *magician*," George Plitt observed.[23] In New York the Democrats split wide apart on the issue and were soundly whipped in the state elections. Their defeat demonstrated to the Democrats of Pennsylvania the necessity for united action. Buchanan's friends wrote: "Our good old State is now the last hope for the party, and if she fails us, through the headstrong perversity of a few leaders, we shall be beaten in the Union for years to come."[24] If, however, New York remained split and Pennsylvania delivered a victory in 1838, there was every prospect that Buchanan could become the key man in the Van Buren Administration. A great deal would depend on the nominating contest for governor in the spring.

121

Buchanan insisted that Muhlenberg and Wolf each withdraw his name as candidate for governor and urged the party to unite on someone previously unconnected with that schism. Wolf, who had protested Muhlenberg's appointment to the Austrian Mission, now promised to stay out of the governor's race and to keep his friends loyal to a convention choice. Buchanan got comforting news from prominent Democrats— "whether it be Porter, Blythe, Carpenter or Klingensmith, that receives the nomination, not a man will demur."[25]

Two weeks before the Democratic nominating convention in Harrisburg, the State Legislature passed resolutions instructing the Pennsylvania Senators to vote against the Subtreasury Bill. Supported by the Whigs and signed by Governor Ritner, the motion pledged "full confidence in Martin Van Buren." These idiotic resolutions, "an absurd medley and damnable humbug," were intended to force Buchanan to resign the senatorship so that he could be replaced by one of the "recreants." As one of the originators of the Subtreasury Bill he could not oppose it; but under the instruction system, he would have to kill his own bill or resign. The Bank crowd thought they had him this time. Whatever decision he made would disrupt the harmony of the Democratic meeting of March 4.

Buchanan thought it over thoroughly, pushed aside the pile of letters appealing to him by all that was holy to tear up the instructions and vote the party line, and wrote out his announcement to the Senate. "If a Senator can look behind his instructions," he declared, "the right is at once abandoned. . . . My only alternative, then, is either to obey or to resign." But, if he should resign, "the right of instruction itself would soon grow into disrepute, and the Senatorial term of six years . . . would terminate whenever such a conflict of opinion should arise. . . . I shall, therefore, obey my instructions honestly and in good faith."[26] He would move to table the Subtreasury Bill in the hope that by next session he could get the support of Pennsylvania for it.

This decision did not precisely delight Van Buren, but he could scarcely protest; it at least offered hope, which was more than he could say for his own state of New York. And, while the announcement disappointed all those who had been engaged in the fight against the Bank, they swallowed it and kept a bold front, praising its forthrightness. Fortunately, it came too late to affect the county meetings to elect delegates to the state nominating convention, or there would certainly have been a swarm of contesting claimants to seats. As it was, there had been numerous Democratic county meetings sponsoring, in one hall, "Van Buren and a new bank," and across the street "Van Buren and down with the bank." The Democrats nominated David R. Porter for governor without difficulty—a tremendous triumph for Buchanan's unity platform; but the convention members made no

122

statement at all on the Bank issue. Their silence on this point might have caused trouble except for the fact that the other parties were even more splintered on the question than the Democrats and could make no capital of the glaring omission.

The Pennsylvania gubernatorial contest aroused more excitement than any event of the preceding decade. The members of all Democratic factions pulled strong enough in harness that Buchanan felt he could afford to keep his distance. He stayed out of the state campaign and immersed himself in the business of the Senate. "Really," wrote an old crony, "you have become public property, and have lost sight altogether of the domestic relation. No one in Lancaster has heard from you since Congress began."[27] There was some reason for this, for the Committee on Foreign Affairs was suddenly confronted with a whole docket full of crises, and many problems corollary to the Subtreasury came up for individual study and discussion.

A new fight arose over a scheme that Biddle had worked out to give the newly chartered Bank of the United States of Pennsylvania millions of dollars which it ought not to have. Under the old federal charter, the Bank had an unspecified period of time to liquidate the bank notes which had been circulating for twenty years. Instead of calling these in, Biddle permitted them to circulate as usual; and on top of them the Bank issued new notes authorized under the Pennsylvania charter. Thus, this "monster," which Jackson thought he had destroyed, now roamed the countryside more than twice as big as ever and exercised a national influence far greater than it had in the heyday of 1828. But worse than this, its note issues were now swollen as badly as those of an old wildcatter, though the public, conditioned by two decades of assurance that these notes were the best security in the nation, took them avidly as if they were solid gold. Biddle expected that he would receive gold for them; he was currently engaged in a quiet endeavor to get a corner on the southern cotton crop, and if he succeeded he would have plenty of specie to cover those "resurrection notes." Even if Congress outlawed them, he would still have the gold. All that was needed was to prevent any sudden resumption of specie payments, and he could certainly protect himself against that at Harrisburg. Biddle was a man of ideas.

Buchanan fought to proscribe Biddle's old notes by means of a federal bill imposing fine and imprisonment on any director, trustee, or officer of a corporation chartered by Congress who permitted notes of a defunct corporation to remain in circulation. He analyzed, with a clarity which should have made Biddle revise his plans, the nature of the cotton speculation then in progress in open defiance of a prohibitory clause in the Pennsylvania charter of the Bank. He pointed out that the Bank never bothered to make the periodic reports to the Auditor General of Pennsylvania which the new charter specified, and that the Bank effectively blocked

123

all efforts to revive specie resumption in the Commonwealth. "In vain you may talk to me about paper restrictions," he concluded. "When did a vast moneyed monopoly ever regard the law, if any great interest of its own stood in the way? It will then violate its charter, and its own power will secure it immunity."[28] Biddle, he proclaimed, "like all other men, must yield to his destiny." This was prophetic. He eventually yielded to bankruptcy but never to the United States Government.

By mid-July, the Senate session was over and the critical Pennsylvania gubernatorial election of 1838 drew near. The great day arrived. Votes were counted, recounted, counted again. Great God in Heaven! Between Ritner and Porter the vote was so close that no one knew who had been elected, and each claimed the victory.

THE ROLE OF THE RICH UNCLE

In November, the death of sister Harriet's husband, the Reverend Robert Henry of Greensburg, raised family problems so serious and immediate that James spent the entire month attending to them before going to Washington. The family was like politics. He loved both and felt duty bound to both, but their problems, demands, and feuds were ever on his doorstep. For a long while he had anticipated the difficulties that now faced him. He had already acquired major responsibility for half a dozen young nephews and nieces, and if tuberculosis continued to afflict the family, as he feared it would, he would soon have a whole orphanage on his hands.

He told Harriet that he would come to Greensburg and then tried to formulate some plans. The family problem had several aspects: money, proper care of the children, and the resolution of jealousies and disagreements among the surviving elders. Moreover, he was at this time especially concerned about Mary Snyder. Some of the family opposed the idea of his marriage, particularly Edward who anticipated sharing a goodly inheritance from his brother. Mary herself may have been disturbed by the thought of becoming an unwanted addition to the circle. Buchanan wondered whether he had the right to ask her to undertake the role of foster-mother, and whether it was wise to let his money get out of the immediate family.

He worked late in his study in the King Street house, his mind wandering back over the past to his mother and her ambitions for him and to sister Sarah, who had run off to get married and then died at twenty-seven, leaving a little girl, Elizabeth Huston. Mr. Huston had since died and Elizabeth had been living with the Kitteras in Philadelphia or with Miss Hetty in Lancaster during vacations from the boarding school in

New Jersey which Uncle James had chosen for her. But her school days were nearly over, for she was sixteen, and more permanent provision had to be made. Uncle Edward stuffily announced that he would not have her because she was "too giddy, too fond of company" and too little impressed with the responsibilities of life. What would the parish think? It put Buck in a quandary. He could not leave her with Miss Hetty. John N. Lane, a relative of his sister Jane's husband, lived in Lancaster and would have liked to keep Elizabeth, but James feared that this arrangement would "raise a talk here which might be injurious to Edward or his wife." But, he said, "if it becomes my duty to fix her in this County, they must take the consequences of their own conduct, and should it become necessary that I should express an opinion on the subject, it will be against them and in favor of Elizabeth."[29]

Robert Henry's death left sister Harriet with very little money, an advanced case of tuberculosis, and a five-year-old boy, James Buchanan Henry. Buck wrote to her urging her to take care of her health "for the sake of your child and other relatives. You are welcome, most welcome to a home with me where I think you may promote my happiness as well as your own." In his distraction, he addressed the letter to "My dear sir" from force of habit, and dated it 1837 instead of 1838.[30] Harriet would now have to go to live with her sister Jane in Mercersburg for a while and then move to Edward's home in Lancaster County until the end of the next Congress, when Buchanan could have things ready for her in the King Street house.

Jane posed an equally distressing problem. She was confined to her room, spit blood copiously, and was resigned to death in a matter of months. She had four children: James Buchanan Lane, who was already in his twenties; Elliot Eskridge, thirteen; Mary Elizabeth, twelve; and Harriet, eight.

Sister Maria, now married to Dr. Charles Yates of Meadville, had her troubles. The Doctor was her third husband. By her first, Buchanan's old school teacher, Jesse E. H. Magaw, she had had one daughter, named Jessie. She had four more children by Dr. Yates, their house was cramped, their income small, and Jessie was suffering from tuberculosis and needed to get out of the Meadville climate. Of all his nieces, she was probably Buchanan's favorite. Jessie went to live with her Aunts Harriet and Jane at Mercersburg for a time, until she could be sent to school. James told Maria that he planned to send Jessie "to the *very best* country female school I can find. I have seen enough of the effects of sending country girls whose expectations are moderate to Philadelphia Boarding Schools." Jessie, he thought, "will make a fine woman, if she lives. If not very smart, she is very good, and that is better."[31] He would send her to school at Mt. Joy, near Lancaster, but Jessie was so fond of

Aunt Harriet that it might be best if all stayed at the family homestead at Mercersburg, and she attended school there.

Finally there was Edward, his only surviving brother, who seemed increasingly to resent the contrast between his own poverty and James's affluence. Edward was ready for college when his brother William died, and it was this event which influenced him to gratify the wish of his mother that one son would study for the ministry. George and James had already prepared for law, and no one was left but him to follow the cloth. Now that George had died, he and James had to take care of the family. Edward complained that he had more expenses than James and scarcely income enough to keep himself in clean shirts; why should he take care of the family wanderers while James kept an empty house in Lancaster and had other quarters in Washington. James had been kind but strict with Edward. "You shall not be at any loss for money," he often said but he always kept track of the loans, and when there was a little estate to divide, he acted as executor and deducted the amount of his advances. "Rely upon your own judgment in all things, and I shall be content," he would write, but took occasion to disapprove strongly of the judgments Edward had made.[32]

James thought wryly of Edward, the "baby brother." He was even now only twenty-seven, proud, impatient, suspicious, and consumed with ambition. He had wanted to make a big impression on his superiors by making a fine donation to help endow a chair of theology at one of the church colleges, but the parish had contributed only $6. James sent him $144 more to enable him to forward a thumping check for $150—that would help make them remember where Pequea Church was.

Now there was trouble over Harriet's desire to sell the old Dunwoodie property, "Bridge farm," near Mercersburg. The income from this would be shared by all the children, but they had to agree to its sale. Edward felt that it should be held until prices improved, but Harriet needed money so desperately that she could see no other solution. James had then proposed to buy it himself, matching the best offer they could get from the outside. After a general family conference at Mercersburg, he concluded the purchase, much to Edward's dissatisfaction. "Nothing but family pride," James wrote, "induced me to purchase your farm. I could not bear to see the last vestige of father's property in Franklin County go into the hands of strangers." Significantly he added, "You will at last probably get my property or the greater part of it among all of you."[33] Whatever hopes he may have had of marrying were not very bright when he wrote that sentence.

On the same trip to Mercersburg he had a long talk with his sister Jane and made all arrangements for the distribution of her property after her death. She named him trustee of her inheritance (some $6,000).

He was to hold it during her life and use it later to pay for the care and education of the children. The remainder was to be apportioned and paid to them with interest when they reached maturity. Elliott T. Lane, her husband, agreed to this plan and signed a release which was recorded at Chambersburg.

James was glad to see Maria at the family conclave. Like her daughter Jessie, she was very good, but not very smart. Fortunately her latest husband was both and he managed to keep the household in order. Buchanan had grown to be very fond of him, and the doctor reciprocated by getting into politics in Meadville. He endorsed every Buchanan movement so enthusiastically that he insulted patients who disagreed with him and almost ruined his practice. Buchanan had loaned them the money to buy a house years before and had gotten his first taste of Maria's financial capabilities. On the strength of his guarded assent to make a loan, she had gone right out and bought a place, without ever having the title checked. He had upbraided her for her negligence and withheld his aid until his friend Henry Shippen, county judge in Meadville, had recorded a clear title and prepared a first mortgage. "It is my inflexible rule in life," he had told Maria, "never to invest a dollar in any property except it has a clean title and is free of every incumbrance."

Maria soon complained that the new house was too small. "That which I feared has come to pass," he wrote back. "It seems you are now dissatisfied with the use of the front room as a shop and are anxious that Dr. Yates should build one. I confess I am somewhat astonished at this. Besides your promise to me, you ought to reflect that your circumstances are very limited and that your expenses will be increasing annually. Were I residing in that house myself, I should never think of any other law office but the front room."[34]

As the years passed, odd little incidents occurred. Dr. Yates bet one of his patients $200 that Buchanan would be elected Senator in 1833, lost both the wager and the patient, and thus the means of paying the bet. Buchanan got him out of trouble in his usual way, not by sending money but by giving Yates a receipt for $200 which he said he had deducted from the sum the doctor already owed him. His letter had the qualities which his relatives came to recognize and to dread; it was at once both kind and nasty. "Be firm in politics, but avoid giving personal offence," he admonished. "I did not know you were in debt to anyone but myself, but if you do owe to others, you ought to pay it."[35] Once in a while, he would ask Dr. Yates to send only two thirds of the usual $150 instalment on the mortgage and give the other third to Maria. On such occasions he would not enter the credit until he got a formal receipt from Maria that she had actually received her fifty.[36]

127

James knew what the family thought of him, and wondered if their view was not justified. Often he wondered just what he thought of himself. He felt kindly to nearly everyone, but he could scarcely believe that anyone felt kindly toward him. Any manifestation of friendship or appeal to his better nature set little red flags flying in his mind; what was this person after? No one ever surmounted his suspicion; no one in his family ever expected from him other than what decency, bounded by the letter of the law, absolutely required. But to give to one would raise a howl from all the others. To make gifts to the family with no strings attached would make them wasteful and dependent, and soon the time would come when he would necessarily have to refuse. Then they would hate him. He knew that much about human nature. No, the best course was to give only when the need was critical, and then in a way that showed he expected to be paid back. That method would keep them all independent and self-respecting, it would protect him from voracious demands, and while it might not promote any outburst of emotional gratitude, it would maintain a long-range family stability. As he told Edward, they would all probably share everything he had, anyway. And right now, he had $120,000 of his own at work for interest, and some $25,000 of funds in trust for the various children. He hoped that if they let him manage, they would all some day have financial security.

10

WISE AS THE SERPENT • 1838 - 1841

TRIAL BALLOON

According to unofficial election returns, David R. Porter led Governor Ritner by 5,540 votes in the election of 1838, but the seats of eight Assemblymen and several State Senators were in dispute because of frauds in Philadelphia. The award of these contested seats would determine which party controlled the Legislature, and the Legislature would control the outcome of the election for governor, for it certified the vote. Secretary of the Commonwealth Burrowes issued a circular advising the public to "treat the election as if it had never taken place," and Thaddeus Stevens proclaimed emphatically that Porter would never be governor.

At Harrisburg the anti-Masons and the Democrats each organized an Assembly and a Senate and proceeded independently to business. At one stage a mob invaded the House chamber, threw the anti-Masonic speaker from the rostrum into the aisle and then rushed into the Senate, chasing Stevens and Burrowes "out of a window twelve feet high, through three thorn bushes, and over a seven foot picket fence." As excitement mounted, the anti-Masons seized the Harrisburg armory and Governor Ritner called out a militia battalion to sustain him. These troops, by stopping for a supply of buckshot at the Frankford arsenal, gave the name "Buckshot War" to the fracas. Meanwhile the Democrats mobilized thousands of volunteer "minutemen" who now began a march on Harrisburg to defend their rights.

When the militia officers refused to obey Governor Ritner, he wrote to President Van Buren, of all people, demanding the aid of U. S. troops, presumably to prevent a Democrat from assuming the governorship to which he had been duly elected! Van Buren felt that Pennsylvania ought to take care of its own troubles. At length, several of the Whigs became so thoroughly disgusted with proceedings that they announced they would vote with the Democrats, a switch that deprived the anti-Masons of even a phony majority in the House and enabled the Democrats to proceed legally.

129

The Senate continued its turmoil for ten days longer when it, too, organized. The Legislature now declared David R. Porter to have been elected governor, barely in time to meet the January 1 inauguration date.

Buchanan did not join the throng of Democrats which descended on Huntingdon to press claims on the governor-elect. He had long since impressed upon Porter that his nomination had resulted from the voluntary retirement from the field of both Wolf and Muhlenberg, and that the new Administration ought to conciliate these two factions. If Porter should ally with either one or try to create his own Democratic machine, he would surely wreck himself and jeopardize the national prospects of the party in 1840. Porter recognized the problem and did his best to steer a middle course, giving important jobs to representatives of all the major Democratic segments. Buchanan urged him to support the Van Buren program and promised to promote appropriate federal appointments.

Buchanan now began to work out the details of a plan which he had been toying with for the past several years. Van Buren would certainly run for a second term as president, but he would probably not demand the renomination of Richard M. Johnson as his running mate. As Johnson had dragged down the ticket in 1836, a number of men were already openly canvassing for his place, among them Senator Thomas Hart Benton and Secretary of State Forsyth. Buchanan proposed William R. King of Alabama for the vice-presidency.

King's nomination would have multiple advantages. It would eliminate both Forsyth and Johnson; it would put on the ticket a man whom Buchanan's partisans in Pennsylvania could consider to be his choice, and this belief would help to bring out the vote; and it would please the South. But most important of all, it would pave the way for the election of James Buchanan as president in 1844. King frankly told his roommate that if he became vice-president, he would not permit the consideration of his name for the presidency in '44. Furthermore, he would use his influence to promote Buchanan's nomination.

This plan looked good to Buchanan. Pennsylvania's Democrats were closer to real unity than they had been since the governorship of Simon Snyder; if Porter played the game he would be re-elected and the state administration would support Buchanan in the 1844 convention. New York Democracy was in the midst of schism; but New York, like Pennsylvania, would have learned its lesson and would be back on the Democratic track in five years. New York by then would have had the vice-presidency and the presidency for twelve years: she would be compelled to relinquish further claims and support a neighbor. The border states, too, had been favored: Virginia, Tennessee, and Kentucky. Van Buren was the only uncertain part of the program. What would he think?

130

Would he deliver the goods in Pennsylvania to men who would work for King?[1]

At Buchanan's suggestion, Democratic editors began puffing King and laying the propaganda groundwork for a formal movement. The appearance of their articles, however, touched off countermoves. The Dallas men of Philadelphia and the pro-Bank Democrats of western Pennsylvania, who were hostile to Buchanan, boomed Forsyth as the Pennsylvania choice for vice-president.[2] By the summer of 1839, Buchanan thought that the Forsyth movement had failed and that King would be nominated unless "Old Tecumseh" (Richard M. Johnson) should insist upon running again.[3] The Democratic members of the Legislature even gave Buchanan a testimonial dinner, together with the governor and other dignitaries, an unprecedented mark of party harmony.[4]

This happy augury failed to take into account the vagaries of state politics. Governor Porter did his part, giving Buchanan's friends a fair share of the patronage, but the leaders of the factions refused to be disciplined.[5] The governor, for example, bestowed favors on the Harrisburg *Keystone*, which had been in the past a violent anti-Muhlenberg, anti-Buchanan sheet. The *Keystone* kept pounding at the anti-Buchanan line and spread abroad a conclusion, quite erroneous, that the governor had gotten into a fight with the Senator. As a result, the Buchanan journals began to lambast the *Keystone* and from here it was natural to go on to attack the governor. The Dallas men took advantage of this presumed rupture to promote their interests by cultivating the anti-Buchanan movement centering on Forsyth. Cameron, just back from his Winnebago Indian Mission, saw a chance to trouble the waters to his advantage and quietly encouraged all Pennsylvania Democrats to insist upon a free and easy Bank program, the very thing against which Porter and Buchanan had pledged themselves. By September, Buchanan was discouraged. "My name has often been mentioned in connection with the Presidency in 1844," he wrote, but Pennsylvania would never unite on one of her own sons "with such energy and enthusiasm as to make him successful. . . . They care little for their own men."[6]

Felix Grundy, Attorney General of the United States, resigned in December. After the various factions got in their bids, Van Buren offered the post to Buchanan "although," he added, "I have no reason to suppose that it would be desirable to you."[7] It was not. Buchanan saw no use in exchanging the senatorship for a belated invitation to take a one-year job in the lowest Cabinet place. In declining he earnestly urged the appointment of the governor's brother, James M. Porter, but the president next offered the appointment to George M. Dallas, recently back from Russia. Dallas refused and the office went to Henry M. Gilpin of Philadelphia, a gentleman unpopular both with Porter's and Buchanan's friends.

"The President's disposition towards myself is proclaimed upon the house-top," Buchanan wrote to Porter. The King movement in Pennsylvania never recovered from this blow to Buchanan's prestige at the critical moment, and Vice-President Johnson embraced the opportunity to announce that he would run again. Porter could have used aid and comfort from the national administration and with such aid he might well have been influenced by Van Buren's wishes, but without it he would have to go ahead and settle the state banking problem on the basis of local interest. As a result, the state administration ran head-on into a policy collision with the national administration in a critical election year.

Both Democratic party policy and state law required that distressed banks should resume specie payment after a given date. This deadline had passed, but the Pennsylvania banks insisted that they could not pay specie; let the governor enforce this law, and a new panic would immediately ensue. Porter agreed that summary specie resumption under existing conditions would be foolhardy, but he had a variety of courses he could have taken which would have protected both the party and the banks.

His decision, announced in the message to the Legislature in January, 1840, emphasized the necessity of the resumption of specie payments, but Porter declared his intention not to force this until it could be done with safety to the general economy. Letters quickly piled up on Buchanan's desk. Anti-Bank Democrats were "out in full cry against the Message. . . . Many are looking to you for an expression of opinion."[8] Buchanan replied to Porter, "You have perhaps never witnessed anything like the exaltation, either felt or affected, of the Whigs here when the first news of your special message arrived." He knew the necessity which prompted the message, but he hoped that the Legislature would settle an early date for resumption; if it adjourned without action, leaving the banks without any mandate for resumption, "the integrity of our party will be in great danger."[9]

THE WHIGS ATTACK

The Whigs exploited the Bank controversy in Pennsylvania at a "union and harmony" meeting at Harrisburg in September and by holding their national nominating convention at the same place on December 4, where they chose General William Henry Harrison for president and John Tyler of Virginia for vice-president. So diverse were the elements of Whiggery that the delegates decided to issue no platform statement at all; if they concentrated on hatred of Van Buren and made a hero of "Old Tippecanoe," they could bring in Masons and anti-Masons, slaveholders and abolitionists, friends and enemies of the banks, high and low tariff men, manufacturers

132

and employees, radicals and conservatives. "The Whig party is very Catholic," Buchanan declared. "It tolerates great difference of opinion."[10]

The situation was, indeed, ridiculous. The party which but a few years before had acknowledged its descent from the Federalist tradition of government by the rich and well-born, now turned on the party of the "common man," and tried to make it appear a regime of royalty. The Whigs contrasted King Van Buren, riding in an English-made coach more sumptuous than a coronation carriage and dining regally from platters of gold, with Old Tippecanoe, who had been reared in a log cabin. The Whigs simply took the pro-Jackson campaign program of 1828, used it for themselves, and created a wildly exciting canvass with hard cider, coonskins, and log cabin festivals all over the country. The Democrats vainly tried to stem the tide with sweet reason and sarcasm.

The program of attack on Van Buren presupposed attacks on all his lieutenants. In Pennsylvania there was a very effective propaganda campaign to prove that Buchanan had urged a banking program that would reduce the wages of labor to ten cents a day. "Ten Cent Jimmy," the pamphlets were labelled. Buchanan, in formal debate, always presented as strongly as he could the case of the opposition, and then proceeded to demolish it systematically by his own arguments. In supporting the Independent Treasury Bill, he had outlined the terrible conditions which would prevail unless banks were reformed and had then gone on to show how much better all would fare under the proposed bill. Senator John Davis of Massachusetts took the first section of this speech, and offered it as Buchanan's reasons for supporting the Independent Treasury. He took the "10 cents a day" phrase and quoted it out of context, asserting that Buchanan supported the Independent Treasury Bill in the hope that it would reduce wages, destroy banks and deflate property values. Davis's speeches, when circulated in print, had tremendous political impact.

Forney reported from Pennsylvania: "I do not know when I have been so much disgusted with the course of any political opponent as with that of this Mr. Davis—. . . He must be either a mere catspaw of others, or a weak, addle-brained man, or a malignant and unscrupulous ruffian. . . . When I see the effect they are making here, by means of his villainous perversion of your intelligible *Defence* of the laborer, I cannot but put such a construction upon his unworthy conduct. Why, Sir, they have flooded this county with his so-called Reply to you. . . . A copy has been sent to nearly every Democrat. . . . His whole speech is the assumption of the broad ground that the people are ignorant, and unable to discriminate between right and wrong."[11]

The human mind has not yet discovered the way of counteracting promptly the effect of the bold lie propagated by the prominent man. History is full of pertinent illustrations. If representative government has a nemesis, this is probably it. The "Ten Cent Jimmy" lie seriously weakened Buchanan in Pennsylvania.

Forney proposed that the Democrats "challenge any responsible member of the opposition here to join in the republication of both yours and Davis' speeches, both of which are to be published *correctly* and . . . *bound together*, and so circulated. . . . If they do not accept, they are *down* forever."[12] The opposition did not accept, nor was it down forever. Instead, it proceeded to improve its advantage by reviving the "drop of blood" smear and sending that out with the "Ten Cent Jimmy" pamphlets. Editor Middleton, of the *Lancaster Examiner*, did much of the printing. He had recently distinguished himself by shooting James Cameron when Cameron came in to beat him up for other lies he had published.[13] Buchanan was for "carrying the war into Carthage," but his friends advised against it. "It's only giving tone to falsehoods by heeding them," wrote Judge Champneys.

Buchanan made several long defensive speeches in the Senate on the "Ten Cent Jimmy" accusations. "If the most artful and unfair man in the world had determined to destroy any public measure," he asked, "in what manner would he most effectually damn it in public estimation? It would be to enumerate all the terrible consequences which would flow from it, according to the predictions of its enemies, and put them into the mouth of its friends as arguments in its favor. There could not by possibility be any stronger admission of its evil tendency. . . . This is the ridiculous attitude in which I am placed by the Senator's speech. If these imputations were well founded, I must be one of the most ferocious men in existence. Destruction must be my delight. No wild agrarian in the country has ever thought of waging such an indiscriminate war against all property, my own among the rest, as that which has been attributed to me by the Senator."[14] But Buchanan's exposure of Davis's fraud proved a futile effort. People found it easier to say "Ten Cent Jimmy" than to read a rebuttal, and the nickname stuck.

Meanwhile the Pennsylvania Democratic convention met on the 4th of March. Except for the Lancaster County delegation which cast its votes for William R. King as vice-president in token of esteem for Buchanan, the convention voted for Van Buren and Johnson and passed a resolution of confidence in Porter. But it did not dare to bring upon the floor any of the current issues and adjourned, like the Whigs, with no statement of policies.

The United States Senate kept Buchanan in Washington until its adjournment late in July. He tried to manipulate the strings of politics in the Keystone State by correspondence, but he grew more and more discouraged because of the attacks on him. Furthermore, it seemed utterly hopeless to reconcile the Democratic factions by patronage, though both he and Governor Porter were in full agreement on "the absolute necessity of union and harmony between the state and national administrations" and the wisdom of apportioning the state offices. Pittsburgh and Philadelphia were the two great centers of trouble. In the West, Buchanan's friends fought Porter and demanded that a new name be introduced for governor in 1841.[15] In the East, the pro-Bank party of Dallas knifed both Buchanan and Porter on every occasion. Yet both groups professed their solid support of Van Buren. The president had contributed some of the trouble by appointing several anti-Porter Democrats in the Pittsburgh area. In order to offset these, Buchanan induced Van Buren to select a staunch Porter man, Calvin Blythe, for the collectorship of the Port of Philadelphia, a position left open by the recent death of George Wolf. Porter gave evidence of his solidarity with Buchanan by naming some of his particular friends to Philadelphia judgeships.[16] As a result the Philadelphia Democrats were so furious with these two that they organized gangs to break up political rallies held by the friends of Buchanan and Porter in that city. The leading Democratic journal in Philadelphia, the *Pennsylvanian*, refused to publish any of Buchanan's replies to the Whig attacks on him, charged him by the line for every Senate speech which he wished printed, and purposely omitted the complimentary toasts given him in the lists of those reported from various meetings.[17]

The Muhlenberg Democrats of Berks County invited Buchanan to appear on a huge program they had arranged for the 4th of July. Vice-President Richard M. Johnson was to be the main attraction. With intention to insult, the arrangements committee failed to invite Governor Porter, but Buchanan replied sharply that he would appear on no program of such general interest which ignored Porter and thus forced the committee to send him an invitation.[18]

The Fourth of July celebrations demonstrated that the assaults on Buchanan had begun to boomerang. "Look at the East—at the West—at the South—and here in the middle states," wrote Forney. "Their celebrations are full of your name. You are right when you say that this attack upon you has done you good. It has been a god-send, indeed!"[19] Whether this was true or not, the Whig campaign against Buchanan only increased in intensity. Simon Cameron, playing a game of political blackmail, dug out a copy of an old 1814 handbill headed "We as Federalists," signed by Buchanan as president of the old Washington Association, and sent this for dissemination to Charles B. Penrose, one of the Democrats who had sold himself to the Bank several years before, and was now presumably a Whig.[20]

But more was yet to come. In a campaign speech in Lancaster Buchanan spoke of the efforts of the anti-Masonic Whigs to steal the election of 1838 by the Buckshot War in Pennsylvania and of a similar

135

affair in New Jersey the same year. He then quoted Whig Senator William C. Preston of South Carolina who had stated in a recent speech that "he believed Mr. V. Buren's election would be defeated by Constitutional means, yet if those means were insufficient—if the ballot box should fail him — he, for one, was willing to resort to the rights and arms that Nature gave him." A few days later the Philadelphia Whig papers came out with an article quoting Buchanan as saying,

> I believe General Harrison will be defeated by Constitutional means, yet if these means are insufficient, if the ballot box should fail, I for one would resort to the rights and the arms which nature gave me.[21]

Though never very enthusiastic about stump-speaking around the circuit, Buchanan now set out on a six-weeks tour of the Commonwealth, speaking nearly every day. He opened the campaign at a huge Democratic jamboree in Lancaster which attracted some 25,000 people. For two hours, he poured fire and brimstone into the enemy. With his speech in hand, he set out for the West: Chambersburg, Greensburg, Pittsburgh, Meadville, Erie. He also visited the northern counties and returned home by the end of September. "I arrived here from Western Pennsylvania," he wrote Van Buren, "broken down in voice and so hoarse that I fear I shall not again be able to take the field until after our first election. The effort of frequently addressing immense multitudes of people in the open air is more severe than I could have anticipated."[22] It took some stamina to be a working politician. Buchanan much preferred his usual method of campaigning with the pen. When someone chided Clay for a particularly cutting remark to Buchanan in the Senate, he replied: "Oh, damn him, he deserved it. *He writes letters!*"[23]

The state elections of October brought uncertainty, for state politics commanded allegiances and represented issues so distinct from the national contest that all predictions based on it were shaky. The excitement continued hot up until the balloting for presidential electors in November, which drew almost twice as many voters to the polls as had the fight of 1836. The final Pennsylvania tallies showed that the Whigs had a grand majority of 350 votes out of a total of nearly 300,000. The returns were heartbreakingly close; in several counties a few dozen votes spelled the difference between victory and defeat; but across the nation Harrison captured the presidency by an electoral vote of 294 to 60, and the Whigs won control of both houses of Congress.[24]

"I never was so much astonished or disappointed as at the result in Pennsylvania," Buchanan wrote to Van Buren. "But it is useless to indulge in vain regrets. . . . The Whigs & Anti-Masons are now gloating

136

over the prospect of driving me from the Senate. . . . Let them instruct me to vote for a national Bank, and I shall glory in my political martyrdom."[25]

A REGULAR CHINESE PUZZLE

Buchanan found the meaning of the election peculiarly hard to decipher. His own county of Lancaster and that of his birthplace, Franklin, had given huge Whig majorities; in Huntingdon, home county of Governor Porter, the Whigs had also won. The opposition, of course, had put all the money and men it could into these particular areas, which had been in the uncertain column since 1828. But Philadelphia had gone Democratic, if only by a whisker. Here the pro-Bank Democrats did better against the Whigs than anti-Bank Democrats—a regular Chinese puzzle. Did the election mean that Van Buren would have to be run in 1844 to vindicate his program, or did his defeat mean that he should not run again? Did the election mean that Porter should step down in 1841? What was the political aspect of the State Legislature? The anti-Masonic Whigs controlled the Senate, but in the House the control lay in the hands of Philadelphia Democrats, who agreed with the Whigs on almost all financial questions. Would the Legislature instruct Pennsylvania's Senators to destroy the Independent Treasury and create a new national Bank? And what bearing had these matters on Buchanan's chances for the presidency in four years? He was sure he did not know, but he did know one thing: they were a great deal less promising than they would have been if Little Van were in the White House with King as his vice-president.

For the time being there was nothing to do but wait. "Everything here is quiet," Buchanan wrote in December. "Our true policy is for the present to leave the Whig party to themselves. This party contains in itself the seeds of its own destruction, if they are permitted to germinate and bring forth their natural fruit."[26] "The Whigs are composed of such heterogeneous materials," he assured his brother, "that they will probably fall to pieces."[27]

Actually, the election of Harrison helped the Pennsylvania Democrats to solve their major problem, the Bank issue, for the state politicians could now proceed to act on this without facing pressure and loyalty-tests from a national administration. Buchanan had long agreed with Porter on the common sense course, though the two had been forced to pull in opposite directions because of the political requirements of their respective positions. Now Buchanan went to work for the renomination of Porter for governor, as the move best calculated to promote his own interests in 1844.

William Henry Harrison died exactly one month after taking the oath of office, leaving the presidency in the hands of Democrat John Tyler

137

who had been placed on the Whig ticket as part of a weird horse-trade in Virginia to get William C. Rives into the Senate. Rives, elected by Virginia Democrats, joined with the Whigs in Congress; Tyler, elected by the Whigs, now rejoined the Democrats.[28]

To compound the shock, Biddle's Bank suffered a run shortly after resuming specie payments and closed its doors with such a resounding crash that few expected they would ever open again. "The third crash of the Bank of the United States so soon after its resumption," wrote Buchanan, "has taken us all by surprise. I sincerely hope it has made its last struggle. . . . As long as it shall continue to exist, it will continue to derange the business of the country."[29]

What, in January, had looked like a bleak and hopeless prospect for the Democrats, by April had blossomed into a whole garden of new political promise. Porter was renominated for governor with the united support of Buchanan, Muhlenberg, and the Philadelphia Democrats, a "devilish strong team."[30] There was scarcely a canvass; the Democrats sent him back for a second term in November, 1841 by a huge majority over his Whig opponent, John Banks.

Porter continued to be the key to Buchanan's revived aspirations for the presidency in 1844, for the fall of the Bank would flatten Dallas in Philadelphia, leaving the Commonwealth solidly in the hands of the governor and senator in alliance, a combination that seemed to be the condition precedent to a serious bid for the White House. Porter, under the terms of the new state Constitution, would have to retire at the end of his second term and leave the field clear for Muhlenberg.

By August, 1841, the prospects looked even better than they had in the spring. President Tyler had just vetoed the darling measure of the Whigs, a bill for a new Federal Bank. His message had produced "prayers and thanks to God on the one side; and imprecations and eternal vows of vengeance on the other."[31] "Never was there a party so completely used up as the Whigs have been in so short a time," wrote Buchanan. "A Manifesto . . . will appear tomorrow from the Whigs in Congress reading John Tyler out of the Whig Church and delivering him over to Satan to be buffeted."[32]

Still, there were plenty of thorny problems to solve. Pennsylvania had gone bankrupt; it could not pay the interest on its bonds. Porter had delivered a strong message on banking reform which coincided with Buchanan's favorite views: prohibition of speculation in commodities by banks; state supervision of note issues to keep them within the limits permitted by charter; elimination of bank notes under $10 or $20 in order that employers would have to pay workmen in coin; and the summary revocation of the charter of any bank which refused to redeem its notes in specie on demand.

138

But the Legislature, still closely balanced between Whig and Democratic control, drew up its own bill and proceeded, with the usual support of pro-Bank Democrats, to pass it over the governor's veto. By the new measure, Pennsylvania borrowed $3,100,000 from the various banks for which they were permitted to issue paper currency against the promissory note of a bankrupt state! There was no requirement of specie payment, no control of bank issues, no curtailment of small notes— nothing that was desired. Buchanan hit the ceiling. "My public life has been stormy and tempestuous," he wrote, "but no political event has ever made me despond before. The last night was the first which I have ever spent in sleepless anxiety. . . . It would seem that whether the Democratic party are successful or defeated in the popular elections, the result in regard to Banks is always the same. . . . The value of this new currency will fluctuate with the ever fluctuating value of [the State loan] on which alone it rests . . . . What a standard of value! . . . The State gives . . . the Banks . . . the privilege of perpetual suspension. What miserable hum-buggery! What could have been the reason why twelve Democrats deserted us and voted against the veto?"[33]

The same combination of Whigs, anti-Masons and pro-Bank Democrats at Harrisburg used their tenure up to the election of October, 1841, to embarrass Buchanan by instructing him to vote against the Independent Treasury, in favor of Clay's Bank Bill, in favor of a resolution to expunge the expunging resolution, and in favor of the Whig land program. He obeyed the obnoxious instructions to avoid the necessity of resigning, but debated vigorously in every case against the view he had to support on roll call, justifying himself by the declaration that he spoke his own views but was bound to respect his instructions.

The 1844 presidential race began the moment General Harrison's coffin was lowered into the grave. Van Buren? Calhoun? Benton? Buchanan? Tyler? R. M. Johnson? Who would lead the Democracy? The field looked so large and the results so uncertain that the friends of Dallas and the Bank got up their own private movement in favor of Commodore Charles Stewart as Pennsylvania's favorite son. "The Commodore has money enough," reported Forney, "as those fellows know, and if he is willing to bleed to have his name in print everyday, why let him enjoy the novel immortality."[34]

Ridiculous as the drive was, Buchanan got quite excited about it. The Stewart mangers bought up a whole string of editors who divided their efforts between belittling Buchanan and puffing Stewart. If anything could upset his prospects, Buchanan thought, just such a program might do it; you could meet an antagonist who was well known, but how could you handle a man with no political record? As the rash of "Old Ironsides" Clubs spread, Buchanan marshalled his editors into defensive line. The battle turned out to be mainly a newspaper fight, but in the course of it the Buchanan and Porter journals resumed their old-time feud and spread abroad the suggestion that Porter would oppose Buchanan's bid for re-election to the Senate which was just a year away.[35]

From Pittsburgh Buchanan got the warning: "Porter is no friend of yours and a dishonest politician." He would trample his best friend to get ahead and was covertly promoting a southern candidate for president to get the second office himself.[36] But Philadelphia reported that "Porter is opposed to Stewart, and will take bold ground for you. . . . The Stewart business is directed *entirely* against you."[37]

Buchanan's friends worked desperately to bolster him up. "*You must drive through!*" they told him.[38] "Put your hand fairly to the plough and play the game. Lay aside your usual modesty and neither look back nor hesitate."[39] "*Pennsylvania will be all right,*" they assured him. "Stewart is hung at the political yardarm, and knows you are the rising and strong man." Forget about them all, even Van Buren. People were "furiously at loggerheads" about him, and as for Tyler, "he don't go with the democrats."[40]

These men had some reason for their concern, because Buchanan had developed a reputation for being unwilling to fight on his own behalf. This trait governed much of his political thinking, and no phase of his character bred more doubts, misunderstanding, and contempt among his contemporaries. Buchanan had a phenomenal capacity for detachment; he could view himself from outside himself and criticize freely what he saw. He even wrote his memoirs in the third person. He continually placed himself and his friends on stage and went to the back of the theater to look the cast over and figure out, with total lack of appreciation of the personal impulses of the actors, what they ought to do to perfect the play. He was the very opposite of John Forney, his excitable, hotly emotional, young editor of the Lancaster *Intelligencer.*

Forney lived in cycles of stygian gloom or celestial happiness; all men were either his bosom friends or bitter enemies; insults had to be promptly avenged, if possible by a fist fight, and favors had to be promptly repaid by favors. His was a life of lavish generosity and bankruptcy, of jubilation and hangover. Forney's life depended upon Buchanan's political success; he attached himself like a leech, worked his heart out, and frankly admitted that his object was to get future patronage.

Because of his violent temper, Forney continually got Buchanan into trouble. He would see an insult where none was intended, and frequently took the bait of a sly remark purposely tendered to get a rise out of him. An able and powerful advocate, Forney regarded himself as Buchanan's confidential political manager, explosively attacked any presumed rival, and caused a great deal of resentment among Buchanan's other friends. For years Buchanan kept the tight rein on Forney, writing him to stop his attacks on editors or politicians whose support he needed. Why, Forney complained, did he not stick 100 per cent with his true friends and throw the others out of the window? Because, Buchanan would explain patiently but with tart precision, no man had enough 100 per cent true friends to elect him dogcatcher; only united effort could win; union could only be achieved by compromise, never by force. Force only achieved two things: either the total destruction of one part of those who disagreed, or a fight which destroyed both parties. Both results lost elections. Forney must curb his personal feelings or Buchanan would lose; and if Buchanan lost, Forney would certainly lose. Could anything be plainer?

Buchanan used the dependence of others on him by threatening, when they became insubordinate, to withdraw from politics or from Pennsylvania. When he felt that his editors were not active enough in repelling the "drop of blood" and "Ten Cent Jimmy" canards, he used this technique and received the answer he expected from Forney: "I am sorry, indeed I may say *alarmed* at the intimation you threw out of leaving Lancaster. . . . The whole county have taken you to their heart of hearts; defending you the more you are assailed. . . . Depart from Lancaster! Besides the shock it must be to your friends—and I confess I speak interestedly—it would be, as a matter of policy, . . . wrong in the extreme. Pardon me when I say that we look up to you as our stay and support."[41] Time and again Buchanan resorted to this technique, but Forney caught on quickly and in times of crisis would play the same game, announcing his intention to quit his newspaper and take up law, a threat usually good for a kind letter and a loan of several hundred dollars from his patron.

Buchanan wanted the presidency but in a peculiar way; he did not want to win it, he wanted to be invited into it. In September, 1841, he wrote, "I would not wish you to bring out my name as a candidate for the Presidency. It is yet too soon to agitate this question in the Public Journals; and any premature movement would only injure the individual it was intended to benefit. Besides I have no ambitious longings on this subject. Let events take their course; and my only desire is that at the proper time, the individual may be selected as our candidate who will best promote the success of the party & its principles."[42] He, of course, would be this person but a gentleman could not say so. "In regard to the Presidency," he told Reynolds, "the real contest would seem to be between Van Buren & myself; & if the Democracy of Penna. would sustain me with an unbroken front I think my chances are fully equal if not superior to his. . . . Should there be even the appearance of a serious division in Penna., I shall make my bow and retire."[43]

141

11
THIS I BELIEVE • 1834 - 1845

THE CREED OF A CONSERVATIVE

By the time the election of 1844 drew near, Buchanan had already served twenty years as a legislator. The decade he spent in the Senate brought him into daily contact with probably the most distinguished group of American statesmen ever assembled there, a company including not only five future Presidents of the United States (Van Buren, Tyler, Polk, Fillmore, and Pierce) but also such parliamentary giants as Webster, Clay, Calhoun and Benton. In this remarkable galaxy of American politicians, Buchanan always stood on the periphery. He never, in all his legislative career, had his name attached to an important bill or became the focal point of public interest in a debate. He had talent for clear thinking but none for self-dramatization. He brought to the senatorship great seriousness of purpose, readiness to debate and forensic ability, loyalty to party, diligence in seeking facts, and a consistency of view which made his stand on public questions easily predictable and gained him the nickname "friend of the obvious." With these tools of his trade he quietly exerted a great deal of influence on important legislation, but his steady craftsmanship attracted little public attention. It did, however, gain the respect and often the admiration and thanks of his colleagues.

The well-ordered intellectual world of James Buchanan rested upon principles behind which he rarely probed, and upon them he logically developed his political views. "Abstract propositions," he once said, "should never be discussed by a legislative body," and he might have added that concrete propositions should never depart very far from the *status quo* or anticipate any very rapid change of society.

Buchanan believed that the essence of self-government was restraint. Written constitutions, he thought, were the most useful invention of his age, but what were constitutions "but restraints imposed, not by arbitrary authority, but by the people upon themselves and their own representatives?" "Restraint," he said, "restraint. . . . Sir, this Federal

142

Government . . . is nothing but a system of restraints from beginning to end." That alone could preserve a Union of several dozen states which differed from each other in their institutions, their people, their language, their soil, climate, and products. In an enlarged view their interests might appear to be identical, but "to the eye of local and sectional prejudice," he noted, "they always appear to be conflicting." Therefore, jealousies would perpetually arise which could be repressed only "by that mutual forbearance which pervades the Constitution."[1] Mutual forbearance, mutual accommodation, the avoidance of extremes, the willingness of a majority to extend some consideration to the minority, the acceptance of compromise as the only method short of war or despotism for settling political disputes, these attitudes alone could perpetuate self-government and the federal system.

In his senatorial career, Buchanan approached most closely the role of statesman, for here he uniformly took the long view. His recommendations on domestic and foreign policy, though attacked at one time or another by every geographic section, were consistent and have remained remarkably sound. At the base lay the conviction that political power, in whatever form it existed, must always be held in check, and that the United States Constitution provided all the machinery necessary for this purpose.

Buchanan remained continually alert to partisan attacks upon the delicate balances which the Constitution provided. As a Representative he had led the battle to prevent Congress from emasculating the power of the Supreme Court by repealing its authority to review state legislation. As a Senator, he vigorously and successfully fought an effort of Clay and Webster to deprive the president of the power to remove executive officers, presenting arguments which raised him to eminence among serious students of constitutional law. To give the Senate power to pass on executive removals would subordinate the president to the Congress, "a position," said Buchanan, "in which the Constitution of the country never intended to place him."[2]

In the debate to expunge the Senate's resolution censuring President Jackson, he pointed out the constitutional problem: the Senate by convicting an executive officer without a hearing, witnesses, or counsel had destroyed its competence to act later as a court of impeachment. But if the resolution condemning the president as a tyrant and usurper had any basis of fact, then the executive should stand trial. Buchanan warned that the procedure of legislative censure could easily lead to a star-chamber substitute for impeachment, enable the Senate to destroy at will any executive officer, and thus overthrow the structure defined in the Constitution.[3] On another occasion he jumped to the defense of the veto power of the president which angry Whigs, after Tyler's veto of the Bank Bill, tried to amend out of the Constitution. Throughout his political career, Buchanan could be found among those who tried to define clearly and to keep strong the delicate lines which separated the three branches of government and the functions of state and federal administrations. He did not, like Calhoun, propose state supremacy; or like Webster, seek a consolidated national government; but he sought to keep the state and federal entities in their separate orbits, revolving without collision around the sun of the system, the Constitution.

The great national economic issues of the 1830's were the tariff, banking, and public land. Buchanan condemned both free trade and prohibitive tariffs because either system would impoverish one or another part of the nation. Why should the northern Whigs and Democrats want to bankrupt the South by the protective tariff of 1842? And why should the southerners think it sensible to hold conventions in favor of free trade, which would only put northern manufacturers out of business? Thus he addressed the Senate, complaining all the while that he was "exposed to fires from both sides, Mr. Clay and Mr. Calhoun."

Buchanan voted, under instruction, for the high protective tariff of 1842 but stated that he disapproved of the bill. He predicted, accurately, that the measure would be replaced by another bill sponsored by the South which would be too low, and that both enactments would prove contrary to the best public interest. Why not split the difference and permit both sections to share in a modest local prosperity, instead of using partisan politics to aid one section to grow rich upon the ruins of another? Such a political program he would always resist. Let people call him a trimmer, or vacillating, or whatever they wished; he would sustain a balanced tariff as constructive policy for the United States, and he would urge it in the face of Webster, Calhoun, the Pennsylvania ironmasters, and the Mississippi planters. "I am viewed," he said, "as the strongest advocate of protection . . . in other States: whilst I am denounced as its enemy in Pennsylvania."[4]

Buchanan took the same middle-ground position on the Bank question. He strongly opposed unregulated state banking but, with equal vigor, opposed the control of banks by the state. He wanted enough hard money in circulation to pay workingmen's wages, but he was enough of a businessman and banker himself to know that an expanding national economy demanded an elastic currency. His proposals for banks showed there was a wide range of alternatives between wildcat banking and total control.

Tariff and banking problems became entangled with the public land policy of the federal government. Demand for public land encouraged rash overissues of state bank notes; this currency, when paid into the public treasury for land, created a surplus on the government books; and

144

when a surplus showed, pressure mounted to cut down the tariff rates. Then, when the paper money forwarded by the treasury to the state banks for redemption proved worthless, the surplus was wiped out and the treasury could not pay its bills with the tariff duties alone. Thus, tariff, banks, and public land formed parts of a single economic problem.

For years the politicians had agreed to distribute any surplus arising from the sale of federal land to the individual states in order to draw off this eccentric source of revenue and to render the tariff fixed and certain. In opposing this practice, Buchanan shrewdly observed that no legislator would vote money for federal projects if he knew that a share of any unspent money went to his home state. "Man at his best is but a frail being," he said. If you placed his interest on the one side and his duty on the other, he would generally promote his private advantage. Buchanan also foresaw a fight over the terms of distribution, whether pro rata to the states or in proportion to their population, the very question which had nearly wrecked the Constitutional Convention of 1787. To avoid all these problems he proposed to apply the surplus to the national defense establishment. "With this money," he said, "you might increase your navy, complete your fortifications, and prepare for war; and you would thus distribute its benefits more equally and justly among the people than you could do in any other manner."[5] This proposal, side-tracking local interest and concentrating attention on a new and larger objective, typified Buchanan.

FOREIGN AFFAIRS

Buchanan's reference to preparing for war reflected the agitated state of foreign affairs in the 1830's. A war with France had narrowly been averted; war with Mexico over Texas seemed a real possibility; and relations with England were strained by a succession of events: the *Caroline* affair of 1837-1838, the Aroostook War in 1839, the *Creole* affair of 1841, and the Oregon Question.

Buchanan, chairman of the Senate Foreign Relations Committee for five years before the election of Tyler and an active member of the Committee thereafter, brought in several reports on the Maine boundary dispute before Webster became Secretary of State and began formal negotiations with the British.

Buchanan reported that the Committee did not "entertain a doubt of the title of the United States to the whole of the disputed territory," but three years later Secretary of State Webster, considering the maintenance of friendly relations with Britain to be more important to the United States than the acquisition of a small segment of Maine, met

145

Lord Ashburton in a conciliatory spirit and agreed to a compromise settlement.[6]

The Webster-Ashburton Treaty passed the Senate in 1842 by a large majority, but Buchanan voted against it for reasons which he explained at great length. After detailing the voluminous evidence sustaining the American claim, he denounced Webster for failing to use his bargaining power to advantage. If he had insisted on America's rights in this matter, he might have won concessions in others. He might have negotiated a settlement of the Northwest Boundary Dispute, obtained redress for the *Creole* and *Caroline* outrages, and forced Britain to abandon her policy of impressment on the high seas. Webster had not used diplomacy. He had given up American territory for nothing, and prospects for settling other Anglo-American problems were now no better than ever. Buchanan called the treaty "an unqualified surrender of our territory to British dictation."[7]

At the opposite end of the country, along the southwestern border, tension had risen nearly to the breaking point. The Mexican government found it difficult to maintain order and could not protect the lives and property of foreigners. Claims of injured United States citizens against Mexico multiplied rapidly and American business there, once estimated at $3,000,000 per year, dropped to $300,000. Then Texas revolted. The Texans, most of them emigrants from the United States, set up the Lone Star Republic, invited diplomatic recognition, and petitioned for admission to the United States.

The Texas revolution of 1836 and the Canadian revolution of 1837 soon demonstrated the need for a stiffening of the American neutrality laws, for American citizens became involved in both affrays. Buchanan now proclaimed the doctrine of the good neighbor. "We have three neighbors on our frontiers," he said, "Canada, Texas and Mexico; and the duties of good neighborhood require something more from us in relation to them than could be strictly demanded under the law of nations. . . . It is our duty to prevent our citizens from aiding in every revolutionary movement against a neighboring government. . . . It is against all reason and justice that in case of a sudden commotion in a neighboring country . . ., the citizens of the United States should be permitted to take part with the insurgents."[8]

Carrying this doctrine one step further, he urged a policy of nonintervention in the domestic affairs of foreign nations. Petitions had been flooding the Senate in the spring of 1836 praying Congress "to recognize the independence of Texas, and . . . to interpose to terminate the conflict which now rages in that country." It was natural, Buchanan admitted, for the sympathies of American citizens to be "earnestly enlisted in favor of those who drew the sword for liberty," but to act on such feelings was to ignore the teaching of the wisdom of the past. "We should

146

never interfere in the domestic concerns of other nations," he asserted. The people of every nation had the absolute right to adopt any form of government they thought proper, and the United States ought to preserve the strictest neutrality. "The world must be persuaded," he insisted. "It could not be conquered." Acting on these principles, the United States had "always recognized existing Governments *de facto*, whether they were constitutional or despotic. It was their affair, not ours."[9]

But should the United States render aid to Americans struggling for freedom in Texas? No, answered Buchanan, lest there be "suspicion that we have got up this war for the purpose of wresting Texas from those to whom . . . it justly belongs."[10] Should the independence of Texas be recognized? Yes, "when the fact of their actual independence was established—then—and not till then." Was any act of the United States required during the period of uncertainty? Yes, the United States Government should rigorously prosecute "all persons who might attempt to violate our neutrality in the civil war between Mexico and Texas" and should inform Mexico and Texas that the United States would require them both to scrupulously respect American territory.

On March 3, 1837, President Jackson recognized the independence of the Republic of Texas. The Texans had already voted in favor of immediate annexation to the United States. These acts brought the American people face to face with the two most crucial problems of the age: territorial expansion and slavery.

EXPANSION AND SLAVERY

Buchanan vigorously urged territorial expansion. "This I believe," he said. "Providence has given to the American people a great and glorious mission to perform, even that of extending . . . liberty over the whole North American continent. Within less than fifty years, there will exist one hundred millions of free Americans between the Atlantic and Pacific oceans. . . . What, sir! prevent the American people from crossing the Rocky Mountains? You might as well command Niagara not to flow. We must fulfill our destiny."[11]

But how could the nation fulfill this destiny without spreading abroad the slavery system? "I feel a strong repugnance by any act of mine," wrote Buchanan, "to extend the present limits of the Union over a new slave-holding territory." The acquisition of Texas, he hoped, might "be the means of limiting, not enlarging, the dominion of slavery." In every state not dependent upon cotton culture, economic pressure would force gradual abolition. Where grain became a staple, slavery would bring bankruptcy, and "if the slave don't run away from his master, the master must run away from the slave." In Texas, slaves would run off into

147

Mexico and there "mingle with a race where no prejudice exists against their color." Buchanan thought that if Texas should be annexed, it would be divided into four or five states, in only one of which the soil and climate would support slavery. But the annexation treaty itself ought to determine the proportion of free and slave states. "Should this not be done, we may have another Missouri question to shake the Union to its center."[12]

The Senate, in Buchanan's day, was full of the sound and fury of debates on slavery. He entered prominently into the discussions about the circulation of abolitionist propaganda, presided over the committee which had to solve the controversy over the right of petition, and acted as spokesman for the North against Calhoun's proposal to outlaw all "intermeddling" with slavery in the national capital or the territories.

Several southern states, facing an inundation of abolitionist writings which they considered an incitation to riot, outlawed the circulation of such literature. The Senate considered a bill authorizing postmasters to withhold mail they knew to be prohibited by state law and destroy it if it were not claimed by the sender. Buchanan and Webster debated this measure. The latter argued that it infringed the freedom of the press and that mail, as private property, could not be destroyed. Buchanan defended the freedom of the press, but he stoutly maintained that the government had the right to refuse to distribute pamphlets intended to destroy it. He asserted that no person could have any property right in articles which the law forbade him to possess, whether the prohibitory law was state or federal. It was, said Buchanan, "a question not of property, but of public safety," applicable only in states where the people had declared, by law, that their safety was threatened.[13]

The discussion of the mails linked the cause of abolition with the cause of civil liberties. This connection, so exasperating to the defenders of the Union, was further emphasized by the long struggle over the right of petition. The House of Representatives, faced with a mountain of petitions from some 500 antislavery societies, eventually adopted a resolution to table them all. This so-called "Gag Resolution" seemed a clear denial of the right of petition guaranteed to citizens by the Constitution.

Buchanan became the center of the Senate fight over abolition petitions when his colleagues made him chairman of the Committee to consider the question of the prohibition of slavery and the slave trade in the District of Columbia, the subject of most of the petitions. Buchanan fought strenuously against an outright gag, but at the same time insisted that no splinter group of citizens should be permitted to stop the machinery of government by abuse of the petition device. As the debates on the circulation of abolition mail had brought him into conflict with Webster and the antislavery forces, the debates on petitions now brought him into conflict with Calhoun and the proslavery advocates. "I have not found, upon the present occasion," he noted wryly, "the maxim to be true, that 'in medio tutissimus ibis.' "

When Buchanan presented a petition from the Caln Quarterly Meeting of the Society of Friends, referring to the abolition of slavery in the District of Columbia, Calhoun moved not to receive it. Buchanan replied: "Let it once be understood that the sacred right of petition and the cause of the abolitionists must rise or fall together, and the consequences may be fatal. . . . We have just as little right to interfere with slavery in the South, as we have to touch the right of petition."[14]

Calhoun alleged that the people of no state were aggrieved by conditions in the District of Columbia; what went on there was none of their business; it was the concern only of Congress and the local inhabitants. But who, asked Buchanan, is to judge "whether the People are aggrieved or not? Is it those who suffer, or fancy they suffer, or the Senate. The Constitution secures the right of being heard by petition to every citizen; and I would not abridge it because he happened to be a fool."[15]

Buchanan asked Calhoun to withdraw his motion. "Why select the very weakest position, one on which you yourselves will present a divided front to the enemy," he asked, "when it is in your power to choose one on which you and we can unite? . . . You place us in such a position that we cannot defend you, without infringing the sacred right of petition. Do you not perceive that the question of abolition may thus be indissolubly connected . . . with a cause which we can never abandon?"

Buchanan proposed that the Senate should accept the petitions but reject their prayer. To those who could not see any difference between tabling and rejecting the prayer, he suggested the difference between inviting a man into the house, hearing his proposition, and then declining to accept it or kicking him downstairs before he had a chance to speak. And why should the prayer be rejected? Only because the nation was bound in honor to respect the promise to the original donors of the District, that slavery would not be disturbed there so long as it existed in Maryland and Virginia.

After two months of heated discussion, Buchanan's motion to accept the petition but reject its prayer finally came up for a vote on March 9, 1836, and passed 36 to 10. "I rejoice at the result of the vote," he wrote. "Abolition is forever separated from the right of petition. The abolitionists . . . must now stand alone."[16]

Buchanan's mail had been heavy during the height of the controversy. A Quaker wrote him that the question had broken up the Caln meeting.[17] Another wrote that the North ought to thank God it was rid of slavery and be satisfied.[18] Buchanan's roommate, King of Alabama, told him frankly that if the North persevered in its current course, "then we will separate from them."[19] On hearing this, Thomas Elder commented:

"Let them withdraw and wade in blood before six months."[20] "It is rapidly becoming a question of union or disunion," wrote Buchanan to the mayor of Pittsburgh. "If the progress of the abolition societies cannot be arrested, I fear the catastrophe may come sooner than any of us antici- pate. . . . Would it not be well to get up counter-societies of friends of the Union?"[21]

John C. Calhoun now presented to the Senate an inflammatory resolution:

> That the intermeddling of any State or States, or their citizens, to abolish slavery in this District, or any of the Territories, . . .; or the passage of any act or measure of Congress, with that view, would be a direct attack on the institutions of all the slave- holding states.[22]

Buchanan, Benton, and most of the northern Democratic Sen- ators labored to get these resolves buried in a select committee as rapidly as possible, for they promised nothing but another acrimonious and fruitless debate which would spread its poison throughout the nation. Why, asked Buchanan, are our southern friends continually "driving us into positions where their enemies and our enemies may gain important advantages." Were not the abolition attacks enough? Did the South, too, have to assault the Union men of the North? "Abolition thus acquires force," he said. "Those of us in the Northern States who have determined to sustain the rights of the slave-holding states at every hazard, are placed in a most embarrassing position. We are almost literally between two fires."[23]

But what irked Buchanan most was the fact that the abolitionists were preventing the achievement of the very result which nearly everyone sought, the ultimate solution of the slavery problem. "Before this un- fortunate agitation commenced," he said, "a very large and growing party existed in several of the slave States in favor of the gradual abolition of slavery; and now not a voice is heard there in support of such a measure. The Abolitionists have postponed the emancipation of the slaves in three or four States of this Union for at least half a century." If they continued urging their mad schemes, they would "cover the land with blood." "The Union is now in danger, and I wish to proclaim the fact," Buchanan warned.[24]

He reiterated this theme. "This question of domestic slavery is the weak point in our institutions," he insisted. "Touch this question of slavery seriously . . . and the Union is from that moment dissolved. . . . Although in Pennsylvania we are all opposed to slavery in the abstract, yet we will never violate the constitutional compact we have made with our sister states . Their rights will be held sacred by us. Under the Consti- tution it is their own question; and there let it remain."[25]

150

12

AN OFFICE NOT TO BE SOUGHT • 1844

NO PEACE FOR PENNSYLVANIA

Buchanan hoped to complete the first stage of his plans for the presidential nomination, firm control of Pennsylvania, before he came up for re-election to the Senate in December, 1842. He had stated clearly that he would bid for the presidency only if the Pennsylvania Democracy united solidly back of him. With the Pennsylvania votes to manipulate in the national convention, his prospects might be good, especially if the convention came to a deadlock.

The State Legislature in the spring of 1842 eliminated the main cause of Democratic schism by passing a banking act which provided for gradual resumption of specie payments and conformed closely to Buchanan's ideas. The new law would, he wrote, enable the people "to enjoy the advantages of well-regulated specie-paying Banks, without being cursed by the evils of the present unrestricted system." Biddle's "monster" lay dead, Tyler's veto had put an end to the threat of a new Federal Bank, and the Democrats after ten years were at last relieved of the ordeal of party tests on the Bank question.[1]

The Dallas party was weakened because it had lost its chief source of funds, and it could no longer create dissension by intruding the banking issue; Buchanan was strengthened among the working classes because their pay envelopes would now contain sound money rather than depreciated shinplasters. As his popularity grew among the Irish Catholic laborers, the millworkers and clerks, his managers in metropolitan areas urged him to get busy and capitalize on his advantage. "If we now had a paper in Philadelphia, what an impression we could make!" cried Forney.[2] Cameron advised Buchanan to move permanently to Philadelphia.

Buchanan wrote noncommittal replies. He would not promote his own elevation; he would not run away from home for political reasons; he would let his friends work for him if they thought he was worth it, and if not, he would be satisfied. He would do all he could to unite the party,

151

but would not stir a finger for the presidency. He would follow Jackson's motto: The presidency is an office not to be sought.[3]

Such replies went down hard with those in the field who were spending their days making contacts and writing articles, and their nights attending strategy meetings. They were spending their money, too, keeping bankrupt editors out of the hands of the sheriff and entertaining for the party. They agreed heartily with Benjamin F. Brewster of Philadelphia, but few had the guts to write, as he did: "Mr. Buchanan, we do need some action. We do need some concert. We do need some decided proclamation."[4]

Forney urged Buchanan to take a political barnstorming trip, for work was needed in New York, Ohio, Indiana, and the southern States; but instead, Buchanan got out his two "little black books" in which he kept annotated lists of state and national politicians and campaigned by direct mail.[5] Within Pennsylvania, a friend reported, "everything looks bright, very bright. The ball has rolled on with a force and velocity alike gratifying and astonishing. The feeling in your favor in this State is very strong." The Pittsburgh *Manufacturer*, a Whig paper, the *Erie Observer*, formerly against Buchanan, and the *Spirit of the Times*, which had been Stewart's chief mouthpiece, all joined the Buchanan movement.[6]

But trouble developed in the quarter where Buchanan had tried hardest to prevent it. At the beginning of Porter's second term, Buchanan's enemies tempted the governor to set up his own party, to try to get control of the state delegation in the 1844 convention, and to use it to promote himself. He would be out of a job in January, 1845; why give everything to Buchanan when he might very well capture the vice-presidency? He held Buchanan's future in the hollow of his hand. Irritated by some of Buchanan's friends who made excessive demands for their fidgity support, Porter succumbed.

The game would be to have the state Administration evince interest in all the prospective presidential candidates so that when the field narrowed, Porter could name his price for the Pennsylvania delegation. Rumors had been flying about that the governor's henchmen had been cultivating Vice-President Richard M. Johnson, and in January, 1842, the truth erupted with dramatic suddenness in a breakup of the state Cabinet. Secretary of the Commonwealth Shunk resigned rather than obey Porter's order to transfer the state printing in Harrisburg from a Buchanan paper to a journal which had been praising Johnson. Henry Petrikin, Shunk's deputy, also resigned, as did the Auditor General, the Treasurer and the Librarian, all of them friends of Buchanan.

Porter's new Cabinet became a kind of electioneering headquarters for Johnson during the summer. The governor arranged to have "Old Tecumseh" visit Pennsylvania in October, ostensibly to celebrate the anniversary of his victory at the Battle of the Thames. Buchanan received an invitation to join the official party under an assurance that the occasion was a historic observance, "entirely non-political," but of course he declined. Long before the celebrations at Williamsport and Danville, however, Porter himself admitted that the Johnson movement had burned out.[7]

Porter continued to write cordially to Buchanan, explaining his Cabinet changes with the comment, "I would as soon attempt to control the wind as manage some of these people."[8] He renewed his promise to treat all factions fairly and Buchanan, for his part, tried to calm his associates, which was not an easy matter for they were wild with rage at the governor.

The Porter men now turned their interest to General Lewis Cass of Michigan, who had just returned from his diplomatic mission in France. A bluff westerner who had served as Secretary of War under President Jackson, Cass aroused American chauvinism by his violent Anglophobia and his ardent support of expansion. "Pennsylvania is the soil for President-making," wrote Buchanan. He did not fear Cass as a presidential rival, for the Pennsylvania Cassites, he predicted, would "damn any cause in which they embark," but he did fear that the local Cass movement would be used to influence the coming senatorial election.[9]

Toward the end of 1842, Forney ferreted out a plot. Buchanan's organization had decided to hold a convention at Harrisburg on Jackson Day, 1843, in order to place Buchanan's name officially in nomination for the presidency. This meeting would convene just before the Legislature began balloting for his re-election to the Senate. Governor Porter's friends now prepared to bring General Cass to Harrisburg for a demonstration immediately on the heels of the Buchanan convention, and to use the general's visit as a means of obtaining the senatorship for one of themselves. The Cass men demanded that Buchanan should make his re-election conditional upon his withdrawal from the presidential race or, if he wanted to run for president, get out of the senatorial race. "If," they said, "Buchanan's friends insist on filling every office . . . at Harrisburg . . . with none but his adherents, we will unite with the Whigs to defeat *his* election."[10]

The answer rested with the Legislature and, as Buchanan freely admitted, "our past experience in Penna. has proven that the Representative does not always obey the will of his Constituents. . . . Our security now is that the Whigs have no money to pay the wages of iniquity."[11] It would be close, for the "rebels" could count on the votes of ten Democratic Cassites. "They must have Thirteen, at least, to effect what they desire," reported Forney. *"This they never can get."*[12]

Forney's prediction proved correct. By Christmas, the Cass-

153

Porter men gave up and publicly announced their readiness to support Buchanan. The Buchanan convention met on January 8, endorsed its man and adjourned to await the action of the Legislature. That body quickly re-elected Buchanan to the Senate and the convention then immediately resumed its sessions.[13] Forney made the address and introduced resolutions proposing Buchanan for the presidency. The convention "closed in a burst of such enthusiasm as never was known in Harrisburg, except during the Jackson campaign."[14]

With the senatorial election past and the presidential struggle just beginning, what were Buchanan's prospects? Van Buren had gone on a western tour during which he had visited Jackson at the Hermitage and received the general's blessing. The people, said Old Hickory, would survey Little Van's record and on "sober second thought" repair their error of 1840. Buchanan's friends, however, asserted that "every fool will see that a course more destructive to the party [than the renomination of Mr. Van Buren] could not be recommended by its most decided enemy."[15] But Van Buren would run, and Jackson wanted James K. Polk of Tennessee to go in as vice-president. Calhoun, too, would run with any assistance he could get. He would promote the aspirations of as many competitors as possible in order to throw the election into the House of Representatives. Cass, with Pennsylvania's aid, planned to take advantage of a convention deadlock between Calhoun and Van Buren. Tyler saw the same prospect and made a bid for Buchanan's support, offering him a seat on the Supreme Court. When Tyler failed to enlist Buchanan, he turned to Porter.

The best Buchanan could make of it was that Van Buren and Polk, endorsed by Jackson, had the lead and would be supported by Dallas. This ticket was sure to lose Pennsylvania and with it the national election, but if Van Buren insisted, all would have to go along; the party could survive a defeat better than a split. Calhoun would try anything and remained an uncertain quantity. Tyler wanted to start a third party, but he would discover he had no party at all, and anyone who played his game would go down with him. Cass might prove formidable. Buchanan had fewer enemies than any, but he lacked a national organization and had to depend upon the effect of a united Pennsylvania delegation introduced into a confused and uncertain convention. With the support of his home state delegates working in harmony, there was a possibility that he would be nominated. Otherwise, his chances were hopeless.

Buchanan predicted that Tyler would take the governor's brother into his Cabinet and "we shall have a Tyler party in Pennsylvania."[16] On March 4, the president exploded his political bomb by naming Judge James M. Porter Secretary of War, thus blasting Buchanan's hopes of a united Pennsylvania. Governor Porter now dismissed the few remaining "Buchanan men—by God!" from state offices and tried to force Tyler down the throats of his followers, but here he got a shock. Even the old faithful Harrisburg *Keystone*, long Porter's mainstay, refused to endorse Tyler. When Porter took the state printing from it, Editor Orville Barrett quit and joined Buchanan. The governor had written his political death warrant. "His fall," wrote Buchanan, "has been more sudden than that of any other public man I have ever known."[17]

From New York came the word that Van Buren was regularly in the field. "You are aware," Buchanan wrote, "that he never has been popular in Pennsylvania and that feeling which was formerly one of indifference has been converted into positive dislike. I am sincerely sorry for it; because should he be nominated he shall receive my decided support."[18] By midsummer the Van Buren band wagon began to pick up speed in many states. The Philadelphians (Dallas, Gilpin, Henry Horn, John K. Kane and others) jumped aboard. They invited Buchanan to be their speaker at a celebration but he declined politely. Certainly his chances had gone hopelessly overboard. The state administration had become his enemy, Philadelphia had slipped out of his grasp, he had no trustworthy support left but his own fraction of the party, and that was committed, by his own orders, to Van Buren. And who would control if Van Buren won? Dallas! After Congress adjourned on March 3, Buchanan returned to Lancaster and went to bed with a bilious attack which tormented him until the middle of June.[19]

Buchanan took his usual tour through western Pennsylvania during July and August, going to Mercersburg, Bedford, Pittsburgh and Meadville. He had family business and political affairs to look after but most of all he needed a rest cure. He thought of making a trip to the deep South and stopping at the Hermitage to pay his respects to Jackson, but ruled out the southern visit for fear of exposing himself to the charge of electioneering.

The family visits gave welcome diversion, but not exactly relief. The Mercersburg establishment was gloomy and beset with difficulties; Jane Lane had passed on, and soon thereafter her husband had died very unexpectedly. They left four more orphaned children in Buchanan's charge: two boys who were grown and could manage and two young girls, Mary and Harriet, who needed homes. They were now in Charlestown, Virginia, with their father's relatives, where Buchanan would stop to see them on his way home.[20]

Harriet Henry's death a year after that of her husband left nothing in Greensburg but melancholy memories. Her only son, ten-year-old James Buchanan Henry, now lived in Lancaster under Miss Hetty's care. Harriet Lane would also move in very shortly, and possibly her sister. He had prepared for them by buying a lot of Henry Slaymaker's furniture at a sheriff's sale and would set up quarters for half a dozen permanent or wandering family guests. It was time the King Street house was fully furnished; he and Miss Hetty had used only a few rooms. He hoped Miss Hetty would enjoy managing seven bedrooms and taking care of the new kitchen equipment; and he hoped little Harriet would enjoy the piano. He had paid $17.50 for it.[21]

Since the breakoff with his "intended" of the Kittera household, Buchanan had become seriously interested in young Anna Payne who lived with her famous aunt Dolly Madison in the gray house on Lafayette Square in Washington, a popular resort of capital society. He grew quite devoted to her and would in all probability have married her except for the disparity in their ages. It had become a vogue in this period for young girls to marry men old enough to be their grandfathers, but the results did not always prove happy. Letting his better judgment overrule his heart, Buchanan gave her up in an outburst of poetry.

> In thee my chilled & blighted heart has found
> A green spot in the dreary waste around.
> Oh! that my fate in youthful days had been
> T'have lived with such an one, unknown, unseen,
> Loving and lov'd, t'have passed away our days
> Sequestered from the world's malignant gaze!

> A match of age with youth can only bring
> The farce of 'winter dancing with the spring.'
> Blooming nineteen can never well agree
> With the dull age of half a century.
> Thus reason speaks what rebel passion hates,
> Passion,—which would control the very fates.

> Meantime, where'ere you go, what e're your lot
> By me you'll never, never be forgot.
> May Heaven's rich blessings crown your future life!
> And may you be a happy, loving wife![22]

His growing responsibilities as a guardian for nieces and nephews and his increasing preoccupation with politics at length banished all expectation of a marriage for love. He put his thoughts very frankly to his old friend, Mrs. James J. Roosevelt, some years later. "I feel that it is not good for a man to be alone," he wrote, "and should not be astonished to find myself married to some old maid who can nurse me when I am sick, provide good dinners for me when I am well, and not expect from me any very ardent or romantic affection."[23]

THE DEMOCRATIC NOMINATION OF 1844

By 1843 his political prospects looked almost as forlorn as his prospects for romance. Davy Lynch, for example, had been charged with accepting overpayments from the government for rent of the Pittsburgh post office building. He faced trial and wanted Buchanan to get him out of trouble. In the meantime Tyler would certainly remove Lynch and probably appoint in his place J. B. Moorhead, who had voted against Buchanan's re-election to the Senate and had been working hard to seize control of the western Pennsylvania Democrats.[24]

But Moorhead's threat was only one of many worries. The Democrats had to select a candidate for governor in the spring, and Henry A. Muhlenberg, just back from the Austrian Mission, expected Buchanan to help him get the nomination. Muhlenberg, however, tried to fit back into the associations of years before, allying with the old "improvement men," now friends of Porter; the old Van Buren men, now the Dallas party; and the Moorhead faction in Pittsburgh. "I believe," Buchanan said, "I have not a personal enemy in the Democratic party of the State who is not a devoted friend of Mr. Muhlenberg."[25]

Francis R. Shunk also wanted to be the gubernatorial candidate and demanded Buchanan's help. Had he not resigned as Secretary of the Commonwealth in order to conduct the fight against Porter in Harrisburg? Were not all of Buchanan's friends in the present canvass solidly back of Shunk and against Muhlenberg? Could Buchanan withhold his support under these circumstances?

The difficulty reached its most acute stage in Lancaster County where all the jarring elements came into close contact. Buchanan stalled Muhlenberg, explained the local events of the past several years, and expressed a wish to stay entirely out of the contest. He would, however, as an evidence of good faith, promise to deliver Lancaster County to Muhlenberg. But he would take no part in the contest between his two friends. Muhlenberg went back to Reading where his local party promptly nominated delegates pledged to Van Buren to the coming state convention.

Van Buren's partisans won so sweeping a victory in the organization of the national Congress that his subsequent nomination now seemed assured. Buchanan was prepared for this eventuality, but not for the angry reaction of his friends at home. Despite his repeated pledges that he would not contest the nomination against Van Buren and that he would not take sides between Muhlenberg and Shunk, he learned two weeks before Christmas that his Lancaster newspaper was flying from its masthead the slogan: "Win with Buchanan and Shunk!"[26] The game was up. He closed himself in his Washington room and worked all night on the draft of an important letter; the most important, he knew, that he had ever written.

Pushing aside half a dozen scratched over and interlined copies, he took up a fair draft and read it. "Washington, December 14, 1843. To the Democrats of Pennsylvania. Fellow Citizens: After long and serious

157

reflection, I have resolved to withdraw my name from the list of presidential candidates to be presented before the democratic national convention. This resolution has been dictated by an anxious desire to drive discord from the ranks of the party, and secure the ascendancy of democratic principles, both in the state and throughout the union. In arriving at this conclusion I have consulted no human being. It is entirely my own spontaneous act, and proceeds from the clearest and strongest conviction of duty."

Now, what else? He must thank his friends for their work and show where the fault lay. When he had accepted the state nomination a year ago he had said plainly that he would run only if the Democracy of Pennsylvania "should resolve to offer my name to the national convention . . . with that degree of unanimity which could alone give moral force to their recommendation." Anyone who had observed current politics would have to grant there was now no unanimity, and that "the moral force of Pennsylvania with her sister states would be exerted in vain." It would be a hopeless contest; even his friends must admit it. He expected by his withdrawal to "purchase harmony and unanimity in the selection of a democratic candidate." After sealing the letter, he addressed it to the editor of the Lancaster *Intelligencer*.[27]

During January and February of 1844, Buchanan essayed the awkward task of remaining on friendly terms with both Muhlenberg and Shunk. Lancaster County did not help when it elected delegates committed to Shunk to the state nominating convention, contrary to Buchanan's wishes and his earlier promise to Muhlenberg. On March 4, the Democrats meeting at Harrisburg nominated Muhlenberg for governor by a close vote on the first ballot, thus giving at least an indirect endorsement to Van Buren for president. Under pressure from Buchanan, Shunk agreed not to split the party and promised his support to the settled ticket.

The road ahead now seemed clear for Van Buren, but that was reckoning without Calhoun, Tyler, and Texas. On February 28, Secretary of State Abel P. Upshur was killed by the explosion of the great gun "Peacemaker" aboard the U.S.S. Princeton. Within a week, President Tyler had determined upon a stroke of policy which, he hoped, would promote a second term for himself. He would appoint John C. Calhoun to the State Department and annex Texas. Calhoun had already withdrawn from the presidential race, but he had not yet committed his support to any of the remaining aspirants; as a member of the Tyler Cabinet he might be induced to support his chief.

John Calhoun accepted the State Department on April 1, and by the 16th had completed a Texas Treaty, which Tyler submitted to the Senate for action on April 22, 1844.[28]

The acquisition of Texas under the leadership of Tyler and

Calhoun by means which seemed sure to provoke a war with Mexico put every presidential aspirant on guard. To the North it appeared crystal clear that a southern plot was afoot to spread slavery. To the South it seemed equally apparent that her only future security lay in expansion. Thus the questions of slavery and expansion were locked together and thrust into the midst of the presidential canvass.

On April 20, Van Buren had written a letter to Congressman W. H. Hammet of Mississippi, published a week later, stating that the United States ought not to annex Texas. Clay came out the same day with a letter taking essentially the same stand. Historians assume that this simultaneous pronouncement by leaders of the two opposing parties had been prearranged between them. Tyler, by his submission of the treaty of annexation on April 22, stood before the country as the champion of expansion.

Buchanan's friends immediately urged him to reconsider his withdrawal and to fight actively for the nomination. Cameron and J. M. Read called a hurried meeting of the Pennsylvania Democratic Central Committee to have delegates to the Baltimore Convention reinstructed for Buchanan but failed because frenzied efforts of the Van Buren men prevented the appearance of a quorum.[29] Many begged Buchanan only "to say one word to give the Baltimore Convention a chance to nominate him" and Pennsylvania would swing into line, carrying other states with it.[30]

By the middle of May, he had decided on the position he would take, although it was not all that his friends demanded. He would not compete with Van Buren for the nomination. But should the latter voluntarily withdraw either before or during the convention, Buchanan's supporters could offer his name.[31]

Many Pennsylvanians considered his attitude craven, but they did not know the national picture as well as Buchanan did. General Jackson disapproved of Van Buren's stand on Texas, and was pressing the name of James K. Polk openly for vice-president and covertly for the first place if a convention deadlock should develop. Buchanan could expect no favors or public support from Jackson, and should he run independently he would be flying in the face of both Van Buren and Jackson. "I confess," he said, "that if I should ever run for the Presidency, I would like to have an open field & a fair start. The battle has already been more than half fought . . . and it would be difficult for any new man to recall the forces which have already gone over to the enemy."[32]

The Democratic Convention opened at Baltimore on May 27, elected Hendrick B. Wright of Pennsylvania to the chair, and adopted the two-thirds rule for nominations. With this regulation, Van Buren could not be nominated; without it, he would go in on the first ballot. Pennsylvania's delegates, who were instructed for Van Buren, voted nonetheless

159

for the two-thirds rule which they well knew would exclude their candidate. Having sabotaged Van Buren, these gentlemen then proceeded to vote for him on the roll call for nominees, but after the first few ballots the Pennsylvanians went over to Buchanan, giving him the unanimous vote of the state on the fifth ballot. Lewis Cass of Michigan ran strongly on the sixth and seventh ballots, while Van Buren's strength declined, but none of the candidates came near the 178 votes needed.

The convention adjourned overnight, and by morning leaders of the Pennsylvania and Massachusetts delegations had completed plans to introduce Polk's name to the deadlocked meeting. Polk drew 44 votes on the eighth ballot, but before the ninth could be taken, the New York delegation retired for consultation. Upon its return, Benjamin F. Butler got the floor and read a letter of withdrawal from Van Buren. The convention, in riotous confusion, then gave its unamimous approval to James K. Polk as the presidential nominee. The vice-presidency went almost unamimously to Silas Wright of New York as a peace offering to the Van Burenites, but he declined the offer in order not to profit from his friend's defeat. George M. Dallas gladly accepted the vice-presidential nomination.

RED HERRING

Along with other Senators who remained in Washington during the convention, Buchanan learned the news from Baltimore via the first official trial of Samuel F. B. Morse's telegraph instrument, which the inventor himself was operating in the basement of the Capitol Building. The Democratic platform included all the principles of 1840 with two additions, the "re-annexation of Texas and the re-occupation of Oregon." The key issues would be expansion and the tariff.

The Whigs had already nominated Henry Clay on May 1, and had adopted a platform which significantly failed to mention Texas and which took a stand on the tariff just about as vague as that of the Democrats. In Pennsylvania, at least, this issue, above all others, required clarification.

Polk amplified his views on the tariff in a letter to John K. Kane of Philadelphia, stating that "in adjusting the details of a revenue tariff I have heretofore sanctioned such moderate discriminating duties as would produce the amount of revenue needed, and at the same time afford reasonable protection to our home industry."[33] This stand was weak enough, to be sure, but it could be made to serve if editors like Forney harped enough on the last phrase. The campaign ground was also defined by the Senate's rejection of the Texas Treaty, June 8. At that time Buchanan made a long speech in support of the treaty and urged annexation for many reasons. Chief of these was his fear that Britain would take control if the United States failed to annex.[34] Polk's letter to Kane and the defeat of the Texas measure enabled Buchanan to sidetrack the two main sectional issues of the canvass. He would simply state that Polk was sounder on the tariff than Clay and merely point to the speech on Texas.

It was a busy and perplexing summer. Congress adjourned late in June, and Buchanan took the usual fortnight's vacation at Bedford Springs. In the meantime, all manner of complications vexed the campaigns of both parties. A Native American party grew strong in urban centers and became involved in violent anti-Catholic riots in Philadelphia during midsummer, requiring the presence of the governor and the state militia. The Liberty party, with James G. Birney as its candidate, posed an uncertain threat both to Whigs and Democrats. Clay befogged his position by hedging on his antiannexation stand, and Tyler, supported by office holders, was running independently for re-election.

Cameron urged Buchanan to campaign vigorously for Polk in Pennsylvania. "He must owe the state to you; and you can . . . command the nomination in '48."[35] Judge John Catron of the Supreme Court, a Tennessean, wanted Buchanan to stump through the West for Polk. He could pay a final visit to General Jackson, establish the personal contacts he needed in that region for 1848, and place himself in debt to Polk who, Catron added, especially wanted him to make the trip. There was added appeal in the invitation because Buchanan was an intimate friend and great admirer both of Mrs. Catron and of Mrs. Polk, and these charming ladies repaid his good opinion of them with flattery and kindness.[36]

The canvass in Pennsylvania changed rapidly. Henry Muhlenberg died on August 11, and Shunk immediately became the Democratic candidate for governor. On August 20, President Tyler announced his withdrawal from the presidential race, blasting Governor Porter's hopes of future eminence. Buchanan at once sought to pacify the disappointed friends of Muhlenberg by obtaining pledges from Shunk that he would divide the patronage with them. Buchanan's next task was to persuade Cameron to agree to call off his attacks on Shunk and obtain Shunk's promise not to proscribe Cameron's friends for adhering to Muhlenberg.[37]

Buchanan left on a speaking tour of northern Pennsylvania during the first week of September. He was much worried by Polk's desire to make himself too clear on some things. "For Heaven's sake let our friend . . . write nothing more on the subject of the tariff," he pleaded. "Let us alone & we shall do it."[38] He then proceeded to Danville, Milton, Williamsport, and on up to Towanda where he addressed large crowds. "I have raised an excitement everywhere I have gone on the Bank question," he wrote on September 18, the day after his return. "Our friends in that portion of the state will denounce the Bank as loudly as the Whigs do free trade. One excitement will countervail the other."[39] The Bank was a red herring to distract the attention of these people from the tariff, which posed the most serious threat to the party. He advised Polk, cautiously, that Pennsylvania would probably be safe, but by no huge majorities. As for himself, he would have nothing to ask of the new president, but would "expect much from the President's lady. During her administration I intend to make one more attempt to change my wretched condition, and should I fail under her auspices I shall then surrender in despair."[40]

In the October elections, Shunk carried his ticket for governor, and in November Polk won the presidency. It was a close election; but the Democrats had squeaked through, and Buchanan deserved credit for right guessing and canny manipulation in achieving the result. The next four months would see the distribution of the rewards.

13

POLITICS UNDER POLK • 1845 - 1846

THE STATE DEPARTMENT

Buchanan wrote to Polk immediately after the election, urging him to make "young Democrats" the core of his Administration. "The old office holders," he said, "generally have had their day & ought to be content."[1] This advice may possibly have been intended for self-protection in case the president-elect ignored him, but it also meant to flatter Polk, the nation's youngest president, and it might serve to eliminate some of the old party hacks.

The Pennsylvania electors unanimously recommended Buchanan for the State Department, but Polk seemed in no hurry to move.[2] There were those who said that General Jackson had explicitly warned Polk against including Buchanan in the Cabinet.[3] By the end of January Buchanan could stand the suspense no longer and asked Judge Catron, a neighbor of Polk's, to find out how matters stood. Catron replied that Polk had "not indicated to *any one* the appointments he intends to make."[4]

In the meantime, Buchanan tried desperately to achieve unity within the new state administration, insisting that Shunk should appoint a Muhlenberg man to a prominent cabinet post and avoid participating in the election for United States Senator which would take place in Harrisburg just after the governor's inauguration. He advised Shunk "not to take part in favour of any candidate for the Senate, but to express your opinion strongly and decidedly in favour of an adherence to caucus nominations."[5] Shunk tried to foster a union of the state factions by his appointments, but he achieved only the curses of both sides for his efforts.[6] The Democratic caucus for Senator ran into a deadlock between George W. Woodward, the Shunk candidate, and Nathaniel B. Eldred of the Muhlenberg faction with the result that the Legislature elected Daniel Sturgeon, the incumbent.

Shortly thereafter, on February 17, Buchanan got a letter from Polk inviting him to be Secretary of State. The form letter, which Polk sent to all appointees, was unique in the history of presidential invitations to Cabinet service. It read, "Should any member of my Cabinet become a Candidate for the Presidency or Vice-Presidency of the United States, it will be expected . . . that he will retire from the Cabinet. . . . I will myself take no part between gentlemen of the Democratic party who may become aspirants or Candidates to succeed me in the Presidential office, and desire that no member of my Cabinet shall do so." Polk wanted no Department head to use the federal patronage to promote the interests of his personal political machine.[7]

Buchanan's letter of acceptance clearly demonstrated his fitness for the diplomatic post. "I cheerfully and cordially approve the terms on which this offer has been made," he wrote. But he could not control what others might do in his behalf, and he could not in justice to his friends take the office "at the expense of self-ostracism." "I cannot proclaim to the world that in no contingency shall I be a candidate for the Presidency in 1848," he continued. But in that event, he would retire from the Cabinet, unless Polk asked him to remain. "If under these explanations, you are willing to confer upon me the office of Secretary of State, I shall accept it."[8]

Buchanan terminated his senatorial career with a ringing speech in favor of the resolutions for the immediate annexation of Texas. These contained a provision applying the Missouri Compromise line to all land which should be acquired under the term "Texas." "I am not friendly to slavery in the abstract," he said. "I need not say that I never owned a slave, and I know that I never shall own one." But the price of continued unity rested on the willingness of all to recognize the plain constitutional rights granted to each part. "The constitutional rights of the south, under our constitutional compact, are as much entitled to protection as those of any other portion of the Union." If it was a question of slavery south of 36° 30' or the end of the Union, he would "never risk the blessings of this glorious confederacy."[9] Three days before the inauguration, President Tyler signed the joint resolution for Texan annexation.

In the weeks remaining between the profer of the State Department and the date of assuming his new duties, Buchanan worked day and night, writing letters, seeing visitors, consulting upon the political problems of Pennsylvania, and arranging for new quarters befitting the social obligations of a Cabinet member. On the advice of Mrs. Stephen Pleasanton he eventually decided upon a house on F Street, between 13th and 14th, next to the residence of John Quincy Adams and just a block from the State Department building. He could rent it for $2,000 per year, elegantly furnished and with nearly enough chinaware for state occasions. He sent to Paris immediately for an ornament for the center of the table for, as the ladies informed him, "you cannot set a handsome dinner without one and they are not to be had in this country."[10]

But most pressing of all, he had to master the details of the work of the Department. Handling the diplomatic functions gave him little concern, but the State Department was not only a diplomatic office; it had become a receptacle, so to speak, for all kinds of odd jobs which Congress for thirty years had been dumping into it, without providing sufficient personnel.

The Department had been divided into the Diplomatic, the Consular, and the Home Bureaus. In the Diplomatic Bureau, five clerks handled the correspondence with all the American embassies, but none of them had the authority to sign a paper or to decide any question, however trivial. In the Consular Bureau, three clerks tried vainly to keep in touch with over 150 American consuls, with the result that almost all the information the consuls forwarded was useless because there was no one to digest, arrange, or publish it. But the third bureau was the one most understaffed. It had the functions of accounting and disbursing funds for diplomatic agents, receiving bills from Congress and transmitting them to the president, filing official papers, printing the laws, and translating diplomatic correspondence. The Home Bureau was also in charge of issuing patents and copyrights, taking the federal census, affixing the seal of the United States on innumerable documents, keeping the government archives, issuing passports, preparing and filing correspondence relating to pardons, and handling various other tasks which made its functions an administrative monstrosity. Seven clerks were assigned to handle this mountain of business. "The consequences of this accumulation of business upon the head of the department," Buchanan wrote after brief acquaintance with his task, "must be manifest to everyone. He must either neglect the national interests or the subordinate but pressing business involving the rights of individuals."[11]

After an introduction to the mechanics of his office, Buchanan requested Calhoun to assist him for a while after inauguration day and the South Carolinian courteously remained for an extra week. Buchanan asked Caleb Cushing to take the Chief Clerkship with the explanation that he hoped to have it made an Assistant Secretaryship soon, but Cushing declined.[12] William S. Derrick, who had served in the Department since 1827, remained Chief Clerk until August when Buchanan selected Nicholas P. Trist, former consul at Havana, for the post. He appointed Robert Greenhow, husband of the young, beautiful and impish Rose O'Neal Greenhow, as Librarian and Translator, and Lund Washington, Jr. as Archivist.

James Knox Polk ushered onto the American scene a program known as the "New Democracy." He called to its standard men whose devotion to national causes outweighed their sectional loyalty, men who believed that it was better to achieve a large growth of national power along with a small growth of slavery than to stop American expansion in order to prevent any further extension of the slave labor system. Most of them would have agreed with Buchanan's statement that slavery could not be treated in politics as a matter of general morality affecting the consciences of men but only as a question of constitutional law. The New Democracy sought the development of commerce by promoting free trade; advocated the acquisition of Oregon and California; and tried to minimize the slavery issue.

The giants of Jackson's day found no place in Polk's Cabinet. Van Buren's Barnburners had already become strongly tinged with political antislavery and opposed Texan annexation. Calhoun had gone too far on the subject of the slave system as a positive good, alienating many who had once politically defended the South, even if they deplored the system of slavery. Old Benton, fearing a fight over slavery in new lands, opposed expansion. These leaders represented the three strongest factions of the old Democracy.

Polk appointed Buchanan to utilize his diplomatic experience and placate his faction in Pennsylvania. Robert J. Walker of Mississippi, a shrewd financier with a keen interest in Texas bonds and transport speculations, became head of the Treasury. He was a commercial man and a staunch advocate of free trade. He had married a niece of Vice-President Dallas and favored his party. William L. Marcy of New York, Secretary of War, was one of the Hunker leaders, an open enemy of Van Buren. George Bancroft of Massachusetts, Secretary of the Navy, had led the movement to introduce Polk's name to the Baltimore convention. John Young Mason of Virginia, Attorney General, and Cave Johnson of Tennessee, Postmaster General, completed Polk's Cabinet.

THE PERILS OF THE PATRONAGE

Polk's early decision not to seek re-election made it more difficult for him to restrain Cabinet members from working for the 1848 nomination. He had to give close personal supervision to prevent the improper use of the patronage by any individual who might try to start a presidential band wagon for himself by making strategic federal appointments. Also the president had to maintain the strength and vitality of the Democratic party in critical states by a careful distribution of jobs. Otherwise, his party would lose the election in the next presidential campaign.

Pennsylvania and New York were politically the two most important states in the Union. Together they controlled an electoral vote nearly equal to that of the total area south of the Ohio and Potomac Rivers

166

and elected one-fourth of the Congressmen of the whole nation. In both of these vital states the Democracy was critically split. In New York the differences were so great that there was no hope of early unity; in Pennsylvania, however, the factions were not so divided as to rule out the possibility of achieving harmony.

When Buchanan accepted the State Department and resigned his seat in the Senate, this prize came into contest between the friends of Shunk and the Muhlenberg men who knew, by this time, that Shunk would not meet their demands for state patronage. Had Polk issued his invitation to Buchanan early in January the Pennsylvania Democrats might have taken a long step toward reunion by electing to the Senate at the same time a representative of each of the two rivals. As it was, neither faction had won the January election and now both were bent on having the remaining place. On March 12, most of the Democratic legislators held the usual caucus and named as their candidate George Woodward, whose low tariff and expansionist views agreed with Polk's. Buchanan avoided committing himself to any person, but he did advise all Democrats to follow the time-honored procedures, which could be interpreted as a pat on the back for Woodward.

But Cameron's friends boycotted the caucus and laid their own plans. Cameron had already told Buchanan that he wanted to be a Senator, but having gotten no encouragement he planned to win on his own.[13] Two weeks before the March election he wrote to a colleague, "Strange as it may seem, I can be the successor of Mr. Buchanan. . . . The election will not . . . be made by a caucus this time."[14]

Cameron assured the Whigs in the Legislature that he ardently wished to retain the tariff of 1842 and got the backing of more than a dozen Democrats who favored high protectionism. To the Native Americans, he confided his earnest wish to restrict foreign immigration and to curtail the political power of the Catholics. On March 14, Cameron won the senatorship by a combination of 44 Whigs, 16 Democrats, and 7 Native Americans. It was a blow to Polk, a blow to Shunk, and nearly a knockout to Buchanan who had just gone on record in support of caucus decisions. He could not condone Cameron's action but, with the Senate almost evenly divided, he could ill afford to declare open war on him and forfeit a vote. Buchanan's friends raged like wild animals. "Simon Cameron's the Senator! God save the Commonwealth," groaned Forney. With this inauspicious beginning, the fight for federal patronage started.[15]

The infuriated Democrats of the caucus wrote to Vice-President Dallas and to Buchanan, asking them to lend their weight to the Democratic condemnation of Cameron and to read him out of the party. But Dallas, while decisively condemning the breach of party usage, refused to censure a man who now would sit in the legislative body over which he had to preside. Buchanan replied in terms even more discreet, deploring the breakdown of the caucus system but declining to condemn the state Legislature "for electing whom they pleased to the senate of the United States." He hoped that this experience would be convincing proof that legislators ought "to go into caucus and be bound by its decision."[16] Cameron's position, to be sure, was not enviable. Shunk broke with him and ousted his followers from the state administration. Neither Dallas nor Buchanan would seek patronage for him, and Polk considered him, properly, to be an enemy. Henceforth, Cameron offered himself for sale to any faction that would purchase his power and sought to wreck the plans of those who repulsed him.[17]

Buchanan determined to play the waiting game with Cameron, neither breaking with him nor giving him aid. His experience with politics convinced him that little would be gained by declaring factional war. Time after time he had seen such struggles sap the energy of the party without any further result; in fact the principal contenders had often become political bedfellows within a few years. Furthermore, Cameron could be counted upon to get on the band wagon when it was apparent that there was no other place to stand. He was an opportunist and would support Buchanan for president when the time came. The real struggle would be to define the terms of his support. He would make the price as high as possible by demonstrating his capacity with the monkey wrench; Buchanan would keep it as low as possible by showing the power of his position. But Cameron had too keen a talent for mischief for Buchanan to risk open battle with him; he, if anyone, could wreck the plans for '48.

To reduce the heat of the indignation against Cameron, Buchanan removed Forney from Lancaster by providing him a surveyorship in the Philadelphia customhouse. In return, Forney pledged cooperation. "If you can keep Cameron your friend," he wrote, "my course will keep his enemies, and they are legion, on your side!"[18] Forney henceforth worked valiantly but not very successfully, to dissuade Champneys and Frazer in Lancaster from flaying Cameron in their local newspaper.[19]

Buchanan also sought to conciliate Cameron by getting his first lieutenant, Ben Brewster, a job. For weeks, Brewster had been writing letters, ending with the demand, "I want the District Attorneyship!" Polk gave the place to a Dallas man, whereupon Brewster sent a scorching letter threatening "woe to the public man" who would cross his path. Buchanan then offered to make Brewster secretary of the Legation at London. Brewster replied that he might have taken the British Mission itself, if he had been given command of the Oregon negotiations but he would have none of the secretaryship. Horace might accept ivy as a reward, he wrote, but a politician needed money and wanted to hear the jingle of cash. Buchanan eventually found him a place, appropriate for a Cameron disciple, settling Indian claims.[20]

For a number of months, Buchanan's desk was piled high with requests for jobs as clerks, postmasters, inspectors, sutlers, mail agents, auditors, consuls, registers, district attorneys, prison wardens, chaplains, storekeepers, lighthouse keepers, and the like. His careful record of judgments and recommendations survives in a small black notebook which he considered of sufficient importance to exclude it from his political papers and deposit with his executor.[21]

He had more success in promoting jobs than Dallas or the Pennsylvania Senators even though Polk suspected his designs for the presidency. Nonetheless, he fell so far short of the demands that the rumor began to circulate that every jobless politician was a Buchanan man. Forney wrote: "Ousted officers all say they have been sacrificed for being your friends, and you may rely upon it, there is quite a lot of them."[22] Buchanan's pattern of appointments left Cameron so perplexed that he asked point blank in September: "I wish you would tell me whether there is to be peace or war."[23]

On September 23, 1845, Thomas Ritchie, an editor of Polk's official paper, the Washington *Union*, confided to the president that Buchanan wished to quit the Cabinet and go to the Supreme Court. A week later Buchanan asked Polk for the appointment, assigning as his reason the trouble that was brewing in Pennsylvania over the tariff.[24] Buchanan assured the president, however, that he would not leave the Department if war broke out with Mexico.

Three vacancies had occurred on the Court between 1843 and 1845. Justices Smith Nelson and Henry Baldwin died and Joseph Story resigned. The Baldwin and Story seats were still open, and Polk wished to place in them men who were strict constructionists, "who would be less likely to relapse into the Broad Federal doctrines of Judge Marshall & Judge Story."[25] President Tyler, upon Baldwin's death in April, 1844, had offered this place to Senator Buchanan, but he had then declined it. Polk appointed Levi Woodbury to the Story vacancy but reserved Baldwin's place for a Pennsylvanian.

Buchanan's request to go into the Court raised anguished howls from his political friends. "For God's sake, stay where you are," wrote Ben Brewster, who accused Dallas of trying to put Buchanan on the shelf in order to oust his friends from their jobs.[26] Forney hit where it would hurt most. He wrote that "it would be regarded by the world in a light that must place you in a very unpleasant position. That the evident *free trade* tendencies of the administration had made you feel uncomfortable in the Cabinet, and had induced you to retire from it, to an office conferred by the very power which *struck down Pennsylvania interests*—thus showing

169

that although you could not stay in the Cabinet, yet you took your office from the administration, and refused to sacrifice yourself for the cause of the state, leaving her to take care of herself. . . . Others say that you are about to 'desert your friends again' and that you *fear* to face any great crisis."[27]

While such views had their influence, it is also probable that Buchanan decided to remain in the Cabinet because of encouraging developments in the Oregon negotiation, a story to be told a little later. On November 19, he informed Polk that he could not take the Court appointment and recommended John M. Read, of Philadelphia, whom he had earlier suggested to Tyler and who would have been agreeable to Cameron. But on December 23, Polk, without consulting either Buchanan or Cameron, and with the assent of Dallas, nominated George Woodward. Polk rejected Read because he feared appointing "a former Federalist to a lifetime position where he could fall back upon Federalist doctrines," and thought that Woodward might prove pleasing to Buchanan and Shunk, since both had supported him for the Senate.[28]

Cameron considered the appointment a direct insult to him, and hastened to Washington to discuss the matter with Buchanan, despite the fact that the two had neither been seeing each other nor corresponding, except on essential public business, for five months.[29] On Christmas Day, while Cameron wrote complaints to Buchanan, Buchanan called on Polk to complain. He had been absent from Cabinet when the appointment was announced, he said; he was directly involved in Pennsylvania appointments but had not been consulted; his friends grumbled that the patronage was being wielded against him; and he would not have recommended Woodward. Polk, surprised by this outburst, rather curtly stated that he preferred Woodward to Read, had the power to appoint without consultation, and would take the responsibility for his act.[30]

The matter rested there until January 22 when Cameron, finding a number of Democrats absent from the Senate, managed to get Woodward's confirmation up for a vote and defeated it 29-20 by an alliance of six Democrats and the entire Whig membership.[31] James Shields, of the Land Office, told Polk of the Senate's action late on the afternoon of the 22nd, and added that both he and Senator Cass now advised the appointment of Buchanan who had expressed a desire for the office a few days previously. Benton wrote the next day, recommending Buchanan and promising immediate Senate confirmation.[32] "I thought it strange," wrote Polk, "that Mr. Buchanan should have expressed a wish to anyone pending the nomination of Mr. Woodward before the Senate."

The next night Buchanan held a grand ball at which all the rumors and gossip centered on his leaving the Cabinet and going upon the Bench. To whisperings that he had been working with Cameron to sabotage

170

Woodward, Buchanan replied that this was "such stuff as dreams are made of."[33]

The ball, held at Carusi's Saloon, was attended by more than a thousand guests. Mrs. Marcy aided Buchanan in receiving. On an elevated platform at the end of the hall sat Mrs. Madison, "a young lady of fourscore years and upwards," and the aged widow of Alexander Hamilton who talked sensibly about her husband although her memory of current events had entirely ceased. Daniel Webster came accompanied by his wife and a Mrs. Jandon of New York, and William H. Seward, who was in town arguing a patent case before the Supreme Court, promenaded with Mrs. John Adams, widowed daughter-in-law of John Quincy Adams. Old Baron Bodisco's lovely teen-aged Georgetown wife wore a stunning set of diamonds that excited the envy of her sex. Buchanan had attended her wedding as escort for fourteen-year-old Jessie Benton, one of the bridesmaids.[34] The famed Gautier served venison, hams, beef, turkey, pheasant, chicken, oysters, lobster, ice cream, water ice, charlotte russe, punch, fruit and cake pyramids, blanc mange, apple toddy, kisses, chocolate, coffee, 300 bottles of wine, 150 bottles of champagne, and harder beverages for harder drinkers.[35]

On January 28, Representative David Wilmot called on Polk to accuse Buchanan of having brought about the rejection of Woodward's nomination. Polk was greatly disturbed. He reported that Buchanan had been in a "bad mood . . . since Judge Woodward's nomination, . . . and since he has discovered that he cannot control me in the dispensation of the public patronage." The president believed that Buchanan was differing unnecessarily with him in Cabinet meetings and was seeking some public ground for making a break with the Administration.

Shortly thereafter Buchanan had another skirmish with Polk; it was over the appointment of a collector for the Port of Philadelphia, a particularly juicy plum of the patronage. The president determined to appoint Henry Horn, a member of the Dallas wing of the party. Buchanan at first opposed this choice, but he acquiesced eventually. When Horn's name went to the Senate, however, Cameron demanded to see the list of Pennsylvanians who had recommended that name, stated that he had been denied "senatorial courtesy," and defeated Horn's appointment by the same trick he had used to block Woodward: a thin Senate, and a union of Whigs and a few balky Democrats. Polk now arranged a Washington conference of Horn, Cameron and Buchanan, in which the latter was to play the arbitrator between the first two. Then he resubmitted Horn's name, but Cameron persuaded the Senate to reject it a second time. Polk wrote down Cameron as "a managing tricky man, in whom no reliance is to be placed."[36] But how was Buchanan involved? Polk could not be

171

sure; nonetheless, he determined to let the Supreme Court appointment rest for a few months. Horn, meanwhile, was furious with Dallas for failing to push him through.

THE WALKER-McKAY TARIFF

As summer approached, Buchanan grew increasingly restive in the Polk administrative family. The McKay tariff, framed largely by Secretary Walker, had passed the House and was headed for an extremely close contest in the Senate. The bill proposed that no duty should be placed on any article above the rate which would produce the maximum revenue, and that ad valorem duties should replace all specific duties. The bill essentially proposed free trade for the nation. The former duty on shaped iron products dropped from 163 per cent to 30 per cent; on shirting from 95 per cent to 30 per cent; on pig iron from 72 per cent to 30 per cent; and on coal from $1.75 per ton to $.40.

Polk considered the passage of this tariff bill by the Senate as "the most important measure of my administration,"[37] an opinion shared by thousands of Americans. Many of these, particularly the coal and iron men of Pennsylvania and the textile makers of New England considered it the death knell of all business, a "misshapen and monstrous scheme," a "fatal measure which strikes at the root of all industry of the country."[38]

Buchanan knew not what to do. He could not attack the Administration; less could he endorse its favorite measure. On Sunday, June 28, when the passage of the tariff seemed certain, he wrote to Polk about the judgeship, "I have concluded, though with much hesitation, to accept it."[39] At a conference several days later Buchanan asked Polk to appoint him immediately, but the president wished him to stay with the Department until the end of the Congressional session. Buchanan had to be satisfied with this plan, and he wrote his brother Edward in mid-July that he would probably go into the Court at the close of Congress.[40] Forney, too, was reconciled to the inevitable, though he still insisted that Buchanan's chances for the '48 nomination were brighter than ever and added that there was no return from the political grave of the Supreme Court.[41] Dallas wrote of the matter: "Thousands of reports about Mr. Buchanan are in circulation. His retreat from the Cabinet is spoken of as certain and soon— and he is said to be destined for London. This all smoke—a method of keeping up his importance, resorted to by his partizans. . . . There is a growing discontent against the nomination of Mr. Buchanan as Judge, and I think the Whigs are moving in a body against him. The 54.40's will, of course, go with them."[42]

In the Senate, where the fate of the tariff hung on a vote or two, it began to look as if there would be a deadlock. "Did I not say so?" wrote

172

Forney. "It would be fun if Dallas had to *untie* the tariff knot! Rare fun!"[43] Because Senator Spencer Jarnagin of Tennessee refused to vote on the motion to bring up the bill for its third reading, Vice-President Dallas had to cast the deciding vote. He supported the Administration at the risk of his own political future and was so fearful of the reaction in Philadelphia that he urged his wife to move the whole family to Washington at the first sign of trouble.[44] He justified his course at length in a letter to the *Washington Union;* nevertheless, he suffered public condemnation by county meetings all over Pennsylvania.[45] Of the state's entire delegation, only Dallas and Wilmot voted for the Tariff of 1846.

The Pennsylvania Whigs made war on Buchanan by republishing his few remarks in favor of the 1842 tariff, and quoting him as saying, during the 1844 campaign, that Polk was sounder than Clay on the tariff. There was enough truth in the charges to be extremely dangerous, and Buchanan wrote quickly to Forney, sketching out his "new line" on the tariff. He would stand by his remarks on the 1842 tariff: he liked a revenue tariff, with incidental protection, and specific duties. He considered the ad valorem feature of the 1846 tariff faulty and an invitation to fraud, a ruination of mechanics who lived by processing foreign raw materials, and a heavy blow to Pennsylvania's coal and iron industries. He would follow a middle course so long as he could, but if forced to the wall, he would prefer the 1842 bill to the current one.[46]

Within two days, Buchanan knew that this position would not do. He now discarded the 1842 tariff as dead and urged manufacturers not to get excited until they were hurt; they could depend on the Democracy to recognize, in a future session, the special needs of Pennsylvania. "Repeal is not the word, but modification. A protective tariff is not the word; but a revenue tariff with sufficient discriminations to maintain our home industry."[47] Hammering at this line, he wrote a series of articles for Forney's newly purchased *Pennsylvanian* of Philadelphia, which spread abroad the theme of "modification."

But panic and economic collapse did not ensue. In general, the tariff had not much effect on the formerly protected industries, most of which continued to grow and prosper as a result of many contemporary encouragements other than a tariff—the demands of a foreign war, a European famine, heavy immigration, rapid expansion of railroads, and a booming merchant marine. In fact, the tariff issue quickly took a back seat because of the exciting events of the Mexican War. Dallas had been momentarily wrecked, but Buchanan's prospects were so much the better for that. Having completed his carefully drawn statement for Forney on "modification," Buchanan paid an early evening call on Polk and informed him "that he had decided to remain in the Cabinet and not to accept the offer . . . of the Supreme Court." He urged the appointment of his friend, William B. Reed, but Polk had already decided on Judge Robert Grier. Buchanan supported this decision, the nomination went to the Senate on August 3, and the Senate approved it the next day.[48]

14

CONQUERING A CONTINENT • 1845 - 1849

TEXAS

President Polk, shortly after his election, confided to a friend that he proposed to complete the annexation of Texas, to settle the Oregon boundary dispute, and to acquire California. The last objective had not been mentioned in the Democratic platform, but it represented the president's personal commitment to Manifest Destiny.

This term, which became a synonym for the years of Polk's Administration, reflected a variety of ideas. Many antislavery people thought it a mere ruse to hide a slave conspiracy under the cloak of national patriotism, a trick "so's to lug more slave states in." Some feared that territorial expansion to the Pacific would dangerously upset the sectional balance of politics, and others that it would weaken the nation because of the difficulty of ruling distant lands. Those who enthusiastically supported Manifest Destiny, especially in the South and West, saw advantage in changing the balance of political control and expressed no fears about slavery or political administration. Land speculators welcomed expansion, and commercial men eagerly hoped for national control of the deep-water harbors of the Pacific, from Puget Sound to San Diego. Ownership of these strategic bays would prove the key to unlock the trade of the Orient and gain mastery of the Pacific.

England and France both were alive to the prospects of such commercial advantage, and although their governments placed no high priority on imperialistic adventures in the Americas, their diplomatic, commercial, and military representatives scattered from Argentina to Alaska conducted themselves aggressively enough to raise serious apprehensions in the United States. Particularly in Texas, in Mexico, and in California these agents acted in ways that created in Washington a fear of Europe which became one of the most powerful justifications of Manifest Destiny. Buchanan repeatedly said that unless the United States established dominance in the American Hemisphere, England or France would do it. This

175

theme became a powerful weapon of the spread-eagle "Young Democrats" of the day, for it placed territorial expansion on the ground of national security and made Manifest Destiny the slogan of patriots.[1]

Polk stated in his inaugural that no foreign power had any right to interfere with Texan annexation. "None can fail to see the danger to our safety and future peace," he said, "if Texas remains an independent state or becomes an ally or dependency of some foreign nation more powerful than herself." A year earlier Buchanan had warned that Texas "must cast herself into the arms of England," unless the United States accepted her. Even if Texas only formed a commercial alliance with England the result would be that the United States would confront the British to the north and to the south; "and British power and British influence will thus be increased at our expense." On the other hand, if the United States annexed Texas and obtained this great barrier to the west, "the whole European world could not, in combination against us, make an impression on our union."[2]

On March 6, 1845, Brigadier General J. N. Almonte, Mexican Minister to the United States, protested the annexation of Texas as "an act of aggression the most unjust which can be found recorded in the annals of modern history" and demanded his passports. Buchanan replied that Texas had long since achieved her independence, and that nothing but the refusal of the Texans could prevent annexation. He instructed A. J. Donelson, the American Chargé d'Affaires in Texas, to avoid "even the least appearance of interference with the free action of the people of Texas on the question of annexation. This is necessary to give its full effect to one of the grandest moral spectacles which has ever been presented to mankind, and to convince the world that we would not, if we could, influence their decision except by fair argument. We desire that our conduct shall be in perfect contrast to that pursued by the British Chargé d'Affaires."[3]

Despite these assurances, neither Polk nor Buchanan had any notion of leaving matters up to the Texans alone. On March 27, Polk appointed Charles A. Wickliffe as special agent to Texas, with orders to counteract by every means at his command the efforts of Great Britain and France to defeat annexation. Buchanan cautioned Wickliffe to reveal his official character to no one except Donelson.[4]

The process of annexation involved several stages: first, approval of the joint resolutions of the United States Congress by the Congress of Texas; second, the calling of a Texas convention to accept the terms of annexation; third, the calling of a Texan convention to frame a state constitution; fourth, the ratification of the Texan state constitution; and fifth, the approval by the United States Congress of this constitution. A slip in any of these steps might prove disastrous.

The Texans worried about the danger of a Mexican attack in the transition period. This contingency also disturbed Buchanan who had to admit that he did not know what status Texas would occupy between the time of approving the joint resolution and of admission as a state. For practical purposes, however, he informed the Texan government in May that the United States had ordered 3,000 troops to the border, "prepared to enter Texas and to act without a moment's delay" as soon as "the Existing Government and the Convention of Texas" had accepted the joint resolutions.[5]

Matters remained so uncertain throughout June, due largely to the intrigues of Charles Elliott, the British Chargé d'Affaires in Texas, that Polk rejected Donelson's request for leave on the grounds that "nothing ought to be left to accident."[6]   Captain Elliott had fabricated the story of a trip to Charleston, but he had gone instead to Vera Cruz where, acting in the guise of a secret Texan agent, he made an agreement with the Mexican government that Mexico would recognize Texan independence on condition that Texas would never join the United States. He then returned to Texas where he informed the inhabitants that Mexico had massed 7,000 troops on the Rio Grande and would immediately invade unless his proposal was adopted. Buchanan agreed with Polk that such trickery demanded active resistance. On June 15, the president ordered General Zachary Taylor to move from Fort Jesup to the Sabine River and be ready, the moment Texas approved the annexation resolutions, to "consider her territory as belonging to the United States." Buchanan pointed out that Elliott's worst act had been, in obtaining the consent of Mexico to the independence of Texas, to deprive that power "of the only miserable pretext which it had for a war aginst the United States," although at the same time he had stirred up such hatred in Mexico that war doubtless would result.[7]

The Texan Congress assented to annexation on June 23, and a convention at San Felipe de Austin accepted the terms on July 4. In August General Taylor moved his camp to the west bank of the Nueces River. The Texans, meanwhile, drew up their state constitution, and ratified it on October 13. On December 29, the United States Congress approved the constitution, thus finally bringing Texas into the Union as the twenty-eighth State. Taylor now transferred his army to the north bank of the Rio Grande, opposite Matamoros, a region which since 1836 had been claimed by the Texan Republic. During these years the Mexicans had made no effort to exercise authority there. For the moment, the Texan problem was solved.

177

OREGON

The negotiation with Britain for the Oregon region rested on a twenty-year-old contest in which the foreign secretaries of each country claimed a legal right to the entire territory but talked of a compromise around the 49th parallel which would divide the region approximately in half. An agreement of 1818 provided for the joint occupation of Oregon, and another of 1827 permitted termination of the joint occupation upon one year's notice by either party. Proposals of settlement at 49° had already been made by every president since Monroe, the latest under the Tyler Administration. Such a project was pending when Polk came to office but he pronounced in the inaugural that "our title to the Country of Oregon is 'clear and unquestionable.'" Americans were soon shouting a new battle cry: "Fifty-four forty or fight."[8]

Actually, the practical aspects of the Oregon question offered little difficulty. Neither government regarded the land as particularly valuable, each had its own strong reasons for wishing a settlement without war, and both seemed agreeable to the 49° line. This arrangement would give the two countries access to the ports around Vancouver. The real difficulty on both sides lay in the realm of national prestige and of domestic politics. Britain worried about rising tension with France, needed American grain to combat the potato famine, and planned a major reversal of economic policy by repealing the Corn Laws, the success of which would depend upon growing American friendship and trade. The Polk Administration worried about its partisan commitment to expansion, needed to bring in northern territory to balance Texas, planned to repeal the protective tariff, and anticipated a war with Mexico. Notwithstanding, the United States could not afford to appear soft in dealing with Britain. The interplay of these forces, rather than legal claims to Oregon or estimates of its intrinsic value, governed the negotiations.

In March 1844, Lord Aberdeen, British Foreign Minister, had instructed the British Ambassador at Washington, Richard Pakenham, to try to settle for the Columbia River boundary, but if he failed in that to "draw from the American Negotiator a proposal to make the 49th degree of latitude the boundary." Pakenham should also make an effort to obtain free ports for Britain south of the 49th parallel and free navigation of the Columbia River. This proposal, incidentally, had been made to Aberdeen by Edward Everett, the American Minister at London, on November 29, 1843.

But Polk's strident inaugural and the swaggering talk of "54° 40' or fight" in the American press complicated and slowed the plans for settlement and required some British bluster to redress the balance of honor. Aberdeen told a cheering House of Lords, in reference to Polk's claims, "We too, my Lords, have rights which are clear and unquestionable,

178

and those rights, with the blessing of God and your support, we are fully prepared to maintain."[9]

During the early Cabinet meetings, Buchanan had a chance to size up both the traits of the president and the aspect of his own job. Buchanan felt himself superior to Polk in understanding of international affairs, but he soon learned that Polk outranked him and intended to use his authority. The two continually disagreed on matters of policy, of timing, of procedure, and of emphasis. Polk sensed condescension in Buchanan which toughened his own attitude. Buchanan, confident of his ability, forced Polk to take full responsibility for crossing him. During the spring of 1845, while Polk debated whether to affirm directly a claim to all of Oregon, Buchanan advised against it. To claim all without once more attempting a compromise solution, he argued, would lead inevitably to war, invite the condemnation of the civilized world, and destroy the support of the nation. On the other hand, if compromise were offered and rejected by Britain and war followed, then the Administration could "appeal to all mankind for the justice and moderation of our demand . . . and our own citizens would be enthusiastically united in sustaining such a war."[10]

Buchanan's rivals urged that the negotiation be transferred to London, but upon the appointment of Louis McLane of Delaware as Minister to Britain, Polk directed Buchanan to take charge and to continue the talks on the Calhoun proposal of compromise. On July 12, Buchanan sent Pakenham a brief project for settlement at 49°, explaining that Polk "would not have consented to yield any portion of the Oregon territory," except for the acts of his predecessors who had agreed to compromise. Pakenham, not bothering to refer the offer to London for advice though its contents were very close to Aberdeen's own wishes of March, 1844, rejected it. Probably he reacted to a recent letter from Aberdeen, commenting upon the indignation with which Polk's inaugural had been received in England and stating that "we are still ready to adhere to the principle of an equitable compromise, but we are perfectly determined to cede nothing to force or menace."[11] Consistent with the firmness of Aberdeen's stand, Pakenham concluded his note of rejection with the statement that he hoped the United States would "be prepared to offer some further proposal . . . more consistent with fairness and equity, and with the reasonable expectations of the British government."[12] This insulting response brought the Oregon question suddenly to a crisis.

Polk directed Buchanan to prepare a full argument for the American title to all of Oregon, withdraw the compromise proposal, and leave the rest to the British. Buchanan agreed but urged that some statement to the effect that the United States would consider a British counterproposal should be included. Polk overrode him, arguing that to invite a proposal from Britain, when she had just rejected an eminently fair one,

179

would suggest that he might be willing to settle for less than had already been demanded. Buchanan then asked for a postponement of the reply until passions had cooled. He stood firm in his opinion that to close the door to negotiation would lead to war and that war with England for northern Oregon would not be sustained by the country. Furthermore, it would be rash to take such a risk at a time when conflict with Mexico loomed.[13] Polk declared he would "firmly maintain our rights, and leave the rest to God and the country," to which Buchanan replied that he thought God would find difficulty in justifying us in a war over the country north of 49°.[14]

Nonetheless, he proceeded to draw up a detailed statement of claim to all of Oregon. It was lawyer's work, and in it he excelled. On August 30, he delivered to Pakenham a powerful justification of the American demands, together with information that the compromise offer was withdrawn. Attending Cabinet at half-past twelve he announced, "Well, the deed is done," but said he still thought it was bad policy to rule out further talks.

While paper arguments provided no key to settlement, Buchanan's Oregon letter served to strengthen greatly the American position. Cave Johnson, after listening to it in Cabinet, said if he had heard it before he never would have sanctioned the earlier compromise. Bancroft commented on the vast superiority of Buchanan's paper over Pakenham's, and McLane reported from London that the clear enunciation of the American claim had counteracted the idea that the American demands were sheer brass and much softened the British attitude.[15]

Very shortly word arrived from McLane in London that Aberdeen strongly disapproved of Pakenham's rejection of the American compromise offer and would like to negotiate further. Buchanan thought this eminently sensible, and again tried to convince Polk to let him pass along a hint that the United States would receive a British proposal. He then suggested the possibility of informing Pakenham that a proposal from Britain would be submitted directly to the Senate, for its previous advice, thus relieving Polk of the embarrassment of altering his position. Polk thought this procedure would be improper. Discouraged, Buchanan told the president that by diplomatic means, he might get Oregon; but "by strong measures hastily taken, we would have war and might lose it."[16]

Polk's annual message calling upon the Senate to denounce the joint occupation agreement of 1827 caused excitement but no surprise for it was an inevitable consequence of the decision to assert the total American claim. Aberdeen welcomed it, telling Pakenham that "as the crisis becomes more imminent, the chance of settlement improves."[17]

Through December and January, Buchanan, the ministers on both sides of the water, and United States Senators tried to break through

180

Polk's intransigence. The problem by this time seemed clearly to be that of saving face for the president. Ex-minister Everett wrote directly to Aberdeen, and sent the replies to Polk's Cabinet via George Bancroft. Buchanan discussed the business informally with Pakenham. McLane talked freely in London. All agreed that both nations would welcome a 49th parallel settlement. The problem was to persuade Polk to change his position and agree to accept a British proposal of this line.

Pakenham, trying desperately to break through the impasse, sent an angling note to discover what Polk might assent to, with the proviso that it should be considered "official" or "unofficial" depending on the reply. Buchanan endorsed this strategem as practical and harmless, but Polk would have none of it. Pakenham next proposed arbitration, a stale solution previously rejected by the United States, and rejected by Buchanan and Polk twice more. It was a time-wasting device to keep up appearances of a negotiation and was so understood by all concerned.

Buchanan dragged his feet in every possible way and invented such schemes as he could to break Polk's will. He harassed the president on appointments, threatened to resign, blew hot and cold on the Supreme Court appointment, which would have injured the Administration had he taken it in the midst of the fight on Oregon, and continually urged objections to Polk's ideas. Polk wrote him down as differing with all the Cabinet and laboring to upset the presidential policy in his anxiety to leave the door open for further negotiation,[18] and in this opinion Polk was precisely right.

On December 13, Buchanan presented for presidential approval a dispatch to McLane containing the sentence that "if the British Government chose to offer as a compromise the 49° line, the president would be strongly inclined to submit it to the Senate for their advice." Polk struck it out, and substituted the statement that if Britain wished to proceed further toward a settlement, "the President would judge of the character of any new proposition." Buchanan said that if the dispatch went as amended, there had better be some preparations for war. Polk told him to send it.[19] On the same day that Buchanan forwarded this official message to McLane, he wrote a private letter assuring him that practically everyone in Congress wanted to settle at 49° and that a real war threat might possibly bring some constructive results. Aberdeen, in a letter to Everett, stated that if McLane had full powers the whole problem would be settled in an hour.[20]

In England, Sir Robert Peel declared, "We shall not reciprocate blustering with Polk, but shall quietly make an increase in the Naval and Military and Ordnance Estimates." But while the Prime Minister and the Foreign Office prepared for war and announced, "if you desire war, as assuredly you will have it," the London *Times*, mouthpiece for the government, came out strongly for compromise at 49°. Buchanan, long since in possession of information which Polk refused to take seriously, proposed on February 6 that the McLane correspondence relative to British war measures be sent to Congress.

Finally, on February 21, the stalemate broke. Buchanan received a letter from McLane stating positively that Aberdeen had approved the use of force and decided to send a naval force to Canada consisting of "thirty sail of the line besides steamers and other vessels of war of a smaller class."[21] Buchanan took the letter immediately to Polk, who observed that the British were "not altogether of so pacific a character as the accounts given in the English newspapers had led me to believe." Most of the Cabinet saw the letter on Monday, and discussed it on Tuesday, February 24. Buchanan read the McLane letter and then his reply to McLane informing Aberdeen that if the British proposed a settlement at the 49th parallel, the president would submit the offer to the Senate for its previous advice. Polk called on each Cabinet member individually before expressing his own view. All agreed with Buchanan except Cave Johnson.

Polk now yielded. Buchanan sent the dispatch on February 26, accompanying it as usual with an unofficial letter in which he urged a hasty response from the British because of the likelihood of a political change in Congress by fall. He had already canvassed the Senate and knew he could count on approval there. In fact, several Senators had threatened to bring in a resolution forcing Polk to reopen negotiations on Oregon.

From this point, the Oregon settlement was merely a matter of time. Everyone could guess what would be proposed and how it would be received; the question was not what, but when. On June 6, Pakenham delivered a British proposal to Buchanan which almost exactly duplicated the settlement proposed by Buchanan to McLane in February. Polk sent it to the Senate which, on June 12, approved it by a vote of 37 to 12, and on the 15th of June the Oregon Treaty was signed. The negotiation raised Buchanan's prestige in foreign courts and drew from Queen Victoria the statement that she liked Mr. Buchanan's treaty.[22]

Between February and June, after Buchanan knew that he had won the compromise settlement, he assumed, in Polk's words, "a most warlike disposition," taking strong ground against England and heckling the president for giving in. Polk attributed this marked change of attitude to presidential politics and accused Buchanan of being more concerned "with '48 than with 49° or 54° 40'." He may have been partly right in this judgment, but he missed the main point. Polk wrote in his diary that regardless of how his secretary differed with him on public questions, the president held the responsibility. "I will control," he wrote. "If I would yield up the government into his hands and suffer him to be in effect President, . . . I have no doubt he would be cheerful and satisfied. This I cannot do." Buchanan sensed that Polk often appeared to differ with him

182

more to protect the presidential prerogative and to assert command than for reasons substantially bearing on the subject at issue.

Buchanan thought that he could easily have settled the Oregon boundary at 49° months earlier, but because of the prestige the accomplishment might have given him, Polk had obstructed the natural procedure, had made a great show of bearding the British lion, and had sought to focus attention on himself. Now that the public had come to think of a division of Oregon at 49° as a retreat, Polk wanted his Secretary of State to bear the onus of it. Buchanan would not do it. When Polk asked him to help prepare the presidential message for submission of the treaty, he refused, and in Cabinet meeting remarked to the president "that the 54° 40' men were the true friends of the administration and he wished no backing out on the subject."[23] If Polk saw no humor or irony in this statement, some of the Cabinet did, for Buchanan had merely paraphrased what the president had so often said emphatically to him. Buchanan eventually did make a little political capital out of the Oregon question, but not until after the solution he wanted had been guaranteed. And he undoubtedly derived some satisfaction from making Polk take some of his own medicine.

MEXICO

Polk proposed, after the admission of Texas as a state with the Rio Grande boundary, to acquire the Mexican provinces of New Mexico and California. The acquisition of new territory meant the readjustment of the sectional balance in Congress and introduced the explosive political issue, slavery in the new lands. Oregon would presumably form a huge addition to the free region and thus balance Texas. How could a similar balance of power be achieved in New Mexico and California? The Whigs and many northern Democrats would balk at any further extension of slavery. The person who could participate conspicuously in acquiring New Mexico and California and prevent at the same time a striking triumph of either the slave or antislavery forces held the key to the presidential succession. So, at least, Buchanan thought.

Wilson Shannon, United States Minister to Mexico, received his passports on March 28, 1845, ending diplomatic relations between the two countries. Before anything further could be done, Buchanan had to reestablish communications. He sent William S. Parrott of Virginia as a secret agent to discover whether Mexico would continue negotiations. Parrott reported, on August 26, 1845, that if an envoy were sent, he would be well received and "might with comparative ease settle, *over a breakfast table*, the most important national problems." Under the government of President José Joaquín Herrera, a kindly, peaceful man who had replaced Santa Anna shortly after Polk's inauguration and represented the peace party of Mexico, a Mexican declaration of war against the United States seemed very unlikely.[24]

This report directly contradicted other information Buchanan possessed, namely, that the war spirit ran high in Mexico and that her troops had begun to mass along the Texan border. However, Parrott's statement received confirmation through Col. Benjamin Green, Secretary of Legation at Mexico City, who knew the party situation intimately. Green gave assurance that Herrera wished to settle peaceably all questions at issue, not only claims and the Texan boundary but also the cession of New Mexico and California. The Mexican government would have difficulty in sustaining itself if the United States sent a regular minister and attempted to reopen diplomatic relations in the usual way, but if a special commission were appointed to discuss immediate problems, Herrera would receive it.[25]

Uncertain what to believe, Buchanan questioned John Black, U. S. Consul at Mexico City. Black replied that the Mexican Foreign Office was "disposed to receive the Commissioner of the United States . . . with full powers . . . to settle the present dispute."[26]

Buchanan left for Bedford Springs at the end of July. Though not disposed to worry, the heavy responsibilities of his office had begun to tell on him, and he needed rest. "To be Secretary of State is not 'what it is cracked up to be,'" he wrote to a friend before he left Washington. "Here I am sitting in a hot room, engaged from morning till night & often after night at a season of the year when I had ever been as free as mountain breezes. I never much fancied a Cabinet appointment & now less than ever."[27] But he was not to get his vacation. Polk ordered him back to advise on threatening new developments in Mexico and cautioned him to leave Bedford "in a way to produce no public sensation."[28] Bancroft wrote that Mexico probably would start guerrilla warfare across the Rio Grande, but he saw no cause for worry, since Marcy had ordered an increase in Taylor's army. Referring to the continual fight in Cabinet, he told Buchanan that the president "will grow fat in your absence, he sleeps so well *now*."[29]

Polk, with unanimous agreement of his Cabinet, decided on September 16 to make the effort to reopen diplomatic relations with Mexico. Buchanan picked as negotiator John Slidell of New Orleans, who spoke Spanish fluently and had both diplomatic and political qualifications for the work. His appointment was to be kept a close secret, lest the French and British Ministers in Washington or elsewhere should undermine the mission in advance.

Continued uncertainty whether the mission would be received by the Mexicans delayed its dispatch for two months more. In November, Buchanan urged that Slidell be sent immediately with the instructions that had been prepared. Polk, disregarding Col. Green's advice, commissioned Slidell as a regular minister. As such he would have full authority, and rejection of him by the Mexicans would suggest their rebuff of a peace effort.

Buchanan's instructions to Slidell opened with several pages emphasizing the duty of the United States to protect the Americas from European intervention. "The march of free Government on this continent must not be trammelled by the intrigues and selfish interests of European powers. Liberty here must be allowed to work out its natural results; and these will, ere long, astonish the world."[30] Polk, in his annual message of December 2, 1845, elaborated the same point, quoting nearly verbatim from Buchanan. These statements created an impression that the contemplated acquisition of Mexican territory along the Pacific was, in fact, a protection of all America from the military intrigues of Europe and placed the expansion program on the ground of national security.

Buchanan's practical directions to the new envoy rehearsed the long standing grievances of the United States against Mexico, the unsatisfied claims, the breach of treaty obligations, the legal justification for reprisals, the widely acknowledged independence of Texas, and the failure of Mexico to attempt any exercise of authority in the region claimed by Texas. Buchanan then proposed a sequence of settlements: should Mexico approve the boundary as defined by the Republic of Texas in 1836, the United States would pay claims of United States citizens against Mexico; for the cession of New Mexico, Slidell could offer $5,000,000; for the cession of California, "money would be no object," but $25,000,000 should be offered.[31]

First the Herrera government and then that of General Paredes, who had ousted Herrera, refused to receive Slidell. Having little hope that any government would undertake to negotiate with the minister, Buchanan instructed him to make an effort "to throw the whole odium of the failure . . . upon the Mexican government,"[32] and to act in such a way that "it may appear manifest to the people of the United States and to the world that a rupture could not honorably be avoided."[33] A little later, when the Paredes regime was on the brink of bankruptcy, Buchanan authorized Slidell to offer cash to the general "if he would do us justice and settle the question of boundary between the two republics."[34]

In the meantime Col. A. J. Atocha came to Polk with the proposal that the United States should help the exiled dictator Santa Anna return to Mexico. Once re-established in power, Santa Anna would make the treaty of cession to the United States, if that country could stage enough of a military show to convince the Mexican people that their leader was forced into the demand. Atocha suggested that, as a preliminary, Slidell should call for the satisfaction of claims against Mexico from the deck of a warship moored off Vera Cruz.[35]

185

Although Polk put little trust in Atocha, he did take the bizarre scheme to the Cabinet. Buchanan, who had not known of it before, immediately judged it unacceptable. It would give the impression, he said, that the United States had made Slidell the spokesman of aggression rather than a peace commissioner. The Secretary of State, irritated and angry, left the meeting.

That night Buchanan wrote Polk two notes in which he explained in detail his objections to the Atocha plan. "When I differ with you," he continued, "it is always with reluctance and regret. I do not like to urge arguments in opposition before the whole Cabinet. . . . A little previous consultation with me on important questions . . . would always obviate this difficulty."[36] Buchanan hoped that the Administration would not make any move that might lead to war until it had convinced the American people that resort to hostilities had become the only means of preserving the national honor.[37]

Polk wanted action and considered the unpaid claims sufficient excuse for a war with Mexico, but Buchanan pleaded with him to wait until the Mexicans should commit some act of hostility.[38] Private reports he had been receiving from General Taylor's camp near Matamoros led him to believe that Mexican soldiers would soon attack.[39]

On May 9, the day after Slidell returned to Washington for a conference with Polk and Buchanan, news came of a skirmish between the Mexican forces and Taylor's little army during which several Americans lost their lives. Polk immediately called a Cabinet meeting and added to a war message which he had already prepared the statement that Mexico had "invaded our territory and shed American blood upon the American soil." Congress promptly responded to Polk's message by a nearly unanimous vote for a declaration of war.

Buchanan meanwhile prepared a circular for distribution to foreign governments explaining that the United States did not fight to dismember Mexico but only to defend her own territory as far south as the Rio Grande boundary. Polk refused to tie his hands with such a proclamation and rewrote the paragraph to read, "We go to war with Mexico solely for the purpose of conquering an honorable peace."[40] Buchanan argued earnestly for his own version, for he wished to distinguish clearly between initiating a war of aggression and fighting a defensive war. If people believed that the object of hostilities was to make a conquest, the war would be rendered "utterly odious" at home and European intervention might follow.[41] But the Cabinet thought otherwise and Buchanan reluctantly sent out Polk's explanation.[42]

From the day war was declared, Buchanan asked for a clear definition of what territory the Administration proposed to demand from Mexico, in order that he could continue peace negotiations on such a basis even while the war proceeded. Secretary Walker wanted all Mexican territory north of the 26th parallel, from the mouth of the Rio Grande to the Pacific. Buchanan preferred to demand only upper California, from the 37th or 38th parallel, including San Francisco or possibly Monterey, and the province of New Mexico north of the 32nd parallel. To seek southern California or the region south of Texas would, he feared, raise a storm over slavery and "be the means of dissolving the Union."[43]

On July 27, Buchanan sent a note under a flag of truce to the Mexican Foreign Minister inviting further negotiations either in Washington or Mexico. Polk asked Congress to appropriate $2,000,000 for an immediate payment to Mexico upon ratification of a treaty. He hoped that the Paredes government, now nearly bankrupt, would accept this sum as a means of self-preservation.

Buchanan warned Polk that a request to Congress for such an appropriation would only start a bitter debate over slavery. Representative David Wilmot attached to the Administration money bill the "proviso" that slavery should forever be excluded from any territory that the United States might acquire from Mexico. The Wilmot Proviso killed the bill. Richard Rush commented to Buchanan that the rejection of the treaty fund would cost the nation a hundred million dollars in war expenses.[44] Meanwhile, the Mexican Foreign Minister chose to interpret Buchanan's peace offer as an insult. Buchanan answered that no alternative remained but to prosecute the war until Mexico proposed to stop it.[45]

Although still hopeful of peace by negotiation, Buchanan began an effort to direct war strategy into channels which would bring the kind of peace he wanted. He supported the "defensive line" policy which advocated military seizure of only the territory desired. He bounded that region by the Rio Grande to the western edge of Texas and from there by a line along the 32nd parallel to the Pacific. This amount, he hoped, would be reasonable compensation for claims and indemnity for war expenses. Furthermore, its acquisition would cause no serious division in the Democratic party on the question of slavery.

The Administration feared that a full-scale war carried to the heart of Mexico would make Generals Zachary Taylor and Winfield Scott, both Whigs, popular heroes and permit them to set themselves up as presidential candidates. So probable did this development appear that Polk, with Buchanan's hearty approval, tried in vain to persuade the Senate to commission Thomas Hart Benton a lieutenant general so that he would outrank both Taylor and Scott. Polk then offered Benton a major-generalship, which he refused. Therefore, the Whig generals held the field and largely controlled the military policy of the war.

Meanwhile, the army and navy, in a series of signal victories, had won control not only of New Mexico and California but also of the heart of

187

Mexico. The news excited the admiration and enthusiasm of all Americans, silenced much of the Whig and abolitionist condemnation of the war, and converted into howling patriots those who had earlier remained indifferent. Even from abroad came expressions of praise for the conduct of American arms.

The tidings of victory from Buena Vista and Vera Cruz induced Polk to try the olive branch again. The Cabinet approved and Buchanan set to work to draft a peace treaty. His proposal of April 13, 1847, provided for cession of the provinces of New Mexico and Upper and Lower California, together with a right of passage across the isthmus of Tehuantepec. For this, the United States would pay all claims of American citizens against Mexico and $15,000,000 in addition. Against Buchanan's persistent opposition, Polk and the rest of the Cabinet revised the purchase price upwards to $30,000,000.[46]

For a time Buchanan considered going to Mexico as peace commissioner, but he decided that the negotiations might keep him away from Washington too long. The Cabinet felt that domestic politics ruled out General Scott, otherwise a logical choice, or any prominent Democrat. Buchanan suggested the appointment of the Chief Clerk in the State Department, Nicholas Philip Trist, for the task. He had no political aspirations and his open suspicion of Scott's designs on the presidency made Trist even more acceptable to the Cabinet.

Appointed on April 15, Trist set out under an assumed name and arrived in Mexico in May. He opened negotiations through the British embassy on June 6; not, however, before becoming involved in a violent quarrel with General Scott who complained, "I see that the Secretary of War proposes to degrade me." Trist, on his part, reported to Buchanan that Scott was "decidedly the greatest imbecile I have ever had anything to do with."[47] But within a few weeks, both men patched up their futile quarrel and soon became good friends. Scott, too, quickly realized that Trist would be much better than some politically ambitious Democratic Senator in the role of peacemaker.

During the summer Scott, with consummate military skill, struck out from Vera Cruz and fought his way to Mexico City. Trist now for the first time showed Scott the peace proposals and the general, impressed by their fairness and restraint, began actively to assist in the negotiation. Santa Anna had promised that he would negotiate for $10,000 in advance and $1,000,000 upon signing a treaty. Scott put up the $10,000 out of the army secret service fund, but Santa Anna, with the money safely in his pocket, backed out of the bargain. Therefore, Scott had to carry the war to its final conclusion. On September 14, after the thrilling but costly victories at Molino Del Rey and Chapultepec, Scott and the American army marched into the Mexican capital. By this time Santa Anna had fled and the Mexican government was so demoralized that for the moment there was no one with whom to negotiate.

When news of these events arrived in Washington, Buchanan, Walker and others repented their willingness to accept a peace so easy on Mexico as the one outlined in the original instructions to Trist. Buchanan paved the way for stiffening terms as early as June by writing to Trist that "the object of a war, at any period of its continuance, is not necessarily that for which it commenced."[48] During the summer, Buchanan progressively altered his stand on the amount of territory which ought to be demanded of Mexico as indemnity, increasing the area in correlation to American military success and the rising popular demand for all of Mexico.

At the time of drawing up Trist's instructions, Buchanan had written to a friend that to annex most of northern Mexico "would not be in accordance with public opinion," and wanted to limit the acquisitions to Upper and Lower California.[49] In July, however, he informed Trist: "The more I reflect upon the subject the better I am convinced of the importance of running the boundary line between the Rio Grande and the Gulf of California along the thirty-second parallel."[50] In September, when Polk raised the question whether Trist should not demand more territory, Buchanan proposed again that the offer of money be cut from $30,000,000 to $15,000,000, that the cession of the province of Lower California and the right to transit across the Tehuantepec isthmus now be made a *sine qua non* of settlement, and that the northern boundary of Mexico be cut from the 32nd parallel to the 31st.[51]

Polk and Buchanan continued to disagree on war policy. Polk thought the army ought to occupy the whole country, but Buchanan wanted the troops withdrawn from all territory except that which was to be annexed.[52] Polk complained that Buchanan had increased his demands on Mexico. Buchanan explained that the invasion of the interior of the country (which he had opposed) had cost many lives and a great deal of money; therefore, it was foolish to assume that previous terms would now apply. But Polk thought that Buchanan's change of position was due to his desire for the presidency and his unwillingness "to incur the displeasure of all those who are in favor of the conquest of all Mexico."[53]

Military success rapidly changed the tenor of public opinion. All the leading Democratic newspapers of the West and South now insisted on the acquisition of all of Mexico, or a very large slice of it, and even the more conservative eastern papers supported the same policy.[54] Some of the British expressed the opinion that the Anglo-Saxon race inevitably would appropriate North America, and the usually unfriendly Palmerston was heard to remark: "They are going to take two-thirds of Mexico. Why don't they take the whole?"[55] One of Buchanan's military informants wrote: "All Mexico must soon be ours—notwithstanding the wish of the

President and the country for Peace. . . . Thousands of the present generation will live to see the whole of North America under one Confederated Government, and the sooner the better."[56]

In October, 1847, when rumors seeped to Washington that Trist planned to make a treaty recognizing the Nueces boundary of Texas and giving up other vital American demands, Buchanan ordered Trist to return home, treaty or no treaty. Trist, however, determined to defy his instructions. In a 65-page letter of explanation and apology to his chief, he stated that he would stay and conclude a treaty because he felt it was the only way to prevent the summary seizure of the entire country. Polk denounced Trist as arrogant, impudent, insulting, destitute of honor, a scoundrel, and a worse public servant than he had ever known.[57]

Under these unhappy circumstances, Trist proceeded to negotiate the Treaty of Guadalupe Hidalgo, which reached the astounded Administration in Washington on Saturday, February 19. Trist clearly wanted to make Polk take the responsibility for accepting or rejecting a treaty conforming to his original instructions. The treaty itself set the present southwestern boundary of the United States, excepting the Gadsden Purchase, in return for $15,000,000 and payment by the United States of claims against Mexico.

Buchanan sharply opposed submitting this treaty to the Senate. He wished to capitalize, in the months before the Democratic nominating convention, on the political effect of advocating a larger cession. Polk accused him of trying to undermine the treaty in the Senate, but in this the president was mistaken; as in the case of Oregon, Buchanan worked hard to make sure that the treaty would be ratified and privately wanted it ratified.

An exact transcript of the treaty and of confidential correspondence regarding it appeared in the New York *Herald* while it was still under discussion in secret sessions of the Senate. A young Irish reporter named John Nugent who was known to be a close friend of Buchanan sent in the story. Nugent had for some years been writing for the *Herald* under such pen names as "Nous Verrons," "Felix," "Galviensis," and "Chee-Wah-Wah." Just a few weeks before, "Galviensis" had published several articles abusing the President, and Polk suspected Buchanan of complicity. "If I can obtain any reliable proof that Mr. Buchanan has given countenance to Galviensis," he wrote in his diary, "he shall not remain in the Cabinet." Buchanan vigorously denied any connection with the articles. The Senate called for an investigation of the treaty leak and questioned Nugent for two weeks, but he refused to disclose anything except that he had copied all the documents in his own room, and that his informant had no connection either with the Senate or the Department of State.

Buchanan's enemies built a strong case of circumstantial evidence against him as the informer and Polk accused him outright, but Buchanan positively asserted both his own innocence and the trustworthiness of every member of his Departmental staff. He then addressed a letter to the Senate declaring that the secretary and all the Department clerks, waiving every privilege which might exist, would appear before the Senators to undergo examination until every trace of suspicion had been removed.[58] Buchanan suspected that the leak had originated in the Senate.[59] The name of Nugent's informant, however, remains a mystery to this day. The affair had no effect on the Treaty, which was ratified by the Senate and proclaimed by Polk on July 4.[60]

THE LIFE OF A GALLEY SLAVE

Beyond the major problems of the Department, Buchanan directed innumerable minor negotiations. He sought to induce Emperor Dom Pedro II of Brazil to join other nations in abolition of the international slave trade. He challenged the Anglo-French intervention in the war between Argentina and Paraguay, accusing both nations of flagrant violation of the Monroe Doctrine and the principles of nonintervention. In 1846 he concluded a treaty with New Granada which granted the United States a right of transit across the Isthmus of Panama. This important agreement underlay the building of the Panama Railroad and later the construction of the Canal.

After three years of correspondence, he managed to draw up a postal convention with Great Britain which provided for uniform transatlantic mail rates, and he adjusted satisfactorily a dispute with Britain over the "most favored nation" clause of the commercial treaty which had been violated by illegal customs collections on both sides of the ocean. Through Henry Wheaton, he negotiated six commercial treaties with German states to eliminate the old feudal dues and to put these states on the basis of trade reciprocity with the United States.

The European revolutions of 1848 kept the State Department busy. The United States took the lead in recognizing the new French Republic less than a week after the revolution started and promptly recognized the new German Confederation with headquarters at Frankfort. Buchanan successfully urged, against considerable American opposition, the establishment of a diplomatic Mission to the Vatican as a means of developing commerce, for the new Pope, Pius IX, was a strong advocate of a European commercial federation.

In May, 1848, Buchanan saw in the developing revolution in Cuba an opportunity to acquire that island, though he wanted to wait until

191

after the presidential election to initiate the purchase. Polk enthusiastically supported the plan to offer Spain $100,000,000 for Cuba and authorized Buchanan to instruct his Minister at Madrid to explore the possibilities. Spain indignantly rejected the idea, but Buchanan blamed the Minister, Romulus M. Saunders, for some responsibility for the failure. "A more skillful agent might have been selected to conduct the negotiations in Spain," he wrote, "as our present Minister speaks no language except English, & even this he sometimes murders."[61]

Hawaii showed signs of responding to American influence. Buchanan dispatched Anthony Ten Eyck of Michigan as Commissioner to Hawaii early in 1845 with instructions to make a commercial treaty and thwart European influence there. Ten Eyck wrecked his mission by asking for special privileges for white American citizens, to which the Hawaiians replied that such demands reminded them of what happened to Texas. Ten Eyck then stated flatly that he thought what was done in Texas ought to be repeated in Hawaii and appealed to a United States naval commander in the waters to force his treaty on the king. Buchanan roundly rebuked the minister and called for his resignation.[62]

Buchanan did not find his situation in the Cabinet as satisfying as he had hoped or as enjoyable as his activities in the Senate. To be sure, he relished the prestige which the premiership brought him, but he never quite gave himself wholeheartedly to the job. In Cabinet he played the lone wolf rather than the organization man, with his eye constantly straying from the main task to possible alternative prospects for himself, particularly the presidency. He worked tirelessly, but under a continual sense of aggravation, at the archaic structure of the Department which he, in vain, tried to persuade Congress to correct.[63]

But he found himself especially irritated by President Polk. It seemed to Buchanan that the Tennesseean, not entirely sure of himself and fearful lest he become a puppet of the Cabinet, went out of his way to emphasize his determination to wield the scepter. Polk's voluminous diary reflects throughout a deep-seated distrust of Buchanan and is filled with uncharitable comments about him. Yet, though the Secretary of State disagreed with him on almost every important diplomatic decision, Polk retained him. In fact, Polk for the most part arrived ultimately at the judgments Buchanan had offered in the beginning. "Mr. Buchanan is an able man," wrote the president.[64]

Toward the end of his term, Buchanan developed a nervous tic in his leg and a painful tumor in his nose, the latter requiring a series of operations. It took Doctor Foltz and two other Navy surgeons over a year and a half to conclude the surgical treatment of the nasal polyp.[65]

A diligent and laborious worker, Buchanan rarely ever complained of tasks except while he was Secretary of State. "I am an overworked man," he wrote to John Reynolds. "No man, I care not what may be his talents & acquirements, is fit for the office under its present organization, unless his constitution will enable him to work and see company from ten to fifteen hours out of every twenty-four.[66] To another he complained, "My life is that of a galley slave. I have not read thirty consecutive pages in any book since I came into the Department of State."[67] Near the end of his term, he told Arnold Plumer, "I have wished 1,000 times that I had never entered this Dept. as Secretary. I have had to do the important drudging of the administration without the power of obtaining offices for my friends. . . . *I have no power. I feel it deeply.*"[68] One of the things that kept him going was his respect for the president. Although Buchanan frequently mistrusted Polk's judgment, he respected his conscientious and unremitting application to duty.

When Polk died but a few months after the end of his Administration, Buchanan commented: "He was the most laborious man I have ever known; and in a brief period of four years had assumed the appearance of an old man,"[69] and the Secretary wondered how much he had had to do with it. He left Washington with the statement: "I am happy and contented . . . . I would not for any consideration return to the State Department."[70]

15

STILL HUNT FOR THE PRESIDENCY • 1848

RECIPE FOR POLITICAL PIE

However little he may know about James Buchanan, almost everyone has encountered the comment of Ben Perley Poore that "never did a wily politician more industriously plot and plan to secure a nomination than Mr. Buchanan did, in his still hunt for the Presidency."[1] What truth there may be in this statement applies most forcefully to the campaigns of 1848 and 1852, for in these Buchanan seriously set out to bag the game. He proceeded methodically, according to practices which years of experience had impressed upon him as necessary. Had someone asked him to enumerate the rules by which a man might achieve the presidency, he might have listed these: the appearance of disinterestedness, the support of the home constituency, and national rather than sectional views on burning issues of the day.

Buchanan preferred the role of the statesman to that of politician. He stayed aloof from rough and tumble meetings, he avoided public debate and stump speeches, and stayed close to home to confer with party leaders, leaving it to subordinates to work with the voters and pay the campaign bills. He still agreed with Jackson that no man could achieve the presidency who appeared actively to seek it and that the successful candidate must display utter indifference until he was called to duty.

For this reason he felt that an aspirant should have wealth enough to be careless of his political fortune. He confided to J. Glancy Jones that he had never yet known a public man "who had abandoned his profession for politics before he had accumulated something like a competency that did not regret his course."[2] It was the urgent need of money that made men like Forney and Lynch and Brewster scramble for political jobs, and sparked the ambitions of many at a much higher level, like Clay and Webster. Buchanan had no financial cause to seek a government salary; he had made his competency, was proud of the fact, and could in good conscience assure his friends that the loss of political office would not cost him "a night's rest or a meal's victuals."

The appearance of disinterestedness could also be used with political effect. Buchanan had made the prospect of a Supreme Court appointment pay full dividends. The offer stimulated to action all those who looked to him for political patronage and attracted national attention. His decision to decline it created exactly the effect Buchanan wanted, the image of a man personally inclined to retire from active politics but prevailed upon by his friends to remain in harness.

Buchanan always believed that a presidential aspirant, to be successful, had to have firm political control of his own county and state. A man defeated at home had little prospect of developing strength abroad. For this reason he devoted an inordinate amount of his time and energy to petty politics in Lancaster and the contest of factions in Pennsylvania.

The aspiring candidate must subordinate sectional objectives and loyalties to national principles. This was not merely an ingredient for personal success but a requirement for the continued existence of the Union. By 1847 it seemed probable that only a northern man who viewed southern problems with sympathy and understanding could meet this requirement, for there remained little hope, since the Wilmot Proviso and the Tariff of 1846, of finding a southern man with political sympathy for the North on either of these issues. But there were many northerners who, though disliking slavery and free trade, thought that the South should share in new territory and subscribed to a moderate tariff. Buchanan held this position, believing it to be both the surest guarantee of the preservation of the Union and the stand most likely to gain broad support for the presidency. The chief competition would come from the West where men like Cass and Douglas would take national ground by offering to act as mediators in the growing strife between the North and the South.

DISCIPLINING DEMOCRATS

It was impossible to know even where to begin drilling Pennsylvania's demoralized Democrats into something like a strong and dependable organization. In fact, Buchanan had not made up his mind positively to face the task until he knew the local reaction to the Walker Tariff. Providentially for him business remained good, industrialists began to admit that the new tariff would not ruin them and the Pennsylvania Democrats, applauding Buchanan's proposal to modify rates on iron and coal, calmed down. Having cleared this hurdle, which had temporarily tripped Dallas, Buchanan decided to stay in the presidential race.

He had a block of influential friends who would stick with him through thick and thin: Forney, Lynch, Wilson McCandless, Arnold

195

Plumer, Jeremiah S. Black, George W. Barton, W. A. Stokes, William Bigler, J. Glancy Jones, Christian Bachman, W. Hutter, and many others, although they were not enough to control the state. He faced the powerful opposition of the followers of George Dallas, primarily in Philadelphia. Between these major factions were others, generally for sale to the highest bidder, and some of them led by men who were violently detested by Buchanan's friends. Buchanan had to augment his certain support by enough strength purchased from political roustabouts like Cameron to insure his control of the state delegation.

A major test of strength would come in 1847, when Pennsylvania faced another governor's election. Buchanan had supported Shunk before and strongly backed him for renomination, despite the opposition of Cameron and the lukewarm adherence of Forney's friends to whom Shunk had shown no favor.[3] Forney wanted Buchanan to run in order to disentangle himself from the embarrassments of the Polk Administration and to command a larger patronage to consolidate his party than he could obtain in the State Department.[4]

The Harrisburg Democratic Convention of March 4, 1847, quickly renominated Shunk for governor but ran into a bitter fight to decide between Buchanan and Dallas as the "favorite son" of Pennsylvania. The delegates finally stalled to a deadlock and adopted an innocuous statement expressing pride in both the Vice-President and the Secretary of State.[5]

Senator Cameron discovered in this impasse an opportunity to make a show of strength which might improve his bargaining power later. He publicly pronounced General Zachary Taylor to be a Democrat and endorsed him for president. Taylor had enough of the legendary appeal of Andrew Jackson to become immediately formidable, but even Cameron's own partisans acknowledged that to call the general a Democrat was "political prostitution."[6] Nonetheless, the movement grew apace. Cameron set up his brother James as editor of the Democratic *Sentinel*, a new pro-Taylor newspaper in Lancaster, and took a leading part on the floor of a convention at Harrisburg on June 26 which endorsed Taylor and lauded Senator Cameron.[7]

Polk was worried about the increasing popularity of Taylor, and some Congressmen considered a resolution censuring him for what they considered disobedience of orders. Buchanan complained that Taylor should never have consented to an armistice after the battle of Monterey but soon changed that tune when public resentment rose against Polk's charge that Taylor was "incompetent to command a large army." Davy Lynch wrote that it reminded Pittsburghers of the attempts to censure General Jackson, and if Taylor could not command a large army, he still had "the knack of flogging a *larger one* with a very small one," which answered the same purpose.[8] By early fall, the Democratic drive for

196

Taylor in Pennsylvania had still further embittered, if that could be possible, the relations of Buchanan's friends with Cameron's. Forney told Buchanan: "As for Cameron, he pollutes Taylor with his prostituted praises. . . . Every enemy that you now have was made in some way more or less connected with that bold intriguer. God in Heaven knows you have paid a dreadful penalty for the court which he has professed to pay you. My deliberate opinion is now that you have not an enemy who is not a more trusty friend than Simon Cameron."[9] Cameron's endorsement wrote finis to Taylor's candidacy among Pennsylvania Democrats.

In a very different way, Cameron's move also threatened Buchanan's candidacy by infuriating the Frazer-Champneys men in Lancaster to the final breaking point. Since Buchanan still refused to renounce Cameron, they at last repudiated Buchanan and came out strongly for Dallas. This movement had been brewing ever since Cameron's tricky capture of the senatorship, but until now Forney and others had been able to prevent an open and formal break. The truce abruptly ended. Frazer declared war by announcing that Buchanan had refused to pay his personal tax to Lancaster County for the preceding several years, on the ground that he was now a resident of Washington. He had disclaimed his state to save a paltry ten-dollar bill and now wanted to be called a "favorite son." This story, developed in many forms by Frazer, ran the rounds of the opposition press.

Frazer's charge was partly true. A county official had asked Buchanan whether, since he would reside in Washington permanently while he was Secretary of State, he should be billed for local taxes. He had replied that he understood from other Cabinet officers that such tax was usually remitted under these circumstances. The question was still not settled when Frazer gave out the story. Buchanan's friends begged him to ignore the fracas and by all means to avoid a newspaper controversy with Frazer, but Buchanan was more nettled than usual and wanted to clear himself. He wrote a long exposition of his relationship with Frazer, concluding with the facts of the tax matter, and then wisely sent it to Forney, who read it to selected politicians but kept it out of print.

Frazer's father had befriended Buchanan, presented him with a law library, and helped him build up a practice. Buchanan rewarded this kindness over the years by using his influence to secure political jobs for most of the family, both the Frazers and their in-laws, the Steeles. Half a dozen of them were drawing salaries, thanks to Buchanan, by 1845. Reah Frazer wanted more. As Buchanan told the story, Reah's break with him coincided not with the Cameron election, but with Buchanan's refusal to promote another sinecure for one of the clan. This, claimed Buchanan, was the source of Frazer's hostility; the other matters he raged about merely served as convenient excuses to cloak his personal spite.[10]

197

Private circulation of this story served to keep the effects of the attack localized, and leading politicians recognized that Buchanan's estimate of Frazer's motive was perfectly defensible; they understood also that the tax episode reflected a problem common among men who spent years away from home in government service. But how would the voters of Lancaster County react? Frazer, Champneys and Stambaugh could very likely control them and vote Buchanan down in his own ward and precinct, unless someone took prompt action, and this result would kill him off in the Pennsylvania contest for delegates to the nominating convention.

The Pennsylvania convention at Harrisburg to pick delegates to the national convention of the Democratic party was scheduled for March 4, 1848. Counties held their local meetings to choose delegates to Harrisburg at various times. Lancaster County Democrats picked September 1, 1847, for their meeting, a month in advance of the date of the state election for governor. At that meeting one of Cameron's friends, by prearrangement, submitted a resolution in favor of Buchanan. Frazer, as Cameron had anticipated, denounced the resolution and had it voted down. He then obtained approval of a slate of delegates to Harrisburg, all but one committed to Dallas for president, and concluded by ramming through a resolution that Buchanan ought to be read out of the Democratic party![11]

The attack shocked and frightened Frazer's own colleagues, for it suddenly dawned upon them, as upon Buchanan, that the Lancaster County movement might defeat Shunk. The Lancaster group had identified itself intimately with him, and if it now appeared that a vote for Shunk meant a vote against Buchanan, they both might ultimately lose. Buchanan came out strongly for Shunk and the governor cut himself entirely loose from the conflict, while Forney did his best to soften the damage by making Frazer look ridiculous and threatening to "lug him out by the throat" and expose the family salary grab. The suspense ended on October 14, when Shunk routed his Whig opponent by a comfortable majority. Forney wrote to Buchanan the next day that he would come to Washington to prepare for the future and "to see how we shall dispose of Frazer. The fight for the nomination will begin from the jump. I see Dallas and his folks at work."[12]

Buchanan hoped for some help from Governor Shunk, but that worthy, pressed equally hard by the friends of Dallas, prayed good God, good Devil, not knowing which way to turn, and finally declared his emphatic neutrality. He still had his troubles, however, because the presidential question whittled away his own friends until there were "devilish few of them left to be neutral."[13]

All efforts now centered on control of other county delegations to the Harrisburg Convention which would select the Pennsylvania delegation to Baltimore. Buchanan felt confident of strong support in all but a few scattered counties outside of Philadelphia, but the key to success lay

198

in that city, with its huge quota of 85 delegates. Forney, aided by half a dozen aggressive workers devoted to Buchanan, undertook to reduce this stronghold and beat Dallas on his own ground. It was a bold game for a newcomer to that aloof and aristocratic region and deserved more of Buchanan's active political and financial aid than he gave.

Forney began by holding weekly meetings with two or three dozen workers at his own home. He instructed them on policy and tactics and inspired them with "cold cuts and liquid refreshment." Here the leaders set up finance, ward and publications committees, inaugurated a "Buchanan Fund," and named two persons from each ward to promote meetings called "political Wistar Parties" in sarcastic reference to the legitimate ones held by the city's aristocracy. After much debate they agreed to campaign by "quiet, silent exertions" in preference to parades, drum-beating, mud-slinging, and other blatant methods.[14] Forney printed 100,000 copies of the proceedings of the Buchanan Convention of 1843 and mailed out quantities of Buchanan engravings, but he felt that they did not match in effect a book dedicated to Dallas who had bought up the whole edition and franked it all over the state. Cameron, too, created a stir by exhibiting in a Philadelphia store window a huge painting of himself resplendent in a flaming scarlet cloak. In response to Forney's pleas to send documents to the back-country editors, Buchanan planned a mailing of Frémont's report on his western explorations, but since he did not have the franking privilege he concluded that the cost would be prohibitive.[15]

A few weeks before the Philadelphia election of December, both factions staged huge mass meetings. To the first of these, called a "War Meeting" and appealing to all Democrats, the Dallas supporters came early and organized the proceedings half an hour before the Buchanan men arrived. A fight promptly ensued which lasted until 10 o'clock and ended with the ejection of the Dallas partisans. Plitt assured Buchanan: "We had all the decency and, what is better, the rough fellows who do the voting and the fighting. The battle being now begun openly, nothing remains but to fight it out."[16]

The Philadelphia election was heartbreaking: Dallas carried the city by *three votes*. If Buchanan had received them, he would have won Philadelphia Ward and enough candidates to control the balance of the city delegation. The final tally gave Dallas 47 delegates and Buchanan 38. It was, said Forney, no disgrace to lose by such a small majority, considering that they had had to contend with the customhouse phalanx and hostile municipal judges who threatened not to renew the license of any tavern keeper who favored Buchanan.

Forney had done a good job, and his aides thought it so remarkable a showing that they printed a detailed account of the election returns for statewide distribution. Forney, in truth, had nearly worn himself out.

"My whole soul is so absorbed in this fight," he wrote, "that I can think of nothing else. I dream of it at night. I do not go out into company, for it makes me chill and distracted. I have even quit drinking—and almost ceased eating."[17]

A sidelight, at this point, will illustrate the difference between Buchanan's campaign methods and those of his managers and expose the handicaps under which the latter had to work. While the Philadelphia campaign flamed to white heat, Forney took time to try to save Lancaster County, where Frazer now dominated the editor of the Lancaster *Intelligencer*, Forney's old paper. May, the editor, wanted to get out and Forney arranged that W. Hutter of Easton, a man of editorial courage and political stature, should take the paper. This would cost money, $2,425 to be exact, and furthermore May demanded some guarantee of other employment.

Buchanan arranged the loan by the devious means of asking James B. Lane of Lancaster to advance the amount to Christian Bachman, who would sign it over to Nathaniel W. Sample, who would then give it to Hutter and receive a note in return. Buchanan would then privately make good to Lane, thus both hiding and postponing his participation in the transfer.[18]

As to May, Forney wrote: "James B. Lane and myself only got May out of the paper by promising him our influence to get him a clerkship. You . . . I hope, . . . will not hesitate to sustain us in all we have done. Bold and prompt measures are now of the utmost importance, and ordinary delicacy must not be suffered to interfere with stern duty. We acted for you." Buchanan replied: "I fear the Clerkship will be a great obstacle in the way. Suppose May would insist upon this promise. Its recognition & performance on my part would do me more harm than ten Intelligencers would do me good, greatly as I esteem the value of the paper. On the other hand, suppose he should not obtain the clerkship, he might publish the fact that you had got him out of the paper on this promise. A clerkship I shall not procure for him, at least not for the present. The money is nothing when compared with an independent and erect course of conduct."[19] By midsummer, May still had no clerkship.

The Harrisburg Convention of March 4, far from being a resounding triumph for Buchanan, turned out to be a two-day wrangle in which Cass and Dallas each came off very strong. Buchanan got a majority of delegates to the national convention, and the pledge of the minority to support him until the majority should yield; but the Dallas delegates, committed to Cass as second choice, greatly weakened Buchanan's bargaining position. The convention rejected a resolution favoring Buchanan's major political plank, extension of the Missouri Compromise line to the Pacific, and in its place accepted a resolution complimenting Cass and Dallas. Cameron threw everyone into confusion by suddenly proposing a whole slate of national convention delegates chosen from among his own followers, and no one quite knew whether this move had been sanctioned by Buchanan or was merely another Cameron fishing expedition. Forney, chagrined at the outcome after all his work, had at least the satisfaction to report that he could deliver the solid vote of the state to Buchanan on the opening ballots at Baltimore.[20]

While Forney's crew worked their hearts out to capture Pennsylvania, Buchanan tried to develop the broader pattern of support from his headquarters at Washington. Here he analyzed public opinion and designed policy to fit its general trend. We have already seen how he attempted to disassociate himself from unpopular policies of the Polk Administration while preserving his party regularity by remaining in the Cabinet. But the big issue which dominated the thoughts of every party and every section as the Mexican War drew to a close was what to do about slavery in the new territories. It was not enough to condemn the Wilmot Proviso; a workable solution, widely acceptable, had to be devised. Buchanan gave his proposal for solving the puzzle in a letter to a Harvest Home celebration of Democrats in Reading, Pennsylvania, in August, 1847.

In this "Berks County letter," as it came to be known, Buchanan stated that he did not expect any northern Democrats to approve of slavery, but he did expect them to honor the Constitution which left the slavery question up to the states where it existed. In new territories the problem had been settled, with great difficulty, by the Missouri Compromise in 1820, and since then Texas had come into the Union under the same rule. For the future, "the line of the Missouri Compromise should be extended to any new territory which we may acquire from Mexico." While this would safeguard the rights of the South and keep faith, it would not, nevertheless, result in the extension of slavery. None of the new territory was adapted to slavery, there would be no means of recovering fugitives to Mexico, most of the settlers would certainly come from the North and West, and the population already in residence had long since abolished slavery under Mexican law.

He concluded: "The question is, therefore, not one of practical importance. Its agitation, however honestly intended, can produce no effect but to alienate the people of different portions of the Union from each other; to excite sectional divisions & jealousies; and to distract & possibly destroy the Democratic party, on the ascendancy of whose principles & measures depends, as I firmly believe, the success of our grand experiment of Self Government."[21]

The concluding paragraph has been quoted in full because writers generally ignore it as a mere platitudinous peroration, whereas Buchanan considered it the main element of his idea. To him the problem was not slavery but the agitation it caused. Slavery had not destroyed the nation

201

and need not destroy it, but the contest over slavery very likely would. He selected the Missouri Compromise proposal as best suited to answer the fundamental need—to end the agitation, because it had back of it the force of tradition. It would permit the Southerners to take slaves into part of the Mexican cession, but it would not threaten the addition of any new slave states to the Union.

This letter, the first formal pronouncement by a major political figure on the touchiest question of the day, got fairly wide and favorable notice, but it raised the most dust in Pennsylvania because of the Wilmot Proviso. Lewis Cass professed himself to be surprised. Buchanan's letter, he said, "was well written, but there was no call at that particular moment for its appearance; rather there was none for his writing it, and all experience shows that politicians had better write as little as possible."[22] But it took Cass only four months to hear the call himself. In December, he announced his own policy, popular sovereignty, in the "Nicholson letter."

No one will ever know how much these competitive views influenced the coming Democratic nomination, but it is worth pointing out that the popular sovereignty idea was peculiarly western in its inception and appeal. To those who would live in the newly acquired area, the Missouri Compromise seemed a restriction imposed by the East; popular sovereignty was a freedom initiated by the West. Buchanan never got this point, for he never saw the West. He worked out the practical operating details of his Missouri line proposal with a clarity and simplicity not matched by the advocates of popular sovereignty, but he failed to appreciate that frontiersmen would prefer a do-it-yourself policy to a rule imposed from Washington.

It was an oddity of Buchanan's life that he never travelled very much in America. He saw more of the continent of Europe during his Russian Mission than he saw of the United States in his whole lifetime. Up to 1848 his travels in his own country, with the exception of his jaunt to Kentucky as a youth, could be circumscribed by a line drawn from Philadelphia, to Boston, to Buffalo, to Pittsburgh, to Richmond, and back to Philadelphia. He had no physical aversion to travel, but he hated to lose touch with his affairs or break his routine. Perhaps most important, he believed it politically dangerous to roam, and particularly so to make a pilgrimage for political purposes.

He had no dearth of invitations to go south or west but he turned them all down. Even in his own restricted orbit, he kept a tight schedule and visited little. Forney continually complained of his "comet-like" trips through Philadelphia, reporting "our boys here are very sore because they did not see you." He spent some time in New York State in the fall of 1846 trying to patch up an agreement between the Barnburners and the Hunkers, and joined President Polk on his New England trip the following summer, exasperating his friends by skipping Philadelphia and joining Polk in New York City. He vacationed at Bedford Springs, visited his sister in Meadville, and spent the rest of the time in Lancaster or Washington.[23]

Even if Polk had been willing to permit political touring, Buchanan would have stayed home. He feared what he had seen happen time after time to prospective presidential candidates who travelled widely. They were first of all written down as office seekers out to curry additional favor; then they were pounced upon by contending factions in each locality. As a result, they more often gave offense than they built up support. Buchanan purposely avoided going to Philadelphia with Polk in 1847 because the president had made arrangements to stay with Vice-President Dallas. When factionism reached its height in the North, he wrote, "*under existing circumstances*, . . . I could not visit the States of New York & Massachusetts unless it might be to pass through them quietly & rapidly."[24]

Buchanan knew he could confer with all the important politicians at Washington, and he believed that conferences with them were more effective than public appearances at the grass roots. Buchanan had many firm friends at the common level whom he cherished throughout his life, but he had little talent for making friends and influencing people on a political junket. One might say that he was democratic only in his personal life. He usually declined invitations to speak at public meetings, sending a letter instead, and avoided party caucuses and conventions. If these methods constituted a "still hunt for the presidency" then Perley Poore was right.

Buchanan had no national political organization but utilized his many friends in a kind of hit or miss program of promotion. In one of his thriftiest maneuvers he had graciously permitted the Ottoman Porte to finance part of his campaign. The ruler needed "two or three agriculturists" who were willing to come to his country as technical assistants and teach the people to raise cotton. He sent $2,500 with which to pay the agent who would find these technicians. Buchanan gave the assignment to George Plitt, who travelled over the South in the search and conferred with politicians along the route.[25]

Starting on Christmas Day, 1847, Buchanan undertook his most strenuous and expensive enterprise in personal politics, a series of dinners which he gave every week or ten days until the end of Polk's Administration. Some of these parties were only for members of the diplomatic corps, but most of them were purely political gatherings. During this period of entertainment, he wined and dined nearly all the Democratic Senators and Congressmen, many of the Whigs, and innumerable visiting politicos. Ordinarily he played host to twenty or thirty at a time. On one occasion he invited the entire Pennsylvania Congressional delegation, but only half

203

of the members came, and several never had grace enough to acknowledge the invitation. He invited Judge Stephen A. Douglas regularly, but he declined, as did Daniel Webster who in former years had often shared the festive board with Buchanan. The brandy flowed freely, and of champagne and fine old Madeira there was plenty; but of the conversation, alas, there is no record. Buchanan considered these dinners a better medium for airing his views and putting them into circulation than public speeches or the effusions of a controlled press.[26]

CONVENTION BLUES

The Baltimore Convention assembled on May 22. Buchanan's friends had arrived on the ground ten days in advance to hire a large headquarters room and caretakers for it. They placed their chief hope in the strategy of holding off Cass, the strongest contender, until the convention admitted he could not win. This tactic would bring a contest between Buchanan and Levi Woodbury of New Hampshire, in which Buchanan stood by far the better chance. The delegates adopted the two-thirds rule and then ran into a two-day wrangle over New York which had sent full delegations both of Hunkers and Barnburners. Upon a decision to admit both, but with the voting strength of only a single delegation, the Barnburners withdrew angrily and the Hunkers refused to take part in the voting. On the first presidential ballot, Cass polled 125, Buchanan 55, and Woodbury 53. On the third ballot, Virginia shifted from Buchanan to Cass and practically settled the issue, for Cass won on the next ballot. Cameron attributed the result to Pennsylvania's promotion of the futile effort to compromise the New York dispute, when strong support of either side might have purchased at least a part or possibly all of the New York vote. Buchanan blamed Virginia. "To trade me off," he wrote, "for the chance of making [John Y.] Mason vice-president & then to fail signally in the attempt was unworthy of the ancient Commonwealth." But it was all over, and when the Whigs nominated Taylor a few weeks later Buchanan felt he was lucky to be out of the contest.[27]

George Plitt echoed Buchanan's own thoughts when he wrote: "So soon as the present campaign shall have ended, I shall go to work for that of '52. . . . I shall not rest until you are in the Presidential chair."[28] Buchanan worked for Cass in 1848, but there is no evidence that he over-exerted himself in the cause. He may very possibly have felt that a Whig victory would exercise a salutary effect upon his chances in 1852, for it would demonstrate that the Democracy would have to hearken to the Keystone State's demands if it wished to win.

The summer brought surprising and disturbing developments. The disappointed New York Barnburners held their own convention on

June 22 at Utica, nominating Martin Van Buren for president on a Wilmot Proviso platform. In August, a convention of antislavery men at Buffalo also named Van Buren as their presidential candidate and launched the Free-Soil party in a blaze of enthusiasm and righteous indignation under the slogan: "Free Soil, Free Speech, Free Labor, and Free Men."

In Pennsylvania, Governor Shunk grew desperately ill of tuberculosis and resigned on July 9, making William F. Johnston, Whig Speaker of the Senate, the acting governor. Arrangements were then made to fill the office at the state election of October 10. The Whigs promptly nominated Johnston, but the Democrats fell into a welter of confusion. Leaders of all the factions now converged on Buchanan, demanding that he accept the nomination. Cameron wrote that "it can be presented in such a shape as to make your acceptance the result of a wish to save the party—as Wright did in 1844." Plitt predicted that "were we allowed to use your name for Governor . . . we would give the ticket an overwhelming majority."[29] Forney was torn between his wish to see Buchanan become governor or return to the Senate, inclining somewhat to the latter because he thought Cameron wanted Buchanan in Harrisburg to prevent a contest for his own seat in the Senate. The public hue and cry developed so fast that Buchanan had to make up his mind quickly.

In a letter to A. H. Reeder, he declined and gave the reasons for his decision. He wished to return to private life and do some writing. He had already received his share of political honors and did not wish to stand in the way of others. He must take care of some important affairs pending in the State Department. He could now gracefully retire with the good wishes of the party but might not be able to do so later.[30] He privately expressed the hope that Arnold Plumer, Jeremiah S. Black, or William Bigler might be nominated. But Cameron controlled the issue, and the nomination went to Canal Commissioner Morris Longstreth.

In the October elections, the Pennsylvania Whigs won the governorship by a majority of 297 votes of the 336,747 cast; with this advantage, Taylor was able to carry the state in November by a margin of 13,000. In New York, the Democratic party was so divided by the Van Buren ticket that all 36 of the state's electoral votes went to Taylor. When the contest was over, Buchanan's friends admitted they were glad that he had not been in it. "I do not regret the defeat of Genl. Cass," wrote Davy Lynch, "for I sincerely believe that it will be a *useful* lesson to the *Huckstering* politicians by which his nomination was brought about."[31]

16

THE SAGE OF WHEATLAND • 1849-1852

COUNTRY SQUIRE

When he retired from the State Department, Buchanan had reached the age of fifty-eight. He had gained weight and his hair had turned white, but he still walked with a spring in his step. He now habitually wore a high cloth collar with a flowing white neckerchief which emphasized his height and gave a kind of distinction to his appearance. Nathaniel Hawthorne described him as "heavy and sensible, cool, kindly and good humored, with a great deal of experience." Indeed, he had completed nearly thirty years of continuous public service. What should he do when he left Washington?

He returned to Lancaster, but because of the recent political bitterness which had erupted into fist fights between Frazer's men and his own friends, he did not want to remain in the King Street house. He certainly would be a contender for the presidential nomination in 1852, and to entertain political visitors in this exposed location adjacent to the newspaper offices would be unthinkable.

Furthermore, he needed a larger house. By this time he had acquired twenty-two nephews and nieces, and thirteen grandnephews and grandnieces. Seven of these children were full orphans in his immediate care, and several of the rest were half-orphans. They could no longer be farmed out at boarding schools, nor could he, the "rich uncle," continue to depend upon friends like the Plitts and the Kitteras to act as foster parents. Brother Edward, still a poor country pastor, had too large a family himself to assume any extra burden and plainly told James that he now ought to devote his time and money to his less fortunate kinfolk.

Consequently, when Buchanan learned in the summer of 1848 that Wheatland, a lovely country estate situated a mile west of Lancaster, was for sale, he seized the opportunity to buy it. The mansion had many personal associations. William Jenkins had built Wheatland and lived there until recently. His daughter, Martha, had married James B. Lane. To have Wheatland would keep Buchanan in Lancaster but out of the center of the city. Its spacious rooms, broad lawns and well-kept groves of oak would provide a happy playground for his wards, enable him to assume the politically strategic role of the simple, dignified country squire, and give him facilities for entertainment in keeping with the station of an aspirant to the presidency. He purchased the estate from William Morris Meredith in December, 1848, and took up residence there the following spring after retiring from the Cabinet.

No sooner had he established himself at Wheatland in mid-May, 1849, than he began to invite his political friends to visit. To a politician who addressed a letter for him to Washington, he replied, "I presume you may have supposed I would be in that City, now the grand theatre of President making. But this is not my way." His way was to sit in the study at Wheatland; to write letters day after day; to receive calls quietly; and to keep himself in a position to say: "I leave my claims to an intelligent and patriotic Democracy." More than once Miss Hetty found him, late at night, seated at his desk, his head fallen onto the paper and the candle guttering by his side.

But all was not politics at Wheatland. Buchanan soon discovered that a country gentleman has more to do than write letters. "I have a large and excellent garden," he said, "that is, it would be excellent if properly cultivated." He eventually got a gardener, one Edward Bolger, and promptly set him to work setting out 1,200 strawberry plants. He needed a coachman and general handy man on the place, but the first man he hired soon grew dissatisfied with his $8.00 per month and keep. The second, a coachman by the appropriate name of William Whipper stayed for many years.

After he discovered that weeds grew on the grounds of a country home in summer, he soon learned that cold winds howled round it in winter and that Wheatland's equipment suited it far better for summer than for winter living. He installed a new furnace, put in a new kitchen, had bookcases built, and enjoyed for the first time in his life the novelty of house renovation.

By the end of his first year, he had become thoroughly delighted with his new life, and he assumed with pride and gratification the title which politics now bestowed upon him: "The Sage of Wheatland." To Eliza Watterson he wrote, "We proceed in the same 'John Trot' style as when you were here, without your charming society to enliven the dullness of a winter in the country." He took great pleasure in sleighing, and many a crisp wintry morning when the snow crunched underfoot the horses came prancing down the lane of Wheatland, their bells ajingling, to take him for a trot out the Marietta Pike. But even more he liked the company of a few congenial spirits with whom he could crack a bottle of Madeira, talk freely, and "have a cozy time in the country."

In the springtime he made it a practice to get up with the sun to enjoy the cool beauty of the day's first hours. "The place now begins to look beautiful," he wrote in April, "and we have concerts of birds every morning." In summer the house and grounds came alive with children and young people encouraged by Harriet Lane, now a vivacious and beautiful young lady of nineteen, who lived at Wheatland and became the focal point of social activities there. She liked children and welcomed those of the neighborhood: Anna, Ella and Eddie Gable, Sue Ripley, and others. They hunted eggs in the barn, went on straw rides, knocked peaches and pears from the trees with sticks, or invaded the kitchen for fresh-made apple pie and milk. It pleased Harriet to go into town with her uncle and call at his favorite tavern, The Grapes, on North Queen Street where, shortly after their arrival, "the boys" would casually start dropping in.[1]

Buchanan visited on Harriet all the care and affection and discipline of a doting father on a favorite child, and she responded with love and pride, although she chafed at the firm restraints he placed on her impetuosity. When she was fourteen, soon after becoming his ward, he wrote to her: "I would give almost anything in the world for a niece whom all could love for her amiability & all respect for her intelligence, nor would I be severe in my requisitions." Harriet came to doubt the last phrase, but could not deny that Uncle James, or "Nunc" as she playfully called him, gave her nearly all a young girl could desire. During her vacations from school, while he was in the State Department, he sent her on summer vacations with various of his friends, the Walkers, the Bancrofts, the Pleasantons, Adele Cutts, the Plitts and others to the fashionable resorts at Rockaway Beach, Saratoga Springs and Bedford.

After her first visit to Bedford Springs with her uncle, he expressed his regret that he had given permission, disapproving of her "keen relish for the enjoyments there." He turned down her request to spend Christmas with him in Washington because "it would turn the head of almost any girl your age to engage in the dissipations of this city & particularly one of your ardor for pleasure. Your day will come. . . . After your education shall have been completed & *your conduct approved by me*, . . . I shall be most happy to aid in introducing you to the world in the best manner." At the moment she was in a scrape at school for having started a "clandestine correspondence" with a boy she met at Bedford. Her teacher had intercepted and destroyed his letters and she, too, vetoed the Washington trip. "With Harriet's peculiarity of temper," she wrote, "indulgence is subversive of all discipline . . ., one gratification excites a wish for a second until the exactions become wholly unreasonable."[2]

In 1846, Buchanan brought Harriet to the Convent School at Georgetown. "Your religious principles are doubtless so well settled that you will not become a nun," he assured her. "My labors are great; but they do not *way* me down as you write the word. Now I would say *weigh*; but Doctors differ on this point."

Shortly after Buchanan moved into Wheatland, Harriet came of age and into her inheritance. For a time she travelled about, spending weeks with friends in Baltimore, Philadelphia and Pittsburgh. She charmed everyone she met, from crusty old Davy Lynch in Pittsburgh to Martin Van Buren, who took her to dinner in Philadelphia and drank her health first at a formal party. His son, debonair "Prince John," paid her active court, but soon was left far behind in the crush of her admirers. Buchanan began to refer to her lovers in groups of three to keep it simpler, but he worried much about her making a suitable marriage.

As Harriet turned twenty-one, he gave her counsel which he repeated at intervals for the next ten years: "I wish now to give you a caution. Never allow your affections to become interested or engage yourself to any person without my previous advice. You ought never to marry any man to whom you are not attached; but you ought never to marry any person who is not able to afford you a decent & immediate support. In my experience, I have witnessed the long years of patient misery & dependence which fine women have endured from rushing precipitately into matrimonial connexions without sufficient reflection. Look ahead & consider the future & act wisely in this particular."[3]

Harriet's brothers were now on their own. James B. Lane ran a mercantile business in Lancaster and had acquired wealth. Elliot Eskridge Lane also lived in Lancaster, boarding around the town and helping his uncle and his brother, by turns, until he should decide upon a profession. Harriet's older sister, Mary Elizabeth Speer Lane, lived with the Plitts in Philadelphia, and in 1848 married George W. Baker. She stayed for a while in Lancaster until her husband went to California with the 49'ers. Buchanan was delighted to learn that she had turned out to be "a grand housekeeper. . . . There is no spectacle more agreeable to me than that of a young married woman properly sensible of the important duties of her station."[4]

Sister Maria, of Meadville, had two children and little money. Her son James Buchanan Yates held an appointment on board a revenue cutter. Her daughter by the first marriage, Jessie Magaw, married a young man named Weaver who had no job. Uncle James hired him as a clerk in the State Department, getting him a salary equal to those who had served there for a decade by the device of promoting an $800 raise for the others. Upon retiring from the Department, Buchanan urged his successor, John M. Clayton, to retain Weaver, to which Clayton replied: "as to young Weaver, he minds his business and will be contented & happy, provided his great uncle will let him alone."[5]

James Buchanan Henry, orphan son of sister Harriet, was seven years old when Buchanan became his guardian. Until now, he had lived in the King Street house in Lancaster cared for by Miss Hetty. All of his uncle's diplomacy failed to induce the youngster to eat vegetables. Buchanan promised him a magic lantern for Christmas, and young James replied in childish scrawl: "I am trying hard for it & think it will please you when you hear that I eat vegetables," but the flesh proved weak. Three years later, he still had made no progress. Buchanan wrote Harriet from Washington: "James Henry is here. I intend to commence with him tomorrow & make him eat vegetables or he shall have no meat. I have not yet determined on a school for him." He later sent Buchanan Henry to Princeton and in 1851 arranged to have him study law under John Cadwalader of Philadelphia.[6]

Brother Edward jealously resented James's wealth and rarely visited him, although his children often summered at Wheatland and had a wonderful time. Edward dutifully named one of his boys after his famous uncle, but this was no longer a novelty. Forney did likewise, and Dr. Foltz, and James M. Hopkins among many others.

In 1851 the students of Dickinson College called upon the ex-Secretary of State to negotiate a peace treaty between them and the College administration after an incident had provoked a mass dismissal of the junior class. Buchanan, acting as mediator, extracted from the outraged students a pledge of good behavior and from the faculty a retraction of the penalty. In 1853 when Marshall College in Mercersburg merged with Franklin College at Lancaster, Buchanan accepted the presidency of the Board of Trustees of the new institution, gave $1,000 to it, and spent considerable time helping to select a suitable location in Lancaster for the campus. His renewed associations with academic people led him to expand his library and to do more reading. He at last had time to look at the five volume *Life of Washington* by Jared Sparks, and to study Madison's newly published notes on the Constitutional Convention and Elliott's *Debates* on its ratification. He dipped into the works of Byron and read a good many of Sir Walter Scott's novels and the writings of Charles Dickens.

Buchanan could not forsee it, but these days of temporary political retirement at Wheatland were to be the happiest and most carefree of his life. His prestige was secure, his friends loyal and confident, and his future bright. The world came to his door, constantly filling Wheatland with gay society and the fascinating discussion of politics. He had money to spare, a good appetite, and a wonderful vaulted wine cellar fit for the vintages he now began to collect with the appreciation of a connoisseur.

The press often commented upon his "resisting power against the fumes of intoxicating drinks." He performed feats that would have startled the statistician. "The Madeira and sherry that he has consumed

210

would fill more than one old cellar," wrote Forney, who was a good judge of such matters, "and the rye whiskey that he has 'punished' would make Jacob Baer's heart glad." The wine was none of your thin potations, but stout and heady; wine that "would make an old British sea captain weep joyful tears." He was no single bottle man, either. He would dispose of two or three at a sitting, beginning with a stiff jorum of cognac and finishing off with a couple of glasses of old rye. "And then the effect of it! There was no head ache, no faltering steps, no flushed cheek. Oh, no! All was as cool, as calm and as cautious and watchful as in the beginning. More than one ambitious tyro who sought to follow his . . . example gathered an early fall."[7]

When his stock ran low, Buchanan could use the Sunday drive to church as an excuse for a trip to Jacob Baer's distillery for a ten-gallon cask of "Old J. B. Whiskey," which he considered finer than the best Monongahela. He also liked the name and enjoyed the comments of guests who thought that the initials stood for James Buchanan.

When Miss Hetty began to entertain gentleman friends, and a Mr. Evans bid fair to capture her excellent services, Buchanan again thought about marrying, though we do not know the lady he had in mind. Possibly it was Mrs. Benson, Mrs. Catron's pretty niece, whom he regarded highly at the moment. "Should Miss Hetty marry Mr. Evans," he confided to Harriet, "I shall bring this matter to a speedy conclusion one way or the other. I shall then want a housekeeper, as you would not be fit to superintend; and whose society would be so charming as that of—."[8]

But rich and satisfying as were the maintenance of a family homestead and the epicurean delights of the life of a country squire, politics absorbed Buchanan's deepest interest and thought.

THE COMPROMISE OF 1850

The gold rush and California's application for admission as a free State in 1849 brought the slavery issue again to the forefront in Congress. The Free-Soilers and many Whigs favored excluding slavery from the remaining territories by Congressional mandate based on the Wilmot Proviso. Most of the Democrats preferred the doctrine of popular sovereignty, which denied by implication the right of Congress to legislate on slavery in the territories. Buchanan thought Congress should act by extending the Missouri Compromise line to California, thus prohibiting slavery north of 36° 30' and leaving the problem south of that line "to be decided by the people." He had formally proposed this solution in his Harvest Home letter of August, 1847. Southern extremists demanded federal protection of slave property in all of the territories, while a good many people of all

211

sections and parties hoped that the Supreme Court might finally decide the status of slavery in the territories.

Congress had been bringing new states and territories into the Union at a record pace during the previous four years. It had admitted Florida and Texas to statehood in 1845, Iowa in 1846 and Wisconsin in 1848, but Oregon proved a stumbling block and California a major crisis because of the slavery question. The bill to organize Oregon as a free territory, introduced in January, 1847, touched off a long and acrimonious debate that lasted until August, 1848. A year later, when the Californians set up a free state government and applied for admission, skipping entirely the territorial stage, neither Congress nor the country was in a frame of mind to consider the petition calmly. The South feared that it would now lose the traditional balance of free and slave states in the Senate and fall into the status of a perpetual minority. This risk it refused to take, and declared that California should not be admitted unless the South got guarantees which a hostile majority would have to respect: adequate provision for the return of fugitive slaves; continuance of slavery in the District of Columbia; and the right of southerners to carry their slave property into at least some of the territories.

The Thirty-first Congress, which was almost evenly divided between Democrats and Whigs, met in December 1849 and prepared to seek an adjustment of the slavery question. Failure would bring disunion. Both sides joined in deadly battle from the very outset, casting sixty-three ballots before they could elect a Speaker. Buchanan participated indirectly in the fight to organize the House, strongly pushing for Speaker young Howell Cobb, a Union Democrat from Georgia, and supporting Forney for Clerk. Forney reported that terrible scenes were enacted. Congressmen shouted "Liar" at each other on the floor and exchanged challenges to duel. "I fear the crisis is at hand, as you have so long predicted," he wrote to Buchanan. The southerners declared "that they would secede if the Wilmot Proviso were passed."[9] Cobb at length won and Forney lost, but slavery had dominated the organizational proceedings to the extent that even the opinions of the doorkeeper had to be investigated.

After Congressional debates that lasted throughout the spring of 1850, Henry Clay reported out of committee the Senate plan of compromise. This proposed that California should be admitted as a free state; that Congress should enact a stricter fugitive slave law; that New Mexico and Utah should be admitted as territories whose inhabitants would decide about slavery at the time of application for statehood; that the slave trade in the District of Columbia should be abolished; and that the Texas boundary should be reduced, in exchange for federal assumption of the Texan debt.

212

In June southern fire-eaters, meeting at Nashville to discuss secession, displayed such division of opinion about the proposed compromise that they weakened the effect of their earlier threats. In July, President Taylor, an opponent of the compromise measures, suddenly died. His successor, Millard Fillmore, supported them. Friends of the compromise worked energetically in its behalf, none more effectively than Senator Stephen A. Douglas of Illinois who had earlier preferred the Missouri line proposal. By the end of September the plan had been passed in the form of separate acts of Congress which Fillmore speedily signed. Many people believed that the crisis had passed.

James Buchanan was not one of these. Throughout the contest he had been in and out of Washington for conferences and had been writing letters incessantly to leaders in the Senate.[10] He had condemned the course of Democratic editors, like Ritchie of the Washington *Union*, for singing the siren song that "all will be well." "My firm conviction is," he told Dr. Foltz, "that in four years from this time the union will not be in existence as it now exists. There will be two Republics . . . there will be no civil war. . . . I sincerely and fervently hope I am [wrong], but such are my deliberate opinions. Nous verrons."[11]

Few northerners, for example, knew that the moment California entered as a free state, the Governor of Georgia, in obedience to an act of the Legislature, had to call a convention to consider secession. South Carolina was pressing Virginia to join her in issuing resolutions in favor of secession. Buchanan gave effective support to John A. Parker who played a leading role in side-tracking this movement in the Virginia Legislature in 1850.[12] Two days after California became a state, a rump session of the Nashville Convention denounced the Compromise of 1850 and asserted the right of secession.

Buchanan had to announce his own position on the compromise measures in preparation for the presidential race of 1852. He thought that Congress had both the right and the duty to define the status of slavery in the federal territories, a view he maintained in opposition to the Democratic party platform of 1848, the Nicholson letter, General Cass's speeches, and formal declarations of the Pennsylvania Democratic caucus. Buchanan contended that the Constitution assigned to Congress power over the territories. Congress had asserted its rightful power in the Missouri Compromise and ought to keep control. In the vast reaches of the West, without settled communities and the means of law enforcement, there was not the slightest possibility that slavery could take root. If the inhabitants voted, they would vote slavery out; if they did not vote, the slaves would clear out themselves. The same result would follow whether the Wilmot Proviso, the extended Missouri Compromise line or popular sovereignty became law. No kind of legislative mandate could establish slavery in such

213

a region; economics and not politics would kill it. But Congress could declare the *right* of the South to migrate with slaves to part of the federal domain, and such legislation would have the advantage of abating the current agitation.

Southerners, in the tentative exercise of their right to carry slaves west, would find out for themselves the economic ineffectiveness of slavery outside the cotton and rice belt. Such a discovery, proceeding from the experience of southerners, would undermine the slave system and gradually confine it to South Carolina and the Gulf Coast states where, at last, it would succumb to overwhelming public pressure no longer entirely sectional. By the extension of the Missouri line, the South would have its "rights," but slavery would not be extended except experimentally. The experiment would bring in no new slave state but rather prove conclusively that slavery could not endure in the West. This economic determinist view underestimated the potency of the white-supremacist dogma among southerners.

But Congressional abdication of control, as proposed by the popular sovereignty doctrine of Cass and now written into the Utah and New Mexico territorial laws would, Buchanan feared, raise the devil. Congressional nonintervention would only establish new fighting zones in the West where the opposing parties would go to war over slavery during the period of territorial status. Since the question of right was left undefined, slavery would exist or not exist as a result of might, as a result of the power of whatever local force could subdue the opposition in any territory. Southerners would demand federal protection from attacks on their property in the territories; antislavery settlers would claim that the question was local and no business of Congress; the abolitionists would provoke atrocities; and the combination of excitements would inflame sectional passions and consume the nation.

Much as he disliked the popular sovereignty provisions of the Compromise of 1850, Buchanan acknowledged the need for some kind of settlement. He told Glancy Jones, "I have passed a month in Washington. . . . The deep and bitter feeling among the Southern members in regard to the Slavery question cannot be justly appreciated except by those on the spot, and not even by them unless admitted behind the scenes."[13] To his friend J. M. Read he confided that the southerners "say with truth, that whilst the agitation of the Slave question in the North may be sport to us, it may also prove death to them . . . the feeling of the South on this subject . . . is not a political feeling; but one that is domestic & self-preserving."[14]

After the adoption of the compromise, Buchanan met the mounting public demand for his opinion of it in a letter to a Democratic meeting in Philadelphia on November 19, 1850. He took no direct issue with the

214

compromise, but by restricting himself to an attack upon the continued agitation of the slavery issue and a plea for obedience to the Fugitive Slave Law he expressed by implication his lack of confidence in the agreement of 1850. The fanatical abolitionists, he said, had wrought more damage to the Negro, both slave and free, in North and South, than any group in the nation. They had postponed the course of regular and constitutional emancipation, raised anti-Negro sentiment in the North, forced more rigorous control of slaves and free Negroes in the South, and brought the Union into imminent peril. "They have done infinite mischief," he said, and by their fanatical folly had prevented the achievement of the very result they claimed to seek.

He pointed out that the new Fugitive Slave Law was exactly the same as the law of 1793 except that its enforcement now became the responsibility of federal instead of state officers. He hoped the North would faithfully enforce it, for it was all that the South had salvaged from the entire compromise. Buchanan concluded with an impassioned plea for the Union, "this, the grandest and most glorious temple which has ever been erected to political freedom on the face of the earth!"[15]

This letter constituted Buchanan's opening bid for the presidential nomination in 1852. A week after its publication, he wrote to Robert Tyler: "I have rarely known anything to take as my letter to the Union meeting has done. Every mail brings me papers from the South containing favorable notices of it & some of them speak in very strong terms in regard to the Presidency. . . . Letters from Washington speak confidentially of my prospects. If the Pennsylvania Democracy were anything like unanimous, there could, I think, be no doubt of the result."[16]

Buchanan anticipated that Lewis Cass would be his most formidable rival. Therefore he had to make a clear distinction between his position and that of Cass on the compromise, not an easy task. A strong movement had developed within both Whig and Democratic parties to lay to rest the slavery issue by declaring the recent compromise a "finality." Buchanan the statesman acknowledged that the country needed a period of calm after the storm of 1850; but Buchanan the politician distrusted popular sovereignty and declined to endorse this panacea devised by his chief competitor. While he determined not to attack the Compromise of 1850 outright, explaining that he saw no prospect of an early modification of it, he did express doubts that popular sovereignty would work, and stated that it would give the southerners no protection of slavery in the territories. Southern extremists applauded this view and flocked to Buchanan's standard; he welcomed their support though he had no sympathy with their secessionist talk.

When Union Whigs and Democrats invited Buchanan to participate in a great "peace meeting" at Baltimore where the delegates proposed to banish the slavery question from the 1852 canvass by jointly accepting the Compromise of 1850 as final, he declined. Nothing would be worse, he thought, than a bipartisan agreement on slavery at this moment, for such a jointure would stimulate the formation of sectional factions based on the slavery issue in both the North and the South, exactly the result he had been trying to prevent. Let the Whigs and Democrats remain enemies on the old, traditional ground that had divided them from the beginning. The Democrats stood for strict construction of the Constitution and the reserved rights of the states. The Whigs stood for consolidated central government. Let them fight the campaign on this issue which transcended sectionalism and would emphasize the national scope of each party.

At length, Buchanan recognized that his continued endorsement of the 36° 30' line cast him in the role of an opponent of the Compromise of 1850 and threatened his chances of nomination. Although he remained convinced that popular sovereignty would break down the first time it got a practical trial, he saw no alternative except to let the trial proceed. Then, perhaps, the nation would learn its lesson and adopt the other plan. In February, 1852, Buchanan told a public meeting: "The Compromise measures are now a 'finality'—those who opposed them honestly and powerfully, and who still believe them to be wrong, having patriotically determined to acquiesce in them for the sake of the Union."

THE BAND WAGON ROLLS AGAIN

On the Pennsylvania front, Cameron declared open war on Buchanan. He cultivated anti-Catholic prejudice to raise a Protestant counterweight to Buchanan's Irish vote, agitated antislavery excitement, and cried out for a high protective tariff. He gained influence in the Dallas faction, added Congressman Richard Brodhead to his bag, and persuaded his followers to elect Whigs to the State Senate. Buchanan wrote that Cameron had done him more political injury than "any man living."[17]

In the Pennsylvania Democratic convention to nominate a governor in 1851, however, Buchanan's friends won a victory for their candidate, William Bigler, against the Cameron favorite. On the other hand, the Pennsylvania Legislature named Richard Brodhead to fill Sturgeon's senatorial seat. The other Pennsylvania Senator, James Cooper, had been elected by the triumphant Whigs in 1849. Thus, in the Senate, Buchanan had to contend with a Whig and a Cameron lieutenant, a difficult plight for a presidential aspirant claiming to be the "favorite son" of his state.[18]

The campaign for the governorship of Pennsylvania in 1851 engrossed the interest of the nation and became the subject of excited editorials throughout the land because of the Christiana Riot of September

216

11. At this little village in southern Lancaster County, a group of Negroes and local whites prevented a United States Marshal from serving papers on a fugitive slave, shot the slaveowner and assaulted others of the official party. Buchanan, in all his recent speeches, had warned that the effectiveness of the Compromise of 1850 depended upon the willingness of northerners to abide faithfully by the terms of the new Fugitive Slave Law. Now, twenty miles from Wheatland, Pennsylvanians had committed murder and interfered with agents of the Federal government who had sought only to enforce the law. A student of the event wrote, "Many Americans felt the Christiana Riot tested crucial matters: the sanctity of law; the existence of peace and order; the ethical course of the country; and the very existence of the nation."

Extremist newspapers, north and south, printed frenzied editorials to voice their views. The Lancaster *Saturday Express* headlined: "Civil War—The First Blow Struck," and called the Christiana affray the "murder fruit" of the horrid "tree of slavery." Southern journals characterized the riot as "wanton," "atrocious," "horrible," "a most foul and damning outrage," and said that if northerners were going to shoot down slaveholders "like wild beasts," they would have to leave the Union. But most papers hoped, like the New Orleans *Picayune*, that the "sober and conservative spirit" which had always distinguished Pennsylvania in sectional crises would "crush within her borders the desperate faction whose teachings have produced and encouraged these lawless acts." The Christiana Riot gave national significance to the forthcoming state election.

Bigler's opponent, William F. Johnston, represented the views of Seward and Scott who favored the Wilmot Proviso, desired a repeal of the Fugitive Slave Law, and welcomed agitation of the slavery issue. Wrote Buchanan, "The eyes of every true patriot in the Nation will look . . . to the result in Pennsylvania. Should her people . . . re-elect Johnston, this would be a fatal index." Bigler's election in October, Buchanan believed, did more "to tranquilize the South, to restore peace & harmony between the Slave and the non-slave-holding States & to preserve the Union, than any event which has occurred since the commencement of the unfortunate agitation."[19]

Bigler's victory proved a powerful antidote to the rumors which Cameron had spread of Buchanan's inability to carry Pennsylvania and augured the selection of a strong Buchanan delegation to the Baltimore Convention, a delegation which would be named at a Harrisburg state convention on March 4. The usual local fights preceded this. In Berks County, a meeting unanimously rejected a resolution in Buchanan's favor. "Just the thing for Brodhead to frank around," wrote Buchanan with a grimace.[20] In Philadelphia, the Buchaneers moved an amendment to a Cass resolution, substituting Buchanan's name. The chairman put the

217

motion to a voice vote, declared the amendment carried without any marked evidence to support his decision, received a motion to adjourn, and then jumped out of the window one leap ahead of the enraged Cassites, who got a piece of his coat but no endorsement of their candidate.[21]

At Harrisburg, the convention gave Buchanan 94 votes; Cass, 31; Sam Houston, 2; and Robert J. Walker, 2. On a motion to make it unanimous for Buchanan, the vote came out 103 yea and 30 nay. The next day Buchanan sat down at his desk and wrote in his "Little Black Book" the name of every delegate to Harrisburg, endorsing after each the letter "B" or "C" (Buchanan or Cass), and to make sure he would never forget the traitors, he made an entry four pages later headed "Protesters at the 4 March Convention, 1852," under which he wrote again the names of the thirty whom Cameron controlled.[22] But a ray of sunshine broke through in the decision that the majority would impose the unit rule at Baltimore. Buchanan could therefore announce to the world that he went into the Baltimore convention with the solid support of the delegation of his home state. Privately he predicted that "the Cameron clique will resort to every trick to diminish the force of the State nomination," and these rebellious delegates, "while instructed to support me, will stab me under the fifth rib whenever an opportunity may offer."[23]

In many other states Buchanan had not exactly an organization but a coterie of friends who actively campaigned for him. Anyone who reads Polk's diary will gather from it the impression that his Cabinet had no very high regard for Buchanan; yet most of its members joined the effort to nominate him in 1852: Clifford of Maine, Toucey of Connecticut, Bancroft of Massachusetts, Mason of Virginia, and Johnson of Tennessee. Walker stood off, but Marcy would have come along except for the fact that the New York Barnburners fired his own ambition for the nomination as a means of bringing themselves back into the party. Slidell thought Buchanan ought to come to Saratoga in the summer for missionary work among the New Yorkers, but this he declined to do.[24]

The state conventions in Pennsylvania, Mississippi, Tennessee and Alabama favored Buchanan, but there the good news stopped. California and Maryland rejected him and New Jersey, because of a local fight, went for Cass. In Louisiana Slidell, in order to defeat the Soulé forces who were pledged to Douglas, had to join the Cass men.[25]

Virginia held the key. Here Buchanan's friend, John A. Parker, persuaded Henry A. Wise, the energetic, hot-headed leader of the dominant Democratic faction in the Old Dominion, to back Buchanan. Wise saw in him a means to combat his rival, R. M. T. Hunter, who ran with the fire-eaters and supported Douglas. If Virginia did not support Buchanan at Baltimore, Wise said he would "break up the Democratic organization in the State."[26] John Y. Mason, Thomas Ritchie and other Virginia worthies worked with Wise, but Buchanan felt that so much depended upon success here that he visited Richmond for a few days in the spring of 1852.

When he learned that Cameron had sent several deputies to Richmond, he dispatched Lynch and David R. Porter to the scene. They arrived and helped Wise run the meeting, which proved something of a job as most of the county delegates had never attended such a gathering before and had no idea what to do. Wise almost destroyed his own plans by demanding a pledged Virginia delegation, contrary to all prior party procedure, but he soon backed down and delivered to Buchanan an unpledged delegation friendly to him. Lynch had to write to Buchanan for money to get out of Richmond, and with the $40 he received proceeded to Washington. From there he wrote: "Your friends have no organization in this place. The friends of all the other candidates have."[27]

This news stimulated Buchanan to more letter writing. He sought in this last month before the nomination, to convince the friends of Douglas that their hero could not possibly win in 1852, but that he could be chosen in 1856 if he supported Buchanan now. Buchanan warned that Cass could never win Pennsylvania, and if nominated he would be sure to lose the election.

Delegates poured into Washington during the last two weeks of May to sniff the political atmosphere before going to Baltimore where the nominating convention would open on June 1. There the motley crowd overflowed all the hotels. People slept where they could, if not in beds then on bare boards. It had recently dawned on some states that by sending large delegations they might carry added influence through sheer mass. Pennsylvania had doubled its delegation, and Virginia sent 69 delegates to cast 15 votes. On opening day nearly 700 delegates scrambled for the 296 chairs.

By the next morning the local arrangements committee had provided adequate seating facilities, and the convention finally got underway with its organization. Buchanan's supporters fought a motion to ballot immediately for the nominees, demanding that the platform should be submitted for adoption first, for they wished to make every candidate toe the line on details of the Compromise of 1850. But the convention, 155 to 123, decided to name the candidate first, and then to endow him with principles. Cass led on the early ballots, and Buchanan ran second with between 90 and 100 votes. Douglas and Marcy had 20 or 30 each, and half a dozen favorite sons polled scattering votes. By Friday, Cass had declined and Douglas had strengthened his position, but no decision seemed near. Then John W. Davis, chairman, after a heated debate, ruled that each delegation might retain or reject the unit rule, as it saw fit.

After this ruling, Buchanan jumped to the top with 104 votes; Cass dropped down to 33; Douglas came up to 80, and Marcy held on to his

New York votes. Here the procession stopped. Buchanan's friends begged, bargained, and bullied to get Marcy to lend a hand and push the Buchanan band wagon, but the New Yorkers refused, feeling sure that Buchanan could not go further without them. After this, Buchanan's poll declined, and his bid collapsed. Hearing the news in Lancaster, he immediately wrote to Porter, the head of his delegation: "From the result of the ballotings yesterday, I deem it highly improbable that I shall receive the nomination." He thanked his friends, declined positively to be considered as vice-president, and announced his determination to go into final retirement without regret.[28]

Meanwhile Douglas went through the cycle, neared 100 votes, and then came down. Cass, down to 27, made a comeback to 131 votes, but could get no more. Marcy then began to climb, running his score of votes to 98 on the forty-sixth ballot. New York now came in sackcloth and ashes to beg Pennsylvania and Virginia for Buchanan's votes, but received stony glares and curses, punctuated by tobacco juice. The Buchaneers had already decided the next move: to bring in by easy stages the name of Franklin Pierce of New Hampshire. On the forty-ninth ballot, the under-cover work of the Pierce men, supported by Buchanan delegations, came into play. After a number of small states had voted for Pierce, the delegations from New York, Indiana, and Pennsylvania retired to caucus. At the critical moment, Pennsylvania returned to cast for Pierce the ballots that pinned down his nomination. By the time the roll call was complete, Pierce had amassed 282 of the 296 convention votes.[29]

Buchanan and his friends collected their reward in the nomination of William R. King of Alabama as vice-president. It constituted more a personal tribute than a political triumph, for King had an incurable disease which made it nearly certain that he would not survive another administration.

Dejected, Davy Lynch wrote that "if New York had not acted the 'Dog in the Manger' you would have been the nominee."[30] At Wheatland, the Sage sat at his desk reading scores of letters of condolence, and drafting appropriate replies. Of these, his remarks to Robert Tyler contained the gist of all: "I have received your favor of yesterday, condoling me on my defeat. You ought rather to congratulate me on the ability, devotion & energy of my friends. They have fought a good fight & have deserved success. It was not their fault if they could not command it. For the first time, I have had a fair trial & have been fairly defeated . . . . I give you now your final discharge after long, able & faithful service, but live in the hope that I may yet be able to manifest my gratitude to you by something more decisive than words."[31]

17

A MISSION FOREDOOMED • 1852-1854

ADVICE AND DISSENT

Buchanan took little part in the contest between Franklin Pierce and Winfield Scott until the autumn of 1852 when the activities of the Free-Soilers threatened to upset the interparty truce on slavery and split the Pennsylvania Democrats. The publication of Harriet Beecher Stowe's vivid and inflammatory novel, *Uncle Tom's Cabin*, during the campaign, the Christiana Riot, and the Free-Soil convention at Pittsburgh, which nominated John P. Hale for president on a platform that "Slavery is a sin against God and a crime against man," fanned the slavery question in the Keystone State to white heat.

Some of Buchanan's friends advised him to remain aloof. "Avoid the crowd," they urged, "and in the dark hour . . . you will be brought in 'to calm the troubled waters & allay the storm'. . . . Much evil will grow out of the Pittsburgh Convention, and four years hence, you will be wanted."[1]

But Buchanan felt otherwise. In September he presided at a Democratic rally at Reading, Pennsylvania, sharing the platform with Senator Stephen A. Douglas, Governor Bigler, and visiting worthies from Massachusetts, Maryland, and Tennessee.[2] In October he addressed a mass meeting at Greensburg where, in a ninety-minute speech, he assailed Scott and warned against "elevating to the highest civil trust the commander of your victorious armies." General Scott and the northern Whigs had been hedging on their pledge to respect the finality of the 1850 Compromise, and some of them insisted on repeal of the Fugitive Slave Law, regardless of the consequences. Buchanan hit the keynote of the Democratic campaign when he said, "I view the finality of the Compromise as necessary to the peace and preservation of the Union. . . . The great political question . . . is, . . . will the election of Scott, or the election of Pierce, contribute most to maintain the finality of the Compromise?"[3]

Franklin Pierce won the presidency, carrying all but four states.

221

Pierce had great personal charm but little administrative experience. Affable and sincere, he tried earnestly to please and made promises in the enthusiasm of the moment which later he either forgot in the press of events or found impossible to fulfill. The forty-eight-year-old president represented the "Young America" wing of the Democrats and hoped to free his party from the control of the "Old Fogies."

Before the inauguration, Pierce asked Buchanan for counsel on the launching of the new Administration. His letter had the ring of the dedicated young man seeking advice from the elder statesman, but it contained one peculiar sentence. "I think," Pierce wrote, "I am expected to call around me Gentlemen who have not hitherto occupied Cabinet positions." This plan not only excluded Buchanan but rejected his entire leadership, for it ostracized the whole Polk Cabinet. Buchanan advised Pierce not to take the "Young America" idea so seriously as to abandon all the experienced men of the party. This action "could not be very gratifying to any of them," and would appear to be an intentional rebuke to the Polk Administration. Buchanan counselled delay in choosing the Cabinet and disagreed with Pierce's proposal to incorporate all political viewpoints in it. *"The Cabinet,"* he said, *"ought to be a unit. . . .* General Jackson, penetrating as he was, did not discover this truth, until compelled to dissolve his first Cabinet on account of its heterogeneous & discordant materials." He recommended either Judge James Campbell or David R. Porter as the Pennsylvanians who most deserved a Cabinet post.[4]

It suddenly occurred to the Sage of Wheatland that he was getting old. He enjoyed joking about himself as a "Middle-Aged Fogy," but he now wrote to Forney: "I am surely becoming an old fogy and have got far behind the rapid march of the age."[5] His teeth bothered him, and he had suffered the worst bilious attack of his life just before the election. Staying at hotels aggravated him, and travel wore him out. "I am rapidly becoming a petrifaction," he told saucy Eliza Watterson. "In truth I daily become more and more fond of my retirement, and always feel reluctant to leave home, though this I am often compelled to do."[6] He was already more than threescore, and had lived longer than his father. It seemed a long while since anyone had called him "Jimmy"; now he was "Old Buck."

The winter dragged on and there was no word from Pierce about Cabinet appointments or policies. Not until after the inaugural address, in which the only Buchanan influence seemed to be a statement that the Administration would "not be controlled by any timid forebodings of evil from expansion," did the country at last learn who would form the Cabinet: William L. Marcy of New York would take the State Department; James Guthrie of Kentucky, the Treasury; Jefferson Davis of Mississippi, War; James C. Dobbin of North Carolina, Navy; Caleb Cushing of Massachusetts, the Attorney-Generalship; Robert McClelland of Michigan, Interior; and James Campbell of Pennsylvania, the Post Office. These men represented friends of all the prominent contenders of 1852 except Douglas.

Buchanan was deluged with Pennsylvania requests for letters of recommendation to the president. His "Application Book" for the spring of 1853 contains pages of names of applicants and the jobs they sought. But instead of appointments, Buchanan got disappointments. To Robert Tyler he wrote: "I urged the appointment of Governor Porter with all my might as collector; but my strong recommendations were disregarded by the President *as they have been in every instance. . . .* I not only recommended Porter, but opposed Brown. How, then, can I ask Brown for appointments for my friends? . . . I expect daily to hear of the sacrifice of Van Dyke & the appointment of Dallas. I now know exactly my position. . . . I shall bear all philosophically, but take an outside seat & observe the Grand Drama."[7]

THE MAN WHO WAS ORDERED TO FAIL

On the same day that he posted this letter, Buchanan received a note from Pierce asking him to accept the Mission to England. Obviously he could not, in view of the prior rejection of so many of his Pennsylvania friends, nor did he relish Marcy as his boss; but he could, perhaps, make some capital out of the offer. He sent a noncommittal reply. At dinner with Pierce and Slidell on April 8, Buchanan raised questions which had been disturbing him. Would not the important negotiations be conducted at Washington, as was customary? "No," Pierce replied. "It is my intention that you shall settle them all in London."

"What will Governor Marcy say to your determination?" asked Buchanan.

"I will control this matter myself," replied the president.

Buchanan thought that this arrangement would create trouble, but Pierce disagreed. The Cabinet had understood that negotiations would center in London when they unanimously endorsed Buchanan.

Buchanan then complained that "in all your appointments for Pennsylvania, you have not yet selected a single individual for any office for which I recommended him ... and if I were now to accept the mission to London, they might with justice say that I had appropriated the lion's share to myself. . . . I could not and would not place myself in this position." Pierce emphatically assured him that Pennsylvania would receive "not one appointment more or less" on account of the British mission, which would be considered "as an appointment for the whole country."

With a clear understanding of all these matters, Buchanan felt inclined to accept the post, but on Sunday, when he learned that the Senate planned to adjourn the next day, he assumed that his name would not be proposed, probably because Marcy did not want to relinquish the negotiations. That noon Jefferson Davis told him that Pierce would make the appointment after adjournment, and the Senate would confirm it at the fall session. Buchanan immediately announced that he had no intention of departing on a mission without prior Senate confirmation. By evening couriers had spread word that Senators should not leave town but be on hand in the morning to transact business. Pierce sent in Buchanan's name, and the Senate confirmed the appointment on Monday morning. After another call on the president to make sure all arrangements were clear, Buchanan felt that he stood on solid ground. Pierce even approved on the spot his request to have his friend, John Appleton of Maine, for Secretary of Legation.[8]

After a few weeks had passed, Buchanan knew he had let himself in for a bad bargain. Pennsylvania got no appointments. His three strongest recommendations were all turned down on the ground that the London Mission filled the state quota for jobs. On May 17 he went to Washington. The president could not explain what had happened, but he did reaffirm the guarantee that Buchanan's job should not be counted as any part of the quota of Pennsylvania patronage. But Buchanan observed, "I had not been in Washington many days before I clearly discovered that the President and cabinet were intent upon his renomination and re-election. . . . It was easy to perceive that the object in appointments was to raise up a Pierce party, wholly distinct from the former Buchanan, Cass, and Douglas parties; . . . and I readily perceived . . . why my recommendations had proved of so little avail."[9]

For several weeks, Buchanan worked daily in the State Department, conferring frequently with Marcy and occasionally with the president, and soon he began to suspect that neither intended to transfer negotiations to London. In fact, it became apparent to Buchanan that Marcy intended to keep for himself in Washington those negotiations which promised a successful conclusion, and to transfer to London questions which seemed hopeless of settlement.

During June, Buchanan worked harder at diplomacy than ever in his life. Personally he wanted no part of a mission prearranged to fail, but neither did he want to sacrifice the chance for a full-scale settlement of the controversies with Great Britain merely to give Marcy the credit for concluding a few minor treaties. He went over the whole area of Anglo-American relations time after time with both Pierce and Marcy, protesting against handling some questions in Washington and others in London, and said he would stay home unless Pierce kept his promise to transfer negotiations to London.

Three diplomatic questions pressed for attention. First, Great

224

Britain, in defiance, Buchanan believed, of the Monroe Doctrine and of the Clayton-Bulwer Treaty, had seized the Bay Islands off the coast of Honduras and established a protectorate of the Mosquito Coast in the vicinity of Greytown. These two points, insignificant as they looked on a map, commanded the entrance to any isthmian canal which might be built across Nicaragua. Second, fighting threatened in Nova Scotia and Newfoundland over the rights of Americans and Englishmen to catch fish in coastal waters and dry them on uninhabited shores. Third, the British government wished to negotiate a reciprocal trade treaty between Canada and the United States.

Marcy and Pierce wanted to use a treaty of reciprocity as the *quid pro quo* to achieve privileges for American fishermen and planned to conduct these negotiations at Washington. Buchanan could handle the Central American business in London. But he argued that Britain's foray into Central America constituted a breach of treaty and an insult to the national honor, and that prior abandonment of these colonies "ought to be a *sine qua non* in any negotiation on any subject with the British government." Said he:

> With what face could we ever hereafter present this question of violated faith and outraged national honor to the world against the British government if whilst, *flagrante delicto*, the wrong unexplained and unredressed, we should incorporate the British North American provinces, by treaty, into the American Union, so far as reciprocal trade is concerned? How could we, then, under any circumstances make this a *casus belli*? If a man has wronged and insulted me, and I take him into my family and bestow upon him the privileges of one of its members, without previous redress or explanation, it is then too late to turn around and make the original offense a serious cause for personal hostilities.[10]

Beyond this, he denied that fishing rights constituted an equivalent for a free-trade agreement with Canada. Let reciprocal trade be used as the lever to force England out of Central America, with war as the alternative if she should refuse to withdraw. As to fishing grounds, the United States had as much right to the ocean as England.

Buchanan postponed his departure, released Appleton from his appointment as Secretary of Legation, and flooded the State Department and the White House with arguments, facts, international law, and threats to resign. Pierce neglected to answer some of the letters, but he continued to hold out the prospect that Buchanan might possibly be given the chance to run the show in London.

Buchanan had not yet picked up his commission from the State Department. When Pierce ignored two of his letters in June asking for

225

definite instructions, Buchanan wrote a third requesting that he be permitted, "in case your enlightened judgment has arrived at the conclusion that Washington & not London ought to be the seat of the negotiations, most respectfully to decline the mission." Pierce answered, still keeping the door open. Finally, on July 7, Buchanan for the first time saw the instructions which had been drawn up for him. As he expected, he got only the Central American negotiation. Marcy would keep the leverage at Washington for his own purposes.

Buchanan wrote back to Pierce that he wanted to confer with him during a forthcoming presidential visit to Philadelphia, and that in the meantime, he should look out "for some better man to take my place." But he had lost the game and knew it. Marcy knew it, too. "Old bachelors as well as young maidens do not always know their minds," he told Edward Everett. "If he ever meant to go he can assign no sufficient cause for changing his purpose."[11] Pierce said to Forney, who thought Buchanan ought to decline: "Why should he not go? The greater the obstacles thrown in his way, the greater will be his triumph when he succeeds."[12] But to resign now would make Buchanan look like a querulous old man, quitting in a pet because he could not have everything his own way. Pierce had trapped him and there was no way out. He had given him a mission foredoomed to failure, robbed him of his patronage, and put a gag in his mouth. Had anyone ever been so taken to the market![13]

The now vacant Secretaryship of Legation brought a request from Henry A. Wise who had first urged Buchanan's appointment and had his heart set on the selection of his son. Pierce had a different suggestion, and Henry W. Welsh also wanted the job. Forney learned to his amazement that Daniel E. Sickles of New York would like to go to London. Sickles was a wealthy and influential Democrat, a "hard" Hunker, a good friend of the president, and had married a beautiful young wife. Buchanan interviewed him at Wheatland and within a week had him appointed. If he counted upon the pleasure of a cozy time with Mrs. Sickles in London he was destined to disappointment, however, for the new secretary left her at home and travelled abroad with his mistress, Fanny White.[14]

Buchanan turned his business affairs over to his nephew, Elliott Eskridge Lane of Bellefonte, Pennsylvania, and James L. Reynolds of Lancaster, giving them power of attorney to handle some $150,000 in bonds, mortgages and stocks. Another $50,000 he assigned to his brother Edward, his nephew James B. Henry, and agents in New York and Washington. He kept smaller sums of ready cash on deposit with Riggs and Corcoran of Washington and the Chemical Bank of New York, and transferred some funds to Rothschild's in London. Having completed these arrangements, he informed his agents: "I believe I do not owe a debt in the world. . . . My pew rent in the Presbyterian Church is to be paid, this date." He had arranged to have tax payments made for James B. Henry and Harriet. She was to stay, first with friends in Virginia and later with the Plitts in Philadelphia, until he could bring her to London the following summer. Lane and Reynolds should give Miss Hetty any cash she requested for the care of Wheatland, should pay 7 per cent interest for any money put in their keeping by his brother or nephews, and collect at least 5 per cent on money put out on loan.[15]

Declining a farewell dinner in Lancaster, he left quietly on August 3, disappointed his Philadelphia friends by failing to stop to say goodbye to them, and proceeded straight to New York where he embarked on the steamer *Atlantic*. After a stormy passage of ten days, he arrived at Liverpool where the Legation Attaché met him and took him to the Clarendon House in London.

For the first week he could scarcely believe he was in England. Slidell was there, and John Ward of Boston, and Robb of New Orleans. With Ambassador Ingersoll and the New England philanthropist, George Peabody, Buchanan called on the Marchioness of Wellesley, the former Miss Caton of Baltimore, now residing at Hampton Court. She had two sisters, one of them now Lady Stafford and the other the Duchess of Leeds. Buchanan had known them all in earlier days when they were Baltimorean belles and through them gained an immediate entrée into the circle of British nobility. On August 23 he went to the Isle of Wight with Ingersoll where the Earl of Clarendon, British Secretary of Foreign Affairs, presented him to Queen Victoria.

THE COURT OF ST. JAMES

Buchanan arrived in England just a week after Parliament had adjourned, and the nobility had already scattered to country estates or to the Continent, leaving London dull and deserted until the "season" should begin again in February with the opening of Court. Thus he had several months of very welcome freedom which he used to find quarters for the Legation and to familiarize himself with his new situation. For the time being he continued to live at the Clarendon House, but by November 1 he had rented an establishment at 56 Harley Street which became the United States Legation during his ministry. On November 11, all hands turned out in noise and confusion to move the Legation files and equipment into the new quarters.[16]

John William Cates was dean of the Legation servants by virtue of eighteen years' service at the American Embassy. His son, William John Cates, served as butler. Buchanan had a housekeeper who had worked for several previous ministers. He reported diplomatically to Miss Hetty at Wheatland that he was "satisfied with her, without being greatly pleased." In addition to these old hands, Buchanan had brought along Frederick

William Jackson, a mulatto manservant he had hired in New York a day before he sailed. While at first dubious of the wisdom of this impetuosity, he soon discovered that Jackson was very much of a "find," for he turned out to be a first-class valet and made something of a hit in London. "I have been diverted," Buchanan wrote, "to witness the attention he receives here where the same prejudices do not exist against color as in the United States. And yet he is homesick & thinks as I do, that there is no place in in the world to be compared with our Country."[17]

A problem of Court etiquette arose as soon as Buchanan had been accredited because a Court Dress Circular issued by Secretary Marcy in June ran counter to the ceremonial procedure of most European courts. Marcy asked American diplomats to perform their duties "in the simple dress of an American citizen," and to avoid the gold lace, ribbons, jewels, patent-leather boots and aristocratic gewgaws that custom prescribed for diplomats at ceremonies where a sovereign presided. Buchanan had often ridiculed the peacock parade and urged the adoption of such a rule, but at the Court of St. James it gave him serious trouble.

Sir Edward Cust, Master of Ceremonies of the Court, pointed out that to appear before her Majesty in street clothes would signify a lack of respect and that the outfit Marcy prescribed would put the minister in precisely the costume worn by the Court servants, subjecting him unintentionally to indignities from everyone. The American rule, Cust said, would raise a storm of indignation among the British people who would view it as presumption. He had no alternative but to require the customary dress and if Buchanan could not wear it, to deny him admittance to the opening of Parliament and to Court balls and dinners.

Buchanan appreciated the force of these arguments and the penalty he would pay for refusing to follow the local code. He would receive no invitations from Court, and thus would receive none from the courtiers. As he said, he would be "socially placed in Coventry here," a condition which would not bother him personally but which might ruin the mission, for it would cut him off from all normal sources of information. He considered a variety of costumes that might solve the problem. Someone suggested the military uniform of George Washington, which he promptly cast out as a recipe for subjecting him to everlasting ridicule. He thought about a plain blue coat with gold buttons embossed with the American eagle, but he soon abandoned that idea. Having found no answer when Parliament convened, he did not attend the opening session and thereby raised a public storm in the press of both nations. The Americans lauded his independence, and the British condemned this act of "Republican ill manners" and "American Puppyism." The London *Times* erroneously reported that Buchanan sat in evening dress amid the blaze of stars, ribands and crosses in the diplomatic box, "unpleasantly conscious of his singularity." Only with difficulty did Buchanan dissuade Parliament from making the incident the subject of a formal inquiry.

Political pressures raised by the outbreak of the Crimean war at length brought a calm to this tempest in the wardrobe. The Ministry had no intention at this time of promoting a breach with the United States over such trifling absurdity. Buchanan agreed, at British suggestion, to equip himself with a plain black-handled sword, everywhere the mark of a gentleman, a visible token of respect to the queen, and a ready means of identification among the servants.

Dan Sickles, who disliked Marcy's circular because it curtailed his chance to strut, donned the gaudy uniform of the New York State Guards, daring Marcy to call it an un-American costume. Buchanan reported of his first appearance under the new dispensation: "Having yielded, they did not do things by halves. As I approached the Queen, an arch but benevolent smile lit up her countenance—as much as to say, you are the first man who ever appeared before me at Court in such a dress. I must confess that I never felt more proud of being an American."[18]

For two months after his arrival, Buchanan heard nothing from the British Foreign Office. He spent his time familiarizing himself with Legation procedure, mastering the details of the subjects of negotiation, and writing letters home. To politicians he uniformly emphasized his decision not to be a candidate for president in 1856. He exchanged letters weekly with Harriet, who was beside herself to know how soon she could come to London to see a duke and meet a queen. She said the trip would be "the future realization of a beautiful dream." Buchanan responded, "Like all other dreams you will be disappointed in the reality." He wrote to Miss Hetty that she gave him "more interesting news than any other friend" and asked her for a full report on Wheatland and the neighbors. How was Lara, his Newfoundland dog, and what of the new calf, and who would fill the icehouse? He sounded a little homesick.

Forney sent him a tirade against President Pierce and ended it with the prophecy that Buchanan would next occupy the White House. He replied,

> In answer to the last suggestion contained in your letter, I now say to you in writing what I have repeatedly said in conversation, that I have neither the desire nor the intention 'to play a very prominent part in politics for the next seven years.' On the contrary, this mission is alone tolerable because it will enable me gracefully and gradually to retire from a strife which is neither suited to my age nor my inclinations. . . . I should have been highly gratified had I been nominated & elected President in

1852; but the office has no longer any charm for me. I write thus explicitly to you; because the warmth of your friendship might otherwise induce you to take part in again bringing me forward as a candidate.[19]

At last Buchanan received the awaited summons to the Foreign Office and Clarendon's apologies for the long delay. In the opening interview, the two ran over the problems that might involve their countries: the Russo-Turkish crisis, the Central American issue, the pending fishery and reciprocity treaties, and the movement developing in Cuba to liberate the slaves and set up a Negro government. They agreed that the Central American question was first in importance, but Clarendon confessed that he was not familiar enough with the subject for serious discussion. A few days later Buchanan prepared a summary of the American position and submitted it to Clarendon.

THE CARIBBEAN CRISIS

By 1850 the British occupied much of the coastal area of Honduras and Nicaragua. From the time of the Polk Administration, the United States had protested English intervention in that part of the New World. After the acquisition of Oregon and California, there was a greater need than ever for some kind of passage across the Central American isthmus, and in 1849 the United States negotiated a treaty with Nicaragua for the exclusive right to build a canal. But the English now held the points of entry on the Gulf: Greytown, at the head of the San Juan River in Nicaragua, and Ruatan Island off the Honduran coast. The conflicting interests of the United States and Great Britain became a threat to peace, and in 1850 the Clayton-Bulwer Treaty was drawn up for the purpose of removing the danger of an outbreak of hostilities.

By the terms of the agreement neither nation would ever assume exclusive control of any future canal or fortify any portion of Central America. Buchanan condemned this pact from the start. "The Treaty," he said, "altogether reverses the Monroe Doctrine, and establishes it against ourselves rather than European Governments."[20] Some day, he feared, there would be "a bloody war with England should she remain as powerful as she is at present."

Despite the cordiality and freedom that marked the early conversations with Lord Clarendon, Buchanan soon learned that back of the Foreign Secretary's smile lay the hard rock of British policy. Ruatan, largest of the Bay Islands and the British protectorate of the Mosquito Indians represented elements of this policy. Ruatan Island, Buchanan declared, "is one of those commanding positions in the world which Great

Britain has been ever ready to seize and appropriate. It enables her to control our commerce in the Caribbean Sea and on its transit to California and Oregon." As a point of commercial power Great Britain intended to keep it, treaty or no treaty.[21]

The British protectorate of the Mosquito King involved the point of international prestige. Buchanan chided Clarendon for making so big an issue of so petty a territory, when friendship with the United States stood at stake over it, but the Foreign Secretary expounded the duty of a nation with native protectorates all over the world to make good its promises, even more scrupulously to the small than to the large princes. As a point of honor, England would sustain the Indian King.[22]

Without any *quid pro quo* to induce the abandonment of these positions, Buchanan had to establish that the British posture in Central America constituted a breach of treaty with the United States. Success in this effort would have to bring British capitulation, or an American retreat, or war. He was therefore astonished when Clarendon introduced casually into the conversation one day, as if it were a matter of common assumption, that the Clayton-Bulwer Treaty was entirely "prospective in its operation."[23] Buchanan, while recovering from the shock, introduced the newly arrived fisheries and reciprocity treaty as a manifestation of American friendship and generosity to compensate for British adjustment of the Central American dispute. Clarendon rejoined that the treaty drove too hard a bargain with the Canadians and doubtless would be rejected by England.

With negotiations at an impasse during the spring of 1854, Buchanan turned his efforts to building a recognition in England of the tremendous potential of good relations with America. He propounded the theme of Anglo-American friendship based on kindred speech, culture, and principles of government. These two nations, he thought, should jointly face the continual threat of world despotism. "There have never been two nations on the face of the earth," he said, "whose material interests are so closely identified."[24] Britain annually exported to the United States as much as to all of Europe.

By the end of March, the Crimean War became a reality and England and France, in an *entente cordiale*, faced the Russian power in the eastern Mediterranean. Not until mid-April could Buchanan get Clarendon back on the Central American problem, so busy had he been with duties connected with the war. At this meeting, the Foreign Secretary, with marked embarrassment, finally explained to Buchanan the official British position. Britain considered the Clayton-Bulwer Treaty "prospective," that is, it guaranteed all British rights as they existed at the time of ratification and applied its restrictions only to subsequent acts. Buchanan pointed out that according to this contention the treaty confirmed Great Britain's right to remain in Central America and excluded the United States from it.

231

He acidly asked his Lordship if he really expected anyone to take seriously this ridiculous interpretation. He had the impression that Clarendon very reluctantly asserted this view. Buchanan then pointed out that England had occupied the Bay Islands after the conclusion of the treaty, and even accepting the "prospective" interpretation—which he never would—the British would have to get out of Ruatan. Clarendon promised to check the date of the occupation of the islands, and the interview ended awkwardly.

For the next two months, Buchanan applied himself to the preparation of a long reply rebutting the British contention. In such an effort he showed at his best, and his argument won the warm commendation of Pierce, Marcy, and the Cabinet in Washington, but it brought no reply from Clarendon.

Whatever hope remained of softening the British stand collapsed under the impact of the Greytown affair. Punta Arenas, across the river from Greytown, was occupied by Americans working for the Accessory Transit Company, an enterprise of Cornelius Vanderbilt to build a road across the isthmus. The captain of a Vanderbilt ship shot a Greytown native who sought to board his vessel. When some of the residents tried to arrest the captain for murder, Solon E. Borland, the United States Minister, joined a party to prevent his capture, a fight ensued, and someone slashed Borland's face with a broken beer bottle. President Pierce sent Captain G. N. Hollins, of the U. S. S. *Cyane* to Greytown to exact apologies and reparations for the insult to Borland; Hollins, upon rejection of his demands, bombarded Greytown until not a mud wall or thatched roof remained intact. The inhabitants, warned in advance, had all retired to a safe distance, and no one was hurt.

News of this affair arrived in London just a few days after Buchanan had submitted his paper on Central America. With no information except what he got from British sources, Buchanan expressed the hope that Pierce would disavow the act, and Clarendon observed that unless he did, the outlook would be bleak for a settlement of the Central American problem. Much to their displeasure, Pierce defended the action of Captain Hollins as necessary and justifiable. Buchanan tried to sustain his government, according to the policies outlined by Marcy, but made as poor a show of this as Clarendon did in support of the "prospective" interpretation of the treaty.

Buchanan had long felt that Clarendon sincerely wished to compromise the issues in Central America but that the Ministry would not permit it. After Greytown, he changed his mind and suspected that Clarendon himself prevented a settlement. In one conversation, he told Clarendon that Britain could end the whole Central American dispute in a note of twelve lines, if the Foreign Office really wanted it settled. "If I did that," said Clarendon, "our American cousins would say, we have discovered the mode of dealing with the British—we went down to Greytown and *smashed* it, whereupon they became alarmed and gave us all we wanted." Buchanan replied that he would now have to talk directly with Lord Aberdeen, the Prime Minister, who might perhaps be willing to treat America with fairness. Clarendon angrily seized Buchanan by the coat lapels and, shaking him, declared: "I am as good a friend of the United States as Lord Aberdeen; or any man in the Three Kingdoms." Possibly so, Buchanan replied, but the friendship had certainly produced no results.[25]

Lord Aberdeen was polite but adamant; Britain would remain in Central America. With this interview, except for several more excited sessions with Clarendon over Greytown, Buchanan's Central American negotiation came to an end. Clarendon never officially replied to Buchanan's statement of the American position. All that remained was to await Pierce's decision whether to let the matter rest, or to issue an ultimatum.

233

18

PLAYING THE OLD TROUPER • 1854-1856

CUBA—PEARL OF THE ANTILLES

While the Central American negotiation stagnated, Buchanan kept up a steady campaign to promote the purchase of Cuba. The more he examined August Belmont's idea of persuading the Spanish bondholders to press for the sale of the island, the more he liked it. He had described the outlines of the proposal to Pierce before leaving Washington and had recommended that Belmont be made Minister to the Kingdom of the Two Sicilies. At Naples he would come into contact both with many of the bondholders and with members of the Spanish royal family who ruled there. Buchanan felt that Pierce had made a mistake by sending Belmont to the Hague, but he still believed that with judicious management Spain might be induced to sell Cuba to the United States. The main problem would be to prevent interference from the governments of England and France. Buchanan told Pierce in the spring of 1854 that he had shaped his course ever since his arrival in England "with a view of reconciling Great Britain to that great object."[1] Clarendon had already confided to him that "if Spain lost Cuba it would be their own fault for the wretched manner in which they governed the island."[2]

In May, Buchanan wrote to Slidell that the British were prepared for the acquisition of Cuba by the United States and that the British newspapers had on several occasions foreshadowed the event. His only fear was France. He urged Pierce to define a policy on Cuba and to prepare instructions for its acquisition. England and France had their hands full with the Crimean war. The Republican revolution which broke out in Spain in July further threatened the chaotic finances of that country and presaged the abolition of slavery in Cuba. Buchanan now prodded Marcy to decide what steps ought to be taken "to give a direction to the impending revolution in Cuba," an outbreak which certainly would follow the insurrection in Spain.

234

In Europe, the fate of Cuba became a pawn in the great revolutionary movements then in progress under the leadership of Kossuth, Mazzini, Louis Blanc and Ledru Rollin who, though differing with each other on most things, agreed that it would mightily advance their crusade if they could enlist the support of the United States in their assault on monarchy and aristocracy in the Old World. They held out the inducement that if the United States would assist Spanish Republicans in overthrowing the queen, the new democracy would then agree to Cuban independence and subsequent annexation.

Many "Young Americans" worked actively with the European revolutionaries. George Sanders, United States consul in London, maintained a rendezvous for political exiles from the Continent and used the diplomatic pouch for sending inflammatory letters, stamped with the Legation seal, throughout Europe. Some of these fell into the hands of the French authorities and caused a commotion. Victor Fronde, an important figure in the plan to subvert the Spanish monarchy, used a United States courier's passport, which he had obtained by fraud, to aid in his travels as an agent of the revolutionaries. Legitimate governments in Europe soon learned of his activities and protested. Pierre Soulé, American Minister to Spain, loudly proclaimed his sympathies with the antimonarchists. He made himself thoroughly obnoxious to the Spanish queen by his arrogant and insolent manner in dealing with her ministers. Worst of all, he seriously damaged American-French relations by shooting the French Minister to Madrid in a quarrel over the latter's wife.

The Spanish government was facing bankruptcy. Its bonds, now nearly worthless, were held by the Barings, the Rothschilds, and other international bankers who were reported ready to sanction the sale of Cuba for something over $100,000,000 if the money could be kept out of the hands of the royal family and used in the development of Spanish resources. The bankers were prepared to act as receivers, so to speak, of the nation and work to put the economy on a sound basis. The Church also had an interest in such a program, for the monarchy had threatened to confiscate ecclesiastical properties as one means of solving its financial problems. Leading churchmen seemed willing to join the financiers in the effort to convince the queen that the sale of Cuba was the only way to save her regime.

Pierce and Marcy had to fit Buchanan's plans for Cuba into the general Administration program which, in the spring of 1854, had become dependent upon the fate of the Kansas-Nebraska Bill. Douglas had introduced this in January, Pierce adopted it as an Administration measure, and Congress did almost nothing but debate it until the end of May. Its passage aroused terrible political hatreds and split the Democrats. Men were "afraid to unbosom themselves, lest they reveal the secrets of their hearts to an

235

enemy, in disguise," wrote a Congressman, "while scarcely a man knows to a certainty whether he is or is not a friend of the Administration."[3]

Around Washington no one seemed to know what course the Administration planned to take in regard to Cuba; Pierce and Marcy remained "mum" but not idle. Pierce proposed to send a three-man commission to Spain to try to purchase Cuba, with the warning that if they failed, American filibusters might seize the island. He then ordered strict observance of neutrality laws and put port officials under special instruction to prevent the departure of suspicious vessels, but presumably he would revoke these orders if Spain refused to sell Cuba.

Buchanan approved of the idea of the commission, but not of the threat of filibusters as a lever to the negotiation. Filibustering he opposed under any and all circumstances, and thought that any mention of the subject to Spain except in terms of a promise to prevent it would be fatal to the Cuban purchase. Sickles learned what was afoot, and wrote to Howell Cobb sentiments which he never uttered to Buchanan. "I sincerely hope the rumor that you are to go to Madrid is true. *Now* is the time for us to get Cuba—*Europe expects it & is prepared to endure it.* The present condition of Spanish politics . . . is peculiarly favorable for a *row* or a *negotiation to purchase.*" If Cobb should come, Sickles wanted a week with him to tell him what wires to pull at Madrid, and requested an appointment as his secretary. He planned to return home in autumn. "I have had enough of London," he wrote. "It would suit me better to stay away another year on account of the present condition of N. Y. politics, but I am tired of London and *of this mission.*"[4]

If Sickles was bored with London, Buchanan was tired of Sickles. While he envied and admired the young man's dash and zest for life and personally enjoyed his company, he found him not only useless but harmful to the embassy. He paid little attention to business, and wrote so wretched a hand that he imposed an added burden of copying on the rest of the staff. These faults Buchanan would have tolerated had Sickles lent the weight of his dynamic personality to the policies of the Legation, but he did the contrary. He balked on the program of republican austerity and lived both extravagantly and ostentatiously. When Buchanan was in the midst of his campaign to foster Anglo-American friendship, Sickles raised a furor by remaining seated during the toast to the queen at a public dinner because Victoria rather than Washington came first on the list. Later he wrote anonymous letters to the British newspapers condemning his host, George Peabody, for toadyism to the queen and implicated Buchanan in the same thing. The controversy, touching the tender nerve of national honor in both countries, caused a newspaper storm on both sides of the Atlantic and put Buchanan, a guest of honor at the dinner, in an embarrassing position.

When the Spanish Revolution broke out during July as the Sickles controversy reached its height, Buchanan seized the opportunity to send him to Washington to report the news directly and to urge immediate action on Cuban policy.[5]

Sickles arrived at the White House on August 8. By this time Pierce knew that Congress would ignore his request of August 1 for an emergency appropriation to support a special commission to Spain. With elections coming on and the Democrats weakened by the Kansas-Nebraska struggle, the Senate Foreign Relations Committee decided not to risk another sectional upheaval and declined to report out a Cuban bill. Pierce joyfully welcomed Sickles and moved him into the White House as a personal guest for a week of conferences. The president already had letters from Soulé and Mason, Minister to France, stating that the Spanish Republicans would sell Cuba if the United States contributed funds to help their cause and that the British and French planned no intervention to sustain the Spanish government.

On August 16, after numerous Cabinet discussions, Marcy sent out instructions to Soulé. Instead of the creation of a special commission, Soulé, Buchanan, and Mason, should meet in Paris "to adopt measures for perfect concert of action in aid of your negotiations at Madrid. . . . This whole subject in its widest range is opened to your joint consideration." The explanation of this vague proposal lay in a disagreement between Marcy and Pierce about Soulé. Marcy had tried repeatedly to have him removed for conduct unbecoming a minister and defiance of instructions, but Pierce would not let him go. Forney, now an editor of Pierce's organ, the Washington *Union*, wrote Buchanan at this time: "It is said here that Mason has gone to meet Soulé, and the idea is laughed at in all quarters, for if ever a man has fulfilled the prophecies of his enemies, disappointed the hopes of his friends, that man is Pierre Soulé. . . . He has put back the acquisition of Cuba fifty years, . . . made Spanish Republicanism a jest, and . . . by his folly and conceit he has enabled the enemies of our country to hold him up as a sample of American statesmen & Diplomatists. It is only we who must defend this artificial & hollow effigy of Democracy, that can realize most sensitively the difficulty of making a silk purse out of a sow's ear."[6]

Saddled with Soulé but required to act at Madrid, Marcy believed that Buchanan and Mason might serve as a check on Soulé's wildness and somehow guide a negotiation along rational lines. This might, indeed, have happened except for two other factors. The first was Marcy's instruction of April 3 to Soulé, still in force, which authorized him to offer as much as $130,000,000 for Cuba. If Spain appeared unwilling to sell, this instruction continued, "you will then direct your efforts to the next most desirable object, which is to detach that Island from the Spanish dominion and from all dependence on any European power."[7] It is now clear that Marcy *meant* to say that the independence of Cuba was the object, next to purchase, most desired. But the ambiguity of the dispatch left some question about the explicit meaning of the important words *to detach.*

Second, Pierce in his enthusiasm and with his usual carelessness of phrase, filled Sickles's mind with ideas never communicated to Marcy or any of the ministers. Sickles formed the impression that Pierce wanted him to act as a confidential agent to explain, verbally, to all the ministers that the government wanted some really drastic action on Cuba and was ready to face the consequences. His impression received reinforcement from the wording of the instructions of August 16, inaugurating the meeting of ministers: "You are desired to communicate to the government here the results of opinion or means of action to which you may in common arrive, through a . . . confidential messenger, who may be able to supply any details not contained in a formal despatch." Pierce wrote to Buchanan that Sickles would "have much to communicate verbally with regard to home and other affairs."[8] Sickles thus became in effect spokesman for the president and could turn the meaning of the general instructions in any direction. This freedom nullified the moderating influence of Marcy, Mason, and Buchanan.

Buchanan protested. He wrote to President Pierce on September 1:

> I can not for myself discover what benefit will result from a meeting. . . . It is impossible for me to devise any other plan for the acquisition of Cuba . . . than what I have already presented to you. We are willing to purchase, and our object is to induce them to sell. . . . I am glad, therefore, that our *meeting for mere consultation and not for decisive action* is left to [Soulé's] discretion. . . . P. S. Since the foregoing was written, I have had a long conversation with Col. Sickles, and am sorry to say this has not changed my views concerning the policy of a meeting. . . . No more unsuitable place than Paris could be devised for such a meeting. . . . Every object which you have in view can . . . be accomplished by correspondence.[9]

Sickles had already ruined Buchanan's hopes, having blared his way through continental Europe before ever reporting to London. At Paris he found Dudley Mann, assistant Secretary of State, John L. O'Sullivan of "Manifest Destiny" fame and currently minister to Portugal, Pierce's friend John A. Dix, and John Van Buren. Sickles elaborated his plans to all, and then proceeded to Spain where he found Soulé in the haunts of the revolutionaries in the Pyrenees. European newspapermen sensed something big in the wind and broadcast their conjectures. Buchanan pointed out to Pierce that he could quietly get the names of the Spanish bondholders and unite with them in an effort to persuade Spain to sell Cuba, but "Capital and Capitalists . . . are proverbially timid, and nothing of this kind ought to be attempted until after the *éclat* by the public journals to Col. Sickles' journey to Paris and Madrid shall have passed away. Matters of this kind, in order to be successful in Europe, must be conducted with secrecy and caution."[10]

Buchanan succeeded in vetoing Paris and Basle as the scene of the meeting, agreeing on Ostend, and with this small success resigned himself to obeying distasteful orders. The conference, he wrote his nephew, "will probably make noise enough in the world." After three days at Ostend, the glare of publicity drove the ministers to Aix-la-Chapelle where, on October 18, they completed drafting the Ostend Manifesto.

Buchanan bore the chief responsibility for restraining Soulé during the conference. Mason looked on the whole procedure as senseless and, so far as he was concerned, "a chance to loaf." At the very start, Buchanan turned down the request of Sickles to act as secretary of the meeting and after the first few days at Ostend, pointedly gave him to understand that he need not come to Aix-la-Chapelle. Soulé, who had the instructions from Marcy, shaped the ideas that he thought should be included, and jotted them down in notes. Buchanan then wrote out a rough and later a finished draft of the document. Its first sentence placed responsibility directly on Pierce. "The undersigned," it began, "in compliance with the wish expressed by the President in the several confidential despatches . . . addressed to us" &c. &c. This meant that Marcy's "to detach" letter lay on the table, for the only other official instruction on Cuba was the one calling the conference. The argument contained nothing new. The United States should promptly approach the Supreme Constituent Cortes of Spain with a proposition to buy Cuba, openly, frankly, through regular diplomatic procedures, and in such a way "as to challenge the approbation of the world." This would benefit Cuba, provide Spain a golden opportunity to return to solvency and prosperity, and prevent the recurrence of troubles between the United States and Cuba such as had marred the past. If the Cubans should rebel, continued the Manifesto, "no human power could . . . prevent the people and Government of the United States from taking part . . . in support of their neighbors and friends."

So far, the report constituted an accurate statement of Buchanan's purchase plan and of Pierce's concept of the role of filibusters. The final section added the views of Sickles and Soulé, modified, or at least phrased, by Buchanan in such a manner as to pull their teeth. "After we shall have offered Spain a price for Cuba, far beyond its present value, and this shall have been refused, it will then be time to consider the question, does Cuba

239

in the possession of Spain seriously endanger our internal peace and the existence of our cherished Union? Should this question be answered in the affirmative, then, by every law human and Divine, we shall be justified in wresting it from Spain, if we possess the power." This version substituted the words "to wrest" for Marcy's "to detach" and thus followed orders, but Buchanan believed that he had interposed an effective barrier to the extremist hope of acquiring Cuba by force. He had named a number of conditions precedent to seizure which he felt certain would never arise: freeing of the Cuban slaves, Africanization of the island's government, and the beginning of a race war in the United States. Buchanan thought he had successfully spiked the guns of the Young Americans and would-be filibusters. Roy Nichols, biographer of Pierce, notes that the final text of the Manifesto was "not a direct threat," as Soulé wanted, but a "laborious attempt at a guarded hint," which Buchanan phrased as a means to balk rash action while still obeying Marcy's instructions.

Buchanan believed that he had managed to salvage a little from his plan for purchase and had undermined the policy of seizure. But Buchanan did not know that Soulé sent a private letter to Pierce along with the Manifesto, stating that if Spain would not sell Cuba, the United States ought to take it by force while England and France were engaged in a war and would not be likely to interfere. This message reversed the policy Buchanan intended, but Soulé's sentiments could be inferred from the text of the Manifesto.

At home the Whigs and Know-Nothings routed the Democrats in the North and West at the October elections. Hence, when the Ostend report arrived in November the Administration sat on it; and Marcy, shocked at the outcome, wrote to Soulé to proceed with the greatest caution in broaching the idea of purchase and to avoid any threats.

As might have been expected, the New York *Herald* soon got hold of a garbled version of the Manifesto which it further distorted with the paraphrase "that our safety demanded and our interests required we purchase or take Cuba at once." Some newsmen went so far as to state that the ministers had acted on their own initiative. Pierce offered no explanation or refutation; in his annual message he did not even mention Ostend. Buchanan finally wrote to Marcy: "I observe in a number of American Journals the statement made positively that the Conference at Ostend was the *voluntary* action of the American Ministers. Surely this ought to be corrected. *Never did I obey any instructions so reluctantly.*" Marcy wrote privately that the report itself did not sustain Soulé's interpretation, but still made no public pronouncement. "I am glad to perceive that you exonerate us from the charge . . . that we had recommended to offer Spain the alternative of cession or seizure," Buchanan replied. "How preposterous and suicidal would have been such an idea! . . . It would

240

have defeated the great object we had in view—the peaceful acquisition of Cuba."[11]

Marcy, just as badly caught as Buchanan by the unwanted publicity, made his stand at least officially clear by writing to Soulé, tearing to shreds his private proposals about Cuba and condemning his conduct as minister. Thus he achieved what he had long wanted, Soulé's resignation, and took his stand with Buchanan and Mason against the "sell or seize" doctrine.

But the end was not yet. The new anti-Administration Congress called for publication of the Cuban correspondence. Thus, for the first time, the correct version of the Ostend Manifesto became public property. Unhappily for Buchanan, the Administration, after several discussions in Cabinet, decided that it could not afford to permit the publication of the "detach" paragraph of Marcy's instructions. His biographer says: "It was a bad business, either way, and the expedient path was chosen. . . . The reaction of the public, which did not know of the ambiguous "detach" item, was mostly favorable to Marcy; the 'three wise men of Ostend,' . . . were lashed unmercifully for their part."[12] Slidell attributed Marcy's course to his eagerness for the presidency. He told Buchanan, "He fancies that he sees in you the only obstacle to the realisation of his dreams."[13] The public impression, however, was that James Buchanan stood for the highwayman's principle that "if Spain will not sell Cuba, we will take it." He should have known that people would grasp the simple, dramatic, but false cliché, rather than try to understand the complex logic back of the manifesto itself. But whatever he thought, he played the old trouper and made no defense. "I continue to be entirely satisfied with our report," he said.

AN UNTHINKABLE WAR

The remainder of Buchanan's mission brought diplomatic frustration, political soul-searching, and social triumph. In the months following Ostend it appeared that everything at the Legation had been going wrong. Sickles had been using the Legation seal and diplomatic pouch to send around all manner of personalia. Miller, the London dispatch agent whose business it was to receive diplomatic mail for all the continental embassies and forward it via courier had been using his official seal to cover and protect from routine censorship correspondence of a very undiplomatic character, much of it propaganda of the European revolutionists. On one occasion the British Customs at Liverpool charged Buchanan with petty smuggling. It had discovered six pounds of American cigars, undeclared, wrapped into a package of books on international law which were addressed to Buchanan. After much unpleasantness in England and voluminous correspondence, Buchanan concluded that a courier from New York, who had boasted on board ship what privileges awaited him in Liverpool and complained loudly that he could not accompany the mail boat to shore, had perpetrated the deed.[14]

After the Ostend conference Sickles again returned to the United States, thoroughly disgusted with Buchanan. Forney had added to the trouble by printing some observations Buchanan had written him in confidence condemning Sickles for his attack on the Peabody dinner and disparaging his competence as a Legation officer.[15] Buchanan made a clean breast of it to Sickles and told him to submit his resignation. To his great satisfaction, Sickles complied and Pierce appointed John Appleton. Appleton arrived in March and managed so competently that Buchanan assured Marcy that he was "well qualified to perform the duties of any Diplomatic station under the Government." "He is a *perfect* secretary," he wrote, "as well as an excellent friend." At this time he also got a new Legation clerk, Benjamin Moran of New York, whom he paid $800 a year out of his own pocket since federal statute forbade the government to hire a clerk at a foreign mission.[16] Moran made himself indispensable. He could receive visitors, handle most of the tourist problems, and translate foreign languages, in addition to keeping meticulously ordered files of correspondence and dispatches. In this latter regard he was very like Buchanan, and the two quickly achieved mutual respect which ripened into warm friendship. It was a pity Buchanan did not have such a staff at the start, for by the time he got competent help the negotiating was done. A final blow came when Marcy informed him that Congress had passed a law substantially reducing his salary and the allowance for outfit.

In April, 1855, Buchanan wrote that he wanted to leave England on August 23, and requested his letter of recall as of that date. The Central American negotiation had grown futile with the elevation of Palmerston to the Premiership in January. Buchanan talked occasionally with Clarendon, who remained in the Foreign Office, but the old rapport had dissolved. Whenever Buchanan mentioned Ruatan, Clarendon brought up Greytown, and just before Buchanan sent in his resignation they had a very disagreeable altercation.

During the summer of 1855, when the British began to see a triumphal end to the Crimean War, their relations with the United States rapidly deteriorated. Marcy noted it from the tone of the British press, and Buchanan reported to him that "there begins to be an uneasy feeling . . . that all is not well in the relations between the two countries."[17]

Nevertheless, President Pierce, on August 6, sent instructions to Buchanan to ask Palmerston for an explicit statement of the final British position on Central America, in reply to the American statement of the previous July. This demand invited a showdown and Palmerston considered it an ultimatum. He responded in a tart communication condemning the American position and reasserting British claims in Central America. This reply he supported by ordering a fleet of 84- and 60-gun battle cruisers, with auxiliary vessels, to Bermuda and the West Indies, allegedly to assume routine stations.

More than ever, Buchanan wanted to go home. He wrote to Marcy on October 3 that he had received dispatches 108, 109 and 111, but not 110 which contained his release. He urged the appointment of J. Glancy Jones as his relief and a search for the missing letter of recall. He also wrote to President Pierce, assuring him that Appleton could handle the Legation business indefinitely. But by the end of October, Appleton was no longer willing to take the responsibility of handling the mission. Buchanan wrote: "The aspect of affairs between the two countries has now become squally." Two weeks later, he received his letter of recall which, although dated the 12th of September, had not been mailed from the State Department until October 22. "It has arrived," he told Marcy, "at a time when the relations between the two countries have assumed so threatening an aspect . . . that I cannot at the present moment retire."[18]

Buchanan now enlisted all his energies to reduce the growing war fever. So far the planned movement of the British fleet to the Caribbean had not reached the press. When Buchanan asked the reason for the naval orders, Clarendon cited the attacks on J. F. T. Crampton, the British minister in Washington, for recruiting troops in America, a letter of Attorney General Cushing which had labelled British recruiters "malefactors," information that an American built steamer was about to leave New York as a Russian privateer, and a report that thousands of Irish-Americans were plotting a descent upon the Emerald Isle to free it from Britain. As Buchanan already knew the privateer rumor to be false and the Irish invasion pure speculation, he was forced to the conclusion that the British were looking for a fight.

This attitude drew the issue sharply. If the United States wanted war, they could now have it. The historian might well speculate what result might have emerged from such a conflict; whether, perhaps, it might have side-tracked sectionalism, united the American nation, and postponed or even averted the Civil War—at possibly an even higher price. Buchanan expounded the situation thus to Clarendon:

> The news of the sending of the fleet . . . would most probably excite much public indignation. . . . It would find the people calm and tranquil in relation to their foreign affairs and wholly unprepared for it. It would burst upon them suddenly, and they would doubtless manifest their feelings in strong and defying

language. This would return to England and react upon the people here . . . until at last by degrees the two countries might find themselves at war, although . . . there was no question of very serious importance between them. And such a war! . . . I would not have it on my conscience for any human consideration to be the author of any act which might lead to such consequences.[19]

The British, in response to the American retreat, cut in half the strength of the proposed West Indian squadron. Clarendon informed Buchanan "that three ships had been sent to Bermuda & one to Jamaica" which would be "on their guard against all dangers, . . . let them come from what quarter they may." Buchanan answered in two sentences that this reply fell far short of his hopes and would not "exert that happy influence in restoring cordial relations . . . which . . . I shall always so earnestly desire." For several weeks the possibility of war depressed the Stock Exchange and Buchanan reported that "an incautious word from me would either raise or sink the price of consols." Palmerston held his position and backed it up by force; unless the United States attacked there was nothing to fight about. By the end of November the leading British journals deprecated the idea of war and condemned the Ministry for risking it. On December 14, Buchanan reported to Marcy that the storm had blown over. "I hear this sentiment everywhere I go," he said. "There is certainly no disposition at present on the part of the British people to have serious difficulties with the United States."[20]

Buchanan had a respite of exactly two weeks. On December 28 Marcy sent him word that the United States had asked for the recall of Lord Crampton and of the British consuls at Cincinnati, Philadelphia and New York, who had been illegally recruiting troops for the Crimean War. When Buchanan informed Clarendon of the contents of this dispatch, the latter jumped up and declared in angry surprise, "We will not do it." During February, Buchanan felt sure that a diplomatic rupture impended. "As soon as the news shall arrive in this country, that you sent Mr. Crampton his passports," he informed Marcy, "I shall receive mine from Lord Clarendon."[21]

Viscount Palmerston presented a one-sided picture of the recruiting controversy to Parliament and raised a storm of indignation in the press. With the end of the Crimean War in sight and British military strength at its peak, the Premier rattled the saber against America as a means of maintaining himself in power; at least so Buchanan thought. He immediately responded that the Viscount had falsified the facts by withholding details that justified the American position. When Lady Palmerston later gave a diplomatic dinner and omitted Buchanan's name from the guest list, he assumed that his time had come. But Britain delayed any official reply to the request for Crampton's recall, and Marcy postponed dismissing him. Meanwhile, British public opinion slowly turned against Palmerston. Lord Bulwer announced that he agreed with Buchanan and not the Ministry on the interpretation of the treaty he himself had negotiated with Clayton.[22]

During all this time, Buchanan pleaded with Marcy for another letter of recall. "I consider this mission as a sort of waif abandoned by the Government," he complained. "Not a word even about a secretary of Legation. . . . I have to labor like a drayman. Have you no bowels?" In February he learned that George M. Dallas had been appointed his successor, and by the middle of March he had the "long looked-for, come at last"—his final letter of recall.

After the October elections of 1854, when the Kansas-Nebraska Act had split the Democracy, destroyed the Whigs, raised up the new Republican party and given a fleeting prominence to the Know-Nothings, Buchanan's friends began to bombard him with petitions, prognostications and praises that no man could ignore. Pierce could not succeed; his Administration had fallen lower than Tyler's. No candidate but Old Buck could be trusted; Kansas-Nebraska had dirtied all the others. The country was fearful to the verge of panic and would not accept a "speculative candidacy." Everyone wanted the next president to be a statesman, a man whose integrity and experience had been proven over the years. In short, Buchanan was the only man who could win for the Democracy. There was no doubt that he would be drafted.

By January, 1855, Buchanan caved in and admitted to confidential friends that they could have him if they wanted him. Having decided to be "available," he laid a little of the groundwork in England. He asked Sir Emerson Tennent to arrange a dinner at which Cardinal Wiseman would be present. In July, 1855, after Tennent's banquet, Buchanan held a long conversation with Wiseman, and told the prelate of his admiration for Archbishop John Hughes of New York. Thurlow Weed later asserted, *"That dinner made Mr. Buchanan President of the United States!"* Weed exaggerated, but the Cardinal's good opinion of Buchanan doubtless had some influence on Archbishop Hughes and the American Catholics.[23]

Buchanan wrote to Marcy shortly before his recall,

> I know . . . that you would consider me in a state of mental delusion if I were to say how indifferent I feel in regard to myself on the question of the next Presidency. You would be quite a sceptic. One thing is certain: that neither by word nor letter have I ever contributed any support to myself. I believe that the next Presidential term will be perhaps the most important and responsible of any which has occurred since the origin of the

245

Government; and whilst no competent and patriotic man to whom it may be offered should shrink from the responsibility, yet he may well accept it as the greatest trial of his life.[24]

DEAR MISS LANE

Although British society was something of a strain on his constitution, Buchanan thought it very congenial. The formality of the Court did not invade the drawing room where he found the nobility as simple and unpretentious as his Lancaster neighbors. It took him some time, however, to become accustomed to dinners at eight and parties at eleven when he should have been going to bed. He looked forward to Harriet's arrival in the spring of 1854, though he knew her visit would double his social activities.

Harriet, now in the full bloom of young womanhood, flippant, gay, flirtatious yet well-mannered and well-read, became a favorite in the diplomatic social world. She dined with Victoria, danced with Prince Albert, and received a marriage proposal from the enormously wealthy, fifty-eight-year-old Sir Fitz-Roy Kelly. At Oxford, where "Nunc" and Alfred Lord Tennyson received honorary degrees at the same ceremony, the students paid only cursory attention to the dignitaries and shouted and whistled their approval of Hal Lane. She flitted from castle to castle, attended fashionable weddings, and kept the Legation in constant turmoil with preparations for parties. Buchanan loved the gaieties.

He also worried, for Harriet seemed to be succumbing to the glamor of British titles. At the same time a Philadelphia suitor by the name of Tyson was confidently planning to come to England and marry her, although she had treated him so badly during their long courtship that he had well earned the name Job.

Harriet did not even let Tyson know that she planned to return to America a few weeks after his scheduled arrival in England. She saw him briefly in London to tell him "No." Buchanan was angry, not at the decision but at the cruel and thoughtless manner of her refusal.

In the fall of 1855, Buchanan received news that Harriet's older sister, Mary Baker, had suddenly died in California. Harriet fell into unconsolable grief, confined herself to her room for weeks, and threatened to join a convent. Buchanan gave her some of his own philosophy: to mourn the dead at the expense of the living is sinful. Heart-rending afflictions are the common lot of humanity, man's duty on earth is to submit with humble resignation. "In all calamitous events, we ought to say, emphatically, 'Thy will be done.' " He himself was as much distressed by the recent death of another niece, Jessie Yates Weaver. Poor Jessie. What would he do with *her* children.

246

George Dallas arrived in England on March 13, 1856, accompanied by his wife, his sister, three unmarried daughters, and a son, who was to be Secretary of Legation. Buchanan wrote, "The Legation will be a family party."[25]

Before his audience of leave, Buchanan dined with the queen who, with the princess royal, talked mostly about "dear Miss Lane." He spent two convivial weeks with Mason in Paris and then returned to England to sail for home aboard the *Arago*.

19

THE RIGHT MAN FOR THE TIMES • 1856

THE SHAPE OF THINGS TO COME

The steamship *Arago* slipped her cables and edged slowly out of her dock at noon on Wednesday, April 9, 1856. By midafternoon Buchanan had affably acknowledged the greetings of many of his fellow passengers, finished his constitutional around the deck, and retired to his stateroom where he took off his greatcoat, removed his cutaway, and then opened his travel chest to get his old leather slippers and a bottle of Madeira. After some puttering about he found the cork puller and a glass, lit a "segar" and then settled back on his bed, drew a long sigh of solid comfort, and relaxed.

Had he been less nervously exhausted, the soft movement of the ship might have lulled him to sleep. Instead, it set him musing, haphazardly at first and then with increasing focus and plan. Well, thank God that job was done. He had never wanted the mission; yet he had to admit that he had enjoyed the experience, had done his duty, and had emerged better off politically than if he had stayed at home. He could not help wondering about the freak fate which had kept him out of Congress during each of the four most violent sectional controversies of the century: the Missouri Compromise, the nullification struggle, the 1850 Compromise, and now the Kansas-Nebraska Bill. If he should become president, he feared he would not escape the next outburst. He sipped some Madeira and continued his reverie. With fair weather he might reach New York on his sixty-fifth birthday.

At that thought he roused himself, went to his portfolio, and extracted a packet of letters. Sorting through he picked out half a dozen and settled back to read, for he wanted to catch up on the state of political affairs, particularly in Pennsylvania and Kansas. The Pennsylvania Democrats had suffered from the Kansas-Nebraska controversy, and James Pollock, a Know-Nothing, Whig free-soiler now sat in the Pennsylvania governor's chair. Men who had predicted Bigler's re-election in 1854 by a 50,000 majority woke up to find him defeated by 37,000 votes.[1]

248

Buchanan felt sure that the Know-Nothing movement, like anti-Masonry, would pass as quickly as it had appeared, but for the moment it was dangerous. He read a letter from Jeremiah S. Black:

> Here is a party less than one year old which has already triumphed in half the states of the Union. Its members are sworn to secrecy and to fidelity. . . . It conceals its secrets not merely by silence but by positive falsehood. When men are seduced into its lodges they are instructed to conceal the fact and preserve their previous party attitude. Know-Nothings continue to speak at Democratic meetings, to argue for Democratic principles, to act as members of Democratic Committees, to run as Democratic candidates. The consequence of this is terrible. The obligations of truth are treated with an awful frivolity. . . . A majority of the legislature have obtained their seats by false pretenses which would send them to the penitentiary if they got 5 dollars by similar means. Cameron was nominated for Senator by a system of secret voting inside the secret order—the cheats were cheated. . . . 28 members . . . certified that he had got his nomination by 'wholesale corruption and individual bribery.'[2]

Forney, in another letter, stated that he did not see how Cameron could be beaten "unless they fix the charge of Bribery upon him, and it looks as if they would."[3] But Cameron had angered even the Know-Nothings, and William Bigler won the senatorship.

Matters looked better than usual in Pennsylvania; the Buchaneers, except for the governorship, held control. Forney was confident that Buchanan could win the presidency and in order to induce him to accept the nomination, promised to relinquish all rights to patronage.[4] From all he read in his correspondence, Buchanan judged that at last Pennsylvania was "right."

He wished that he could feel as optimistic in regard to the situation in Kansas. The trial of popular sovereignty had brought civil war to that territory. Settlers had gone there to claim land and fight for political control. These immigrants, from the North and the South, carried with them a deep sense of mission and bitterly hated each other. New Englanders, because of better organization and financing back home, came in greater numbers and with more armament than the Southerners, but the latter had the sympathy of the Missourians who cast ballots for the first Kansas territorial legislature and elected candidates favorable to the South. The New Englanders called the invaders "border ruffians," but they do not appear to have been very different from any of the frontier inhabitants of their day. The Missourians thought that they had as much right to enter Kansas as did armed mercenaries from Massachusetts. Those tenderfoots would not show them how to run the frontier.

When Pierce removed Kansas Governor Andrew H. Reeder, for fraudulent dealings in land, the antislavery men charged that he had been fired for denouncing the territorial election. The free state men set up a legislature of their own at Topeka, elected Reeder as Congressional representative, and drafted a constitution. This, incidentally, was an anti-Negro rather than an anti-slavery constitution; it established white supremacy by forbidding any Negroes to live in Kansas. In January, 1856, when they elected their own governor, Pierce, in a special message to Congress, denounced the Topeka regime as revolutionary and Congress sustained him by affirming the legality of the original Kansas government, with its capital at Lecompton.

But the Topeka government defied the United States and continued to rule wherever its guns could enforce submission to its decrees. Neither Pierce nor the new territorial governor, Wilson Shannon, would risk use of federal troops to enforce local law, but they ordered the army to prevent violent collision between the contesting factions and to avert the outbreak of full-scale war. The troops, however, could do little about sporadic outrages perpetrated by small groups. Beatings, shootings, housewrecking and arson became so common that the press began to write of "Bleeding Kansas." The ordeal of Kansas would not be easily ended. Few settlers wanted coexistence; each side determined to rule, and to rule meant to eliminate the enemy.

The trip of the *Arago* proved calm and peaceful, but hardly a vacation for Buchanan. He recognized that it would very likely be the last fortnight he would have for a long time to collect his thoughts and formulate his course of action without constant interruption. If he became president, he would look back longingly at this cruise. What were his chances, and how should the cards be played?

It seemed very unlikely that Pierce or Douglas could be nominated, but they might be strong enough to deadlock the convention and pave the way for another dark horse. Plenty of willing spirits hoped for this kind of result—Hunter, Davis, Walker, Marcy and others. A little management ought to prevent such an occurrence, particularly emphasis on the risk to the country of an accidental nomination in the hour of danger. A nation in crisis needed an experienced and dependable candidate. Pennsylvania, which had three times failed Buchanan, now promised him full support, for the Harrisburg Convention of March 4 had given him its unanimous endorsement. Finally, the disruption of the Whig party over the Kansas-Nebraska Bill might be turned to advantage. The Whigs in in 1854 and 1855 had split along north-south lines into rump segments which stood helpless in a national contest. Whig leaders and voters were looking for a new home, some of them joining the Republicans, some the Know-Nothings, some the Southern Americans and some the Democrats. Many Whig leaders saw that under the new conditions they stood closer to the conservative Buchanan wing of the Democrats than to any of the other parties. Buchanan already had a sheaf of encouraging letters from prominent Whigs stating that they considered their party dead and would join the Democrats if he were nominated.

Since Forney had become obligated to Pierce, John Slidell actively undertook management of Buchanan's political future. He planned to cultivate the growing popular demand for Buchanan's nomination to give it the aspect of a spontaneous movement. Dr. Foltz assured Buchanan in November, 1855, "The People have taken the next Presidency out of the hands of the politicians. . . . The people, and not your political friends will place you there."[5]

Slidell seized this idea and promoted his candidate as the people's own choice. He did not create the force, but he saw and used with intelligence the latent public sentiment which needed only a little cultivation to start it growing. Little by little, he and his co-workers induced back-country editors to puff Buchanan until, by late in 1855, scores of Democratic newspapers and quite a few of Whig persuasion carried Buchanan's name on the masthead. The "puffs" followed the theme that Buchanan's name had attained prominence without the aid of the machinery of politics and almost without the help of politicians. "The fact that he has become formidable without effort has gone far to inspire a wide and almost universal confidence in his strength."[6]

During 1854 Slidell earnestly counselled Buchanan to stay in England as long as he could. "The political atmosphere at Washington is malarious," he wrote, "and those who are not compelled to inhale it had better keep away." A year later, when the newspaper chorus had swelled to national proportions, Slidell thought it time for Buchanan to express to some discreet friends his willingness to be a candidate. Instead of doing this, Buchanan sent off a batch of letters reiterating his indifference but explaining with care his views on the slavery crisis. Slidell warned him to stop this. "You cannot well be in a better position than you are now," he said, "& those who are not satisfied with your antecedents cannot be made so by any explanations."[7] Buchanan never did throw his hat in the ring. He did, however, admit that others had taken him up. As late as February, 1856, he could still write,

> In the present canvass, strange as it may seem to you, I have had no part, either directly or indirectly. In the beginning I did all I could to prevent any movement in my favor, & what has since been done has been entirely spontaneous, at least so far as I am personally concerned.[8]

251

This statement was delicate, prudent, and as technically correct as a Philadelphia lawyer could have made it, but it was scarcely open and candid. Buchanan could have stopped the movement in its tracks any time he wished, but instead he kept the door open. For a time he certainly went through an agony of indecision. Wheatland beckoned strongly, and life there looked heavenly in comparison with the presidency of a country in political shambles and with a civil war at its center. He summed up his state of mind to Harriet in a maxim from La Rochefoucauld: *"Les choses que nous desirons n'arrivent pas, ou, si elles arrivent, ce n'est, ni dans le temps, ni de la manière qui nous auraient fait le plus de plaisir."*[9] But a man could not turn down the presidency when his friends threw it at him, and the family would never forgive him if he rejected it. He had been in on all the phases of planning and knew how much "spontaneity" there was. He had discouraged, but not killed off, the promotion; and now, just as with the diplomatic mission, he was caught.

After a survey of the whole scene, Buchanan determined to do nothing to injure or embarrass the efforts of his friends. He would keep his mouth shut and make no promises. He would stay at Wheatland and let those who wished come to see him. He would put his record on the block and let people take it or leave it. That would be the fall of the cards until the convention. "Sufficient unto the day is the evil thereof." With the matter settled in his mind, he gave himself up to the pleasures of the voyage. Mrs. Plitt amused him. She had sent a newspaper clipping reporting that he would return via New Orleans in order to go on to Tennessee to marry Mrs. Polk. Jokingly, she said she wished it were true. She was sure he would find it "an agreeable way of Polking your way into the Presidency."[10]

THE PEOPLE'S CHOICE

The *Arago* failed to make port on Buchanan's birthday, but she docked at New York the next day, ahead of schedule, taking the local dignitaries so much by surprise that the welcome fell far short of what some had predicted —"such a triumph as the Caesar's only have seen."[11] At the Astor House Buchanan received visitors until a formal reception committee could be mustered at City Hall. He firmly declined the tender of a public dinner and supped quietly with the mayor and a few friends. The New York arrival confirmed the wisdom of his determination to remain aloof. The dinner would have been dynamite. It would have widened the split between the Democratic factions, required a speech that could not possibly have suited both, and provoked charges that Buchanan started electioneering the moment he set foot on home soil. His arrival without notice and the refusal of ceremony brought members of both factions out to see him,

252

enabled him to avoid saying more than that he was glad to be back, and strongly sustained the key idea that he was a simple citizen who had earned and wished no special honors. His scheme worked beautifully and he was off to Philadelphia before his enemies realized that he had scored a tremendous psychological triumph.

Philadelphia was more exciting, though its celebration, too, fell considerably short of a Roman holiday. Booming cannon welcomed Buchanan's train, and the official escort took him to the Merchant's Exchange where he made a three-minute speech to a crowd of about three thousand. The City Council had rejected a request that Independence Hall should be opened that night for a formal reception, but the Merchant's Hotel served as well. From its portico Buchanan reviewed a parade, watched a fireworks display, and patiently endured a band serenade.[12]

Joseph B. Baker, superintendent of the state railroad, had a special train ready the next morning. The locomotive bore the name "Young America" and had been draped with bunting and signs reading "Welcome Home, Pennsylvania's Favorite Son." On the trip to Lancaster the train stopped at local stations while Buchanan stood on the back platform waving his hat. They made a short stop at Baker's home in Gap, along the main line, where the engine took on water and the official party champagne.

Buchanan's home town of Lancaster gave him a rousing reception. The "Wheatland Club" fired the "Old Buck Cannon," and for two days the town celebrated with bands, transparencies, torchlight processions, and fireworks. Two weeks later Adam Reigart, the wine merchant, brought to Wheatland an itemized bill for $809.65 for liquor merchandise. The front porch campaign was underway.[13]

The first few weeks of May passed auspiciously. Forney, whom Pierce had released from allegiance, wrote almost daily from Washington with late details on the expected convention vote at Cincinnati on June 2. Buchanan's strength lay in the middle belt of states from Delaware to Missouri. The New England Democracy was for Pierce, and the South favored Douglas, but both of these could be stopped by making strategic promises to favorite son candidates. Buchanan interrupted a trip to Washington to report on the English Mission in order to make a speech in Baltimore. "Disunion is a word which ought not to be breathed amongst us even in a whisper" he warned. "Our children ought to be taught that it is a sacrilege to pronounce it. . . . There is nothing stable but Heaven and the Constitution."[14]

On May 22, Congressman Preston S. Brooks, of South Carolina, strode into the Senate Chamber after hours, attacked white-haired Senator Charles Sumner of Massachusetts and beat him into unconsciousness with a heavy rubber cane. The Senator had invited trouble by subjecting a relative of Brooks to one of the vilest and most insulting diatribes ever heard in Congress. But regardless of the provocation, responsible southerners were shocked by the caning and wrote of it: "unjustifiable, unmanly, ill-timed, ill-advised, cowardly, dastardly. Mr. Brooks has outraged decency, and dishonored the South—expel him." That was the word from Savannah. From Boston came the same cry, and Brooks in all likelihood would have been turned out except for the events of two days later.

About 11 p. m. of May 24, John Brown, his three sons, and four henchmen headed for Pottawatomie Creek in Kansas and later knocked at the door of James Doyle, a southerner whom none of the party had ever seen before. Doyle, half dressed and unarmed, asked them to come in, but Brown's men drew pistols and invited him to come out. When Doyle's sons, William aged 22, Drury, 20, and John, 16 stepped to their father's side, Brown ordered them to come along. A few minutes later Mrs. Doyle and her youngest son, who had remained with her, heard screams and pistol shots outside the cabin, and then there was silence.

After midnight Allen Wilkinson, who was up late because his wife Louisa was sick with measles, went to answer a thunderous pounding on the door. "In the name of the Northern Army, open up," came a deep voice. Brown's party entered and ordered Wilkinson outside.

Shortly thereafter the raiders visited James Harris, who was in bed with his wife when the door burst open and the Brown gang entered. For some inexplicable reason, they ignored Harris and dragged out William Sherman, a guest.

Not until the next morning did anyone dare to go out and investigate. James Doyle and two of his sons lay near the cabin, with bullets through their heads, their skulls split in two with a broadaxe, their sides hacked open, and their fingers cut off. A neighbor found Allen Wilkinson shot in the head, his skull chopped apart and his side pierced. Bill Sherman was lying face down in a small creek, shot in the head, his skull laid open and the brains trailing down the stream but still attached to the bone, his side stabbed full of sword wounds and his hands cut off.

The Democrats reacted with a howl of rage and fury, and had the Republicans equally expressed their horror of the savage insanity which prompted this blind slaughter, Brooks might have been punished and the country might have become calmer. But antislavery extremists hailed Brown as a hero. Slavery was a sin, and the wages of sin was death. God had ordained Brown to smite the wicked. When this kind of report began to percolate into the South, it became the fashion there to "present a cane" to Preston Brooks wherever he made a public appearance. It is no wonder James Buchanan returned to Wheatland less optimistic than when he left.

At Cincinnati, as convention time approached, there was great activity on the part of the advance guard of Pierce and Douglas supporters, but no Buchanan team was in evidence. Rather quickly it became apparent that Buchanan's uncoordinated managers had taken too literally the "spontaneous" idea, and that no one was in command of the organization. Slidell got busy, rounded up his colleagues—Judah P. Benjamin of Louisiana, Jesse D. Bright of Indiana, and James A. Bayard of Delaware—and the.four Senators hastened to Cincinnati. Forney arrived soon after, and began negotiations to detach the Douglas forces from their agreement with Pierce. Pierce and Douglas planned to hold on to their own delegations at all costs and block the Buchanan bid.

The Democratic National Convention opened noisily on June 2 when rival delegations from Missouri and New York overpowered the doormen and pummeled their way onto the convention floor. After order had been restored, the convention chose John E. Ward of Georgia, a Buchaneer, as permanent chairman. Buchanan's friends succeeded in gaining early control of most of the convention machinery and began to execute their strategy. Admit all contesting delegations in order to split the vote of the states from which they came. This plan would give Buchanan at least fifty per cent where he might otherwise get nothing. Adopt the platform first and include in it a popular sovereignty resolution to propitiate Douglas. Promise Bright the patronage of the Northwest, and let him use this to seduce weak Douglas delegates. For those strong on Douglas, promise the patronage to him and remind them that the Little Giant, still only 43 years old, might expect to be favored in 1860 if he played the game now. Win Michigan by showing to her delegates evidence that their favorite son, Cass, had been knifed by Douglas in 1852. Tell everyone who had failed to secure a job under Pierce that his only hope lay with Buchanan. Have the Buchanan Committee continually circulating about the floor, visiting with each state delegation. These visits might not accomplish much directly but would create a constant disturbance with Buchanan's name at the center. Speaker Ward promised not to interrupt this unparliamentary procedure.[15]

In a dozen ballots Buchanan led but did not approach a two-thirds majority. Then Pierce withdrew, throwing his votes to Douglas, and stray votes began to drift over to Buchanan. On the sixteenth ballot Buchanan polled a two-to-one majority over Douglas from New England, the middle States, and the West, and Douglas ran two-to-one ahead of Buchanan in the South, a conclusive refutation of the fallacious story of later years that the South had picked Buchanan.[16] Douglas finally withdrew, hoping to promote his chances for 1860, and on the seventeenth ballot the convention nominated Buchanan by acclamation. It chose John C. Breckinridge of Kentucky as vice-president, an honor which came as a total surprise to him.

The Democratic platform, nearly identical with the previous one, added a new plank: opposition to further agitation of the slave question, a firm stand on the Compromise measures of 1850, and recognition of "the right of the people of all the Territories . . . acting through the legally and fairly expressed will of the majority of the actual residents . . . to form a constitution with or without domestic slavery, and be admitted into the Union."

The Republicans named John C. Frémont, a choice of expediency. Their strongest candidate, William H. Seward, did not want to risk the defeat which he anticipated the party would suffer in its first national campaign. Frémont had tremendous romantic appeal, no political record, and would bring the northern Know-Nothings along with him.

The Republican platform promised to promote the building of a railroad to the Pacific, to make big appropriations for rivers and harbors, and to prohibit in the territories "those twin relics of barbarism, polygamy and slavery." One resolution broke sharply from the old pattern of party platforms and took the form of a revolutionary manifesto. It accused the Pierce Administration of every crime in the human calendar, charging it with murder, robbery, arson, confiscation of private property, false imprisonment, and the tyrannical subversion of the Constitution in Kansas. The platform labelled as "spurious and pretended" the territorial government of Kansas which Congress had recognized as legal and called the revolutionary Topeka government, whose members soon would be under federal indictment for treason, the "constitutional government." But the last sentence was the serious one. It arraigned the Administration, the president, his advisors, agents, supporters, apologists, and accessories for crimes against humanity and concluded "that it is our fixed purpose to bring the actual perpetrators of these atrocious outrages, and their accomplices, to a sure and condign punishment hereafter."

Had this been the platform of some insignificant, crackpot party, the people of the country would have laughed it off as pure moonshine, something like the ravings of the suffragettes or the phrenologists. But Kansas was no laughing matter, nor did the Republicans appear as a harmless lunatic fringe in 1856. They might win.

If they were victorious, the platform pledged them to arrest, jail, and possibly execute those who disagreed with them on Kansas. People might easily brush aside the Democrats' sense of outrage at such threats as mere partisan prejudice but northern Whigs discovered the same import in the Republican platform. Said they: "Can [the Republicans] have the madness or folly to believe that our Southern brethren would submit to be governed by such a chief magistrate? I tell you that we are treading on the brink of a volcano."[17] People who still loved their country were frightened.

Frémont posed no great problem to the Democrats. The political sophisticates passed him off as "a man whose only merit, so far as history records it, is in the fact that he was born in South Carolina, crossed the Rocky Mountains, subsisted on frogs, lizards, snakes and grasshoppers, and captured a woolly horse."[18]   A good many agreed with Sophie Plitt: "Frémont to run in opposition . . . *What a farce!* Poor ignoramus. And Dayton too—they want a burlesque!"[19] It amused Buchanan to remember how he had first brought Frémont into the public eye by persuading the Senate to print and distribute thousands of copies of the *Exploring Expedition to the Rocky Mountains.* Frémont did not worry him; the real issue was the Republican threat of disunion and civil war. Buchanan feared this possibility, not only as a candidate but also as a private citizen. "In case of a dissolution of the Union," he wrote to Howell Cobb in July, "Maryland and Pennsylvania would most probably be frontier states; & whilst we and generations yet to come would have bitter cause to deplore the dreadful catastrophe, these two states would suffer more than any other members of the Confederacy."[20]

CONSERVATIVES TO THE RESCUE

Buchanan stated the keynote of his campaign in these words, "*The Union is in danger and the people everywhere begin to know it.* The Black Republicans must be, as they can be with justice, boldly assailed as disunionists, and this charge must be reiterated again and again." Forget the past, bury the bank, the tariff, and the rest as historical fossils. The Democrats must publicize the statements of "the abolitionists, free soilers and infidels against the Union," to show that the Union was in danger. "This race ought to be run on the question of Union or disunion."[21]

The Democratic press generally adopted this campaign theme, and devoted columns to the antiunion pronouncements of prominent Republicans. Ohio's Representative Joshua R. Giddings had announced "I look forward to the day when there shall be a servile insurrection in the South; when the black man . . . shall assert his freedom, and wage a war of extermination against his master; when the torch of the incendiary shall light up the towns of the South, and blot out the last vestige of slavery; and though I may not mock at their calamity, nor laugh when their fear cometh, yet I will hail it as the dawn of the millenium." New York's Governor William H. Seward asserted that "there is a higher power than the Constitution," and hoped soon to "bring the parties of the country into an aggressive war upon slavery." Speaker of the House Nathaniel P. Banks said frankly that he was "willing . . . to let the Union slide." Judge Rufus S. Spalding declared that if he had the alternatives of the continuance of slavery or a dissolution of the Union, "I am for dissolution, and I care not how quick it comes."

Editor James Watson Webb predicted that if the Republicans lost the election, they would be "forced to drive back the slavocracy with fire and sword." Horace Greeley of the New York *Tribune* wrote that "the free and slave states ought to separate." The Union, he editorialized, "is not worth supporting in connexion with the South." A Poughkeepsie clergyman prayed "that this accursed Union may be dissolved, even if blood have to be spilt." A group of Republicans petitioned Congress to take "measures for the speedy, peaceful, and equitable dissolution of the existing union." O. L. Raymond told an audience in Faneuil Hall, "Remembering that he was a slaveholder, I spit upon George Washington." (Hisses and applause) "You hissers are slaveholders in spirit!"[22]

Almost every day during the campaign, Democratic newspapers ran a column of such quotations as evidence of Republican doctrine. But Buchanan and the Democrats incorrectly assessed the fundamentally revolutionary nature of the Republican party. While the Democrats published this material to expose the determination of the Republicans to break up the Union, the Republicans joyfully welcomed all the free publicity and published the same material in their own newspapers as bright banners of the glorious crusade. About 175,000,000 copies of newspapers circulated annually in the North, and about 50,000,000 annually in the South. The southerners got only the Democratic viewpoint, the terrible threat; the certainty that the Republicans planned for them just what their platform promised: fire and sword. The northerners got four times as much material on the same theme, in the papers of both parties, and the Republicans believed it was helping them more than Buchanan. In fact, the word "disunion" so dominated the campaign that it began to take hold of Democratic minds. So solid a Union Democrat as Jeremiah S. Black, in urging Howell Cobb to prevent the South from acting politically without prior consultation with friends in the North, concluded: "If you will do this, even the election of Frémont may result in nothing worse than turning New England with her ignorance, bigotry, and superstition out of the Union; and that is a consummation most devoutly to be wished."[23]

Buchanan made no speeches during the campaign; he stayed at Wheatland conducting a prodigious correspondence. Every question of the election dwindled to trifling insignificance, he wrote, "when compared with the grand and appalling issue of union or disunion." If Frémont won, he said, disunion "will be immediate and inevitable. . . . We have so often cried 'wolf,' that now, when the wolf is at the door, it is difficult to make people believe it." From the South came letters from men who had once opposed nullification and secession but who now said "that the election of Frémont involves the dissolution of the Union. . . . Many now deem that it would be for the mutual advantage of the parties to have a Southern Confederation."

British newspapers were "all for Frémont . . ., and a dissolution of the Union." French journals assumed that there would be an immediate declaration of war between the sections if Frémont should win, and expressed surprise that the word "disunion," once so horrifying to Americans, was now spoken openly in all parts of the country. The Abolitionists and Radical Republicans of New England and Ohio shrilled to the same chorus. When a convention in Cleveland, called for the purpose of northern secession, failed to accomplish that object in the fall of 1856, Garrison, Wendell Phillips and their partisans called another to meet in Worcester, Massachusetts, in January, 1857, where they proposed to secede from a union with slaveholders. "It is now with nine-tenths only a question of time," said Phillips. Garrison defiantly cast a copy of the Constitution into a bonfire with the exclamation: "So perish all compromises with tyranny." "Boston is a sad place," wrote Buchanan. "In that city they have re-elected to Congress a factious fanatic, . . . who, in a public speech, said that we must have an anti-slavery Constitution, an anti-slavery Bible, and an anti-slavery God."[24]

The Democratic campaign and the adherence of many prominent Whigs to Buchanan's cause seemed to guarantee success in November. That supposition got a rude shock in September when Maine held its state election. While the Democrats had no real expectation of winning the state, they had spent money and sent speakers in the hope of keeping the Republican victory small. But Maine went Republican by an overwhelming majority. This smashing defeat aroused the Democrats to energetic action. Southerners, in a panic, mobilized hurriedly, declaring in the meantime that if the Republicans won they would have to secede immediately to save their lives. Pennsylvania now became crucial, for careful analysis showed that Buchanan had to carry his home state to win. But every electoral vote became critically important. To bolster California, Buchanan wrote a letter endorsing the construction of a Pacific railroad to counter the Republicans' strongest propaganda weapon there. Forney discovered, to his horror, that Buchanan had never even written to President Pierce or to Senator Stephen A. Douglas, enlisting their aid in his campaign. Buchanan recognized it as a stupid oversight, but he found himself unable to repair it, for to write at this late date would be an insulting insinuation that these gentlemen had been dragging their feet. Douglas became so excited that on his own volition he sold some land and gave the money to the campaign chest: $100,000 according to a biographer of Douglas, and $100 according to a Buchanan biographer. In a thank you letter for this, Buchanan unfortunately addressed the envelope to "The Hon. Samuel A. Douglas."

The Democratic party leaders converged on Pennsylvania where the state election in October would determine the fate of the presidential balloting. They had two weeks in which to work. Cobb came from Georgia and made ten speeches in ten days to huge audiences from Philadelphia to Erie. At Meadville he talked to a crowd of 3000 for an hour and a half in a driving snow storm, then drove by buggy to Erie in the off-season blizzard and spoke another hour and a half. For a Georgian, this was the supreme sacrifice.[25] From the South came the word: "Concentrate your entire force of every kind upon Pennsylvania until the 15th—even the day of election have speakers everywhere. Success here will carry more votes . . . than can possibly be accomplished by direct efforts in other states. Carry every speaker to Pennsylvania. . . . Don't waste your time replying. Carry Pennsylvania."[26]

The week before election Lancaster staged the greatest effort of the campaign. Some 50,000 people descended on the little Dutch community to hear the sons of Henry Clay and Daniel Webster (both Whigs) and all the prominent Democrats. There was a huge parade with booming cannon and innumerable bands, and placards were displayed at every little distance bearing the legend:

> Nail up the Flag, aye, nail it fast;
> The Union First, the Union Last.
> We hail no flag—no party own
> That any of the States Disown.[27]

Only one mishap marred the occasion. The first section of the special train carrying 2000 Philadelphians wrecked, blocking all following traffic, with the result that the Dallas contingent never got to Lancaster.[28]

The Democrats won Pennsylvania by a slim majority on October 15 and everyone relaxed. A Democratic presidency was assured. The election would not go to the House of Representatives. Frémont could not win. In the November elections, Buchanan polled through the nation some 1,800,000 votes, Frémont 1,300,000, and Fillmore 900,000. South of the Mason-Dixon line, Frémont drew less than 8000 votes. The Electoral College gave 174 votes to Buchanan, 114 to Frémont and 8 to Fillmore.

The Union was saved. "I believe now," wrote Howell Cobb's brother, "that no other man but Mr. Buchanan could have been elected with the opposition we have encountered at the North. He was The Man . . . the most suitable man for the times."[29] Back at Wheatland, his "segar" lit and the Madeira bottle open, President-elect Buchanan agreed.

20

CHARTING THE COURSE • 1856-1857

A NATIONAL AND CONSERVATIVE GOVERNMENT

On March first, 1857, James Buchanan, clad in a dressing gown and slippers, sat alone in his study trying to calm his nerves and itemize a list of incidentals which needed attention. They must all be ready in the morning when he would leave for Washington. He could hear Harriet and Miss Hetty walking about in the room directly above him; the murmur of their conversation and the occasional thump of a trunk lid annoyed him. Going to the door, he asked one of the servants to call J. B. Henry who had been acting as his private secretary during the past hectic months.

Buchanan gave him a few instructions and went upstairs to his bedroom where he removed his dressing gown and tried on the vest and coat of his inauguration suit. Mr. Metzger, the tailor on East King Street, had delivered it the week before, and it showed the signs of his fine craftsmanship.[1] Outwardly it was unobtrusive; a plain black coat of French cloth, but into the lining was worked a magnificent design of thirty-one stars representing the states of the Union, with Pennsylvania dominating the center. It would fit, he thought to himself. A man ought always to be plain, dignified, and restrained on the exterior, but he ought to wear beneath this external coat the knowledge of his true talents and character. Let there be more hidden in reserve than outwardly shows. Thus would a man always be competent to the tasks assigned to him.

As he tried on the flowered satin vest, he ruminated about his inauguration ceremony. For him, it would be no inauguration at all; it would be more like a culmination. What would it be for the Union? The election of 1856, for the first time in American history, had probed down to the bedrock question of union or disunion; survival or disruption. The cliché of editors and orators had become the *bona fide* statement of the fundamental problem: the Union *was* in danger.

After his election, Buchanan wrote: "The great object of my administration will be to arrest, if possible, the agitation of the slavery

261

question at the North, and to destroy sectional parties. Should a kind Providence enable me to succeed in my efforts to restore harmony to the Union, I shall feel that I have not lived in vain."[2] He re-echoed the theme to Mr. Justice Grier.[3] To the students of Franklin and Marshall College, who visited at Wheatland a few weeks after the election, he confided that "the object of my administration will be to destroy any sectional party, North or South, and harmonize all sections of the Union under a national and conservative government, as it was fifty years ago."[4]

UNION ABOVE SECTION, PARTY ABOVE FACTION

In the interval between the election and the inauguration Buchanan could do little or nothing about the slavery dispute, but even before taking the oath of office he could strike a blow against sectionalism by carefully picking his Cabinet. He would not incorporate into it men of different political opinions. He would choose only those who had proved their party regularity and demonstrated their devotion to nation above section. There would be no extremist in the Cabinet.

As soon as Buchanan received the facts and figures of the election, he made a study to determine the proper dispensation of office and political favor. He wanted to unite the national Democrats with the Union Whigs and to destroy the subversive league of northern fanatics and southern rebels. The election returns showed that Buchanan had won all the slave states except Maryland (which went for Fillmore), and had carried the free states of Pennsylvania, Indiana and California. Frémont had won the six New England states plus Michigan and Wisconsin. Elsewhere Buchanan and Frémont had run a tight race and neither had achieved a popular majority.

The election strongly highlighted the sectional nature of the Republicans and the national appeal of the Democrats.[5] Frémont commanded a majority in only one of the geographical sections of the nation; he scarcely had any vote south of the Mason-Dixon line. Buchanan beat Frémont in seven of the eight geographical sections.[6] But the American party, by running Millard Fillmore, had complicated the election and induced a critical 21 per cent of the voters to dodge the issue on which the safety of the nation rested. There was no way of knowing what these voters stood for.

Buchanan knew definitely what kind of Cabinet he wanted. To keep a Democratic bastion in the heart of the enemy's country, he needed a New Englander. Either Nathan Clifford of Maine or Isaac Toucey of Connecticut would meet the requirements of experience and party regularity. New York might as well be left out; the two Democratic factions of the state were, after a generation of feuding, hopelessly irreconcilable. He could pick no New Yorker without widening the split. Pennsylvania had to have a Cabinet post, but the selection here would be as difficult as in New York. The Democrats remained so faction ridden that the selection of any veteran might wreck the party. Buchanan planned to avoid trouble by appointing a personal friend who was a newcomer to Pennsylvania politics, J. Glancy Jones of Reading, who had once lived in the South and commanded confidence and respect there.

Virginia, which had loyally supported Buchanan, had earned a place. He promptly offered one to Henry A. Wise, but the governor turned him down. He also offered John Slidell a Cabinet appointment but he, too, declined because he preferred to remain in the Senate.

As an antidote for northern suspicion, Buchanan wanted in a position of high responsibility the most outspoken southern unionist he could find. Howell Cobb of Georgia was that man. He had stumped the North during the campaign and had given to thousands a thrilling demonstration that the South contained some of the most aggressive and determined champions of union in the land. After Slidell's refusal, Buchanan wanted Cobb to have the State Department, and Cobb let it be known that he would serve only in that station.

The Union Whigs had contributed so many votes to Buchanan's election that he wished to confirm their conversion to Democracy by including one of their leaders in his official staff. Other needs, however, would have to be taken care of first.

The Northwest presented the worst problem. Here, in the upper Mississippi Valley, Senator Stephen A. Douglas of Illinois and Jesse D. Bright of Indiana were locked in mortal combat for control of the power and patronage of the party. Buchanan detested Douglas, considering him the irresponsible destroyer of the slavery settlement of 1850. To Buchanan, the stupidity of the Kansas-Nebraska Bill was overshadowed only by the avaricious personal ambition of its author. Unhappily, Douglas could not be ignored for he had nearly taken the 1856 nomination, and with a strong following in the South he commanded a power essential to the party. Bright had brought in the vote of Indiana for Buchanan when Douglas had failed to deliver Illinois, but Douglas threatened to wreck the party if Bright went into the Cabinet. Bright was determined that no friend of Douglas should receive an appointment. Under these circumstances, Buchanan felt he dared not commit himself to either for the time being.

At this point in his planning, Buchanan received the reports from California. They gave him an increased majority and suggested one new idea. He could not give California a position, but he could again endorse a federally-built railroad to the Pacific which would gratify the westerners and weaken Douglas, who was working in political team with Jefferson Davis in the South. The renewed prospect of a Pacific railroad

263

would trip one or the other, for each was determined to have the eastern terminus of any such road in his own back yard. He advocated the railway in a letter which he sent to the press December 8.

Wheatland was open house during November and December, though the stream of visitors never reached the 400 daily that some of the newspapers reported. John Appleton of Maine, whom Buchanan planned to install as the editor of an Administration newspaper in Washington, even lived at Wheatland for a time, to the great distress of John Forney, who wanted the editorial job. Forney rushed in and out continually in the early weeks, until he learned that he was not considered for the Cabinet and would not be awarded the Washington editorship.

Buchanan did not know what to do with Forney. He had supported Pierce up to the very last moment before the Cincinnati Convention. Although he had cleared the position with Buchanan beforehand, this did not mollify Buchanan's friends; and nothing would ever make Forney acceptable to Virginia Democrats. He had gotten into a violent fight with the Wise faction while Buchanan was in London, and had expressed himself with such abandon that he was lucky to have escaped a duel. Buchanan's Virginia friends would have preferred the devil to Forney in any responsible position, and Buchanan needed Virginia back of him. Forney wrote that he was staying close to the foot of the throne to counteract the southern insistence that he should not edit the Washington *Union*. "I can be elected Senator," he said, "but I will not be. I will go into the Union, or I will stay home and —. I confess I am sick at heart. Met Mr. Glancy Jones. He is for the Cabinet. God save us."[7]

During November, Buchanan went on a brief trip with Lewis Cass of Michigan, and visited Governor Wise and Senator Douglas in Philadelphia. The more he listened and the more mail he read, the more complex his Cabinet problem became and the more secretive he grew about it. By early December he knew that Wise and Slidell would not serve, that Bright was blocked, that Clifford was unacceptable to Pierce, that Jones would be rejected by the Democrats of Pennsylvania, and that none of the Democratic leaders was willing to give up a Cabinet place to a Union Whig. Only Cobb remained a certainty, and he insisted on the State Department or nothing.

On December 1, Buchanan wrote that he was still "wholly uncommitted about the cabinet,"[8] and stated that he intended to keep his own counsel on the subject "even after I shall have formed a decided opinion, so that if circumstances should require a change, this may be made without giving offence."[9] By the end of the month Buchanan asked his friends to keep out of Lancaster because "everybody is now looked upon with a jealous & suspicious eye who visits Wheatland."[10] Howell Cobb, who should have been first in Buchanan's confidence, at last abandoned his curiosity and told his wife that he was ready "to let Old Buck fix up his Cabinet to suit himself—as . . . he will do anyhow."[11]

Perhaps Buchanan was wise to be silent, and to postpone any appointment until he had worked out a scheme incorporating all. But unhappily for him, his secrecy multiplied his difficulties. In the absence of a public announcement, every clique and faction of the Democracy which had a candidate to push or a trade to make got into the game. Manufacturers of public opinion to influence Buchanan's choice set up in every hole and corner of the nation.

False rumors refueled all the old factional fights. Forney raged against Virginia, "For Hunter we never will or can go. Against him we shall wage war to the knife and the knife to the hilt . . . by the Great God they shall find that if we are Democrats we are not negro slaves and dogs . . . anybody before Hunter."[12] Wrote another: "If the Free Soilers at the North have been as busy as the Southern Rights men . . . his Cabinet will have to be taken from the extremes of the party, leaving all the national men out."[13]

Buchanan hoped that the first week of the New Year would settle one worrisome deadlock, the problem of Forney and Jones. The Pennsylvania Legislature would soon elect a Senator to replace Richard Brodhead who for the past six years had made it a kind of religious mission to vilify and discredit the Sage of Wheatland. Buchanan had hoped to send Jeremiah Black to the Senate, but Forney now had his heart set upon that place. Something had to be done for Forney. He was now in a state of near frenzy, and if he ever lost control of himself he could and would play havoc with the Democracy in Pennsylvania. Buchanan could not possibly have him in the Cabinet and he could not trust him with the Washington *Union*, but he would be pretty safe in the Senate; at least a vast improvement over Brodhead. If Forney went into the Senate, there would be no resistance to Jones in the Cabinet.

After much prodding Buchanan wrote a letter to Harrisburg stating his personal preference for Forney as Senator. The letter was both restrained and belated, but it was nonetheless a direct endorsement, 'which was more than Buchanan had ever before given to anyone in a Pennsylvania senatorial race.[14]

A few days later the telegraph wires hummed with the news of the election of Simon Cameron as Senator. "My God, what a scene of public corruption and wholesale bribery it was," exploded Forney.[15] The Democrats nominated Forney but Cameron, after mobilizing the opposition, discovered he needed only a handful of votes to win. He first utilized David Taggart, a state senator from Northumberland County, whose bank Cameron had threatened to close and then relented on a promise of political subservience. He also enlisted the aid of Charles Penrose. These two successfully appealed to three Democrats who were looking for a chance to square old scores with Forney. For Buchanan it was the worst thing that could have happened; it destroyed the very keystone of his plan. Pennsylvania Democracy was to have been the model and the guide; the symbol of national spirit and forbearance in the party. Now it was a laughing stock. Howell Cobb wrote to his wife "that Simon Cameron, an abolitionist, was elected. . . . It is a hard blow not only upon Forney but upon Mr. Buchanan and the democratic party. I have never felt more deeply a result than I do this."[16]

Forney's defeat raised a strong wave of sympathy for him which broke in the form of demands that Buchanan now put him in the Cabinet on the principle "that great generals ought to care for . . . the gallant and true-hearted that nobly fell with their face to the enemy, particularly when treason worked their fall."[17] But if Buchanan had decided nothing else, he had determined not to have Forney in the Cabinet. He now reconciled himself to another firm conclusion: he could not have Jones, either, and in great embarrassment sat down to ask Jones to release him from his former promise.[18] Angry and hurt, Jones tried to maintain his claim, but he ultimately gave Buchanan a written release and intimated that he might accept a mission to give the appearance of party harmony.

Knowing that Forney, with five children, mounting debts, and no job, desperately needed money, Buchanan urged that he take the Liverpool consulate, the richest place he could find in the non-policy making branch of the government, but Forney would have none of it. He would not go abroad, and he refused to serve at home in any subordinate position.[19] Unable to find any post he could conscientiously give which Forney would accept, Buchanan temporarily gave up the effort; but when he learned that his old friend was drinking heavily and had threatened to mortgage the Washington property which was the only remaining security for his family, Buchanan stepped in, arranged to act as trustee of the property for Mrs. Forney and the children, and devised a temporary income for Forney as paid correspondent for various Democratic papers.[20]

In January it was rumored that Buchanan was seriously considering Robert J. Walker for the State Department, proclaiming him for Pennsylvania. Walker had been born in Bellefonte, Pennsylvania, and grown up in Pittsburgh, but he was now a resident of Mississippi. He had strong national views and personally opposed slavery, although he was reconciled to it politically as a system sanctioned by law and tradition. The rumor concerning Walker disturbed Cobb and set in motion his enemies, Jefferson Davis and Stephen Douglas, who now began to push Lewis Cass for the top post in the Cabinet. They sought by this scheme to block Cobb and Bright so that Davis could gain control in the South and Douglas in the Northwest.[21] But Cobb, with great magnanimity and political astuteness, endorsed their candidate, "and that knocked all their calculations into 'pi.' "[22]

Buchanan neither liked nor respected Cass, but he did recognize him as an ideal symbol of his policy and saw in his appointment an opportunity to resolve several of his most embarrassing problems. Cass would undoubtedly accept, for he had just been voted out of his job as Senator from Michigan and would be reluctant to return home in defeat. He was a thorough nationalist, an undeviating party regular, an old-time Jacksonian, and a former presidential candidate. He would not make a good Secretary of State, for he was a notorious Anglophobe, and he was so old, lethargic, and indolent that Buchanan planned to instruct others to do the work. But Cass would reinforce the idea of party unity. Cobb had agreed to defer to him, though to no other, as head of the Cabinet and would take the next position, possibly the Treasury.[23] Cass's installation would break the critical stalemate; confound Davis and Douglas without giving them cause for resentment; pacify Bright who had won his Senatorship and would not contest the issue with Cass; permit Buchanan to have Cobb in the Cabinet; and make room for maneuver in other selections because the greatest pressures were removed. So far nothing had been given to Pennsylvania, but she would have to wait. At this point Buchanan decided to go to Washington and finish the Cabinetmaking.

He arrived in Washington on January 27 during the worst cold wave in decades and went immediately to the National Hotel. Forney reported in the *Pennsylvanian* that President Pierce and Senator Douglas sent Buchanan dinner invitations, which he declined,[24] but certain persons who were on the scene stated that he dined with Pierce, Douglas, and others on the night of January 31 and the next evening attended a dinner party given by Mrs. Douglas.[25] One thing is known; he talked with Douglas, and the Little Giant reported afterwards that the atmosphere was chilly. He was not referring to the weather.[26]

Buchanan consulted at length with men he particularly trusted; Cobb, Wise, Slidell, and others. Cobb wrote to his wife on January 31 that "Old Buck still avers he has not communicated to anyone" his Cabinet plans, but he included in the same letter a list of probabilities. His accurate "guessing" leads one to suspect that the decisions were made during these consultations.[27]

Buchanan returned home on February 3. A cryptic note in the Wrightsville *Star* reported that the president-elect "footed it" the 10 miles from Wrightsville to Lancaster.[28] The visits to Wheatland continued: Bright, Douglas, Dan Sickles, and a stream of Pennsylvania Democrats. All reported that Buchanan was still planning Cabinet appointments, but more likely he was giving most of his time to the inaugural address.

Forney's friends were furious that Glancy Jones was going around blabbing that he had been invited for an advance perusal of the address and was acting very uppity about it.[29]   Of the Cabinet, Buchanan wrote in mid-February: "Applications are pouring in to me recommending different gentlemen for the Cabinet; but they are too late . . . the testimony is closed and the case ready for judgment. . . . I shall announce it in a few days."[30]

On February 17, Buchanan wrote the first of a series of letters that would settle the composition of the Cabinet.   He informed Glancy Jones that he would definitely be out, and that Jeremiah Sullivan Black was to have the only place available to a Pennsylvanian.[31]   On the 18th he had it out with Forney, who wrote to Cobb of the interview: "Just from Lancaster where I have heard *my doom*. . . . It wounds me like a blow."[32] On the 20th and 21st, Buchanan was "mysteriously missing," according to the local press, but it is certain that he was at Wheatland, for he wrote to Cobb from there on the 21st and formally asked him to accept the Treasury Department.

The same day he wrote to Cass, offering the State Department under conditions which would let Cass have the honor but place the work and responsibility in the hands of assistants named by Buchanan.   He then invited Aaron V. Brown of Tennessee to take the Post Office, and Jacob Thompson of Mississippi the Interior Department.   The Navy Department and Attorney-Generalship were still unfilled; into these places he wanted to put a Pennsylvanian and a New Englander, one of them, if possible, a Union Whig.   Buchanan felt he could go no further at the moment.   On February 25 he published in the newspapers a notice that positively no more visitors would be received at Wheatland until after the inaugural ceremonies.

To close the door to callers was very much out of character for Buchanan, even when he had a presidential inaugural address to finish. His "mysterious absence" and his subsequent seclusion resulted from something a good deal more serious than a wish for peace and quiet. James Buchanan, along with dozens of other guests, had gotten a bad case of the "National Hotel disease" during his recent visit to the Capital.   The disorder was a kind of dysentery, accompanied by violent diarrhea, severe intestinal inflammation, and distressing persistence.   The affair was partially hushed up, but rumors amplified the brief reports which attributed the cause to frozen plumbing which in some way had contaminated the water supply.   Some averred that rats, driven from the walls by the cold, had sought refuge in the attic and there tumbled into the open vats in which rain water was collected for the hotel system.   This explanation expanded into the tale that poisoned rats were purposely placed in the water tanks.   Other experts concluded that poisonous gas from sewers which were connected with the kitchen sinks had been stopped up by the freezing of sewer outlets and had poisoned the food.   The probable reason was that sewer waste had backed up into the kitchen, contaminated the area, and infected the servants, who passed the infection on to the guests. At such time it was inevitable that there should be an ugly rumor of an attempted assassination.[33]

Whatever the cause of the epidemic, Dr. Jonathan Foltz, who treated Buchanan after his return to Wheatland, ordered him to live elsewhere during the preinaugural period, preferably the President House where all the water came from a tested spring.[34]

Buchanan felt he had nearly completed the first part of his task. The Cabinet would represent national interests and the inaugural would emphasize the same theme. Every extremist from Maine to Florida and every faction from New York to California had had a go at him and been given a fair hearing. They had forced him to alter some of his personal choices, but he had held firm on the principle governing the final selections. There would be not one factionist or one sectional fanatic among his advisors; all were devoted to the Union above section; to the party above faction; and to a desire to preserve the *status quo* at least long enough to calm the public mind. The Cabinet would be national and conservative.

Buchanan had expected to defer the second great task, dealing with slavery, until after the inauguration. But during February he was drawn into a correspondence which gave him hope that part of the problem might be solved at a stroke. While in Washington he had learned that the Supreme Court was nearly ready to bring in a decision on the Dred Scott case. Eager to have the backing of the Court, he wrote to Justices John Catron and Robert Grier about the wisdom of having the Supreme Court issue a thorough expository opinion on the power of Congress over slavery in the territories. Buchanan knew what the majority decision would be— that Scott had no right to sue because he was not a citizen—and he knew that two dissenting Justices would prepare a statement supporting their views. Should not the majority do likewise, and make explicit that Congress had no power over slavery in the territories; therefore, the Missouri Compromise had been unconstitutional? Buchanan strongly urged this action as the best possible way to get the slavery debate out of Congress and settle once and for all the sectional contention. If the country was so far gone that it would attack the Supreme Court, then the Union was already cracked beyond repair.[35]

Buchanan stirred and shook his head as the room came back into focus and his rumination turned into the realities of March 1, 1857. The inaugural coat still lay upon the bed. Tomorrow morning he was leaving for Washington.

"I DO SOLEMNLY SWEAR"

Lancaster was up betimes on the cold, snowy morning of March 2. The church bells began ringing at six to inform the people it was time to begin the march to the depot. The marshals, in their gaily colored silk scarfs and white rosettes, cantered about waving their batons and shouting lustily at the straggling crowd along West King Street to form a line and close ranks, in readiness to follow Buchanan's carriage the moment it arrived. After half an hour of shivering and foot stamping, the marshals very sensibly abandoned their pride of organization to the need of action and started a parade toward Wheatland to intercept the president-elect. The band fell to its work with zest but after about five minutes had to give up the attempt because of the cold, and clambered aboard the wagon provided for its use. At Wheatland it was learned that Buchanan's party was still not ready to leave. At last, to the echo of rousing cheers, the carriage came round to the front portico. Buchanan, Miss Lane, James Buchanan Henry, and Miss Hetty Parker stepped into it, and without further ado the procession, with Captain John H. Duchman's Lancaster Fencibles proudly leading the way, was off to the railway station.

Superintendent Joseph B. Baker had provided a special train of four cars the sides and windows of which had been decorated with patriotic symbols and scenes from Wheatland. The presidential party boarded, acknowledged a last rousing ovation, and left for Baltimore. There a change of stations required passengers to go to the other end of the city for the Washington trains.

En route a message was delivered warning that a rowdy mob of about 1000 anti-Buchanan Know-Nothings was swarming around the Calvert Street Station looking for trouble. The party therefore got off at the Charles Street Station, where several companies of cavalry, sabers drawn, waited to accompany the presidential party to Barnum's Hotel for a huge midday banquet. But Buchanan was so ill that he retired immediately until three o'clock when he boarded the train for the capital. Meanwhile, the Lancaster Fencibles, who had to walk between stations, ran into the foiled Know-Nothings, had to fight their way through, and were so much harassed during their march that they missed the train.[36]

Despite the specific orders of Dr. Foltz and the urgent pleas of Senators Slidell, Bigler, and others, Buchanan went to the National Hotel as a mark of confidence in its proprietor, an old personal friend. He still had two Cabinet appointments to make and the address to finish. The politicians assembled at Washington took up every minute he would spare them and tried to "help" him complete these tasks. At one stage he added a sentence to the inaugural implying that settlers in Kansas and Nebraska had no power over slavery in the territories until the time of framing a

270

state constitution. News of this opinion leaked out to General Cass who, as an originator of the popular sovereignty idea back in 1848, could not swallow this interpretation and told Buchanan bluntly that he would refuse to serve in the Cabinet if this statement appeared in the speech. Buchanan cut it out. He concluded that he could not complete the Cabinet in such turmoil and decided to postpone the work until the day after the inauguration. Furthermore, he was very sick with a recurrence of the dysentery, and he was shocked to learn that the disease had broken out again with increased virulence among the guests at the hotel.

A faultless spring day dawned on March 4 to grace the inauguration festivities. The thousands who had poured into the city were glad to be up early from their makeshift beds in the parlors, dining rooms, and public lobbies which had been pressed into service to accommodate the overflow crowd. The bells began to ring, and slowly members of military companies in gay uniforms appeared on the streets, citizens hung flags and bunting from windows along the line of march, and members of the Twelfth Ward Democratic Club of Philadelphia redoubled their efforts to sell more tickets at five dollars a head to the Inauguration Ball.

By noon the three groups of parade marshals, with their white, yellow or blue scarfs and saddle cloths trimmed with rosettes had the thirty-odd fire companies, militia battalions, bands, floats, and groups of artisans in line; and the procession started down Pennsylvania Avenue to the National Hotel. There Buchanan was joined by vice-president-elect Breckinridge, and all were ready to proceed when it was found that President Pierce was not on hand. A twenty-minute delay ensued until someone on the arrangements committee discovered that through an oversight, Pierce had been completely forgotten. After a flurry of excitement and consultation, the committee picked Pierce up at the Willard Hotel and at last the waiting crowds were relieved of their impatience by the sight of an elegant, four-horse barouche, containing the president and the president-elect. Ahead of them, leading the procession, was a huge float drawn by six white horses bearing a lady symbolizing the Goddess of Liberty on a high platform. Members of the Keystone Club rode beside the open presidential carriages, and behind them came a float with a large model of a warship.

At the Capitol, the group which was to share the inauguration platform gathered first in the Senate Chamber where Vice-President Breckinridge took the oath of office. All then filed out onto the stand in front of the east portico. In the shuffle of getting seated, Buchanan and Chief Justice Taney met momentarily at the front of the rail and held a brief chat. Some of those who witnessed this exchange swore to their dying day that at this very moment Taney told Buchanan how the Supreme Court would decide the Dred Scott case, and that Buchanan instantly added this information to his address. What they did not know was that he had more than a week before learned the news from one of the Justices.[37]

The address was soon over and the oath of office administered. Buchanan felt thankful that his queasy stomach had responded to the brandy and medication which Dr. Foltz had given him just a half hour before and that he had been able to complete the ceremony with dignity. The address had been sincere, if unexciting; that was its purpose, his purpose, and the country's need. Below, hawkers were already selling a kerchief-sized edition of it, printed on silk.[38] The audience discovered nothing new in it except two statements—that Buchanan would not run again, and that the Supreme Court would soon settle the issue of slavery in the Territories. Foreign correspondents wrote that the new Administration would be a compromise, a postponement of the solution of gripping issues.

That night the whole of Washington seemed determined to crowd into the Inauguration Ball. The managers had built a temporary structure 235 feet long and 77 feet wide on Judiciary Square for this function. Gold stars winked against the white ceiling, and bunting of red, white and blue festooned the walls. "Such a jam, such heat," wrote a lady who was there, "I never either saw or felt before. . . . The members of Congress got so over-excited with wine that they had to be locked up in the upper rooms lest they should reappear in the ballroom."[39]

Miss Lane, hailed by enthusiastic newsmen as "Our Democratic Queen," appeared resplendent in a white dress decorated with artificial flowers and wearing a necklace of many strands of pearls. President Buchanan and Harriet mingled with the crowd, talked to members of the diplomatic corps, and enjoyed the cheers and gaiety. But they soon left and shortly thereafter the doors of the White House closed gently upon the new tenants.

Back at the Ball, the Russian Minister, Baron de Stoeckl, was trying valiantly to dance with Madame Sartiges, wife of the French Minister. He remarked to her that the current situation in Washington reminded him of Paris just before the Revolution of 1830. There, at a ball given by Louis Philippe, Talleyrand whispered to the monarch, "Sire, we are dancing on a volcano."[40]

21

THE PRESIDENT'S FAMILY • 1857

BACHELOR IN THE WHITE HOUSE

Glamorous as the White House has always seemed to those who have imagined the day when they might occupy it, the reality of moving in has brought many a new president back to the workaday world with a thump. He finds himself, after the tumult of inauguration, just another human being walking into a strange house hastily vacated by the previous tenants. Buchanan, to be sure, fared better than Pierce who, after receiving visitors until past midnight of his inauguration day, fumbled his way upstairs to his living quarters to discover that they were a shambles and no beds had been made up. Recalling this experience, Pierce graciously moved out of the White House a day early so that Miss Hetty could prepare a more homelike reception for Buchanan upon his return with Harriet from the inaugural ball.

Most of Pierce's White House staff stayed in service. Miss Hetty and Harriet for a time tried joint superintendence of household operations, but the experiment soon raised such a fuss that Buchanan faced a domestic crisis. Miss Harriet intended to be Mistress of the White House; if not, she would pack her trunks and get out. Miss Hetty said nothing but continued quietly to give instructions to the servants. Buchanan then began to understand Martin Van Buren's recent advice that the most important appointment he would make in his Administration would be a good White House steward. The new president found one and told Miss Hetty to return to Wheatland, but he invited her to visit the White House as one of the family whenever she wished. He agreed that Harriet should dictate all matters of social protocol, leaving the execution of details to the steward.

The White House family included James Buchanan Henry, Elliott Eskridge Lane, and for a time Dr. Foltz. As Buchanan suffered severely from the effects of the National Hotel disease for six weeks after the inauguration, Foltz stayed until the affliction had run its course. Eskridge Lane, too, had caught the infection, thought he had it under

273

control, and then suddenly died of a violent attack during April. It was a dreadful setback for Buchanan, who had come to rely heavily upon Eskridge, and another crushing blow to Harriet. She determined at this time to devote her life to "Nunc" and become a much more serious-minded young lady than she had been in the past.

The domestic routine slowly worked itself out. The household arose about 6:30, and finished breakfast by eight. The president retired to his second floor office, where he spent most of his time until noon receiving visitors. In an adjoining room, J. B. Henry read through all the incoming mail, sorted it for forwarding to the Departments or to the president, wrote a digest of contents on the outer leaf of each letter, and entered receipt of it and the name of the person to whom it was forwarded in his day book.

After lunch every day except Sunday and reception days, Buchanan met with the Cabinet and then went for an hour's stroll about Lafayette Square and through the residential district north of the White House. He bought a new carriage with trappings, but he never used it except on infrequent state occasions or during the midsummer months. In July and August he stayed at the "Soldiers' Home," a stone cottage near Georgetown, and each morning drove in to Washington where he worked in a room at the State Department. Harriet pretty much ran her own life, spending the mornings planning or gracing social functions and the afternoons riding out on a beautiful white horse she had recently acquired. Riding side-saddle and accompanied only by her groom, she came to be a familiar and striking sight in Washington.

In the evening the whole White House family, including Miss Hetty when she was there, dined informally about seven. Buchanan invited one or two Cabinet families and a few chosen friends to small weekly dinners with rarely more than fifteen present. Once a week he also gave a "state dinner" for about forty persons to entertain the members of the Supreme Court, the diplomatic corps, Senators, Representatives, governors, army and navy dignitaries, and important visitors. Buchanan made up the guest lists for these affairs, Harriet worked out the details of precedence at the table, and Buchanan Henry had the duty of pairing each gentleman with the lady he should escort to dinner. Harriet's task was perhaps the most difficult, for members of all political parties came to these dinners, and it was a matter of some delicacy to achieve the right order of precedence without seating mortal enemies next to each other. Her London training stood her in good stead and she managed her part with great cleverness and tact. After the guests left, the president retired to his study to read over the correspondence which his nephew-secretary had digested and sorted into appropriate folders. He wrote his own orders on papers he wished personally to attend and sent the rest back to the secretary's room for filing or forwarding. Before retiring he often read in the Bible or some religious work and then went to bed around midnight.[1]

THE CAPTAIN AND THE CREW

The members of Cabinet, too, had to establish their households and define their role in the new Administration. Everyone sensed that the capital faced the gayest social season in its history. Little social leadership had come from the White House since the days of Van Buren. Tyler had been restrained by Harrison's death, political schism, and the loss of his wife. Mrs. Polk had governed social functions by the sternest rules of Presbyterian morality. She banned dancing, liquor, and even nonalcoholic refreshments at White House functions. She disapproved of cards, horse racing, betting and loose joviality. "This is a very genteel affair," a Congressman once remarked at one of her parties. Without a smile, she replied, "I have never seen it otherwise." Mrs. Taylor, a Maryland blue blood, thought commerce with politicians was degrading and declined to appear publicly with the president. Taylor's death threw a pall over social activities which Fillmore's shy school-teacher wife did nothing to raise. Mrs. Pierce never recovered from the sudden death of her son, Benny, and avoided public appearances. The election of Buchanan had brought release from the terrible tensions which gripped the nation during the campaign of 1856 and put into the White House a wealthy Epicurean, a gay bachelor with a flair for society and a Chesterfieldian knowledge of its ways. And Harriet Lane, lovely, sprightly and eager for the fun of social competition promised to bring an enchantingly new tone to White House festivities. The president unofficially confirmed the public expectation in a note to his liquor merchants, a few weeks after inauguration, rebuking them for sending champagne in small bottles. "Pints are very inconvenient in this house," he wrote, "as the article is not used in such small quantities."

Although the members of the Cabinet held similar political opinions, none of them had known each other or Buchanan very well prior to March 4, 1857. Lewis Cass, who had been a general in the War of 1812, was by 1857 a ponderous but feeble old fellow with a massive bald head which he kept covered with an ancient brown wig. He held the State Department only as a symbol of old-time Democracy, while the president and John Appleton did the work. Cass enjoyed the prestige of his station. He rented two adjacent houses, furnished them regally, and gave his daughters Mrs. Henry Ledyard and Belle Cass free rein to entertain on the grand scale. Buchanan had never liked Cass since their days of rivalry and the old general, though grateful for his rescue from oblivion, would have been less than human had he not felt a little uncomfortable playing the subordinate. Black wrote, "They never spoke evil of one another, but

275

Buchanan learned to think unpleasantly of Cass's faults and was not kind to his virtues."[2] At Cabinet meetings Cass rarely said much, but kept opening and shutting his mouth, and sucking his breath between his teeth as if he constantly tasted something disagreeable.

Howell Cobb became the acknowledged premier of the Cabinet. Buchanan formed a warm attachment to the chubby, good-natured, forty-one-year-old Georgian who had come to Congress in 1842, served as Speaker of the House during the 1850 crisis, and then returned to Georgia to fight down the secessionists there by allying with Union Whigs and capturing the governorship. He returned to the House in 1855 as an anti-Douglas, pro-Union Democrat. Buchanan found many ideas and experiences they shared in common. The University of Georgia had kicked Cobb out for about the same reasons that Dickinson had expelled Buchanan, too much enthusiasm and not enough respect for the professors and the rules. They often laughed about the escapades of their college days. Cobb, like Buchanan, never could gain solid political control of his own county, but he never had any trouble carrying the district or state. He disliked the principle of slavery and hoped the system would slowly die from economic pressure. Cobb calculated that he would have more net income if he sold his plantation and invested the money, but he refused to cast his slaves adrift as freed men with no one responsible for their care and did not want to sell them because this would break up the families.

It pleased Cobb to be the favorite, but he soon learned he had to pay for it. Buchanan gave him "the duty" every time he went on vacation to Lancaster or Bedford, often called him for special consultation, and had him move into the White House for weeks at a time when his wife was in Georgia. Howell tried for three months to get back to Athens to bring Mary Ann Cobb and a newborn son (their fourth child) to Washington and told his wife he would come "whether the President will permit me or not." But he feared to defy Buchanan and finally sent his assistant, Philip Clayton, for the family. Howell rented a house from Corcoran at 15th and I Streets which he christened the "Widower's Den" before the arrival of his wife in the autumn of 1857. A number of the new members of the Cabinet who had not yet moved their families to Washington held impromptu stag parties there in the early months of the Administration.[3]

Mary Ann Cobb possessed qualities which Buchanan much esteemed in women. She was unpretentious and inclined to domesticity. She enjoyed society but had no particular ambition to cut a figure in it. She talked with frankness, wit, and good sense, although she felt a little inadequate in small talk and gossip. Buchanan admired her a good deal more than she did him; she complained that he worked Howell too hard and acted too dignified, making her nervous for fear she would not do or say the right thing.

Mrs. Cobb brought with her a sprightly young widow, Mrs. Elizabeth C. Craig, who had achieved some notoriety by detonating a local civil war on the issue whether she or a rival was the most beautiful lady of Athens, Georgia. This grave crisis split the university, realigned county politics, and led to combat between citizens of the town. Mrs. Craig quit the fray with a flourish, announcing that she would go to Washington and snare the president. "Nothing short of the first man in office will answer," she wrote to Howell in advance of her arrival. When Buchanan invited her to live at the White House some months later, betting odds began to turn in her favor.[4]

Jacob Thompson of Mississippi, Secretary of the Interior, proved to be one of the most popular members of the Cabinet circle. "Winning, able, persuasive in argument, affectionate, and warm hearted, he melted opposition rather than destroyed it."[5] Such a man was after Buchanan's own heart, and the two achieved a mutual respect which even the passions of civil war could not wholly destroy. Thompson was well acquainted with land policy and Indian affairs, though he had little public experience outside Congress. He moved into a house at Eighteenth and G Streets where he let his vivacious wife, Kate, and her niece, Miss Wiley, run social events to suit their fancy. Buchanan preferred Kate Thompson above all the Cabinet wives, possibly because she was so much of a flirt and turned her best coquetry on him, or perhaps because she was so impetuous and passionate, qualities that he particularly admired in others, having so little of them himself. Mrs. Cobb called her "an easy and free-hearted woman."[6] Buchanan used to drop in unexpectedly at her house when her husband was out of town, but she played the game and generally walked him over to Cobb's where they bantered away the night. She was scatterbrained and bubbly, but she knew how to get favors out of the Old Chief when others had failed.

Postmaster General Aaron V. Brown and his wife brought with them from Tennessee more wealth than they knew what to do with and determined to show it off to Washington society. Mrs. Brown fancied herself above the standing rules of etiquette and brashly gave dinners without thought of protocol or precedence. She seated guests where she pleased, and if the French Minister found himself at the wrong end of the table and beside some territorial representative, it did not trouble the hostess. Mrs. Brown and her daughter soon became known in Washington as "the diamonds." "They are the only ladies of the 'priory council' who *patronize* jewels and trains," wrote an acquaintance. "Entre nous, they evince something of the *vulgarity* of wealth."[7]

Other members of the Cabinet lived more modestly and engaged only in the social activities which their station demanded. Jeremiah S. Black did not even know he was to be included in the Cabinet as Attorney

General until after the Senate had confirmed him. Black's wife and his daughter Mary may have had social ambitions, but they had neither the money nor the personal graces to gratify their hopes. Black was a curious combination of brilliant lawyer and miscast dramatic actor. He loved to toss compliments to pretty ladies and could call Milton, Shakespeare, or Shelley to his aid at will, but he lacked the feather touch and seemed to caress with a sledge hammer. Some women thought him disgusting and others, foolish, but closest to truth was the remark of one recipient of his gallantry who remarked that he reminded her of an elephant trying to dance a hornpipe. He was honest as the day, and decisive as a thunderclap. As the Administration wore on, Buchanan more and more leaned upon the strength of his mind and will. Black got on better with the Cabinet than did his family and was always welcome at formal or informal gatherings. Howell Cobb's young son paid him the ultimate compliment by naming his new dog "Jerry Black."

John Buchanan Floyd, governor of Virginia as his father had been before him, participated little in the whirlwind of society. His wife had a bad fall shortly after he assumed the War Department which incapacitated her, and Floyd himself was plagued by illness. Even had health permitted, they would have found no pleasure in the social round. Buchanan liked Floyd and granted him favors and privileges not extended to others, insisting that he take time off to regain his health. But he worried about Floyd's fitness for his job, and found it necessary to reprimand him more often than any other Cabinet member.

At the beginning of the Administration, Buchanan knew Isaac Toucey, Secretary of the Navy, better than any of his staff, for he had served with Toucey in the Polk Cabinet. Toucey was mild, quiet and industrious. Because his wife suffered ill health, he stayed home most of the time he was not busy with office work.

This group comprised the "Administration." "The cabinet ladies," wrote one of them, "are all pleasant and promise to be as one family. They are called here 'The President's Family,' and surely the gentlemen are as much at ease as several sons with a kind, indulgent father. The President, I think, is the greatest man living."[8]

PAYDAY FOR POLITICIANS

Buchanan had expected a wild scramble for patronage, but the reality far exceeded even what he had steeled himself to endure. Not only were there more applicants than ever before but also fewer jobs. Not since the inauguration of Van Buren, twenty years before, had one Democratic Administration succeeded another. Now the offices were filled with Pierce

278

men who could not be swept out without disrupting the party. Furthermore, Buchanan for a generation had been accepting political aid but never had achieved any office that gave him power to pay off party debts. In the Secretaryship of State his influence on appointments had been slight. Now, when he found himself for the first time in an administrative position with direct control over patronage, his obligations had grown larger and the expectations greater than he had realized. All his old-time friends came for jobs, and they all brought long lists of *their* friends who had been promised their rewards. Even if these requests had not created an impossible situation, Buchanan's ancient policy of amalgamation and the reconciliation of contesting groups would have done so. He had long advocated a division of the spoils between Democratic factions, and in the recent elections he had promised to let the Whigs come in for a share. Thus, he probably doubled the number of those who felt justly entitled to patronage. In addition to all these pressures there was still another: the ambition of presidential aspirants for 1860, whose appetites had been whetted by Buchanan's inaugural pronouncement that he would retire after a single term. Douglas, Hunter, Walker, Davis, Cobb, and others all demanded special consideration and were ready to fight for it. It required no wizard to foresee the result. Whatever patronage policy should be developed, there would be unprecedented disappointment and discontent throughout the Democratic ranks, and no "administration party" at all. Had Buchanan taken the governorship of Pennsylvania in 1848, he might have been better prepared to solve the problem he now faced, but he came to the presidency with almost every kind of public service experience except executive.

Buchanan adopted the general rule that Pierce appointees who were good men and held commissions for a specified time should retain their offices until their terms expired. In the case of ministers and consuls, the incumbents should have an automatic tenure of four years from the date of their original appointment unless they requested relief earlier. Appointees with indefinite tenure would have to be judged on the merits of each case. Buchanan hoped to spread the availability of many choice jobs throughout his term. Pierce had installed a good many of his friends in the last two years of his Administration when he hoped to promote his own renomination. By leaving these men in office, Buchanan could hold their jobs as prospects and have some important gifts to offer in the latter stages of his term, without need to remove his own appointees to create vacancies.[9]

The Cabinet, meeting for four or five hours nearly every day, considered little but the patronage for the first several months. Buck Henry sorted out the thousands of requests and recommendations which came directly to the White House, and the individual Cabinet members got hundreds more daily to add to the pile. Cobb reported returning to the Treasury office late at night after a hard day's work to find a bushel basket of unopened mail on the floor beside his desk.[10]

Even had these men been endowed with peculiar genius, they would have faced several grave disadvantages in making appropriate selections from this mountain of requests. In the whole Cabinet group there was not one "big city" politician; there was no son of the new West; there was no "Young American;" there was no representative of industry; there was no spokesman for the free-soil Democrats. Buchanan could not have had a unified Cabinet with these elements included, but by surrounding himself with rural politicians and lawyers who frankly accepted the America of Andrew Jackson as their ideal he got only a partial and antiquated view of the forces astir in the land. Buchanan's supreme confidence in himself might have been his greatest asset had he become president in 1844 or 1848, for he then was in touch with the national scene. But for a decade he had been either out of office or out of the country, and lightning changes had been in progress. The friends he trusted and the enemies he understood had died or passed from view: Clay, Calhoun, Webster, Benton, Jackson, Adams, Polk, King, Shunk, Reynolds, Muhlenberg—nearly all those he had known in the House and Senate and in state politics—were gone. He did not know the new generation, and it did not know him except by reputation. The president had become very nearly a political stranger in his own country. But he had the confidence of rectitude and past success and hoped to proceed serenely. Otherwise he would not have remarked to a friend who warned that he would be hounded to death by job-hunters: "I'll be damned if I will."

Every one of the thirty-one states had its peculiar problems of faction. The Administration considered each in its turn, trying always to figure out some way to keep the party intact.[11]

The New York Democracy since 1848 had gone from schism to chaos. The Softs, erstwhile friends of Pierce, had split; the Hards had been weakened by loss of office, and an entirely new faction master-minded by New York City's upstart mayor, Fernando Wood, had taken over Tammany Hall with brass knuckles and clubs wielded by a crudely disciplined army of Bowery thugs. Not knowing quite what to do with this hell's brew of faction, Buchanan gave his old friend, Augustus Schell the key federal job, Collector of the Port of New York. Schell was rich, pious, aristocratic, pompous and, by comparison with those over whom he was expected to exercise control, a paragon of honesty. He does not, however, seem to have been very bright, and certainly could not supply the fight and leadership that his job demanded. He was much more at home presiding over the New York Historical Society than over the water-front gang in his charge. Within a few months the slippery Wood had talked him into an alliance which split the Hards, creating faction worse confounded. The New York Postmaster, Isaac V. Fowler, who presumably was to work in harness with Schell, now became head of the opposition to him, and Buchanan found that he had four Democratic factions knifing each other in the Empire State.[12]

Pennsylvania's problems proved peculiarly exasperating. The Keystone State had been crying foul play for its small share in federal patronage ever since the days of Jefferson. Buchanan tried to redress the balance, appointing so many Pennsylvanians that the appearance of another on the confirmation list came to be the signal for a roar of laughter in the Senate. Nevertheless, he brought no peace to the Democracy of Penn's land. To gratify Forney's faction, he appointed Joseph B. Baker as Collector of the Port of Philadelphia and made G. G. Wescott, one-time editorial assistant to Forney, postmaster of the city. But when he appointed Francis J. Grund, former henchman of Cameron, to a foreign post, rumblings began. And when he made George Bowman of the *Bedford Gazette* the editor of the Washington *Union*, lightning flashed. The great objection to Buchanan's appointments was his failure to give office to his political laborers of twenty and thirty years standing, notably Lynch, Forney, Plitt, and Foltz.

Each of these cases was different, yet every one was important. Davy Lynch was very insignificant in politics by 1857, but he remained a symbol of loyalty to Buchanan dating back to the 1820's. He had proved an inefficient public servant and could not be trusted with any place of responsibility, but he spurned any minor situation. Of late his condition had become pitiful; he drank incessantly and lived in abject poverty. He would not beg, but his wife wrote letters constantly asking for loans and Buchanan sent money to Lynch regularly. Davy talked with the quivering emotion of the loyal veteran, abandoned in the hour of need by the man who had climbed to fame and fortune on his bowed shoulders.[13] In the western region he greatly damaged Buchanan's reputation, for the enemy publicized his plight as a symbol of Buchanan's selfishness and ingratitude.

Forney presented a problem peculiarly painful. Buchanan never believed in giving important posts in the public service to persons who depended on politics for their living. To favor and encourage them would make them utterly dependent upon the vagaries of political fortune and sooner or later, in these days before Civil Service protection, place them in a position of such insecurity that they would always be for sale to the highest bidder. A sound party demanded men who could stand on their own feet, come success or failure at the polls. Forney was not in that category; he always needed a post.

Having been excluded from the Cabinet, denied the editorship of the Washington *Union*, and defeated in the race for the Senate, Forney raved wildly in his humiliation. The president, he complained to Black, has "never asked my counsel since the election." When Forney indignantly rejected the Liverpool consulate because he refused to be "exiled," he should have remembered that on two occasions Buchanan reluctantly accepted foreign "exile" for party purposes. Nor had the salary been as attractive as the one now offered to Forney.

Forney continued to clamor. "Read this letter to Mr. B.," he wrote Black, his intermediary. "Ask him if he is dead to the past in which I have served him almost like a slave. Ask him if he forgets the dark hours when his friends fled from him & I stood alone a monument of fidelity. . . . I speak not for myself alone, but for hundreds of thousands."[14] But Buchanan could offer nothing that Forney would take. "I mourn for Forney," he wrote. "I repeat, I mourn for Forney." It was misplaced pity, as Buchanan soon learned.

By mid-June, when Forney finally realized that Buchanan would not give him the trust and recognition he demanded, he all unknowingly wrote the real truth in an excited scrawl to Black. Mr. Buchanan insists, he said, that "if I succeed, it is to be as before, on my own merits."[15] Forney decided to go back to managing the *Pennsylvanian*. For this he needed money. Would Black please help him sell his wife's property in Washington? Then he learned that Buchanan had placed that property, in trust, out of his reach. There are those who still maintain that John Forney broke with Buchanan over the principle of Lecompton. Actually they had reached the point of rupture a year before; Lecompton would serve as a convenient excuse. Buchanan offered him no more prospects; if Forney could not influence this Administration, he had better get on the right track for the next. By September he was in the Douglas camp.[16]

George Plitt and his wife Sophie had acted as foster parents to the Lane children. Mary Lane made her home with them, and Harriet stayed at the Plitt "Shantee" in Philadelphia with as much freedom and an even warmer welcome than she found at Wheatland. Plitt, whom Buchanan had installed as clerk of the Philadelphia federal circuit court in 1846, was a quiet, unambitious, dutiful, and devoted friend. Before long the Dallas Democrats of Philadelphia began an attack on him, for their man Hopkinson had been ousted to make a place for Plitt. Buchanan offered him a different position, but he enjoyed the clerkship and declined. Later, faced with the ultimatum "fire Plitt or lose four votes in Congress," Buchanan asked Justice Grier to explain matters to Plitt and solicit his resignation. Grier emphasized the absolute necessity of vacating the clerkship and assured Plitt that "As [Buchanan's] *friend* you *deserve at his hands & should receive* some appointment of far greater value."[17] Plitt resigned, as requested, but Buchanan could not immediately find an appropriate opening for him. By the time there was one Buchanan could no longer command Senate confirmation for personal friends. Late in 1860, Sophie wrote ruefully to Harriet about the coming presidential election: "I don't care who is Prest. I worked for one nearly all my life—my husband was removed from office, & we have been ever since *counting every dollar to keep our home.* I despise politics. . . . There is too much ingratitude in political men & *I am not a spaniel.*"[18] George viewed it more calmly and remained friendly; he recognized at last the truth of Buchanan's oft-repeated advice to build his security on a firmer rock than party patronage. But Plitt's many friends wrote off Old Buck as an ungrateful wretch.

Buchanan had recommended Dr. Foltz's appointment as a Naval Surgeon back in 1829. Since then the effusive and emphatic young doctor had kept up a steady correspondence with Buchanan from ship and shore, and on numerous occasions had served as his personal physician. Since 1840 he had been keenly interested in politics; and whenever he was in Pennsylvania, he had worked hand in glove with Forney.

When Buchanan became president, Foltz demanded appointment as Chief of the Bureau of Medicine and Surgery. As the office was already in the capable hands of Dr. Whelan who, according to the patronage policy, would continue to serve until his term expired, Buchanan declined to replace him; and even had he done this, he almost certainly would not have selected Foltz. Foltz then began attacks on Dr. Whelan, sending proofs that he was a Douglas man and alleging that Buchanan retained him only because he was Catholic and could protect the Irish vote. Buchanan gave Dr. Foltz an appointment as physician to the Philadelphia Lazaretto, a respectable sinecure which permitted him to stay in the city with his family and conduct private practice along with his supervisory work at the hospital. Foltz took the job, but in anger and disappointment. Within a short time he became one of the most violent and abusive of all Buchanan's enemies.[19]

Buchanan spent much thought and emotional energy trying to solve the patronage problems of New York and Pennsylvania. His failure to satisfy the wishes of his four old-time Pennsylvania friends, whose names for over a quarter century had been synonymous with loyalty to him, damaged him politically. Knowing what he did of these men, he would have been wiser to break with them years before than to let himself into the situation he now faced. The rationalization of his course seemed perfectly sound to him; he offered all he conscientiously could; but in calmly believing that a rational excuse would satiate men who had waited so long in anticipation of their reward in his day of triumph, he proved that he had been living alone too much. He had lost touch with human feelings and reactions.

Buchanan left appointments in most of the other states to those who best knew the requirements, but he insisted upon reviewing in Cabinet all the major proposals. He appointed a Chicago postmaster recommended by Douglas but selected other federal officers in Douglas's territory without even consulting the Senator. He appointed J. Madison Cutts to a federal position against the written protest of Douglas and the advice of the entire Cabinet. Buchanan had known Cutts long before the Senator ever dreamed of politics, and had been fond of his daughter Adele, now Mrs. Douglas, as early as the Tyler administration. He replied to the Senator with calculated and insulting frankness. "Should I make the appointment, . . . it will be my own regard for Mr. Cutts and his family, and not because Senator Douglas has had the good fortune to become his son-in-law."[20]

In Louisiana, Slidell insisted that Buchanan should dismiss the old director of the New Orleans mint, regardless of the tenure rule.[21] Slidell was in trouble because the New Orleans postmaster he had recommended had been caught in a defalcation by Postmaster-General Campbell, an appointee of Pierce. Campbell charged that Kendall had been forced to steal post-office money to pay his gambling debts to Slidell. The Senator challenged Campbell to a duel but got no satisfaction.[22] Slidell now demanded the elimination of all remnants of the Pierce Administration in Louisiana.

Buchanan weakened rapidly under the strain. Many of his notes and letters of April, 1857, far from the methodical, delicate, and precise penmanship which is the trademark of his manuscripts, present a hurried, sloppy scrawl. Cobb remarked that the president had been so "annoyed and harassed" during April that he feared to request Georgia appointments until the air had cleared.[23] For all the routine procedure that Buchanan tried to establish, appointments continued to be made by hook or crook. In order to rush one through the Interior Department, Cobb took the original letter of application, endorsed on it "Request granted—J. Thompson, Sec'y. of Interior" and slipped it quietly into the "approved" pile in Thompson's office.[24] Thompson apparently never did know about it. When the male applicants had worn themselves out, they hired the ladies to try. "They take it for granted that we become so hardened that we can resist the importunities of men—but cannot withstand the plaintive entreaties of the fairer portion of God's creation," wrote one of the Cabinet.[25]

By midsummer the available jobs had been assigned, and the hungry, unsatisfied horde went home. Some monumental decisions had been made, chief among them the selection of Robert J. Walker as Governor of the turbulent Kansas Territory. Slidell would be the Administration leader in the Senate; J. Glancy Jones would be the House whip and Chairman of the Committee on Ways and Means. With a majority in both branches, it began to look by June as if the Administration had gotten off to a fair start.

THE OLD CHIEF

After the first few months of daily conferences and contention, what had the Cabinet come to think of their chief? They agreed with Black's pronouncement: "He is a stubborn old gentleman—very fond of having his own way, and I don't know what his way is."[26] Floyd told a friend that "Mr. Buchanan was different from Genl. Jackson; . . . Genl. Jackson could be *coaxed* from his purpose, but . . . Mr. B. could neither be coaxed nor driven."[27] One Cabinet member remarked that they all stood in awe of him like boys in the presence of their schoolmaster and called him "The Squire" behind his back;[28] another said that he "overhauled the Secretary of War" so scorchingly that they were all afraid of him.[29] Floyd, on this occasion, had sold Fort Snelling in Minnesota to a New York syndicate for a fraction of its value, and although he had not profited or broken any law, Buchanan gave him a lashing for being a dupe. Mrs. Craig, after a month in the White House, began calling Buchanan "The Grand Turk."

The president's colleagues found him extremely nosy. He flustered Cobb one day by inquiring in great detail about his wife's fortune and finances. After getting the information, Buchanan asked abruptly, "Well, if you are so rich, why don't you pay that $15,000 you owe?" Taken aback, Cobb almost replied, "I will, if you will loan it to me," but restrained the impulse. "Don't you think the old gentleman is quite curious about such matters?" he asked.[30] The busybody habit, not only in matters of private affairs but in the activities of all the departments bred secretiveness in the Cabinet that contributed to Buchanan's ignorance, later in his term, of some very irregular proceedings that went on under his nose. But as a whole, the Cabinet had great respect for and confidence in the chief. Jerry Black, in characteristic phrase, wrote in July, 1857, after a flurry of trouble in Kansas: "This being the first little gale we have had, those who have the handling of the ship are a little awkward for the moment. I speak of lieutenants & sailing masters. The great old captain looks calmly up into the sky and gives his orders quietly—orders which will keep her head steady on true course."[31]

285

22

KANSAS — A TRAGEDY OF ERRORS • 1854-1857

CRISIS IN KANSAS

One cannot imagine a more unfortunate place to have precipitated a crisis between the North and the South in 1854 than Kansas, for here centered the greatest hopes of each section. And what hopes they were! Fifty million acres of level farm land; a strategic location for the eastern terminus of a transcontinental railroad which would tap the enormous trade of the Pacific coast; the promise of rich political offices which might determine the future supremacy of a party or section. And this region of golden opportunity lay at the junction of North, South and West, easily accessible to adventurous crusaders from each. Why did Douglas propose the Kansas-Nebraska Bill? Why did Congress by a large majority sustain him? And where did the results leave James Buchanan in March, 1857?

Senator Douglas, as Chairman of the Committee on Territories, had sweated his way through many Congressional struggles over the organization of the federal domain. In 1847 he had proposed the extension of the Missouri Compromise line to the Pacific. In 1850 he backed popular sovereignty for New Mexico and Utah. His main interest lay not in method but in speed. The West would grow as fast as Congress would let it grow; did there need to be a year's discussion every time a new territory was to be created?

In January, 1854, Douglas reported out of Committee a bill to divide the Nebraska Territory. When the two parts were admitted as states they should be "received into the Union, with or without slavery, as their Constitution may prescribe at the time of their admission." This rendered void in Kansas and Nebraska the Missouri Compromise restrictions against slavery north of 36° 30'. Having attacked the Missouri line, Douglas decided he might as well eliminate entirely the idea of Congressional control and added to the bill the explicit statement that the Missouri Compromise was "inoperative and void . . . it being the true intent and meaning of this act not to legislate Slavery into any Territory or State, nor to exclude it therefrom, but to leave the people thereof perfectly free to form and regulate their domestic institutions in their own way, subject only to the Constitution of the United States." He suspected this part would raise a "hell of a storm" but thought it would please the South without hurting the North. After a violent debate, Congress passed this dangerous measure. A little later Douglas's friends reported that he looked "like a man who sorrows for a misdeed."[1]

Douglas assumed that no more slave states would come in under his bill. The climate of Kansas was unfavorable to crops which slaves could profitably cultivate; slavery could not rapidly be moved into an unsettled region; free men by the score could easily establish themselves in the new territory before a single slaveholder could transport his unwieldy property to it. At the same time, the South would gain its right to settle the common domain and therefore would permit the rapid admission of western states. Douglas was "groping for a new center of gravity in politics," the Great West. It would make him rich, and unless he misread his future, it would make him president.[2]

Evidence that Douglas had made a mistake soon poured in from every side. Forney, then Clerk of the House, reported that a number of Buchanan's friends had supported the measure in the very hope of killing Douglas off for the presidency.[3] The abolitionists promptly formed a "New England Emigrant Aid Society" to free-load settlers into Kansas, and the South organized competitive companies to stimulate immigration. Douglas helplessly appealed to Congress to outlaw such "perversion of the provisions of the Kansas-Nebraska Act."

In Kansas settlers sympathetic to slavery established a Territorial government with headquarters at Lecompton which President Pierce recognized as legal. Antislavery settlers set up a competing government at Topeka which both President Pierce and Congress declared illegal and revolutionary, but its adherents refused to disband. Open warfare between the two governments soon broke out and continued in Kansas up until Buchanan's inauguration. Federal troops supported the Lecompton officials, but General Jim Lane's private free-state "army" provided effective defense of the Topeka rebels. Two sets of public officers and competing legal codes made Kansas, in effect, not one but two territories, one lawful and the other at war with the United States government. Supporters of both engaged in wholesale ballot-box frauds, graft, claim-jumping, intimidation, and settlement of debatable questions by bullet and bowie knife.

While "bleeding Kansas" symbolized the struggle over slavery to most people in the United States, to Kansans this issue was incidental to the main one—land. Whoever controlled the government distributed the political jobs, and the holders of these supervised the disposition of land.

287

Governor Geary reported: *"the* greatest obstacle to overcome in the production of peace and harmony in the Territory, is the unsettled condition of the claims to the public lands," and the *Squatter Sovereign* concurred. "It is a historical fact," wrote the editor, "that almost all the contentions which result in bloodshed . . . have their origin in some dispute over land claims." Another paper said: "Each week adds to the list of murders . . . mostly growing out of this one thing; and there is no law to come to the rescue."[4]

Slavery became an excuse for dissensions in Kansas, and for the artificial promotion of settlement, but as Paul Gates writes, "The first objective of most people who went to Kansas . . . was to secure land claims which might be sold profitably."[5] The New England Emigrant Aid Society of Connecticut sent out settlers to take up land for resale, and this company quickly invested three times more cash in Kansas land claims than any other syndicate. The Missouri "Border Ruffians," who allegedly invaded Kansas to vote illegally and make it a slave state, mainly wanted to protect their land interests. Only 3% of the Missourians of the region held slaves, but nearly half of them staked out claims the moment the Kansas Territory was opened. It should be added that the Missouri-Kansas boundary had not yet been marked, and frontiersmen near the uncertain border thought they had better vote; they might be Kansans. The entire border population, when the opportunity arose, claimed to be residents of Kansas, and prior to a federal survey there was no way to prove they were not. They felt, at least, that they had as good a title to residence in Kansas as the peripatetic mercenaries of the Emigrant Aid Society who showed up en masse at land auctions as *bona fide* resident "settlers" but left by boat the day after the sale for their residence elsewhere.[6]

But outside Kansas the slavery question dominated the headlines. By the time of Buchanan's inauguration, a variety of points of view had become clearly discernible. The Republicans used the "bleeding Kansas" theme as party propaganda. Any atrocities they could pin on the Democrats strengthened their cause in the North. The Free-Soilers and later the Republicans jumped like grasshoppers from one territorial policy to another, espousing any one which at the moment seemed best calculated to weaken their Democratic opponents. In 1848, the antislavery partisans wanted the Wilmot Proviso and opposed both the extension of the Missouri line and squatter sovereignty. In 1854, they upheld the Missouri line as if they considered this the ideal policy, and blasted popular sovereignty. By 1857 they championed popular sovereignty more ardently than Douglas, and vilified Buchanan for permitting frauds in its operation.

But despite their capricious territorial policies, the Republicans proclaimed and exploited to the fullest a fundamental principle that stood immovable: that the doctrine of human slavery could never be reconciled to the tenets of free government. Let there be no further extension of slavery. In the realm of theory, in political ideology, and in moral propriety they stood impregnable. They themselves never seriously proposed acting on the basis of racial equality, however. The antislavery party demanded the exclusion of Negroes from their society. Northern leaders frankly said that they wanted Kansas as a "white man's country."[7] Many Republicans had little practical interest in ameliorating the lot of the Negro. Primarily they wanted to seize political control from the Democrats. When the Republicans in Kansas could not direct the legal government, they seceded and lived under their own revolutionary regime. So soon as they were sure they could control the legal government, they adopted that. The main issue with them was not slavery, nor the Negro; their prime objective was political power.

Southern extremists, or fire-eaters, held very much the same aims. *"Kansas must come in as a slave state or the cause of southern rights is dead,"* they thundered. "If Buchanan should secretly favor the free-state men of Kansas . . . he will richly deserve death, and I hope some patriotic hand will inflict it," wrote T. W. Thomas of Georgia.[8] These defenders of slavery and uncompromising foes of the Yankees told their constituents that Kansas would come in as a slave state. By some means or other, they had to make good their promise or lose their following. For them, too, the issue, stripped of the verbiage of propaganda, was political control.

Conservative Democrats, both north and south, emphasized the need for admitting Kansas to statehood, free or slave, as the quickest way to quiet the abolitionist furor in the North and the secession clamor in the South. After the passage of the Kansas-Nebraska Bill, many of the moderate southern journals deplored it as of no practical use whatever to the South. No one there had been asking a repeal of the Missouri line when Douglas proposed it, and the result had been a disastrous revival of the agitation which had nearly wrecked the country in 1850. "All agree," said the *Richmond Enquirer*, "that slavery cannot exist in the territories of Kansas and Nebraska."[9]

These Union Democrats wanted to achieve not a free or a slave Kansas, but a Democratic Kansas. With the Whigs defunct and such odd political makeshifts as the Southern American and the Know-Nothing parties picking up thousands of voters set adrift by the Kansas storm, it was of first importance that the Union Democrats get clear of the sectional dispute as speedily as possible. Then and not until then could they begin to regroup their scattering forces.

What did James Buchanan think of Kansas when he entered the White House other than that it would be the critical problem of his Administration? Personally he disapproved of the Kansas-Nebraska Bill and his friends assumed that had he been in Congress in 1854 he would have fought against its passage.[10] He had clearly defined his reasons for opposition to popular sovereignty in his comments in 1850 on the New Mexico and Utah bills. The nation was a republic, not a pure democracy; the citizens did not rule, could not rule by direct vote; they delegated authority to representatives.

Popular sovereignty not only denied the competence of Congress and the validity of the system of representative government, it actually invited local war. The popular sovereignty bills were drawn so loosely that they did not provide any legal mechanism for the expression of the public will. They left undefined the rules for voter qualification, registration, control of polls, official count, election officers, jurisdiction over disputed ballots, and the limits of matters to be voted on. Finally, they made the colossal assumption that a group of unlettered frontiersmen could settle in a peaceful, orderly, and effective way the slavery problem which had defied the intelligence of Franklin, Washington, Jefferson, Hamilton, Clay, Calhoun, Benton, Jackson, Webster, Seward, Douglas, and every other political figure who had grappled with it. Buchanan's letters to Toucey, Foote, Davis and others in 1850 had predicted the result of asking first settlers to decide this old question of slavery "in their own way." They would rush in from opposite sides and murder each other.

Buchanan's official endorsement of the Kansas-Nebraska Act accounts for the odd response he made to the Keystone Club upon learning of his nomination in June, 1856. He was no longer "simply James Buchanan," he said, but the "representative of the great Democratic party" and had to square his conduct with the platform.[11] He would support the bill as his public duty, but that did not mean he thought privately it was a good law.

During the election canvass the northern Democrats developed the idea that Buchanan would achieve fair play in Kansas, and this would bring it in as a free state. "Buchanan, Breckinridge and Free Kansas," read the banners at party rallies. In the South the electoral line was, obviously, not "free Kansas" but a quick and fair settlement which would end the agitation and write finis to the Republican party. These elements of the campaign impressed on Buchanan the lines of policy which he should follow: first, a fair settlement, which meant submission of a Kansas constitution to an open, peaceful vote; second, a quick settlement; and third, the creation of a Democratic Kansas which would silence the few southerners who would complain because it came in as a free state. That a fair vote would create a free Kansas James Buchanan never doubted—not, at least, in the early months of his Administration.

A GOVERNOR OF NATIONAL STATURE

In consultation with the Cabinet and Senator Douglas, Buchanan decided to appoint a Kansas governor of outstanding prestige. Ex-Governors Reeder, Shannon, and Geary, hard as they had tried, had failed to unify the Territory, and the Kansans had broken them one after the other. It would be interesting to know whether Buchanan offered the job to Douglas, for he would admirably have met the requirements and would have gratified many by taking personal charge of the hornet's nest he had stirred up. But Buchanan picked Robert J. Walker, a politician of national stature— even a possible future president. Walker wanted no part of the job, but Buchanan argued so earnestly that the safety of the Union depended upon him that he eventually accepted the governorship as a public duty. To pin down explicitly the terms of the appointment he wrote to Buchanan: "I understand that you and all your Cabinet cordially concur in the opinion expressed by me, that the actual *bona fide* residents of the Territory, by a fair and regular vote, unaffected by fraud or violence, must be permitted in adopting their State Constitution to decide for themselves what shall be their social institutions."[12]

Frederick P. Stanton, secretary of the Territory and acting governor in Walker's absence, departed for Kansas on April 2 to assume responsibility until the governor should arrive at the end of May. Buchanan also ordered General William S. Harney to take over the 1,500 troops in Kansas and prevent civil disorder there. Walker in the meantime conferred in Washington to clarify further his policy and then left for Kansas via New York where, at a public dinner, he explained his purposes in language that stretched considerably the proposals which had been cleared in Washington. Instead of promising a fair vote to permit Kansans "to decide for themselves what shall be their social institutions," (that is, to vote on *slavery*) he now declared his determination to secure a full vote upon *any constitution* which might be offered for adoption.[13]

Walker arrived in Kansas on May 24, hobnobbed for two days with the free-state men at Leavenworth and Lawrence, and then proceeded to the ramshackle, clapboard capital village of Lecompton where he delivered his inaugural address to a restless and uninterested assemblage of frowzy frontiersmen. The address had two parts, one describing the political and the other the economic prospects. "In no contingency," he said, would Congress admit Kansas as a state without a popular vote on the adoption of a constitution. Unless the entire constitution should be submitted to direct vote, it "will and ought to be rejected by Congress." There should be no cause for quarrel about slavery, he continued. Nature had already decided that issue; the thermometer drew an "isothermal line" beyond which slavery could not possibly exist, and Kansas lay north of this line. Climate, not politics, would inevitably make Kansas free.

Kansas had unlimited promise of economic growth, he said, if only the people would cease their quarrels. The government would recommend an enormous land grant upon the admission of Kansas to statehood. There was everything to gain and nothing to lose by voting on a constitution and petitioning promptly for admission.

If the New York address had stretched instructions, the inaugural broke entirely away from them. Buchanan had talked with Walker, but he had never seen a draft of the inaugural.[14] He had not committed himself to submission of the whole constitution but only of the slavery question; and he certainly never dreamed that the governor would tell the territorials how to adopt their constitution, under threat of rejection by Congress if they did not follow his advice. Buchanan disapproved of this part of the inaugural; nevertheless, he prepared to make the best of it. He agreed with Walker that Kansas inevitably would become a free state, but he felt that the governor's indiscreet speech at a time when the Administration wanted to emphasize its rigid impartiality in guiding the two sections of Kansas toward statehood would cause trouble.

Walker had reasons for his address. He had become convinced in the weeks before going to Kansas that his main task would be to persuade the free-state people to vote. Many of these were Democrats, and he gambled on the hope that they would join with the Lecomptonites in a movement to make Kansas a free Democratic state in preference to a Black Republican and abolitionist state. He assumed that the proslavery minority would come along. The Republicans could be mollified by special considerations in land distribution. Walker foresaw himself as conqueror of the Kansas dragon and soon to be Senator from the new state. He wanted the free-state people to trust him, to abandon their Topeka organization, and to vote. He offered everything: a free Kansas, control of the new government (which would follow a full vote), and land. If this prospect did not gain their cooperation, nothing would.

Walker had expected his frank and undiplomatic remarks to raise a few dust devils, but not the tornado which swept the land. He did not yet know that Stanton had told the Lecomptonites that only the slavery question had to be put to a public vote, and that it would be wise to handle this issue independently of the constitution. Let that document be on the regular pattern, without mention of slavery. "Then," he said, "the convention ought to prepare a separate article on the subject of slavery" for the voters.[15] This proposal apparently came right from headquarters and did, in fact, accurately represent Buchanan's view.[16] Nor did Walker know that before he even left Washington some of the proslavery men of Kansas who had come east to interview him had returned home with the report that he was dangerous and would have to be "broken" like the other governors. One of them, hulking, red-headed L. A. Maclean of the

292

surveyor's office, got up after the inaugural banquet and towering over the shrivelled little man in the governor's chair, ridiculed him as a "pigmy" and told him to mind his own business or be run out of the territory.[17]

But the reaction in Kansas was mild compared to that of the southern fire-eaters who had only with the greatest difficulty been brought to a grudging and distrustful support of Buchanan in 1856. "*We are betrayed!*" they roared. "Our victory is turned to ashes on our lips, and before God I will never say well done to the traitor [Walker] or to his master who lives in the White House." "I wish Walker had been hung before he went [to Kansas] to try & make himself next President."[18] The letters flew, damning Buchanan's "vile treachery" and Walker's harlotry with free-soilers and abolitionists. Then came the direct pressure for Walker's summary dismissal; if he were not dismissed, southern Senators would block his confirmation. This was no bluff, for five southern states held congressional elections in midsummer, and if the fire-eaters beat the Union Democrats in them, the whole Administration policy of creating a strong Democracy would crumble. But Buchanan could not possibly remove Walker after one speech, and particularly when the northern Democrats hailed that speech as straightforward, manly, and honest.[19]

Buchanan tried to calm the storm, inserting in the Washington *Union* an article explaining that the people of Kansas *ought* to vote on their constitution but disclaiming the right of anyone to make them do this. He then put Cobb to work writing letters intended to pacify the southern extremists. To clear the Administration, Cobb pointed out that Walker's instructions did not demand submission of the constitution to a vote; only the slavery question required a plebiscite. The governor in his initial enthusiasm had overstepped the mark. To justify Walker, the Administration emphasized "that it was better to make [Kansas] a Constitutional Democratic state than to let it be Black Republican," and Walker therefore had taken the free-state Democrats into the movement.[20]

Alexander H. Stephens, a strong southern Unionist and keen interpreter of the Constitution, complained that those who applauded Walker's address always overlooked the main point. They thought only of the *propriety* of submitting the constitution for ratification. On this all could agree. But suppose the convention chose not to do it? Who had the *right* to tell a constitutional convention what to do? The governor certainly had not, and if Congress should try to exercise such a power, it would "strike at the foundation of our government" and extinguish "everything recognized as States Rights and State Sovereignty."[21]

No one could dispute the correctness of Stephens's contention that the ultimate sovereignty in the United States lay in the people in their constitution-making capacity, in convention assembled. The exercise of outside control over a constitutional convention meant subversion of

293

the basic principle upon which the government rested. Some of Stephens's friends, however, observed that his comments came with very bad grace from a man who had recently "voted for that clause in the Minnesota bill requiring that the Constitution *shall* be submitted to the people."[22]

Buchanan, deep in the midst of patronage problems and pestered to distraction by office seekers, gave little attention to the uproar about Kansas. He would sustain Walker, but he would not endorse his foolish talk. In the meantime finicky southerners in and out of Kansas, resentful of Walker's "arrogant and insolent threats," began to think that *because of Walker*, the convention "ought never under any circumstances to comply with his demand." Its refusal would not only establish the sovereignty of the people but also force Walker "to carry out his threat, and join the free-soil traitors."[23] On the other hand, word spread that the free-state men in Kansas would never vote in an election administered by the Lecompton government. If there were no submission and no vote on slavery, it would be a double catastrophe.

Walker continued to make the bold and unequivocal speeches which he believed necessary to promote his program, and they naturally aggravated partisanship. He told the free-state people that if the coming constitutional convention did not submit the slavery issue to a vote, "I will join you, fellow citizens, in lawful opposition to their course. And I cannot doubt, gentlemen, that one much higher than I, the chief magistrate of the Union, will join you in opposition." From this statement, the southerners assumed Walker had completely gone over to the free-soilers. It should be carefully noted, however, that this time Walker had pledged himself and Buchanan to a submission only of the slavery question. After this encouraging pronouncement from the governor, the free staters in Lawrence proceeded to ignore the Lecompton government and framed their own city charter without authorization from anyone. Walker now spoke again but in terms that cheered the hearts of the proslavery men. Any citizens who defied the legal government at Lecompton would be guilty of treason, and Walker would not hesitate to use the army to impose the usual penalty for it. "If you have wrongs," he said, "redress them through the instrumentality of the ballot box." Otherwise, Walker would declare them rebels and use the army "to perform the painful duty of arresting your revolutionary proceedings."[24] In the face of this threat, the city fathers of Lawrence backed down, and the free-soilers modified some of their earlier hopes for Walker.

The governor wrote to Buchanan on June 28, taking full personal responsibility for his pledges to achieve submission of the forthcoming constitution and for his assertions that Kansas would have to be a free state. He apologized for taking this position and outlined in detail the conditions in Kansas which required him to do so. He believed that had he not come out for submission and acknowledged the "axiomatic truth" that the "existence of slavery here is preposterous," he would have faced a renewal of bloodshed. "The expression of these great truths . . . was a solemn duty," he told Buchanan. "Now unless I am sustained thoroughly and cordially by the administration here, I cannot control the convention, and we shall have anarchy and civil war."[25]

Buchanan had to make a decision. Walker had gone beyond his instructions and initiated a new policy; could the Administration support it? The president replied that Walker's letter which he had just read to the Cabinet contained views which "were not calculated to assure us of your success." Buchanan's position was extremely awkward. He could not come out in opposition to Walker, for this would wreck all chance of uniting the Democrats in Kansas. On the other hand, to sustain the policy that the constitution had to be submitted was to deliver the Administration into the hands of the delegates who soon would meet at Lecompton to do whatever they pleased.

Buchanan collected as much information as possible from other sources. He received assurances from people he trusted that Walker was merely echoing the opinions that prevailed in Kansas when he arrived. It seemed likely that the convention would draw up a constitution in which there was no mention of slavery and submit it to the voters. The question of slavery would be decided separately. Walker said he planned to visit every delegate. Even the southerners admitted that the only reason for not submitting was the fear that the majority ballot would make Kansas free, for it was presumed that most of the 9,251 persons legally registered to vote for delegates favored submission and a free state.

Buchanan finally wrote Walker, "On the question of submitting the Constitution to the bona fide residents of Kansas, I am willing to stand or fall."[26] He put his Administration on the line with this statement and explained very carefully to the Cabinet what he meant by it. He would sustain as party policy Walker's unfortunate pledge to achieve submission of the whole constitution to a public vote. He did not say that if the constitutional convention ignored this policy and failed to submit, he would as president defy and oppose their action. That would be a different matter, a matter not only of policy but also of law, to be handled if the problem arose. "Sufficient unto the day." Howell Cobb wrote that the possibility of the convention refusing to submit its work to a vote was "full of difficulty. . . . With all my heart, I trust that such an issue will not come upon us. I am not authorized to say what course the Administration will pursue. We have not anticipated it and have made no programme."[27] With the matter temporarily disposed of, Buchanan left for a much needed two weeks' vacation at Bedford Springs.

POPULAR SOVEREIGNTY IN ACTION

Meanwhile, Kansas officials had begun the long process of calling a constitutional convention. Those of the modern age who deplore the skullduggery which both sides practiced ought now to pause and reflect upon the nature of the problem. Nothing has so taxed the ingenuity or so frustrated students of human affairs as the conduct of a plebiscite to determine by a fair vote the fate of a locality inhabited by people of antagonistic loyalties and ideologies, supported by strong and equally matched outside allies. In the case of Kansas, the balloting would be administered and the results tabulated by one of the parties to the contest, the Lecompton government. If the people of Kansas achieved less than a quiet and peaceful delivery of the presumed rights of one party into the hands of the other by a vote, they at least did better than might have been expected.

Buchanan had hoped, by the most rigid observance of impartiality and technically correct application of legal form, to play the part of umpire. Walker thwarted the president by publicly appearing to take sides with the free-state party. Black reported in July that Buchanan would apply the law and "take no care who frets, who chafes, or who the conspirers are."[28]

On February 19, 1857, the Lecompton legislature provided for an election in June of delegates to a constitutional convention to meet in September. A census was taken during March. Kansans were given the month of April in which to correct errors, and registration of voters followed. Rules of eligibility were stricter than they were for ordinary elections. Each person had to show proof of three months' continuous residence and a receipt for payment of some territorial tax. Quite a few illiterate squatters thought the census takers were checking land claims and drove them away. Others sought to avoid taxation by keeping their names off the list. The census officials did not visit several remote counties, assuming that only Indians lived in them. The Republicans caused serious trouble. Apparently the majority of them felt that their registration would signify acknowledgment of the legitimacy of the Lecompton government, and they therefore boycotted the listing.[29]

Obviously the census and registration were incomplete. But the statement, repeatedly made, that only nineteen of the thirty-four counties got representation in the Lecompton convention does not convey a correct picture. Because of widely scattered population, Kansas counties had been grouped into units for electoral purposes. In several units where no white population existed, no census was taken; in other units, census work went normally in some counties but ran into opposition in others so that the electoral unit got representation, even if some counties did not. The convention, however, was not a rump affair from which the Republican half of Kansas was intentionally excluded, as some charged. Anyone not

296

registered had an opportunity to add his name to the rolls, but the Republicans wanted to keep the registration down to create the appearance of of foul play and an unfair vote.

Despite Walker's inaugural promises to the free-state people, only about 2,000 Kansans voted for delegates, nearly all of them proslavery adherents. The free-state Republicans who had purposely refused to qualify for voting apparently convinced the free-state Democrats not to exercise their right after getting it. The election was peaceful, no flitting border ruffians or floating New England Emigrants appeared to stuff the ballot boxes, and all those registered had an opportunity to vote. The delegates who would meet at Lecompton on September seventh were duly and legally authorized to act for the people of Kansas.

While at Bedford, Buchanan drafted an answer to forty prominent educators and preachers of Connecticut who had protested his "tyrannical" use of the army to "force the people of Kansas to obey laws not their own, nor of the United States." In his reply Buchanan exposed some of the misinformation being circulated about Kansas and explained his policy. The Topeka regime, he reminded them, was "a usurpation of the same character as it would be for a portion of the people of Connecticut to undertake to establish a government within its chartered limits, for the purpose of redressing any grievance . . . against the legitimate State government." He emphasized the fairness of the Kansas election law which sought to make every *bona fide* resident a qualified voter, and the efforts to achieve a full vote. When "lawless men . . . refused either to register or to vote," the convention members "were elected, legally and properly" by those who were willing to exercise their voting right. He would use the Army in Kansas, he concluded, only "to resist actual agression." In words clearly prophetic of his policy in 1861, he continued: "Following the wise example of Mr. Madison towards the Hartford convention, illegal and dangerous combinations, such as that of the Topeka convention, will not be disturbed, unless they shall attempt to perform some act which will bring them into actual collision with the Constitution and the laws. In that event they shall be resisted by the whole power of the government."[30]

When Buchanan returned to Washington in August the future of his Administration looked bright. He had just about disposed of the patronage, the southern state elections had brought a triumph of the Union Democrats over the secessionists, it seemed a certainty that the Kansas convention would submit its work to a vote, and the "Silliman letter" to the Connecticut preachers satisfied most northern Democrats, and brought cheers from the South. Howell Cobb's brother wrote "that B.'s letter to the Forty Fools from Connecticut is *the greatest state paper for the South*, that has ever emanated from the executive chair since the days of Washington."[31]

297

The days of peace and good will proved to be short. On August 24 the New York Stock Exchange collapsed from a rush to unload securities that signalled the Panic of 1857. For the next two months the financial problems of the nation and the task of preparing his first annual message occupied Buchanan's attention. He kept in touch with Kansas affairs, but ceased to worry about them for he believed that the trouble there had nearly come to an end. The Lecompton Convention met on September 7, but agreed to adjourn until after the election of Territorial officers so that no one could accuse the delegates of playing politics. A month before the October election of a new Territorial legislature, Walker asked Buchanan for information to help him handle conflicts over interpretation of the election laws. Cass replied that a Territorial governor had no authority to judge the qualification of voters; this power by law belonged to election judges who were appointed by County Commissioners. Nor did the governor have legal authority to pass judgment on disputed election returns. Members of the legislature had jurisdiction over disputed returns for their own members; and judges of the courts had jurisdiction if returns for court officers were in dispute. The governor ought to express no opinion on the elections.[32]

The Territorial law permitted "free" voting; that is, neither proof of residence nor tax receipt was required. Walker disposed his troops with the utmost care to keep order and assure a fair contest, but his effort failed. McGee County, which had polled 14 votes in June, showed 1,226 in the October returns. It was in a remote region, and for this reason no troops were sent there. In Oxford County, boasting a total of 11 shacks, 1,828 votes mysteriously appeared. Outraged and shocked, Walker personally examined the polling districts of these two counties. He could find no population. On these fraudulent returns depended the complexion of the new legislature: with them it would be proslavery; without them, free-state. After hearing about the McGee-Oxford trickery, the adherents of the Topeka government quickly formed their army under General Jim Lane and marched on Lecompton. The fraud was so palpable and the probability of armed conflict so imminent that the governor, on October 19, issued a public proclamation: he would transmit no returns from McGee and Oxford Counties.

The proslavery delegates to the constitutional convention called their adjourned session to order at Lecompton the very day of Walker's pronouncement on the voting frauds. Furious at his breach of instructions, they determined never to be guided by his wishes. Understanding that his presence was a detriment, Walker departed from Lecompton, leaving Surveyor General John C. Calhoun to work with the convention.

Calhoun had the able assistance of Colonel H. L. Martin who had recently arrived, ostensibly to check some land records. Actually he had come as an agent of Buchanan to propose that the convention draw up two constitutions: one would protect slavery; the other would not. The White House sponsors thought this plan would please Douglas and create a free, Democratic Kansas. Calhoun and Martin believed they had won over the convention, but it suddenly voted to draft a proslavery constitution and send it directly to Washington.

Working frantically to prevent such a bombshell from landing on Buchanan's desk, Calhoun induced the convention to adjourn for a few days and reconsider the two-constitution scheme. Almost by a miracle, he persuaded the delegates to approve his proposal by a vote of 27 to 25. Kansas would have some kind of constitution and could, therefore, become a state. In case the vote went antislavery, as Calhoun presumed it would, the owners of the 200 slaves in the Territory were to be temporarily protected by the anticonfiscation feature common to the abolition laws of the northern states, and slavery would vanish as speedily in Kansas as it had in Massachusetts or Pennsylvania. Calhoun felt, with reason, that he had prevented a renewal of civil war, guaranteed the political loyalty of Kansas to the Democrats, and saved both Douglas and the Buchanan Administration from certain ruin.[33]

23

LECOMPTON — PYRRHIC VICTORY • 1858

"BY GOD, SIR, ANDREW JACKSON IS DEAD!"

News of the action of the Lecompton Convention brought shouts of "swindle" from all parts of the country. Free-state men were outraged at the refusal of the convention to permit a vote on the constitution and Douglas told the Senate that "all those who are in favor of this Constitution may vote for or against slavery as they please; but all those who are against this constitution are disfranchised." The Republicans rejoiced that the convention had offered them so inviting a target and asserted, erroneously, that Kansas would remain a slave state whether people voted for the pro-slavery or antislavery constitution. Southern extremists also jumped hard on the Lecompton Convention for submitting anything to a popular vote, and damned Buchanan for sustaining a free-soiler like Walker as governor. "Nothing short of seeing the Holy Ghost descending on Old Buck in the shape of a dove patent to my eyesight," wrote one of them, "could ever make me trust him again."[1]

Governor Walker never revisited the convention and soon left the territory. Far from returning home in triumph, he would be ruined unless he could make out of the unexpected rebellion of the convention an issue that would vindicate his mistaken judgment. In Chicago, Walker found Douglas much troubled by the events in Kansas. But Buchanan occupied the most difficult position of all; he would be denounced for the Lecompton Constitution whichever side he took. Political capital might be made of his certain discomfiture if it were known what course he planned. Walker proceeded to Washington to find out.

He found Buchanan greatly distressed but still hopeful that the people of Kansas would go to the polls, take one constitution or the other, achieve statehood and end the controversy. After that they could do what they pleased with their constitution. Buchanan said he would urge this course in his forthcoming message to Congress. Walker pressed him to reject the Lecompton trick and join in a demand for a new convention, but

300

Buchanan would have none of it and Walker left, declaiming with fire and brimstone that the president had betrayed him.

Douglas called at the White House on December 3, angry because Buchanan had already released the Kansas portion of his message without having consulted him. Buchanan, thinking that the Calhoun compromise at Lecompton had the support of Douglas and sure that the product of the convention, provocative as it was, nevertheless met precisely the terms of the Kansas-Nebraska law, had not expected the Little Giant to be up in arms. But Douglas believed that he could not possibly survive in Illinois politics unless he denounced the Lecompton Constitution; fifty-five of fifty-six Illinois newspapers were out against it. The president and the senator discussed the problem, dispassionately at first, but with increasing impatience and rancor, since each remained blind to those features of the issue which appeared most obvious and compelling to the other. Buchanan maintained that unless Kansas came in promptly, the Republicans would keep it stirred up for the next three years and undoubtedly win both Kansas and the national election of 1860. That would bring civil war. He granted there had been fraud and trickery draped all around Kansan political affairs, but the constitutional elections had been honest. The basest action in these had been the opposition's refusal to register and to vote. The constitution-making procedure had been scrupulously legal and the president was under oath to execute the law. He had no right to use his authority to force a constitutional convention to comply with his private wishes. Lecompton *had* to be sustained; there was no other course.

Douglas said he would have to oppose it; his people would never accept so palpable a fraud. It was a dirty business and a breach of the basic principle of majority rule. A minority had swindled the majority and made popular sovereignty a joke. Finally, with positions solidified by argument and tempers mounting, Buchanan rose and said: "Mr. Douglas, I desire you to remember that no Democrat ever yet differed from an Administration of his own choice without being crushed. Beware of the fate of Tallmadge and Rives." Years before, Jackson had destroyed the careers of these two men who had opposed him. "Mr. President," replied Douglas, "I wish you to remember that General Jackson is dead!" and with this he stalked out.[2]

Buchanan, in his first Annual Message on December 8, explained why he would be duty bound to transmit the Kansas constitution to Congress, no matter which one the voters chose. The convention had been legally elected, and federal law only required submission to a public vote of the question "with or without slavery." The citizens of Kansas had been given every opportunity to register and vote, and the refusal of any of them to avail themselves of their right could in no manner affect the legality of the convention. Under the existing government, said Buchanan, "a majority of those who vote—not the majority who may remain at home, from whatever cause—must decide the result of an election." Abraham Lincoln, faced with a similar case in West Virginia in 1863, wrote that "it is universal practice in popular elections in all of these states to give no legal consideration whatever to those who do not choose to vote, as against the effect of the votes of those who do choose to vote."[3]

Buchanan approved of submission, and he had hoped that the convention would agree. But he had never suggested that he would require it. Douglas himself, in his Springfield speech of June 12, 1857, had declared that submission was not at all necessary. The convention had done what it had a right to do, and the president could not reject its work because he had preferred a different decision. Under these circumstances Buchanan questioned "whether the peace and quiet of the whole country are not of greater importance than the mere temporary triumph of either of the political parties in Kansas."[4]

Next day in the Senate, Douglas attacked the legitimacy of the Lecompton Constitution. On December 15, Governor Walker resigned, charging Buchanan with betrayal. On December 21, the people of Kansas cast 6,143 votes for the constitution "with slavery" and 569 "without slavery." Meanwhile, in mid-December, acting governor Stanton called a special session of the newly elected territorial legislature which otherwise would not have met, Buchanan hoped, until after the admission of Kansas as a state. Buchanan immediately removed Stanton and appointed Indian Commissioner James W. Denver, but the damage had already been done. The legislature quickly called for another vote on January 4 on the whole Lecompton Constitution. The results of this referendum showed:

Against the Lecompton Constitution 10,226
For it, with slavery 138
For it, without slavery 24

Despite this blow, Buchanan remained firm and on February 2 transmitted the Lecompton Constitution to Congress accompanied by a long explanatory message. "I am decidedly in favor of its admission, and thus terminating the Kansas question," he concluded.

What, exactly, was the issue raised by Lecompton? Douglas and his allies said it was a question of morality: the vote on the constitution had been fraudulent and unfair, and violated the principle of popular sovereignty. Buchanan and his allies said it was a question of administrative law and practical politics: a scabby and unfortunate affair, but legal, constitutional, and, given the antecedents, inevitable. These differing points of view augured an irreconcilable conflict from the start. The argument of those who emphasized the moral issue quickly degenerated into ridicule and vilification of Buchanan. The president pointed out the futility of trying to settle political questions by appeal to moral principles.

"The Bible for Heaven, the Constitution for earth," he would say; or, "You cannot legislate morality." Douglas agreed with these maxims when he talked of slavery, for he declined to discuss its moral aspects, but not when he talked of Lecompton and popular sovereignty.

A great many reasons combined to make Buchanan take the position of "no parley with Douglas," and Douglas to threaten, "By God, sir, I made Mr. James Buchanan, and by God, sir, I will unmake him." Their personalities clashed. Buchanan was the kind of man who tried to avoid risk, Douglas the kind who welcomed it as a relish and stimulus. No amount of arbitration could alter these differences in their nature. Buchanan had little ambition for further political honor, but he was tremendously eager to achieve a "historical" reputation. He would attain this, he thought, if he could settle the problem of slavery in the Territories by the swift admission of Kansas. Thus would he not only preserve the Union but also encourage a final solution of the sectional problem, for he thought that slavery would die out in time "by the silent operation of economic and moral forces."[5]

Furthermore, Buchanan took a certain spiteful satisfaction that Douglas's principle of popular sovereignty had turned out to be such a catastrophe. Finally, as a party politician, Buchanan knew that 36 of the 39 Democratic Senators and probably 110 of the 130 Democratic Congressmen would vote to admit Kansas under the Lecompton Constitution. The president could not reject the Lecompton Constitution without renouncing the Democratic party.

Douglas, on the other hand, believed that he would lose the senatorship in 1858 if he supported Lecompton, and he had to stay in the Senate to attain the presidency in 1860. By denouncing Lecompton as a fraud, he could make a case for popular sovereignty and at the same time embarrass Buchanan.

"I ACKNOWLEDGE NO MASTER BUT THE LAW"

The anti-Lecompton forces brought six indictments against the constitution and the Buchanan Administration: that the principle of majority rule had been violated; that the constitution was invalid because it had not been ratified by popular vote; that the people had no opportunity to choose between slavery or no slavery; that the constitution could not be amended until 1864; that Buchanan had betrayed Walker; and that the president had become the captive of a southern "Directory."

The debate on majority rule ran wild and revealed that Americans could not agree on a definition of it. Buchanan held that a majority meant a plurality of votes cast by legally registered voters in an election called by proper procedure to decide a question that had a legitimate place on the ballot. According to this definition, the Lecompton Constitution met every challenge.[6] Anti-Lecompton newspapers variously defined a majority as "fifty-one percent of all the potential voters," "a preponderance of those registered," "most of those who actually voted," or "a plurality of the representatives" of any of these three groups.[7]

If Douglas meant to protest a violation of the Kansas-Nebraska Act because the Lecompton vote failed to comprise a majority of all the potential voters, then he had to admit that the October vote for the free-state Legislature and the January 4 vote against Lecompton also violated the principle, as none of these comprised a plurality of the 24,000 bona fide male inhabitants of voting age. That Douglas believed sincerely in majority rule seemed refuted by the fact he disregarded the overwhelming majority of his own party in opposing Lecompton. Backed by twenty-two colleagues, he defied 150 Democratic Senators and Congressmen, using every power and parliamentary trick at his command to obstruct the policy of seven-eighths of his party's legislators.

The opponents of the Lecompton Constitution complained of fraud and harped on the term "fair vote." Douglas wanted resubmission, but Buchanan thought that another election would only produce more confusion; it would be an unwarranted admission that the first ballot was dishonest and permit the Republicans to prolong the agitation and again sabotage the effort of the Lecompton government to get out the vote.[8]

The Douglas bloc declaimed: "We must stand on the popular sovereignty principle," but when Buchanan proposed to implement this procedure they all repudiated his proposal. If they wished the people to act for themselves in their sovereign capacity, said Buchanan, place them immediately in a sovereign capacity. Make Kansas a state and then, indeed, its people could vote all of their domestic problems up or down. But Douglas, emphasizing that his doctrine applied only to the territorial stage, jettisoned the main principle and feared to admit Kansas to statehood. Buchanan, by urging the speedy admission of Kansas and inviting its people to scrap the Lecompton Constitution immediately thereafter, placed more faith in the basic principle of popular sovereignty than Douglas. Buchanan freely admitted that the proslavery part of the constitution ought to be thrown out, but the president could not do it. This was a job for the people of Kansas. Admit them to statehood and let them act.

Some historians, while admitting that the procedures of the Lecompton Convention were "quite legal," have airily dismissed this fact as a "lame technicality" and condemned Buchanan for his failure to "cling to principle."[9] Buchanan would have admitted privately that many of his arguments for Lecompton were expedient and shallowly political, but not his defense of its legality. He would not subvert the law just because the law happened to be, in his judgment, bad. The game of government had to be played by the rule book no matter how the crowd reacted. Said he, "I acknowledge no master but the law."

Douglas repeatedly accused Buchanan of trying to "force" the Lecompton Constitution on the people of Kansas "against their will, in opposition to their protest," and with foreknowledge that they would have voted it down if given the chance. "It does not mitigate the evil," Douglas argued, "that you are forcing a good thing upon them."[10] Buchanan thought it odd that there should be such violent resistance to an invitation to be free. It seemed to him that the protesting Kansans did not really want statehood and a chance to make whatever kind of constitution they wished; they liked the political effect of continued agitation. "Everybody with the least foresight," wrote Buchanan, "can perceive that, Kansas admitted, and the Black Republican party are destroyed; whilst Kansas rejected, and they are rendered triumphant throughout the Northern States. . . . I very much fear that the fate of the Union is involved."[11]

The second charge, that the Lecompton Constitution had no validity because the convention had not submitted it to a popular vote for ratification touched an interesting phase of the Kansas controversy. Buchanan stated that "under the earlier practice of the government, no constitution framed by the convention of a Territory . . . had been submitted to the people." The Philadelphia *Press* said that "Most State Constitutions have been submitted." Southern journals and letters emphasized that submission, while not wrong, was entirely unnecessary and contrary to general practice. Many western newspapers asserted that only popular ratification gave validity to a constitution.[12]

Historically, out of the 63 constitutions which had been adopted by the 33 states from 1776 to 1858, 30 had been ratified by popular vote and 33 had been proclaimed in force by a constitutional convention. Each section developed a different method. In the South, 21 of 30 constitutions had come into being by convention edict. In the West, 11 of 14 constitutions had been ratified by a vote of the people. In the New England and Middle Atlantic States, 10 constitutions had been submitted to popular vote, and 9 declared in effect by a convention. Thus, in the contest over Lecompton, each section reacted in conformity with its own historical tradition. Southerners fumed with rage when Douglas charged that the nonsubmission method of constitution-making was a cheat and a fraud. Westerners, so accustomed to popular ratification that they thought of it as a "right," immediately smelled a crooked deal when Kansans failed to use this practice. By 1858, only 9 of the states still lived under charters never ratified by the people, but of these 8 were in the South.[13] There was

305

no historic basis for the assertion of Douglas that the validity of a constitution depended upon its ratification by the people, but it would have taken more than a different personality in the White House to overcome the prejudices arising from the differing constitution-making traditions of the two sections.

The third charge was that the "slavery" or "no slavery" plebiscite offered no choice but protected slavery no matter how the vote went. This certainly had all the appearance of a swindle. The facts were these: if the voters chose the "constitution with slavery" a four paragraph article sustaining slavery would be inserted; if the other option won, the constitution would be silent on slavery. But a "schedule" accompanied the constitution, defining the details of procedure for setting up the new state. It stated that "property in slaves now in the territory shall in no manner be interfered with" and that the constitution could not be amended before 1864, and only then by a vote of two-thirds of both houses of the legislature confirmed by a popular election. These provisions were foolish and provocative, but they were not nearly so ironclad or tricky as the anti-Lecompton propaganda made them out to be. Had the free-state people of Kansas voted for the "no slavery" option, they would have agreed not to confiscate summarily the 200 Negro slaves then in residence, but they would not have secured to the owners any right to hold the newborn children in slavery. No court proclaimed a natural right in slavery—that is, its automatic existence without any creative law. Most northern states had abolished slavery when a few slaves still remained in their region and had avoided outright confiscation. The Pennsylvania abolition law of 1780 had projected for some years into the future the point when complete abolition would occur. This period gave opportunity for compensated emancipation, manumission by slaveowners or the removal of slaves from the state, but the law did not annihilate property rights.

The Lecompton Convention could easily have devised a plan for eventual emancipation that would have been less obnoxious to the North, but defenders of the Kansas Constitution could maintain with truth that the version "without slavery" would have made Kansas a free state just as quickly as the laws of Pennsylvania or New Jersey had brought free statehood. If Kansas was perpetrating a swindle, nearly every other northern state had done the same thing years before.[14] Furthermore, the Kansans could change the "schedule" after admission to statehood if they wished.

The next charge was that by means of the "schedule" a trifling minority had prevented the majority from making any changes before 1864. Buchanan's repeated assertion that no power on earth could keep the people of Kansas from amending their constitution or making a new one whenever they wished, once they had statehood, was confirmed by the practice of

306

other states. The president contended that the fastest conceivable way to enable the Kansans to create exactly the constitution they wanted would be to admit them to the Union.

Did Buchanan betray Walker? One will read in vain to find any statement from Buchanan that he considered the Lecompton Convention bound to submit its product to a public vote, or that he would reject a constitution not so submitted. He said on many occasions that he hoped the convention would submit; that he assumed it would; and that it should be encouraged to do so, but this was a far cry from a presidential order that the convention had to do it. Walker and many others read into Buchanan's letters a mandate where only a hope had been expressed.

Even the "stand or fall" letter to Walker on July 12 did not pledge the rejection of a proclaimed constitution. It read, "On the question of submitting the Constitution to the bona fide residents of Kansas, I am willing to stand or fall." Walker repeatedly broke instructions during May and June by committing Buchanan to the total submission policy, a position the president had never approved or authorized. Buchanan would have removed Walker for his insubordinate actions, but a dismissal at the time was politically impossible. To have broken with him so soon after all the effort to induce him to accept would have indefinitely wrecked any Kansas program. Moreover, no one else of similar stature would take the governorship under such circumstances, unless it would be an ardent partisan, and such a man could not administer the policy Buchanan deemed essential.

The president, therefore, took the calculated risk, gave Walker the "stand or fall" pledge, and hoped that the governor might succeed. Had Buchanan, at the risk of national safety, supported Walker in the abortive policy which the governor himself had originated, this support indeed would have demonstrated a weak and spurious consistency. Instead, Buchanan reaffirmed the policy he had instructed Walker to observe in the first place and philosophically accepted the abuse which came when the governor, with White House backing, failed to deliver what he promised. Walker did not seem to feel very seriously that Buchanan had "betrayed" him. After blustering for a while he came to dinner at the White House and a little later tried his best to persuade Douglas to return to the support of the Administration.[15]

A final aspect of the "betrayal" charge rests on an allegation that Buchanan had promised a "full and fair vote" in Kansas and, by accepting a partial vote, had reneged on his pledge.[16] But Buchanan never promised anyone that he would produce a full vote in Kansas; he could provide only the opportunity for a full and fair vote, and this he did.

Lastly, many historians have charged that Buchanan, in accepting Lecompton, weakly capitulated to a "Directory" composed of southern members of his Cabinet and the fire-eaters. "Through his career," says one,

"Buchanan had been a 'dough-face'—now the Fire-Eaters' threats filled him with unquenchable alarm . . . if he had not abandoned Walker, the Southern States would carry out their threats 'either to secede . . . or take up arms against him.' " Another writer states: "He was swayed by timidity: he quailed before the Southern menaces transmitted to him by Cobb, Thompson, and a hundred others." A third asserts that the southern clique "bent the president at will."[17]

There is no valid evidence that before 1860 any members of Buchanan's Cabinet were fire-eaters, nor did the president timidly give in to his advisors. Buchanan had included no extremists in his Cabinet; the aggressive antislavery wing of the Democracy had no representative in it, nor did the fire-eaters. Prior to the election of Lincoln, Cobb was one of the leading antisecessionists of the South. His political rivals there were the fire-eaters. Buchanan respected him, and it was Cobb, the Union Democrat who influenced him, if anyone did.

If Buchanan deferred to his Cabinet, that was one thing; but it was not deference to southern extremists. But did he defer to the Cabinet? He picked men who he knew already agreed with him. His ideas on southern rights and the supremacy of law had been demonstrated and stated by him for a generation. His support of Lecompton and the arguments in behalf of it were not prompted by threats or sweet talk, for he merely restated his old policy. No one needed to bend him into a shape he already held. He was going to enforce the letter of the law in Kansas, without regard to the advantage of one side or the other. None but the blind missed the irony of Buchanan's reply to Walker's bitter and denunciatory letter of resignation. The president had learned with pleasure, he wrote, that Walker in all his speeches had "refrained from expressing any opinion whether Kansas should be a slave or a free state."[18] If Walker had ruined his usefulness as an umpire by publicly declaring he would make trouble unless the northern team won, Buchanan would not follow him; and threats from the South did not govern the decision.

Why, we may ask, was Buchanan in the camp of the southern extremists in the fight over the Lecompton Constitution? The answer is simple: he was a legalist. He based his decision on the legality of the Kansas document. At that time his stand happened to favor the practical interests of the South. Cobb wrote, in the midst of the Lecompton struggle, that Buchanan could not be driven from his course "by the clamor either of the South or North—for he has encountered and resisted both."[19]

DRIVE THIS BILL "NAKED" THROUGH THE HOUSE

Buchanan carefully canvassed the Congress and found that the Lecompton Constitution would get a large majority in the Senate, and about 100 of the 118 votes needed for passage in the House. The prospects looked so good and the end to the infernal Kansas question seemed so near that he decided to make support of the admission bill a party measure and crack the whip to drive the few necessary stray votes into the fold. The opposition of Douglas might prove less serious than it had at first appeared. Political insiders guessed that he and Walker were "both throwing *high dice* for the Northern Democracy for Pres," and that they wanted to destroy Cobb, who seemed to have the inside track to the succession.[20] When this word got around, the Douglas crusaders for the "great principle of majority rule" might begin to lose their zeal and Douglas, when all the chips were down and the Democracy was mobilized for action without him, might give up the fight. He could not reach the White House with only the vote of Illinois.

In the South, the Legislatures of Alabama and Georgia had adopted resolutions requiring their governors to call state conventions to consider secession in the event that Congress denied admission to Kansas under the Lecompton Constitution. To quiet down some of the most excited southern Senators, Buchanan unwisely let them know some weeks in advance that he planned to transmit the Lecompton Constitution to Congress with his blessing as soon as the official copy should arrive from Kansas. This tied him down completely, and denied him the freedom of action which he could possibly have used to advantage later. He received a letter from Acting Governor Denver shortly thereafter advising him that angry Republicans in Kansas had developed a new scheme which might deprive Buchanan of all of the advantages he anticipated from quick admission. They had worked up a kind of "murder incorporated" to assassinate systematically all officers who might try to serve under the Lecompton Constitution. Kansas would be bloodier as a state than it had been as a Territory, and the Republicans would continue to have their campaign ammunition. Denver reported that most influential Kansans preferred the passage of a Congressional enabling act which would start the constitution-making process over again under clear authority and specified procedure. Buchanan probably regretted that he could not take up this plan which he had favored when it was first proposed some years before, but he had committed himself beyond recall. He had chosen the course which seemed to offer the best chance of success.[21]

Buchanan sent the Lecompton message to Congress on February 2. In it he tried to put the best possible face on a bad business, emphasizing that by no other means than admission to statehood could Kansas achieve peace and the nation be spared further agitation over slavery. In a letter to Arnold Plumer, he said,

> I am now thoroughly convinced that the question of the union is directly involved. . . . Should the Kansas Constitution be

309

rejected by Congress then the Topeka rebels will send a constitution here, not merely providing for a free state, but stuffed with all manner of abominations, . . . and everything which can be offensive to the South. . . .

There is much talk about the Lecompton 'swindle.' I have no doubt frauds were committed by both parties at contested elections, but none of these can be charged at any election necessary to give validity to the constitution. . . . These elections went by default. . . . It was the law & order party voting & the revolutionary mob headed by Jim Lane refused to vote. I have pursued the path of duty which I saw clearly from the beginning and I shall pursue it to the end. . . . I believe . . . that Kansas will be admitted; but upon a question involving the life or death of the union neither my anxiety nor my exertions shall cease until we are saved.[22]

The Senate would be safe with 39 Democrats; Douglas would oppose Lecompton, but would carry with him only David C. Broderick, George E. Pugh and Charles E. Stuart. But in the House the fate of Lecompton hung by a hair. Here there were 92 Republicans, 14 Americans, about 100 Administration Democrats and 21 rebellious anti-Lecompton Democrats, although the exact number of the latter remained uncertain from day to day. Buchanan's friends wanted the Lecompton message referred to the House Committee on Territories, but knowing in advance that this motion would not pass they proposed creating a select committee which Speaker James L. Orr would appoint. The anti-Lecomptonites moved to invest this committee with power to investigate. The Administration wanted at all hazards to avoid an investigation, for it could produce nothing but free propaganda for the Republicans and might delay action indefinitely. After an excited week of parliamentary maneuver, including a filibuster and a fist fight on the floor, the critical vote was called. The Administration lost, 113-114. One Buchanan Democrat, who straggled in a few minutes late, might have changed the course of American history. The House then proceeded by another close vote to authorize the appointment of a select committee with power to investigate but Speaker Orr packed it with pro-Lecompton men.[23]

Buchanan had to find some way to weaken and divide the Democratic anti-Lecompton bloc by just a few votes in order to win. The House committee waited for the Senate to act. During February and March a Senate proposal to admit Kansas and Minnesota as a "package," and a plan by Senator John J. Crittenden to submit the Lecompton Constitution to another vote in Kansas both failed. On March 23 the Senate passed a bill to admit Kansas under the Lecompton Constitution, specifying the right of immediate amendment and cutting down the proposed mammoth land grant of over 16,000,000 acres to the customary size of about 4,000,000 acres.

Douglas busied himself to prevent a single adherent from wavering or quailing under Administration threats. He did this organizational work so well that Buchanan at length despaired of breaking down the House opposition. The president used every means he could to pick up the few votes needed, dismissing friends of Douglas wholesale, holding up new appointments, and offering patronage, contracts, commissions, and in some cases cold cash. The women, wives of Senators and Cabinet members, used their charms to soften up opponents of the Administration.

President Buchanan held conferences continually, called for unselfish patriotism, and when all the softer means failed, invoked massive retaliation against Douglas. But one factor nullified much of this monumental Administration effort: the approaching elections of Congressmen in the North. These men feared they would not be re-elected if they sustained Lecompton.

Buchanan got some encouragement from Pennsylvania, whose legislature endorsed the Lecompton proposal. "God bless my good & great old State," he wrote. "They have not deserted me in my last political trial nor deserted the cause of Union & Democracy. *I say the cause of Union*, because if the Lecompton Constitution should be defeated in the House, . . . I apprehend it will be the beginning of the end."[24] But by the end of March he knew he could not succeed in his original purpose, to drive Lecompton "naked" through the House. Some compromise would have to be developed, and until it was ready the Senate bill had to be kept on ice in the House Committee room.

Buchanan's managers had to prevent a House vote on the Senate bill, for if it were defeated there could be no hope for further action. But if the House would add amendments, then possibly a conference committee could work out a compromise. Little risk would attach to the work of such a committee, for the Administration would control the appointment of its members. Buchanan cagily selected Representative William H. English of Indiana, an anti-Lecompton Democrat who favored some compromise solution, to initiate the move. "It will be your fate," the president wrote to him, "to end the dangerous agitation, to confer lasting benefits on your country, & to render your character historical."[25] Buchanan and Cobb fed ideas to English which he in turn proposed to his colleagues. In due course, the House sent the Lecompton bill back to the Senate with the Montgomery-Crittenden amendment for resubmission. The Senate voted this down and asked for a conference. The Administration used all the discipline it could muster, and English worked on some of his friends to support the plan which now had come to bear his name. After one of the

311

most dramatic roll calls in the history of the House, the clerk at last read the tally: 108 to 108. Speaker Orr broke the tie.

The conference adopted the expedient of a referendum on the land grant. If the people of Kansas voted to accept a reduced grant, the English Bill provided for immediate admission under Lecompton. If they rejected the offer, they could not reapply for statehood until the population had grown larger.

This proposition put Douglas in a difficult position, for it was, in the final analysis, the equivalent of resubmission. Douglas agreed to support the measure, but his anti-Lecompton colleagues forced him to change his mind and fight the referendum on the grounds that it was not the same as resubmission. His aboutface calmed the rising fear of some southerners that they were being betrayed by Buchanan into some kind of bargain with Douglas. Finally, on April 30, the English Bill passed, in spite of Douglas's opposition.

Of course Douglas and his supporters would continue as a separate faction, at least for a while, but Buchanan was not worried. "I have never known the Democratic party in Congress more united & compact than they were during the last three or four weeks of the session," he wrote. "From what I learn, Douglas has determined to come back to the party with a bound & to acquiesce cordially . . . in the English Bill."[26] With gratitude and a sigh of relief, Buchanan wrote to English, "It is painful even to think of what would have been the alarming condition of the Union had Congress adjourned without passing your amendment."[27]

24

A FLOOD OF INNOVATIONS • 1857-1860

PANIC AND WAR

When the new Democratic nominee told well-wishers at Wheatland in June, 1856, that he was "no longer James Buchanan, but the representative of the Cincinnati platform," he spoke not in jest. Buchanan considered the presidential office not as a place of leadership but as a post of executive agency. The president should faithfully implement and enforce the policies defined by deliberative bodies: the party convention, the Congress of the United States, and the federal courts. He should shoulder the responsibility not of invention but of action; he should not initiate policy but execute it with skill and efficiency. Party delegates distilled the hopes and fears of their constituents into a platform; the lawmakers of the winning party sought to translate this statement into statute; the president set up the administration of these laws, reporting from time to time the results of his efforts and calling for further legislation if needed to achieve the proper execution of the will of the legislature.

The Cincinnati platform did not provide much of a program. Except in the realm of foreign affairs, it spoke in the negative. In great detail it expounded all the things that the federal government could not do: assume state debts, inaugurate a system of internal improvements, aid private industry, give proceeds from sale of public lands to the states, establish a bank, or interfere with domestic slavery in any of the states. The platform urged vigorous opposition to all parties based on prejudice against foreigners and non-Protestants and pledged resistance to all attempts to revive the agitation of the slavery question. It endorsed the Kansas-Nebraska Act, promised a fair vote to the people of Kansas, and proclaimed "adherence to those principles and compromises of the Constitution—which are broad enough and strong enough to embrace and uphold the Union as it was, the Union as it is, and the Union as it shall be."

But the platform endorsed a vigorous foreign policy: the establishment of "free seas" and "progressive free trade" throughout the world,

313

the building and control of interoceanic trade routes in Central America, and the imposition of "our ascendancy in the Gulf of Mexico."

This program of the status quo at home and active diplomacy in the Caribbean well suited Buchanan's talents and desires. It had been his hope to settle the Kansas issue quickly and peaceably; he would then divert public attention from sectional interests by such foreign adventures as would raise the United States to the first rank among the powers of the world, and in so doing renew the flagging spirit of national pride and patriotism. So he hoped. But even had Kansas gone more nearly according to plan, Buchanan's timetable would have been interrupted. In August, out of the blue sky, the Panic of 1857 hit, and in September came word that Brigham Young's Mormons proposed to fight the United States army then en route to the new Zion.

In late July, Dr. Foltz wrote from New York: "The money market is easy, and on all sides we have health, abundance, and prosperity. We are truly a favored people." A month later the banks were popping like crackers, and fear and terror gripped Wall Street where crowds of trembling depositors jammed against the locked doors of banks and brokerage houses to read the notices posted there. Specie payments stopped, making the notes of some 1,400 state banks worthless; investment businesses went into bankruptcy, mills closed, and before long crowds of hungry workmen flocked to the public squares of northern cities chanting "Bread or blood."[1]

Though the causes of the panic were manifold, a few outstanding abuses seemed obvious. Americans had been buying goods from Europe at such a rate that specie was drained off. Railroads, in frenzied competition, built lines where for years there would be little likelihood of revenue; land speculators mortgaged themselves to the hilt for vast, vacant ranges which for decades could not be resold at a profit. The state banks, in aggregate, loaned $7.50 in their own notes for every $1.00 of gold or silver they had. Buchanan attributed the panic to "the vicious system of paper currency" and "wild speculations and gamblings in stocks." Northern industrialists blamed the tariff reduction of 1857, which Congress had passed the day before Buchanan took office.

Cobb immediately concentrated a large stock of subtreasury gold in New York and won a memorial of thanks from New York merchants for his prompt action. Other Departments, when revenue from customs and land sales dried up, ordered curtailment of public works. "*Not* at this time of crisis," came the anguished howls. "Labor needs the work. The Government can get the money. This is exactly the wrong time for retrenchment, for party and humanitarian reasons."[2]

In his Annual Message of December, 1857, Buchanan announced his policy: reform not relief. The government sympathized but could do

314

nothing to alleviate the suffering of individuals. It would continue to pay its obligations in gold and silver; it would not curtail public works, but it would start no new ones. To prevent recurrence of these periodic upheavals, Buchanan recommended that Congress pass a uniform bankrupt law which would provide for the immediate forfeiture of the charter of any bank that suspended specie payments. He urged the states to require their banks to reserve one dollar in specie for every three issued as paper and to prohibit the issuance of bank notes of less than twenty dollars so that employers would have to pay the weekly wages in coin. Buchanan held to the bullion theory of credit, not credit as value or prospects. He thus discouraged the use of federal or state bonds as security for bank note issues, for he feared that putting the civil debt into circulation would inaugurate an endless spiral of inflation.

This view of the panic conformed not only with the party platform but with Buchanan's personal attitude. Men who respected property would not put it out to work except with sound collateral; those who took the speculative risk deserved the gambler's fate. As to the innocent victims, rugged individualism would triumph over adversity; the buoyancy of youth and the energy of the people would enable them to recover. The prophecy proved correct, but not before untold thousands had suffered the misery of broken lives, imminent starvation, and despair.

Two ideas which would loom large in the future, grew out of the panic. In the North the factory workers, abandoned by the Democratic Administration, listened with eager belief to the vehement assertion of Republican leaders: they could blame their plight on the reduction of the tariff; with the Republicans in power the tariff would go up; and wages, in the ensuing prosperity, would go up, too. In the South, where the panic scarcely touched the cotton economy, James Hammond of South Carolina began to preach that "Cotton is King." "Thirty-five million dollars, we, the slaveholders of the South, have put into the charity box for your magnificent financiers," he said. The North, with its business gamblers, beggars, paupers, and so-called free-labor, "the very mud-sill of society" he named it, could not exist without the South. Wrote *DeBow's Review*: "The wealth of the South is permanent and real, that of the North fugitive and fictitious."[3]

In the western territory, Buchanan inherited an incipient war. The Mormons, viciously persecuted during their early existence and abominated by most Americans, had trekked to their State of Deseret only in time to be reincorporated into the United States by the Mexican cession. The Compromise of 1850 made their Zion the Territory of Utah, but for five years the government at Washington, except for appointing Brigham Young as governor, left the Mormons to themselves.

The Mormons had legitimate grievances. Congress had twice ignored their request for an enabling act to form a constitution and when they finally drew up an unauthorized document, President Pierce gave it no consideration. There might have been some chance of recognition if the leader of the Mormons had been willing to outlaw polygamy. Another cause of resentment was the refusal of the government land office to grant title to Mormon lands. The reason was that the Indian title had not yet been extinguished, but the Mormons feared that the government would eventually deprive them of their homes. There was bitter conflict between federal judges and local magistrates.

In 1855 President Pierce appointed three federal judges to Utah Territory. Two were renegade Mormons and the third a brutal, dictatorial Mormon-hater. They soon had the Territory in a turmoil. In the spring of 1857 several Mormon emissaries and the judges came to Washington carrying conflicting stories. The former charged the judges with conspiracy and attempts to defraud them of their land; the latter complained that they had been prevented from performing their duties, their official papers had been confiscated and burned, and they themselves had been driven from the Territory.

Buchanan should have verified these tales, but Mormon defiance of federal authority was traditional and he took the judges' version at face value. He appointed a new governor, Alfred Cumming, and in May ordered Colonel Albert Sidney Johnston to proceed to Utah with 2,500 troops to act as a *posse comitatus* to uphold federal law. It was to be one of the best equipped and best provisioned expeditions in American history, but flaws marred the planning. Through the pleas of Walker, the cavalry was ordered to stay in Kansas, leaving the Utah expedition a helpless target for the mounted Mormon guerrillas. Furthermore, the official letter informing Brigham Young that he was to be replaced by a new governor never arrived because the Pierce Administration had annulled the Utah mail contract.[4]

Young, knowing only that a large military force was moving against the Mormons, mobilized his own army and ordered a scorched earth policy. "There shall not be one building, nor one foot of lumber, nor a stick, nor a tree, nor a particle of grass and hay that will burn, left in reach of our enemies," he said.[5]

Among the miseries that were to be the lot of the Mormon expedition it will suffice to mention the destruction of the wagon trains, the ambushes, the theft of the oxen, the snow, and the gruelling two weeks that it took to struggle the last thirty miles to Fort Bridger. "It was a scene," said the *Atlantic Monthly*, "which could be paralleled only in the retreat of the French from Warsaw."[6]

At this point in the ridiculous little war, Buchanan's friend Thomas L. Kane of Philadelphia convinced the president that the Mormons were a peace-loving people and that Brigham Young would cooperate in any honest program of the Administration. Kane asked permission to go as a private agent to Utah and try to make peace. His mission was a success and the newly appointed governor was soon in office.

Cumming made the mistake of bringing the troops into Utah Territory. Thousands of Mormons fled before the army and burned their buildings and crops as they went. Buchanan offered amnesty to all inhabitants who would respect the authority of the government and moved the troops to a point forty miles away where they remained throughout his term in the presidency. Peace came to Zion, but it was a year before the Mormons who had left their homes in ruins began to return.[7]

POLICEMAN OF THE CARIBBEAN

Buchanan viewed the panic, Kansas and the Mormon War as unfortunate interruptions of his main administrative program. It was in the realm of foreign affairs that he proposed especially to engage the interest and attention of the nation. In his inaugural address he announced, "No nation will have a right to interfere or to complain if . . . we shall still further extend our possessions."[8] In what direction would this expansive force flow? "It is beyond question the destiny of our race to spread themselves over the continent of North America, and this at no distant day. . . . The tide of emigrants will flow to the South. . . . If permitted to go there, peacefully, Central America will soon contain an American population which . . . will preserve the domestic peace, while the different transit routes across the Isthmus . . . will have assured protection."[9]

Buchanan had outstanding qualifications for conducting foreign policy. No president since John Quincy Adams had had such wide diplomatic experience or had been personally acquainted with so many foreign heads of state, and none until Theodore Roosevelt would propose so aggressive a policy in the Caribbean. The first step would be to sweep European influence out of Central America; the second, to establish American control by purchase, annexation, or intervention. If the United States insisted that Europe should get out, it would have to assume responsibility for protecting the lives and property of European nationals in Central America. Buchanan urged an interpretation of the Monroe Doctrine which would provide for that protection. He assumed personal direction of the State Department, maintained an office there, and, with John Appleton, administered the diplomatic work of the Secretary of State. Cass, however, shared Buchanan's views; he was a rabid expansionist who for years had fought against European influence in the Americas, and the two worked in close cooperation on most matters of foreign policy.[10]

317

When Buchanan took office the Central American question had been substantially settled by the Dallas-Clarendon Treaty which the Senate ratified on March 12, 1857. This treaty provided that Great Britain would withdraw from her several Central American positions by agreements with the countries immediately concerned. But the Senate amended the treaty to include immediate British withdrawal from the Bay Islands and the British countered with another amendment unacceptable to Buchanan who would consider no proposal that left the fate of the Bay Islands to be settled later. He wanted no British base athwart an isthmian canal route.[11]

"That unfortunate Clayton & Bulwer Treaty must be put out of the way," he wrote directly to Lord Clarendon, with whom he maintained a frank and amiable private correspondence throughout his Administration. "It will be the bone of contention & a root of bitterness between the two Governments as long as it exists." Lord Napier, British Minister at Washington, had already admitted that the British could no longer maintain their "prospective" interpretation of the treaty.[12]

To prevent Buchanan from recommending summary abrogation of the treaty in his Annual Message of 1857, Britain appointed a special envoy to make the necessary withdrawal from Central America and instructed him to discuss his plans with Buchanan in Washington before proceeding south. The selection of the envoy obviously aimed at conciliation. Sir William Gore Ousley, brother-in-law of Mrs. James Roosevelt, had been an intimate friend during Buchanan's tenure at the Court of St. James. Ousley came to Washington on November 18, 1857, and told Buchanan that he would arrange cession of the Bay Islands to Honduras, place the Mosquito Indians under Nicaraguan sovereignty, and define clearly the boundaries of Belize. This met all American demands. But despite these assurances, Buchanan recommended abrogation of the Clayton-Bulwer Treaty. "The fact is," he said, "that when two nations like Great Britain and the United States . . . have unfortunately concluded a treaty which they understand in senses directly opposite, the wisest course is to abrogate such a treaty by mutual consent and to commence anew."[13]

This attitude irritated the British, who thought they had leaned over backwards to agree, even to the point of raising no formal objection to the recently negotiated Cass-Yrisarri treaty between Nicaragua and the United States which gave the latter the right to traverse the isthmus and protect the route with troops. This treaty was a violation of the Clayton-Bulwer pledges.

British interests in Central America had changed since 1850. Originally England sought control, or at least participation in control, of transisthmian routes; now she sought primarily commercial development in Central America itself. As there could be no exploitation of commerce so long as Central America remained the scene of political chaos, the British had little objection if the United States wished to bring order to these troubled nations and give them the benefit of stable government. "Pray believe," wrote Clarendon," .·. . that we neither wish nor want to have anything to do with Central America." "We would not accept such a *'damnosa possessio'* as Central America," he said, "if it could be offered to England as a gift."[14]

But Britain proposed to keep the treaty and accept the American interpretation of it. Thus the United States was still bound by its own interpretation, and that included the self-denying ordinance. The United States could not seize Central American territory or set up protectorates; the procedure would have to be more subtle. Buchanan thought that the canny use of claims and the peaceful migration of North Americans into the region might accomplish the desired results without raising an issue with England. Hence he violently attacked filibustering, which nourished hatred and excitement and discouraged peaceful immigration.

Just about the time of Ousley's arrival, the notorious filibuster, William Walker, "eluded" the vigilance of federal officers and set sail for Nicaragua with a fully equipped private army aboard his ship and the best wishes of southern sympathizers ringing in his ears. Buchanan assured the nation that he had alerted military and peace officers to prevent Walker's escape and pointed out that they had in fact apprehended him in New Orleans, but in accordance with existing law he gained his freedom on $2,000 bail and set out again on his military adventure. The president emphatically denounced such buccaneering enterprises as "robbery and murder" and called for stricter laws to hold and punish their leaders.

By the end of December word arrived that Commodore Hiram Paulding of the U. S. Navy had traced Walker's ship, the *Fashion*, to San Juan de Nicaragua, had seized Walker, and had brought him back. A federal marshall took Walker to Washington, where the State Department set him free on the ground that it had no jurisdiction and no charge against him. This was true, though why Attorney General Black did not promptly develop a charge of violation of the federal neutrality laws remains a mystery.

Buchanan reprimanded Commodore Paulding for exceeding his authority by leading an armed force into the territory of a friendly nation. Under international law, he could scarcely avoid disavowing this act; the United States would probably have declared war had a European naval vessel forced an entry into New Orleans to seize one of its nationals in that city. The sectional issue immediately arose, the North commending Paulding and the South condemning his rash violation of Nicaraguan soil to prevent Walker from doing the very same thing. After his release, Walker went to Mobile and in a public address told the wild and bizarre story that Buchanan had secretly encouraged him to seize Nicaragua but

319

had then changed his mind and double-crossed him. Within two years Walker met the fate he courted: death before a firing squad in Honduras.[15]

In Central America, the heads of state of Nicaragua and Costa Rica issued the Rivas Manifesto. In it they accused the Buchanan Administration of directing the attacks of filibusters because of Nicaraguan resistance to the Cass-Yrissari treaty. The Central Americans now put their countries under the protection of France, England, and Sardinia, against the "barbarians" of the United States.[16] In response to this outburst, Buchanan urged the American envoy to work unceasingly for the creation in Central America of "a federal system, resembling . . . that of the United States." Unless the Central Americans acted properly, said the president, reparations for the insulting Rivas Manifesto would be demanded and, if necessary, collected "by . . . efficacious means." Furthermore, the American government would resist at all times the European intervention and protection which had been requested.[17]

Sir William Ousley lingered long in the United States and joined Buchanan at Bedford Springs in August, 1858. There they enjoyed the ovation which the little town provided upon hearing the news that the Atlantic Cable had been completed. Two weeks later, Victoria sent to Buchanan the first official message to be carried by the cable. American newspapers which printed the brief, almost insultingly brusque text, thought that the queen had cast an intentional slur upon the nation, and they called on Buchanan to respond with indignation. Assuming that some mistake had occurred, he prepared a highly complimentary reply. For a time Americans grumbled about Buchanan's "toadyism," but it was announced a short time later that the cable had failed before the queen's communication was completed.

Victoria was highly pleased that Buchanan had, by an act of trust, sustained the good will between the countries and saved her from personal embarrassment. The incident was small; yet it may be counted among the series that gradually diminished rancor and bred better Anglo-American relations. Perhaps the most significant development in the changing British attitude was their abandonment, in 1858, of the right of search on the high seas.

Ousley eventually went to Central America, but instead of concluding the anticipated treaties, he "succeeded in raising the very D—l," as Buchanan complained to Clarendon. The envoy not only failed to negotiate the treaties which the British government had desired but also contributed to the Nicaraguan rejection of the Cass-Yrissari treaty. Britain replaced him with another diplomatic agent, who quickly completed his assignment. In his last presidential message, Buchanan was able to report: "Our relations with Great Britain are of the most friendly character. . . . The discordant constructions of the Clayton and Bulwer Treaty . . . have resulted in a final settlement entirely satisfactory to this government."[18] Buchanan erred in his prediction that a rapid flow of emigrants would now move southward into Central America, but he correctly assessed the importance to the United States of control of isthmian transit and laid the foundation for the building of the Panama Canal.

Corollary to the effort to drive European influence from Central America, Buchanan proposed to project American power into the region. He firmly believed that the political and economic ideology of the United States would bring peace, prosperity, and happiness to these neighboring lands, and he expected that unless the United States maintained law and order in Central America, the major European powers would intervene to do so. The imperative need to provide speedy and safe travel between the East and the West called for prompt action.

Buchanan urged, in successive annual messages, that Congress should authorize the president "to employ the land and naval forces of the United States in preventing the transit from being obstructed or closed by lawless violence, and in protecting the lives and property of American citizens travelling thereupon."[19] As incidents multiplied, Buchanan used the claims of American travellers as a club to obtain either money reparations or privileges, under the threat of reprisals. This technique Buchanan applied to troubles with New Granada, Costa Rica, Nicaragua and Mexico. Congress, however, regularly declined to authorize the use of troops at the president's discretion, and the Administration had to work almost entirely by diplomacy.

During his term of office, Buchanan negotiated a treaty with New Granada in which the latter acknowledged its responsibility for claims arising out of the Panama riot of April 15, 1856, and induced Costa Rica to refer claims against that republic to a board of commissioners. Furthermore, he persuaded Nicaragua to grant transit rights to the United States and bullied Mexico into submitting to American military occupation in times of civil disorder. But before these diplomatic objectives had been fully achieved, the hostile 36th Congress came in, and to win a two-thirds majority for any Administration-sponsored treaty proved impossible. Even the South now withdrew from cooperation in an aggressive foreign policy, for the southern leaders, already thinking of secession, did not want to help strengthen the federal government. Therefore Buchanan's hope of preponderance in Central America died a victim of sectionalism.

The Administration's Mexican policy went a good deal beyond the proposals for intervention which characterized efforts to impose law and order on the central republics. Buchanan wanted Mexican territory, either by purchase or by the creation of a protectorate of Mexico which might, in time, lead to the annexation of the northern provinces of Chihuahua and Sonora.[20]

321

The Mexican government presented a scene of utter chaos. John Forsyth, American Minister to Mexico, warned Buchanan that unless the United States swiftly offered Mexico her aid, help would come "in the form of a French Prince supported by ten thousand bayonets, or British gold, effecting that floating mortgage on her territories which we decline." Mexico had to lean on some power. "Shall it be Europe or the United States?" he asked.[21]

After Zuloaga seized control in Mexico in January, 1858, Forsyth immediately broached the topic of territorial cession. "You want Sonora?" he wrote to Cass in April. "The American blood spilled near its line would justify you in seizing it. . . . Say to Mexico . . . Give us what we ask for in return for the manifest benefits we propose to confer upon you for it, or we will take it."[22] This undiplomatic language reflected American reaction to the recent murder of the Crabbe expedition, the slaying by Mexicans of a group of Americans inside the United States border, the summary execution of three American physicians in Tacubaya, and a host of less spectacular executions, arrests, property seizures, and studied insults to official American agents. When Zuloaga, in May, 1858, began enforcement of a new decree taxing foreign property in Mexico, Forsyth on his own initiative broke diplomatic relations.[23]

In his message of December, 1858, Buchanan reviewed the Mexican situation and concluded that it was the duty of the United States "to assume a temporary protectorate over the northern portions of Chihuahua and Sonora, and to establish military posts within the same." The Senate Committee on Foreign Relations favorably reported a bill, but the Senate defeated it in February, 1859, by a vote of thirty-one to twenty-five.[24]

One other prospect remained. A special agent informed Buchanan that the newly established Juárez government might, if the United States backed it, part with some land. Forsyth was replaced by Robert McLane, who had instructions to deal with any government that seemed able to rule. McLane recognized the Juárez regime but soon found that he could expect no territorial cessions from it; the best he could do without upsetting the government, he reported, would be to buy transit rights and get authorization for the United States to use its own troops for protection of the right of way. While he labored to draw up a contract, the advocates of stronger measures, some American and some Mexican, bombarded Buchanan with pleas that he send soldiers to the border.[25]

In December, 1859, Buchanan urgently requested the power to send a military police force of volunteers to Mexico. Such troops, he thought, might settle there and become the nucleus of an American colony that would lend stability to the Sonora-Chihuahua region and promote its annexation. Congress did not grant the request. Early in 1860, Buchanan received the McLane-Ocampo Treaty in which Mexico agreed to give the

United States transit rights and the privilege of policing the route for a payment of $4,000,000. More important than the treaty itself was the "convention to enforce treaty stipulations" which Ocampo signed reluctantly after McLane assured him that the United States would keep the treaty in force, with or without the Mexican's signature.[26] The convention bound each government to send military forces, on request, to the aid of the other when internal disorder threatened violation of the pact.

The fate of Juárez lay in the treaty. If it should be rejected and Juárez should collapse, McLane reported, "anarchy will be the order of the day, and American influence will cease here." "Let us take the constitutional government firmly by the hand," he urged, "and we will in a twelve-month drive out of Mexico every anti-American element and pave the way for the acquisition of Cuba. Indeed, if Spain should execute the threats she is now making . . . against Vera Cruz, American privateers will soon make their anchorage under the Moro."[27]

The treaty received wide discussion in the newspapers; the North generally condemned it as another Administration plan to strengthen the slave power, and the South in general favored it. The Senate debated and rejected the proposal in May, 1860. European nations, except Spain, had expressed the hope that the United States might bring order to Mexico, but with this prospect now dead they had to consider a plan to collect their own claims and protect their interests. Buchanan saw that this meant foreign intervention, which the United States could not, under these circumstances, oppose. In order to make his position perfectly clear, Buchanan sent a circular to Mexico stating the determination of the United States to prevent by arms any attempt of Europe to intervene in Mexican politics, but he added that his government could not deny "their right to demand redress for injuries inflicted on their respective subjects."[28] Not for a half century would any president of the United States try as hard to establish his country as the policeman of the Caribbean. Buchanan's forewarning of European intervention proved true when Prince Maximilian with a French army took control of Mexico during Lincoln's presidency.

Far to the south Buchanan achieved very quickly the settlement of claims and protection of American citizens by a show of force. The Paraguayans in 1855 had fired on the American steamer, *Water Witch*, and had killed a sailor. In addition, a number of United States citizens claimed that Paraguay had seized their property in violation of the 1853 treaty. Buchanan obtained authorization from Congress to send commissioners, backed by a strong naval force, to Paraguay to demand redress. "We must not fail," Buchanan instructed Secretary of the Navy Toucey. "Better take time than run any risk."[29] Toucey sent nineteen warships mounting 200 guns to convince Paraguay, which had next to no navy, that the power of the United States must be respected. The desired redress was speedily forthcoming. It must be added that Buchanan saw more at stake than the national reputation in Paraguay. The European countries had begun to manifest as much interest in the growing economy of the area around the La Plata as earlier they had in Central America, and the show against Paraguay was put on for a wider audience; its real theme was that the United States had the will and the power to enforce the Monroe Doctrine.

Of all the elements of his Latin-American policy, Buchanan personally had most interest in the acquisition of Cuba. He had advocated its purchase since the 1830's and as president he called again for money and political support to attain the "Pearl of the Antilles." In his efforts to persuade Congress to back the renewal of negotiations, Buchanan emphasized Cuba's strategic importance as the Gibralter of the Gulf of Mexico, the continual annoyance it had caused the United States, and the confusion of its government and economy. Most of the claims against Spain arose from injuries to United States citizens by Cubans; the African slave trade centered in Cuba, producing incidents which inflamed partisan hatred in the United States and kept the American Navy busy in efforts to apprehend slave ships; and finally, there existed the ever-present prospect of political revolt and race war in Cuba. "If I can be instrumental in settling the slavery question . . ., and then add Cuba to the Union," Buchanan said after his nomination, "I shall be willing to give up the ghost."

The president did not mention Cuba in his first annual message, but he did authorize the American Minister to Spain to make cautious inquiries as to the best way of opening a negotiation to acquire the island.[30] The next year, however, he came out strongly for its purchase and asked Congress to appropriate funds with which to pay Spain the long-standing debt that resulted from the old *Amistad* case. In addition, he requested a much larger sum to be used as an advance payment immediately upon the conclusion of a treaty with Spain. He termed the remittance prior to ratification "indispensable to success."

On January 1, 1859, Slidell introduced a bill in the Senate calling for an appropriation of $30,000,000 "to facilitate the acquisition of the Island of Cuba by negotiation." The bill was referred to Committee, and reported back favorably within the month, accompanied by a full account of prior negotiations. The report concluded that there were but three solutions for the Cuban problem: control by some European power other than Spain; independence, which would probably result in some form of protectorate; or annexation to the United States.

Official introduction of the bill brought a long debate in Congress and a full-scale newspaper war in America and Europe. The opposition made Buchanan the chief target of its attack. Zachariah Chandler called the money "a great corruption fund for bribery." Doolittle of Wisconsin

324

said the whole bill was a fraud; the millions were never intended for Spain but rather for the Democratic campaign chest.[31]

Others argued that Buchanan had presented "the subjugation of Mexico, the taking of Central America and the acquisition of Cuba" as the means to secure his renomination in 1860. Crittenden of Kentucky thought it was a "mere piece of fanfaronade—a sort of political fireworks set off . . . to amuse and entertain the people."[32] The southerners described Cuba as "panting for liberty," pointed to the advantages of making the Caribbean a *mare clausum* for the United States and banishing European influence from the Americas, and stated their readiness to acquire territory from Alaska to the Horn.[33] To this, Collamer of Vermont replied: "If you take Cuba, you must take Jamaica; you must take San Domingo; you must take the Bahama Islands," for each of these would prove as much an "annoyance to Cuba, if part of the Union, as Cuba was to the United States."[34] A statement from the Spanish government that it would never abandon "the smallest portion of its territory," arrived in the midst of the debate and was exploited to the fullest by enemies of the Cuban purchase. The opposition proved so strong that Slidell withdrew the bill, fearing to wreck the project by letting it come to an adverse vote.

Buchanan recommended the purchase of Cuba in his messages of 1859 and 1860, but the proposal never again got to the floor of Congress. The Senate even rejected a Spanish offer to pay claims it owed to the United States, fearing some deal about Cuba. Buchanan's determination reflected his Scotch pertinacity and his seriousness of purpose. "We must have Cuba," he was in the habit of saying, but his enemies took delight in translating his statement into the words, "We must have slavery."

AN EXTRAVAGANT LIST OF MAGNIFICENT SCHEMES

Buchanan projected his interest in territorial expansion not only to the south, but also to the Pacific northwest. When a contest arose over ownership of San Juan, off Vancouver Island, and American settlers challenged at gun point the efforts of agents of the Hudson's Bay Company to drive them out, he ordered navy units and an army force under General Scott to hold possession and negotiated a joint-occupation agreement until final settlement could be arranged. His own papers of the 1845 Oregon negotiation led to British withdrawal from the disputed area.

But of much more importance was Alaska. During the Crimean War, Russia had approached the Pierce Administration with the offer to sell the huge Arctic peninsula. In the fall of 1857, the Russian Minister, Baron de Stoeckl, talked with Buchanan about it. Since the Mormons seemed determined to set up an independent nation in Utah, Buchanan

325

toyed with the idea of colonizing them in Alaska. There was a rumor that they might go there, anyway; and when Stoeckl asked the president whether they would go as conquerors or colonists, Buchanan replied with a laugh that it mattered little to him, provided he got rid of them.

Two years later the Alaskan question was revived. Senator Gwin of California discussed it with Buchanan and they agreed that an offer ought to be made. Gwin informed Baron de Stoeckl that the United States proposed five million dollars as a base of negotiation and urged that he begin talks with the State Department. Stoeckl called the price too low for serious consideration, but Buchanan would not go higher because the treasury was depleted and the Congress hostile to him; he might carry through a bargain but felt he could not indulge in an extravagant outlay for rocks and ice.[35] Seward later took up the proposal where Buchanan had left it.

The Buchanan Administration greatly extended American commercial opportunities, and opened the door to diplomatic relations with Asia. Reciprocal trade privileges in selected commodities were arranged with Brazil and with France. An exchange of ministers was projected with Persia and initiated with Japan as a huge and colorful Japanese delegation visited Washington to officiate at the signing of the first treaty. Buchanan sent two of his most trusted friends to China, William B. Reed of Pennsylvania and later John E. Ward of Georgia. These gentlemen represented the interests of the United States during the Anglo-French war against China and, coming in at the end, succeeded in obtaining for their country trade privileges equivalent to those won by the French and the English. Within a year of the signing of the Chinese Treaty, American trade with the Orient leaped upward. Buchanan's Asiatic policy represented an extension of his program to achieve rapid, safe transcontinental transit and looked to the fulfillment of Asa Whitney's dream of the United States as the funnel of Oriental trade to Europe. Had Congress been as much interested in this as it was in sectional politics, the United States might have entered actively into the commercial and political development of Asia a half century before it did, and this participation might have altered considerably the course of later international events.

Buchanan's accomplishments in diplomacy fell far short of his early hopes and expectations, and he held Congress chiefly responsible for his failures. But he had recommended the party program and almost without legislative aid carried out a good deal of it. He induced England to give up the long-asserted right to search American vessels on the high seas; he developed trade by treaty on three continents, and he established rights of transit in Central America. Beyond these things he firmly maintained the rights of American citizens abroad, by force in Central and South America, and by treaty in Europe where France finally acknowledged

326

French-born naturalized citizens of the United States as expatriates, no longer subject to French military service or jurisdiction when visiting in that land. He enlarged the scope of the Monroe Doctrine by asserting the responsibility of the United States, "as a good neighbor," to keep order in the Caribbean, and by professional diplomacy Buchanan enhanced the the reputation of the country in foreign circles.

Modern Americans hear little of Buchanan's diplomatic efforts which, after the outbreak of the Civil War, appeared insignificant enough. Yet, during his Administration, the nation considered his foreign policy aggressive and adventuresome. Wrote the *National Intelligencer:*

We must retrench the extravagant list of magnificent schemes which has received the sanction of the Executive. . . . The great Napoleon himself, with all the resources of an empire at his sole command, never ventured the simultaneous accomplishment of so many daring projects. The acquisition of Cuba . . .; the construction of a Pacific Railroad . . .; a Mexican protectorate; international preponderance in Central America, in spite of all the powers of Europe; the submission of distant South American states; . . . the enlargement of the navy; a largely increased standing army . . . what government on earth could possibly meet all the exigencies of such a flood of innovations?[36]

25

CHAOS AT CHARLESTON • 1860

A FATAL FEUD

With the passage of the English Bill, Buchanan renewed his hope of achieving an end to the violent agitation of the slavery question. Only Douglas stood in the way, and he would have to be conciliated or thrown out of the party. Buchanan knew which course would be wisest; he wished to end the feud. Although he let the anti-Douglas Democrats in Illinois, led by Isaac Cook, go ahead with their preparations to name an anti-Douglas senatorial ticket, he cut off further favors to Cook's faction and hinted that he would stop fighting Douglas as soon as Douglas stopped fighting him.

By June, 1858, many Democratic editors wrote as if they could not recall that there had ever been any differences between the Little Giant and Old Buck, and even Abraham Lincoln observed that Douglas and Buchanan had buried the hatchet.[1] The anti-Lecomptonites began to drift back to the Administration fold; only the few consumed by personal hatred of Buchanan, such as Forney, Broderick, and Shields, remained adamant. Their refusal to return to the party worried Douglas, for he perceived that he might, indeed, share the fate of Tallmadge and Rives. For a time he tried to concoct a deal with Illinois Republicans to run for Senate on both the anti-Lecompton and Republican tickets. He took "steep free-soil ground" but soon found that this position seriously damaged him in the South and failed to persuade the Illinois Republicans. At length he acquiesced rather unhappily in the decision of the stiff-backed anti-Lecomptonites that the little phalanx should continue as a distinct political bloc.

On June 9, Cook's convention of Administration Democrats in Illinois produced so weak a ticket that even Buchanan admitted the hopelessness of trying to beat Douglas on his home ground. Howell Cobb, who had been in charge of firing Douglas officeholders during the spring, now strongly urged reconciliation and Slidell agreed.[2] Buchanan remained agreeable but wary. He told the Cabinet that Douglas had betrayed the Administration once and would not scruple to do it again, but he would not block Douglas's return to the party. The door stood open; Douglas would have to move if he wished to enter. He made that move on June 15, announcing in the Senate that he hoped to rejoin the regular Democracy. A tentative agreement was reached: if Douglas would approve of the English Bill and stop attacking Buchanan, Buchanan would withdraw Cook's Democratic ticket in Illinois and give Administration backing to Douglas's senatorial campaign.[3]

In the meantime, the Illinois Republicans, on June 16, named Abraham Lincoln as their nominee for Senator. This meant formidable opposition to Douglas and a campaign that would center on the Kansas issue. Douglas, on his trip back to Illinois in early July, encountered such marked evidence of northern disgust with the English Bill that his conciliatory mood weakened. In a moment of dramatic inspiration he determined to run for the Senate against the Republicans and the Buchanan Democrats and take them both into camp. *That* should make him president. On his arrival in Chicago, on July 9, while telegrams completing the peace treaty were already speeding toward him from Washington, he delivered a harsh public tirade against President Buchanan.

Buchanan thought the ensuing campaign in Illinois a tragedy. Lincoln challenged Douglas to a series of debates and these contests throughout the summer of 1858 drew the excited attention of the nation to the very questions which the president hoped he had removed from the realm of campaign politics. Lincoln, in order to widen the Democratic split, said that Douglas "had a great deal more to do with the steps that led to the Lecompton Constitution than Mr. Buchanan."[4] Douglas spent nearly as much effort assailing Buchanan as he did fighting Lincoln.

Both men scattered firebrand statements about in the heat of debate which seemed to serve their immediate local purpose, and some of these caught the public imagination and set the nation ablaze. Lincoln's friends had made him promise not to use the provocative "house divided" argument, but he used it anyway. Lincoln could never thereafter persuade fearful southerners that he would not aggressively attack slavery. Douglas, with equal lack of reserve, declaimed: "All you have a right to ask is that the people shall do as they please."[5] Buchanan observed that such careless talk only inflamed public opinion. It would soon destroy all reason, render powerless the tools of practical politics, and terminate in national disaster. He might heal the split in the party, he might do without Douglas in the Senate, but he perceived no way to calm the tempest of sectional hatred and bigotry which these debates were regenerating at the very moment when the storm seemed at last to be receding. Buchanan condemned both men for sacrificing the public interest to their personal ends.

Governor Wise of Virginia summed up Buchanan's problem succinctly. Douglas's success in Illinois, he said, "*without* the aid of the

Administration will be its rebuke; his defeat with its opposition will be the death of the Administration; and his success with the aid of the Administration might save it and the Democratic party."[6] The president agreed with Wise. He had offered his help, but Douglas had decided that Buchanan's enmity was more valuable politically than his support.

Howell Cobb spoke the view of the Administration:

> If Judge Douglas had done as he promised . . . all of us ought to have sustained him. Such has not been his course. *Publicly* he attacks the administration. . . . *Privately* he indulges in the coarsest abuse of the President. . . . Under these circumstances to ask our support is in my opinion asking too much. . . . [Douglas is] determined to break up the Democratic party. . . . Forney announced in plain language his purpose . . . to unite with anybody and everybody to defeat us.[7]

Buchanan followed the election returns with nervous apprehension. Late summer reports raised his hopes, but by the time the October tallies had come in the outlook became bleak as the approaching winter. Douglas made good his threat to beat the Republicans and the Administration Democrats in Illinois, and his astounding triumph expanded both his reputation and his ego. In Pennsylvania, New York, New Jersey, Ohio, Indiana, and New England the Congressmen who had sustained the English Bill were generally defeated. Worst of all for Buchanan, J. Glancy Jones, the Administration "whip" in the House, had been beaten in Pennsylvania by the frantic efforts of the "Forney mob." Who could replace him?

He wrote to Harriet after the election, "Well! we have met the enemy . . . & we are theirs. This I have anticipated for three months. Yesterday . . . we had a merry time of it, laughing among other things over our crushing defeat. It is so great that it is almost absurd. . . . The conspirators against poor Jones have at length succeeded. . . . With the blessing of Providence, I shall endeavor to raise him up & place him in some position where they cannot reach him."[8]

In addition to Jones, there were many other defeated candidates for whom some new post had to be found. Just at this moment the terms of many Pierce appointees in the foreign service came to an end. Buchanan might have filled the vacancies with disturbers of the peace or he might have used these choice appointments as a means of purchasing needed support, in accordance with his patronage policy of 1857. But now he had to give the jobs to his wounded friends. In so doing he would gain no additional strength and would send out of the country the very people who were most valuable on the domestic scene. Within the year he had shipped out of the combat zone the strong leaders of the Democratic organizations in the northern states whom he needed as delegates to the nominating convention at Charleston. One after another, he had placed them in positions where they were safe from their enemies and at the same time unable to help him. Buchanan had made an error in tactics the magnitude of which became apparent only in the spring of 1860. His consolation was in the thought that he had rewarded his friends.

The exact complexion of the 36th Congress would not become clear until the last state elections in the summer of 1859. The Democrats still might control if Douglas behaved himself. With his usual optimism, Buchanan wrote to Hiram Swarr in Lancaster: "Politically the prospects are daily brightening. From present appearances the party will ere long be thoroughly united. Douglas will stand alone in the Senate if he does not come back fair & square." Apparently less confident of his personal future than of his party's, he enclosed an unsolicited check for $500 for Swarr's church.[9]

Buchanan's second annual message of December, 1858, painted the picture of a virile nation which had weathered the storm of financial panic and the hurricane of Kansas, and now sailed a calm sea of unlimited opportunities. Britain had renounced the right of search and would soon be forced to withdraw from Central America; commercial treaties were being completed with China, Japan, and other countries of the Far East. To encourage rapid expansion of the economy Buchanan asked for an increase in the navy, authority to protect transport routes through Panama, Nicaragua, and Mexico, the construction of a Pacific Railroad, and a revision of the tariff to increase revenue. Most important of all, he urged the purchase of Cuba to gain dominance of the Caribbean. Through this program, the United States would "attract to itself much of the trade and travel of all nations passing between Europe and Asia" and would soon become the wealthiest and most powerful nation on the globe.

Except for the sectional passions aroused over Lecompton and the refusal of Douglas to rejoin the Administration party, this program might have aroused national pride and patriotic enthusiasm. Instead, it served only to intensify the sectional contest. The themes of slavery and sectional advantage sooner or later came to dominate every Congressional debate. The North killed Cuba, the South killed the tariff, and strange combinations of vengeful and frustrated lawmakers prevented action on the other proposals. The president's program failed either to command the needed votes in Congress or to arouse enthusiasm outside. The people back home seemed to have lost interest in national glory and achievement; led on by their local representatives, they could be excited only by the intramural contest.

Some people imagined that a stirring voice from the White House at this juncture might have interrupted such petty bickering and enlisted powerful support behind a president willing to act without reference to Congress or the Constitution. Others admitted that even the voice of Andrew Jackson could scarcely have united the discordant factions of Democrats or altered the sectional bias of Republicans. But Buchanan had no desire to rule without Congress, and Congress did nothing.

By March 3, 1859, the day before adjournment, Congress had not even passed the routine Treasury bills. Buchanan, in an agony of frustration, sent in a hurried message warning that the government could not pay federal salaries unless Congress provided the means. The bill passed only after an all night battle, but it failed to include any provision to pay a large post-office deficit. Postmaster General A. V. Brown, though desperately ill of pneumonia, conducted the fight for his Department from his sickbed, but Congress adjourned without passing the post-office bill. Brown, defeated and exhausted, died four days later.[10]

While Buchanan continued to express optimism, he knew that worse was still to come. If this was a sample of control by the Democrats, what would happen when the Republicans commanded the House in December? He could scarcely tolerate the thought and sought distraction in administrative work, visiting around the Department offices to check up on the activities. As others began to lose confidence in him, he boasted greater confidence in himself. A newspaper reported, "Mr. B. is delighted at the idea that any member of his Cabinet should get sick, and is in the habit of saying every day, 'I never was in better health in my life; I can take my glass of Old Monongahela, dine heartily, indulge in Madeira, and sleep soundly, and yet my Cabinet is always dilapidated.' "[11] When Secretary Thompson asked for some time off, Buchanan told him that "he thought all his Cabinet had better leave and he and the different clerks would manage matters till their return."[12]

THE LONELIEST JOB IN THE WORLD

But despite this bold front, the impending collapse of his party weighed heavily on him and changed his conduct in ways which nearly everyone saw except himself. In the privacy of the White House he became more irritable, impatient, fussy, and dictatorial. Harriet complained and chafed under the need to suppress all her feelings for "Nunc's sake." Sophie Plitt urged her to marry at once, for if she felt lonely in the White House, she would be utterly forlorn when they all returned to Wheatland.[13] After completing her duty as hostess until Congress adjourned, Harriet left for a three months' visit to New York, Philadelphia, and Lancaster. When Buchanan's friends asked if he did not miss her, he replied, "I do not care how long she stays. I can do very well without her." Responded Kate

Thompson, "Who can expect anything better from such a *hardened* old Bachelor!"[14]

The row with Harriet arose in part from Buchanan's rigid discipline for White House social events—no cards or dancing—but more especially from his nosiness about his niece's private affairs. Harriet found it particularly exasperating that "Nunc," either from suspicion or preoccupation, often opened her mail. On such letters he would endorse the words, "Opened by mistake. I know not whether it contains aught of love or treason." Harriet at length discovered a way to communicate in security with Mrs. Plitt. Buchanan received fresh butter regularly from Philadelphia in a locked, brass-bound kettle. Harriet obtained the White House steward's key, sent a duplicate to Sophie, and during the last years of the Administration the two sent their private mail "via the kettle," as they wrote on the envelopes.[15]

After quitting his job as secretary, James Buchanan Henry went to New York and proceeded to marry without his uncle's blessing. To celebrate his independence, James Henry raised a huge black moustache which, one guest reported, "looked awful" and which the president would have made him shave off had he been present, but Buchanan did not attend the wedding and sent no gift—at least none was on display, from which the guests concluded that none had been given.[16]

The widow Craig, who had been living at the White House during December and January, also departed. She had affected Buchanan more deeply than most women; he confided to Cobb, much to the latter's amusement, that he spent restless nights dreaming of her. The president kept up a bold front and proclaimed his indifference, but he felt hurt and lonely. During May he practically took possession of Howell Cobb, whose wife had returned to Georgia, having him to meals at the White House every day and calling on him "to give an account of himself" whenever he was absent.[17]

By mid-May Buchanan's social life had dwindled to informal parties with his official family, notably the Thompsons, the Blacks, Cobb, Cass, the Gwins, Judge Mason and Bob Magraw. Toward the end of the month he accepted an invitation from the Mayor of Baltimore to select a site for the new courthouse and submit designs for the main courtroom. Accompanied by a dozen of the "regulars," he made a frolic of the visit to Baltimore. The men toured likely spots, the women window-shopped, and all concluded the affair by a sumptuous dinner at Barnum's, enlivened by plenty of wine at $10 a bottle. They returned on the evening train, much to the annoyance of the younger members of the party, who wanted to stay for the theater, but the "old Chief" would have none of this. The inside circle considered it something of a triumph to have gotten "Old Pub Func" out of the capital at all. "Who urged him up to it?" inquired Mrs. Cobb. "Mrs. Gwin or Mrs. Ledyard?"[18]

333

Buchanan at length got on the nerves of his associates. Thus it was that some of the Cabinet tried to get him out of Washington and cooked up a presidential tour to the South in June. There came to be something pathetic in the way the Cabinet bobbed, curtsied, and put on the "happy family" act in Buchanan's presence and ridiculed him in private. They respected his talent and feared his wrath, but they hated his sanctimoniousness. Kate Thompson called him "Old Gurley" (for Phineas Gurley, the Senate Chaplain) or "The pride of the Christian World." Mrs. Cobb wrote in the broadest sarcasm of "The greatest President that we have had since *Washington* and *Jackson!* And Miss Lane, the *model* of an American girl!!"

On Monday, May 30, President Buchanan accompanied by Thompson and Magraw left Baltimore by boat for Norfolk; from there they went to Raleigh and Chapel Hill. The newspapers reported the president "gay and frisky as a young buck," and Cobb said that "the old gentleman was perfectly delighted with his trip. . . . There has not been since the days of Genl. Jackson such an ovation to any President." Even Kate Thompson admitted, after hearing the report of her husband, "truly I think the old Rip Van Winkle waked up for this occasion. . . . He had a good time in N. Carolina for Mr. T. says he kissed hundreds of pretty girls which *made his mouth water!*"[19]

Buchanan returned to Washington on June 7, and Harriet came back from her vacation shortly thereafter. Since the heat of the summer was beginning to set in, the household moved to more comfortable quarters at the Soldiers' Home. At this time Buchanan was interested in a wealthy grass widow, Mrs. Bass from Virginia. One afternoon she drove out to the presidential retreat for a visit. When her rig came in full view of the group on the piazza, according to a report of one of the guests, "the President immediately left. In a few moments after we had said howdy & got seated the Old Chief came tripping and smiling out, dressed in an inch of his life— & Mrs. Gwin declares he changed his coat, pants & shoes in that short time—to see the widow. Now, did you think any woman could make him do that much?"[20]

Toward the end of July, Buchanan set out for his regular fortnight at Bedford Springs, taking the widow Bass and her three young children with him. The pleasant interlude was marred by only two incidents. Buchanan found himself placed in rooms next to Simon Cameron, and the abolitionists ran away with Mrs. Bass's Negro servant girl. People at the Springs generally assumed that Cameron had arranged the episode to spite Buchanan. Apparently, some people of Bedford had persuaded the girl to leave and had given her money with which to travel farther North. But Mrs. Bass took it calmly, announcing that the girl was honest and capable, and had taken none of the money and jewels available in the rooms. She hoped only that others would care for her and treat her kindly, which she feared they would not.[21]

Buchanan and his "Court" returned to Washington on the first of August. It had been a gay, restful summer, a far cry from the nerve-wracking pressure of congressional politics. Now it was time to get back to business. The last elections for the 36th Congress had been held and the exact nature of that body stood revealed. The Democrats would control the Senate, but they were a minority in the House whenever the Republicans allied with Douglas Democrats or Whig-Americans. What kind of a program could possibly achieve cooperation from such a legislative body? Buchanan had to figure out the answers to that question in the preparation of his next annual message.

DOWNGRADING THE PRESIDENCY

While the year 1859 outwardly looked peaceful and calm in comparison with the two previous years, it bred its share of ugly incidents. Seward's dark prophecy of "irrepressible conflict;" the angry Congressional debates on Cuba, the tariff, and public land; the Ohio trial of the Oberlin-Wellington prisoners whose crime had been to rescue a human being from slavery; the cases of the *Echo* and the *Wanderer*, highlighting the overseas slave-trade; the Vicksburg Convention proposals to reopen this brutal traffic under law; the calculated murder of Senator Broderick in a California political duel; and the pamphlet war between Douglas and Attorney General Black in August and September—all these kept tension high and slavery in the spotlight. The October elections brought the worst kind of news for Buchanan: more Republican victories in Pennsylvania, Ohio, and Iowa.

Late on Monday morning, October 17, Buchanan received word of some trouble at Harpers Ferry. The crew of the night train from Wheeling to Washington had telegraphed the news that an armed force of abolitionists at the Ferry had captured the bridge and town, shot a watch-man, killed a Negro porter, and apparently intended to terrorize the countryside. Buchanan hurriedly met with Secretary Floyd and ordered a force of artillery and marines under the command of Col. Robert E. Lee to the scene. By two p. m. he had on his desk a copy of the *Baltimore Sun Extra* with headlines: "Negro Insurrection at Harpers Ferry. Headed by 250 Abolitionists. The Armory Seized—Trains Stopped—Cars Fired Into— One Man Killed" and a more detailed account of events. Not until the next day did he learn that old John Brown, the Kansas murderer, led the rebel band. His few dozen followers soon capitulated to the state and federal troops, and Brown himself was captured alive. Floyd made an investigation but found no need to proclaim martial law. Governor Wise of Virginia was on hand and laid claim to Brown as a state prisoner. A Virginia court found him guilty of murder and treason within two weeks of the affair and the authorities hanged him on December 2.

One can scarcely imagine an episode better designed to arouse the worst passions of Americans than John Brown's raid. The South soon learned that the idea of the attack had not been confined to the diseased mind of the perpetrator. Half a dozen prominent and wealthy New England abolitionists who had at least a partial knowledge of Brown's plans had financed the arming of the raiders. In addition to the "Secret Six," other distinguished northerners had helped Brown and now glorified him with their pens. Some northern extremists exploited him as a latter-day Christ and set him up as a martyr.

Governor Wise saw to it that Brown's trial should be conducted with the utmost dignity and decorum. He talked at length with Brown, pronounced him entirely sane, and made clear to southerners what they had scarcely dared to believe before—that a perfectly normal antislavery partisan of the North, financed by the "best people" there, could calmly plot mass murder as if it were a part of the day's business. Although Republican leaders scurried to disassociate themselves from all connection with Brown, the southerners set him up as a stereotype of northern Republicans.

John Brown's raid strengthened the Republican party by bringing to a dramatic focus the moral issue of slavery. Lincoln and his partisans might later pledge that they wished to save the Union, with slavery or without it, but after Harpers Ferry no one south of the Ohio or Potomac would ever believe them. The disturbance also widened the rift in the Democratic party. Congress met three days after John Brown's body stretched hemp. What now would southerners think of Douglas Democrats who, through the whole past session, had linked hands with Republicans on the slavery issue? How could they tolerate men who had made war on the Democratic party by alliance with the promoters of Brown's foray? Southerners now called the anti-Lecompton bloc the "Black Republican Reserve." Douglas might have perceived more clearly than he did the depth and conclusiveness of this southern attitude. Finally, the raid made the idea of secession, hitherto a radical or "ultra" notion, thoroughly respectable in the deep South. To resist Republican rule now meant simply to resist surrender to self-confessed conspirators and murderers. The insurrection answered the question whether the South could remain in a Union controlled by Republicans. The reply was no.

The House met on December 5 and tried to organize. From that day until February 1 the Congressmen ballotted angrily and in vain to select a Speaker. After two months of wrangling which occasionally boiled over into fist fights, the Representatives chose their officers. The situation

336

was foreboding. The Administration party and the southern Democrats had lost; the Republicans and the Douglas Democrats were in.[22] Douglas, it appeared, still accepted membership in the Black Republican Reserve. This appearance hardly coincided with the truth, but the impression gained currency in the South.

Buchanan, laboring over his message, tried to pierce the darkness of the future and to plot some safe course. He feared that John Brown's raid and the wild enthusiasm with which some northerners welcomed the news had "made a deeper impression on the southern mind against the Union than all former events." The Cabinet was gloomy. Cobb wrote that "the North seems determined to force upon us the issue of Sewardism or disunion." "The days of the union are numbered," he said. "I write this as my unwilling conviction."[23]

The president sent his message to the Senate on December 27, but no one in or out of Congress paid much attention to it. "The message has been here a week and I have not yet seen the first person who has read it," reported a Georgia politician. It was dull enough, to be sure, to deserve this fate, but there lay embedded in its routine comments some ideas that were startling: the presidential warning that the Harpers Ferry incident was a symptom "of an incurable disease in the public mind, which may . . . terminate, at last, in an open war by the North to abolish slavery in the South;" the assertion, in direct defiance of Senator Douglas's doctrine, that the Supreme Court explicitly promised protection of slavery in the Territories; the statement that "without the authority of Congress" the president could not fire a gun in any "species of hostility however confined or limited," except to repel the attacks of an enemy; the charge that in failing to pass deficiency bills, Congress had arrested the action of government and could, by this means, "even destroy its existence." None of these points was, in itself, momentous; but all taken together, they showed clearly that the president placed squarely on the shoulders of Congress the responsibility for solving the problems which confronted the nation.

By doing so, Buchanan weakened the presidential office. His purpose, however, was to keep responsibility clearly defined. Throughout his Administration the opposition in Congress had attacked him as a dictator, a tyrant, a James the First. But he had always emphasized that his duty as executive was only to carry out the will of Congress. He recalled the dictum of Governor Simon Snyder, "My duty is to execute the laws . . . and not my individual opinions." He now reiterated this idea and called national attention to it; he had no intention to be the scapegoat for Congressional inattention to business. At the same time that Buchanan circumscribed the presidential powers, the lawmakers labored ardently to the same end. Enemy Congressmen, hating Buchanan and fearful of his dictatorial use of power against them, determined to destroy him by

337

destroying the power of the office he held. Between them, they succeeded all too well.

On March 5, 1859, the House adopted a resolution to investigate whether the president had tried to influence the votes of Congressmen on the English Bill by improper means. Speaker Pennington appointed the originator of the resolution, John Covode of Pennsylvania, as chairman of the investigating committee. Buchanan assumed that John Forney had been the real author of the scheme, for he had proposed something of this sort in a violent speech just before Pennington's election.[24] He further suspected that the Covode investigation was tied up with Douglas's plans to carry off the Democratic nomination at Charleston in April.

But other factors were at work. In the Senate a Democratic committee had been busily compiling testimony which linked the Republican party with complicity in the John Brown raid. Now the Republican-controlled House would offer to the public a countervailing exposé of Democratic corruption. Also, John Covode had a personal grudge to settle with Buchanan. As a prominent member of a railroad company which wanted a huge land grant from several western states, he had taken the responsibility to put through Congress a federal land donation act, cloaked as a bill to establish agricultural colleges. Buchanan vetoed this bill on February 24. "Hence," said the Buchanan press, "the bitter personal hostility of John Covode to President Buchanan."[25] Finally, the Douglas Democrats saw in the investigation an opportunity to strengthen the prospects of their favorite at Charleston. A re-examination of the Kansas fight and the handling of patronage in Illinois would certainly damn the Administration and strengthen Douglas.

Unlike most partisan investigations, this one would bring damaging testimony from members of both parties. Even Douglas may not have realized how serious a blow the Covode inquiry might deal to the nation, for it aimed at discrediting not only a man, but the power and prestige of the whole executive machinery. Buchanan promptly protested. "Mr. John Covode," he said, "is the accuser of the President. . . . The House have made my accuser one of my judges. . . . Since the time of the Star Chamber and of general warrants there has been no such proceeding. . . . I defy all investigation. Nothing but the basest perjury can sully my good name."[26]

The Committee went enthusiastically about its business, questioning all kinds of witnesses, both those in office and disgruntled ones who had been dismissed. Forney who in an earlier day had been an active influence peddler now planned to tell all. "God knows what he will swear," groaned Buchanan when Forney took the stand. "If he should tell anything like the truth, I have nothing to fear."[27]

338

The investigators unearthed practices common to every Administration since the days of Andrew Jackson, namely, that politicians used public offices and certain types of public funds for political purposes. Government printing contracts for decades had been a source of party income. Partisan editors received printing contracts as a reward for editorial support and then improved their situation by overprinting, overcharging, or farming out work for a commission. Buchanan's Administration permitted this well-established procedure to continue. The Committee thoroughly overhauled the activities of the notorious Ike Cook faction in Illinois and spent a lot of time examining the peculiar machinations of Cornelius Wendell, financial manager of the Washington *Union*, the Administration paper.

There was evidence that naval contracts had been awarded for political reasons and that War Secretary Floyd had offered to sell government property cheap and to buy dear. Buchanan himself had intervened to prevent the payment of $200,000 for a site in California which he thought a poor bargain. Such matters formed the burden of testimony before the Covode Committee. In May, the Buchanan Administration itself gave the Committee an extra boost when the Postmaster General discovered that the postmaster of New York City, I. V. Fowler, had stolen $160,000 of federal funds. Fowler promptly fled to Europe to escape arrest.[28]

The Committee concluded its work in June, had the hearings printed, bound them in with previous hearings on naval contracts, and franked the results all over the country. Even those who did not read must have felt that such a huge tome would record a comparable volume of corruption. Had the report been a mere partisan attack, like the censure of Jackson in the 1830's, it might have been less damaging; but this time there was a difference. The Republicans said that the report showed the hand of treason at work, a slave conspiracy pulling the strings on a puppet president. The Douglas Democrats pointed out that the Administration had used its power to defraud the voters in Illinois, a kind of continued Lecompton swindle. Both ideas set Buchanan before the public as a willing tool of the slave power, ready to use the public treasure to crush votes for freedom.

Buchanan addressed a spirited reply to the House after the investigation, asking why Congress had failed to recommend any resolutions of impeachment or even of censure of himself or any executive officer. The House had discovered no abuse of executive authority, nor had it proposed any corrective legislation. After spreading a drag net over the nation "to catch any disappointed man willing to malign my character," after listening to every coward that wished to insult the president under guaranteed immunity, after hearing all the witnesses who wanted to swear away their character before the Committee, after proceeding for three

339

months in secrecy without permitting any testimony on behalf of the accused, the Committee had found nothing on which to ground a specific complaint. Such procedure, Buchanan said, violated public and private honor, it denied to the president a fair trial and the right of self-defense, it instituted a "reign of terror," and degraded the presidential office to such a degree that it became "unworthy of the acceptance of any man of honor or principle." "I have passed triumphantly through this ordeal," he concluded. "My vindication is complete."[29]

DEMOCRACY DIVIDING

While the Covode Committee met, the Democrats held their nominating convention at Charleston, S. C., April 23 to May 3. For over a year the Douglas press had made a concerted effort to create the notion that Buchanan wished to have the nomination. Buchanan's own friends had helped foment the foolish idea through an article in the *Pittsburgh Post* on July 19, 1859. Immediately on seeing it, the president wrote a statement that he positively would not accept a renomination. He called B. F. Meyers, editor of the *Bedford Gazette* to his room at the Springs Hotel at midnight on the 20th and gave him the article with instructions to print it the next day. Then he sent copies to the *Pittsburgh Post*, the *Pennsylvanian*, and the Washington *Constitution*.[30] He wrote privately to Howell Cobb, J. B. Baker and Wilson McCandless during July, expressing his "final and irrevocable" determination to retire.[31]

As the second-term publicity would not stop, he wrote to Baker again in February, 1860, denying his candidacy and, before the Charleston Convention met, sent to Arnold Plumer, one of the delegates, a letter in which he restated that he would not "in any contingency" be a candidate. He also sent a copy to another delegate. There is no reason to believe he was not sincere. He told Mrs. Polk, "I am now in my sixty-ninth year and am heartily tired of my position as President."[32]

The talk of another term afforded certain presidential aspirants a weapon for their own cause. The New York *Herald* published a letter of Governor Wise of Virginia stating that "Mr. Buchanan himself is a candidate for renomination, and all his patronage and power will be used to disappoint Douglas and all other aspirants."[33] The Philadelphia *Press*, a Douglas organ, alleged that Buchanan swore to his friends that he "had to be" the candidate at Charleston; the times demanded it.[34] This had been the whole object of the Chapel Hill junket. Ever since the Harpers Ferry raid, he had been trying to frighten the nation about secession, "manufacture a disunion panic," and thus render the nomination of any northerner, except himself, impossible.[35] In the South, Toombs of Georgia wrote that

"Old Buck is determined to rule or ruin us. I think he means to continue his own dynasty or destroy the party" and in another letter said, "I think Mr. Buchanan would like to prevent the nomination of another in order to make himself necessary."[36]

This identity of hostile views from opposite sections highlighted Buchanan's lack of rapport with either. He thoroughly disapproved of Douglas and equally opposed the nomination of any ultrasoutherner, but he had strong hopes that a southern Unionist, particularly Howell Cobb, might succeed him. Cobb, however, had become discouraged after the John Brown affair. He would not be a candidate, he told his brother-in-law, unless strongly pressed by Georgia, and even then he felt gloomy about the future of the country. "For that reason," he said, "I feel less solicitous about the matter. . . . I am more desirous of obtaining the full confidence of the people of Ga.—that I may serve them in the crisis that is before us— than I do to obtain even presidential honors."[37] On March 15, the Georgia Convention in a close vote declined to support Cobb as the favorite son, and he publicly announced his retirement from the race. Buchanan now placed his hopes in such men as Vice-President Breckinridge or James Guthrie of Kentucky or Joe Lane of Oregon. These men represented the border-state or moderate point of view on the major question that would face the Charleston delegates: popular sovereignty as defined by Douglas's Freeport Doctrine or federal protection of slaves in the territories, according to Jefferson Davis's slave-code resolutions. There was ground for compromise between these extremes, and on this ground Buchanan stood. Few others did.

At Charleston, Murat Halstead, a newspaperman, observed that Douglas was the pivotal figure. "Every delegate was for or against him. Every motion meant to nominate him or not to nominate him. Every parliamentary war was *pro* or *con* Douglas." He and his friends intended, by focussing attention upon him as the central figure of the party, to force everyone who opposed him into the position of schismatics. Only thus could Douglas free himself from his reputation as chief apostate of his party. He would so crowd the center of the stage that he would force Buchanan, Cobb, Bright, Slidell, and all others who opposed him into the wings. The more fighting that ensued, the better; it would further emphasize his importance.[38]

Buchanan had some influence among the delegates. He had achieved a reconciliation with Governor Packer and thus controlled a part of the Pennsylvania delegation. The patronage had dictated the choice of Administration delegates from California, Oregon, Massachusetts, New Jersey, and a scattering from other states. Senator Bigler became Buchanan's chief spokesman on the floor, and Caleb Cushing, a loyal

341

Buchaneer, presided over the meeting and guided the selection of committees. Cobb, Bright and Slidell, none of them delegates but all bitter enemies of Douglas, assumed local direction of the Administration plans for the convention. The president could now have used the help of those friends he had sent away on foreign missions.

Buchanan's plan had grown out of a careful study of Douglas's letter of June 22, 1859, explaining his views on slavery in the territories. Buchanan had conferred at length with Slidell about it and had come to the conclusion that Douglas intended to stick to the Freeport Doctrine and to deny the right of the Supreme Court or of the Congress to speak the last word on the question of protecting slave property in a federal territory. He also thought that Douglas would not accept a nomination unless the convention "shall first erect a platform to please himself." Slidell viewed the candidacy letter as "an unequivocal declaration of war."[39] Buchanan endorsed the strategy of insisting upon the adoption of the platform first; Douglas would then have to modify his views to suit the party or abandon his candidacy.

Douglas, surprisingly, accepted the "platform first" idea which passed the day after the convention assembled. The convention then split wide open over the platform itself. His supporters bent furthest toward a compromise, agreeing at last to say nothing whatsoever about popular sovereignty and stand on the old Cincinnati Platform. But the southerners demanded more of Douglas than silence; they wanted some positive statement to the effect that Congress had a right to protect property in the territories, and this wish Douglas would not grant. Bigler, heading a conference committee, tried his best to translate the middle ground into acceptable words but failed, like the rest.

Even in the face of this impasse, something might have been salvaged from the convention had the southern delegates kept their tempers and their seats. But during the vote on the Douglas minority platform, which reaffirmed the Cincinnati Platform, the delegates of eight southern states walked out leaving the Douglas men in charge. These, unable to muster a two-thirds majority of the whole to nominate their candidate, adjourned the convention to reconvene in Baltimore on June 18. The southerners had done exactly what Douglas wanted, but not in the way he had anticipated. By voluntarily assuming the position of bolters, they had made Douglas the leader of the regular party. They had torn the apostate's cloak from his shoulders and wrapped it around themselves. Had only a few withdrawn, the Douglas strategy might have worked; but instead of the secession of a mere lunatic fringe, a major portion of the party had walked out and made a legal nomination impossible.

Buchanan read the results with anger. The ground he occupied had now been entirely cut away. He could join the knaves or the fools.

Well, be damned if he would; he would join neither of them. He would continue to urge the only course he could devise which might unite the Democracy and bring victory in November. He believed that neither section should demand both platform and candidate but should be willing to give in on one to get the other. If Douglas would accept a modified guarantee of protection to slaves during the territorial period, or Davis would run on the Cincinnati platform, either might win; if each wanted everything for his own section and would concede nothing to the other, then the party would lose and the Republicans would take over the government.

May and June brought such a press of official duties that Buchanan had little time to devote to election politics, although he emphasized his plan of give and take whenever opportunity offered. During May the moderates of the border states organized a Constitutional Union party and nominated John Bell of Tennessee for president and Edward Everett of Massachusetts for vice-president. Their platform was: "The Constitution of the country, the union of the States, and the enforcement of the laws." A week later the Republicans at Chicago nominated Abraham Lincoln and Hannibal Hamlin to lead them on a program of high tariff, free homesteads, and no extension of slavery. Finally, in mid-June, the Democrats met again for their adjourned session in Baltimore. The split persisted; the Douglas faction placed him in nomination and the Charleston seceders retired to a separate hall to nominate John C. Breckinridge for president and Joe Lane for vice-president. By June 28, four tickets were formally in the field, but only one of them, the Republican, represented a clear-cut party organization.

Tragic irony marked the final disintegration of the Democratic party at the Baltimore Convention. At the end Douglas formally asked that his name be withdrawn in the interest of party harmony, but his managers ignored his request and shoved him through. At the same time they adopted the very platform which Buchanan had urged upon them all along and which, had it been accepted earlier, might have achieved peace. Douglas would run on a promise to let the Supreme Court determine the "subject of domestic relations" in a territory, thus abandoning the principle which he had made the central theme of all his former battles. On the other hand the southerners, long champions of the Supreme Court principle, now considered its adoption by Douglas sufficient cause to bolt. Even so, their own platform on which Breckinridge would run considerably modified the slave-code proposal of Jefferson Davis. It stated merely that the Federal Government had the duty "to protect, when necessary, the rights of persons and property in the Territories." It thus became very clear that the issue went much deeper than a formula for slavery in the territories. It had come to the point that southern Democrats would not trust their northern colleagues, regardless of principle or party, and the northern Democrats reciprocated the feeling.

Theoretically, Buchanan might even now have saved the party by coming out strongly for Douglas. He had no further ambitions to gratify for himself and could scarcely have imagined any phraseology of condemnation that had not already been directed against him. Douglas, with Administration support, might possibly have united the Democratic voters of the upper South and the lower North, the middle belt which could command an electoral college majority. Had the Douglas men not been at this very moment busily engaged in upsetting the tar barrel over the Buchaneers in the Covode inquiry, such a move might have been conceivable. Under these conditions, it was not. Buchanan had to agree with the Republican editor who wrote: "A penitent prostitute may be received into the church, but she should not lead the choir." He decided for the time being to withhold the power of his influence from either side. Whatever persuasiveness he possessed he would use to promote a withdrawal of both Democratic candidates, and to achieve a new and legal nomination supported by the border states whose inhabitants could still talk to each other as friends and neighbors. As for the future, sufficient unto the day. . . .

26

MR. LINCOLN IS ELECTED • 1860

WAR ON THE WHITE HOUSE

The end of the Congressional session reminded Buchanan very much of the days of the John Quincy Adams Administration. Bills were manufactured or side-tracked, it seemed, for the particular purpose of damning the Administration. Both Republicans and Democrats joined in the game. The tariff bill, which Buchanan favored as a means of strengthening the Treasury, was left to rot in Committee. The appropriations bills were kicked back and forth between the Republican House and the Democratic Senate. The Senate Democrats sabotaged proposals to make American influence count in Central America, and the two Houses adopted a Homestead Bill which all knew Buchanan would have to veto.

Buchanan needed the Morrill Tariff both to get more revenue and to conciliate the demands of manufacturers. He had gratified the South by vetoing earlier some river and harbor bills which would have spent federal funds largely in the northwest, and he deserved southern Democratic support for his firmness during the Lecompton fracas. The Morrill Bill conformed to his ideas of a moderate tariff and would have greatly eased his administrative problems, but the southern Senators defeated it.

He needed appropriation bills to maintain the functions and services of government. When services had to be curtailed the Administration bore the brunt of the complaints. The political opposition, by headlining the shocking fact that Buchanan inherited a $4,000,000 surplus from Pierce and by 1859 had a deficit of $27,000,000, drummed home the idea that the public funds had been wasted in graft and corruption. But the figures were misleading.

Pierce had enjoyed a rich revenue from land sales and customs receipts amounting to $273,000,000 during his term of office. In Buchanan's Administration, because of the panic of 1857 and the near cessation of land sales, due partly to the Lecompton fight, the federal income dropped to $223,000,000. Thus Buchanan had the task of running the government for four years with $50,000,000 less than Pierce. He did this, conducted a war with Paraguay and a war with the Mormons, increased the navy, and established two new transcontinental postal routes. At the end his net deficit was $7,000,000. He had, with rigid economy, actually run the country for $39,000,000 less than his predecessor, and therefore deserved credit for efficient management of public funds.[1]

Buchanan refused to give away the public domain for fear of threatening the financial stability of the nation, since that land formed the collateral for public loans. Hence his veto of the Homestead Bill on June 22, 1860, which has often been cited as the act which elected Lincoln. The Republican press proclaimed that "this act of oppression . . . would sink the administration of James Buchanan in infamy as long as it will be remembered."[2] A modern writer says that Buchanan acted as "a tool of the slave power," and that the veto message was "perhaps the most irrational, ill-conceived and amazingly inaccurate veto message that has ever emanated from an American President."[3]

The message may properly be called labored and in some places specious, for it never mentioned the real reasons for the veto; but neither did the framers of the bill publicize their real reasons for pushing it through. It was actually framed to draw a veto and embarrass the president, for Buchanan had earlier made public his antagonism to its provisions. The fundamental purpose was to manufacture Republican votes in the 1860 election and new Republican states thereafter. No one doubted that any party which offered free land to small farmers would gain favor principally in the North and among antislavery people in general. As had been shown in Kansas, these would inundate the new region and, in the continuing uncertainty about the controls over slavery, might well reopen the half-healed wounds of Kansas. Buchanan thought that the worst thing he could possibly do at this moment would be to encourage a frenzied migration into the new West. That had been the mistake of the Kansas-Nebraska Bill and he aimed not to repeat it.

He interpreted the Homestead Bill as a Republican effort to reactivate the slavery furor, a demagogic device to buy northern votes with public treasure, and a cheat because it would give mainly to northerners land which had been acquired in great part through the sacrifice of southerners during the Mexican war. In the end even the northern farmers would be cheated, Buchanan believed, for as the bill had been written, railroad promoters would wind up with most of the land. He paid dearly for the veto, for it placed the Administration in the position of condemning the West to stagnation and of trampling the wishes of northern freemen to gratify the South. It hurt Douglas, and it gave the Republicans the chance to stand as champions of free workingmen and free farmers, a combination

346

hitherto the backbone of northern Democracy. The veto may well have elected Lincoln. But if Buchanan had signed the bill, he would have repudiated his whole presidential policy by endorsing a measure that he thought fiscally unsound, sectional in its benefits, productive of renewed slavery agitation, condemned by his own party platform, and formally sponsored by the Republicans.

HOW TO STOP LINCOLN

After Congress adjourned, many of the Democrats lingered to try once again to achieve union between the Douglas and Breckinridge men. The Administration or Breckinridge wing of the party succeeded in persuading Senator Benjamin Fitzpatrick to surrender his place as vice-presidential candidate on the Douglas ticket and promised that if Douglas, too, would quit the race, both Breckinridge and Lane would withdraw, and a new nomination would be sought. To induce Fitzpatrick to make the initial sacrifice, the Buchaneers suggested that he might very well be selected as the ultimate presidential nominee, in recognition of his disinterested patriotism. But Douglas would not retire, and his managers soon named Herschel V. Johnson of Georgia to take the place of Fitzpatrick.

Buchanan's hope from this point on lay in working out such fusion tickets in various states as might possibly prevent an election and throw the decision to the House of Representatives. No other plan promised the slightest chance of defeating Lincoln. He wondered whether he had not erred in refusing to support Douglas at Charleston. Here had been the great opportunity for, although nominating Douglas would not have kept the Gulf States from walking out and naming their own candidate, it might have united the border states back of the Little Giant. These states, if they voted en bloc, could triumph over the Yankee North and the fire-eating South. Douglas, with Administration support, stood a good chance of capturing 161 electoral votes. It took 152 to win.

That chance had now gone by. Douglas would squander his strength where Lincoln was stronger; his prospects were hopeless. Breckinridge would command the whole South and just might get Pennsylvania and the Far West, a combination that would produce 146 electoral votes— enough to spike Lincoln if either Douglas or Bell captured a few electors from him. If this happened and the election went to the House, it seemed likely that a deadlock would ensue. The voting would be by states, and it would require seventeen states to name a president. The Republicans had only fifteen; the Democrats could be sure of only thirteen; Douglas would have one; Bell, one; and three states would probably divide and not vote.

If the House failed to elect, the Senate would proceed to ballot for a vice-president and, because of its strong Democratic majority, would undoubtedly choose Joe Lane. He then would take the helm, in the absence of a president. This was a guessing game, to be sure, but it was educated guessing upon which the fate of the nation seemed to depend. Buchanan thought it the best prospect.

He did not actively campaign, but stated his position to a Breckinridge rally in front of the White House on the night of July 9. He condemned breaches of traditional procedure by both Democratic factions. Neither nomination had been according to rule and therefore, he said, "every Democrat is at perfect liberty to vote as he thinks proper." He planned to vote for Breckinridge because he believed that property was guaranteed protection by the Constitution, and that this guarantee could could not be thrown out by a local vote in a territory as Douglas claimed. He would not interfere between the factions in their state campaigns. His main object was to defeat the Republicans.

The implication of this speech was clear. Buchanan would let Douglas do all the damage he could to Lincoln in the North. He would try to protect the southern vote for Breckinridge and most particularly try to save Pennsylvania where he still held a strong working force. To fight Douglas and Lincoln would be to scatter his strength.

IMPERIAL VISITORS

Buchanan found himself distracted, in the critical period between the Charleston and Baltimore Conventions, by a large delegation of Japanese dignitaries who had come to the United States for the signing of the first commercial treaty to be negotiated by this mysterious Oriental Empire. The Nipponese visitors took the country by storm. "They are really a curiosity," wrote Harriet Lane. "All the women seem to run daft about them."[4] Buchanan held a state dinner for them, arranging them in small groups at separate tables with one or another of the Cabinet. The Dutch Minister gave a garden party, Mrs. Slidell a matinée dansante, and others plain receptions. "And still," said Mrs. Cobb, "curiosity is not satiated." At the White House the Japanese left a whole room full of gifts which were placed on exhibit for the edification of the public.[5]

No sooner had the Japanese left Washington than the president undertook other social responsibilities. At the wedding of Madame de Bodisco, widow of the Russian Ambassador, to a British Army Captain, he gave the bride away. About the same time he learned, with a shock, that his old flame, Mrs. Craig, had married and was now living in Chicago.[6]

By midsummer the four-year-old fight between Secretary Floyd and Captain Montgomery C. Meigs had reached the breaking point. Meigs had been superintending a number of construction projects in the Washington area, including new wings and a new dome for the national capitol. He had been entrusted with this work by Jefferson Davis, Secretary of War under Pierce, and deserved his reputation as an honest officer. He immediately ran into trouble with Floyd who tried to use the supply contracts for these enterprises as political favors.

The fight between Meigs and Floyd eventually engaged the interest of Congress. The anti-Administration legislators now framed appropriation bills to prevent the War Department from spending money on these projects except through Meigs. Buchanan had several times listened patiently to the story from both men and had tried to patch up matters, but eventually Meigs lost his temper. He wrote Buchanan a letter sharply accusing Floyd of shoddy practice and demanding that one or the other be dismissed. Meigs had justice on his side, but he might have realized that his Commander in Chief would have considerable difficulty in removing his Secretary of War on complaint of a Captain with a long record of insubordination. Buchanan agonized over this episode longer than he should have, considering the weight of other matters crying for his attention. At length he dressed down Floyd, but at the same time he agreed that Meigs would have to be transferred. The latter now entered the growing ranks of those who attacked Buchanan as a pliant tool of the South, an ingrate, and a corruptionist. Meigs's name had become well known throughout the country, and his outraged voice carried wide and clear, assisted on its way by Forney's sympathetic pen in the Philadelphia *Press*.[7]

At the end of August Buchanan went to Bedford Springs for a rest. The townspeople there, thinking that this might be his last visit as president, prepared a huge celebration for him. The promoters, who wished to surprise Buchanan, did not notify him of the plans. He did not arrive as expected on Friday and the crowd, after a four-hour wait, went home disappointed. Next day he came to the hotel without fanfare and promptly went to bed.[8]

During his vacation Buchanan had a serious private talk with the Rev. William M. Paxton of the First Presbyterian Church of New York City on the subject of religion. Paxton related that the president questioned him "closely as a lawyer would question a witness upon all points connected with regeneration, atonement, repentance, and faith." At the end of the conversation, Buchanan said, "Well, sir . . . , I hope I am a Christian. I think I have much of the experience which you describe, and as soon as I retire, I will unite with the Presbyterian Church." Paxton asked him why he delayed, to which he replied, "I must delay for the honor of religion.

349

If I were to unite with the church now, they would say 'hypocrite' from Maine to Georgia."[9]

Upon learning that the Prince of Wales planned a visit to Canada in September, Buchanan wrote to Victoria and suggested that her son conclude his trip with a tour of the United States and a stopover in Washington. The queen approved. The first visit to the United States of a member of the British royal family created great excitement throughout the country, but especially in high social circles.

Harriet wanted to have a huge ball for the prince, but the president said, "No dancing in the White House," and when he spoke thus, his decision was as irrevocable as the law of the Medes and Persians. He also ordered Harriet to remove her picture from the prince's bedroom and put it in the library. The evening of his arrival, Buchanan held a grand state dinner. Toward the end of it the president grew fidgety and told the waiters to hurry up the courses, for he thought that young Edward Albert was about to fall asleep at the table. Later the guests played cards, a great concession, since Buchanan detested card games and had never before allowed them in the White House. At the end of the day, after the royal party had been accommodated, Buchanan discovered that all the White House beds were full and he had to sleep on a sofa.

Next day the prince toured the public buildings, appeared at a public reception, and in the afternoon visited a gymnasium with Miss Lane where he swung on the rings, climbed a rope ladder, and lost to Harriet in a game of ninepins. To gratify the ladies, Buchanan arranged a party on board the revenue cutter *Harriet Lane* to enliven the prince's cruise to Mt. Vernon. Gautier superintended a splendid lunch on deck, and on the return voyage there was music and dancing. The prince first led out Miss Lane and as he seated her at the end of the dance he was heard to whisper, "Now, Miss Lane, who must I dance with next?"[10]

In New York, where the dance floor caved in during the grand ball, Edward was rumored to have escaped the eye of the Duke of Newcastle and to have spent the night disporting himself riotously in the city's most luxurious brothels.[11]

After her son's return home, Victoria expressed her pride and gratification at his reception and described the visit as "an important link to cement two nations of kindred origin and character."[12] The occasion seemed to symbolize an end to the traditional hatreds of Revolutionary days and marked the beginning of stronger Anglo-American friendship.

THE ELECTION OF 1860

The royal visit could scarcely have come at a worse time. The most critical election in American history was surging to its climax, and Buchanan

350

should have been devoting all of his time to it. Three of the candidates, Lincoln, Breckinridge and Bell, had been following the traditional procedure; they stayed home and said nothing. But Douglas, though sick, proved he was still the same old "Steam engine in breeches." Breaking precedent, he began to stump the nation. Starting with a trip to Boston on the pretense of visiting his mother, he then carried his campaign all through the South. Here he boldly proclaimed that the election of Lincoln should give no excuse for secession, but at the same time he accused the Breckinridge and Lane partisans of being bent on secession should Lincoln be elected. Presumably he intended by this means to frighten pro-Union southerners into voting for him in preference to Breckinridge. However, Douglas underestimated southern hatred of his past course, and sowed broadcast seeds of the very movement he was trying to avert. By smearing the Breckinridge party with the tar of secession he weakened Union sentiment in the South, and he strengthened the secessionists by harping on the probability of a Lincoln victory.

William M. Browne, editor of the Administration's Washington *Constitution*, wrote angrily in midsummer, "I am almost crazy at the shilly-shally, dilly-dally policy being pursued. Make a holocaust of Douglas men and even now build an organization and elect Breckinridge."[13] Cobb thought the only chance to defeat Lincoln lay in the withdrawal of Douglas.[14] Buchanan, worried but calm, concentrated his efforts on control of Pennsylvania whose electoral vote held most promise of deciding the issue and worked for an agreement that all the Pennsylvania electors would vote as a unit for either Douglas or Breckinridge—whichever choice would defeat Lincoln.

In late August Breckinridge's home state of Kentucky defeated the Administration party's local ticket by some 22,000 votes and plunged the president in gloom. "All may perhaps depend upon Penna.," Buchanan now wrote. "Should Lincoln be elected, I fear troubles enough though I have been doing all I can by conversations to prevent them."[15] The October elections in Pennsylvania gave the governorship to Andrew Gregg Curtin, candidate of the People's party which backed Lincoln.

Hope now seemed nearly dead. Cobb told his wife that Georgia would "not stand for the election of Lincoln. Regard that as a fixed fact."[16] A few weeks later he wrote his son that when Lincoln became president, "the true remedy is to withdraw from the Union on the 4th of March. As the government passes into the hands of the Abolitionists—we should pass out. To secede while the Government is in the hands of our friends would be wrong and unjustifiable."[17]

In the November elections, Lincoln polled some 1,800,000 votes to win over the 2,800,000 votes of the combined opposition. He would get 180 electoral votes; Breckinridge, 72; Bell, 39; and Douglas, 12. The

351

Democrats got little solace from the fact that only 39.8 per cent of the voters had cast ballots for Lincoln. Even had all the anti-Lincoln electoral votes been concentrated on one candidate, the Republicans would still have won in the electoral college.[18]

"Lincoln is elected and we are alive to tell it. J. B. must be in an agony of suspense," wrote Sophie Plitt to Harriet. In Georgia a hysterical politician cried: "The voice of the North has proclaimed at the ballot box that I should be a slave! At the same time I hear the voice of God command, 'Be free! Be free!' "[19] In Columbia, South Carolina, Lawrence Keitt orated hoarsely at midnight, "South Carolina will either leave the Union or else throw her arms around the pillars of the Constitution and involve all the States in common ruin. Mr. Buchanan is pledged to secession and will be held to it."[20] Slidell wrote to the president from New Orleans, "I deeply regret the embarrassments which will surround you during the remainder of your term. I need scarcely say that I will do everything in my power to modify them . . . and to arrest any hostile action during your administration. I see no possibility of preserving the Union, nor indeed do I consider it desireable."[21]

Buchanan retired to the White House library where he thumbed abstractedly through his Bible till he came to Ecclesiastes. "Vanity of vanities! All is vanity. What does man gain by all the toil at which he toils?"

27

THE IMPENDING CRISIS • 1860

SPOTLIGHT ON CHARLESTON

South Carolina moved swiftly after hearing the news of Lincoln's election. Her leaders had long since proclaimed that this event would be their signal to withdraw her from the Union, and they had taken public action to implement this threat in advance. On October 20, the Washington Light Infantry of Charleston mobilized, and on the 25th the leading politicians of the state met at the Charleston home of Senator James H. Hammond to plan the details of procedure for secession. By November the machinery of withdrawal had been constructed. News of the election of Lincoln would be the only impulse needed to set the wheels turning.

The day after election the federal grand jury at Charleston quit, and all officers of the federal district court resigned. Federal activity ceased in South Carolina except in the post offices, the customhouse, and the military posts. No one could be charged with breaking federal law, since there were no federal courts to which anyone could be brought for trial. The resignation of court officers created a kind of sit-down strike against the federal authority for which, at the moment, no constitutional remedy existed.

Also on November 7, South Carolina's Governor William H. Gist appealed to his compatriot, William H. Trescot, Assistant Secretary of State, to find out informally what action President Buchanan planned for the federal forts around Charleston. There were four of these. Castle Pinckney, inhabited only by an old ordnance sergeant and his family, occupied a small island well inside the harbor and close to the Charleston city docks. Fort Johnson and Fort Moultrie stood on tips of land about three miles apart which formed the neck or entrance to the harbor, and between them, in the middle of the channel, was Fort Sumter. Fort Johnson, an abandoned barracks and hospital area, had no proper claim to the term "fort." Sumter, a brick pentagon fifty feet high resting on a rock foundation no bigger than the structure, was in the charge of a lieutenant

353

of engineers who daily supervised the work of 120 civilian laborers engaged in completing the interior construction of the massive pile. A few cannons were scattered about the parade ground; the fort contained no military stores.

Fort Moultrie housed the main defense command of some seventy-five officers and men. It was a strong work, well supplied with heavy guns facing seaward, but not designed to repel an attack from the rear. At the moment it was short on small arms; 22,000 of these were stacked at the federal arsenal a few blocks from the docks in Charleston. The people of Charleston felt that they lay at the mercy of these federal forts, and the army garrison felt that it was at the mercy of the Charleston merchants who supplied the food. Here was the recipe for trouble.

Within twenty-four hours after Lincoln's election the federal troops nearly ran into a fight with the people of Charleston. Col. J. L. Gardner, who commanded Fort Moultrie, sent a squad of soldiers in civilian dress to get some military stores at the arsenal. They were in the process of loading boxes at a private wharf when the owner ordered them off and threatened to raise an alarm unless the supplies were returned. As the soldiers wished to avoid a riot, they carried the ammunition back and reported the affair to their colonel. Next morning the mayor gave him permission to load the supplies he needed, but the colonel would not acknowledge the right of the city authorities to exercise any jurisdiction over this matter.

Meanwhile, the South Carolinians telegraphed W. H. Trescot to learn whether Gardner had acted on War Department orders. Trescot went to the White House and caught Floyd, Cobb and Toucey as they were leaving a Cabinet meeting. Floyd told him that no orders had been issued to move ammunition from the arsenal to the fort, and none would be given. He had, in the meantime, sent Major Fitz-John Porter to Charleston to observe conditions at first hand and report back.[1]

STRATEGY AND TACTICS

These events formed the Charleston background of the important Cabinet meeting of November 9. Buchanan wished to have Cabinet advice on the message that he had cogitated for weeks, in anticipation of the situation which now confronted the nation. He planned at this point to make clear before the world how little cause any southern state had to secede and to portray the act contemplated by South Carolina as rash, foolish, and precipitate. Buchanan had no great hope of preventing South Carolina from adopting a secession ordinance, but he hoped to deter others from following her, at least during his Administration. No one could properly charge him with hostile intent toward the South, and he would keep this attitude. Secession in the face of it would throw the burden of guilt squarely on the seceders and would strengthen the forces of Union in both the North and the South. But if Buchanan assumed a menacing posture by threatening illegal executive action, this in itself would add justification for secession, strengthen its appeal, and hasten its accomplishment.

In addition to such considerations of strategy, Buchanan had to weigh the tactical military situation. For advice on this he depended upon Lieutenant General Winfield Scott, now aged seventy-four and in ill-health. Scott had not forgotten insults, both real and fancied, that he had suffered at Buchanan's hands during the Mexican War and the bitter political campaign of 1852. From his headquarters in New York City, Scott, on October 29, had addressed a long communication to the Secretary of War entitled "General Scott's Views" on the approaching crisis. He sent a copy to Buchanan and to others. "To save time," Scott began, "the right of secession may be conceded." He thought that the president had no power to use force to prevent any coastal state from exercising that right. After describing the horrors he anticipated from civil war, he added that "a smaller evil would be to allow the fragments of the great Republic to form themselves into new confederacies."

This statement a week before election, coming from the commander of the Army, still a towering national hero, could scarcely fail to encourage and delude the southern ultras. Buchanan thought it imbecilic in its ideas and highly improper politically. Only the final few pages of the "Views" addressed themselves to the southern forts. Scott warned that some rash, southern filibuster-type raid might overpower any one of the dozen forts scattered along the Atlantic and Gulf coasts. Few of them were manned, and not one garrisoned to the recommended strength. Buchanan read this with astonishment having assumed that it was the general's particular business to keep them garrisoned to the strength he thought proper. "In my opinion," Scott concluded, "all these works should be immediately so garrisoned as to make any attempt to take any one of them by surprise or *coup de main* ridiculous."

Scott suggested no means for strengthening the forts, but the next day he sent a supplement to the "Views" covering this oversight. Said he, "There is one (regular) company at Boston, one here (at the Narrows), one at Pittsburg, one at Augusta, Ga., and one at Baton Rouge— in all five companies only, within reach, to garrison or reenforce the forts mentioned in the 'Views.' " Although Buchanan later claimed that because of their "strange and inconsistent character" he had dismissed the "Views" from his mind without further consideration, he worried much about their import on his policy. He could not replace Scott, but how far could he trust him if an armed clash should, by some accident, occur? Buchanan

355

feared the "Views" would convince the people of the South "that they might secede without serious opposition from the North."[2]

The army was in deplorable condition through no fault either of Scott or of Buchanan, for both had been continually calling upon Congress for the means of improvement since 1857. Some 15,000 men were in active service in 1860, but only 1,000 of these had been assigned to the Department of the East at any time during Buchanan's presidency. The wide-flung frontiers called desperately for more troops than were ever available. To withdraw any western company meant almost certain death to the nearby inhabitants, for these military posts provided their only protection against hostile Indians. General Scott told the Senate that "as often as we have been obliged to withdraw troops from one frontier in order to reenforce another, the weakened points have instantly been attacked or threatened with formidable invasion."[3] Troops had been moved, not only from the South but also from every point safe from Indian raids, in order to protect the frontier.

The morale of the army had suffered for years from the excessive demands made upon the soldiers. Long marches, hard labor, continued Indian fighting against heavy odds, and perpetual sickness were routine. Since there were no replacements, there were no furloughs.

Buchanan urged Congress to make provisions for a decent retirement system for disabled officers, advocated laws to provide penalties for assisting a deserter, asked that volunteers be allowed to select the branch of service they wished to join, and pleaded for a reform of the system of promotion which had become, in fact, a system of non-promotion; but Congress rejected each of these pleas in turn. The Senate even passed a bill to decrease the pay of officers and enlisted men, but it was buried in the House.[4]

In 1859 and 1860, the legislators rejected Administration requests for more military funds and voted a general cut in this part of the national estimates. When Buchanan called for an increase in military man power in 1858, the Senate proposed an addition to the regular army, and the House favored building up the force temporarily with volunteers. Buchanan fought strongly for the Senate Bill, but only a House measure which restricted the use of volunteers to the Utah area passed.[5] This was the history of military legislation in Buchanan's term, up to the election of Lincoln. The president believed, on the basis of his past experience and his knowledge of the political temper of the 36th Congress, that no recommendation for strengthening the army had any prospect of being approved. His policy necessarily had to take the hostile attitude of Congress into consideration.

The navy was in somewhat better shape. Although twenty-three ships were on foreign duty, the home squadron was in 1860 exceedingly large. Twenty-three warships and forty-five steamers cruised the eastern waters or lay at anchor at Boston, New York, Annapolis, and Norfolk.[6] These would form an important deterrent to southern rashness and a firm argument against attacks on the coastal forts. These tactical facts Buchanan carried with him into the Cabinet meeting of November 9.

The Cabinet was no longer the confident, comradely body that had earlier stood in awe of the Chief and united back of his policies. Cobb and Thompson had already decided that their active future must lie with their states, but Buchanan expected that they would use their influence to delay the threatened secession of Georgia and Mississippi until after March 4. Floyd had no patience or sympathy with the secessionists and might have helped Buchanan, except for the personal difficulties that had arisen between them.

During the Mormon War Floyd had hired the firm of Russell, Majors and Waddell to transport supplies for the army. Congress would not appropriate money until the job was done, and the firm could not complete the task without an advance, because it had tied up its funds in other ventures. Floyd, therefore, received bills from the company for services not yet performed, signed or "accepted" them, and returned them to the company to use as collateral for loans. Floyd assumed that Congress would meet the obligation by passing deficiency bills at the end of the session. In 1859 Buchanan asked Floyd by what law he issued the acceptances. Floyd replied there was no law, but the procedure had always been used in emergencies. "Well," replied the president, "discontinue it at once. If there is no law for it, it is against the law."[7] The two had many disagreements. Buchanan had on several occasions rebuked Floyd for being careless with Department funds, and Floyd had become sullen and bitter.

Joseph Holt of Kentucky now served as Postmaster General. He, with Black and Cass, represented the outspoken Union element in the Cabinet. Cass, usually lethargic, aroused himself to active participation in Cabinet discussion on the preservation of the Union. While these three agreed on the need for a firm stand against secession, they did not get along well personally. Black had a light spirit and a keen sense of humor, but Holt was dour, bitter and unhappy. Cass mildly resented Black's increasing influence in the Cabinet and his tendency to meddle in the affairs of other Departments. Mild-mannered Toucey got along with everybody. He held no sympathy for secession, but he considered a civil war to be a worse catastrophe and inclined to whatever policy seemed most likely to avert an armed collision. Thus the Cabinet, by the fall of 1860, had lost both its old political unity and its personal *esprit de corps*.

Buchanan told his Department Heads on November 9 that "the business of the meeting was the most important ever before the Cabinet since his induction into office." The question at issue was "the course to

357

pursue in relation to the threatening aspect of affairs in the South, and most particularly in South Carolina."[8] Two days earlier Buchanan had conferred with Floyd about the danger of attack on the Charleston forts, and had told him that "if those forts should be taken by South Carolina in consequence of our neglect to put them in defensible condition, it were better for you and me both to be thrown into the Potomac with millstones tied about our necks."[9] Black now "earnestly urged sending at once a strong force into the forts at Charleston Harbor, enough to deter if possible the people from any attempt at disunion."[10] Buchanan assured him that he intended to protect the forts and had already instructed Floyd to supply them with such provisions, arms, and men as were necessary. He then asked the question uppermost in his mind: how to prevent general secession, at least during the remainder of his Administration?

Buchanan thought that only a constitutional convention could override Congressional politics, bring popular sentiment to the forefront, and succeed in averting disunion. But should such a policy be immediately proposed by proclamation, or should it form the theme of the presidential message in December? The Cabinet split on both the proposal and the alternate methods of publicizing it.

As the meeting broke up, W. H. Trescot brought news of Gardner's abortive effort to remove arms and ammunition from the arsenal at Charleston. Buchanan now conferred with Black and asked him to investigate the legal powers of the president to deal with secession and state opposition to federal law. At the Cabinet meeting of the 10th to discuss the problems raised by the Gardner incident, Buchanan declared his intention to state in his message that he would not acknowledge any "right" of secession and would protect federal property. Cass, Black, Holt and Toucey thought this a sound position, but Cobb, Thompson, and Floyd thought it too strong and wanted to consider the more immediate question of the arsenal incident. Floyd had talked to Fitz-John Porter, who had just returned from Charleston with the suggestion that new commanders be assigned to Fort Moultrie and the arsenal. The Cabinet agreed to send Major Robert Anderson, a former native of Charleston, to replace the aged Col. Gardner and to put Col. Benjamin Huger, a Carolinian, in charge of the arsenal. The government would thus gain a more alert command and at the same time demonstrate to the Charlestonians by these appointments the needlessness of their fears of any attack on them. General Scott sent orders effecting these changes on November 15.

Buchanan talked with Black about his investigations of the legal powers of the executive and soon discovered that the Attorney General had drawn up a set of policy recommendations for a president faced with secession. Buchanan rather tartly told him that he had not requested advice but information. What legal powers had the president? Black then asked Buchanan to define exactly what he did want, and the two framed a set of questions. Black wrote them down and, in order to avoid any mistake and fix responsibility, had Buchanan endorse them in his own hand. The questions were:

1. In case of a conflict between the authorities of any State and those of the United States, can there be any doubt that the laws of the Federal Government . . . are supreme?

2. What is the extent of my official power to collect duties on imports at a port where the revenue laws are resisted by a force which drives the collector from the custom house?

3. What right have I to defend the public property (for instance, a fort, arsenal, and navy yard), in case it should be assaulted?

4. What are the legal means at my disposal for executing those laws of the United States which are usually administered through the courts and their officers?

5. Can a military force be used for any purpose whatever under the Acts of 1795 and 1807, within the limits of a State where there are no judges, marshal or other civil officers?[11]

To these questions Black replied on November 20. First, a state, while still in the Union, could not absolve her citizens from obedience to laws of the United States. Second, federal law required the president to collect import duties at specified points. A collector, if denied the use of buildings at the port, could collect duties from the deck of a government vessel in the harbor. Third, the president had a clear duty to protect public property, a duty which included the right of recapture if the property had been unlawfully taken by another.

The last two questions proved more difficult. Black thought them "of the greatest practical importance," for they involved the executive use of the army to enforce federal law in a case where no state or federal officer asked for any help or made any complaint that a law had been violated. In this respect the case differed markedly from the Whiskey Rebellion or from the Nullification affair of 1832. Black found that the act of 1807 merely authorized the use of military force in cases "where it is lawful." This was no help. The Act of 1795 provided that the militia could be called "whenever the laws of the United States shall be opposed . . . by any State, by combinations too powerful to be suppressed by the ordinary course of judicial proceedings." It was up to the president to decide when such a condition existed. Buchanan could readily have mobilized militia to achieve enforcement of federal laws under this statute, but he would have had to use the troops first against Massachusetts, Wisconsin and the other northern states whose Personal Liberty Laws had undermined enforcement of the federal Fugitive Slave Act. These states had committed overt acts of defiance; South Carolina as yet had not. The president could not march against people who only talked against the federal government, ignoring states which had for years been actively obstructing the course of federal law.

Black cautioned Buchanan that the "whole spirit of our system" was opposed to any method of law enforcement other than that of the courts, "except in cases of extreme necessity." The resignation of federal officers did not constitute such necessity and did not give legal cause to send troops. "You can use force only to repel an assault on the public property," he said. If revenue could not be collected and the laws executed by normal means, Congress would have to legislate new means. Black advised Buchanan that if a state tried to secede, he should try to execute the laws only by means clearly provided by federal statute and should assume that "the present constitutional relations between the States and the Federal Government continue to exist until a new code of laws shall be established either by force or by law." The general government had a right to preserve itself by repelling "a direct and positive aggression upon its property or its officers," but, he concluded, "this is a totally different thing from an offensive war, to punish the people for the political misdeeds of their State Government."[12]

Both the Cabinet and the country debated the problems of the "right of secession" and the "coercion of a state," questions which probed to the very root of the federal idea. The southerners generally assumed a "right" to secede and denounced coercion, as was to be expected. But it was remarkable that many northern journalists, including leading Republican editors, agreed with this view and for six weeks after the election of Lincoln contended that the principle of government by the consent of the governed made secession a natural right. Horace Greeley editorialized on November 9, "We hope never to live in a Republic whereof one section is pinned to the residue by bayonets."[13]

Curiosity about Lincoln's ideas ran high, but he said very little, and that little augmented sectional tension. On October 23 Lincoln told a southern editor that he would not "disclaim all intention to interfere with slaves or slavery in the states."[14] In mid-November he said in a public speech that he welcomed a "practical test" of the issue of State Rights and was "glad of this military preparation in the South." It would, he thought, tend to unite southern Unionists.[15] Pennsylvania Republicans assured the president-elect that although Republicans would be in a minority in Congress, "the Union element of the South will naturally act with us."[16] Buchanan considered such optimistic views completely at odds with reality.

Getting no leadership or policy statement from Lincoln, the country anxiously speculated on Buchanan's forthcoming message. The

360

president kept very quiet about it, refusing as late as November 28 to send an advance copy to his confidential friend, Hiram Swarr. "The circumstances of the Country," he wrote, "require the retention of the message, for possible modification, up to the latest hour."[17] But Buchanan did tell a group of secessionists exactly where he stood. In a long conference at the White House during the third week of November, he said that he would deny any "right" of secession and oppose it strongly. He assured the southerners that the "mighty West" would never permit the closing of the mouth of the Mississippi by a foreign power, which would be the case if Louisiana tried to withdraw. "South Carolina," he said, "wishes to enter into a conflict with me—a conflict with myself—and upon the drawing of the first drop of blood to drag other Southern States into the secession movement." Buchanan admitted that the South had suffered ill-treatment at the hands of the North, but he said that these wrongs did not yet constitute just cause for disunion. He planned first to "appeal to the North for justice to the South," and if it was denied, "then," said he emphatically, "I am with them." But terminating the interview, he cautioned his visitors that the recent flamboyant statements of Keitt and Yancey to the effect that he was "pledged to secession" were entirely false, and that the South ought not to assume any sympathy for secession from the Administration.[18]

THE PRESIDENT PROPOSES

Buchanan sent his message to Congress on December 3. In it he placed the blame for the crisis squarely on the northern antislavery agitators and warned them that unless they left the slave states alone, disunion would be inevitable. One half the nation would not live "habitually and perpetually insecure," and only those who had threatened to bathe the South in blood could dissipate the fears they had aroused. The southerners, on the other hand, had no excuse to break up the Union because a president they distrusted had been legally elected. Even if Lincoln intended to usurp unconstitutional powers and attack the South, which Buchanan doubted, he could not do so because the other branches of the government would restrain him. The Republicans, with a minority president, a minority in both houses of Congress, and a minority on the Supreme Court, had not the strength to act rashly unless the southerners withdrew.

He counselled the South not to secede from "apprehensions of contingent danger in the future." Only "some overt and dangerous act" of the new president would justify their resistance, and previous resistance would be revolution. "Let us wait for the overt act," he urged. In the meantime, he would charge the president-elect to do common justice to the South and try to force a clear expression of intent from him. Let Lincoln's party faithfully execute the Fugitive Slave Law in the states where

Republicans held sway. Should Lincoln refuse to do this duty, then he would have "wilfully violated" the Constitution. In that event, "the injured States . . . would be justified in revolutionary resistance to the government of the Union."

But even in such an eventuality, there could be no "right of secession." The government of the United States was intended to be perpetual and had the duty to preserve itself. The framers had not committed the "absurdity of providing for its own dissolution." "Let us look the danger fairly in the face. Secession is neither more nor less than revolution. It may or may not be a justifiable revolution; but still it is revolution."

And what ought the president do about the crisis? He had taken an oath to execute the laws, but in South Carolina no machinery now existed for administration of the laws. Such machinery could be reestablished only by new laws or by the dictatorial use of military force. No statute gave the president power to use force against South Carolina. Did the Constitution give Congress power to "coerce a State into submission?" Buchanan answered "that the power to make war against a State is at variance with the whole spirit and intent of the Constitution. . . . We could not, by physical force, control the will of the people and compel them to elect senators and representatives to Congress. . . . Our Union rests upon public opinion, and can never be cemented by the blood of its citizens shed in civil war. If it cannot live in the affections of the people it must one day perish. Congress possesses many means of preserving it by conciliation; but the sword was not placed in their hand to preserve it by force."

Buchanan then defined the program he wished Congress to implement. Let Congress call a constitutional convention into being, or recommend that the several state legislatures issue the call. This convention ought to devise an explanatory amendment to the Constitution on three points:

1. An express recognition of the right of property in slaves in the States where it now exists or may hereafter exist.
2. The duty of protecting this right in all the common Territories throughout their territorial existence, and until they shall be admitted as States into the Union, with or without slavery, as their constituents may prescribe.
3. A like recognition of the right of the master to have his slave, who has escaped from one State to another, restored and 'delivered up' to him.

This procedure, said the president, "ought to be tried . . . before any of these States shall separate themselves from the Union."[19]

362

The message commanded praise or censure from the press, depending upon the party of the editor; but the condemnation of it rang much more loudly than the applause for Buchanan pulled the checkrein on both of the major contending groups, and both reacted angrily to the bit. The Lincoln journals commented that never had a message been "cast aside with such unqualified disappointment," and roundly condemned Buchanan's efforts to fix blame for the trouble on the abolitionists as a deadly insult, a "brazen lie," and an "atrocious" perversion of the truth.[20] The Breckinridge sheets considered the message a "calm, patriotic, consistent and convincing" statement of the problem, characterized by "energy, decision and moderation."[21] The Douglas papers generally agreed that Buchanan had been exactly right in "attributing the present unfortunate . . . condition of the country to the general Abolition agitation," but they picked for their target the "absurd" proposition that secession was unconstitutional but that no constitutional remedy existed to prevent it.

The newspaper discussions of this apparent paradox ranged from rant through metaphysics. Buchanan, however, had merely stated an inescapable fact: admittedly, there was a flaw in the structure, and the condition would exist until remedied by some revision of the Constitution. Black had heard Buchanan reply scores of times to southerners who urged a "right" of secession, "I find no such right laid down in the Constitution." To northern advocates of "coercion" (presumably an executive order for the armed invasion of a state in the absence of any call for help or declaration of war by Congress) Buchanan answered with equivalent words. Neither secession nor coercion were comprehended in the federal Constitution, and to say so was not the mere partisan expression of one president.[22]

A CHALLENGE TO MR. LINCOLN

While the message failed to convince anyone to think or act very differently, it placed Lincoln and the Republican party in difficulty. No cause justified breaking the Union, Buchanan said, except continued overt defiance of the Constitution. The North, not the South, had for ,years been practicing such defiance by its Personal Liberty Laws. Unless the northern states repealed these, the South would be equally justified in ignoring or defying the constitutional compact. Buchanan challenged the Republicans to clean their own house before raising the question of obedience to federal law. The northern states, he accused, actively defied the Constitution; so far South Carolina only threatened action. Now it was Lincoln's move.

Buchanan also challenged the Republicans to agree to a national constitutional convention. If Lincoln rejected this proposal, he rejected the whole basis of the constitutional system and took the position that he did not actually want a solution based on the will of the public. Lincoln would have to endorse a convention or appear to admit publicly that his minority party dared not risk using traditional procedures. Buchanan hoped that his message would force the Republicans to face the question of a constitutional convention and to elicit from Lincoln some clear statement concerning it.

But the Republicans, divided among themselves, chose to treat Buchanan's challenge as an insulting political trick designed to destroy them, and they declined to respond to it. One historian has noted that while it was perfectly clear that the Democrats had lost the election, "there was still grave doubt as to who had won it."[23] Wendell Phillips wrote, "Lincoln is in *place*, Garrison in *power*." Who controlled the Republican party: Seward and Weed, the radical abolitionists, the shrewd political mavericks like Cameron and Blair, the old Constitutional Whigs, or Lincoln and the westerners? Would Lincoln run the party, or would someone else run Lincoln? As no one had the answers to these questions, each Republican group laid its own plans to bring Lincoln into camp. Lincoln became the key figure, the target of conquest within his own party, the man to whom the country looked for a statement of the Republican program to meet the crisis.

In the absence of any word from Lincoln, Republican spokesmen published all sorts of contradictory proposals. The Pennsylvanians reported that the state was "thoroughly anti-abolitionist," and wanted no Negro issue raised. They were Republican only because of the tariff, and would support Buchanan's proposed amendments on the slave question, if a vote should be taken, by a majority of two to one.[24] The radicals, like Senator Lyman Trumbull of Illinois, told Lincoln: "Republicans have no concession to make or compromise to offer. . . . It is impolitic even to discuss making them." These men sought to prevent getting up any convention or Congressional committee or private parley to discuss the crisis. "Proposing new Compromises," Trumbull said, "is an admission that to conduct the government on the principles on which we carried the election would be wrong. Inactivity and a kind spirit is . . . all that is left for us to do, till the 4th of March." Congress ought to give no power to Buchanan, for he would not know how to use it.[25] Congressman E. B. Washburne agreed that "what we want most is a 'masterly inactivity,' " but he warned Lincoln that the people in Illinois had not the faintest conception of the depth of secession feeling.[26]

Friends of Douglas reported to Lincoln that the Little Giant had said, "All government is coercion, and I go in for asserting this principle at every hazard. Rather a million men should fall on the battlefield, than that this gov't should lose one Single State."[27] But a Chicago delegate thought that "we can consent to no secession, and yet we must avoid any collision"—queer doctrine for a Republican who denounced Buchanan's message.[28]

Republican Governor E. D. Morgan of New York urged Lincoln to come out strongly in favor of the acquisition of Cuba in order to gain the support of pro-Union Democrats.[29] Thurlow Weed, Seward's spokesman, recommended that Republicans approve the extension of the Missouri Compromise line to the Pacific. John Sherman and other Republicans in Congress applauded this suggestion. David Kilgore of Indiana proposed that the federal government should pay compensation to owners of fugitive slaves. Eli Thayer of Massachusetts thought a reapplication of popular sovereignty in the territories would end the trouble. Sherman, after getting no support on the Missouri Compromise proposal, asked Congress to admit all territories immediately as states, thus ending the national phase of the slavery controversy.[30]

These diverse suggestions to Lincoln gradually tended to define two distinct elements of the Republican party: those who favored a conciliatory policy and admitted the necessity of some compromise and those who rejected compromise and wished to avoid any discussion about it. The first group, led by Seward and Weed, hoped to attract the northern and western Democrats and border-state Whigs by the compromise policy. The radical group, led by Lyman Trumbull, Ben Wade, and the eastern abolitionists thought compromise would wreck the party, and that the secession threat was only a bluff. It might even be good·riddance and strengthen the nation to part company with South Carolina and a few of the Gulf black-belt states. But no one knew who spoke for the Republicans until Lincoln made his choice.

"There is only one man in the United States who has it in his power to restore the country to its happy and prosperous condition," wrote the New York *Herald*, "and that man is the president-elect. . . . If Mr. Lincoln will speak out in a manner to reassure the conservative masses of all the States, the present cloud will pass away like a summer shower." S. L. M. Barlow of New York wrote a letter to John Slidell for "private circulation in D. C.," saying that if Lincoln would come out for a constitutional convention, the trouble would end. If not, or if the Republicans blocked the discussion of compromise, then war would be sure.[31]

But Lincoln made no public announcement, and the substance of his private letters soon got into circulation and spread the impression that he opposed any settlement by conciliation. His enemies assumed that he planned to subjugate the South by force. Lincoln had said almost nothing since the Douglas debates of 1858. He made no campaign speeches, and he wrote only one public letter during the entire election canvass—the one in which he accepted his nomination. "The Chicago Platform," Lincoln wrote, "meets my approval and it shall be my care not to violate or disregard it in any part." To dozens of letters requesting clarification of his policy, he regularly replied by referring the writers to his "previous statements." Everyone could pick what he wished from Lincoln's past utterances. His friends could make him a saint, and his enemies could make him a devil. On November 28 he wrote to Henry J. Raymond of the New York *Times* concerning the advocates of compromise: "These political fiends are not half sick enough yet. . . . 'They seek a sign, and no sign shall be given them.' At least such is my present feeling and purpose."[32]

Lincoln left even so important a partisan as Weed in the dark. Weed wrote on December 11, in preparation for a conference of Republican governors in New York, "I have been acting without knowledge of your view upon vital questions."[33] Lincoln gave him no satisfaction; nevertheless, he invited him to pay a visit to Springfield. Private correspondence showed that Lincoln did have a policy by early December and had advised certain friends of it. "Prevent . . . entertaining propositions for compromise of any sort, on 'slavery extension,'" he wrote E. B. Washburne. "There is no possible compromise on it . . . whether it be the Mo. line, or Eli Thayer's Pop. Sov. it is all the same. . . . On that point hold firm, as with a chain of steel."[34] He later told Weed, "I will be inflexible on the territorial question. . . ."[35]

Lincoln had in fact firmly adopted the radical position which Buchanan had warned would be sure to bring war, a belief shared by most Americans of all parties except for the radical wing of the Republicans. But Lincoln did not publicly announce his position, nor did he believe that it would bring conflict. He thought the threat of secession humbug and war unlikely. Buchanan, in addition to keeping southerners in harness, faced the task of convincing Lincoln that his estimate of the national problem was oversimple and unrealistic and that upon the victorious Republicans rested the issue of union or disunion.

Buchanan had a much more accurate knowledge of the temper of the South than Lincoln, who had not held national office for a decade and who rarely visited outside Illinois. The president prophesied to Hiram Swarr on December 10:

> I am truly sorry to say that South Carolina will secede about the 20th & the other cotton states will, in all probability, speedily follow. The contagion of disunion is fast spreading in North Carolina and Virginia & even in Maryland to a considerable extent. They are proceeding rashly & precipitately & will afford no opportunity of trying the question at the Ballot Box in the North whether the people will or will not agree to redress these grievances. The Black Republicans say nothing & I fear will do nothing to arrest the impending catastrophe. *These remarks are strictly private.*[36]

With such gloomy forebodings Buchanan prepared to face events as they developed. He had laid down certain general rules, a broad strategy to chart his course, but he would have to improvise the details of his program. Of first importance, he determined to avoid initiating a war. He would take no provocative action and would apply force only to repel a military assault on the government. Second, he would observe his oath and act only according to law. He would not usurp power and risk impeachment, giving Congress and the Republican leadership an excuse to dodge their responsibility. He would ask Congress for additional means to act under law; if denied such lawful authority and the public support that legislation represented, he would act within existing law. Third, he would keep open the door to compromise. This gesture would encourage southern Unionists, invite the continuing loyalty of the border states, and permit the president to act as a mediator. If war had to come, it would arise from the obdurate refusal of Republicans to make any sacrifice for the Union or from some rash, aggressive act of the secessionists. The Buchanan Administration would not start it.

28

CURSED ARE THE PEACEMAKERS • 1860

"WE WILL HOLD THE FORTS"

The Charleston forts continued to pose the most perplexing problem for the Administration. Major Anderson, working at top speed to put Fort Moultrie in a condition of readiness, reported at the end of November that he had nearly completed this task. But he still feared an assault from Charleston which would be hard to withstand because of a series of sand hills to the north from which sharp-shooters might fire directly into the fort. He had already started to level these hills. He asked Floyd's permission to repair Castle Pinckney and garrison it lightly with troops from Fort Moultrie. Floyd vetoed the shift of troops, but approved the employment of civilians to repair Castle Pinckney. By this time Fort Sumter had been sufficiently completed to receive a garrison of one company, and Anderson asked the War Department to assign such a force.[1]

During the last week of November, Buchanan called Floyd to the State Department. Black and Cass left when Floyd arrived, and the president then told him that he had decided to reinforce the Charleston forts. "I would rather have my throat cut, sir," he said, "than have Fort Moultrie seized by South Carolina. You must & shall send troops forthwith." Floyd said he would risk his honor and his life that South Carolina would not molest the forts. "That is all very well," responded Buchanan, "but . . . does that secure the forts?"[2] Floyd, who suspected the influence of his northern colleagues, persuaded Buchanan to defer action until both of them talked with General Scott. Floyd later confided to Trescot that he would "cut off his right hand" before he would sign any order to reinforce the forts and would resign if Buchanan persisted in his course, but he would resist any attempt of South Carolina to seize the forts. Cobb and Thompson held the same views, he said.

Trescot wrote this information to Governor Gist, warning him that Buchanan feared seizure of the forts at any moment and intended to strengthen them to resist attack. Trescot urged Gist to pledge South

Carolina to inaction as the only means of preventing the movement of additional troops. Gist replied on November 29 by two letters, one appointing Trescot an unofficial agent of South Carolina to communicate with the Administration, and the other empowering him to assure Buchanan that "everything is now quiet and will remain so until the ordinance [of secession] is passed, if no more soldiers or munitions of war are sent on." The governor added that he would "use all the military power of the state to prevent any increase of troops in these garrisons" and invited Trescot to show his letter to Buchanan. This he did.

In view of these developments, Buchanan asked Trescot to carry an advance copy of his message to Governor Gist. After a long conversation with the president, Trescot felt that Buchanan's aim at the moment was to persuade the Carolinians to postpone secession at least until March 4 and to convince them that he would maintain a *status quo* at the forts if South Carolina would stay in the Union. When Trescot brought this report to Gist, the governor told him to reply that "no scheme of policy, however plausible, could induce delay until the 4th of March, either in deference to Mr. Buchanan's position or with a view to the cooperation of other States."[3]

On the day that the message went to Congress, Buchanan met with the Cabinet to discuss Anderson's request, which had just arrived, for men, ammunition, and supplies.[4] When the Cabinet divided on the question, Buchanan put off making a decision, for it had now become clear that the Cabinet would break up whatever the answer, and this the president wanted to delay until he had news of Trescot's visit with Gist.

Anderson grew increasingly apprehensive of attack and multiplied his reports of danger during the early weeks of December. State troops drilled constantly in the city, he said, and openly boasted of their intent to take Fort Moultrie.[5] He had ordered repair work to begin on Castle Pinckney and in order to protect workmen there and at Moultrie, had prepared a requisition to draw 100 muskets with cartridge belts and ammunition from the Charleston arsenal. Col. Huger at the arsenal would not issue these arms without orders directly from the War Department, and wrote to Floyd for authority. Huger's inquiry reached Washington on December 6 and soon became public knowledge, as there was no security of information going into or out of Charleston. Floyd replied to Anderson that "the increase of the force under your command . . . would . . . judging from the recent excitement produced on account of an anticipated increase . . . but add to that excitement and might lead to serious results," and he informed Col. Huger that authority to supply arms to the forts would be "deferred for the present."[6]

On the same day Floyd tried to relieve Anderson's nearly intolerable situation by sending Major Don Carlos Buell from Washington to explain to him the position of the Administration and to give him "explanatory" orders. Floyd did not put these in writing, nor did he inform Buchanan of the exact conversation. At Fort Moultrie, a few days later, Anderson and Buell both agreed that the instructions ought to be put in writing for Floyd's positive approval and drew up the following memorandum on December 11: "You are carefully to avoid every act which would needlessly tend to provoke aggression. . . . But you are to hold possession of the forts in this harbor, and if attacked you are to defend yourself to the last extremity. The smallness of your force will not permit you, perhaps, to occupy more than one of the three forts, but an attack or an attempt to take possession of any of them will be regarded as an act of hostility, and you may then put your command into either of them which you may deem most proper, to increase its power of resistance. You are also authorized to take similar steps whenever you have tangible evidence of a design to proceed to a hostile act."[7] They sent this note to the War Department, and Floyd authenticated it. Of this exchange Buchanan knew only that Anderson had been instructed to act defensively and hold the forts.

SWIFTLY CHANGING CIRCUMSTANCES

South Carolina had elected delegates to its secession convention on December 6, and two days later the members of the South Carolina Congressional delegation at Washington called on Buchanan. The meeting started on an awkward note because the southerners believed that Buchanan had approved sending reinforcements to Anderson, and Buchanan believed that the Charlestonians intended shortly to assault Fort Moultrie. The Carolinians—John McQueen, William Porcher Miles, M. L. Bonham, W. W. Boyce, and Lawrence M. Keitt—expressed their desire to reach some agreement with Buchanan which would prevent bloodshed until secession had been proclaimed. After that, the independent nation of South Carolina would send commissioners to Washington to discuss the future. Buchanan told his callers to put whatever they wished to recommend in writing. He told them that "he would collect the revenues at all hazards," avowed "his determination to obey the laws," and bitterly denounced the ingratitude of South Carolina in rushing out of the Union before she had been hurt. When someone asked him if he would use force to execute the laws, he responded, "I will obey the laws. I am no warrior —I am a man of peace—but I will obey the laws."[8]

On the same day, Buchanan got Howell Cobb's note of resignation from the Cabinet. This was not a surprise, but no less a blow for that. Cobb had made up his mind to resign shortly after Lincoln's election but had postponed action and continued his work during the last month with a good deal of embarrassment.[9] Black forced him to the wall by proposing that both of them confront Buchanan and state their respective positions on secession. If Buchanan supported secession, Black said he would resign in five minutes; if he opposed it, Cobb would resign.[10] Cobb actually resigned on December 8. "The President and myself parted in the most friendly spirit," he wrote his wife. "We both see & feel the necessity & both regret that it should be so."

Cobb's resignation hurt Buchanan much more than he admitted at the moment. One of his friends wrote, "If 'old Buck' loves anybody in the world, that man is Gov. Cobb. . . . He spoke of the Gov. in great kindness, but with sorrow." The President believed Cobb had made a great mistake and "*believed firmly* Georgia would never secede." Harriet said she thought Cobb was making "the greatest mistake of his life."[11] Cobb had nourished Buchanan's expectation that Georgia would stand as a firm bastion against secession in the deep South. Now both Cobb and Georgia were gone, and the loss would be much more serious than anything which might happen around Charleston. Buchanan appointed Philip F. Thomas of Maryland, commissioner of patents, to the Treasury.[12]

On December 10 the South Carolina Congressmen came back to the White House with their statement about the Charleston forts. This document expressed the belief of the signers that South Carolina would not molest the forts until some "amicable arrangement" had been made between the state and the federal government, "provided that no reinforcements shall be sent into those forts, and their relative military status shall remain as at present." Buchanan did not like the word "provided" and refused to restrict his freedom of action by such a guarantee, particularly since the delegation had no official status and could not bind anyone to the terms of the letter. He stated that although it was his *policy* not to alter the *status quo*, he could *pledge* nothing. The South Carolinians told him that the words "military status" meant that the transfer of the Moultrie garrison to Sumter would be the equivalent of a reinforcement and would be the signal for war on the forts. Buchanan made no comment on this clarification but said, as they were leaving, "After all, this is a matter of honor among gentlemen; I do not know that any paper or writing is necessary; we understand each other." The delegation wanted more than a verbal statement and asked what might happen if Buchanan changed his mind and did send troops. "Then I would first return the paper," he answered.[13] After they had left, Buchanan took the paper and wrote on it his recollection of the verbal exchange.

Why did Buchanan change his policy from a determination to garrison the forts at the end of November to a policy of maintaining the *status quo* on December 10? Cobb's resignation provided the answer. So long as Buchanan could count on Georgia, he could deal strongly with

371

South Carolina as an isolated pocket of disunion without provoking a general reaction. North Carolina and Georgia would bracket her with Union defenders. But with Georgia lost, such a policy would spread the secession movement instead of localizing it. The new situation required a new approach. "What is right and what is practicable are two very different things," he observed.[14]

If December 10 produced a spongy *modus vivendi* between the Administration and the secessionists, the next day brought events that were hard and sharp as flint. On that day Buchanan parted company with his chief advisors on both sides. Secretary of State Cass resigned because he believed "that additional troops should be sent to reinforce the forts in Charleston."[15] Senators Gwin and Slidell called a few hours later to remonstrate against Buchanan's refusal to promise not to reinforce the forts. Buchanan called them disunionists and expressed his regret that he had so long listened to their advice. They left in anger, never again to communicate with him except as enemies.[16]

Buchanan was very much surprised at the resignation of Cass and thought it "remarkable on account of the cause he assigned for it."[17] But he quickly accepted it, to Cass's chagrin, and told Black that he considered it not as a calamity "but rather as a good riddance." Black as well as Buchanan attributed the resignation not to a difference of opinion but to Cass's wish to be "outside when the structure should begin to tumble."[18] The next day Cass asked for reconsideration, but the president said the matter was closed. On December 17, Buchanan appointed Black to the State Department and moved Assistant Attorney General Edwin M. Stanton to the top position. People who had observed Stanton in action on government business in California had warned both Buchanan and Black not to trust him, but they could find no one else who knew so well the background of important land cases then pending before the Supreme Court.

These events discouraged not only Buchanan but also the whole nation, for it began to be clear that the simultaneous break of both Cass and Slidell with the Administration foreshadowed the end. These men were not the "partizans" or the extremists; they were the moderates. Therefore, if Cass found Buchanan's policy too "southern" and Slidell thought it too "northern," what course could Buchanan follow? Thompson said that gloom and depression overwhelmed the capital—"no dinners, no parties, everybody looks sad." "You will read the President's proclamation for fasting and prayer on the 4th of Jan.—that tells whether he sees the danger or not."[19] Buchanan's appeal for a day of prayer gave rise to little except a round of new jokes.[20]

Sunday morning after the Cabinet changes, Washington society was shocked by news of the death of Secretary Holt. People exclaimed to each other, "did you ever see such a fatality attending the administration, two resignations and a death in a week." The wild rumor was dispersed when, lo, Holt appeared at his office on Monday morning.[21]

The day after Cass resigned, General Scott at last came to Washington. Buchanan had received no word from him on defense of the forts since the famous "Views" of October 29 and 30. On December 14 Scott conferred with Lyman Trumbull, who assured the old general that Buchanan had joined the traitors, was plotting the surrender of Fort Moultrie, and ought to be "gibbeted."[22] The next day, Scott urged the president to send a force of 300 men to Fort Moultrie immediately. Buchanan pointed out that this advice came two weeks too late, and that General Scott knew at the time he made this recommendation that it must be rejected. The president could not have complied with it "without at once reversing his entire policy, and without a degree of inconsistency amounting almost to self-stultification."[23] Buchanan's mail indicated that the country solidly supported this view. From Boston came the word: "The first re-inforcement sent there would be the signal of war, & you would be put in the position of initiating it and your successor be able to carry it on without responsibility for its origin."[24] A Georgian wrote, "re-inforcing Anderson would as certainly have produced a collision between the Federal and State Governments . . . as there is a God in Heaven."[25] Congressmen gave him the same advice.

Secretary Thompson chose this moment to make a strange request of the president. The State of Mississippi had appointed him an agent to visit North Carolina to discuss the secession movement, and Thompson wished Buchanan's approval of the mission, offering to resign if the president opposed his going. Buchanan suffered heavy condemnation at the time and for years afterward for allowing Thompson to make this journey while he was still a member of the Cabinet, for it outwardly appeared as if the president were actively promoting the secession movement. Buchanan explained that he had approved "only under the belief that [Thompson's] mission was to *prevent*, not to precipitate secession."[26] Thompson had disagreed with Buchanan's message, insisting that a "right" of secession did exist and expressing his determination to follow his state if it should secede. But he thought that the "right" came into existence only when sufficient cause existed to justify revolution, and that there was no such reason yet. He strongly opposed hasty action or separate action by any state; he was a cooperationist. Before there was clear justification for secession, no southern state ought to secede. With cause, all should go out. This was Thompson's message to North Carolina.[27]

If the Thompson trip had not convinced many that Buchanan had gone over to secession, the course of the Washington *Constitution*, edited by William M. Browne, would have done so. This journal acted as the "Administration organ," and received favored treatment in public printing contracts for playing the party tunes. Browne became a red-hot secessionist who labelled the election of Lincoln "a concentrated expression of the deadly hatred of the North to me and all I value."[28] Assistant Post-master General Horatio King complained to Black on December 14, "I am amazed that some decided action is not taken by the Government to cut itself entirely loose from disunion and disunionists. Look at the *Constitution* newspaper of to-day. . . . *Its whole bearing is for disunion*; and, say what you will, the Government is held, and will be held, in great degree responsible for it."[29]

King told John A. Dix of New York that "the course of the *Constitution* is infamous, but the President, I presume, has no means of controlling it."[30] King complained that the friends of the Union seemed to stay away from Buchanan in the belief that the *Constitution* "speaks the sentiments of the President, which is certainly not the fact."[31]

Buchanan, sensitive to executive interference with the freedom of the press, had Browne insert notices that the newspaper's editorials did not represent the Administration views. At length, on Christmas Day, Buchanan rebuked Browne for an editorial favoring secession, and advised him that he had withdrawn support from the paper. Still, most of January had elapsed before all government patronage to the *Constitution* had been cut off. Buchanan desperately needed accurate reporting of Administration policy in friendly newspapers of national circulation. Of these there were very few, notably the Philadelphia *Pennsylvania* and the Boston *Courier*. After he had had to abandon the *Constitution*, the president wrote to Bennett of the New York *Herald*, asking him as a patriotic citizen to publicize the compromise proposals advocated by the Administration.[32]

Suspicion that Buchanan was in league with the secessionists brought a furious storm of public denunciation upon the president. Abraham Lincoln received numerous warnings. "Buchanan is today as truly a traitor as was Benedict Arnold." "I hope you are preparing—in case that cowardly old imbecile & traitor Buchanan shall go on, & mischief result—to strike out & sharply for his impeachment. If ever a man deserved it, he does. If ever hanging were a proper use to put a man to for his political sins, he really deserves it." "What an ignominious exit from public life of James Buchanan!"[33] Northern Democrats wrote the same sentiments. One was "in favor of hanging Buchanan, his organ grinder, [and] the Sec'y of War." Another warned that Buchanan should never plan to come back to Pennsylvania. "Our people will not treat him with respect." Many called him a traitor who favored secession.[34] Greeley's New York *Tribune* ran a headlined editorial on December 17 which stated that the president was insane, and others reported that he was a coward, an imbecile, and ill from sheer terror. Cass, perhaps to justify his resignation, told people that Buchanan had become "pale with fear" and divided his time equally between praying and crying. But guests at a wedding reception on December 20 which the president attended found him proclaiming that he had never enjoyed better health and looking the part.[35]

In the midst of the festivities, when a commotion started in the hall, Buchanan turned his head and said to a guest, "Madam, do you suppose the house is on fire?" She went to inquire. In the hallway she found Lawrence Keitt "leaping in the air, shaking a paper over his head, and exclaiming, 'Thank God! Oh, thank God!' . . . South Carolina has seceded! Here's the telegram. I feel like a boy let out from school." On hearing this report Buchanan called for his carriage, and drove back to the White House. There he found a telegram waiting for him from South Carolina's new governor, F. W. Pickens, confirming Keitt's report.[36]

The announcement was not exactly news to Buchanan. He knew that action probably would come on the 20th, and during the past week had sent Caleb Cushing to South Carolina to make a last ditch plea for delay. Cushing had informed him that the convention would vote for secession. What worried the president more was a letter from Governor Pickens, dated December 17 and presented to him on the morning of the 20th, demanding that he authorize South Carolina "to take possession of Fort Sumter immediately."[37] The courier wanted an instant reply, but Buchanan told him to come back the next day. In the meantime, W. H. Trescot learned of the contents of the letter. His resignation as Assistant Secretary of State had been accepted only that morning, and he now acted as a spokesman for South Carolina. He saw that Pickens's demand terminated the *status quo* policy that Buchanan had informally stated on December 10 to the South Carolina Congressmen and would give the president practically a mandate to garrison all the forts. He sought out Slidell, Jefferson Davis, and Congressmen Bonham and McQueen, and all telegraphed Pickens to withdraw his letter.[38]

Buchanan drafted his reply that night. He would not surrender any forts or public property in South Carolina, he wrote. "If South Carolina should attack any of these forts, she will then become the assailant in a war against the United States. It will not then be a question of coercing a state. . . . Between independent governments, if one possesses a fortress within the limits of another, and the latter should seize it . . . this would not only be a just cause of war, but the actual commencement of hostilities."[39] By morning Pickens had withdrawn his letter and Buchanan did not send the reply he had prepared.

This incident had grown out of another altercation over the delivery of arms from the arsenal at Charleston. Captain Foster, engineer officer in charge of construction at Castle Pinckney and at Fort Sumter, feared mob action against his workmen and wanted muskets for them. As the War Department had never sent authorization of the request of December 6 for 100 muskets, he went to the arsenal on the 17th and showed a storekeeper the old order of November 1 for 40 muskets—the order which had caused the earlier change of command at Charleston. The storekeeper delivered the guns, and Foster divided them between Castle Pinckney and Fort Sumter. The news enraged the people of Charleston, who demanded the delivering up of Sumter. Pickens wrote his letter to Buchanan that day, under the apprehension that the order had originated in Washington, and thus terminated the "gentleman's agreement." When Col. Huger learned of the transaction he demanded the return of the muskets, but Anderson refused to deliver them. The next day the South Carolina authorities set up a 24-hour patrol of Fort Sumter by gunboats. When news of these events reached Washington, Floyd immediately ordered Anderson to return the guns to the arsenal, and by the end of the day conditions were back to normal. The incident made shockingly clear how tenuous was the December 10th "understanding" and how slender a thread restrained the sword of war.[40]

Only now, the day after secession, did Buchanan learn of the orders which Buell had written out for Anderson ten days before. At a Cabinet meeting on December 21 to consider afresh the position of Anderson, Buchanan asked exactly what orders had been sent to Moultrie. Floyd did not even remember and had to send for his files at the War Office. When Buell's memorandum had been found, Floyd read it and stated that it conformed to his verbal instructions to Buell. Buchanan did not like the sentence which directed Anderson to defend himself "to the last extremity," feeling that this called for a needless sacrifice of life, but otherwise agreed that the directions were sound. The Cabinet approved, and Black then wrote out a revised copy including a statement that Anderson should "exercise sound military discretion" and not make a useless sacrifice of his men. Floyd signed this, making it a formal Department order, and sent it by courier to Anderson at Fort Moultrie.[41]

While the new orders were on their way to Charleston, a letter from Anderson of December 22 was speeding toward Washington. After the proclamation of secession, Anderson momentarily expected an attack on Fort Moultrie. He had five days more work to complete his temporary defenses, but, he wrote, "God knows whether the South Carolinians will defer their attempt to take this work so long as that." He reported that the patrol boats had orders to prevent any military occupation of Sumter. So many civilian workmen there had begun to wear the blue cockade, he said, that construction ought to be halted and the fort left in the charge of a lieutenant and a few picked men.[42] Buchanan also heard, on this day, that commissioners from South Carolina would arrive in Washington on December 26 to discuss the problem of the forts.

THE CABINET EXPLODES

Before the nerve-wracking 22nd of December had ended, Buchanan learned of a Cabinet scandal so shocking that it forced every other concern into the background. Floyd's easy-going management had at last brought disaster growing out of his continuing practice, against Buchanan's explicit orders, of writing "acceptances" for Russell, Majors and Waddell, the army contractors. A relative of Floyd, one Godard Bailey, worked in the office of Secretary Thompson and had access to negotiable bonds worth $1000 each which the government held in trust for the Indians. Russell needed money and hit upon the scheme of offering Bailey Floyd's "acceptances" in return for the bonds. When Congress paid Russell, he would pick up the acceptances and return the bonds. Bailey either wanted to help Floyd or had been offered some inducement by Russell, but whatever the reason, he cooperated until $870,000 had left the Interior Department. The bonds soon came on the market and to Secretary Thompson's attention. He learned the facts from Bailey, who seemed unaware that he had been doing anything wrong, and then set out to find Russell. Within several days he had them both in jail and then broke the disgraceful news to Buchanan. The press reported the story in the most damaging and sensational way. The Covode Committee, it now appeared, had been on the right track, but had quit too soon. As the investigation developed, the public learned (whether with truth or not, no one could be sure) that half a dozen New Yorkers and quite a few Washington officials had been in on the scheme, and that several who might have "leaked" had been paid to hold their tongues. The press also reported that Riggs and Company, Buchanan's bankers, had bought six of the filched bonds for the president's private account.[43]

Buchanan had no alternative but to fire Floyd, but he so hated to do it that he asked Black to convey his request for the resignation. Black declined, and Buchanan finally persuaded Breckinridge to do it. But Floyd angrily refused to resign, and Buchanan had not the heart to dismiss him on Christmas Day.

Apparently, Floyd had known nothing about Bailey's trading and he had certainly derived no profit from it. True, he had disobeyed Buchanan in order to provide for the army whose needs Congress had persistently ignored, but he felt he deserved praise rather than blame for risking his administrative neck to care for the nation's troops. The district court thought otherwise and planned to prosecute him for conspiracy to defraud the government.

Floyd for some weeks had been quite ill and the bond affair completed his breakdown. On the day he first learned about it he ordered his ordnance chief, Captain Maynadier, to send a shipment of heavy guns from the Pittsburgh armory to some unfinished forts in Texas. The charitable view of this was that Floyd, who never had much knowledge of the detailed operations of his department, issued this order without any treasonable intent and as a matter of routine. The less charitable view was that Floyd, nervously awaiting the visit of the South Carolina commissioners and knowing that the bond scandal must terminate his Cabinet career, gave way to despair and decided on the spur of the moment to cast his lot with secession. He abruptly changed his stand during the last week of December and violently denounced in Cabinet the very policies he had formerly supported. It seems most likely that the impact of the Bailey business, his poor health, and the crisis over the forts combined to create in his heart an utter detestation of Buchanan, the Administration, and the Union.

Floyd spent Christmas Day in an emotional torment, but he retained enough balance to reject in anger a scheme proposed to him by Senator Wigfall to kidnap Buchanan and put Breckinridge into the presidency. At Cabinet meeting the next day, Floyd, who had come uninvited, lost control of himself and spoke loudly and discourteously to Buchanan. Black and Stanton did not attend this session, which was perhaps fortunate, for Floyd had come to hate the sight of them; but Thompson was present and he pitched into Floyd for involving the Interior Department in the bond scandal. Thompson said he would prosecute to the limit of the law everyone connected with the affair, and he left no doubt that he thought Floyd was among the guilty.[44]

Buchanan wanted the Cabinet to consider the treatment of the South Carolina commissioners who had just arrived in Washington, but first another problem had to be settled. Black had received telegrams from worried citizens of Pittsburgh protesting the shipment of cannon from the local gun works to the South. Inquiry had revealed that the Texas forts were quite unprepared to receive them, and the transaction aroused suspicion. The Pittsburghers thought it plain treason. Black told Buchanan of Floyd's orders on Christmas Day, and the president instantly cancelled the shipment. No guns left Pittsburgh, but Floyd considered Buchanan's act a direct slap at him.[45] The Cabinet then agreed that it would be permissible for Buchanan to confer with the South Carolina commissioners as "private gentlemen," and perhaps to submit to Congress a proposition which they might make.

William H. Trescot, acting as a go-between, scheduled a procedural meeting for December 27. On the morning of that fateful day news arrived which created wild excitement. Major Anderson had just spiked the guns of Moultrie and had moved his entire command into Fort Sumter under cover of darkness in a brilliant military maneuver carried out under the very eyes of the South Carolina patrol boats and the state militia pickets. The South Carolina commissioners cancelled their visit to Buchanan and

378

waited for more information. Trescot hurried to Floyd's office and obtained from him a promise that he would promptly order Anderson back to Moultrie as soon as he received official confirmation of the reports. Floyd immediately telegraphed Anderson that he did not believe the news, "because there is no order for any such movement," but Anderson replied, "The telegram is correct."[46]

While messages sped back and forth, the southern leaders in Washington headed for the White House. Jefferson Davis arrived first and broke the news to Buchanan. "Now, Mr. President," he said, "you are surrounded with blood and dishonor on all sides." According to Trescot, Buchanan "was standing by the mantelpiece, crushing up a cigar in the palm of his hand. . . . He sat down as Colonel Davis finished, and exclaimed, 'My God, are calamities never to come singly! I call God to witness, you gentlemen more than anybody *know* that this is not only without but against my orders. It is against my policy.' " Senators Hunter, Lane, Yulee, even Slidell called and bore down on Buchanan to order Anderson out of Sumter or face general secession and war. Buchanan paced nervously, telling his excited callers to keep calm and trust him. He gave evidence of sympathizing with their position for it seemed to him at the moment as if Anderson had ruptured the "gentleman's agreement." It certainly was a move the president had not anticipated. But for all his soothing words, he gave the southerners no promise. They left not knowing what Buchanan intended to do. He himself did not know.

The afternoon Cabinet meeting ran over into the night. Black, Holt, and Stanton aggressively defended Anderson's action. "Good," said Black. "It is in precise accordance with his orders."[47] "It is not," said Floyd. The orders were sent for and read—the latest ones in Black's handwriting, signed by Floyd and approved by the Cabinet only five days before. Floyd had brought a paper with him containing his objections to Anderson's move and now read it in a "loud and discourteous" tone, but he got no support from anyone except Thompson. Toucey said little. Floyd asserted that the "solemn pledges of this Government have been violated" and that federal troops should now be withdrawn from all the Charleston forts. Black, with the orders signed by Floyd in his hand, turned livid and, waving the paper in Floyd's face, shouted: "There never was a moment in the history of England when a minister of the Crown could have proposed to surrender a military post which might be defended, *without bringing his head to the block!*"[48]

The president tried to calm his colleagues, for Floyd by this time had risen out of his seat in nearly uncontrollable rage. Buchanan believed that Anderson's orders justified his maneuver. The Cabinet had assigned the major "military discretion" and had authorized him to take defensive action in the face of "tangible evidence of a design to attack him." His

379

report of a few days before had offered such evidence, though no hint that he intended to transfer the troops. Buchanan said he would not order Anderson to return to Moultrie, but he expressed deep concern over the settlement of the question of responsibility. Neither the president nor the Secretary of War had commanded the transfer, but Buchanan and the Cabinet had agreed to the permissive orders under which Anderson could justify his act.

Floyd's sharp difference with the Cabinet provided him the excuse he needed to resign on the pretext of a conflict of principles, rather than to be discharged for malversion in office and conspiracy to defraud the government. Many in Washington believed that he had purposely changed his views to accomplish this result. One wrote that Anderson's action had been "a happy chance" for Floyd, and would "bring the mantle of charity to his aid."[49]

Before the commissioners called on December 28, Buchanan received news that South Carolina had just seized Forts Moultrie, Castle Pinckney, and the U. S. Customhouse. There was some doubt whether Anderson's move had violated the December 10th agreement, but do doubt at all that this act of South Carolina broke it. This put the commissioners on the defensive.

Buchanan had agreed to see the South Carolinians "only as private gentlemen." At their interview, the only one which was to be held, they informed the president excitedly and with asperity that they would not negotiate with him until he ordered all federal troops out of the Charleston area. Buchanan replied that he could issue no such order. He might, however, refer to Congress any communication they might wish to give him. The president reported that he had said very little but had listened with patience.[50] The commissioners then withdrew and that night prepared a statement which they sent to the White House the next morning. Their letter had the tone of a threat. It suggested that South Carolina had made a serious mistake "to trust to your honor rather than its own power," and warned that unless the troops were withdrawn, affairs would speedily come to a "bloody issue."[51]

The Cabinet meeting of December 29 was probably the most important of Buchanan's career, and certainly it was for him the most agonizing, for he held in his mind hopes and plans, privately wrought, that his colleagues did not yet know. This story, which came to its climax on December 30, will be told shortly. Buchanan wrote a reply to the Carolina commissioners which Black, Holt, and Stanton refused to accept, feeling that it granted too much and demanded too little. Although this paper has disappeared, its contents may be reconstructed from the objections made to it in the Cabinet. Buchanan, in his own memoir, states that had the commissioners "simply requested that Major Anderson might be restored to his former position at Fort Moultrie, upon a guarantee from the State that neither it nor the other forts or public property should be molested; this, *at the moment*, might have been worthy of serious consideration."[52] Certainly this was the proposal Buchanan intended to make. And why this? Because he had underway a secret negotiation with the president-elect to obtain his backing for a national constitutional convention, and he expected an answer from Lincoln at any hour. Buchanan later wrote that he had held out the idea of submitting a proposal from South Carolina to Congress, not in any hope of its acceptance, but because he knew Congress would waste some time on it. "This was to gain time . . . to bring the whole subject before the representatives of the people" in a general convention.[53] If he promised enough to South Carolina to keep matters fluid for just a day or two more, he might solve the problem. With this hope he wrote his first answer to the commissioners.

The Cabinet argued the question all afternoon, but the president was inflexible and determined to submit the paper as he had written it, against the will of all except Thompson and Toucey. Black went home to spend a "miserable and restless night." The next morning he made the rounds of the Cabinet expressing his determination to resign unless the reply should be changed. Toucey immediately reported this decision to the White House and Buchanan called Black away from a conference with Stanton. "Do you, too, talk of leaving me?" he asked. Black stated his position firmly. "Your answer to the commissioners leaves you no cause; it sweeps the ground from under our feet; it places you where no man can stand with you, and where you cannot stand alone."[54]

Buchanan did not give up easily and argued at length, but at last he gave in. "Here," he said to Black. "Take this paper and modify it to suit yourself, but do it before the sun goes down." Before Black hurried off, Buchanan added, "I cannot part with you. If you go, Stanton and Holt will leave."[55]

"MR. LINCOLN, WILL YOU HELP?"

Although Buchanan did not want to lose his ministers, their threatened resignation was not the only reason for his change of mind. For a month Buchanan had been quietly trying to isolate South Carolina by forcing conservative Republicans to endorse some kind of conciliatory measure.

Because of the confused party structure of Congress, decisive action there seemed unlikely but not impossible. Unfortunately for compromise hopes, recent state elections showed that the Republicans would lose some seats in the new Congress of December, 1861. A number of Republicans thus believed that their party would benefit if some of the southern states seceded. Without these southern lawmakers, the Republicans would control the next Congress.

The House created a Committee of Thirty-three to report a program of compromise on the sectional crisis. Its early meetings exposed the facts that the Democrats could not agree among themselves and that the Republicans did not want to settle current problems by compromise. Its southern members wrote to South Carolina a week before secession that, so far as they could see, "all hope of relief is extinguished."

The Senate delayed even talking about the secession movement until December 18, two days before it became a fact. On that day Senator John J. Crittenden of Kentucky, a Whig, presented a comprehensive plan of compromise which became the center of national interest from then until March 4. He proposed an extension of the Missouri Compromise line prohibiting slavery to the north of it, but guaranteeing protection in territories to the south; the admission of new states with or without slavery as their constitutions should provide; no abolition of slavery in the District of Columbia or of the local slave trade in the South; payment for fugitive slaves; improvement in the enforcement of the Fugitive Slave Law; and firm suppression of the overseas slave trade. The day South Carolina seceded the Senate appointed a Committee of Thirteen to consider these proposals to avert secession. The nation looked with hopeful anxiety to the Senate Committee, for the Crittenden proposals had brought widespread public approval, and the Committee personnel represented every geographic section and every important political viewpoint. Work was delayed until December 24, however, because Seward was out of town. As chief representative of the Republicans, his views would be essential, for he would bring Lincoln's response to the Crittenden measures directly to the Committee.

By Christmastime Buchanan had despaired of any effective action from Congress and decided to try a behind-the-scenes manipulation of political and financial strings to force a statement from Lincoln. At first he hoped that Lincoln would come to Washington for a face-to-face talk; but the president-elect refused to leave Springfield, and Buchanan had to work through agents.

Lincoln already agreed with Buchanan on some aspects of secession. They both thought that it could be contained within a few states and that these would probably return quietly to the Union in due course if war could be averted. Buchanan could concur with Lincoln's statement of December 17 that "it is the duty of the President, and other government functionaries to run the machine as it is."[56] The real question was: by what means could war be averted? Buchanan had faith in the Crittenden plan, but if that should fail he intended to fall back upon the chief recommendation of his message, a national constitutional convention. Would

Lincoln lend his support to this? Some leading Republicans thought he would. Buchanan also began to hope so.

Thurlow Weed, editor of the Albany *Evening Journal* and a well-known figure on Wall Street, had come out boldly for a restoration of the Missouri Compromise line in his edition of November 24. People assumed that this trial balloon had been released by Seward. From the day Congress convened, Seward had been expressing his fear that five states might secede and his belief that the Republicans would have to act to prevent it. In the absence of any leadership from Lincoln, Seward hoped to take the Republican helm and steer the party to a conservative course, that is, to keep the door open to compromise and thus preserve peace. But the *Journal* editorial raised such a storm among the radical Republicans that Seward repudiated agency in it on December 5. Three days later Lincoln offered him the State Department.

During the first two weeks of December Lincoln wrote many letters declaring that he would not budge one jot on the subject of the further extension of slavery, but the more Seward observed in Washington, the more convinced he became that compromise alone could avert war, and that the Republican party ought to participate in the effort. He had his Cabinet post; he could now act more freely.

On December 10, Lincoln invited Weed to come to Springfield. The next day Weed informed Lincoln of a plan to have Republican governors meet in New York on December 20 to discuss compromise measures and promote harmony within the party. There was a clear hint of political pressure in the announcement.[57] Seward conferred with Weed in Albany on December 15 and 16 and told him to obtain Lincoln's assent to some kind of Republican compromise proposal. On December 17 Weed's paper came out a second time in favor of the Missouri line. This stand, on the heels of Seward's repudiation of the idea, was so ill-timed and so defiant of the Republican party policy that it caused widespread comment. What was behind it? Seward certainly intended to force a statement from Lincoln on the plan that Crittenden was just about to present to the Senate. Weed would bring back the answer.[58]

New York City for the next week became the headquarters for frantic compromise activity. The financiers and merchants who stood to lose some $150,000,000 in long term notes owed them by the South became thoroughly frightened by the news of secession, and a panic ensued. Politics and finance united in New York in the persons of August Belmont, national chairman for the Douglas Democrats; Samuel L. M. Barlow, a Buchanan party leader; Thurlow Weed and others. Judah P. Benjamin, Louisiana financier-politician, and Duff Green of South Carolina also figured in the compromise efforts of the New York businessmen.

383

On the day of secession, several Republican governors met in New York, Weed interviewed Lincoln, and Royal Phelps wrote to Buchanan that Seward had just told him that the Republicans "are doing all in their power to have the Personal Liberty laws repealed . . . and that they are willing for the sake of the peace of the Country, to have the territorial question settled by the Missouri Compromise Bill running it to the Pacific." Many of the most influential Whigs and Republicans had written Tom Corwin, Chairman of the Committee of Thirty-three, "urging him to advocate concessions." The New York Republicans were getting up a meeting to "cut loose entirely from Greeley and the abolitionists." "These doings," he concluded, "are conducted very privately."[59]

Van Buren and Belmont wrote to Crittenden and Douglas that the Republicans had decided to compromise on the Missouri principle. The news was soon abroad, and the abolitionists bombarded Lincoln with warnings. William Cullen Bryant wrote that Lincoln should beware of "a plan manufactured in Wall Street" and that "the restoration of the Missouri Compromise would disband the Republican party."[60] Another letter assured the president-elect that there were "multitudes here who will plunge into blood to the horses bridles" to defend the Chicago Platform— young men full of "a spirit of *fierce rebellion* against any compromise."[61]

Barlow had been conducting a vigorous correspondence with southern leaders, particularly Slidell and Benjamin, counselling patience and reason. The North had not elected Lincoln, he said, but the stupidity of the Democrats; Lincoln would be powerless unless the southerners quit Congress. Peaceful secession was a delusion. The North, in alarm, was receding in horror from the results of abolitionism but if the South started a revolution the North would unite solidly in opposition. A constitutional convention should solve all the problems.[62]

Barlow told Benjamin that Weed's compromise articles had been written by Seward; that the governors had agreed that the slavery issue ought to be decided by the present Congress on the basis of the Crittenden proposals; that Weed had gotten Lincoln's assent to this method of settlement; that Lincoln had assured Weed that he would break with the abolitionist faction of the party if necessary; and that the Missouri line proposal would pass the House with the aid of the needed Republican votes. Seward, Barlow said, would oppose this proposal in order to maintain the appearance of party regularity but would nevertheless deliver enough Republican votes to pass the measure. This report does not agree with Weed's recollections but the discrepancies are less important than the fact that Barlow sent this story to Benjamin on December 26. Important southern leaders had assurance from a source they trusted that the Republicans, led as they presumed by the conciliatory Seward, had committed themselves to an adjustment.[63]

But affairs did not stand as Barlow reported. Lincoln had vetoed the Crittenden plan and had given Weed written instructions to govern Seward's course in the Committee of Thirteen. They constituted more an insult than a compromise, considering the Committee personnel. Lincoln said that Congress ought to pass a new fugitive slave law without the clause which required private persons to assist in its execution, that all state laws in conflict with federal laws "if there be such" ought to be repealed, and that the Union ought to be preserved. Seward presented these terms to an expectant Committee. Editor W. M. Browne wrote that Seward's talk "almost made a disunionist out of Crittenden." Within the Committee, all base for compromise had been wiped out.[64]

Buchanan had not entertained much hope that the Republicans could be moved to accept the Missouri line. "I have no reason to believe," he wrote to Phelps on December 22, "that this is at present acceptable to Northern Senators and representatives, though the tendency is in that direction. They may arrive at this point when it is too late."[65] But Seward's capitulation to Lincoln, and Lincoln's apparent capitulation to the radicals of his party dramatically changed the issue. The Union Democrats who had continually urged compromise and who had been led by Seward to expect help from him, now suddenly found their hopes dashed when they were brightest. There had been as little warning of Seward's change of position as of Anderson's. That they occurred simultaneously confirmed the worst fears of the South. Compromise was dead, killed by false promises of the Republicans and betrayal by the Administration.

Buchanan now considered the time ripe for his final effort. If Lincoln would not compromise, if Congress would not compromise, would the Republicans permit the people of the United States to express their views in a constitutional convention? This would not be a compromise; it would be only a recognition of the validity of constitutional government. He sent Duff Green to Springfield to ask Lincoln about a convention. Green wrote back the night of his interview, Friday, December 28, that Lincoln thought that "the question on the amendments to the Constitution and the questions submitted by Mr. Crittenden belonged to the people and states in legislatures or conventions, and that he would be inclined not only to acquiesce, but to give full force to their will thus expressed."[66] Though foggily phrased, this sounded like good news; Lincoln would back a convention.

Lincoln had asked Green to call again at 9 o'clock the next morning to receive a written statement which Green planned to telegraph to Buchanan. Lincoln wrote the letter on Friday night but apparently did not give it to Green on Saturday, for he had changed his mind. He sent the letter to Senator Lyman Trumbull first, requesting him to deliver it to Green if he approved its message. "I do not desire any amendment to the

385

Constitution," it read. But Lincoln would not permit this statement to be made public unless "six of the twelve United States Senators from Georgia, Alabama, Mississippi, Louisiana, Florida, and Texas shall sign their names to what is written on this sheet below my name, and allow the whole to be published together." The statement pledged the southern States "to suspend all action for dismemberment of the Union" until the incoming Administration had committed some act violating their rights.

No one has reported what Lincoln said at the second interview, but it seems certain that he did not give Green any further encouragement. This in itself should have told Green that the president-elect had backed away from his statement of the previous day. Green had orders to telegraph Buchanan the moment he got a "satisfactory" response from Lincoln. Did he telegraph his fears on Saturday or Sunday, or keep silence until he got Lincoln's written statement? Either course meant bad news to Buchanan.

It seems likely that by Sunday afternoon, December 30, Buchanan had either learned from Green that Lincoln would not endorse a convention or anticipated this result from Green's silence. Certainly if Lincoln, who knew Buchanan's crisis as well as anyone, had not responded by Sunday to Green's plea of Friday morning, he was not likely to respond favorably. With these thoughts running through his mind, Buchanan guessed that he would get no help from Lincoln. This opinion brought him to the end of the first phase of his policy, his attempt to achieve some constructive action to allay southern fears. He now embarked on the second phase and told Black to rewrite the reply to the South Carolina commissioners.[67]

Buchanan soon learned the text of Lincoln's letter to Green. It had been framed, he saw, to repel the pledge demanded of the South, thus keeping secret Lincoln's rejection of a convention. Lincoln had quoted copiously from the Chicago Platform and now asked the southerners to suspend secession in return for an endorsement of the Republican articles of faith. Buchanan could not repress a wry smile at such a transparent "offer." Yet it helped him to interpret Lincoln. The man certainly had a grip on practical politics. He had done exactly what Buchanan himself had done in 1856 when called upon to answer difficult questions as spokesman for a faction-ridden party—quoted the platform. Buchanan now recognized that Lincoln did not dare to support any peaceful move which might settle the crisis for fear of disrupting his own party. But Lincoln had significantly emphasized a particular sentence from the Chicago Platform. "I denounce," he quoted, "the lawless invasion, by armed force, of the soil of any State or Territory, no matter under what pretext, as the gravest of crimes." In short, he could not afford to come out openly for compromise, but he did ot want war. This was language a politician could understand.

Black and Stanton worked over the reply to the commissioners, and on the basis of their recommendations Buchanan rewrote his own draft, mostly by editing out the parts that Black had condemned.[68] He held his ground on the "gentleman's agreement," stating that he had never sent reinforcements or authorized any alteration of the status of the forts. He quoted the orders to Anderson and then wrote, "it is clear that Major Anderson acted upon his own responsibility." His "first promptings" to have Anderson return had been nullified by the summary seizure of the forts by South Carolina, "without waiting or asking for any explanation." Buchanan said he could find no ground for any grievance of South Carolina, accused the state of stealing half a million dollars in federal property, and stated his intention "to defend Fort Sumter . . . against hostile attacks, from whichever quarter they may come."[69] The stunned commissioners replied to this on January 2 in an angry blast which the Cabinet termed "so violent, unfounded and disrespectful" that Buchanan returned it with the endorsement: "This paper, just presented to the President, is of such a character that he declines to receive it."[70]

The simultaneous failure of parleys with the Republicans and with the secessionists unnerved Buchanan more than anything that had yet happened. Importuned, threatened, warned, begged, pushed, pulled, and shoved in every direction, bombarded by plans and propositions until he resentfully complained that he had not time even to say his prayers, the president at length became distraught and despaired of achieving a solution. His two chief hopes—that conservative Republicans might give a little help and that his erstwhile southern friends might continue to trust his pacific intentions—both blew up in his face at once. He believed that he and his advisors represented the views of a vast majority of Americans, but the Administration no longer spoke for any political party. The only two organized parties, the inflexible secessionists and the unyielding Republicans, controlled the issue. Their leaders offered no quarter. Their representatives in Congress united their votes to prevent the registration of public opinion in a convention and to prevent the President of the United States from obtaining any legal means to handle the crisis. There was no New Year's Eve jollification at the White House, December 31, 1860.

387

29
FORTY DAYS AND FORTY NIGHTS • 1861

THE STAR OF THE WEST

During the first weeks of 1861 Buchanan leaned heavily upon the advice of Black, Holt, Toucey, and Scott. At the Cabinet meeting of Wednesday, January 2, they considered again the subject of reinforcing Major Anderson. Scott had written a few days before that he could instantly supply 150 recruits and ample foodstuffs to Sumter and recommended that orders to reinforce be issued. He also urged Buchanan to garrison Forts Taylor, Jefferson, Pickens, Jackson, and others along the Gulf Coast. Some of these, which controlled access to the Mississippi, could be taken, he said, by "a rowboat of pirates."[1] On New Year's Day South Carolina had cut off mail service to Fort Sumter, seized the lighthouse in the harbor, and announced that all United States ships were excluded from the vicinity. It had been during the discussion of these matters that the final reply of the South Carolina commissioners had been delivered and indignantly rejected. As the president's secretary, Adam Glossbrenner, left the room to return the commissioners' letter, Buchanan exclaimed, "It is now over, and reinforcements must be sent."[2] Secretary Thompson later claimed not to have heard this statement, but Toucey and Stanton said they did, and Holt must have, for he immediately acted upon it.[3]

Buchanan, having decided to reinforce Anderson, left the tactical arrangements to Holt, Scott, and Toucey with the understanding that they should observe the utmost secrecy in preparations. They hoped to send the reinforcements in without raising an alarm and encountering resistance. Buchanan and Toucey strongly urged the use of the navy's *U. S. S. Brooklyn*, but General Scott insisted that a ship of lighter draft should be chosen to prevent grounding on the bar. The sidewheel merchant steamer, *Star of the West*, was therefore chartered, quietly loaded with foodstuffs at New York, and then ordered to proceed down the bay to the Narrows where she took on recruits out of sight of the public eye. The men were ordered below decks in order that the steamer might appear to chance observers as a commercial vessel. She weighed anchor on January 5.[4]

On the same day Buchanan got further word from Major Anderson that he considered his command safe in its present position and that the government could reinforce him at its leisure. On hearing this, Scott, with Buchanan's approval, sent word posthaste to stop the relief expedition, but the ship had sailed shortly before the countermanding orders arrived. That night a visitor, after spending an hour with Buchanan, reported, "I have never seen him so solemn. . . . He remarked that nothing but the interposition of all-wise Providence could save our Country—that he had despaired of being able to do anything himself."[5]

Rumors of the expedition soon got into print. In fact, to expect to carry out any government maneuver in secrecy was almost a fool's hope. No war existed; no censorship or martial law had been proclaimed; and government officers felt within their rights to report to their political friends what was going on. Seward, for example, had just assured Lincoln that he had "gotten a position in which I can see what is going on in the Councils of the President." Stanton had agreed to "leak" to him. Others wrote, "I am not sure who are my friends anymore."[6]

The pro-Union Cabinet members kept Thompson and Thomas in the dark about the relief expedition, but they learned of it through the press. Thompson immediately resigned the Interior Department. He had told Black at the end of the Cabinet meeting of January 3 that he would have to do so if Buchanan sent reinforcements. On the day the *Star of the West* sailed, he had telegraphed to friends in South Carolina and Mississippi that no troops had been sent, "nor will be, while I am a member of the Cabinet."[7] Naturally, he felt he had been deceived, and with good reason. Buchanan promptly accepted his resignation, asserting that Thompson had no cause for complaint, since the decision to reinforce had been made openly in a Cabinet meeting. But Thompson had not so understood the meaning of Buchanan's remark at that meeting, and it seems probable that the matter was left vague at that time in order that he should not know the exact plans. Although his resignation would have been unmistakable evidence that more troops were on the way to Sumter, Thompson informed his southern friends of the reinforcements the moment he learned the truth. Many condemned him for treason, but that judgment, if it had been generally applied, would have made a traitor of almost every politician in the land, for practically all of them were passing important news along to their fellow-citizens.

Thompson thought the President had treated him shabbily and Buchanan, while trying to justify himself, knew that Thompson was right. But he had to sacrifice Thompson in order to protect the expedition.[8] Kate Thompson reacted characteristically: "Now you can guess what I think of

389

the President's heart—as black as the man of War Brooklyn. . . . Judge Black is the meanest man living. . . . Stanton . . . a mean low-life Pen-Scamp. I wish I was a *Military Dictator.* I would take his head off to the tune of Yankee Doodle!"[9]

For a few days after his repulse of the South Carolina commissioners Buchanan had been something of a hero in the North. He seemed at last to provide a rallying point for "union-loving men." One of Harriet Lane's correspondents reported that in New York "you could *read* the President's course . . . *on the faces of the people in the streets,*" a deep and patriotic feeling rare in that cosmopolitan city. "Our suburb of Brooklyn," wrote this confident gentleman, "has more population than South Carolina's whites . . . & our fire department would, I think, be able alone to protect the government from her misdeeds."[10]

But after the *Star of the West,* driven off by shore batteries, had returned with its cargo, northern denunciation fell upon Buchanan, and the southern leaders joined the chorus. Mrs. Gwin, who stated at this time, "*I am not yet a secessionist,*" wrote that "The feeling here with the Southern members is most violent against the President. The denunciation of him is fearful. I often wonder how he can stand it. He has given up his evening walk. I think that makes him feel worse. . . . My heart warms to the *President.* I feel for and love him. I think him a better man than the world gives him credit for. He looks badly. His face indicates much unhappiness & when I see him I feel like comforting him, but you know him well enough to know no one could approach him in that way."[11] Phil Clayton, former Treasury official, spoke of the bitterness of the southern Senators against Buchanan, and William Browne, editor of the *Constitution,* was beside himself with rage.[12]

Within a few days Philip F. Thomas, the last of the Cabinet who had any strong southern leanings, resigned from the Treasury Department and Buchanan decided to give that post to John A. Dix of New York. Mrs. Thompson sneered, "Mr. Dix is in his glory with an empty box (no money)."[13] Buchanan could find no one suitable to take the Interior Department and finally assigned the work to the Chief Clerk, Moses Kelly. By January 11 the Cabinet had again become a unit, representing views which coincided with the president's.

WHAT WILL CONGRESS DO?

These views became much more sharply defined during January. The customs collector at Charleston had resigned when Anderson moved to Fort Sumter. On the day of decision to reinforce Sumter, Buchanan had sent to the Senate his nomination for a new collector, one Peter McIntire of York, Pennsylvania, who would be ordered to receive duties from the deck of a naval vessel. The Senate refused to confirm him.

On January 8, Buchanan sent to Congress a special message concerning relations with South Carolina. "The prospect of a bloodless settlement fades away," he warned. He intended "to collect the public revenues and to protect the public property" so far as existing laws permitted, but "my province is to execute, and not to make, the laws." Congress, and Congress alone had the responsibility and the power to authorize the use of troops, to declare war, or to legislate the removal of grievances. "We are in the midst of a great revolution," he said. "The present is no time for palliations; action, prompt action is required." But he added, "the Union must and shall be preserved *by all constitutional means.*" That part of Buchanan's policy infuriated the direct-action men. He repeated that although neither the president nor Congress had any constitutional authority to make aggressive war on a state, "*the right and duty to use military force defensively against those who resist the federal officers . . . and . . . assail the property of the federal government is clear and undeniable.*"

Buchanan appealed again for the question to be "transferred from political assemblies to the ballot box" where the people would soon achieve a solution. "But, in Heaven's name, let the trial be made before we plunge into armed conflict upon the mere assumption that there is no other alternative." From the beginning, concluded the president, he had determined that if the difficulties were to end in war, no act of his should commence it, "nor even . . . furnish an excuse for it by any act of this government. My opinion remains unchanged."[14]

This policy, to collect the revenue, to defend the public property, if assaulted, to avoid any provocative act, and to strive for a full expression of public opinion outside of Congress, constituted Buchanan's program for the remainder of his term. In addition, he determined to give every inducement to the border states to remain in the Union and took action to protect the national capital against any southern effort to prevent the peaceful inauguration of Lincoln.

The inactivity of Congress convinced Buchanan that although the Republicans agreed with his policy and had nothing different to propose, they nonetheless did not wish a solution of the crisis during a Democratic Administration. He presumed that they would proceed with the same program once they came to power and thus take credit for a triumphant result which, if Buchanan achieved it, would annihilate their party. Lincoln's repudiation of the use of armed force indicated that the new Administration would not pursue a course of coercion.[15]

The Senators, north and south, knew that in refusing to confirm Buchanan's nomination for a customs collector at Charleston they deprived the president of the only legal means he had to call up the militia. Had such a federal officer appealed for aid, Buchanan could have mobilized forces under existing law; without such an appeal he could not mobilize troops except by special act of Congress. Proposals to enact such special legislation were repeatedly introduced and voted down in Congress by a combination of Republicans and secessionists. But why, asked some of the proponents of "action" and a "bold policy," did not the president forget about the law and use the army in his own name? Buchanan never dignified such suggestions by a formal answer, but he could have recited the reasons: impeachment, no army, no money, no public support, which even dictators need. But most important, such a course would destroy exactly what he was trying to save—a government under law.

When on January 16 the Senate was asked to consider the least controversial point in the Crittenden plan, whether to initiate a constitutional convention, every Republican voted against letting the question even come to the floor. Thus ended the work of the Committee of Thirteen.[16] Baron Stoeckl, Russian Minister in Washington, commented that the great Congressional leaders of the past had been replaced "by men undistinguished either by ability or reputation. Totally lacking in patriotism, they have but one purpose: the increase of the antislavery agitation. . . . They preach war against the South and demand the extirpation of slavery by iron and fire."[17]

Under these conditions Buchanan had to manage the last two months of his Administration. Because he had no control in Congress, he was forced by the Republicans to follow Lincoln's policy of "masterly inactivity." The Congress rejected *seriatum* each element of Buchanan's active policy: extension of the Missouri line, confirmation of a customs collector at Charleston, a constitutional convention, and a new force bill which would enable the president to mobilize troops for use in federal law enforcement. Buchanan was a seasoned enough politician to know better than to try single-handed to break the stalemate imposed by the disunionists and the Republicans. As the best hope of peace and reunion, he reconciled himself to Lincoln's passive position and continued, by the exercise of that self-control and the art of diplomatic parley he had so long practiced, to try to hold the government together. He hoped, in the six weeks remaining of his term, to avoid further alarms and explosions and to maintain the *status quo*. This in itself proved a task of the utmost complexity and delicacy.

The events of the first week of January gave impetus to the secession movement, for the Gulf States now abandoned hope of any sympathy, even from Buchanan. Georgia elected a prosecession convention on January 2, and the governor seized Fort Pulaski at Savannah the same day. Florida and Alabama took over federal property in their area. At Washington, southern Senators planned the creation of a confederacy of seceding states to be brought into being before the end of Buchanan's term. By the time the *Star of the West* expedition had returned, the secession conventions of Mississippi, Alabama, and Florida had already begun to meet, and popular elections in Louisiana and Texas showed majorities for secession.

Senators of the border states set up a new committee to break the deadlock which Lincoln's orders had created in the Committee of Thirteen and worked out new modifications of the Crittenden plan which Douglas and Buchanan strongly supported, but the usual combination of Republicans and secessionists defeated the resolution to introduce the plan for discussion. Following this, southern Senators telegraphed their state conventions on January 7 and 8, "Secede at once."[18] They planned tentatively to have a general convention of delegates from South Carolina, Georgia, Florida, Alabama, Louisiana, Texas, and possibly others at Montgomery, Alabama, around the middle of February to create a new general government.

Buchanan found no way to stop such activity, but he did see many ways to prevent the upper South from joining the disunion movement and to keep alive hope among the pro-Union people of the seceding states who, because of the prevailing excitement, had little chance to air their views. Buchanan's mail brought scores of letters from the South asserting that most southerners were "not in favor of Secession unconditional—We want our rights in the Union and not secession out of it."[19]

A TEMPORARY TRUCE

But Fort Sumter remained the matter of immediate concern to the president and the Cabinet. Why had not Major Anderson replied to the fire on the *Star of the West*? His guns could have commanded the Charleston shore batteries. When the *Star* came in close to Fort Moultrie in the dawn of January 9, the captain had run a large garrison flag up and down the foremast as a signal for Anderson to protect the ship. But he had no orders to do so. In fact, he had learned only by accident that a relief expedition was afoot. The major had discounted the news as rumor, and when the vessel appeared, he could only guess its contents and mission. After a consultation with his officers, he determined not to fire; but he wrote immediately to Governor Pickens and protested the assault on the flag. He also demanded a disavowal and stated his intention of using the fort's guns to stop all subsequent movement of ships in the harbor.

Pickens responded with the demand that Sumter be surrendered to South Carolina. Still lacking official information of the attempt at reinforcement, Anderson answered that he intended "to refer the whole

393

matter to my Government," and to send one of his officers to Washington for instructions. Pickens also determined to send an emissary to Washington and agreed to respect a local "truce" until his agent returned. Anderson sent Lieutenant Norman J. Hall, and Pickens chose Attorney General Isaac W. Hayne.

Before these gentlemen arrived in Washington, another officer from Fort Sumter had already reported to Buchanan and the Cabinet. On the basis of his statement, Holt wrote to Anderson, approving his decision to withhold fire in the absence of any foreknowledge of the relief mission, and said that the government would not again send reinforcements until requested to do so but would make a "prompt and vigorous effort" the moment Anderson asked for help.[20]

Hayne called on Buchanan the morning of January 12, but the president told him he should communicate only in writing. Before Hayne had a chance to submit Governor Pickens's demand for the evacuation of Sumter, the southern Senators descended on Hayne to force him to delay. They anticipated rejection of Pickens's letter and the immediate opening of hostilities, which would greatly complicate the organization of the new confederacy. For three weeks, Hayne's mission took the center of the stage and arguments about it filled reams of paper. While the "truce" prevailed at Charleston during this long controversy, Anderson busily prepared Fort Sumter for action and South Carolina built up her shore batteries and sank hulks across the entrance to the harbor.

The truce proved both a boon and an embarrassment to Buchanan. It delayed what appeared to be a certain outbreak of war, but at the same time it prevented sending another expedition which the Cabinet now thought necessary. Black particularly insisted upon prompt action to garrison Sumter and wrote a long inquiry to Scott about practical methods of accomplishing it, but the General failed to respond. Instead, without consulting anybody, he released to the press his strange "Views" of October 29th, much to Buchanan's disgust. No document could have given secession more encouragement than this, hitting the newspapers on January 18, 1861.

The southern Senators during the last two weeks of January hounded Buchanan to get a promise from him either to withdraw Anderson from Sumter or to pledge not to send any aid to the fort. They had persuaded the South Carolinians that if they could get this much out of the president, the demand for surrender of the fort could safely be dropped. One of their arguments was that a war started under Buchanan would help only Lincoln, who could escape the responsibility for starting it while gaining the power of a dictator in fighting it. Senator Clay of Alabama called on Wednesday afternoon, January 16, to press again for the return of Anderson to Moultrie, under a Carolina guarantee that he would have access to all the supply facilities in Charleston and would not be molested. It was understood that the current truce would last only until Colonel Hayne returned to the South. Buchanan answered that he "could not & would not withdraw Major Anderson from Fort Sumter."[21] He was not now planning to order reinforcements to Sumter, he said, but would send aid the moment Anderson asked for it. This statement left the matter up to Anderson.

The Cabinet earnestly discussed the reinforcement question at successive meetings during the last two weeks of January. Black, in a letter to Buchanan which he asked the president to keep secret from the rest of the Cabinet, complained about the gullibility of the Administration for believing southern threats of war. The refusal of the *Brooklyn* to engage the shore batteries which were firing on the *Star of the West*, he continued, had made the government "the laughter and derision of the world." Black concluded, "In the forty days and forty nights yet remaining to this administration, responsibilities may be crowded greater than those which are usually incident to four years in more quiet times. I solemnly believe that you can hold this revolution in check, and so completely put the calculations of its leaders out of joint that it will subside after a time into peace and harmony."[22] He hoped for an early reinforcement of Sumter.

Buchanan did not agree, and neither did General Scott. The Anderson-Pickens truce dragged on until January 31, when Hayne finally presented Pickens's letter to Buchanan. Four days later the delegates of the six states that had already seceded met at Montgomery to frame a constitution for the Confederate States of America. Holt replied to Hayne on February 6, commenting on the "unusual form" of Pickens's request— "an offer on the part of South Carolina to buy Fort Sumter . . . sustained by a declaration . . . that if she is not permitted to . . . purchase, she will seize the fort." The United States, Holt said, would keep the fort and reinforce it whenever Anderson made the request. The next day Hayne delivered his answer, which Buchanan termed "insulting," and speedily left Washington.[23] Buchanan maintained his policy on Sumter for the rest of his term. Thenceforth, the Cabinet debated not whether to reinforce Sumter when Anderson should call for aid, but how to do it.

Scott, Toucey, and Holt prepared a relief expedition of four small Treasury steamers which would maintain a ready status in New York. Commander J. H. Ward, in command of this force, had orders to be prepared to sail instantly in response to a call for help from Major Anderson. The Administration also pondered the plan of Navy Captain Gustavus V. Fox who proposed a convoy of several large ships carrying launches and two light-draft harbor tugs. The tugs would load supplies outside the harbor and, protected by cotton bales, make a run for Sumter in darkness, while the launches brought in the troops. Most later strategists agree that Fox's plan had the best chance of success, but by the time it had gotten a fair hearing, the southerners had arranged to buy the two tugs that Fox wanted and the plan had to be abandoned. Scott and several of the Cabinet wanted Buchanan to send Commander Ward's fleet to Charleston before the southern batteries grew too strong; but Buchanan withheld assent, unless Major Anderson should call for relief. There seems little doubt that both the president and the major believed a relief expedition would bring an immediate outbreak of war, and it is equally probable that Buchanan believed, if he did not know, that Anderson would make no appeal. Thus Sumter would be delivered intact, but still the central issue, to the Lincoln Administration. Lincoln had asked for this. Buchanan would give it to him.

THE FINAL EFFORT

Congress all the while continued its private war against Buchanan. The president asserted that Congress, "throughout the entire session, refused to adopt any measures of compromise to prevent civil war, or to retain first the cotton or afterwards the border States within the Union."[24] In addition to sabotaging every compromise proposal, Congress failed to provide for any judicial process in South Carolina after the resignation of all the federal court officers. It then declined to give the president any authority to call out militia or volunteers to help suppress insurrection. Even after Buchanan's message of January 8 which declared the existence of revolution and reminded Congress of its exclusive power to muster troops, no bill authorizing the calling of militia was introduced until three weeks later, and it was immediately withdrawn. Not until February 18, two months after South Carolina seceded and ten days after the formation of the Confederate States, was another more limited militia bill proposed. The House killed this on February 26 by a resolution to postpone.[25]

Even had either of these measures passed, Buchanan could not have used them to advantage because no bill was ever proposed "to raise or appropriate a single dollar for the defense of the government against armed rebellion." The Senate ignored the need for special laws to implement the collection of duties from a warship. Bingham of Ohio, on January 3, had reported a bill similar to the old Force Bill of Jackson's day to enable the president to collect revenue "either upon land or any vessel," but the Senate let it lie dormant until March 2, and then voted down a resolution to consider it. People asked why Buchanan did not act boldly on his own without consulting Congress. He responded that to have done this while Congress sat ready to do business a few blocks away would have been to make war not only on South Carolina but also on the representatives of the whole American nation. Buchanan interpreted the persistent

396

refusal of Congress to act as proof "that the friends of Mr. Lincoln . . . believed he would be able to settle existing difficulties . . . in a peaceful manner, and that he might be embarrassed by any legislation contemplating the necessity of a resort to hostile measures."[26]

But Congressional inaction told only half the story. Congress did act in many ways to embarrass and distract the president. On December 31, 1860, a House Committee began inquiry into the question whether ex-Secretary Floyd had been engaged in a conspiracy to ship huge quantities of arms from northern to southern arsenals. The Committee, after a thorough investigation, found no cause for alarm. It learned that since January 1, 1860, some 8500 of the best army rifles had been distributed among the states, of which the South got less than one-fourth. Of heavy cannon, the South received only one-third of the distribution. Inquiry into the Pittsburgh heavy ordnance shipment revealed facts already told. Despite the failure of the House Committee to find evidence of an arms conspiracy, many northerners preferred to believe that the Buchanan Administration had knowingly tried to arm the South in preparation for secession.[27]

On January 16th the Senate demanded to know why it had not been asked to confirm the appointment of a new Secretary of War. Buchanan replied that he had appointed Holt in accordance with a statute empowering the president to make interim Cabinet appointments for a period of six months without Senate confirmation and implied that the Senators should have been acquainted with their own laws.[28]

An exasperating controversy arose over the defense of Washington. The city seethed with rumors of a southern conspiracy to take possession of the capital before Lincoln's inauguration. An attempt at seizure could be entirely practicable. Buchanan therefore brought extra troops into the city to discourage any such effort. Since the threat to kidnap him, he could take seriously the rumored plan to seize Washington, declare Breckinridge president, and claim the city as the capital of a nation composed of the southern states and such others as would join the new Administration. The Republicans feared an armed southern endeavor to prevent the counting of the electoral votes on February 13.

The Howard Committee, appointed to consider legislation to strengthen the military arm of the president in accordance with his January message, investigated evidence of a conspiracy to capture the capital. Congress got into the peculiar dilemma of fearing an attack on the government if no troops occupied Washington, and fearing an attack by such troops if Buchanan had command of them. They thus belabored the president simultaneously for having too small and too large a force in the city. Buchanan mobilized a force of 653 men to keep the peace. When these troops arrived after the return of the Sumter expedition, tension rose high and frightened observers wrote, "Old Buck has so many soldiers there it looks more like a Camp Ground than a City. I believe the poor old man is crazy."[29] "Constitution" Browne wrote on January 11 that the city had become "a great military camp. . . . In the vacant lots behind the city hall there is an artillery camp, and another on Capitol Hill. . . . Orderly officers are galloping through the streets from morning till night."[30] Kate Thompson reported that "the Departments are all filled this morning with guns and pistols stacked ready for use. Was there ever such *Tom foolery*."[31]

But it did not seem tomfoolery to Buchanan, Black, Holt, or Scott. Black warned the President that "the possession of this city is absolutely necessary to the ultimate designs of the secessionists. . . . If they *can* take it and *do not* take it, they are fools. . . . I take it for granted that they have their eyes fixed on Washington."[32] Buchanan did not answer the Committee's inquiry whether he had actual knowledge of a conspiracy until March 1, and then only under urgent pressure from Holt. After the Committee reported that it could find no support for the rumors, he considered the matter finished. But during the last two weeks of February, reports spread over the country "intended to show that the safety of the capital [had] never been menaced, and of course that all . . . preparations here have been prompted by cowardice, or the spirit of despotism."[33] After Lincoln had come into Washington by stealth in the dead of night to escape a rumored plot to kill him in Baltimore on February 22 and the newspapers took up this story, the attacks on Buchanan for trying to protect Washington diminished. On March 1 he sent Congress a message explaining his reasons for bringing troops to the capital. Of all people to complain about this, he thought the Republicans least entitled to the privilege.[34]

Along with excitement about conspiracy in Washington came suspicion of subversion elsewhere. When Holt learned that the Superintendent of the United States Military Academy at West Point, Captain P. G. T. Beauregard, was a secessionist sympathizer he dismissed him. Slidell stormed into the White House demanding that Buchanan disavow this act; but the president declared that Holt's acts "are my acts for which I am responsible."[35] Slidell never spoke to him again.

In Buchanan's mind these surface flurries assumed much less importance than Virginia's efforts to promote a national expression of opinion through an "unofficial" convention, in the absence of the real thing. The Virginia Legislature, on January 19, adopted resolutions inviting delegates from all states interested in promoting peace to assemble at Washington on February 4. It named ex-President John Tyler a commissioner to the President of the United States and Judge John Robertson a commissioner to the seceded states to obtain from them a pledge to refrain from hostile action until the convention had concluded its efforts.

The convention was asked to consider the Crittenden plan and to recommend constitutional amendments to Congress. The proposal obviously aimed at two things: first, to prolong the "truce" in Charleston harbor which Hayne's imminent return would automatically terminate; and second, to force on the country an expression of public opinion independent of Congress.

Buchanan submitted Virginia's resolutions to Congress on January 28 with his enthusiastic endorsement, but he dulled considerably the impact of his message by stating emphatically that he would not promise during the meeting to abstain "from any and all acts calculated to produce a collision of arms." Such a pledge must come from the seceding states, he said, and "then the danger . . . will no longer exist. Defence and not aggression has been the policy of the administration from the beginning."[36] This was a good deal less conciliatory than the Virginians had hoped, but it at least gave official recognition to their proposal.

Although Congress paid no attention and insulted Virginia by failing even to refer her resolutions to committee, twenty-one states sent delegates to the Virginia Peace Convention. Its work got underway on February 4, the same day that the Confederate constitutional convention began. John Tyler, the presiding officer, took his task very seriously, for he felt that Lincoln's silence, Buchanan's legalistic view of his duties, and the continued inaction of Congress left no remaining point of origin for conciliatory action except this meeting. The conference made its greatest appeal to the border states, but in a remarkable way it furthered the interests of almost everyone. It gave South Carolina a good excuse to avoid terminating the Sumter truce after Hayne's return, the secessionists a way to gain time to perfect their organization and preparations for future resistance, and the Republicans a chance to pose before the country as supporters of conciliation and drive a wedge between the border states and the deep South. Buchanan welcomed any delay which would reduce the danger of war during his Administration and sought all the encouragement anyone could offer to Unionists in the border region.

Tyler recognized these advantages and kept in close touch with Buchanan to prevent the slightest rocking of the delicate balance between the South and the Administration. Even before the sessions began he had questioned the president about the dispatch of the *Brooklyn* on a secret mission and the rumor that the troops at Fort Monroe had turned the guns inland. "When Virginia is making every possible effort to redeem and save the Union," he complained, "it is seemingly ungracious to have Cannon levelled at her bosom."[37] Buck assured him that he would investigate the cannon story, and that the *Brooklyn* had gone on an innocent assignment. Actually she was bound for Fort Pickens with orders to stand by unless Florida tried to take this position.

Tyler later urged Buchanan to prevent any military display in the annual Washington's birthday parade in the capital for fear the appearance of federal troops might emphasize northern preparedness and create an incident. Buchanan explained that he could hardly prevent militia companies from marching in a parade, and that it would appear odd if the United States Government went unrepresented in such an affair, but nonetheless he promised that the army would not appear. Unknown to him, Holt had already issued orders calling out the troops and sent an announcement to the newspapers. When Buchanan learned about it late the night of the 21st, he asked Scott to prevent the assembly of the troops. The citizens of Washington waited impatiently for the parade the next morning, and after an hour's delay got wind of the news that the affair had been cancelled. Dan Sickles rushed to the War Department where he found Buchanan and Holt and soon convinced them that more trouble would arise if the parade were forbidden than if it were permitted. Wearily Buchanan gave in, wearily Scott learned the orders had been reversed again, and most wearily of all, the officers and men who had been dismissed several hours before got back into their uniforms and prepared to celebrate the birthday of the father of their tottering country.[38]

The Peace Convention in the meantime worked out a program which its members believed might meet Republican objections to an extension of the Missouri line. In response to arguments that slavery could not exist in the New Mexico region, the only area affected by an extension of the line, the Republicans had protested that the Missouri principle would legalize slavery in new territory, say Cuba or northern Mexico, if these should later be acquired. The convention therefore agreed to make the acquisition of any new territory nearly impossible. Lincoln termed this the "one compromise which would really settle the slavery question." But so soon as the compromisers met the objections of the Republicans, the latter found new ones to interpose. The Peace Convention made its recommendations at the end of February, but in view of the opposition to them from the radical Republicans, they aroused little interest in the nation and none at all in Congress.

Kentucky proposed that Congress call a convention to amend the Constitution, and Buchanan supported this proposal, as he sustained every attempt to bring a constitutional convention into being, but it got no Congressional consideration. On February 27 the House Republicans voted down even the proposed Thirteenth Amendment which stated a part of their own party platform—that slavery should not be interfered with in the states where it already existed. Some members later changed their votes and this measure did pass at the end of the session, but it accomplished nothing.

Of these events, Roy F. Nichols, historian of the politics of the Buchanan Administration, writes, "compromise had been killed by two power aggregates. The secession Democrats, confronted with loss of power, could see no compromise which would restore their accustomed dominance. . . . The victorious Republicans—the new power—eager to enjoy the fruits of their triumph, could see nothing in compromise but the destruction of that control which they had just won."[39] During the last two months of his term, Buchanan occupied the position of the most important official of the United States government who remained uncommitted to either power aggregate. What influence he had lay in this position; what strength he had lay in seeking areas of honorable agreement and in holding the balance, a tricky, tightrope procedure. That he succeeded seemed clear from the attacks on him by both the secessionists and the Radical Republicans.

In the closing months of his stay in the White House, Buchanan's old southern friends put him down as "against the South."[40] Mrs. Thompson learned with amazement that one of her friends, calling at the White House, found Senator and Mrs. Lyman Trumbull there "on very social terms" with Buchanan and Harriet. "What a change! . . . *Forney wants to make up with* the President. . . . *All their* old friends are thrown off and new ones in their place."[41] Another southerner reported that Buchanan had "allowed Holt & Scott to exercise the powers they have, from a *knowledge* that their acts will conform to Lincoln's policy. . . . There has been for some time a perfect understanding between Lincoln and the War Department." Charles F. Adams regarded Seward as "the guiding hand at the helm of the Buchanan Administration."[42]

Buchanan still maintained cordial relations with such of his former friends as would meet him on purely social ground. Even after the difficulties which led to the resignation of the Secretary of the Interior, he invited the Thompsons to a farewell dinner at the White House, and they reluctantly accepted the invitation. Said the once vivacious Kate, "I went in with the Old Chief. Mr. T. with Miss Lane—& Genl. Dix (who is staying there) with Mrs. Ellis (niece of the late W. R. R. King), who was also staying. . . . There was nothing disagreeable said or done, but I felt very much embarrassed. The President asked me at dinner who was to be *our President*." She told him Cobb. It was Buchanan's last social event of the old style.[43]

During these days many occasions took on the aspect of "the last." Harriet, especially, felt pangs. Her last visit to the "Lyons Den," the last matinee and review, the last dance. "I receive so many evidences of kindness and good feeling," she said, "and so many regrets at my leaving that it makes me feel very sad." Lincoln's arrival to pay his first call at the White House at 11 a. m., February 24, made the departure seem chillingly imminent to Harriet, gloriously close to her nearly prostrate uncle. Of Lincoln she wrote, "the glimpse I caught of him was the image of *Burns*— our tall, awkward Irishman who waits on the door. Burns is the best looking, but I only had a side view. They say Mrs. L. is awfully *western*, loud & unrefined."[44]

The press of last-minute routine came as a welcome relief from the incessant pressure of the past two months. In the few days immediately preceding the inauguration, the Department clerks came to farewell parties for the Old Chief at the White House and the judges and foreign ministers called to pay their respects. Copies of bills had to be hurried to and from Congress which concluded its affairs in a torrent of angry talk that did nothing to reduce the mountain of unfinished business.

The long awaited Fourth of March blew in crisp and windy. Buchanan spent the hour before noon signing the final bills which came from the tumultuous proceedings of Congress. While he was thus engaged in the president's room at the Capitol, Holt came racing in excitedly with a dispatch from Anderson which had just arrived. The major wrote that it would now take 20,000 men to reinforce successfully his command at Sumter! But there was no time to handle this red hot chestnut for the parade would soon begin. Buchanan ordered his carriage and went to pick up the president-elect.[45]

Buchanan and Lincoln drove in procession from Willard's to the Capitol, chatting affably to the astonishment of many onlookers who seem to have expected that they would be pointing pistols at each other's heads. Buchanan, said a reporter, "appeared pale and wearied; yet his face beamed with radiance, for he felt relieved from the crushing care and anxiety he had borne for four years."[46] He turned to Lincoln and said, "My dear sir, if you are as happy in entering the White House as I shall feel on returning to Wheatland, you are a happy man indeed." Lincoln replied with courtesy, "Mr. President, I cannot say that I shall enter it with much pleasure, but I assure you that I shall do what I can to maintain the high standards set by my illustrious predecessors who have occupied it."[47] Of more small talk there is no record. The two entered the Senate Chamber arm in arm and after Hannibal Hamlin had been sworn in as vice-president, the whole party proceeded to the East Portico for Lincoln's inaugural. Buchanan sat quietly breathing in a kind of freedom he had not known for fifty years. He was out of politics. He could go home in peace; peace for himself and his country.

30
ON THE ROCK OF ST. HELENA • 1861-1868

THE OLD PUBLIC FUNCTIONARY

On the night after Lincoln's inauguration, Buchanan should have relaxed and eased his spirits in Old Custom House Madeira at the home of his host, Robert Ould. Instead, he held another Cabinet meeting. Anderson's letter stating that it would require 20,000 troops to relieve Fort Sumter had shocked Buchanan. The next morning he again met with the Cabinet at the War Department where Holt read a letter which he planned to send to Lincoln along with Major Anderson's dispatch. In it he quoted from Anderson's earlier reports that he could easily hold Fort Sumter, and the War Department replies that reinforcements would be sent the instant Anderson should request them. Holt further explained to Lincoln the existence of the force which for over a month had been waiting in New York ready to sail for Sumter on a few hours notice. Before Buchanan left Washington that afternoon, Holt reported that he had sent these documents to President Lincoln.[1]

At two o'clock Buchanan waved farewell to the friends who had gathered at Ould's to see him off and set out with his escort to board the special train prepared for him by the Baltimore and Ohio Railroad. He told the crowd that he felt confident that President Lincoln intended no harm to anyone in the South, and that there was no occasion for the hostile reaction of some of the southerners to his election. At Baltimore he received a wildly enthusiastic ovation and had considerable difficulty getting through the crowds to the home of his host, Zenos Barnum. Although he had already made one speech upon leaving the train, he had to make another at eleven that night. Leaning out of an upstairs window, he thanked the demonstrators for their "attention to an old man going out of office." They responded with a series of cheers which epitomized the political confusion of the city. "Three cheers for Old Buck." "Three more for the last President of the *United* States." "Three for the South." "Three for the Union." "Three for the Border States."

403

Buchanan's party left the next morning at eight for Lancaster in the same decorated car that had carried it to the inauguration four years before. York welcomed the ex-president with a military parade, speeches and a "handsome collation," and Columbia had everything in readiness for a celebration, but the train arrived so late that it stopped there only momentarily to add cars. Lancaster gave its home-town boy a hero's welcome starting with a blast from the "Old Buck Cannon," a 34-gun presidential salute, and the ringing of church bells. There was a two-mile parade from the railroad to the town square for speeches, and another to Wheatland where, as a final flourish, the Baltimore City Guards presented a poetic address and the band played "Home Sweet Home." Buchanan was a little embarrassed. His latch string was always out, he said, but since he had not had time to lay in supplies, he hoped they would all call at some future time.[2]

During the first month after his return to Lancaster, Buchanan savored all the anticipated delights of an honored retirement. Wheatland teemed with visitors who came to bless the "old Public Functionary" for pursuing steadfastly his quest for peace and to wonder at the suddenness with which the Republicans had adopted Buchanan's policy. Musical organizations came out in the evenings to serenade in the hope of being invited in for a crack at Wheatland's newly stocked cellar. Buchanan enjoyed strolling about the estate again. He loved the circular, stone-girt spring with water ten feet deep and so clear that he could nearly read the lettering of a new coin on the white sand at the bottom. He poked into the icehouse, sniffing the wet sawdust; checked on the supply of barked hickory for the fireplace in his study; looked at his horses and wondered what to do with the new carriage he had bought for ceremonial occasions in Washington. He could not use this deluxe conveyance around Lancaster without becoming a butt of ridicule. He missed Lara, his old Newfoundland dog, but was happy that the chained eagles had been disposed of. In the house his library began to take shape again: familiar books back on the familiar shelves, the comfortable chair before his desk, his slippers, the old dressing gown, a good "segar," and a bottle of Madeira. Life was almost worth living.

PRESIDENT LINCOLN'S POLICY

The newspapers and letters on his desk were full of accounts of Lincoln's inaugural. Offhand he could not see much in it that he had not said himself on many occasions, except the part about the Supreme Court. The *National Intelligencer* reported that on the subjects of the right of secession and the coercion of a state, Mr. Lincoln's opinions appeared to be "identical with those announced by Mr. Buchanan in his message to Congress at the opening of the late session."[3]   The *North Carolina Standard* said that "so far as coercion is concerned, Mr. Lincoln occupies the very ground occupied by Mr. Buchanan."[4]

But most editors treated the inaugural with a wild abandon of partisan prejudice that reminded Buchanan of the reception of his own recent messages. Republican papers labelled Lincoln's language "strong, straightforward, manly, plain, terse, all bone and iron muscle, clear as a mountain brook," and characterized by "perspicacity, unmistakable decision, firmness, integrity and will." The Democrats called it "involved, coarse, colloquial, devoid of ease and grace, bristling with obscurities and outrages against the simplest rules of syntax, trite, commonplace, lifeless, cold, phlegmatic, rambling, discursive, questioning, loose-jointed, feeble, and unworthy of a schoolboy." A neutral editor remarked that the Republicans would certainly have denounced the speech had Buchanan, Cass, or Douglas made it.[5]

It interested Buchanan particularly that the Republican press now discovered it a great thing to enforce the laws under a promise "that no blood shall be shed" unless by the act of "those who resist the laws." The idea of a constitutional convention suddenly became respectable.[6]

The Republican somersault made Buchanan laugh, but it angered him, too, and he decided to take a good look at the text of Lincoln's inaugural and to compare it carefully with his own messages. He discovered that the similarities were greater than he had at first suspected. Where he had written, "The Union was designed to be perpetual. . . . Its framers never intended . . . the absurdity of providing for its own destruction," Lincoln had paraphrased, "The Union of these States is perpetual. . . . It is safe to assert that no government proper ever had a provision in its organic law for its own termination." Buchanan had asserted, "No State has a right upon its own act to secede from the Union," whereas Lincoln said, "No State upon its own mere motion can lawfully get out of the Union." Where Buchanan had proclaimed, "My province is to execute the laws. . . . It is my duty at all times to defend and protect the public property . . . as far as this may be practicable," Lincoln said, "I shall take care . . . that the laws . . . shall be faithfully executed in all the States . . . so far as practicable. . . . [My power] will be used to hold, occupy and possess the property belonging to the Government." Where Buchanan had stated, "If the seceding States abstain 'from a collision of arms,' then the danger . . . will no longer exist. Defence and not aggression has been the policy of the Administration," Lincoln declared that "There needs to be no bloodshed . . . and there shall be none, unless it is forced upon the national authority."

Buchanan wrote, "The people themselves would speedily redress the serious grievances. . . . In Heaven's name, let the trial be made before we plunge into armed conflict. . . . Time is a great conservative power."

405

Lincoln urged, "Why should there not be a patient confidence in the ultimate justice of the people? . . . Nothing can be lost by taking time." Buchanan said that disunion "ought to be the last desperate remedy of a despairing people. . . . I earnestly recommend an 'explanatory amendment' of the Constitution on the subject of slavery." Lincoln, who had rejected Buchanan's plea for a convention, now proclaimed in the inaugural, "Whenever [the people] grow weary of existing government, they can exercise the constitutional right of amending it. . . . I should, under existing circumstances, favor rather than oppose [amending the Constitution]. I will venture to add that to me the convention mode seems preferable." Where Buchanan had pleaded, "If, with all the . . . proofs . . . of the President's anxiety for peace, [the South] shall assault Fort Sumter . . . and thus plunge our common country into the horrors of civil war, then upon them . . . must rest the responsibility," Lincoln said, "In your hands, my dissatisfied fellow-countrymen, and not in mine, is the momentous issue of civil war. The government will not assail you. You can have no conflict without yourself being the aggressors." So far as Buchanan could determine, he could have no conflict with Lincoln or Lincoln with him, on the grounds of principle or policy regarding the subjects of these quotations.[7]

During March news poured into Wheatland steadily from the capital. "I need not tell you that the new administration is a failure," wrote Black. "If it made peace its abolitionist force would desert it; & if it made war it would be broken into fragments. . . . Everything wears the aspect of a most painful uncertainty. . . . It now seems to be absolutely certain that Fort Sumter is to be evacuated. *Sic Transit.*"[8] Dix wrote, "I envy you the quietude of Wheatland. There is none here. . . . Fort Sumter will be abandoned."[9] Stanton kept Buchanan as well supplied with inside information about Seward's plans as he had formerly kept Seward acquainted with Buchanan's activities. In half a dozen letters between March 10 and April 10, Stanton repeated the phrase, with the words underlined, "Major Anderson *will be withdrawn.*" "A continuation of your policy *to avoid collision* will be the course of the present administration," he wrote. "The embarrassments that surrounded you they now feel; and whatever may be said against you must recoil against them."[10] Holt also reported that Sumter would be evacuated and advised Buchanan that he need not worry about his policy on Fort Sumter; the Republicans were caught in the same trap and could not adopt coercive measures without reversing their announced policy of peace and losing the border states.

These rumors emerged in part from Seward's frantic negotiation with the emissaries of the Confederate States to whom he gave his word that the Administration would order Anderson to evacuate Sumter as soon as his supplies ran out. His promise proved, however, to be premature, for the counsel of the radical Republicans prevailed and Lincoln took a different course. By April 3, Stanton reported that an effort would be made to reinforce Sumter. By the 10th, talk in Washington centered on the expectancy of an immediate outbreak of war. Senator Bigler wrote on the 11th, "I am convinced that Mr. Lincoln is about to initiate civil war."[11]

One feature in all these reports especially interested Buchanan: the idea that the evacuation of Sumter would be a vindication of his own policy. "I do not believe there will be much further effort to assail you," wrote Stanton. "In giving reasons for their action, they must exhibit the facts that controlled you in respect to Sumter." "I do not think there will be any serious effort to assail your administration in respect to Fort Sumter," he added. "That would imply . . . hostility to your pacific measures." Dix wrote, "I think it is decided to withdraw Major Anderson *without holding your administration to any responsibility for it.*"[12]

Buchanan believed that here lay the very crux of the matter. If the Republicans should abandon Sumter they would indeed vindicate his pacific policy. This might allay the excitement in South Carolina, retain the loyalty of the border states, and avert war; but it would be sure to split the Republican party. Furthermore, a war might still break out somewhere else and in this event the Republicans would have to shoulder the blame for it. Buchanan's name was already indelibly connected with Fort Sumter. Hence his anxiety that the fort should continue a symbol of peace and reunion; hence also the Republican anxiety that if a war had to come, it ought to start at Sumter where they could blame it squarely on the Buchanan Administration.

The adoption of a reinforcement policy could not have been easy for Lincoln in the face of Anderson's recent estimate of forces needed to succeed. General Scott, furthermore, had written the new Administration strongly urging compromise or letting the South go out in peace. A serious effort to coerce, he warned, would take 300,000 trained troops, $250,000,000, and two or three years of hard fighting. Scott advised Lincoln to permit Anderson to evacuate Sumter when his food supplies ran out, which would be around April 15. Seward advocated the same plan; let Sumter go on the ground of military necessity, but hold all the other forts as a proclamation of future policy; and set up a naval blockade. Lincoln acted initially on this policy, gave orders to reinforce Fort Pickens as a sign of federal purpose, and made ready to give up Sumter as a matter of military tactics. But on April 7, Lincoln learned that the relief expedition he had sent to Fort Pickens had failed.

At that moment Lincoln had to make his choice. Against the presumption that full-scale war would follow any attempt to relieve Anderson, he had to weigh other factors: that the abandonment of Sumter at this moment would invite foreign recognition of the Confederacy; that a

407

southern attack on Sumter would unite the North solidly behind the president and ensure the dominance of his party; that a war would not in any event last very long; and that the Republicans could blame it on Buchanan. The Republicans would never have a better chance. If they missed it, they might have to fight a war under much less favorable conditions.

Lincoln notified Governor Pickens that he proposed to reprovision, but not to reinforce, Major Anderson and sent off the relief expedition. Anderson, in the meantime, had already notified the South Carolina authorities that he would have to evacuate Fort Sumter on April 15 because he had no more food. The Confederate Government now ordered General P. G. T. Beauregard to reduce Fort Sumter before the relief ships should arrive. At dawn of April 12, 1861, old Edmund Ruffin yanked a gun lanyard at Fort Moultrie, sending the first shell arching over the water toward the flag at Sumter. He wanted the privilege of initiating the war, but the Republicans had already determined to award that dishonor to James Buchanan.

THE MAKING OF A MYTH

"The Confederate States have deliberately commenced the civil war, & God knows where it may end," Buchanan wrote to his nephew the morning he heard the news. "They were repeatedly warned by my administration that an assault on Fort Sumter would be civil war & they would be responsible for the consequences."[13] People who gathered around the bulletin boards in Lancaster had no idea of the seriousness of the news. They boasted they would go south and wipe out "those damned nigger drivers" in a month. The crowd shouted "Traitor" at a man who said soberly, "Gentlemen, this will be a three years' war." "Why, man, you're crazy," they cried, or "Oh, my God, this means nothing. It'll all be over in a month."[14]

Buchanan had no such optimism. From Lincoln's call for 75,000 volunteers on April 15 and other news he anticipated grim results. During the first weeks of retirement he went into town frequently and spent many pleasant hours at the old Grapes Tavern or in conversation with friends along Lawyers' Row. Now the ugly mutterings that he had better not show his face in the city began to be heard, and every day there were "violent, insulting & threatening letters," especially from Philadelphia. Miss Hetty found anonymous notes stuck under the back door of Wheatland which warned that the house would be set on fire some night. Buchanan refused to hire a guard of detectives because he did not want to broadcast his plight, but he did accept help from the local Masons. Lodge #43 of

Lancaster, of which he had been past master, held a special meeting at which each member pledged "to protect his person and his property from injury." From that day until the course of the war diverted the public interest, several Masons stood guard at his home.[15]

On May 18 Harriet heard from Sophie Plitt that someone in Philadelphia had printed a story in which he said that Dr. Foltz had billed "Nunc" for medical services that dated from 1848. Buchanan had actually received a bill for $1,000 on March 8 and had asked his lawyers to obtain an itemized statement under the physician's oath which he proposed to send to Washington "to be dealt with there under the rules & regulations of the Navy against an officer for abusing and vilifying his Commander in Chief. . . . I think a Naval Court martial would make short work of Dr. Foltz."[16]

Some stores exhibited banknotes which bore Buchanan's vignette, the eyes bunged with red ink, a gallows drawn above his head with a rope around his neck, and the word "Judas" inscribed on the forehead. The Pottsville, Pennsylvania, bank had to call in its issue of these notes, "so unmistakable," said a newspaper account, "are the manifestations of popular indignation against the man who might, had he had the will or pluck, have nipped this rebellion in the bud, as Jackson did before him."[17]

The suddenness of the attacks, their virulence and their crudeness sent Buchanan to bed with a bilious seizure. He had just celebrated his 71st birthday, a day which he had long anticipated as the time when he would begin to enjoy the ease of an honored old age at Wheatland. Now he knew that the greatest fight of his life still lay ahead. These assaults, he believed, were not spontaneous or mere hysteria. They signalled what he had feared during the first month of Lincoln's Administration, a studied, calculated, prearranged campaign against him with the object of making him appear to be responsible for the war. This would be good politics for the Republicans, and some of their editors would do the job with relish and without scruple.

For the next five years Buchanan faced a lonely struggle against overwhelming odds to counteract the lies about him which filled northern newspapers in intervals between the more exciting battle news. The Administration temporarily sealed the lips of those who might have refuted many of these stories with offers of political reward and threats of retaliation.

President Lincoln announced the Republican doctrine on war guilt in his message to the special session of Congress which convened on July 4. Though his language was careful and restrained, he made a number of charges that clearly applied to Buchanan: that "a disproportionate share of the Federal muskets and rifles" had found their way to the South, that quantities of money lay ready for seizure at southern mints, that "the Navy was scattered in distant seas, leaving but a very small part of it within the

409

immediate reach of the Government;" and that the effort to reinforce Fort Pickens had been foiled by "some *quasi* armistice of the late Administration." These statements from such a source carried the strongest implication of foul play by the Buchanan Administration. They inaugurated serious newspaper efforts to foment the idea of a Buchanan conspiracy to aid secession, an undertaking which got a tremendous additional impetus from the shocking defeat suffered by the North at First Bull Run a short time later. This shattered the northern pipe dream of a "three-months war," and brought home brutally an awareness of the titanic struggle which must ensue. The author of such a terrible war must be made to pay. The world should know how President Buchanan brought this holocaust upon his countrymen.

Much of the attack fell in terms too vague to make any short, decisive rebuttal possible. The resolution submitted to the Senate by Garrett Davis of Kentucky on December 15, 1862, put the charges into official language. "*Resolved*, That after it had become manifest that an insurrection against the United States was about to break out in several of the Southern States, James Buchanan, then President, from sympathy with the conspirators and their treasonable project, failed to take necessary and proper measures to prevent it; wherefore he should receive the censure and condemnation of the Senate and the American people." The resolution did not pass, but Buchanan nonetheless received the public "censure and condemnation." Said he, "If two years after a Presidential term has expired the Senate can go back & try, condemn, & execute the former incumbent, who would accept the office?"[18]

Buchanan quickly learned, as the assault developed, that he could not make any public defense while the war lasted. His first short "Letter to the Editor" provoked such a storm of denunciation that he resigned himself to silence. Any explanation he offered would only be seized and turned as a weapon against him. Hence he began collecting documents and letters which he hoped, some day, to publish in vindication of his presidential policies. In the meantime he catalogued the charges against him and jotted down the main errors in them.

Why, the newspapers asked, had not President Buchanan sent troops to Charleston early and, like Jackson, nipped secession in the bud? Because, he noted in the privacy of his study at Wheatland, his Cabinet and the leaders of every political party opposed such a move in the months before Lincoln's election; because General Scott saw no danger until October 29, and at that time he could muster only 300 troops (Congress would not authorize a call for more); because a provocative mobilization of strength at Charleston would most probably activate secession and war rather than avert them; because no one knew how the election would go or what Lincoln might have to say, if he were successful.

410

Why had Buchanan not cracked down immediately when South Carolina seceded, occupying the rebellious state by troops who could enforce obedience to federal laws? Because, Buchanan wrote, no request for troops had come from any federal or state officer; because the government could not attack people for threatening talk; because South Carolina had violated no law; because an order to the army to proceed on an illegal mission in the face of the opposition of Congress while it was in session would be an attack on Congress as much as on South Carolina and would probably have brought deserved impeachment.[19]

Why had Buchanan negotiated with the agents of secession and made one truce after another with them? But he had not negotiated or made any truce, he asserted. He had talked with some United States Senators and told them that his policy would be peaceful, but he had rejected their demand for a pledge of the *status quo* at Sumter. He had talked to some South Carolinians after secession as "private gentlemen," informing them that he would hold Fort Sumter and reinforce it on Anderson's request. With the concurrence of his Cabinet he had honored a limited field truce entered into by his commanders at Forts Sumter and Pickens. In January he told an agent of South Carolina of decisions already made public—that Anderson would stay in Sumter, had orders to resist attack, and would be reinforced whenever he called for help. This was not negotiation but information. If anyone had negotiated with secession agents, that man was Seward.

Why, asked the press, had Buchanan overruled General Scott's demand to send the warship *Brooklyn* to Charleston harbor and sent the unarmed *Star of the West* instead? And why had he vetoed Scott's proposal to send reinforcements after the *Star's* failure? Buchanan assembled records to prove that these assertions exactly contradicted Scott's position at the time. Scott had rejected the *Brooklyn* and insisted on using the *Star*; he had favored restraining the secret relief expedition which lay in readiness at New York until the peace convention ended or Anderson called for it.[20]

Why did Buchanan scatter the navy all over creation and skeletonize the home fleet? Toucey's reports which had already been examined by two Congressional committees showed that the navy 'had been greatly expanded under Buchanan's Administration and that the home squadron had been abnormally large, but the press did not publicize this.[21]

But what about those stolen guns? Republican editors insisted that Buchanan and Floyd had connived to arm the South in anticipation of the rebellion. Scott even published a telegram ("from a high officer—not of the Ordnance Bureau") purporting to show that the South had drawn arms far in excess of her quota in 1860. Buchanan had before him reports from officers still in the Ordnance Bureau, which Congress had examined in February, 1861, showing that the South had drawn far less than her

411

quota of arms; that the transfer for storage of obsolete weapons had occurred a year before the election of 1860; and that he had personally intervened to prevent the first and only suspicious shipment of arms to the South—the cannon from Pittsburgh. As to militia arms quotas, the seven seceded states had drawn an average of only 300 rifles each in 1860, and three southern states had drawn none at all.[22]

Why had Buchanan worked hand in hand with Colonel Twiggs who, the moment Texas seceded, turned over his United States command to the Confederates? Was not this the rankest treason? It was, thought Buchanan. He had cashiered Twiggs before the event and had branded him a traitor after it. Twiggs had threatened to visit Wheatland and wreak personal vengeance on the "Old Pub Func" for the insult. But the press did not report or the public learn it thus. The popular story had Buchanan retaining Twiggs in command so that he could deliver his post to the enemy.[23]

On February 9, 1862, the London *Observer* published an article prepared by Thurlow Weed that galled Buchanan more than any prior attack. It gave a garbled account of a dramatic "cabinet scene" of February, 1861, when Floyd's resignation and Anderson's move to Sumter allegedly came under discussion. Weed related that Buchanan urged Anderson's return to Moultrie whereupon Stanton arose in cold anger, lashed Floyd and the president, and scornfully tendered his resignation. Black, Holt and Dix immediately followed his lead. "This of course opened the bleared eyes of the President," ran the tale, "and the meeting resulted in the acceptance of Mr. Floyd's resignation."[24] Such a story, coming from Weed and involving men who could readily refute it, if false, received international circulation and widespread belief. The article contained enough internal errors to condemn it. Anderson had moved to Sumter not in February but in December; Dix had not yet entered the Cabinet; Buchanan had asked Floyd to resign two days before the Sumter movement took place, and Stanton had not opened his mouth during the tense meeting of December 29—the one obviously referred to by Weed.

Buchanan called Weed's article a "tissue of falsehood" and asked his old Cabinet members to disprove this story. They did, in letters to him; but each in turn insisted that no refutation be made public. "Weed's letter is now *lying* before me," wrote Black. "The story is wholly fictitious." But to Buchanan's plea that he repeat this statement to an editor, Black responded that "this request is more than I can comply with at present."[25] Horatio King, who had attended the meeting, also refused to defend Buchanan, although in later years, after the myth of the president's treason had been firmly established in the public mind, King wrote a book in which he stated the facts that Buchanan had asked him to verify earlier. William Flynn wrote to Buchanan that "fear of Lincoln's and Seward's

412

penitentiary . . . has greatly weakened the power of the pen. . . . I showed the Weed letter to Mr. Horatio King, and asked him to submit it to the criticism of Mr. Holt. He looked scared and began to chaw, remarking that I had better see him myself. . . . Power and patronage have a wonderful and mysterious influence upon men."[26]

General Dix would not state publicly that at the time of the alleged incident he had not yet been invited to join the Cabinet.[27] Stanton, when confronted with the article, "was greatly embarrassed" but made no reply. He knew that Buchanan had a dozen letters from him referring to Lincoln and his policies in the most scurrilous language, but he also knew Buchanan well enough to be sure that he would not put such private correspondence to public use, even to defend himself. Holt, like Stanton, said nothing. Those not in Lincoln's employ, such as Toucey, hesitated to speak out because of hostile public sentiment and fear of summary imprisonment, since the *habeas corpus* privilege had been suspended.

Buchanan wrote, "Is it not strange that four members of my Cabinet . . . should have witnessed without contradiction a statement made by an official of government . . . that they had one after the other offered me the grossest insult? Had such a scene transpired in my Cabinet, they should not have been in office fifteen minutes." "Well, be it so," he concluded philosophically, "*for the present.*" He knew the difficulty. "They all stand mute. They will not contradict Weed, who is powerful & stands high with Mr. Lincoln. They are willing to profit with their new masters by the slander, rather than speak a word of truth in justice to the old President. . . . I was going to say, such is human nature, but I will not say it because the case is without a parallel."[28]

Buchanan often commented upon the peculiar fact that five of his Cabinet officers had been awarded federal jobs by Lincoln while the Republican party editors condemned their prior activity as treasonable. The jobs were not very good, to be sure, but they guaranteed these men some immunity from the Republican tar brush while at the same time they guaranteed the new Administration immunity from the exposure of Republican prewar obstructionism and of the recent fabrications against Buchanan. This was the deal and Buchanan could understand why his old friends took it. They were all still young and had hopes for a political future. Dix, Stanton, and Holt actually had lively ambitions for the White House, and Black for the Supreme Court.[29] For the time being they would serve menially. Dix, appointed a major general of New York militia, received such scandalous treatment from Secretary of War Cameron that he resigned but later accepted command of the Baltimore police.[30] Holt got the dirty job of auditing General Frémont's accounts and exposing the massive thefts of material and supplies in that western command.[31] King consented to appraise Negroes in Washington, work which few would have taken for five times the salary.[32]   Black became reporter for the Supreme Court when he should have sat on the bench.   Stanton alone, master sycophant, achieved high place; he supplanted Cameron in the spring of 1862.

This demonstration that the wartime gag would securely muzzle even the staunchest defenders of Buchanan's Administration, those who had themselves comprised it, marked the point at which Republican editors knew that they could say anything without fear of refutation.   Buchanan now realized that he stood alone in his fight for vindication.   But during the war he would have to keep quiet, "on the rock of St. Helena," as he said, watching the lies piled one on another until they comprised such a mass of uncontradicted vilification that neither his effort nor the passage of a century would sponge it from the public mind.

Now came the petty assaults.   Congress abolished the franking privilege of ex-presidents in order to gag him.[33]   The abolition papers reported that Buchanan was in constant correspondence with foreign governments, urging the recognition of the confederacy;[34] they described in vivid detail fictitious copperhead meetings at Wheatland, complete with lists of all the villainous guests who were supposed to have been on hand for the plotting;[35] and even on one occasion announced, on successive days, that the ex-president was in Leamington, England, selling Confederate bonds, and at Bedford Springs plotting with spies.[36]   Suspicion mounted so high that his outgoing and incoming mail was opened and sometimes pilfered.[37]

The story of the Indian bonds came in for another round of press coverage, with the amount rising to six million dollars allegedly stolen, and Buchanan was made the culprit.[38]   The Commissioner of Public Buildings reported that he had to remove Buchanan's portrait from the rotunda of the Capitol to prevent its defacement.[39]   Thaddeus Stevens told Congress that Buchanan had swindled the government out of $8,000 for private furnishings for the White House.   The Commissioner of Public Buildings, who disbursed these funds, had reported as early as 1862 that Buchanan had kept within the Congressional allowance, but in 1866 Stevens was still franking around public documents containing his charge.   Buchanan sent him a copy of the commissioner's published report.   "Whether you may think proper to correct the error I leave entirely to your own discretion," he said.   Stevens corrected it.[40]   New York papers accused Buchanan and Miss Lane of stealing portraits from the White House and walking off with the gifts brought by the Japanese.   It appeared that the pictures involved were the portraits of the British royal family which Victoria had sent personally to Buchanan.   The gifts had all gone to the Patent Office except a couple of stuffed birds which Harriet had brought home.   Buchanan held on to the portraits and challenged his tormentors to let Lord Lyons or

414

Victoria herself decide the question of ownership. The birds he would send back if Harriet's having them seemed to taint the national honor.[41] A sarcastic squib in the New York *Tribune* announced that Buchanan had forwarded an engraving of Harriet to the publishers of the *Almanac de Gotha*, social register of European royalty, for inclusion among the reigning families.[42] Another report erroneously stated that Buchanan had been fired as President of the Board of Trustees of Franklin and Marshall College. One editor said that Buchanan hoped Lincoln's troops would "die like rotten sheep" in the South. Such trifling but vicious stuff kept appearing, and people made sure he got the clippings in his mail. "If there is anything disagreeable in it," he remarked, "some person will be sure to send it to me."[43]

After Lincoln's death the New York *Post* and the *Tribune* ran a sensational story about the Cincinnati Convention, claiming that Jeremiah S. Black had bought the votes of the southern secessionists for Buchanan by pledging him to work for a southern confederacy during his Administration. Buchanan answered this accusation like a shot. Jeremiah S. Black, he wrote, had not been within 500 miles of Cincinnati at the time the convention met. A Col. Samuel W. Black of Pittsburgh had indeed supported the nomination, but he had since died for the Union at the head of his regiment in the field.[44]

The pattern of the campaign of character assassination convinced Buchanan that it was the deliberate policy of the Republican party. Dix had warned him to expect this when he explained the reasons for Lincoln's decision to draw the issue at Sumter. "The course pursued," he said, "had been the means of fixing the eyes of the nation on Sumter, so that when it fell its fall proved the instrumentality of arousing the national enthusiasm & loyalty, . . . to maintain the honor of the flag."[45] Stanton admitted that "of course, an attempt will be made to cast the responsibility on you," adding at the same time, "But there is a complete defence, as we know."[46] Buchanan wrote of the tide of abuse, "It is one of those great national prosecutions, such have occurred in this & other countries, necessary to vindicate the character of the Government. . . . The world . . . have forgotten the circumstances . . . [and] blame me for my supineness. . . . It will soon arrive at the point of denouncing me for not crushing out the rebellion at once, & thus try to make me the author of the war. Whenever it reaches that point, it is my purpose to indict . . . for libel."[47] That time came very quickly, but Buchanan recognized the futility of lawsuits against a few editors. Forney, Greeley, and Bennett led the pack, and he longed to force them to match their stories under oath against the records he had. By the fall of 1862, he had accepted the inevitable. "The spirit to do me injustice still prevails in the Republican party," he wrote. "They will at last, without the least just cause, endeavor to throw the responsibility of

415

the war on myself. Although this is simply ridiculous in itself, they will endeavor to make it appear a reality."[48]

MR. BUCHANAN'S BOOK

His consuming purpose in life now became the defense of his policy, his character and his reputation—his "vindication," as he called it. "Nobody seems to understand the course pursued by the late administration," he complained.[49] Black at first strongly urged countermeasures. "You owe it to your friends and to your country," he wrote, "to give them a full and clear vindication of your conduct & character. If this be not done, you will continue to be slandered for half a century to come. . . . Nothing is easier than a perfect defence of every important measure which you ever adopted or carried out."[50] Black offered to prepare a biography for $7,000, Buchanan agreed, and Black began the task.

It soon became evident, however, that they could not achieve historical agreement. Buchanan had firmly endorsed the war policy since the attack on Fort Sumter and in September, 1861, sent a letter to a Democratic political meeting in Chester County. He emphasized in this message that the war would have to be loyally sustained until the bitter end and urged the Democrats to stop wasting their time on a futile demand for peace proposals. The minute he saw this letter, Black wrote:

> Your endorsement of Lincoln's policy will be a very serious drawback upon the defence of your own. It is vain to think that the two administrations can be made consistent. The fire upon the Star of the West was as bad as the fire on Fort Sumter; and the taking of Fort Moultrie & Pinckney was worse than either. If this war is right and politic and wise and constitutional, I cannot but think you ought to have made it. I am willing to vindicate the last administration . . . but I can't do it on the ground which you now occupy.[51]

But much as he wanted a "vindication" prepared by so brilliant a thinker and so close a friend, Buchanan would not agree with Black that there was anything but a superficial similarity between the threatening incidents at the end of his Administration and the sustained bombardment and capture of Fort Sumter on April 12. He also disagreed with Black's view that the war itself was unconstitutional, that Lincoln had started it, and that it ought to be stopped as soon as possible by a negotiated peace. Lincoln had no choice, said Buchanan, except to give up Sumter or to strengthen it. This had been his own position: to abandon, which he had refused to do, or to reinforce on request of Anderson, which he had equipped a force to do on two hours' notice. And, said Buchanan, he would most certainly have done it, but no request came from Anderson. "As to

416

my course since the wicked bombardment of Fort Sumter," he told Black, "it is but a regular consequence of my whole policy towards the seceding States. They had been informed over & over again by me what would be the consequence of an attack upon it. They chose to commence civil war, & Mr. Lincoln had no alternative but to defend the country against dismemberment. I certainly should have done the same thing had they begun the war in my time, & this they well knew."[52] After a talk with Black he ruefully wrote Harriet, "I presume the Biography is all over. I shall now depend on myself, with God's assistance."[53] Despite the difference of opinion, the two men remained warm friends.

Buchanan now set himself to the task of compiling a record of his Administration from the published documents of the government and the private correspondence of his administrative associates. He pestered his friends for extracts of letters he did not have, or for confirmation of minor points, or copies of fugitive pamphlets and committee reports. They replied with speed and vehemence, stating generally their temporary inability to find the data he wanted and pressing him in the strongest terms not to publish any defense of his Administration while the war continued. Even Black now wrote, "The breath that kindled those grim fires of persecution has the power to blow them into sevenfold wrath and plunge us into the flames. The tribunal that condemned you against evidence will drown your defense with the sound of its drums."[54] The witch hunt had frightened everyone, and the last thing Buchanan's friends wanted at this moment was the truth about the political events preceding Lincoln's inauguration. The Republicans were equally unwilling to have the facts made public; they would crucify anyone who attempted to give a true account.

In October, 1862, General Scott gave Buchanan a chance to bring part of his defense to the public. The *National Intelligencer* published a long article including Scott's secret letter to Seward of March 3, 1861, and his lengthy "observations" to Lincoln a few days later. Buchanan had been trying unsuccessfully to get copies of these for 18 months. "I view it as a merciful dispensation of Providence," he said, "that the report . . . has been published during my lifetime."[55] The communication obviously invited a reply, and Buchanan set joyfully to the task. It gave him a chance to publicize his defense under the best possible conditions, for Scott's material was full of errors, and it exposed features of Lincoln's early policy which the Republicans in 1862 vigorously denied. Buchanan now learned for the first time that Lincoln had excerpted from Scott's material the misleading statements about Buchanan in the war message of July 4, 1861. He also read with amazement Scott's letter of March 3 urging Lincoln to let the South go out in peace and predicting a long and almost hopeless war as a result of a coercive policy.

417

Within a week Buchanan had his answer in the press. He had not reinforced the southern forts because Scott could not mobilize the necessary soldiers, and Congress would not call up more. He had not refused to issue orders to hold the Charleston forts until he had met with the Carolina commissioners, but had sent Anderson written orders to this effect two weeks before their arrival. He had not refused to send the *Brooklyn* to relieve Sumter, but had reluctantly agreed, at Scott's insistence, to permit the *Star* to be used instead. There was much more, perhaps too much, for people would be too busy to wade through the quantity of refutation presented. But it relieved him to get his story in print.

Scott issued a "Rejoinder" which introduced some new charges but scarcely dented the evidence that Buchanan had compiled. The general said that he had prepared his material "without a printed document and my own official papers" and admitted that "I may have made an unimportant mistake or two." He had indeed made a mistake or two, Buchanan responded, and not unimportant. For instance, Scott had not told Holt to rescind Floyd's order to ship cannon from Pittsburgh to the South during the first week in March, 1861; Buchanan had cancelled that order himself on December 26, 1860, before Holt took the War Office. The interplay of letters introduced the subjects Buchanan wanted most to explain. Scott brought up the topic of the "115,000 extra muskets and rifles, with all their implements and ammunition," which he alleged Floyd had stolen for the South, giving Buchanan his chance to nail that old carcass to the wall. While the affair looked to the public like a spirited controversy, the matters introduced by Scott suggested that the retired commander might have wished to let Buchanan have his day on the front page. Certainly the points the general raised were those against which Buchanan could bring almost conclusive refutation. The "Scott Controversy" became the first public chapter of Buchanan's "vindication."[56]

He finished the draft of his book late in 1862 and sent the copy around for criticism to Augustus Schell, Judge Ellis Lewis and William B. Reed. The latter wrote a preface, but Buchanan rejected it because Reed denied that the bombardment of Sumter offered cause for war. John Appleton published the book in 1866 under the title: *Mr. Buchanan's Administration on the Eve of the Rebellion.* In his own preface, Buchanan explained that he had delayed publication "to avoid the possible imputation . . . that any portion of it was intended to embarrass Mr. Lincoln's administration." The war, he said, grew out of fifty years of persistent hostility and violence between the North and South over slavery. "Many grievous errors were committed by both parties from the beginning," he concluded, "but the most fatal of them all was the secession of the cotton States." Even after secession, Congress had not only rejected compromise but had also "persistently refused to pass any measures enabling him or his successor to execute the laws against armed resistance, or to defend the country against approaching rebellion." This was Buchanan's own considered interpretation of the causes of the Civil War and of his role as president.

The book, like its author, was dignified, restrained and rather dull, but it marshalled the evidence in orderly array, documented it from official records, and presented a powerful case for his presidential policy. It also manifested the anxiety of its author, in common with everyone else of his day, to escape all appearance of agency in promoting the conflict. This preoccupation showed particularly in the sections where Buchanan assigned primary responsibility for the nonreinforcement of Sumter to Holt, Scott, and Anderson. Abner Doubleday, an officer at Sumter, claimed that Anderson had told the War Department that he needed no reinforcement because "he did not want it. . . . Its arrival would be sure to bring on a collision, and that was the one thing he wished to avoid." Buchanan would not have reproached him for this wish, for it was in line with his own policy, but not to the point of abandoning the fort. Buchanan recalled Holt's "tragical face" when he first saw the famous Anderson letter of March 4, and remarked that its publication would "doubtless excite disagreeable, I will not say tragical, feelings in the mind of the major." While Buchanan thus implied that Anderson's political thinking had interfered with his military judgment, he also implied that he had remained satisfied to let an artillery major shoulder a burden of decision which properly belonged to his Commander in Chief.[57]

Buchanan wrote his book as a historical document in the hope that in the years after his death, when passions had cooled, an organized record of his efforts to prevent the war might be available. He also wanted an anecdotal biography. For part of a year James F. Shunk and his wife lived at Wheatland to take notes of Buchanan's reminiscences for a popular account. After they had enough material, the Shunks went back to York but never wrote the book. Buchanan then hired his literary friend, William B. Reed of Philadelphia, to undertake a biography, paying him an outright fee plus a conditional grant to his wife, for he knew that Reed procrastinated and thought that his wife might keep him at work if she knew she would get $5,000 when the job was done. Reed asked Shunk for his notes but never got them; to this day they are missing from the Buchanan papers.[58] Reed never finished the biography, and none appeared based on Buchanan's own papers until 1883 when George Ticknor Curtis completed the two volume documentary *Life of James Buchanan* under a commission from the president's heirs and executors.

OLD MAN DEMOCRAT

Vindication and the protection of his "historical character" constituted Buchanan's major interest in the years of his retirement, but the course of politics ran a close second. From the day of the startling news from Sumter, Buchanan outspokenly supported the war effort. "The present administration had no alternative but to accept the war initiated by South Carolina or the Southern Confederacy," he told General Dix. "The North will sustain the administration almost to a man; and it ought to be sustained at all hazards."[59]

A few weeks after the outbreak of war he addressed a public letter to the *National Intelligencer* condemning military officers who broke their oath by joining the enemy. Unfortunately he also said that Sumter had "lighted a flame which it will require a long time to extinguish," heretical doctrine in May, 1861, and reaped such abuse that he thereafter kept quiet before the public. But privately he contributed to equip volunteer companies ("to keep the mob from hanging him," said Cameron),[60] denounced the Southern attack as "wickedly outrageous," encouraged volunteering ("If I were a young man I should be there myself"),[61] strongly supported the draft law which Democrats generally opposed, and warned against any effort at peace talk in advance of a military decision. The South, he said, "would consent to nothing less than a recognition of their independence, & this it is impossible to grant."[62] After the disastrous battle of First Bull Run he wrote, "I sometimes feel strongly tempted to leave my retirement so far as to take an active part in assisting to rally the people . . . to battle in support of our time honored and glorious flag; but the abuse which I received . . . admonishes me to desist."[63]

Despite the harsh and bitter epithets coined by the party presses for both Buchanan and Lincoln, these two never spoke ill of each other. Each knew, as did no other two people in America, the staggering complexities and uncertainties which the president must bear, and how many forces defied executive control. Buchanan spoke of Lincoln as "a man of honest heart & true manly feelings"[64] and "an honest and patriotic man."[65] "Mr. Lincoln may now make an enviable name for himself," he said, "and perhaps restore the Union."[66] After President Lincoln's assassination he wrote to Horatio King: "I feel the assassination . . . to be a terrible misfortune. . . . My intercourse with our deceased President, both on his visit to me . . . and on the day of his first inauguration, convinced me that he was a man of a kindly and benevolent heart and of plain, sincere and frank manners. I have not since changed my opinion of his character. Indeed, I felt for him much personal regard."[67]

Buchanan kept out of active politics in retirement and willingly passed the torch of responsibility to younger hands. Nonetheless, party managers called on him continually for advice and visited constantly at Wheatland. In the spring of 1863 Congress passed a conscription act which Pennsylvania Democrats attacked as unconstitutional and sought to upset in the State Supreme Court. Judge George Woodward of the State Court had been nominated for governor by the Democrats in 1863 and made opposition to the draft a main feature of his campaign. Buchanan urged strongly that his partisans abandon this policy. "The Constitution confers upon Congress in the clearest terms the power to raise & support armies. . . . It would be very unfortunate if, after the present administration have committed so many clear violations of the Constitution, the Democratic party should place itself in opposition to [the draft]."[68]

As the national election of 1864 drew near, the Democrats hoped to carry the nation with a military hero. They nominated General George B. McClellan whose military potential they thought had been purposely stifled by White House politics. The war had by this time dragged on so long, with so little apparent result, that many northerners grew lukewarm and lost heart in it. Lincoln's Emancipation Proclamation, which seemed to change the war aims from maintenance of the Union to freedom for the slaves and subjugation of the South, contributed to the unhappiness of the Democrats. Many of them now urged the immediate cessation of war by a negotiated peace with the Confederacy.

Buchanan said it was a year too late to raise a storm over the changed war aims, though that might have been a sound issue if it had been joined at once. The party ought not to go on a peace platform. "Peace," he said, "would be too dearly purchased at the expense of the Union."[69] He rejoiced when McClellan stated this idea clearly in his acceptance, but Buchanan anticipated that the Democrats would lose the election. "Have you ever reflected upon . . . the embarrassments of a Democratic administration, should it succeed to power with the war still existing and the finances in their present unhappy condition?" he asked.[70] After Lincoln's second victory he wrote, "They have won the elephant; & they will find difficulty in deciding what to do with him. . . . Now would be the time for conciliation on the part of Mr. Lincoln. A frank and manly offer to the Confederates that they might return to the Union just as they were before . . . might possibly be accepted."[71] This rather more hopeful view than he had expressed during the campaign may have arisen from reports of a meeting between Black and Jacob Thompson in Canada. At this time Thompson believed that the South would settle for the old Union if it could come back in without universal emancipation.

The assassination of Lincoln at the very moment of peace and victory stunned the nation and soon raised horrid apprehensions of continued violence and bloodshed. Buchanan had all along held the view

421

Lincoln later expressed, namely, that the southern states never had left the Union. "I considered the acts of Secession to be absolutely void," he said, "and that the States were therefore members, though rebellious members, of the Union."[72] He was gratified that President Johnson proposed to continue Lincoln's policy "not of reconstruction, but of restoration."[73] Before long, however, it became clear that the radicals intended no such program. Hang Jeff Davis, disfranchise the southern whites, and impose military rule on the conquered region; then reconstitute the states by the rule of the freedmen. That would be the Congressional policy. Johnson wavered and at last defied the program enacted by the radicals. For this, they impeached him. Buchanan's friends in England wrote in bewilderment about the American system of government where "the Chief Justice of the U. S. could not try the President of the Confederate States because he was so busy trying the President of the United States."[74] The Democrats at last had their issue. They had been helpless during the war, but opposition to radical Reconstruction put them on solid ground.

A large body of Philadelphians tendered a public dinner to Buchanan in the spring of 1867 which he had to decline, but for it he wrote his last serious political message. In it he proclaimed the heart of his concept of a constitutional republic, a type of government which, despite the recent military victory, stood, he feared, in imminent danger of destruction by politicians. The unique quality of the United States as devised by the makers of the Constitution had been to define powers of federal and state governments as separate and distinct. "They dreaded lest the vast powers . . . conferred upon the Federal Government . . . might be perverted to . . . usurp the reserved rights of the States. . . . They knew it would be impossible for one Central Government to provide for the ever varying wants and interests of separate people of different lineage, laws & customs, scattered over many States. . . . Consolidation . . . must finally end in Despotism."

"The true touchstone," he said, "as to whether the exercise of any proposed federal power has a warrant in the Constitution is to ask for the specific clause which authorizes it, or, if this cannot be shewn, then to prove that it is 'necessary & proper' without any strained construction. . . . If this cannot be clearly pointed out, then . . . 'The powers not delegated to the United States by the Constitution, nor prohibited by it to the States, are reserved to the States respectively, or to the people.' "[75] For this reason he strongly opposed a federal mandate for Negro suffrage. "Emancipation is now a Constitutional fact," he said, "but to prescribe the right and privilege of suffrage belongs exclusively to the States. This principle the Democracy must uphold."[76]

THE ROAD HOME

The days of retirement, filled as they were with study, writing, politics, and prophecy, were varied by all the continuing threads of a long and active life and rudely interrupted on occasion by the near surge of battle. At the time of Antietam and the first Chambersburg raid, rumor put the Confederate troops on the banks of the Conestoga. Buchanan's friends pleaded with him to vacate Wheatland before the Gettysburg campaign. William Bigler urged, "if the rebels get down to about Port Deposit, your best plan will be to retire to Clearfield"—a town buried inaccessibly in the central Pennsylvania mountains; and Augustus Schell told him to come to New York. Buchanan sent Harriet to Philadelphia, but he stayed at Wheatland. A week after the battle of Gettysburg he wrote to Black, "I felt no alarm at the approach of the rebels & with the help of God should not have removed from Wheatland had I been surrounded by a hundred thousand of them. I have schooled my mind to meet the inevitable evils of life with Christian fortitude."[77] The Confederate advance guard came within ten miles of Wheatland and, except for the demolition of the Susquehanna Bridge at Wrightsville, would very likely have made a bonfire of Buchanan's home.

He enjoyed the opportunity to work at his financial affairs without distraction. Black told him, just before his retirement, that he had discovered in the State Department accounts a record of $1,209 still owing him for per diem salary from the English mission. He verified his claim and sent it to Seward, but no record shows whether he ever got his pay or not. All through the war he tried to take only par funds for returns on his investments. "We cannot use any currency," he wrote his agents. When paper money began to decline, he went in for barter and tried to sell the old family farm for whiskey. Apparently he drove too sharp a bargain, for the distiller replied, "I can not make an exchange of whiskey for your farm because I cannot take those prices for the whiskey."[78] He stuck to his old principle of investment, informing his agent, Swarr, "*I lend no money to any person on a simple bond.*"[79]

He ran the financial affairs of nearly the whole family and not a few of his friends. Between 1855 and 1865 he developed the estate of the Pleasanton sisters from $22,000 to $34,000 and by 1867 had it up to $42,000. They exclaimed that it was "delicious" to get more than 6 per cent.[80] He still kept close track of the financial needs of Dr. Yates and his family, his brother Edward, J. B. Henry, Harriet, and the now married children of his deceased sisters. The family farm he eventually sold to Jerry Black. When Black paid for it and covered a further debt of long standing—something around $15,000—Buchanan looked at the check and said, "You have made a mistake. Your check is ten cents too little." Jerry handed over the extra ten cents.[81]

423

He took great pride in finally terminating the Lucinda Furnace investment, closing out the whole deal after thirty years of accounting for $48.48[82] Buchanan loved bookkeeping. He pored over his bank statements, covered page after page with neat figures in precisely ruled columns and at the end would put the proud endorsement, "Exactly corresponding with their account & balance," or, "Their statement is *exactly correct.*"[83] When the war had ended and the prospects of securities seemed more firm, he meticulously calculated the value of his estate, to which he had been adding at the rate of $15,000 a year from interest since retirement. A list of his total assets showed $205,600 in stocks and bonds, mostly state, municipal, and railroad; $41,190 in personal loans; $46,560 in real estate; and $16,650 owed by members of the family—a total of $310,000. With characteristic caution, Buchanan summed up his calculation with the note: "Dec. 16, 1866—Making all reasonable deductions, I am worth about $250,000."[84]

The household routine at Wheatland had its ups and downs. The staff of half a dozen servants was in continual circulation. One of the gardeners was perpetually in Alderman's court waiting for the master to come and bail him out. Thomas and Rosana Gordon quit and came back to service half a dozen times in as many years, and the house boys seemed always to be drafted shortly after taking a job at Wheatland. The two men in charge of cutting the huge Wheatland lawn received $10 and a gallon and one-half of Buchanan's best whiskey for the job. Miss Hetty kept them all in tight rein, so much so that Buchanan got into the habit of writing at the top of his monthly remittance for household expenses: "Paid to the order of My Lord Chamberlain."[85]

Though the winters were quiet and lonesome, the house in the fair seasons was generally full of guests. Harriet flitted in and out, spending a good deal of time in New York, Philadelphia, Baltimore, and Washington. Annie Buchanan, Edward's daughter, lived at Wheatland more than with her father. Buchanan's neighbor, the Rev. Dr. John W. Nevin, professor of history at Franklin and Marshall College, spent many evenings in the Wheatland study, philosophizing and talking about religion, the war, and the problems of the College of which Buchanan was still President of the Board. Old Lancaster cronies stopped for dinner several nights a week, and frequently his former political associates, ex-Governor Porter from Harrisburg, Judge Cadwalader, and William B. Reed and Joseph Baker from Philadelphia, Henry Welsh and Judge Black from York visited for a week or two. The invitations generally ran in this style: "I am happy that our tastes on so many subjects are the same & that we both delight in the classical dish of sauer kraut. Many pretenders to refinement despise this honest German dish; but we know better. I shall therefore expect you. . . ."

Miss Hetty filled him with sauer kraut till he groaned, but he never complained. He could not do without her, and she knew it. He often told intimate guests that she was the only person in the world who could give him a sound raking over the coals and get away with it.

Buchanan had the usual round of public dinners in Lancaster and nearby towns, and received with regularity the fire companies and glee clubs that came to Wheatland to honor the venerable ex-president and to partake of his liquid hospitality. Whenever he bought a stock of particularly good quality, he anticipated that Wheatland might shortly have such a visitation, for the word always leaked out. He occasionally travelled to Harrisburg, York, Philadelphia, or Baltimore, but apparently he never revisited Washington after Lincoln's inauguration. He went regularly to Bedford where he thoroughly enjoyed himself, for the ladies still made a great fuss over him and the "waters" seemed to ease his gout. Once he tried a New Jersey seashore resort, but the experiment proved a dismal failure. The gout struck while he was there and, for the first time in his life, he could not drink a drop of wine.

At home the mail daily brought nostalgic and saddening news of old friends. For Christmas, 1861, Varina Davis sent him a pair of slippers —"of no value," she wrote, "save that I worked them" as a token of regard and that he might be reminded "of those who love you."[86] Mrs. Bass, an outspoken Unionist, had seen her Virginia estate destroyed by the rebels, and had with great difficulty escaped through the lines under federal military escort to get medical care in New York.[87] Davy Lynch's daughter, Isabel, wrote, "Everything that could be sold out of the house has gone & I am lying on a hard straw bed & my back so sore that every time I move it causes it to bleed." Buchanan sent her $50 immediately and made arrangements to pay her expenses at a convent, but this she refused. He had given her widowed mother nearly $1000 during the war, and eventually did persuade Isabel to enter the Visitation Convent in Brooklyn, giving his New York agents instructions to pay all her bills. But within a year, to his distress, she ran away and was never heard from again. He learned, with sincere regret, of the tragic death of Rose O'Neal Greenhow, a Confederate spy who had drowned while trying to run the Union blockade. The brilliance of her mind and personality had influenced the actions of important men since the days of the Mexican War. Buchanan greatly admired her, and during the period of their intimate friendship in the 1850's he had absorbed from her many of his ideas about the South.[88]

From Washington he found out that most of the White House servants of his term had left. In 1867 he received a pathetic letter from Mary Wall: "I am nearly seventy years old, Sir, I am the old Chamber Maid . . . I write myself as I should not wish your Excellency to think any Imposter had made use of my name, as there are so many bad people in the present day." She wanted money to go back to England. Buchanan tried to discourage her from the trip, but he finally sent her about half the passage money.[89] Leonora Clayton wrote to Harriet of their condition at the war's end. "Do you think of those pleasant Euchre parties in those happy times? How sad now to think of the actors in those scenes. The Thompsons exiles, the Gwins abroad . . . Major McC fills a hero's grave, the Cobbs fallen in power, and only you who are still invested with radiance and hope."[90] Even before the war was half over, one of Harriet's southern friends reported that her children were "playing masquerade—have the character and costumes of darkies, & are ordering the white people out of the way in a style that we may expect to witness some day."[91]

Katherine Ellis, a niece of Senator King, had her own sad tale. King's home had been wrecked, she wrote, and a brigade of Negroes "broke into my home and committed outrages in my sight—I was protected by an officer, but others were not."[92] Buchanan wrote back to her, "*We must meet again, God willing,*" but it was not to be. Harriet met Howell Cobb in Baltimore after the war and immediately wrote to her uncle, inquiring if he wished to see his old friend. With pain, Buchanan replied, "I do not wish to meet him now or hereafter. . . . I wish him well and hope he may obtain his pardon; but this is all. . . . I truly pity him."[93] In January, 1868, he got news of Mrs. Robb's death. Her life in Chicago during the war had been a living hell. Her stepchildren considered her a rebel and would not speak to her, and the political tension eventually broke up her marriage. The hardest blows came from those former friends who had lost a father or husband or son or brother in the war. When General John F. Reynolds fell on the first day at Gettysburg, the family held Buchanan almost personally responsible. All the intimacy of fifty years turned to impassioned hate. Ellie Reynolds, who had been as close as a sister to Harriet and for years had come to Wheatland as one of the family, could no longer abide the mention of Buchanan's name. He wondered painfully how many of the families broken by war felt the same. In Lancaster, he knew, there were many.

It was pleasant, on the other hand, to hear from children who had been named after him and asked for a photograph or an autograph. Literary societies sent him notices of honorary membership, and gifts often came in the mail or were delivered by deputation—canes, poems, wine, books, and a huge liberty pole on one occasion. He was flattered that some people in Mercersburg had bought as an historical relic the log cabin at Stony Batter where he had been born, but he declined the invitation to pay a ceremonial visit. "I am now in my 76th year," he wrote, "and all the friends and acquaintances of my youth in your vicinity have been gathered to their fathers."[94]

Indeed, the allotted time had nearly gone by. A friend wrote that Buchanan now had become "the only surviving member of the House of Representatives as it was on the first Monday of December, 1821." "Truly," he replied, "we both live 'in the midst of posterity.' "[95]

New life started as the old declined. Harriet had married Henry E. Johnston, of Baltimore, in January, 1866, at a private ceremony performed by Uncle Edward at Wheatland. Mr. Johnston, a banker, did not participate in the high society to which Harriet had accustomed herself, but "Nunc" heartily approved of her choice. "You have chosen the wiser part," he said, "in selecting for your husband a gentleman of education, of good manners & of excellent character. . . . You must forget 'the pride, pomp & circumstance' of public life in which you have been raised. In truth, it no longer exists."[96] Buchanan lived to fondle Harriet's first child on his knee at Wheatland and to visit her once at her Baltimore home, but this trip greatly distressed him because his old friends declined to come to see him at the Johnston home, and he vowed never to return to the city.

At Wheatland his thoughts turned increasingly to religion. During the war the Presbyterian Church declined to accept him, presumably over some doctrinal matter. At last, on September 23, 1865, the elders eventually examined him "on his experimental evidence of piety" and admitted him to communion.[97]

In May, 1868, Buchanan took seriously ill of a cold and various complications of old age. He knew the end had come and lay in his upstairs bedroom at Wheatland, spending much time with Hiram Swarr who would be one of his executors. The family came, and Miss Hetty flew about in a panic. The will he had drawn needed revision. Certain stocks ought to be sold while the market was good. He wanted to be buried in Woodward Hill Cemetery, Lancaster, with no pomp, public ceremony, or parade and to have Dr. John W. Nevin perform the burial service, but had no objections if the Masons wished to participate. He carefully specified a plain white marble tombstone and dictated its legend. He talked much at the end about what men in the future would say of him. The day before he died he told Swarr, "I have always felt and still feel that I discharged every public duty imposed on me conscientiously. I have no regret for any public act of my life, and history will vindicate my memory."

Near half-past eight on Monday morning, June 1, 1868, James Buchanan died at the age of seventy-eight. His request to be buried without pomp or parade went unheeded. Lancaster held a public meeting in his honor on Tuesday morning, and later in the day thousands of country folk travelled to Wheatland to file past the casket. Over 20,000 people attended the funeral on Thursday, including official delegations from all over the nation and scores of reporters. Orators recalled his remarkable power of clear and logical argument and bore testimony to his "great private virtues, integrity, charity, kindness and courtesy." One speaker compared him with Lincoln. "Starting at Stony Batter, a barefoot boy climbed to the highest office in the world. A rail-splitter of Illinois did the same thing. The effect of such an example is incalculable. A Republic is the only place on earth where such a thing is possible."[98]

Buchanan's will defined his legacy to his friends and relatives. He gave generous gifts to the Presbyterian Church and to the city of Lancaster for the purchase of fuel for the poor. He provided for Miss Hetty and remembered by small bequests the Wheatland servants. The remainder of the estate he divided carefully among the eleven surviving descendants of his father's family.

What was Buchanan's larger legacy, his bequest to the society to which he had devoted his life? He exemplified in his private conduct simplicity of manners, unfailing courtesy, and a kindly consideration for others. Although proud of his own attainments, he remained familiar and unaffected in his relations with others, treating his barber, his gardener and his poor relatives with no less regard and attention than he gave to people of eminence. In the sense that he appreciated and respected people for their personal qualities, regardless of station, he practiced the republican ideal.

Buchanan believed implicitly that a constitutional republic represented man's greatest invention in the art of government. The success of its trial in America depended, in his opinion, upon the willingness of people in and out of office to exercise self-restraint and to be willing to accommodate their differing ideas and ambitions to the preservation of the system. Neither state nor federal government should dominate; secession or consolidation, each, would wreck the constitutional structure. Nor should any branch of government, executive, legislative or judicial, try to assert an overriding control. A "strong" president, one who overpowered or ignored the Congress and the courts, meant an executive who would destroy the republican form.

Which did James Buchanan regard more highly, the national entity or the principles of free government defined in the United States Constitution? A friend accurately answered this fundamental question on the day of the presidential nomination at Cincinnati. Ever since James Buchanan had been old enough to marry, he observed, "he has been wedded to the Constitution."[99]

Buchanan, in his public and private life, demonstrated mental toughness and moral stamina. Beyond common humanity he was devoted to duty, industrious in ascertaining facts, tenacious of his principles, and nearly always in control of himself. He never approved of the maxim that in the affairs of mankind, while the intellect may persuade, the heart controls. He preferred to hope that in a self-governing society, while the heart might persuade, the intellect would control. Only thus could men curb their passions and achieve peaceful solutions to recurrent crises.

Buchanan assumed leadership of the United States when an unprecedented wave of angry passion was sweeping over the nation. That he held the hostile sections in check during these revolutionary times was in itself a remarkable achievement. His weaknesses in the stormy years of his presidency were magnified by enraged partisans of the North and the South. His many talents, which in a quieter era might have gained for him a place among the great presidents of his country, were quickly overshadowed by the cataclysmic events of civil war and by the towering personality of Abraham Lincoln. Of Buchanan it might be said, as it was later of another, "He staked his reputation on the supremacy of reason, and lost."

NOTES

CHAPTER 1 (pp. 1-12)

1. "Buchanan Chart" by L. D. Buchanan, Houston, Texas, and *Genealogy and History* (Washington, D. C.), Aug. 15, 1940.

2. Records on the lineage of President James Buchanan are incomplete and contradictory. The following sources have been useful: Moore, *Works*, XII, 289; A. W. Patrick Buchanan, *The Buchanan Book* (Montreal, 1911); D. B. Landis, "Rev. Edward Young Buchanan," *Lancaster County Historical Society Papers*, XXXII (1928), nos. 9 and 10; MS. record prepared by Madeline B. Gill, De Land, Fla., in papers of Mrs. B. C. Landis, Lancaster, Penna.; Buchanan papers, YCHS; letters to the author from the Rev. Maurice G. Buchanan, Indianapolis, Ind.; *Genealogy and History*, Aug. 15, 1940, and Sept. 15, 1940; James Buchanan to W. E. Robinson, Feb. 6, 1844, Buchanan MSs., BF; James Buchanan to Charles W. Russell, Apr. 10, 1858, Buchanan MSs., HSP.

3. There is considerable data on Joshua Russell, most of it in the York County Historical Society and in the Office of Public Records, Harrisburg, Penna. In YCHS: Requisition for Recruits, 1781; Tax List, 1783; Tombstone Entries of Black's Graveyard, Cumberland Township; Orphans Court Records, Dec. 1, 1784, E203-204; York County Deed Book, Jan. 7, 1785, 2-C, 1784-1786, p. 33. In the Office of Public Records: Jas. Darah to Joshua Russell, May 5, 1778, Revolutionary Papers, XXI, 14; York County Census (property tax lists), 1783; Post-Revolutionary Papers, XXXV, Dec. 1786; York County Deeds, Grantee Index (microfilm), Feb. 4, 1786, Thomas Armstrong to Joshua Russell. Other data are in Penna. Statutes at Large, XI, 175-177, and XII, 502-509; *History of Cumberland and Adams Counties* (Chicago, 1886), part III, 108, 184, 251-252; Adams County Wills, I, 319, #253, Jan. 5, 1807; Adams County Orphans Court, p. 21, Jan. 7, 1812, and p. 30, Mar. 3, 1812; and Bureau of Census, *Heads of Families at the First Census . . . 1790 . . . Pennsylvania* (G. P. O., 1908), p. 288.

4. On the Speer family: Franklin County Deed Book, Mar. 4, 1802, VII, 428, and Sept. 7, 1804, VI, 328; *The Speer Family Record* (privately printed, Baltimore, n.d.); G. T. Curtis, *Life of James Buchanan* (New York, 1883), I, 3.

5. For the early history of Cove Gap and Stony Batter: J. F. Richard, *History of Franklin County* (Chicago, 1887); Joshua Gilpin, "A Tour from Philadelphia, 1809" in *Pennsylvania Magazine of History and Biography*, L (1926), 169; *Old Mercersburg* (New York, 1912); Sherman Day, *Historical Collections of Pennsylvania* (Philadelphia, 1843), pp. 124-125, 354-355; James Livingood, *The Philadelphia-Baltimore Trade Rivalry, 1780-1860* (Harrisburg, 1947), Chap. II; Historical Commission of Penna., *Frontier Forts* (Harrisburg, 1896), I, 534-550; A. J. Morrison (ed.), *Travels in the Confederation 1783-1784*, by John Schoepf (Philadelphia, 1911), pp. 220, 223.

6. For the John Tom story: Bureau of Census, *Heads of Families . . . Penna. . . . 1790*, p. 114; Franklin County Deed Book I, 371; II, 145-147; article by Thomas W. Lane in scrapbook of John Lowry Ruth, pp. 68-69, in YCHS.

7. Franklin County Deed Book, XVII, 561-562, Dec. 29, 1838. Buchanan paid $7500 for the property. The 1838 deed recites a history of the tract.

431

8. Property of James Buchanan, Sr., is recorded in Franklin County Deed Books II, 145-147; IV, 183; VI, 140, 328; VII, 428; VIII, 110, 413. Also, *Old Mercersburg*, p 55.

9. Alice L. Black, "George Washington at the Carey House, 1794," typescript in YCHS. This thoroughly documented article gives a fairly full history of the Russell Tavern, later the Carey House.

10. Descriptions of James Buchanan's childhood are found in: John L. Finefrock's address on "Stony Batter," delivered at Wheatland, April 27, 1940; Theodore Appel, *Recollections of College Life at Marshall College, Mercersburg, Pa.* (Reading, 1886), pp. 56-59; the autobiography in Moore, *Works*, XII; speech of Dr. Philip Schaff, Carlisle, Spring 1857, described by J. Hassler in *Public Opinion*, Chambersburg, April, 1893; and W. Rush Gillan, "James Buchanan," in Kittochtinny H. S. *Papers*, II, 1901. For the birthplace of James Buchanan and descendants of his parents: *Old Mercersburg*; letter to the Harrisburg *Patriot*, in John Lowry Ruth Scrapbook, p. 64; Reginald B. Henry to R. F. Nichols, Mar. 12, 1937; *Buchanan*, privately printed genealogy of descendants of James and Elizabeth Buchanan, prepared by Reginald Buchanan Henry; J. M. Cooper to O. E. Shannon, Aug. 7, 1866 (photostat in possession of author), relating story of Buchanan birthplace and proposing to buy cabin as historic shrine.

11. Information from conversations with the Rev. E. J. Turner, formerly of the Presbyterian Church, Mercersburg, and church records, including a letter from Buchanan to the Rev. Thomas Creigh, July 10, 1848, describing Dr. King. Also, Alexander Harris, *Biographical History of Lancaster County* (Lancaster, 1872), pp. 341-342.

12. Appel, *Recollections of College Life*, pp. 56-59.

13. Carlisle *Herald*, Oct. 13, 1809; James H. Morgan, *Dickinson College: The History of One Hundred and Fifty Years, 1783-1933* (Carlisle, Penna., 1933), p. 183; Atwater to Benjamin Rush, April 22, 1810; Atwater to the Rev. Ashbel Green, May 11, 1810, Gratz Collection, HSP. For a full account, see Philip S. Klein, "James Buchanan at Dickinson," in *John and Mary's College* (Carlisle, Penna., 1956), pp. 157-179.

14. Morgan, *Dickinson College*, p. 95.

15. *Ibid.*, pp. 170-171. Roger B. Taney's recollections.

16. *Ibid.*, p. 112.

17. Moore, *Works*, XII, 291.

18. Carlisle *Herald*, July 8, 1808.

19. Moore, *Works*, XII, 292.

20. Minutes of the Board of Trustees, I, 348-349, Sept. 28, 1808, DC; Carlisle *Herald*, Oct. 5, 1808; Morgan, *Dickinson College*, p. 196.

21. Buchanan's mathematics workbook, in the Dickinsoniana Collection, DC. Another volume is in the library at Wheatland.

22. Sept. 6, 1809, in Curtis, *Buchanan*, I, 6-7.

23. Moore, *Works*, XII, 293.

24. Carlisle *Herald*, Sept. 29, 1809.

CHAPTER 2 (pp. 13-26)

1. W. U. Hensel, *James Buchanan as a Lawyer* (Lancaster, 1912), p. 2.

2. Day, *Historical Collections*, p. 395.

3. Father to James, Feb. 10 and Mar. 12, 1810, Buchanan Sr. MSs., BF.

4. John, born and died, 1804; William Speer, born 1805; George Washington, born 1808; and Edward Young, born 1811.

5. Father to James, February 7 and April 19, 1811, Buchanan Sr. MSs., BF.

6. Same to same, July 11, 1811, Buchanan Sr. MSs., BF.

7. Same to same, March 18, 1812, Buchanan Sr. MSs., BF.

8. Lucius P. Little, *Ben Hardin, His Times and Contemporaries* (Louisville, 1887), pp. 352-353. The best study of the whole episode is: R. Gerald McMurtry, "James Buchanan in Kentucky, 1813," *The Filson Club Historical Quarterly*, April, 1934, pp. 73-87.

9. Moore, *Works*, I, 1, note 1; 2.

10. Lancaster *Intelligencer and Weekly Advertiser*, Feb. 20, 1813.

11. *Ibid.*, March 20, 1813.

12. Father to James, March 26, 1813, Buchanan Sr. MSs., BF.

13. Curtis, *Buchanan*, I, 15.

14. Buchanan to Smith, Feb. 14, 1814, Dickinsoniana Collection, DC; fragments of legal correspondence mostly on debt collection in Buchanan MSs., BF; and miscellaneous items in the Buchanan MSs. and Cadwalader MSs., HSP. Appearance Dockets of the Courts of Quarter Sessions and Common Pleas, 1812-1821, stored in Lancaster County Courthouse, list Buchanan as counsel in more than 150 cases from 1812 to 1815. In 1819, November term, he was on the docket as counsel in 32 separate actions.

15. Father to James, July 11, 1811, and Sept. 10, 1813, Buchanan Sr. MSs., BF.

16. Lancaster *Weekly Journal*, Aug. 26, 1814, and Oct. 3, 1828; Moore, *Works*, XII, 293.

17. Father to James, Sept. 22, 1814, and Jan. 20, 1815, Buchanan Sr. MSs., BF.

18. Lancaster *Intelligencer and Weekly Advertiser*, Sept. 3, 1814; Moore, *Works*, XII, 294.

19. Members of this troop did not qualify as veterans of the war, and their names will not be found on official rolls. But there is ample evidence of the expedition and of the names of the volunteers. See Lancaster *Intelligencer and Weekly Advertiser*, Sept. 3, 10, 17, 1814; Moore, *Works*, XII, 294; Harris, *Biographical History of Lancaster County*, p. 478; C. S. Foltz, *Surgeon of the Seas* (Indianapolis, 1931), p. 190; H. M. J. Klein, *Lancaster County, a History* (New York, 1924), II, 596.

20. Father to James, Sept. 22, 1814, Buchanan Sr. MSs., BF.

21. Lancaster *Weekly Journal*, Sept. 30, Oct. 21, and Nov. 18, 1814; S. W. Higginbotham, *Keystone of the Democratic Arch* (Harrisburg, 1952), pp. 297-299.

22. Father to James, Oct. 21, 1814, Buchanan Sr. MSs., BF.

23. Philadelphia *Aurora*, Feb. 3, 1815; and Meadville *Crawford Register*, Feb. 23, 1817, give interesting accounts of the daily legislative routine. For Buchanan's proposals, see *Aurora*, Jan. 6, 1815; Lancaster *Intelligencer and Weekly Advertiser*, Dec. 24, 1814, Feb. 10, 1815; Lancaster *Weekly Journal*, Feb. 3, 1815.

24. Father to James, Jan. 20, 1815, Buchanan Sr. MSs., BF.

25. Curtis, *Buchanan*, I, 9-10.

26. Father to James, June 23, 1815, Buchanan Sr. MSs., BF.

27. This sentence may possibly have been the origin of the famous "Drop of Blood" story of 1828. See Chap. 5, note 8.

28. Moore, *Works*, I, 2-8; XII, 316-320.

29. Father to James, July 14, Sept. 1, 1815, Buchanan Sr. MSs., BF.

30. Lancaster *Intelligencer and Weekly Advertiser*, Oct. 14, 1815.

31. *Ibid.*, Dec. 15, 1815.

32. Father to James, Feb. 23, 1816, Buchanan Sr. MSs., BF.

33. *Ibid.* and Curtis, *Buchanan*, I, 15.

34. Buchanan Mss., HSP, contains most of the legal papers, 1816-1835.

35. Hensel, *Buchanan as a Lawyer*, p. 7.

36. Out of this controversy grew the case Moore v. Houston, 3 *Sergeant and Rawle*, 170, in which Justice Tilghman of the Pennsylvania Supreme Court enunciated one of his most famous doctrines: "Where the states are prohibited expressly by the Constitution of the United States, from the exercise of power, all their power ceases from the adoption thereof; but where the power of the state is taken away by implication, they may continue to act until the United States exclude them." Cf. Hensel, *Buchanan as a Lawyer*, p. 8.

37. Curtis, *Buchanan*, I, 17.

38. Lancaster *Journal*, March 1, 1817, et seq.; Lancaster *Intelligencer and Weekly Advertiser*, Mar. 22, 1817.

39. Franklin to Buchanan, March 3, Campbell to Buchanan, March 7, 1818, Buchanan Mss., HSP.

40. John Norvall to Roberts Vaux, March 15, 1818, Buchanan Mss., HSP.

CHAPTER 3 (pp. 27-43)

1. G. F. Reed, *Alumni Record of Dickinson College, passim;* Frank R. Diffenderfer, *History of the Farmers Bank of Lancaster* (Lancaster, 1910), p. 46; William Riddle, *Story of Lancaster, Pennsylvania, Old and New* (Lancaster, 1917), pp. 122-123; invitations to parties and Masonic items in Buchanan Mss., BF; S. R. Fraim, mimeographed history of Buchanan's work in Lodge #43, F. and A. M., dated Sept 13, 1950, Lancaster.

2. For the Coleman family, see Frederic S. Klein, "Robert Coleman, Millionaire Ironmaster," *LCHS Journal*, LXIV (1960), 17-33; Committee on Historical Research, *Forges and Furnaces in the Province of Pennsylvania* (Philadelphia, 1944); H. M. J. Klein and Wm. F. Diller, *History of St. James Church* (Lancaster, 1944); Franklin Ellis, *History of Lancaster County* (Philadelphia, 1883), pp. 305, 465-466 and 911; and Robert Coleman's Will, Book O, 1, pp. 347-352, in Lancaster County Courthouse.

3. Purchased from Christopher Hager, June 18, 1807, Deed Book Y, 3, p. 561, Lancaster County Courthouse. Buchanan later bought this as his home.

4. Ruth Scrapbook, p. 70, YCHS. This item from an undated clipping of the Philadelphia *Press*, notes an oil land title transaction in Warren County, which attorneys had traced back to this deal.

5. Ellis, *History of Lancaster County*, p. 547.

6. Ruth Scrapbook, p. 70, and Annie Gilchrist, "First on the Turnpike," Bedford *Inquirer*, Dec. 30, 1950, quoting the reminiscences of Dr. C. N. Hickok of Bedford.

7. Buchanan to William Wright, President of Columbia Bridge Company, Sept. 13, 1819, Buchanan Mss., BF; the Philadelphia *Union, or United States Gazette and True American*, Nov. 30, 1819; Sheriff's Appearance Dockets, Lancaster entries for autumn, 1819, especially pp. 84-85 which contain notes on the bridge case in Buchanan's handwriting.

8. Lancaster *Journal*, Sept. 16 and Oct. 19, 1818; Oct. 22, 1819, for the local political situation; and Nov. 27, 1819, for the Missouri Resolutions.

9. Hannah Cochran to her husband, Dec. 14, 1819, Slaymaker Collection, Lancaster.

10. Article in Ruth Scrapbook, p. 44, by Blanche Nevin, daughter of the Rev. John W. Nevin and Martha Jenkins Nevin, daughter of Robert Jenkins of Windsor Forge.

11. Sheriff's Appearance Dockets, 1819-1820, pp. 84-85.

12. Nathaniel Chapman (1780-1853). See Charles Morris (ed.), *Makers of Philadelphia* (Philadelphia, 1894), p. 37. Extract from Kittera Diary is in notes of G. T. Curtis, Buchanan MSs., HSP. Extensive search failed to turn up the original of this diary.

13. Samuel Dale to Jacob Hibshman, Dec. 16, 1819, Hibshman MSs., The Pennsylvania State University Library.

14. Hannah Cochran to her husband, Dec. 14, 1819, Slaymaker Collection.

15. Curtis, *Buchanan*, I, 18.

16. Ruth Scrapbook, pp. 56 and 64, undated clippings from the Wyandot *Union* and the Boston *Budget*. Curtis, *Buchanan*, I, 16, says that Buchanan wrote the notice basing this statement on an unidentified diary, presumably that of Judge Franklin.

17. Hannah Cochran letter, *op. cit.* For a more detailed account of the whole Ann Coleman episode, cf. Philip S. Klein, "James Buchanan and Ann Coleman," *Pennsylvania History*, XXI (Jan., 1954), 1-20.

18. Mother to James, Mar. 21, 1826, Buchanan Sr. MSs., BF.

19. In Buchanan MSs., HSP.

20. Story told by Judge Henry G. Long of Lancaster to "Swede" of the Cincinnati *Commercial*, Swarr Scrapbook, Buchanan-Swarr MSs., BF.

21. "Recollections of J. Montgomery Forster," in clippings from the Mercersburg *Journal*, Rankin Scrapbook, Presbyterian Church, Mercersburg.

22. Charles Montelius to Jacob Hibshman, Dec. 11, 1820, Hibshman MSs., The Pennsylvania State University Library.

23. Swarr Scrapbook, Buchanan-Swarr MSs., BF.

24. Buchanan to Cyrus Jacobs, June 9, 1820, Buchanan MSs., BF.

25. Philip S. Klein, "Early Lancaster County Politics," *Pennsylvania History*, III (April, 1936), 98-114, and his *Pennsylvania Politics, 1817-1832; A Game without Rules* (Philadelphia, 1940), Chaps. V-VI.

26. Copy of the "Colebrook" letter is in Buchanan MSs., BF. *The Speer Family Record*, pp. 2-3, refers to earlier portions of the career of the "black girl, Hannah," as do the reminiscences of John C. Finefrock, Mercersburg, in the author's possession.

27. Articles in Lancaster *Journal* and *Pennsylvania Gazette*, and especially article signed "Investigator" in Harrisburg *Republican*, July 21, 1820.

28. July 26, 1820, Buchanan Sr. MSs., BF. This was the father's last letter to James of which we have any record.

29. Lancaster *Journal*, August 11, 1820.

30. *Ibid.*, Aug. 25, Sept. 1, 15, 1820.

31. Commonwealth v. Christian Weldy, Lancaster *Journal*, Jan. 26, 1821.

32. Commonwealth v. William Hamilton, Lancaster *Journal*, May 4, 1821.

33. George McDuffie to Buchanan, March 28, 1823, Buchanan MSs., HSP.

34. Josiah Quincy, *Figures of the Past* (Boston, 1926), p. 241.

35. Curtis, *Buchanan*, I, 29.

36. *Ibid.*, I, 26.

37. Buchanan to Walter Franklin, Dec. 21, 1821, Moore, *Works*, I, 10-11.

38. Notes of Judge John Cadwalader on Buchanan biography, Cadwalader MSs., HSP.

39. Moore, *Works*, I, 11-20.

40. Buchanan to Calhoun, Jan., 1822, Buchanan MSs., HSP; Buchanan to John Reynolds, Jan. 1, 1822, Reynolds MSs., FM.; Lancaster *Journal*, Feb. 15, 1822.

41. Lancaster *Journal*, Mar. 29, 1822.

42. *Ibid.*, July 12, 1822.

43. Buchanan to Hugh Hamilton, Mar. 22, 1822, letter printed in sale catalogue of Alwin T. Sheuer, #5, 1929, filed in New York Public Library.

44. Moore, *Works*, XII, 300-301.

CHAPTER 4 (pp. 44-59)

1. Buchanan to ?, Aug. 18, 1821, Buchanan MSs., HSP.

2. Klein, *Pennsylvania Politics*, pp. 128-130.

3. Marquis James, *Andrew Jackson* (New York, 1938); p. 370.

4. Pleasanton to Buchanan, March 20, 1823, Buchanan MSs., HSP.

5. Buchanan to Pleasanton, March 25, 1823, Buchanan MSs., HSP.

6. Pleasanton to Buchanan and Molton C. Rogers, April 15, 1823, Buchanan MSs., HSP.

7. McDuffie to Buchanan, March 28, 1823, Buchanan MSs., HSP.

8. Klein, *Pennsylvania Politics*, pp. 132-149.

9. Buchanan to John Sergeant, May 9, 1823, Buchanan MSs., HSP.

10. Lancaster *Journal*, August 1, 15, 1823.

11. Hugh Hamilton to Buchanan, Sept. 13, 1823, Buchanan MSs., HSP.

12. Klein, *Pennsylvania Politics*, p. 138.

13. Undated drafts of letters from Buchanan to Mrs. Blake, of 1823, are misfiled in the box containing letters to Buchanan, Nov. 1840, in Buchanan MSs., HSP. Also, George Blake to Buchanan, Mar. 30, 1823.

14. Gibson to Buchanan, Jan. 13, 1824, Buchanan MSs., HSP.

15. Klein, *Pennsylvania Politics*, pp. 161-162.

16. *Ibid.*, pp. 120-124.

17. *Pennsylvania Manual, 1933*, p. 388; the Philadelphia *Democratic Press*, Nov. 18, 1814, gives slightly different returns.

18. Buchanan to Thomas Elder, Jan. 2, 1825, Buchanan MSs., HSP.

19. Markley to Buchanan, Jan. 23, 1825, Buchanan MSs., HSP.

20. Rogers to Buchanan, Dec. 27, 1824, Buchanan MSs., HSP.

21. Marquis James says: "Mr. Buchanan's motive [in interviewing Jackson] seems not to have been more reprehensible than an effort to help Jackson despite himself, and to spare Clay the possible consequences of a dangerous game." *Jackson* (1938 ed.), Chap. XXV.

22. Rogers to Buchanan, Dec. 27, 1824, Buchanan MSs., HSP.

23. A. H. Wharton, *Social Life in the Early Republic* (Philadelphia, 1902), p. 196.

24. Quincy, *Figures of the Past*, pp. 296-298.

25. Buchanan to the editor of the Lancaster *Journal*, Aug. 8, 1827; Moore, *Works*, I, 263-267; Richard Stenberg, "The Corrupt Bargain Calumny," *Pennsylvania Magazine of History and Biography*, Jan. 1934; Curtis, *Buchanan*, I, 41-44; J. S. Bassett, *Life of Andrew Jackson* (Garden City, 1911), I, 356-362; James, *Jackson* (1938 ed.), pp. 414-445.

26. Calvin Colton (ed.), *The Works of Henry Clay* (New York, 1904), I, 418; Bassett, *Jackson*, I, 356-362; Buchanan to Elder, Jan. 2, 1825, Buchanan MSs., HSP.

27. Klein, *Pennsylvania Politics*, pp. 182-183.

28. L. D. Baldwin, *Pittsburgh, the Story of a City* (Pittsburgh, 1937), p. 289.

29. A. L. Hayes to George Wolf, Nov. 9, 1829, Wolf MSs., HSP.

30. Green to Buchanan, Oct. 12, 1826, Buchanan MSs., HSP.

31. Buchanan to Green, Oct. 16, 1826, Buchanan MSs., HSP.

32. Ingham to Buchanan, July 6, 1827, Buchanan MSs., HSP.

33. "To the Editor of the Lancaster *Journal*, August 8, 1827," Moore, *Works*, I, 263-267.

34. Andrew Porter to J. S. Johnston, Aug. 6, 1827, Johnston MSs., HSP.

35. J. H. Pleasants to J. S. Johnston, Aug. 6, 1827, Johnston MSs., HSP.

36. Clay to Francis Brooke, Aug. 14, 1827, Colton (ed.), *Works of Henry Clay*, I, 169.

37. R. P. Letcher to Clay, Aug. 27, 1827, *ibid.*, I, 171.

38. Aug. 11, 1827, Rawle MSs., HSP.

39. Calhoun to John McLean, Sept. 3, 1827, McLean MSs., LC.

40. Daniel Webster to Clay, Aug. 22, 1827, Colton, *op. cit.*, I, 170.

41. Rogers to Buchanan, Aug. 12, 1827, Buchanan MSs., HSP.

42. J. R. Speer to Buchanan, Feb. 1, 1828, Buchanan MSs., HSP.

43. Buchanan to Ingham, Aug. 9, 1827, Buchanan MSs., HSP.

44. Green to Buchanan, July 19; Buchanan to Green, Aug. 17, 1827, Buchanan MSs, HSP.

45. Buchanan to Ingham, Aug. 9, 1827, Buchanan MSs., HSP.

46. Jackson to Kendall, Sept. 4, 1827, J. S. Bassett and J. F. Jameson (eds.), *Correspondence* (Washington, 1926-1935), III, 381.

47. Van Buren to Jackson, Sept. 14, 1827, Van Buren MSs., LC.

CHAPTER 5 (pp. 60-77)

1. William B. Fordney to Buchanan, April 15, 1828, Buchanan MSs., HSP.

2. Moore, *Works*, I, 283-312.

3. Lancaster *Journal*, May 30, 1828.

4. Pottstown *Times*, Mar. 9, 1891 (letter of Thos. J. McCamant).

5. C. F. and E. M. Richardson, *Charles Miner, a Pennsylvania Pioneer* (Wilkes-Barre, 1926), p. 126.

6. J. W. G. Lescure to Buchanan, June 11, 1828; Isaac D. Barnard to Buchanan, July 1, 1828, Buchanan MSs., HSP.

7. Lancaster *Journal*, July 11, 1828.

8. It seems very unlikely that Buchanan made this statement. His 1815 speech was formal, written in advance, and printed from the manuscript immediately after its delivery. No mention of the alleged statement appeared until thirteen years later, during the 1828 election when Buchanan's change of party became the main issue. At that time an anti-Buchanan partisan made an affadavit that he had heard Buchanan make the "Drop of Blood" statement in 1815. Others who had attended the 1815 meeting denied that Buchanan had used the words. No one in 1828 seems to have had access to a printed copy of the address. The complete printed version eluded historians until early in the 20th century when John Bassett Moore unearthed the long-missing second half of the 1815 speech. See Moore, *Works*, XII, 316-320.

The Lancaster *Journal*, July 25 and Aug. 1, 1828, prints the contemporary charge and refutations.
Handbills of the activities of the Washington Society in 1814-1815, listing Buchanan as an officer, are in collections of the LCHS.

9. Lancaster *Journal*, Aug. 1, 1828, Letter of "Volunteer," and Aug. 8, in answer to Marietta *Pioneer*; Joseph Sharp to Buchanan, Aug. 6, 1828; L. Edwards to Buchanan, Aug. 15, 1828, Buchanan MSs., HSP.

10. Lancaster *Journal*, Aug. 22, 1828, cites part of the *Pioneer* article with material to refute charges.

11. Buchanan to E. C. Reigart, Aug. 19, 1828, Buchanan MSs., HSP.

12. E. C. Reigart to Buchanan, Aug. 19, 1828; James Humes to the Public, Aug. 21, 1828, Buchanan MSs., HSP; Moore, *Works*, I, 303.

13. Lancaster *Journal*, Aug. 29, Sept. 5, 1828.

14. Buchanan to Thomas Elder, Feb. 13, 1827, Buchanan MSs., HSP.

15. Harrisburg *Argus*, July 12, 1828. On the tariff, see also: M. R. Eiselen, *Rise of Protectionism in Pennsylvania* (Philadelphia, 1921); Klein, *Pennsylvania Politics*, Chap. IX; and Robert V. Rimini, *Martin Van Buren and the Making of the Democratic Party* (New York, 1959), Chap. XII.

16. Amos Kendall to Henry Baldwin, July 15, 1827, Reynolds Collection, Meadville, Pa.

17. George Buchanan to brother James, July 20, 1827, Buchanan MSs., HSP.

18. J. R. Speer to Buchanan, Feb. 1, 1828, Buchanan MSs., HSP.

19. Buchanan's remarks of June 23, printed in Lancaster *Journal*, June 29, 1827.

20. Lancaster *Journal*, July 20, 1827.

21. Buchanan to Joseph Sharpe, Aug. 9, 1828, Buchanan-Swarr MSs., BF.

22. Lancaster *Journal*, Oct. 17, 1828.

23. *Ibid.*, Nov. 14, 1828.

24. Hugh Hamilton to Buchanan, Jan. 6, 1825, Buchanan MSs., HSP.

25. Buchanan to Thomas Kittera, Jan. 2, 1829, Dickinsoniana, DC.

26. Sam Cochran to Hannah Cochran, Sept. 10, 1828, Slaymaker MSs.; Simon Cameron to Buchanan, Feb. 4, 1829, Buchanan MSs., HSP. The Commencement Program of Dickinson College, Sept. 24, 1828, contains a note that the scheduled address by Buchanan had to be cancelled because of his illness.

27. Louis McLane to Van Buren, Feb. 19, 1829, Van Buren MSs., LC.

28. John Kerlin to W. M. Meredith, Feb. 12, 1829, Meredith MS., HSP; *Franklin Repository* (Chambersburg, Penna.), April 7, 1829.

29. James, *Jackson* (1938 ed.), p. 491.

30. Baldwin to Stephen Simpson, July 21, 1829, quoted in *Franklin Repository*, Dec. 27, 1831.

31. Buchanan to John McLean, June 11, 1829, McLean MSs., LC.

32. *Crawford Messenger* (Meadville, Penna.), April 16, 1829.

33. Buchanan to Barnard, Mar. 11, 1829, Dickinsoniana, DC.

34. Joel Sutherland to George Wolf, May 12, 1829, Wolf MSs., HSP.

35. George Barton to Buchanan, July 16, 1829, Buchanan MSs., HSP.

36. Buchanan to Barnard, Aug. 20, 1829, Dickinsoniana, DC.

37. Buchanan to George Wolf, Oct. 15, 1829, Buchanan MSs., HSP.

38. Group of letters, Nov., Dec., 1829, in Miscellaneous Collection, Office of Public Records, Harrisburg.

39. Klein, *Pennsylvania Politics*, p. 291.

40. *Crawford Messenger*, Nov. 26, 1829, quoting Carlisle *Herald*. The Lancaster papers printed nothing about the local fracas.

41. Buchanan to Wolf, Dec. 12, 1829, Miscellaneous Collection, Office of Public Records, Harrisburg.

42. Sutherland to Wolf, Dec. 20, 1829; Van Amringe to Wolf, Nov. 18, 1829; A. S. Hayes to Wolf, Dec. 9, 1829, Wolf MSs., HSP.

43. Samuel McKean to Benjamin Champneys, April 4 and 26, 1830, Miscellaneous Collection, Office of Public Records, Harrisburg.

44. I. D. Barnard to Buchanan, April 1, 1830, Buchanan MSs., HSP.

45. W. Stewart to Buchanan, June 19, 1830, Buchanan MSs., HSP.

46. H. A. Muhlenberg to Wolf, April 15, 1830; D. H. Miller to Wolf, April 23, 1830, Wolf MSs., HSP.

47. Wolf to S. D. Ingham, April 23, 1831, Miscellaneous Collection, Office of Public Records, Harrisburg.

48. Moore, *Works*, I, 421.

49. Hensel, *James Buchanan as a Lawyer*, p. 15.

50. Moore, *Works*, II, 67-73.

51. Hensel, *op. cit.*, p. 16.

52. C. F. Adams (ed.), *Memoirs of John Quincy Adams* (Philadelphia, 1874-1877), VIII, 306-307. Jan. 31, 1831.

53. Culver H. Smith, "Washington Press of the Jacksonian Era" (Ph.D. thesis, Duke University), pp. 245-246; Klein, *Pennsylvania Politics*, p. 299.

54. Klein, *op. cit.*, pp. 301-310.

55. George Wolf to S. D. Ingham, April 23, 1831, Miscellaneous Collection, Office of Public Records, Harrisburg.

56. Curtis, *Buchanan*, I, 110.

CHAPTER 6 (pp. 78-94)

1. J. H. Eaton to Buchanan, May 31, 1831, Curtis, *Buchanan*, I, 130.

2. Buchanan to Eaton, June 4, 1831, *ibid.*

3. Curtis, *Buchanan*, I, 130-134, prints the correspondence.

4. George Plitt to Buchanan, July 3, 1831, Buchanan MSs., Box I, LC.

5. *Ibid.* and *Crawford Messenger*, July 14, Aug. 18, 1831.

6. Buchanan to John Reynolds, Sept. 25, 1831, Reynolds MSs., FM; Buchanan to Jackson, Sept. 10, 1831, Buchanan MSs., HSP.

7. Buchanan to Jackson, Sept. 10, 1831, Buchanan MSs., HSP.

8. Elizabeth Speer Buchanan to Buchanan, Oct. 21, [1831], Buchanan Sr. MSs., BF.

9. George Wolf to S. D. Ingham, April 23, 1831, Miscellaneous Collection, Office of Public Records, Harrisburg.

10. Buchanan to Wolf, Jan. 31, 1832, Miscellaneous Collection, Office of Public Records, Harrisburg.

11. *Ibid.*

12. Edward Livingston to Buchanan, Feb. 24, 1832, Buchanan MSs., BF.

13. Livingston to Buchanan, Jan. 12, 1832, Moore, *Works*, II, 182.

14. Reynolds MSs., FM., has a series of letters, 1831-1834, dealing with Buchanan's personal finances and Reynolds's management of them.

15. Diary entry of Mar. 21, 1832, Moore, *Works*, II, 182.

16. Stephen Pleasanton to Buchanan, Mar. 30, 1832, Buchanan MSs., Box I, LC.

17. Receipt in Buchanan MSs., HSP.

18. Moore, *Works*, II, 384.

19. *Ibid.*, II, 184.

20. Rental contract, June 17, 1832, between Buchanan and Anna Michavlova, agent for Brockhauser. Document is in Buchanan's handwriting, in French. Buchanan MSs., BF.

21. The dates used by Buchanan in his correspondence from this point until his departure from Russia are according to the New Style Russian calendar. Most of his letters are endorsed (N.S.) to indicate the use of the Gregorian calendar system, 12 days ahead of the Julian calendar which was still used by many in Russia.

22. Buchanan to Livingston, June 12, 1832, Moore, *Works*, II, 194-195.

23. Buchanan to Reynolds, Aug. 6, 1832, Dickinsoniana, DC.

24. Moore, *Works*, II, 195.

25. *Ibid.*, II, 226.

26. Buchanan to Reynolds, Aug. 16, 1832, Reynolds MSs., FM.

27. Moore, *Works*, II, 282.

28. *Ibid.*, II, 288.

29. Reminiscences of J. Montgomery Forster, in the Mercersburg *Journal*. Clipping in Rankin Scrapbook, in possession of the Rev. E. J. Turner, Mercersburg.

30. Moore, *Works*, II, 232.

31. Buchanan to Reynolds, Aug. 16, 1832, Reynolds MSs., FM.

32. Moore, *Works*, II, 198, 199, 218, 265.

33. *Ibid.*, II, 244, 253-254.

34. *Ibid.*, II, 280-281.

35. *Ibid.*, II, 282-283.

36. Buchanan to James Humes, Oct. 13, 1832, Dickinsoniana, DC.

37. Moore, *Works*, II, 288.

38. Reminiscences of J. Montgomery Forster, *loc. cit.*

39. Moore, *Works*, II, 205.

40. *Ibid.*, II, 334.

41. *Ibid.*, II, 302.

42. *Ibid.*, II, 323.

43. *Ibid.*, II, 320.

44. *Ibid.*, II, 329.

45. *Ibid.*, II, 360-366, diary entries of June, 1833.

46. Buchanan to Harriet Henry, Aug. 3, 1832, Buchanan MSs., HSP.

47. Curtis, *Buchanan*, I, 210.

48. Buchanan to John Reynolds, July 3, 1833, Dickinsoniana, DC.

49. Buchanan to Reynolds, Jan. 2, Mar. 20, May 19, 1833, Reynolds MSs., FM.

50. Moore, *Works*, II, 381. For an interesting analysis of the mission, see Joseph O. Baylen, "James Buchanan's 'Calm of Despotism,'" *Pennsylvania Magazine of History and Biography*, LXXVII (July, 1953), 294-310; also Thomas P. Martin, "Initiation of James Buchanan as an American Diplomat—His Mission to Russia, 1832," *Junto Selections* (Pennsylvania Historical Junto, Washington, D. C., 1946), pp. 48-60. See also W. B. Hatcher, *Edward Livingston* (University, La., 1940), Chap. 15, and Francis Rawle, "Edward Livingston," in *American Secretaries of State and Their Diplomacy*, ed. by S. F. Bemis, vol. IV.

CHAPTER 7 (pp. 95-104)

1. August 18, 19, 20, 1833. Packet of endorsed travel folders and itemized bills, Buchanan MSs., BF; Buchanan to John Reynolds, Sept. 17, 1833, Reynolds MSs., FM.

2. Moore, *Works*, II, 387; Buchanan to John Reynolds, Sept. 17, 1833, Reynolds MSs., FM.

3. Moore, *Works*, II, 390.

4. *Ibid.*, II, 394.

5. *Ibid.*, II, 392, 393.

6. Buchanan to John Reynolds, Oct. 7, 1833, Reynolds MSs., FM.

7. Moore, *Works*, II, 267.

8. Lee Crippen, *Simon Cameron* (Oxford, Ohio, 1942), p. 21.

9. Cameron to Buchanan, Dec. 29, 1836, Crippen, *Cameron*, p. 21.

10. Curtis, *Buchanan*, I, 147; Buchanan to John Reynolds, May 19, 1833, Reynolds MSs., FM.

11. Buchanan to Campbell P. White, Jan. 2, 1833, Buchanan MSs., HSP.

12. Curtis, *Buchanan*, I, 152.

13. *Ibid.*, I, 184-185, 192.

14. Buchanan to John Reynolds, Mar. 20, 1833, Reynolds MSs., FM.

15. Buchanan to Reynolds, July 3, 1833, Dickinsoniana, DC.

16. Buchanan to John Reynolds, Jan. 21, May 19, 1833, Reynolds MSs., FM.

17. Buchanan to J. B. Sterigere, May 19, to G. Leiper, July 3, 1833, Curtis, *Buchanan*, I, 189, 206.

18. George Plitt to Buchanan, July 19, 1833, Buchanan MSs., Box I, LC.

19. Buchanan to Reynolds, Nov. 24, 1833, Reynolds MSs., FM.

20. Cameron to Buchanan, Dec. 4, 7, 1833, Crippen, *Cameron*, pp. 22-23.

21. Buchanan to Jackson, Jan. 18, 1834, Buchanan MSs., HSP.

22. Moore, *Works*, II, 397; III, 248.

23. *Ibid.*, II, 398.

24. Obituary notices of Esther Parker, Ruth Scrapbook, YCHS, p. 14.

25. Buchanan to Thomas Kittera, Oct. 9, 1834, Schoch MSs., BF.

26. Agreement of Mar. 10, 1835, in Buchanan's handwriting, Buchanan Mss., HSP.

27. Buchanan to Thomas Kittera, Oct. 9, 1834; Sept. 25, 1837, April 25, 1843, Schoch Mss., BF. Buchanan was on terms of intimacy with the whole Kittera family, from the grandmother (Ann Moore, nee Hopkins of Lancaster) to the grandchildren. Mary Kittera Snyder's sister, Elizabeth, married a close friend of Buchanan, James C. Van Dyke of Philadelphia, in this period. Buchanan regularly stayed at the Kittera or the Van Dyke home when on visits to Philadelphia. For more information on Mary Snyder, see William A. Russ, Jr., "Mary Kittera Snyder's struggle for an Income," in Snyder County Historical Society *Bulletin*, IV, #1 (1959), 1-27.

28. Buchanan to Jacob Kern, et al., Dec. 22, 1834, Curtis, *Buchanan*, I, 229, and Buchanan draft in Cadwalader Mss., HSP.

CHAPTER 8 (pp. 105-115)

1. J. Mitchell to Buchanan, Jan. 15, 1835; John Dickey to Buchanan, Jan. 9, 1835; Henry Buehler to Buchanan, Jan. 15, 1835, Buchanan Mss., HSP. Charles M. Snyder, "Pennsylvania Politics, 1833-1847," Ph.D. thesis, University of Pennsylvania, clearly explains the details of much that is summarized in this chapter. See p. 111 et seq. of the typescript. Though Snyder's work is published as *The Jacksonian Heritage* (Harrisburg, 1958), all my references are to the thesis which is more detailed.

2. Muhlenberg to Buchanan, March 24, 1835, Buchanan Mss., HSP.

3. Buchanan to Thomas Kittera, Mar. 28, 1835; Buchanan to George Wolf, Mar. 28, 1835, Buchanan Mss., BF.

4. Buchanan to Mahlon Dickerson, June 18, 1835, Dickinsoniana, DC.

5. Moore, *Works*, II, 443.

6. Buchanan to ?, Nov. 18, 1835, Dickinsoniana, DC.

7. Buchanan to Ovid Johnston, May 2, 1836, Dickinsoniana, DC; Moore, *Works*, III, 114 ff., quotes the speech.

8. Buchanan to Thomas Elder, Oct. 15, 1836, Buchanan Mss., HSP.

9. Buchanan to Van Buren, Nov. 18, 1836, Moore, *Works*, III, 128-129.

10. Snyder, "Pennsylvania Politics," pp. 154-156.

11. Buchanan to Thomas Elder, Nov. 7, 1836, Buchanan Mss., HSP.

12. Moore, *Works*, III, 147-154.

13. Jan. 12 and 14, 1837, *ibid.*, III, 166-167.

14. Feb. 19, 1837, *ibid.*, III, 220.

15. Feb. 28, 1837, *ibid.*, III, 247.

16. *Ibid.*, III, 213-214.

17. *Ibid.*, III, 220.

18. *Ibid.*, III, 249.

19. J. Fred Rippy, *Joel Poinsett* (Durham, N. C., 1935), p. 168.

CHAPTER 9 (pp. 116-128)

1. Snyder, "Pennsylvania Politics," p. 167.

2. John McCahen to Buchanan, April 7, 1837, Buchanan MSs., HSP.

3. Buchanan to John McCahen, April 1, 1837, Buchanan MSs., HSP.

4. Peter Wager to Buchanan, March 30, 1837, Buchanan MSs., HSP.

5. Bray Hammond, *Banks and Politics in America* (Princeton, 1957), Chap. 12.

6. Moore, *Works*, III, 273.

7. Wager to Buchanan, March 30, 1837, Buchanan MSs., HSP.

8. John Miles to Buchanan, April 7, 1837, Buchanan MSs., HSP.

9. Benjamin Parker to Buchanan, April 4, 1837, Buchanan MSs., HSP.

10. Charles Miner to Buchanan, April 23, 1837, Buchanan MSs., HSP.

11. Buchanan to F. P. Blair, April 22, 1837, Buchanan MSs., HSP.

12. Moore, *Works*, III, 250.

13. Buchanan to James M. Porter, June 9, 1837, Buchanan MSs., HSP.

14. C. J. Ingersoll to Buchanan, June 6, 1837, Buchanan MSs., HSP.

15. Buchanan to F. P. Blair, June 3, 1837, Buchanan MSs., HSP.

16. Moore, *Works*, III, 265; Kittera to Buchanan, May 15, 1837, Buchanan MSs., HSP.

17. Buchanan to James M. Porter, June 9, 1837, Buchanan MSs., HSP.

18. William R. King to Buchanan, April 2, 1837, Buchanan MSs., HSP.

19. Buchanan MSs., HSP.

20. Samuel Parke to Buchanan, April 4, 1837, Buchanan MSs., HSP.

21. Buchanan to Van Buren, June 5, 1837, Moore, *Works*, III, 252-254.

22. Jackson to Buchanan, Dec. 26, 1837, Curtis, *Buchanan*, I, 421, and Moore, *Works*, III, 264-314.

23. George Plitt to Buchanan, Oct. 13, 1837, Buchanan MSs., HSP.

24. George Plitt to Buchanan, Nov. 20, 1837, Buchanan MSs., HSP.

25. J. W. Forney to Buchanan, Feb. 27, 1838, Buchanan MSs., HSP.

26. Moore, *Works*, III, 380-385.

27. William B. Fordney to Buchanan, Jan. 22, 1838, Buchanan MSs., HSP.

28. Moore, *Works*, III, 451.

29. Buchanan to Harriet Henry, Oct. 26, 1839, Buchanan MSs., HSP.

30. Buchanan to Harriet Henry, Nov. 4, 1838 (misdated 1837), Buchanan MSs., HSP.

31. Buchanan to Dr. C. M. Yates, Nov. 21, 1838, Buchanan MSs., HSP.

32. Buchanan to Edward Y. Buchanan, Sept. 1, 1832, Buchanan MSs., HSP.

33. Same to same, Dec. 10, 1838, Cadwalader MSs., HSP.

34. Buchanan to Maria Yates, Jan. 3, 1831, Nichols photostats.

35. Same to same, Dec. 26, 1834, Nichols photostats.

36. Buchanan to Dr. C. M. Yates, Oct. 25 and 30, 1840, Nichols photostats.

CHAPTER 10 (pp. 129-141)

1. Buchanan to John McClintock, Mar. 11, 1839; Buchanan to S. W. Randall, Sept. 16, 1839, Buchanan Mss., HSP; Snyder, "Pennsylvania Politics," pp. 246, 261-262.

2. Buchanan to Dr. C. M. Yates, undated [summer, 1839], Nichols photostats.

3. Ibid.

4. Moore, Works, IV, 121.

5. J. W. Forney to Buchanan, Jan. 16, 1839, Buchanan Mss., HSP.

6. Buchanan to S. W. Randall, Sept. 16, 1839, Buchanan Mss., HSP.

7. Van Buren to Buchanan, Dec. 27, 1839, Moore, Works, IV, 124.

8. J. W. Forney to Buchanan, Feb. 5, 1840, Buchanan Mss., HSP.

9. Buchanan to D. R. Porter, Feb. 24, 1840, Gratz Collection, HSP.

10. Curtis, Buchanan, I, 400.

11. Forney to Buchanan, Mar. 10, 1840, Buchanan Mss., HSP.

12. Same to same, April 11, 1840, Buchanan Mss., HSP.

13. Same to same, Dec. 2, 1829, Buchanan Mss., HSP.

14. Moore, Works, IV, 210.

15. David Lynch to Buchanan, Dec. 3, 1840, Lynch Mss., LCHS.

16. Snyder, "Pennsylvania Politics," pp. 264-266.

17. Buchanan to Benjamin Mifflin, Aug. 20, 1840, Moore, Works, IV, 321.

18. R. M. Barr to Buchanan, June 19, 27, 28, 1840, Buchanan Mss., HSP.

19. Forney to Buchanan, July 13, 1840, Buchanan Mss., HSP.

20. Same to same, April 16, 1840, Buchanan Mss., HSP.

21. Moore, Works, IV, 319, 324.

22. Ibid., IV, 322.

23. J. W. Forney, Anecdotes of Public Men (New York, 1873), p. 182.

24. W. D. Burnham, Presidential Ballots, 1836-1892 (Baltimore, 1955), pp. 704-720.

25. Nov. 18, 1840, Moore, Works, IV, 325.

26. Buchanan to Dr. Edward C. Gazzam, Dec. 11, 1840, Dickinsoniana, DC.

27. Buchanan to Edward Y. Buchanan, Jan. 19, 1841, Cadwalader Mss., HSP.

28. Edward Stanwood, A History of the Presidency (New York, 1898), p. 195, note 1.

29. Buchanan to D. R. Porter, Feb. 9, 1841, Moore, Works, IV, 380.

30. David Lynch to ?, June, 1841, Lynch Mss., LCHS.

31. Jonathan M. Foltz to Buchanan, Aug. 17, 1841, Buchanan-Swarr Mss., Section G, BF.

32. Buchanan to Edward C. Gazzam, Sept. 14, 1841, Dickinsoniana, DC.

33. Buchanan to Francis R. Shunk, May 6, 1841, Moore, Works, IV, 405.

34. J. W. Forney to Buchanan, June 4, 1841, Buchanan Mss., HSP.

35. Snyder, "Pennsylvania Politics," p. 296.

36. David Lynch to Buchanan, Nov. 21, 1841 and Jan. 8, 1842, Lynch Mss., LCHS.

37. Forney to Buchanan, June 16, 1841, Buchanan Mss., HSP.

38. Ibid.

39. David Lynch to Buchanan, Dec. 9, 1841, Lynch Mss., LCHS.

40. Forney to Buchanan, Dec. 10, 1841, Buchanan Mss., HSP.

41. April 16, 1840, Buchanan MSs., HSP.
42. Buchanan to William Flynn, Sept. 5, 1841, Moore, *Works*, V, 72.
43. Buchanan to John Reynolds, Feb. 22, 1841, Dickinsoniana, DC.

CHAPTER 11 (pp. 142-150)

1. Moore, *Works*, V, 117-119.
2. *Ibid.*, II, 421 ff.
3. *Ibid.*, III, 168-194.
4. Buchanan to John Reynolds, Dec. 19, 1844, Reynolds MSs., FM.
5. Moore, *Works*, III, 239-246, 259-264; V, 30.
6. J. M. Callahan, *American Policy in Canadian Relations* (New York, 1937), pp. 148-149, 188.
7. Moore, *Works*, V, 363-364, 368, 383; Curtis, *Buchanan*, I, 505.
8. Moore, *Works*, III, 359.
9. *Ibid.*, III, 61-62.
10. *Ibid.*, III, 64.
11. *Ibid.*, V, 477.
12. *Ibid.*, VI, 15-17.
13. *Ibid.*, III, 86.
14. For the debate, see Moore, *Works*, III, 1, 8, 24, 205, 328; *Congressional Globe*, 24th Congress, 1st session, 78, 85, 95, 182-183, 221-222.
15. Moore, *Works*, III, 14-16.
16. *Ibid.*, III, 18, and *Congressional Globe*, 24th Congress, 1st session, 222.
17. Jeremiah Cooper to Buchanan, Feb. 26, 1838, Buchanan MSs., HSP.
18. P. W. Pell to Buchanan, Jan. 9, 1838, Buchanan MSs., HSP.
19. King to Buchanan, Dec. 20, 1837, Cadwalader MSs., HSP.
20. Elder to Buchanan, Dec. 23, 1837, Buchanan MSs., HSP.
21. Buchanan to Jonas McClintock, Jan. 12, 1838, Buchanan MSs., HSP.
22. *Congressional Globe*, 25th Congress, 2nd session, 55.
23. Moore, *Works*, III, 343.
24. *Ibid.*, III, 344-345.
25. *Ibid.*, III, 27.

CHAPTER 12 (pp. 151-162)

1. Moore, *Works*, IV, 264; Snyder, "Pennsylvania Politics," pp. 294-295.
2. Forney to Buchanan, Dec. 16, 1841, Buchanan MSs., HSP.
3. Buchanan to Dr. Jonathan Foltz, Dec. 14, 1842, Buchanan MSs., HSP.

4. Brewster to Buchanan, Nov. 19, 1843, Buchanan MSs., HSP.

5. David Lynch to Buchanan, April 8, 1842, Lynch MSs., LCHS; Buchanan-Swarr MSs., BF, contains these political notebooks.

6. Forney to Buchanan, Dec. 10, 1841, Jan. 2, 1842, Buchanan MSs., HSP.

7. Snyder, "Pennsylvania Politics," p. 303; Forney to Buchanan, Feb. 7 and Mar. 4, 1842, Buchanan MSs., HSP.

8. Porter to Buchanan, Feb. 20, 1842, Buchanan MSs., HSP.

9. Buchanan to T. L. Hamer, Nov. 29, 1842, Dickinsoniana, DC.

10. Forney to Buchanan, Dec. 5, 1842, Buchanan MSs., HSP.

11. Buchanan to T. L. Hamer, Nov. 29, 1842, Dickinsoniana, DC.

12. Forney to Buchanan, Dec. 5, 1842, Buchanan MSs., HSP.

13. Note, dated Jan. 10, 1843, in Buchanan's County Index book, Buchanan-Swarr MSs., BF, describes these events. Also Forney to Buchanan, Jan. 10, 1843, Buchanan MSs., HSP.

14. Forney to Buchanan, Jan. 13, 1843, Buchanan MSs., HSP.

15. Forney to Buchanan, Dec. 15, 1840, Buchanan MSs., HSP.

16. Buchanan to Benjamin Champneys, Jan. 13, 1843; Forney to Buchanan, Jan. 25, 1843, Buchanan MSs., HSP; Buchanan to Reah Frazer, Feb. 18, 1843, Dickinsoniana, DC.

17. Buchanan to George L. Leiper, July 22, 1843; Buchanan to George Plitt, Mar. 9, 1843, Buchanan MSs., HSP.

18. Buchanan to Dr. Jonathan Foltz, April 21, 1843, Foltz MSs.

19. A. C. Ramsey to Buchanan, Apr. 17, 1843, Buchanan MSs., Box I, LC; Buchanan to Mrs. Heister, June 16, 1843, collection of the late C. H. Martin, Lancaster, Penna.

20. Buchanan to Harriet Lane, July 25, 1843, Buchanan MSs., Box I, LC.

21. List of purchases by Buchanan at sheriff's sale of property of H. Y. Slaymaker in York County, Nov. 3, 4, 1842, Buchanan MSs., HSP.

22. Mar. 18, 1842, draft in Buchanan's handwriting, Buchanan MSs., HSP.

23. Curtis, *Buchanan*, I, 519.

24. David Lynch to Buchanan, Dec. 2, 1842, Lynch MSs., LCHS.

25. Buchanan to John M. Read, Dec. 5, 1843, Dickinsoniana, DC.

26. Snyder, "Pennsylvania Politics," pp. 329-330.

27. Moore, *Works*, V, 437-439.

28. Charles M. Wiltse, *John C. Calhoun, Sectionalist* (Indianapolis, 1951), pp. 158-171.

29. Snyder, "Pennsylvania Politics," p. 310; Henry Welsh to Buchanan, May 20, 1844, Buchanan MSs., HSP.

30. Buchanan to Mr. J. J. Roosevelt, May 13, 1844, Moore, *Works*, VI, 1-3.

31. Moore, *Works*, VI, 4.

32. *Ibid.*, VI, 3.

33. *Niles National Register*, LXVI, 259.

34. Moore, *Works*, VI, 5-44.

35. Cameron to Buchanan, July 2, 1844, Buchanan MSs., HSP.

36. Moore, *Works*, VI, 61.

37. Buchanan to Shunk, Aug. 14, 15, 30, 1844; Shunk to Buchanan, Aug. 17, 1844; Cameron to Buchanan, Sept. 5, 1844, Buchanan MSs., HSP.

38. Moore, *Works*, VI, 70.

39. Buchanan to ?, Sept. 18, 1844, Dickinsoniana, DC.

40. Moore, *Works*, VI, 71.

CHAPTER 13 (pp. 163-174)

1. Buchanan to Polk, Nov. 4, 1844, Moore, *Works*, VI, 72.

2. Penna. Electors to Polk, Dec. 5, 1844, Cadwalader MSs., HSP.

3. Franklin P. Hillman, "The Diplomatic Career of James Buchanan," The George Washington Univ. Ph.D. thesis, 1953, typescript, p. 77.

4. Catron to Buchanan, Jan. 23, 1845, Moore, *Works*, VI, 82.

5. Buchanan to Shunk, Dec. 18, 1844, Moore, *Works*, VI, 76.

6. Cameron to Buchanan, Dec. 7, 1844, Buchanan MSs., Box I, LC; B. F. Brewster to Buchanan, Jan. 19, 1845, Buchanan MSs., HSP.

7. Polk to Buchanan, Feb. 17, 1845, Moore, *Works*, VI, 110.

8. Buchanan to Polk, Feb. 18, 1845, Moore, *Works*, VI, 111-112.

9. Moore, *Works*, VI, 108-109.

10. Mrs. S. Pleasanton to Buchanan, Feb. 1845, Buchanan MSs., LC; Ben Perley Poore, *Perley's Reminiscences* (Philadelphia, 1886), I, 332; Wharton, *Social Life*, pp. 303-304. The Lancaster *Daily Intelligencer*, Feb. 1, 1935, describes a Buchanan residence at 918 E. Street, N.W. in 1845.

11. Moore, *Works*, VI, 411-412, gives a full description of the organization of the State Department which shows that in the previous twenty-eight years the staff had increased 35 per cent; the foreign missions of the U. S., 236 per cent; and the consulates, 153 per cent. An even greater increase in Department functions had taken place in the Home Bureau. See also Graham H. Stuart, *The Department of State* (New York, 1949), Chap. 9.

12. Buchanan to Caleb Cushing, April 26, 1845, Dickinsoniana, DC.

13. Cameron to Buchanan, Dec. 7, 1844, Buchanan MSs., Box I, LC.

14. Cameron to Col. Schoch, Feb. 27, 1845, Cameron item, LCHS.

15. Forney to Morton McMichael, Mar. 14, 1845, Forney MSs., LC; the eruption over the election of Cameron is described in detail in Snyder, "Pennsylvania Politics," pp. 347 ff., and Crippen, *Cameron*, pp. 58 ff.

16. Moore, *Works*, VI, 136-138.

17. Snyder, *op. cit.*, p. 352.

18. Forney to Buchanan, Mar. 21, 23, 1845, Buchanan MSs., HSP.

19. Series of letters, March through October, 1845, Forney to Buchanan, in Forney Box, Buchanan MSs., HSP.

20. Brewster to Buchanan, May 6, July 1, Nov. 12, 1845, Buchanan MSs., HSP.

21. Buchanan-Swarr MSs., BF.

22. Forney to Buchanan, June 28, 1845, Buchanan MSs., HSP.

23. Cameron to Buchanan, Sept. 17, 1845, Buchanan MSs., Box I, LC.

24. Milo M. Quaife (ed.), *Diary of James K. Polk* (Chicago, 1910), I, 39, 45-47. Hereafter cited as Polk, *Diary*.

25. *Ibid.*, I, 138.

26. Brewster to Buchanan, Nov. 7, 1845, Buchanan MSs., HSP.

27. Forney to Buchanan, Oct. 30, 1845, Buchanan MSs., HSP.

28. Polk, *Diary*, I, 137.

29. Snyder, "Pennsylvania Politics," pp. 376-377; Crippen, *Cameron*, pp. 79-81; Cameron to Buchanan, Dec. 25, 1845, Buchanan MSs., Box I, LC.

30. Polk, *Diary*, I, 144-146.

31. Snyder, *op. cit.*, pp. 349-352, notes that the Democrats were Benton of Missouri, Sevier and Ashley of Arkansas, and Yulee and Westcott of Florida. Allan Nevins's short edition of Polk's *Diary* (New York, 1929), p. 44, note 6, states that Woodward was also opposed by two Virginia Senators who hoped to place Buchanan in the Supreme Court and persuade Polk to appoint Virginia's Andrew Stevenson Secretary of State.

32. Polk, *Diary*, I, 189.

33. Buchanan to E. E. Lester, Gratz Collection, HSP.

34. Boston *Journal*, Jan. 26, 1883, "Old Time Washington Gayeties;" Wharton, *Social Life*, p. 278.

35. Accounts of George Plitt, manager of the affair, Jan. 23, 1846, Buchanan MSs., HSP.

36. Crippen, *Cameron*, p. 82.

37. Polk, *Diary*, II, 27.

38. *Niles National Register*, Aug. 1, 1845, p. 345.

39. Buchanan to Polk, June 28, 1846, Cadwalader MSs., HSP.

40. James to Edward Y. Buchanan, July 13, 1846, Cadwalader MSs., HSP.

41. Forney to Buchanan, June 21, 1846, Buchanan MSs., HSP.

42. Roy F. Nichols (ed.), "Mystery of the Dallas Papers," *Pennsylvania Magazine of History & Biography*, LXXIII (1949), 384-385.

43. Forney to Buchanan, July 9, 1846, Buchanan MSs., HSP.

44. Nichols, "Mystery of the Dallas Papers," *op. cit.*, 385-386.

45. *Niles National Register*, Aug. 29, 1849, p. 405.

46. Buchanan to Forney, July 29, 1846, Moore, *Works*, VII, 43-45.

47. Buchanan to Forney, Aug. 1, 1846, *Ibid.*, VII, 46-47.

48. Polk, *Diary*, II, 60.

CHAPTER 14 (pp. 175-193)

1. Norman A. Graebner, *Empire on the Pacific* (New York, 1955), emphasizes the specific commercial objectives of the Manifest Destiny policy.

2. Moore, *Works*, VI, 10-15.

3. *Ibid.*, VI, 165.

4. *Ibid.*, VI, 131.

5. *Ibid.*, VI, 152, 159.

6. *Ibid.*, VI, 165.

7. *Ibid.*, VI, 174.

8. Edwin A. Miles, "Fifty-four Forty or Fight—an American Political Legend," *Miss. Valley Hist. Rev.*, XLIV (Sept., 1957), dates this slogan after Polk's election.

9. Wilbur D. Jones and J. C. Vinson, "British Preparedness and the Oregon Settle-ment," *Pacific Hist. Rev.*, XXII (Nov., 1953), 355; Lady Frances Balfour, *Life of George, Fourth Earl of Aberdeen, K. G., K. T.* (London, 1913), II, 133.

10. Moore, *Works*, VI, 191.

11. Jones and Vinson, *op. cit.*, 357.

12. Moore, *Works*, VI, 220.

13. Polk, *Diary*, I, 2-5, 9-12, 62-65.

14. *Ibid.*, I, 2-5.

15. M. A. DeWolfe Howe (ed.), *Life and Letters of George Bancroft* (New York, 1908), I, 280-281.

16. Polk, *Diary*, I, 62-65.

17. Jones and Vinson, *op. cit.*, 360.

18. Polk, *Diary*, I, 77-82.

19. Moore, *Works*, VI, 341.

20. Jan. 3, 1846. Jones and Vinson, *op. cit.*, 360.

21. *Ibid.*, 361-363; Charles S. Parker (ed.), *Sir Robert Peel*, III, 324.

22. Richard Rush to Buchanan, Oct. 7, 1846, Curtis, *Buchanan*, I, 604.

23. Polk, *Diary*, I, 235, 453-454.

24. Franklin P. Hillman, "Diplomatic Career of James Buchanan," p. 153. Typescript Ph.D. thesis, The George Washington University, 1953.

25. Lyon G. Tyler, *Letters and Times of the Tylers* (Richmond, 1884-1886), III, 175-177.

26. Hillman, *op. cit.*, p. 156.

27. Buchanan to the Hon. F. W. Pickens, June 6, 1845, Dickinsoniana, DC.

28. Polk to Buchanan, Aug. 7, 1845, Curtis, *Buchanan*, I, 589.

29. Bancroft to Buchanan, Aug. 7, 1845, *ibid.*, I, 590.

30. Buchanan to Slidell, Instructions #1, Nov. 10, 1845, Moore, *Works*, VI, 295.

31. *Ibid.*, VI, 296-305.

32. Buchanan to Slidell, Instructions #5, Jan. 20, 1846, *ibid.*, VI, 361.

33. Jan. 28, 1846, *ibid.*, VI, 364.

34. Mar. 12, 1846, *ibid.*, VI, 403.

35. Polk, *Diary*, I, 226-230.

36. Feb. 17, 1846, Cadwalader MSs., HSP.

37. Moore, *Works*, VI, 403.

38. Polk, *Diary*, I, 384-385.

39. From Dr. J. M. Foltz, interpreter for Taylor; series of letters, Buchanan-Swarr MSs., BF.

40. May 14, 1846, Moore, *Works*, VI, 481-485.

41. Polk, *Diary*, I, 397-399.

42. *Ibid.*, II, 254-257.

43. *Ibid.*, I, 496; II, 15-16, 254-257.

44. Moore, *Works*, VII, 66.

45. Sept. 26, 1846, *ibid.*, VII, 88.

46. Polk, *Diary*, II, 229, 234, 240, 432. For Buchanan's original draft, *ibid.*, II, 471-475; for the final instructions, *Senate Ex. Doc.* #52, 30th Congress, 1st session, 81-89.

47. J. G. Van Deusen, *The Jacksonian Era* (New York, 1959), pp. 237-238.

48. Buchanan to Trist, June 2, 1847, Cadwalader MSs., HSP.

49. Buchanan to Gen. James Shields, April 25, 1847, Moore, *Works*, VII, 286-287.

50. July 19, 1847, Instructions #2, *ibid.*, VII, 368.

51. Polk, *Diary*, III, 163-164.

52. *Ibid.*, III, 225-229.

53. *Ibid.*, III, 333-334, 348-350, 400-410, 414.

54. W. E. Dodd, "The West and the War with Mexico," Illinois State Hist. *Transactions*, 1912, p. 23; E. G. Bourne, "The Proposed American Absorption of Mexico," Amer. Hist. Assoc. *Annual Report*, 1899, p. 164.

55. Howe, *Life and Letters of George Bancroft*, II, 23-24.

56. Foltz to Buchanan, May 12, 1848, Buchanan-Swarr MSs., BF.

57. Hillman, "Diplomatic Career of James Buchanan," pp. 198-200; Polk, *Diary*, III, 300-301.

58. Moore, *Works*, VIII, 29.

59. New York *Herald*, May 3, 1848, prints a "Statistical Table of the Leaks of the U. S. Senate."

60. Frederick B. Marbut, "Washington Staff Correspondents before the Civil War." Typescript Ph.D. thesis, Harvard University, 1950, devotes a chapter to the Nugent episode.

61. Buchanan to John Clayton, April 14 and 17, 1849, Moore, *Works*, VIII, 360-361.

62. Buchanan to Ten Eyck, Aug. 28, 1848, *ibid.*, VIII, 181-190.

63. *Ibid.*, VI, 411-422; VII, 154-166.

64. Polk, *Diary*, III, 66, 97-99; IV, 355.

65. Foltz to Buchanan, Nov. 23, 1847, Dec. 12, 1849, and a series of letters, Foltz to Buchanan and Buchanan's executors, 1861-1875, especially March 8 and April 15, 1861, and Buchanan to William B. Reed, Mar. 21, 1861, Buchanan-Swarr MSs., BF.

66. Buchanan to Reynolds, Nov. 12, 1847, Reynolds MSs., FM.

67. Buchanan to Gen. James Tallmadge, Jan. 5, 1846, Dickinsoniana, DC.

68. Buchanan to Plumer, Mar. 19, 1848, Buchanan MSs., HSP.

69. Buchanan to A. J. Donelson, Donelson MSs., LC.

70. Buchanan to Dr. Foltz, April 18, 1849, Buchanan MSs., HSP. Charles A. McCoy, *Polk and the Presidency* (Austin, Texas, 1960), gives a revealing analysis of the relations of Buchanan and Polk in Chap. 4.

CHAPTER 15 (pp. 194-205)

1. Poore, *Reminiscences*, I, 332.

2. Buchanan to Jones, Mar. 30, 1847, Cadwalader MSs., HSP.

3. Buchanan to H. D. Foster, Nov. 19, 1846, Moore, *Works*, VII, 117-118.

4. Forney to Buchanan, Nov. 11, 1846, Buchanan MSs., HSP.

5. Forney to Buchanan, Mar. 7, 30, 1847, Buchanan MSs., HSP.

6. B. F. Brewster to Buchanan, Apr. 11, 1847, Buchanan MSs., HSP.

7. Forney to Buchanan, June 29, 1847, Buchanan MSs., HSP.

8. Lynch to Buchanan, June 15, 1847, Lynch MSs., LCHS.

9. Forney to Buchanan, May 4, 1847, Buchanan MSs., HSP.

10. Many letters and Buchanan's memorandum on the subject are in the Forney Box and the Buchanan letter section of the Buchanan MSs., HSP, summer of 1847.

11. Forney to Buchanan, Sept. 2, 3, 8, 1847, Buchanan MSs., HSP.

12. Forney to Buchanan, Oct. 15, 1847, Buchanan MSs., HSP.

13. Forney to Buchanan, Nov. 8, Dec. 2, 1847, Buchanan MSs., HSP.

14. Plitt to Buchanan, Nov. 23, 1847, Buchanan MSs., Box II, LC; Foltz to Buchanan, Dec. ?, 1847, Buchanan-Swarr MSs., BF.

15. Forney to Buchanan, Nov. 9, 1847, Buchanan MSs., HSP.

16. Plitt to Buchanan, Dec. 9, 1847, Buchanan MSs., Box II, LC.

17. Circular of the Philadelphia Buchanan Committee, Jan. 11, 1848, HSP.; Forney to Buchanan, Jan. 7, 1848, Buchanan MSs., HSP.

18. Forney to Buchanan, Nov. 26, 1847, Buchanan MSs., HSP.

19. Buchanan to Forney, Dec. 10; Forney to Buchanan, Dec. 10, 11, 1847, Buchanan MSs., HSP, and memorandum of Buchanan to James B. Lane, April 15, 1848, E. E. Lane MSs.

20. Plitt to Buchanan, Mar. 4, 1848, Buchanan MSs., Box II, LC; Forney to Buchanan, Mar. 7, 12, 1848, Buchanan MSs., HSP.

21. Aug. 25, 1847, Moore, *Works*, VII, 385-387.

22. Cass to Daniel Sturgeon, Oct. 27, 1847, Ruth Scrapbook, YCHS.

23. Forney to Buchanan, Sept. 1, 1846, Mar. 26, Sept. 17, 1848, Buchanan MSs., HSP; Buchanan to Polk, Sept. 5, 10, 1846, Cadwalader MSs., HSP; Plitt to Buchanan, June 19, Sept. 5, 1847, Buchanan MSs., LC; Buchanan to John Reynolds, June 21, 1847, Reynolds MSs., FM.

24. Buchanan to Miss Lane, Aug. 2, 1848, Moore, *Works*, VIII, 150.

25. Moore, *Works*, VI, 400-402, 433-434, 487. Plitt used only about $400 of the $2,500.

26. Application Book in Buchanan-Swarr MSs., BF, lists all those attending and declining the dinners.

27. Buchanan received reports of the Baltimore Convention from Plitt, May 12, Cameron, May 22, 23, 24, Buchanan MSs., Box II, LC; Foltz, May 19, Buchanan-Swarr MSs., BF; Forney, May 21, 23; Robert Tyler, July 13, Buchanan MSs., HSP.

28. Plitt to Buchanan, May 28, 1848, Buchanan MSs., Box II, LC.

29. Cameron to Buchanan, July 7, Plitt to Buchanan, July 11, 1848, Buchanan MSs., Box II, LC.

30. Buchanan to A. H. Reeder, July 22, 1848, privately owned, Richmond Myers.

31. Lynch to Buchanan, Sept. 21, 1849, Lynch MSs., LCHS.

CHAPTER 16 (pp. 206-220)

1. Philip S. Klein, *Story of Wheatland* (Lancaster, 1936), pp. 19-25; Application Book, Buchanan-Swarr MSs., BF; memorandum of Mar. 28, 1851, Buchanan MSs., HSP; Buchanan to John Cadwalader, Dec. 4, 1851, Dec. 20, 1852, Cadwalader MSs., HSP.

2. Buchanan to Harriet Lane, Dec. 21, 1844, Oct. 14, 1845, Taylor MSs.; Mary E. Merritt to James B. Lane, Oct. 15, 1845, E. E. Lane MSs.

3. Moore, *Works*, VII, 25, 278.

4. Buchanan to Harriet Lane, July 8, 1848, Buchanan MSs., HSP. Also numerous family letters in Taylor MSs. and E. E. Lane MSs.

5. Moore, *Works*, VII, 357-360.

6. J. B. Henry to Buchanan, Nov. 6, 1843, Buchanan MSs., Box I, LC; Buchanan to Harriet Lane, July 3, 1846, Moore, *Works*, VII, 26; Buchanan to Cadwalader, July 16, 1852, Cadwalader MSs., HSP.

7. Philadelphia *Press*, Jan. 24, 1860.

8. Curtis, *Buchanan*, II, 16; Plitt to Buchanan, Jan. 10, 1847, Buchanan MSs., Box II, LC.

9. Buchanan to Cobb, June 12, Nov. 10, 1849, Cobb MSs., UG; Buchanan to Foltz, Dec. ?, 1849, Forney to Buchanan, Dec. 13, 1849, Buchanan MSs., HSP.

10. To W. R. King, May 13, 1850, Moore, *Works*, VIII, 383; Buchanan to Foote, May 31, 1850, *ibid.*, VIII, 385-388; and to Jefferson Davis, Mar. 16, 1850, *ibid.*, VIII, 372-373.

11. Foltz, *Surgeon of the Seas*, p. 140.

12. Buchanan to J. A. Parker, Feb. 3, 1862, Moore, *Works*, XI, 249.

13. Buchanan to J. Glancy Jones, Mar. 8, 1850, Cadwalader MSs., HSP.

14. Buchanan to J. M. Read, Aug. 18, 1849, Dickinsoniana, DC.

15. Letter to a Union meeting, Nov. 19, 1850, Moore, *Works*, VIII, 390-404.

16. Buchanan to Robert Tyler, Dec. 26, 1850, de Coppet Collection, Princeton University Library.

17. Roy F. Nichols, *The Democratic Machine, 1850-1854* (New York, 1923), Chap. 4; Crippen, *Cameron*, pp. 118-128; Moore, *Works*, VIII, 369-376, 416-417; Buchanan to Welsh, Aug. 24, 1850, Buchanan MSs., YCHS; Buchanan to Welsh, Apr. 22, 1851, to John Hastings, Mar. 18, 1851, to ?, Aug. 28, 1851, Dickinsoniana, DC.

18. Buchanan to ?, Jan. 22, 1850, Ruth Scrapbook, p. 71, YCHS.

19. Buchanan to William Hopkins, July 14, Nov. 13, 1851, private, Craig Wylie; R. W. Nash, "The Christiana Riot," *LCHS Journal*, LXV (Spring, 1961), 66-91.

20. Buchanan to Glancy Jones, Sept. ?, 1851, Cadwalader MSs., HSP.

21. New York *Tribune*, Feb. 6, 1852.

22. Buchanan-Swarr MSs., BF.

23. Buchanan to William Hopkins, Nov. 13, 1851, private, Craig Wylie.

24. Buchanan to Cave Johnson, Dec. 22, 1851, Moore, *Works*, VIII, 428-430.

25. Nichols, *Democratic Machine*, Chap. 4.

26. Foltz to Buchanan, Mar. 25, 1851, Buchanan-Swarr MSs., BF.

27. Lynch to Buchanan, April 6, 21, 1851, Lynch MSs., LCHS.

28. Buchanan to David R. Porter, June 4, 1852, Moore, *Works*, VIII, 451-452.

29. Nichols, *Democratic Machine*, Chap. 9; Ivor D. Spencer, *The Victor and the Spoils, A Life of William L. Marcy* (Providence, R. I., 1959), Chap. 16.

30. Lynch to Buchanan, June 11, 1852, Lynch MSs., LCHS.

31. Buchanan to Robert Tyler, June 8, 1852, Dickinsoniana, DC.

CHAPTER 17 (pp. 221-233)

1. Foltz to Buchanan, Sept. 1, 1852, Buchanan-Swarr MSs., BF.

2. Lancaster *Intelligencer*, Aug. 31, Sept. 7, 1852.

3. Speech of Oct. 7, 1852, Moore, *Works*, VIII, 460-491; Plitt to Buchanan, Oct. 20, 1852, Buchanan MSs., Box III, LC.

4. Pierce to Buchanan, Dec. 7, 1852, Buchanan to Pierce, Dec. 11, 1852, Moore, *Works*, VIII, 492-499.

5. Buchanan to Forney, Dec. 15, 1852, Ruth Scrapbook, YCHS.

6. Buchanan to Watterson, Nov. 18, 1852, Moore, *Works*, VIII, 491-492.

7. Buchanan to Tyler, April 1, 1853, Dickinsoniana, DC.

8. Buchanan Memorandum of July 12, 1853, Moore, *Works*, IX, 12-25; Roy F. Nichols, *Franklin Pierce, Young Hickory of the Granite Hills* (2nd ed., Philadelphia, 1958), pp. 256-257; Spencer, *Marcy*, pp. 229-230.

9. Moore, *Works*, IX, 17.

10. Buchanan to Pierce, June 29, 1853, Moore, *Works*, IX, 7-8.

11. Marcy to Everett, July 12, 1853, Spencer, *Marcy*, p. 248.

12. Plitt to Buchanan, July 6, 1853, Buchanan MSs., Box III, LC.

13. Moore, *Works*, IX, 1-25, contains the pertinent letters.

14. H. A. Wise to R. M. T. Hunter, Apr. 16, 1853, in "Correspondence of R. M. T. Hunter," Amer. Hist. Assoc. *Annual Report*, 1916, II, 156; Forney to Buchanan, July 16, 1853, Buchanan MSs., HSP; A. Swanberg, *Sickles the Incredible* (New York, 1956), pp. 89-91.

15. Power of Attorney in Franklin County Deed Book, XXVI, 345; accounts in Buchanan MSs., HSP; bank books and notes on finances in Buchanan-Swarr MSs., BF; Buchanan to Lane and Reynolds, July 30, Aug. 22, 1853, Dickinsoniana, DC.

16. Buchanan to Miss Lane, Sept. 30, Nov. 1, 1853; to Marcy, June 8, 1855, Moore, *Works*, IX, 61, 87, 357; to J. L. Reynolds, Nov. 11, 1853, Dickinsoniana, DC.

17. Moore, *Works*, IX, 103, 114.

18. J. F. Rhodes, *History of the U. S.* (new ed., New York, 1920), I, 507-511; Moore, *Works*, IX, 146, 152, 194; Curtis, *Buchanan*, II, Chap. 4.

19. Buchanan to Forney, Sept. 30, 1853, Buchanan MSs., HSP.

20. Buchanan to Edmund Burke, Dec. 3, 1849, in "Letters of Bancroft and Buchanan," *Amer. Hist. Rev.*, V, 99.

21. Buchanan to Marcy, June 29, 1855, Moore, *Works*, IX, 365.

22. Buchanan to Marcy, Jan. 10, 1854, Moore, *Works*, IX, 135.

23. *Ibid.*

24. April 6, 1854, to the Lord Elgin Banquet, Moore, *Works*, IX, 174-175.

25. *Ibid.*, IX, 250.

CHAPTER 18 (pp. 234-247)

1. Buchanan to Pierce, April 7, 1854, Moore, *Works*, IX, 176.

2. J. M. Callahan, *Cuba and International Relations* (Baltimore, 1899), p. 266; Buchanan to Marcy, Nov. 1, 1853, Moore, *Works*, IX, 83-85.

3. Tom Harris to Howell Cobb, April 10, 1854, Cobb MSs., UG.

4. Sickles to Cobb, June 23, 1854, Cobb MSs., UG.

5. For Sickles affair at Peabody Dinner, cf. memoranda for July, 1854 in Peabody MSs., Box XCI, Essex Institute; Buchanan-Swarr MSs., BF; and Buchanan MSs., HSP;

also Buchanan to J. L. Reynolds, July 14, 1854, Reynolds MSs., FM; and W. W. Stell to Peabody, autumn, 1854, Peabody MSs., Box XCI, Essex Institute.

6. Forney to Buchanan, Sept. 26, 1854, Buchanan MSs., HSP.

7. W. R. Manning (ed.), *Diplomatic Correspondence of the U. S. Inter-American Affairs, 1831-1860* (12 Vols., Washington, 1932-1939), XI, 175-178.

8. Nichols, *Pierce*, p. 359; Spencer, *Marcy*, pp. 320-325.

9. Moore, *Works*, IX, 251-253.

10. *Ibid.* The best accounts of the Ostend affair are found in Amos A. Ettinger, *The Mission to Spain of Pierre Soulé* (New Haven, 1932), Nichols, *Pierce*, and Spencer, *Marcy*.

11. Buchanan to Marcy, Dec. 22, 1854, Moore, *Works*, IX, 289; Nichols, *Pierce*, pp. 368-369.

12. Spencer, *Marcy*, p. 338.

13. Slidell to Buchanan, April 3, 1855, Moore, *Works*, IX, 332.

14. Moore, *Works*, IX, 290, 292, 294, 304, 390, 406.

15. Forney to Buchanan, Nov. 27, Dec. 14, 1854, Jan. 9, 1855; Buchanan to Sickles, Dec. 22, 1854, Buchanan MSs., HSP.

16. Moore, *Works*, IX, 356, 460, 465.

17. *Ibid.*, IX, 354, 365.

18. Buchanan to Marcy, Oct. 3; to Pierce, Oct. 4, 1855; to Miss Lane, Oct. 26, 1855; to Marcy, Nov. 7, 1855, Moore, *Works*, IX, 417-421, 435-437, 447.

19. Buchanan to Marcy, Nov. 9, 1855, Moore, *Works*, IX, 452-453.

20. Moore, *Works*, IX, 459, 469, 476.

21. *Ibid.*, X, 30.

22. Buchanan to Marcy, Feb. 5, 1856, Moore, *Works*, X, 31-32.

23. Wilfrid Ward, *The Life and Times of Cardinal Wiseman* (London, 1897), II, 166.

24. Buchanan to Marcy, Feb. 15, 1856, Moore, *Works*, X, 49.

25. Buchanan to E. E. Lane, Feb. 29, 1856, E. E. Lane MSs.

CHAPTER 19 (pp. 248-260)

1. Lynch to Buchanan, Feb. 16, 1855, Lynch MSs., LCHS.

2. Black to Buchanan, Feb. 17, 1855, Buchanan MSs., HSP.

3. Forney to Buchanan, Feb. 23, 1855, Buchanan MSs., HSP.

4. Forney to Buchanan, Apr. 25, 1856, Buchanan MSs., HSP.

5. Foltz to Buchanan, Aug. 9, 1855, Nov. 22, 1855, Buchanan-Swarr MSs., BF.

6. Lancaster *Intelligencer*, Feb. 26, 1856. The *Intelligencer* at frequent intervals ran a list of all U. S. papers that favored Buchanan.

7. Jan. 17, 1855, Moore, *Works*, X, 8.

8. Buchanan to William B. Reed, Feb. 29, 1856, Moore, *Works*, X, 63.

9. Buchanan to Harriet Lane, Jan. 25, 1856, Moore, *Works*, X, 21.

10. Sophie Plitt to Buchanan, Sept. 17, 1855, Buchanan MSs., Box III, LC.

11. Foltz to Buchanan, Jan. 17, 1856, Buchanan-Swarr MSs., BF.

12. *Intelligencer and Lancastrian*, April 29, 1856.

13. *Ibid.*, and Reigart bill, Buchanan MSs., HSP.

14. Baltimore *Sun*, May 13, 1856.

15. R. F. Nichols, *Disruption of American Democracy* (New York, 1948), Chap. I.

16. *Official Proceedings of the National Democratic Convention . . . 1856*; Gerald M. Capers, *Stephen A. Douglas* (Boston, 1959), p. 142; W. B. Hesseltine and R. G. Fisher (eds.), *Trimmers, Trucklers and Temporizers* (Madison, Wisconsin, 1961), pp. 19, 51.

17. Statement of Millard Fillmore, *Congressional Globe*, 34th Congress, 1st session, App. 716.

18. *Short Answers to Reckless Fabrications* (1856), p. 9.

19. To Harriet Lane, June 16, 1856, Buchanan MSs., Box IV, LC.

20. Buchanan to Cobb, July 10, 1856, Cobb MSs., UG.

21. Buchanan to Jones, June 27, 29, 1856, Cadwalader MSs., HSP.

22. Lancaster *Intelligencer*, July 15, 1856, quoting exchanges. A column of squibs such as this formed a regular feature in many Democratic papers through the nation.

23. Black to Cobb, Sept. 23, 1856, in U. B. Phillips (ed.), "Correspondence of Robert Toombs, A. H. Stephens and Howell Cobb," Amer. Hist. Assoc. *Annual Report*, 1911, II, 383.

24. Curtis, *Buchanan*, II, 180-183, quoting Buchanan to Nahum Capen, Aug. 27, to William B. Reed, Sept. 14, and to Joshua Bates, Nov. 6, 1856; Allan Nevins, *The Emergence of Lincoln* (New York, 1950), I, 345; and box labelled "Clippings" in Buchanan MSs., HSP.

25. Z. T. Johnson, *Political Policies of Howell Cobb* (Nashville, 1929), pp. 147-148.

26. D. H. Branham to Howell Cobb, Oct. 1, 1856, Cobb MSs., UG.

27. Collection of handbills, notices and clippings, Oct. 8, 1856, in Buchanan-Swarr MSs., BF.

28. Reminiscences of Alfred Sanderson, July 1, 1887, in Ruth Scrapbook, YCHS.

29. T. R. R. Cobb to Howell, Nov. 15, 1856, Cobb MSs., UG.

CHAPTER 20 (pp. 261-272)

1. *Intelligencer and Lancastrian*, March 3, 1857.

2. Buchanan to John Y. Mason, Dec. 29, 1856, Curtis, *Buchanan*, II, 185.

3. Nichols, *Disruption*, p. 54.

4. New York *Herald*, Dec. 3, 1856.

5. Lancaster *Intelligencer*, Dec. 9, 1856.

6. Burnham, *Presidential Ballots*, pp. 246-257. The sections referred to are those used by Burnham for analyses of the vote.

7. J. W. Forney to Howell Cobb, Nov. 30, 1856, Cobb MSs., UG.

8. Buchanan to J. Glancy Jones, Nov. 29, 1856, Jones MSs., Philadelphia.

9. Same to same, Dec. 8, Jones MSs.

10. Same to same, Dec. 29, Jones MSs.

11. Cobb to his wife, Dec. 20, 1856, Cobb MSs., UG.

12. Forney to Howell Cobb, Feb. 18, 1857, "Correspondence of Toombs, Stephens and Cobb," in Amer. Hist. Assoc. *Annual Report*, 1911, II, 396-397.

13. John B. Lamar to Cobb, Jan. 24, 1857, Cobb MSs., UG.

14. Buchanan to Henry S. Mott, Jan. 7, 1857, *Intelligencer and Lancastrian*, Feb. 3, 1857; also Recollections of J. Montgomery Forster, undated clippings from the Mercersburg *Journal*, Rankin Scrapbook.

15. Forney to Cobb, Jan. 21, 1857, Cobb MSs., UG.

16. Cobb to his wife, Jan. 13, 1857, Cobb MSs., UG.; Crippen, *Cameron*, pp. 160-165.

17. David Lynch to Buchanan, Jan. 18, 1857, Lynch MSs., LCHS.

18. Buchanan to Jones, Feb. 17, 1857, Cadwalader MSs., HSP.

19. Forney to Cobb, Jan. 21, 1857, Cobb MSs., UG.

20. Recollections of Forster, *op. cit.*

21. John B. Lamar to Cobb, Jan. 21, 1857, Cobb MSs., UG.

22. Cobb to his wife, Jan. 6, 1857, Cobb MSs., UG; "Correspondence of Toombs, Stephens and Cobb," *op. cit.*, 389.

23. Cobb to his wife, Feb. 3, 1857, Cobb MSs., UG.

24. Philadelphia *Pennsylvanian*, Jan. 28, 1857.

25. Leonora Clayton to Mrs. Howell Cobb, Jan. 31, 1857, Cobb MSs., UG; Baltimore *Sun*, Feb. 2, 1857.

26. Nichols, *Disruption*, p. 63.

27. Cobb to his wife, Jan. 31, 1857, Cobb MSs., UG.

28. Quoted in the Baltimore *Sun*, Feb. 7, 1857.

29. David Lynch to Buchanan, Feb. 16, 1857, Lynch MSs., LCHS.

30. Robert Toombs to Howell Cobb, Feb. 18, 1857, quoting letter from Buchanan to Toombs, Cobb MSs., UG.

31. Buchanan to Jones, Feb. 17, 1857, Cadwalader MSs., HSP.

32. Forney to Cobb, Feb. 18, 1857, "Correspondence of Toombs, Stephens and Cobb," *op. cit.*, 396-397.

33. Oliver H. P. Parker to Abraham Lincoln, Sept., 1860, in David C. Mearns (ed.), *The Lincoln Papers* (New York, 1948), I, 284.

34. Jonathan Foltz to Buchanan, Feb. 23, 1857, Buchanan-Swarr MSs., BF.

35. Cadwalader MSs., HSP, contains rough notes in Buchanan's hand, dated 1857, which deal with the concept of the sanctity of law. Some sentences were later incorporated into the Lecompton Message of 1858.

36. Series of clippings in John Lowry Ruth Scrapbook, YCHS.; Nichols, *Disruption*, pp. 69-70.

37. *Intelligencer and Lancastrian*, Mar. 10, 1857, and *Frank Leslie's Illustrated Weekly*, Mar. 21, 1857, give full descriptions of the inauguration ceremonies. *Leslie's* report has many errors.

38. One of these is in the Buchanan MSs., BF.

39. Lillie to Eugene B. Cook, Mar. 4, 1857, Robert J. Walker MSs., LC.

40. A. A. Woldman, *Lincoln and the Russians* (New York, 1952), p. 18.

CHAPTER 21 (pp. 273-285)

1. Sketch by J. B. Henry, Moore, *Works*, XII, 323-333; notes on White House staff in Cadwalader MSs. and Buchanan MSs., HSP; Commonplace Book in Buchanan-Swarr

MSs., BF; Howell Cobb to wife, Mar. 22, 29; Mary Ann Cobb to son, Sept. 7, 24, 1857, Cobb MSs., UG; Harriet Lane to Ellie Reynolds, June 4, 1857, Reynolds MSs., FM; Foltz, *Surgeon of the Seas*, p. 186; Philadelphia *Press*, Aug. 1, Sept. 30, and Oct. 20, 1857.

2. Samuel F. Bemis (ed.), *American Secretaries of State* (New York, 1927-1929), VI, 300-301; Samuel Boykin (ed.), *Memorial Volume of the Hon. Howell Cobb* (Philadelphia, 1870), pp. 28-29; Lancaster *Intelligencer*, June 10, 1856, and March 10, 1857.

3. Howell Cobb to wife, Mar. 8, 22, 19, and June 6, 1857; Mary Ann Cobb to Howell, Mar. 9, 13, and Aug. 4, 1857; Philip Clayton to Mrs. Cobb, Mar. 17; Howell Cobb to son, Apr. 17; J. S. Black to Cobb, Apr. 15; Cobb to Black, Apr. 26, 1857; Cobb MSs., UG.

4. E. C. Craig to Howell Cobb, June 23, 1857, Cobb MSs., UG.

5. Philip G. Auchampaugh, *James Buchanan and His Cabinet on the Eve of Secession* (Lancaster, 1926), p. 115.

6. Mrs. Cobb to son, Sept. 7, 1857, Cobb MSs., UG.

7. Mrs. Cobb to ?, June 17, 1857, Cobb MSs., UG. The Browns lived at 19th and G Streets, William Wirt's old home.

8. Mrs. Cobb to son, Sept. 24, 1857, Cobb MSs., UG.

9. Slidell to Cobb, Apr. 5, 1857, Cobb MSs., UG; Buchanan to Thos. H. Seymour, May 11, 1857, Buchanan Papers, Boston Public Library; J. B. Henry to Father Kenna, June 12, 1857, Cadwalader MSs., HSP.

10. Cobb to wife, Mar. 8, 1857, Cobb MSs., UG.

11. Nichols, *Disruption*, Chap. 5.

12. *Ibid.*, pp. 82-83, 207-209; Dan Sickles to Cobb, July 23, 1857, Cobb MSs., UG.

13. Series of letters in Lynch MSs., LCHS.

14. Forney to Black, May 6, 1857, Black MSs., LC.

15. Same to same, June 15, 1857, Black MSs., LC.

16. Forney papers in the Buchanan MSs., HSP. and Black MSs., LC., for 1856 and 1857 sustain this view.

17. Grier to Plitt, dated only 1857, Buchanan MSs., LC.

18. Sophie Plitt to Miss Lane, Sept. 5, 1860, Buchanan MSs., LC.

19. Buchanan MSs., HSP, and Buchanan-Swarr MSs., BF, contain the correspondence on the subject.

20. Philadelphia *Press*, Sept. 7, Oct. 20, 1857.

21. Slidell to Cobb, Apr. 5, 1857, Cobb MSs., UG.

22. New Orleans *Daily True Delta*, Apr. 4, 1858.

23. Cobb to Black, Apr. 26, 1857, Black MSs., LC.

24. Cobb to son, May 16, 1857, Cobb MSs., UG.

25. Cobb to wife, June 10, 1857, Cobb MSs., UG.

26. Black to Cobb, Apr. 30, 1857, Cobb MSs., UG.

27. C. W. C. Dunnington to R. M. T. Hunter, Oct. 6, 1857, in "Correspondence of Hunter," Amer. Hist. Assoc. *Annual Report*, 1916, II, 236.

28. Mary B. Clayton (ed.), *Reminiscences of J. S. Black* (St. Louis, 1887), p. 106.

29. Dunnington to Hunter, Oct. 6, 1857, *op. cit.*

30. Cobb to wife, June 6, 1857, Cobb MSs., UG.

31. Black to Forney, July ?, 1857, Black MSs., LC.

CHAPTER 22 (pp. 286-299)

1. Tom D. Harris to Howell Cobb, Apr. 10, 1854, Cobb MSs., UG.

2. George F. Milton, *Eve of Conflict, Stephen A. Douglas and the Needless War* (Boston, 1934), p. 183; Capers, *Douglas*, pp. 87-88.

3. Forney to Buchanan, Mar. 19, 1854, Buchanan MSs., HSP.

4. Paul W. Gates, *50 Million Acres* (Ithaca, 1943), pp. 60-61.

5. *Ibid.*, pp. 48-49.

6. *Ibid.*, Chap. 2.

7. Leverett W. Spring, *Kansas, the Prelude to the War for the Union* (New York, 1885), pp. 64-65.

8. T. W. Thomas to A. H. Stephens, Jan. 12, 1857, "Correspondence of Toombs, Stephens and Cobb," Amer. Hist. Assoc. *Annual Report*, 1911, II, 392.

9. Richmond *Enquirer*, March 2, 1854; Henry H. Simms, *A Decade of Sectional Controversy, 1851-1861* (Durham, N. C., 1942), pp. 67-68.

10. Cobb to ?, April 21, 1856, "Correspondence of Toombs, Stephens and Cobb," *op. cit.*, 363.

11. Moore, *Works*, X, 81.

12. Walker to Buchanan, Mar. 26, 1857, quoted in *Intelligencer and Lancastrian*, Mar. 30, 1857.

13. *Intelligencer and Lancastrian*, May 19, 1857.

14. A. Iverson to Cobb, reporting conversation with Buchanan, Sept. 17, 1857, Cobb MSs., UG.

15. Nichols, *Disruption*, p. 105.

16. Cobb to Stephens, June 17, 1857, "Correspondence of Toombs, Stephens and Cobb," *op. cit.*, 402.

17. Nichols, *Disruption*, p. 109.

18. T. W. Thomas to A. H. Stephens, June 15, 1857, "Correspondence of Toombs, Stephens and Cobb," *op. cit.*, 400-401; James Jackson to Cobb, Aug. 27, 1857, Cobb MSs., UG.

19. For many southern letters, cf. "Correspondence of Toombs, Stephens and Cobb," *op. cit.*, 400 ff. and "Correspondence of Hunter," Amer. Hist. Assoc. *Annual Report*, 1916, II, 200 ff.

20. F. W. Pickens to Buchanan, Aug. 5, 1857, Buchanan MSs., HSP.

21. Address by A. H. Stephens, Aug. 14, 1857, in "Correspondence of Toombs, Stephens and Cobb," *op. cit.*, pp. 417-418.

22. William H. Stiles to Cobb, Aug. 26, 1857, Cobb MSs., UG.

23. Robert Toombs to W. W. Burwell, July 11, 1857, "Correspondence of Toombs, Stephens and Cobb," *op. cit.*, 404.

24. Speech of July 15, 1857, at Lawrence.

25. *Covode Committee Report*, 36th Congress, 1st session, #648, pp. 115-119.

26. *Ibid.*, pp. 112-113.

27. Cobb to Stephens, Sept. 19, 1857, "Correspondence of Toombs, Stephens and Cobb," *op. cit.*, pp. 423-424.

28. Black to Forney, July, 1857, Black MSs., I, LC.

29. Spring, *Kansas*, p. 212; Simms, *Decade of Sectional Controversy*, pp. 93-96.

30. Buchanan's reply to a memorial, Aug. 15, 1857, Moore, *Works*, X, 117-122.

31. T. R. R. Cobb to Howell Cobb, Oct. 1, 1857, Cobb MSs., UG.

32. Secretary of State, Instructions to Walker of Sept. 2, 1857, Walker MSs., LC. Proslavery Judge Cato issued a ruling on the election law stating that only tax payers could vote. As few of the Topeka people ever had paid any tax to the Lecompton government, it seemed clear that the object was to prevent the free-state people from voting. Walker immediately protested this decision to Washington, and Attorney General Black promptly overruled Cato's decision.

33. Nichols, *Disruption*, pp. 118-126.

CHAPTER 23 (pp. 300-312)

1. Spring, *Kansas*, p. 223; *Political Textbook for 1860* (New York, 1860), pp. 76-126; T. W. Thomas to A. H. Stephens, Feb. 7, 1858, "Correspondence of Toombs, Stephens and Cobb," Amer. Hist. Assoc. *Annual Report*, 1911, II, 430.

2. Nichols, *Disruption*, p. 130; Milton, *Eve of Conflict*, p. 273.

3. Moore, *Works*, X, 236; C. R. Fish, *The American Civil War* (New York, 1937), p. 337.

4. Moore, *Works*, X, 145-151.

5. Edward A. Ross, in the last 5 chapters of his *Social Psychology* (New York, 1908), sheds much light on the behavior of Americans during the Buchanan Administration.

6. See Buchanan's first three annual messages and the Lecompton Message.

7. *Political Textbook for 1860*, pp. 114, ff. and Forney's *Press* throughout the debate. Issue of Nov. 2, 1857, is a good example.

8. Roberts to Cameron, Jan. 16, 1868, Cameron microfilms, Museum Bldg., Harrisburg.

9. Nevins, *Emergence*, I, 246; Capers, *Douglas*, p. 165.

10. *Political Textbook for 1860*, p. 115.

11. Buchanan to Robert Tyler, Feb. 15, 1858, Moore, *Works*, XI, 514.

12. Moore, *Works*, X, 149; Philadelphia *Press*, Aug. 3, 1857; Nevins, *Emergence*, I, 236, note 19; *Intelligencer and Lancastrian*, July 21, 1857, quotes exchanges on this point from editors all over the country; Philadelphia *Press* of Nov. 2, 1857, has long discussion.

13. Gerald Wagner, "Adoption of State Constitutions to 1860, a statistical study." Typescript, The Penna. State Univ., 1958.

14. Spring, *Kansas*, p. 223.

15. J. B. Floyd to Buchanan, July 31, 1858, Buchanan MSs., HSP., wrote that Walker "intends at all hazards to regain his position, or to throw the blame for his failure upon someone else—either the administration or the War Department." Cass wrote in similar vein on the same date, Buchanan MSs., HSP; Philadelphia *Press*, June 16, 1859.

16. Nevins, *Emergence*, I, 241.

17. Milton, *Eve of Conflict*, p. 271; Nevins, *Emergence*, I, 240; Capers, *Douglas*, p. 155.

18. T. W. Thomas to A. H. Stephens, "Correspondence of Toombs, Stephens and Cobb," Amer. Hist. Assoc. *Annual Report*, 1911, II, 428.

19. Cobb to John B. Lamar, Mar. 10, 1858, Cobb MSs., UG.

20. T. R. R. Cobb to Howell, Dec. 11, 1857; J. W. H. Underwood to Cobb, Feb. 5, 1858, Cobb MSs., UG.

21. Spring, *Kansas*, pp. 230-231.

22. Buchanan to Arnold Plumer, Feb. 14, 1858, Buchanan MSs., HSP.

23. Nichols, *Disruption*, p. 161.
24. Buchanan to Hiram Swarr, Mar. 12, 1858, Buchanan-Swarr MSs., BF.
25. Buchanan to W. H. English, Mar. 22, 1858, Dickinsoniana, DC.
26. Buchanan to Hiram Swarr, June 30, 1858, Buchanan-Swarr MSs., BF.
27. Buchanan to W. H. English, July 2, 1858, Dickinsoniana, DC.

CHAPTER 24 (pp. 313-327)

1. Foltz to Buchanan, July 18, 1857, Buchanan-Swarr MSs., BF; Mrs. Cobb to her son, Sept. 30, 1857, Cobb MSs., UG; New York *Herald*, Oct. 14, 1858.
2. E. B. Hart to Howell Cobb, Oct. 23, 1857, Cobb MSs., UG.
3. *Congressional Globe*, 35th Congress, 1st session, 70-71, 96; *De Bow's Review*, XXIII (Dec., 1857), 592. Best account is G. W. Van Vleck, *The Panic of 1857* (New York, 1943).
4. H. H. Bancroft, *History of Utah, 1540-1886* (San Francisco, 1889), p. 531, note 27; J. B. McMaster, *History of the People of the U. S.* (New York, 1893-1924), VIII, 375.
5. Ray A. Billington, *The Far Western Frontier* (New York, 1956), p. 214.
6. *Atlantic Monthly*, III (Mar., 1859), 369.
7. Billington, *op. cit.*, pp. 206-217; Nichols, *Disruption*, pp. 178-180, 193; *House Ex. Docs.*, 35th Congress, 1st session, Vol. 9, #33; Vol. 10, #71; Vol. 12, #99; Vol. 13, #138; *Senate Ex. Docs.*, 35th Congress, 1st session, Vol. 13, #67. Best account is Norman F. Furniss, *The Mormon Conflict, 1850-1859* (New Haven, 1960).
8. Moore, *Works*, X, 113.
9. *Ibid.*, X, 173-175.
10. Moore, *Works*, XI, 50, 59, 63; Curtis, *Buchanan*, II, 399; Andrew C. McLaughlin, *Lewis Cass* (New York, 1899), pp. 161-162; Frank B. Woodford, *Lewis Cass* (New Brunswick, N. J., 1950), p. 316.
11. Clarendon to Buchanan, Oct. 19, 1857, Moore, *Works*, X, 122; M. W. Williams, *Anglo-American Isthmian Diplomacy, 1815-1915* (Washington, 1916), p. 228.
12. Moore, *Works*, X, 123; Williams, *op. cit.*, pp. 231-232.
13. Moore, *Works*, X, 139-140.
14. Clarendon to Buchanan, Mar. 13, April 22, 1857, Moore, *Works*, X, 114-116.
15. W. O. Scroggs, *Filibusters and Financiers* (New York, 1916), pp. 339-340; Pierce Butler, *Judah P. Benjamin* (Philadelphia, 1907), pp. 185-190; Mobile *Mercury*, Jan. 26, 1858; New York *Herald*, Feb. 2, 1858; New York *Times*, Feb. 2, 1858.
16. Rivas Manifesto, May 1, 1857, in Instruction #9, Cass to Lamar, July 25, 1858, *Senate Ex. Docs.*, 35th Congress, 2nd session, Vol. 1, #1, 62-64.
17. *Ibid.*, 52-53.
18. Moore, *Works*, XI, 26.
19. *Ibid.*, X, 259.
20. J. Fred Rippy, *The United States and Mexico* (New York, 1926) and "The United States and Mexican Policy," *Miss. Valley Hist. Rev.*, VI (1919-1920); J. M. Callahan, "The Mexican Policy of Southern Leaders under Buchanan's Administration," Amer. Hist. Assoc. *Annual Report*, 1910, and "The Evolution of Seward's Mexican Policy," *West Virginia University Studies*, I; H. L. Wilson, "James Buchanan's Proposed Intervention in Mexico," *Amer. Hist. Rev.*, V (1899-1900); Lewis Einstein, "Lewis Cass," in Bemis, *American Secretaries of State*, VI.

21. April 4, 1857. Rippy, *The United States and Mexico*, p. 204.

22. Mexican Despatches, #21, April 12, 1858, Rippy, *op. cit.*, p. 216.

23. *Senate Ex. Docs.*, 35th Congress, 2nd session, Vol. I, #1, 46.

24. *Congressional Globe*, 35th Congress, 2nd session, 1118-1143, *passim; Senate Journal*, 35th Congress, 2nd session, 343.

25. Rippy, *The United States and Mexico*, Chap. 10.

26. Wilson, "Buchanan's Proposed Intervention," *Amer. Hist. Rev.*, V, 197.

27. J. M. Callahan, "Evolution of Seward's Mexican Policy," West Virginia University *Studies*, I.

28. *House Ex. Docs.*, 37th Congress, 2nd session, #100, 17-18.

29. Moore, *Works*, X, 226.

30. Buchanan to Fallon, Dec. 14, 1857, Moore, *Works*, X, 165; Nichols, *Disruption*, p. 228.

31. *Congressional Globe*, 35th Congress, 2nd session, Pt. I, 907 ff., Pt. II, 1079.

32. Callahan, *Cuba and International Relations*, p. 313.

33. *Congressional Globe*, 35th Congress, 2nd session, Pt. I, 541-543, 935-940.

34. *Ibid.*, Pt. II, 1187.

35. F. A. Golder, "The Purchase of Alaska," *Amer. Hist. Rev.*, XXV (1919-1920), 411-417.

36. *National Intelligencer*, Jan. 24, 1859.

CHAPTER 25 (pp. 328-344)

1. Lincoln to Elihu B. Washburne, May 15, 17, 1860, Roy P. Basler (ed.), *The Collected Works of Abraham Lincoln* (New Brunswick, N. J., 1953), II, 447, 455; B. F. Brewster to Buchanan, May 27, 1858, Buchanan MSs., HSP.

2. New York *Herald*, Oct. 26, 1858.

3. Nichols, *Disruption*, p. 214.

4. Speeches at Springfield, July 17 and Galesburg, Oct. 4, 1858, Basler, *Works of Abraham Lincoln*, II, 508; III, 226.

5. Speech at Alton, Oct. 15, 1858.

6. Henry A. Wise to Buchanan, Oct. 12, 1858, Buchanan MSs., HSP.

7. Howell Cobb to A. H. Stephens, Sept. 8, 1858, in "Correspondence of Toombs, Stephens and Cobb," *Amer. Hist. Assoc. Annual Report,* 1911, II, 443.

8. Oct. 15, 1858, Moore, *Works*, X, 229.

9. Buchanan to Swarr, Dec. 31, 1858, Buchanan-Swarr MSs., BF.

10. Nichols, *Disruption*, p. 242.

11. Philadelphia *Press*, April 5, 1858.

12. Jacob Thompson to Howell Cobb, Aug. 7, 1859, Cobb MSs., UG.

13. Sophie Plitt to Harriet Lane, Mar. 18, 1858, Buchanan MSs., LC.

14. Kate Thompson to Mrs. Cobb, June 8, 1859, Cobb MSs., UG.

15. Sophie Plitt to Harriet Lane, Dec. 12, 1859, Buchanan MSs., LC.

16. Leonora Clayton to Mrs. Cobb, Aug. 19, 1859, Cobb MSs., UG.

461

17. Kate Thompson to Mrs. Cobb, May 18, 1859, Cobb MSs., UG.

18. Howell Cobb to wife, May 17, Kate Thompson to Mrs. Cobb, May 18, Mrs. Cobb to Howell, May 20, 1859, Cobb MSs., UG.

19. Howell Cobb to wife, June 7, Kate Thompson to Mrs. Cobb, June 8, 1860, Cobb MSs., UG.

20. Kate Thompson to Mrs. Cobb, July 10, 1859, Cobb MSs., UG.

21. Philadelphia *Press*, July 23, 25, 1859; Philip H. Clayton to Mrs. Cobb, Leonora Clayton to Mrs. Cobb, Aug. 4, 1859, Cobb MSs., UG.

22. Nichols, *Disruption*, pp. 274-275.

23. James Buchanan, *Mr. Buchanan's Administration on the Eve of Rebellion* (New York, 1866), p. 63; Howell Cobb to wife, Nov. 19, 1859, Cobb MSs., UG.

24. Buchanan to Edwin M. Stanton, n.d., 1860, Dickinsoniana Coll., DC.

25. Lancaster *Intelligencer*, April 17, 1860.

26. Moore, *Works*, X, 399-405.

27. Buchanan to Stanton, n.d., 1860, Dickinsoniana Coll., DC.

28. John Cadwalader to Buchanan, Mar. 28, June 12, 1859, Cadwalader MSs., HSP; Philadelphia *Press*, April 1, June 29, Aug. 16, 1859, and issues of the spring of 1860; Report of the Covode Committee, House Report #648, 36th Congress, 1st Sess.

29. Moore, *Works*, X, 435-443.

30. Bedford *Gazette*, July 28, 1859, and reminiscences of the editor, *ibid.*, Sept. 21, 1906.

31. Buchanan to J. B. Baker, July 25, 1859, Moore, *Works*, X, 327; to Cobb, July 23, Cobb MSs., UG; to McCandless, July 25, in "Letters of James Buchanan," *LCHS Papers*, XXXVI, 317.

32. Buchanan to J. B. Baker, Feb. 28, 1860, in Moore *Works*, X, 393; to Swarr, April 13, 1860, privately owned by E. E. Bausman, Lancaster, Penna.; to Mrs. Polk, Meade Minnegerode, *Presidential Years* (New York, 1928), p. 348.

33. New York *Tribune*, Aug. 5, 1859, quoting the New York *Herald*.

34. Philadelphia *Press*, March 24, May 28, 1859.

35. *Ibid.*, Nov. 15, 17, 1859.

36. Toombs to T. W. Thomas, Dec. 4, 1859; to A. H. Stephens, Jan. 11, 1860, "Correspondence of Toombs, Stephens and Cobb," *op. cit.*, 450, 456.

37. Howell Cobb to John B. Lamar, Jan. 15, 1860, Cobb MSs., UG.

38. Milton, *Eve of Conflict*, p. 357.

39. Buchanan to Slidell, June 24; Slidell's reply, July 3, 1859, Buchanan MSs., HSP.

CHAPTER 26 (pp. 345-352)

1. *Historical Statistics of the United States, 1789-1945*, (G. P. O., 1949), p. 297.

2. Gates, *Fifty Million Acres*, pp. 77-79, 89-91.

3. *Ibid.*, pp. 86, 89.

4. Harriet Lane to Ellie Reynolds, July 21, 1860, Reynolds MSs., FM.

5. Philadelphia *Press*, May 31, 1860; Mrs. Cobb to son, May 29, 1860, Cobb MSs., UG.

6. Mrs. E. C. (Craig) Robb to Mrs. Cobb, July 30, 1860, Cobb MSs., UG.

7. Russell Weigley, *Quartermaster General of the Union Army, Montgomery C. Meigs* (New York, 1959), describes the feud fully in the early chapters.

8. Philadelphia *Press*, Aug. 23, 1860.

9. Gillan, "James Buchanan," in Kittochtinny Hist. Soc. *Papers*, II (1901), 196-197.

10. Mrs. Cobb to Lamar Cobb, Oct. 13, 14, 15, 1860, Cobb MSs., UG.

11. L. R. Morris, *Incredible New York* (New York, 1951), pp. 23-24; Edmund O. Stedman, *The Prince's Ball* (New York, 1860).

12. Moore, *Works*, XI, 3.

13. W. M. Browne to S. L. M. Barlow, July 1, 1860, Barlow MSs., HEH.

14. Howell to Lamar Cobb, July 9, 1860, Cobb MSs., UG.

15. Buchanan to Hiram Swarr, Oct. 3, 1860, E. E. Bausman (private), Lancaster, Penna.

16. Howell Cobb to wife, Oct. 10, 1860, Cobb MSs., UG.

17. Howell to Lamar Cobb, Oct. 31, 1860, Cobb MSs., UG.

18. Burnham, *Presidential Ballots*, p. 86.

19. Henry Hull, *Annals of Athens, 1801-1901* (Athens, Ga., 1906), p. 217.

20. Philadelphia *Press*, Nov. 14, 1860.

21. Slidell to Buchanan, Nov. 13, 1860, Buchanan MSs., HSP.

CHAPTER 27 (pp. 353-367)

1. Trescot is also spelled Trescott. The best treatment of the last months of Buchanan's Administration is Kenneth M. Stampp, *And the War Came* (Baton Rouge, 1950).

2. Buchanan, *Mr. Buchanan's Administration*, pp. 99-103.

3. *Sen. Ex. Doc.* #1, 35th Congress, 2nd Session, Vol. III, Pt. II, 761.

4. *Congressional Globe*, 35th Congress, 2nd session, Pt. I, 1032-1038; 36th Congress, 1st session, Pt. I, 1351; Pt. III, 3137; *Senate Reports*, 36th Congress, 1st session, I, 172.

5. *Congressional Globe*, 35th Congress, 1st session, Pt. II, 1425-1427.

6. Nahum Capen to Buchanan, Nov. 8, 1862, Buchanan MSs., HSP, enclosing Toucey's deposition before the Senate Committee on the disposition of the Navy in 1860.

7. Buchanan to Nahum Capen, Jan. 27, 1864, Moore, *Works*, XI, 355.

8. Floyd's Diary, Nov. 10, 1860, MSs., in HSP; William N. Brigance, *Jeremiah Sullivan Black* (Philadelphia, 1934), p. 82.

9. Nichols, *Disruption*, p. 381.

10. Floyd's Diary, Nov. 10, 1860, HSP.

11. November 17, 1860, in Buchanan MSs., HSP.

12. *Opinions of the Attorneys General*, IX, 517; copy in Black MSs., LC, dated Nov. 20, 1860.

13. Howard C. Perkins, *Northern Editorials on Secession* (New York, 1942), I, 18-19 and Chapters II, IV; also Dwight L. Dumond, *Southern Editorials on Secession* (New York, 1931).

14. Lincoln to William Speer, Oct. 23, 1860, Basler, *Works of Lincoln*, IV, 30.

15. David Potter, *Lincoln and His Party in the Secession Crisis* (New Haven, 1942), p. 141.

463

16. J. R. Moorhead to Lincoln, Nov. 23, 1860, Robert Todd Lincoln MSs., LC.

17. A. J. Glossbrenner to Hiram Swarr, Nov. 28, 1860, Buchanan-Swarr MSs., BF.

18. New York *Herald*, Nov. 22, 1860; Philadelphia *Press*, Nov. 24, 1860.

19. Moore, *Works*, XI, 7-25.

20. *Philadelphia North American and U. S. Gazette*, Dec. 5, 1860; Jersey City *Daily Courier and Adviser*, Dec. 5, 1860; New Haven *Morning Journal and Courier*, Dec. 6, 1860; Quincy *Daily Whig and Republican*, Dec. 10, 12, 1860, in Perkins, *Northern Editorials*, I, 125, 133, 136-138, 152-153.

21. New York *Herald*, Dec. 5, 1860; Harrisburg *Patriot and Union*, Dec. 6, 1860; Philadelphia *Morning Pennsylvanian*, Dec. 5, 1860, in Perkins, *op. cit.*, I, 127, 133-134, 142-145.

22. Buffalo *Daily Courier*, Dec. 6, 1860; Cincinnati *Daily Enquirer*, Dec. 6, 1860; Detroit *Free Press*, Dec. 7, 1860; Utica *Daily Observer*, Dec. 7, 1860, in Perkins, *op. cit.*, I, 138-142, 147-152.

23. Potter, *Lincoln and His Party*, p. 39.

24. Francis Blackburn to Lincoln, Nov. 24, 1860, R. T. Lincoln MSs., LC; John Welsh to William Bigler, Dec. 14, 1860, Bigler MSs., HSP.

25. Trumbull to Lincoln, Dec. 4, 1860, R. T. Lincoln MSs., LC.

26. E. B. Washburne to Lincoln, Dec. 9, 1860, R. T. Lincoln MSs., LC.

27. W. G. Snethin to Lincoln, Dec. 13, 1860, R. T. Lincoln MSs., LC.

28. P. A. Hackleman to ?, forwarded to Lincoln, Nov. 27, 1860, R. T. Lincoln MSs., LC.

29. E. D. Morgan to Lincoln, Dec. 16, 1860, R. T. Lincoln MSs., LC.

30. Potter, *Lincoln and His Party*, pp. 93-94.

31. Barlow to Slidell, Nov. 27, 1860, S. L. M. Barlow MSs., HEH.

32. Lincoln to H. J. Raymond, Nov. 28, 1860, R. T. Lincoln MSs., LC.

33. Weed to Lincoln, Dec. 11, 1860, R. T. Lincoln MSs., LC.

34. Lincoln to E. B. Washburne, Dec. 13, 1860, Basler, *Works of Lincoln*, IV, 151.

35. Lincoln to Weed, Dec. 17, 1860, *ibid.*, IV, 154.

36. Buchanan to Hiram Swarr, Dec. 10, 1860, E. E. Bausman (private), Lancaster.

CHAPTER 28 (pp. 368-387)

1. Samuel W. Crawford, *Genesis of the Civil War* (New York, 1887), pp. 66, 75.

2. Barlow to Butterworth, Dec. 3, 1860, quoting a report of the incident, Barlow MSs., HEH; Auchampaugh, *Mr. Buchanan's Cabinet*, p. 150.

3. Crawford, *Genesis*, pp. 30-35.

4. W. M. Browne to S. L. M. Barlow, Dec. 1860, Barlow MSs., HEH.

5. Crawford, *Genesis*, p. 68.

6. *Ibid.*, p. 76.

7. *Ibid.*, p. 73.

8. Philadelphia *Press*, Dec. 8, 1860.

9. Cobb to J. C. Lamar, Nov. 16, 1860, Cobb MSs., UG.

10. Brigance, *J. S. Black*, p. 90.

11. Cobb to wife, Dec. 10, 1860; Leonora Clayton to Mrs. Cobb, Dec. 30, 1860; Mrs. Thompson to Mrs. Cobb, April 15, 1861, Cobb MSs., UG.

12. Auchampaugh, *Mr. Buchanan's Cabinet*, pp. 66-69.

13. Crawford, *Genesis*, pp. 38-39.

14. Moore, *Works*, XI, 56-57, 358.

15. Cass to Buchanan, Dec. 12, 1860, Moore, *Works*, XI, 58.

16. Philadelphia *Press*, Dec. 11, 1860.

17. Buchanan's memorandum of Dec. 15, 1860, Moore, *Works*, XI, 59-60.

18. Black to G. T. Curtis, Sept. 16, 1881, Buchanan MSs., HSP; Buchanan to Cass, Dec. 15, 1860, Moore, *Works*, XI, 59-65.

19. Mrs. Thompson to Mrs. Cobb, Dec. 15, 1860, Cobb MSs., UG.

20. W. M. Browne to S. L. M. Barlow, Dec. 16, 1860, Barlow MSs., HEH.

21. Mrs. Cobb to a "friend," Dec. 19, 1860, Cobb MSs., UG.

22. Trumbull to Lincoln, Dec. 14, 1860, R. T. Lincoln MSs., LC.

23. Curtis, *Buchanan*, II, 367.

24. Levi Woodbury to Buchanan, Dec. 17, 1860, Buchanan MSs., HSP.

25. E. G. W. Butler to Buchanan, Dec. 17, 1860, Buchanan MSs., HSP.

26. Lancaster *New Era*, Sept. 29, 1872. Harriet Lane's letter to the editor.

27. Mrs. Thompson to Mrs. Cobb, Dec. 15, 1860, Cobb MSs., UG, and newspaper letter from Thompson in Ruth Scrapbook, YCHS.

28. W. M. Browne to S. L. M. Barlow, Nov. 24, 1860, Barlow MSs., HEH.

29. Horatio King to J. S. Black, Dec. 14, 1860, Horatio King, *Turning on the Light* (Philadelphia, 1895), p. 34.

30. King to Dix, Nov. 25, 1860, *ibid.*, p. 27.

31. King to Nahum Capen, Nov. 25, 1860, *ibid.*, p. 29.

32. Buchanan to Bennett, Dec. 20, 1860, Moore, *Works*, XI, 69-70.

33. C. S. Henry to Lincoln, Dec. 23, 1860; G. G. Fogg to Lincoln, Dec. 13, 1860; A. J. Randall to Seward, Dec. 15, 1860, R. T. Lincoln MSs., LC.

34. S. L. M. Barlow to H. D. Bacon, Dec. 29, 1860, Barlow MSs., HEH; F. P. James to William Bigler, Dec. 15, 1860, Bigler MSs., HSP.

35. Mrs. Roger A. Pryor, *Reminiscences of Peace and War* (New York, 1905), pp. 110-111.

36. *Ibid.*, p. 111. Telegram is in Buchanan MSs., HSP.

37. Crawford, *Genesis*, pp. 81-83.

38. *Ibid.*, p. 84.

39. Buchanan to Pickens, Dec. 20, 1860, in Moore, *Works*, XI, 71-72.

40. Crawford, *Genesis*, pp. 77-78.

41. *Ibid.*, p. 75; Nichols, *Disruption*, p. 423.

42. Crawford, *Genesis*, pp. 93-94.

43. Barlow Letterbook, VI, 863, HEH; Philadelphia *Press*, Dec. 31, 1860.

44. Leonora Clayton to Mrs. Cobb, Dec. 30, 1860, Cobb MSs., UG.

45. Memorandum of Black to Buchanan, Dec. 27, 1860. Copies of this and of the orders are in Buchanan MSs., HSP; Brigance, *J. S. Black*, pp. 92-93.

46. Crawford, *Genesis*, p. 145; Nichols, *Disruption*, p. 428; Brigance, *J. S. Black*, p. 94.

47. Crawford, *Genesis*, p. 144. Memorandum of Black dated 1861 in Black MSs., LC.

48. Memorandum of Black in Black MSs., LC.

49. Leonora Clayton to Mrs. Cobb, Dec. 30, 1860, Cobb MSs., UG.

50. Moore, *Works*, XII, 160.

51. *Ibid.*, XI, 76-77.

52. *Ibid.*, XII, 161.

53. *Ibid.*, XII, 162.

54. Brigance, *J. S. Black*, p. 98.

55. F. A. Burr in Philadelphia *Press*, Sept. 10, 1883; Brigance, *J. S. Black*, p. 98.

56. Basler, *Works of Lincoln*, IV, 154.

57. Weed to Lincoln, Dec. 11, 1860, *ibid.*

58. Seward to Lincoln, Dec. 16, 1860, R. T. Lincoln MSs., LC; Potter, *Lincoln and His Party*, pp. 163-164.

59. Phelps to Buchanan, Dec. 20, 1860, Buchanan MSs., HSP.

60. Bryant to Lincoln, Dec. 25, 1860; Lincoln to Bryant, Dec. 29, 1860, in Basler, *Works of Lincoln*, IV, 163-164, and note.

61. Horace White to Lincoln, Dec. 22, 1860, R. T. Lincoln MSs., LC.

62. Barlow to Slidell, Nov. 27, 1860; Barlow to Bayard, Nov. 27, 1860, Barlow MSs., HEH.

63. Barlow to Benjamin, Dec. 26, 1860, Barlow MSs., HEH; Harriet A. Weed (ed.), *Autobiography of Thurlow Weed* (Boston, 1883), pp. 603-614.

64. W. M. Browne to Barlow, Dec. 26, 1860, Barlow MSs., HEH.

65. Moore, *Works*, XI, 73-74.

66. Duff Green to Buchanan, Dec. 28, 1860, Curtis, *Buchanan*, II, 426-427; Green to Jefferson Davis, May 26, 1863, J. G. Nicolay and John Hay, *Abraham Lincoln* (New York, 1904), III, 286-288.

67. Lincoln to Green, Dec. 28, 1860; Lincoln to Trumbull, Dec. 28, 1860; Green to Lincoln, Dec. 31, 1860, Basler, *Works of Lincoln*, IV, 162-163.

68. Black file, Buchanan MSs., HSP.

69. Moore, *Works*, XI, 79-84.

70. *Ibid.*, XII, 162.

CHAPTER 29 (pp. 388-402)

1. Scott to Buchanan, Dec. 28, 1860, Buchanan MSs., HSP.

2. Buchanan to Thompson, Jan. 9, 1860, Moore, *Works*, XI, 191.

3. Nichols, *Disruption*, pp. 434-435.

4. Crawford, *Genesis*, pp. 169-171.

5. Mrs. Gwin to Mrs. Cobb, Jan. 5, 1861, Cobb MSs., UG.

6. L. K. Bowen to Howell Cobb, Jan. 3, 1861; Seward to Lincoln, Dec. 29, 1860, R. T. Lincoln MSs., LC.

7. Crawford, *Genesis*, p. 178.

8. Thompson to Buchanan, Jan. 8, 1861; Buchanan to Thompson, Jan. 8, 1861, in Moore, *Works*, XI, 100-101.

9. Mrs. Thompson to Mrs. Cobb, Jan. 13, 1861, Cobb MSs., UG.

10. T.'Bailey Myers to Miss Lane, Jan. 3, 1861, Buchanan MSs., LC.

11. Mrs. Gwin to Mrs. Cobb, Jan. 5, 1861, Cobb MSs., UG.

12. Clayton to Cobb, Jan. 4, 1861; Browne to Cobb, Jan. 11, 1861, Cobb MSs., UG.

13. Mrs. Thompson to Mrs. Cobb, Jan. 14, 1861, Cobb MSs., UG.

14. Moore, *Works*, XI, 94-99.

15. Lincoln to Duff Green, Dec. 28, 1860, Basler, *Works of Lincoln*, IV, 162-163.

16. Potter, *Lincoln and His Party*, p. 184.

17. A. A. Woldman, *Lincoln and the Russians* (Cleveland, 1952), p. 17.

18. Nichols, *Disruption*, pp. 440-443.

19. A. T. W. Lytle to Buchanan. These are in the "Letters to Buchanan," Dec., 1860, Buchanan MSs., HSP.

20. Crawford, *Genesis*, p. 205.

21. Moore, *Works*, XI, 109-111.

22. Black to Buchanan, Jan. 22, 1861, Buchanan MSs., HSP.

23. Moore, *Works*, XI, 126-143, gives the correspondence.

24. *Ibid.*, XII, 134.

25. Nichols, *Disruption*, p. 478.

26. Moore, *Works*, XII, 134-141.

27. Curtis, *Buchanan*, II, 413-417.

28. Moore, *Works*, XI, 106-109.

29. Sarah R. Cobb to Mrs. Howell Cobb, Jan. 20, 1861, Cobb MSs., UG.

30. W. M. Browne to Howell Cobb, Jan. 11, 1861, Cobb MSs., UG.

31. Mrs. Thompson to Mrs. Cobb, Jan. 14, 1861, Cobb MSs., UG.

32. Black to Buchanan, Jan. 22, 1861, Buchanan MSs., HSP.

33. Holt to Buchanan, Feb. 20, 1861, Moore, *Works*, XI, 154-155.

34. *Ibid.*, XI, 152-154.

35. Slidell to Buchanan, Jan. 27; Buchanan to Slidell, Jan. 29, 1861, Buchanan MSs., HSP.

36. Moore, *Works*, XI, 116-118.

37. Tyler to Buchanan, Jan. 28, 1861, Moore, *Works*, XI, 120-121.

38. King, *Turning on the Light*, pp. 52-54.

39. Nichols, *Disruption*, p. 491.

40. Philip Clayton to Cobb, Jan. 4, 1861, Cobb MSs., UG.

41. Mrs. Thompson to Mrs. Cobb, Jan. 14, 1861, Cobb MSs., UG.

42. Richard H. Clark to Cobb, Feb. 16, 1861, Cobb MSs., UG; C. F. Adams Diary, Jan. 15, 1861. Microfilm, The Pennsylvania State University Library.

43. Mrs. Thompson to Mrs. Cobb, Feb. 3, 1861, Cobb MSs., UG.

44. Miss Lane to Sophie Plitt, Feb. 24, 1861, Buchanan MSs., LC.

45. Moore, *Works*, XI, 156; memorandum of Mar. 4-9, 1861.

46. Auchampaugh, *Mr. Buchanan's Cabinet*, p. 188.

47. Asa E. Martin, *After the White House* (State College, Penna., 1951), p. 225.

CHAPTER 30 (pp. 403-429)

1. Moore, *Works*, XI, 156.
2. Lancaster *Intelligencer*, Mar. 12, 1861; *Baltimore County Advocate*, Mar. 23, 1861.
3. *National Intelligencer*, Mar. 9, 1861.
4. Raleigh *North Carolina Standard*, Mar. 9, 1861.
5. Perkins, *Northern Editorials*, Chap. XV, "The Inaugurals, South and North."
6. Indianapolis *Daily Journal*, Mar. 5, 1861.
7. Excerpts are from Lincoln's first inaugural; from Buchanan's 4th annual message and his special messages of January 8, 28, 1861.
8. Black to Buchanan, Mar. 8, 1861, Buchanan MSs., HSP.
9. Dix to Buchanan, Mar. 14, 1861, Curtis, *Buchanan*, II, 533.
10. Stanton to Buchanan, Mar. 10, 12, 14, 16, and April 3, 1861, Moore, *Works*, XI, 163-178.
11. *Ibid.*, XI, 176-178; Bigler to Buchanan, April 11, 1861, Buchanan-Swarr MSs., BF.
12. Stanton to Buchanan, Mar. 16, 1861; Dix to Buchanan, Mar. 28, 1861, Moore, *Works*, XI, 170-171, 176.
13. Buchanan to J. B. Henry, April 12, 1861, Moore, *Works*, XI, 181.
14. Harris, *Biographical History of Lancaster County*, p. 485, note.
15. Buchanan to J. B. Baker, April 26, 1861, Moore, *Works*, XI, 186; Buchanan to James L. Reynolds, May 8, 1861, Buchanan MSs., HSP; Gillan, "James Buchanan," Kittochtinny H. S. *Papers*, 196.
16. Sophie Plitt to Harriet Lane, May 18, 1861, Buchanan MSs., LC; J. M. Foltz to A. J. Steinman, June 16, 1868, Foltz MSs., FM; Buchanan to W. B. Reed, Mar. 21, 1861, Buchanan-Swarr MSs., BF.
17. Lancaster *Examiner and Herald*, Aug. 1, 1863.
18. Moore, *Works*, XI, 323-324.
19. *Ibid.*, XI, 192; Curtis, *Buchanan*, II, 501, 506.
20. Moore, *Works*, XI, 163, 171-172, 211, 280-293.
21. *Ibid.*, XI, 215, 363; Curtis, *Buchanan*, II, 513.
22. Moore, *Works*, XI, 229, 316, 322.
23. *Ibid.*, XI, 179, 182.
24. Curtis, *Buchanan*, II, 518-519.
25. Buchanan to J. H. Dillon, Oct. 24, 1865, May MSs. (private); Curtis, *Buchanan*, II, 520; Moore, *Works*, XI, 263, 266, note.
26. Flynn to Buchanan, May 14, 1862, Moore, *Works*, XI, 269.
27. *Ibid.*, XI, 266.
28. *Ibid.*, XI, 271-272.
29. *Ibid.*, XI, 266, 269.
30. *Ibid.*, XI, 252.
31. *Ibid.*, XI, 244.
32. *Ibid.*, XI, 267-268.
33. *Ibid.*, XI, 340.
34. *Ibid.*, XI, 275.
35. *Ibid.*, XI, 318.

36. Lancaster *Intelligencer*, Aug. 25, 1864.

37. Moore, *Works*, XI, 256, 337, 382, 412.

38. *Ibid.*, XI, 243.

39. Report from the Commissioner of Public Buildings, July 20, 1860, Buchanan MSs., HSP.

40. Moore, *Works*, XI, 251, 418-419.

41. *Ibid.*, XI, 235, 239, 240; Curtis, *Buchanan*, II, 524.

42. *Ibid.*, II, 526.

43. Lancaster *Intelligencer*, Sept. 12, 1865; Moore, *Works*, XI, 412.

44. Lancaster *Intelligencer*, May 24, June 7, 1865.

45. Dix to Buchanan, May 24, 1861, in Moore, *Works*, XI, 197.

46. Stanton to Buchanan, Mar. 14, 1861, in Moore, *Works*, XI, 168.

47. Buchanan to J. B. Henry, May 17, 1861, Moore, *Works*, XI, 192.

48. Same to same, Dec. 19, 1862, Moore, *Works*, XI, 325.

49. *Ibid.*, XI, 183.

50. Black to Buchanan, June ?, 18, 1861, Moore, *Works*, XI, 198.

51. Same to same, Oct. 5, 1861, Moore, *Works*, XI, 224.

52. Buchanan to Black, Mar. 4, 1862, Moore, *Works*, XI, 261.

53. *Ibid.*, XI, 226.

54. Black to Buchanan, Mar. 1, 1862, Moore, *Works*, XI, 258.

55. *Ibid.*, XI, 352.

56. Both Scott's and Buchanan's letters appear in Moore, *Works*, XI, 280 ff.

57. Preface to *Mr. Buchanan's Administration on the Eve of Rebellion*; Abner Doubleday, *Forts Sumter and Moultrie* (New York, 1876), 129; Moore, *Works*, XI, 248.

58. Moore, *Works*, XI, 450, 457.

59. *Ibid.*, XI, 183-184.

60. Mrs. Gwin to Mrs. Cobb, May 5, 1861, Cobb MSs., UG.

61. Buchanan to William B. Rose, Sept. 14, 1861, Ruth Scrapbook, YCHS.

62. Moore, *Works*, XI, 216.

63. Buchanan to the Hon. J. C. G. Kennedy, July 24, 1861, Ruth Scrapbook, YCHS.

64. Buchanan to Charles V. Pene, Dec. 21, 1861, Dickinsoniana Coll., DC.

65. Buchanan to John A. Parker, Feb. 3, 1862, Moore, *Works*, XI, 250.

66. Buchanan to Dix, Mar. 1861, Moore, *Works*, XI, 173.

67. *Ibid.*, XI, 386.

68. *Ibid.*, XI, 341, 346.

69. *Ibid.*, XI, 373.

70. Buchanan to Nahum Capen, Mar. 14, 1864, Moore, *Works*, XI, 358.

71. Buchanan to Dr. J. B. Blake, Nov. 21, 1864, Moore, *Works*, XI, 377.

72. *Ibid.*, XI, 385.

73. *Ibid.*, XI, 405.

74. William B. Reed to Buchanan, May 2, 1868, Buchanan MSs., HSP.

75. Moore, *Works*, XI, 440-441.

76. Buchanan to Schell, Nov. 9, 1867, Moore, *Works*, XI, 455.

77. Buchanan to Black, July 17, 1863, Buchanan MSs., HSP.

78. David Unger to Buchanan, Oct. 21, 1861, E. E. Lane MSs.

79. Buchanan to Hiram Swarr, Mar. 24, 1864, Buchanan-Swarr MSs., BF.

80. Accounts in Buchanan MSs., HSP.

81. Gillan, "James Buchanan," in Kittochtinny H. S. *Papers*, 199; J. Montgomery Forster Recollections, Rankin Scrapbook, Mercersburg, Penna.

82. Correspondence is in Reynolds MSs., FM.

83. In Buchanan's Commonplace Book, Buchanan-Swarr MSs., BF.

84. In Buchanan's passbook for the Chemical Bank of New York, N. Y., Buchanan-Swarr MSs., BF.

85. Commonplace Book, Buchanan-Swarr MSs., BF.

86. Varina Davis to Buchanan, Dec. 1861, Buchanan MSs., HSP.

87. Sophie Plitt to Harriet Lane, Oct. 18, 1863, Buchanan MSs., LC.

88. Letters of Feb. 12, 1862, and July 17, 1866, from Buchanan to Isabel Lynch, Buchanan MSs., HSP; also correspondence in Lynch MSs., LCHS; Ishbel Ross, *Rebel Rose* (New York, 1954), p. 53.

89. Wall to Buchanan, Aug. 26, 1867, Buchanan-Swarr MSs., BF.

90. Leonora Clayton to Harriet Lane, Jan. 23, 1866, Buchanan MSs., LC.

91. ? to Miss Lane, Jan. 6, 1863, Buchanan MSs., LC.

92. Mrs. Ellis to Miss Lane, Oct. 1, 1866, Buchanan MSs., LC.

93. Buchanan to Harriet Lane (Mrs. Johnston), Feb. 22, 1867, Taylor MSs.

94. D. M. B. Shannon to Buchanan, Aug. 7, 1866, in author's possession; Buchanan to Shannon, July 6, 1866, Turner Scrapbook, Mercersburg.

95. Buchanan to Daniel Sturgeon, April 23, 1866; Ambrose Dudley to Miss Lane, Jan. 18, 1866, Ruth Scrapbook, YCHS.

96. Buchanan to Harriet Lane, April 5, 1866, Taylor MSs.

97. Commonplace Book, Buchanan-Swarr MSs.; Theodore Appel, *Life of John Nevin* (Philadelphia, 1889), pp. 601-604, analyzes Buchanan's religious views.

98. Lancaster *Intelligencer*, June 3, 10, 1868.

99. Hesseltine and Fisher (eds.), *Trimmers, Trucklers and Temporizers*, p. 57.

BIBLIOGRAPHY

ABBREVIATIONS

The following abbreviations have been used to designate manuscript repositories frequently mentioned in the notes:

BF   Buchanan Foundation for the Preservation of Wheatland, collections in the Lancaster County Historical Society.

DC   Library of Dickinson College, Carlisle, Penna.

FM   Library of Franklin and Marshall College, Lancaster, Penna.

HEH   Henry E. Huntington Library, San Marino, California.

HSP   Historical Society of Pennsylvania, Philadelphia, Penna.

LC   Manuscripts Division, Library of Congress, Washington, D. C.

LCHS   Lancaster County Historical Society, Lancaster, Penna.

UG   Library of the University of Georgia, Athens, Ga.

YCHS   York County Historical Society, York, Penna.

The printed correspondence of Buchanan, fully cited as John Bassett Moore (ed.), *The Works of James Buchanan*, 12 vols. (Philadelphia, 1908-1911), will be abbreviated in the notes as Moore, *Works*.

MANUSCRIPTS

Library of Congress, Manuscripts Division (LC)
    Jeremiah S. Black MSs.
    Buchanan-Johnston MSs.
    Simon Cameron MSs.
    W. W. Corcoran MSs.
    A. J. Donelson MSs.
    Joseph Holt MSs.
    Andrew Jackson MSs.
    Horatio King MSs.
    Robert Todd Lincoln MSs.
    John McLean MSs.
    William L. Marcy MSs.
    Edwin M. Stanton MSs.
    Martin Van Buren MSs.
    Robert J. Walker MSs.

Historical Society of Pennsylvania (HSP)
    William Bigler MSs.
    James Buchanan MSs.
    John Cadwalader MSs., Buchanan section
    Lewis S. Coryell MSs.
    John B. Floyd MS. Diary
    Gratz Collection
    J. S. Johnston MSs.
    W. M. Meredith MSs.
    William Rawle MSs.
    George Wolf MSs.

Library Company of Philadelphia, Ridgway Branch
    John M. Read MSs.

Dickinson College Library, Carlisle, Penna. (DC)
    Minutes of the Board of Trustees, 1807-1809
    Dickinsoniana, Buchanan section

Fackenthal Library, Franklin and Marshall College, Lancaster, Penna. (FM)
    Jonathan Foltz MSs. and diaries
    John Reynolds MSs.
    Minutes of the Board of Trustees, 1853-1868

Houghton Library, Harvard University
    Autograph Collection
    Buchanan MSs.
    Jared Sparks MSs.

Historical Society of Massachusetts
    C. E. French Collection
    Presidents of the United States Collection
    Edward Everett MSs.
    W. B. Washburne MSs.

Essex Institute, Salem, Massachusetts
    N. P. Banks MSs.
    George Peabody MSs.

Princeton University Library
    de Coppet Collection

Henry E. Huntington Library and Art Gallery
    S. L. M. Barlow MSs.

473

Buchanan Foundation for the Preservation of Wheatland (BF). Collections maintained in the Historical Society of Lancaster County, Penna.
James Buchanan Sr. MSs.
James Buchanan MSs.
Agnes Selin Schoch Collection of Buchanan-Kittera MSs.
E. E. Bausman Collection of Buchanan-Swarr MSs.

Lancaster County Historical Society (LCHS)
David Lynch MSs.

York County Historical Society (YCHS)
Buchanan-Russell family MSs.

Wyoming Historical and Geological Society, Wilkes-Barre, Penna.
Hendrick B. Wright MSs.

Pennsylvania Historical and Museum Commission, Division of Public Records, Harrisburg, Penna.
Simon Cameron MSs.
County records (microfilm)
Papers of the governors, MSs.
George Wolf MSs.
Miscellaneous Collection

Pattee Library, The Pennsylvania State University, University Park, Penna.
Adams MSs. (microfilm)
Jacob Hibshman MSs.

Private Collections
Howell Cobb MSs. (UG), courtesy of William Erwin, Esq., Athens, Georgia. Collection maintained in the Library of the University of Georgia

Buchanan MSs., courtesy of Mrs. Charles S. Foltz, Lancaster, Penna.

Harriet Lane MSs., courtesy of Mrs. Edmund Taylor, Charlestown, West Va.

Charles M. Yates MSs. (photostats), courtesy of Roy F. Nichols, Philadelphia

J. Glancy Jones MSs. (photostats), courtesy of Roy F. Nichols, Philadelphia

Elliot Eskridge Lane MSs., courtesy of Patty Lane Fay Eldridge, San Luis Obispo. Papers now at Buchanan Foundation.

Henry and Jasper Slaymaker MSs., courtesy of Samuel C. Slaymaker, Lancaster, Penna.

Henry Baldwin MSs., courtesy of John Reynolds, Meadville, Penna.

Fugitive Buchanan material was made available to me by C. H. Martin, William Worner, H. M. J. Klein, and Richmond Myers, Lancaster, Penna.; Craig Wylie, Boston, Mass.; Oliver Keller, Springfield, Ill.; E. J. Turner, Mercersburg, Penna.; Gilbert, McClintock, Wilkes-Barre, Penna.; John Lowry Ruth, York, Penna.; H. Hanford Hopkins, Baltimore, Md.; Maurice G. Buchanan, Indianapolis, Ind.; William Hubley Potter, Alexandria, Va.; Herman Blum, Philadelphia, Penna.; George D. Harmon, Bethlehem, Penna.; and Asa E. Martin, Tuscon, Ariz.

NEWSPAPERS

Most of the newspapers listed are located in the Pennsylvania State Library, Harrisburg; the Historical Society of Pennsylvania; the Library Company of Philadelphia, Ridgway Branch; the office of Lancaster Newspapers, Inc.; the Lancaster County Historical Society; or the Library of Congress. A number of items, however, were found in the file of clippings preserved by Buchanan which form a part of the Buchanan MSs. collection of the Historical Society of Pennsylvania, or in the John Lowry Ruth Scrapbook, York County Historical Society, or the Hiram Swarr Scrapbook, Buchanan Foundation.

Baltimore, Md.
Niles National Register
Sun

Bedford, Penna.
    Gazette
    Inquirer

Boston, Mass.
    Budget
    Herald

Carlisle, Penna.
    Herald

Chambersburg, Penna.
    Franklin Repository
    Public Opinion

Cincinnati, Ohio
    Commercial
    Enquirer

Doylestown, Penna.
    Democrat

Harrisburg, Penna.
    Argus
    Keystone
    Patriot (and Union)
    Republican

Indianapolis, Ind.
    Daily Journal

Lancaster, Penna.
    Express
    Intelligencer
    Intelligencer and Lancastrian
    Intelligencer and Weekly Advertiser
    Intelligencer-Journal
    Journal
    New Era
    Weekly Journal

Marietta, Penna.
    Pioneer

Meadville, Penna.
    Crawford Register

Mercersburg, Penna.
    Journal

Mobile, Ala.
    Mercury

New Orleans, La.
    Daily True Delta
    DeBow's Review
    Picayune

New York, N. Y.
    Frank Leslie's Illustrated Weekly
    Herald
    Times
    Tribune

Philadelphia, Penna.
Aurora
Democratic Press
Pennsylvania Gazette
Pennsylvanian
Philadelphia North American and U. S. Gazette
Press
Union, or United States Gazette and True American

Pottstown, Penna.
Times

Raleigh, N. C.
North Carolina Standard

Richmond, Va.
Enquirer

Towson, Md.
Baltimore County Advocate

Washington, D. C.
Constitution
National Intelligencer
Telegraph
Union

York, Penna.
Gazette

OFFICIAL DOCUMENTS

Party Documents
James Buchanan, His Doctrines and Policy as Exhibited by Himself and his Friends, n.p., 1856

Leaven for Doughfaces or Threescore and Ten Parables Touching Slavery, Cincinnati, 1856

Official Proceedings of the National Democratic Convention . . . 1856, n.p., 1856

Old Line Whigs for Buchanan and Breckinridge, n.p., 1856

Political Textbook for 1860, N. Y., 1860

Republican Campaign Documents of 1856, a Collection, Washington, D. C., 1857

Short Answers to Reckless Fabrications, n.p., 1856

Pennsylvania
Appearance Dockets, Courts of Quarter Sessions and Common Pleas, 1812-1821, Lancaster County Courthouse

Deed Books and Will Books, Adams, Cumberland, Franklin, Lancaster and York County Courthouses

Pennsylvania Archives, Fourth Series, "Papers of the Governors," 12 vols., Harrisburg, 1900-1902

Journal of the Assembly of Pennsylvania, 1814-1819

Journal of the Senate of Pennsylvania, 1814-1819

United States Government
"Compilation of Reports of the Committee on Foreign Relations, United States Senate, 1789-1909," *Senate Executive Document* #231, 56th Congress, 2nd Session

Correspondence in Relation to the Proposed Interoceanic Canal, the Clayton-Bulwer Treaty, and the Monroe Doctrine, Washington, D. C., 1885

Correspondence Relative to the Negotiations of the Question of Disputed Right to the Oregon Territory . . . *1842*, London, 1846

Department of Commerce and Labor, Bureau of the Census, *Heads of Families at the First Census of the U. S., taken in the Year 1790, Pennsylvania*, Washington, D. C., 1908

——, *Historical Statistics of the United States, 1789-1945*, Washington, D. C., 1949

Diplomatic Correspondence of the United States, Inter-American Affairs, 1831-1860, W. R. Manning (ed.), 12 vols., Washington, D. C., 1932-1939

Hasse, Adelaide, *Index to United States Documents relating to Foreign Affairs, 1828-1861*, 3 vols., Washington, D. C., 1914-1921

Official Records of the Union and Confederate Navies in the War of the Rebellion, ed. by Richard Rush *et al.*, 30 vols., Washington, D. C., 1894-1914

Register of Debates in Congress and *Congressional Globe*

War of the Rebellion: a Compilation of the Official Records of the Union and Confederate Armies, R. N. Scott *et al.* (eds.), 130 vols., Washington, D. C., 1880-1901

Committee Reports and Executive Documents of the Congressional Series of Publications of the United States, cited fully in the notes, are not listed individually here.

BIOGRAPHICAL

I have incorporated under this heading not only biographies, but diaries, memoirs and the major published writings of persons included in the section.

ABERDEEN: Balfour, Lady Frances, *Life of George, Fourth Earl of Aberdeen, K. G., K. T.*, 2 vols., London, 1913

ANDERSON: Crawford, Samuel W., *The Genesis of the Civil War, The Story of Sumter, 1860-1861*, New York, 1887

Swanberg, W. A., *First Blood, The Story of Sumter*, New York, 1957

BANCROFT: Howe, M. A. DeWolfe (ed.), *Life and Letters of George Bancroft*, 2 vols., New York, 1908

Nye, Russell B., *George Bancroft, Brahmin Rebel*, New York, 1944

BARLOW: Gerton, Richard M., "The Political Activities of Samuel Latham Mitchell Barlow, 1856-1864," M. A. thesis, Columbia University, 1947

BELL: Parks, J. H., *John Bell of Tennessee*, Baton Rouge, 1930

BELMONT: Belmont, August, *Letters and Speeches of August Belmont*, New York, 1890

BENJAMIN: Butler, Pierce, *Judah P. Benjamin*, Philadelphia, 1907

Meade, Robert D., *Judah P. Benjamin*, New York, 1943

Osterweis, R. G., *Judah P. Benjamin, Statesman of the Lost Cause*, New York, 1933

BENNETT: Seitz, Don C., *The James Gordon Bennetts*, New York, 1928

BENTON: Benton, Thomas H., *Thirty Years' View* . . . *1820-1850*, 2 vols., New York, 1854-1856

Chambers, William N., *Old Bullion Benton, Senator from the New West*, Boston, 1956

Meigs, W. M., *Life of Thomas Hart Benton*, Philadelphia, 1904

BIDDLE: Govan, Thomas P., *Nicholas Biddle*, Chicago, 1959

BLACK: Brigance, William N., *Jeremiah Sullivan Black*, Philadelphia, 1934

Clayton, Mary B., *Reminiscences of J. S. Black*, St. Louis, 1887

Nichols, Roy F., "Jeremiah S. Black," in *American Secretaries of State and Their Diplomacy*, ed. by S. F. Bemis, 10 vols., New York, 1929

BRODERICK: Lynch, Jeremiah, *Life of David C. Broderick*, New York, 1911

BRECKINRIDGE: Stillwell, Lucille, *John Cabell Breckinridge*, Caldwell, Id., 1936

477

BUCHANAN: Auchampaugh, Philip G., *James Buchanan and His Cabinet on the Eve of Secession*, Lancaster, 1926

―――, *James Buchanan, a Political Portrait, 1856, according to his Friends and Enemies*, Reno, Nevada, 1946

Buchanan, James, *Mr. Buchanan's Administration on the Eve of the Rebellion*, New York, 1866

―――, *The Works of James Buchanan*, ed. by John Bassett Moore, 12 vols., Philadelphia, 1908-1911

Buchanan, Patrick A. W., *The Buchanan Book*, Montreal, 1911

Butler, Thomas J., *Wheatland, 1848-1868, the Home of James Buchanan* (mimeo), Dover, Del., 1957

Curtis, George T., *The Life of James Buchanan*, 2 vols., New York, 1883

Hensel, William U., *James Buchanan as a Lawyer*, Lancaster, 1912

―――, *The Religious Convictions and Character of James Buchanan*, Lancaster, 1912

―――, *The Attitude of James Buchanan . . . towards the Institution of Slavery*, Lancaster, 1911

―――, *A Pennsylvania Presbyterian President*, Philadelphia, 1907

Henry, J. B. (comp.), *The Messages of President Buchanan with an Appendix Containing Sundry Letters from Members of His Cabinet*, New York, 1888

Henry, Reginald B., *Buchanan*, n.p., n.d. (genealogy)

Hillman, Franklin P., "The Diplomatic Career of James Buchanan," Ph.D. thesis, The George Washington University, 1953

Horton, R. G., *Life and Public Services of James Buchanan*, New York, 1856

Irelan, John R., *History of the Life, Administration and Times of James Buchanan*, Chicago, 1888

Klein, Philip S., *The Story of Wheatland*, Lancaster, 1936

Sioussat, St. George L., "James Buchanan," in *American Secretaries of State and Their Diplomacy*, ed. by S. F. Bemis, 10 vols., New York, 1929

Speer, Talbot T., *The Speer Family Record*, Baltimore, n.d.

CALHOUN: Boucher, Chauncey S. and Brooks, Robert P. (eds.), "Correspondence addressed to John C. Calhoun," Amer. Hist. Assoc. *Annual Report*, 1929, Washington, 1931

Calhoun, John C., "Correspondence of John C. Calhoun," ed. by F. Franklin Jameson, Amer. Hist. Assoc. *Annual Report*, 1899, II, Washington, 1900

―――, *Works of John C. Calhoun*, ed. by Richard K. Crallé, 6 vols., New York, 1854-1857

Wiltse, Charles M., *John C. Calhoun*, 3 vols., Indianapolis, 1944-1951

CAMERON: Crippen, Lee F., *Simon Cameron, Ante-Bellum Years*, Oxford, Ohio, 1942

McNair, James B., *Simon Cameron's Adventure in Iron*, Los Angeles, 1949

CASS: McLaughlin, Andrew C., *Lewis Cass*, New York, 1899

Woodford, Frank B., *Lewis Cass, the Last Jeffersonian*, New Brunswick, N. J., 1950

CLAY: Clay, Henry, *The Works of Henry Clay, Comprising his Life, Correspondence and Speeches*, ed. by Calvin Colton, 10 vols., New York, 1904

Eaton, Clement, *Henry Clay and the Art of American Politics*, Boston, 1957

Van Deusen, G. G., *The Life of Henry Clay*, Boston, 1937

COBB: Boykin, Samuel (ed.), *Memorial Volume of the Hon. Howell Cobb*, Philadelphia, 1871

Johnson, Zachary T., *Political Policies of Howell Cobb*, Nashville, 1929

CRITTENDEN: Coleman, A. M. B., *Life of John J. Crittenden*, 2 vols., Philadelphia, 1871

DALLAS: Beck, Virginia, "George M. Dallas," M.A. thesis, University of Pittsburgh

Dallas, G. M., *A Series of Letters from London, written during the Years 1856-1860*, Philadelphia, 1869

DAVIS: King, Willard L., *Lincoln's Manager, David Davis*, Cambridge, Mass., 1960

Davis, Varina, *Jefferson Davis, a Memoir*, New York, 1890

Strode, Hudson, *Jefferson Davis*, 2 vols., New York, 1955-1959
Steiner, B. C., *Life of Henry Winter Davis*, Baltimore, 1916
DOUGLAS: Capers, Gerald M., *Stephen A. Douglas*, Boston, 1959
Milton, George Fort, *The Eve of Conflict, Stephen A. Douglas and the Needless War*, Boston, 1934
FILLMORE: Rayback, Robert J., *Millard Fillmore*, Buffalo, 1959
FLOYD: Ambler, C. H., *Life and Diary of John Floyd*, Richmond, 1918
FOLTZ: Foltz, Charles S., *Surgeon of the Seas: The Adventurous Life of Jonathan M. Foltz*, Indianapolis, 1931
FORNEY: Forney, John W., *Anecdotes of Public Men*, New York, 1873
FRÉMONT: Nevins, Allan, *Frémont, Pathmarker of the West*, New York, 1955
GREENHOW: Ross, Ishbel, *Rebel Rose, Life of Rose O'Neal Greenhow*, New York, 1954
HARDIN: Little, Lucius P., *Ben Hardin, His Times and Contemporaries*, Louisville, 1887
HAYNE: Jervey, T. D., *Robert Y. Hayne and His Times*, New York, 1909
HUNTER: Hunter, R. M. T., "Correspondence . . . 1826-1876," ed. by C. H. Ambler, Amer. Hist. Assoc. *Annual Report*, 1916, II, Washington, 1918
Simms, Henry H., *Life of Robert M. T. Hunter*, Richmond, 1935
JACKSON: Bassett, John S., *Life of Andrew Jackson*, 2 vols., Garden City, N. Y., 1911
Jackson, Andrew, *Correspondence*, ed. by J. S. Bassett, 7 vols., Washington, 1926-1935
James, Marquis, *Andrew Jackson*, New York, 1938
Parton, James, *Life of Andrew Jackson*, 3 vols., New York, 1860
JOHNSON: Flippin, Percy S., *Herschel V. Johnson of Georgia*, Richmond, 1931
Meyer, L. W., *Life and Times of Col. Richard M. Johnson*, New York, 1932
Steiner, B. C., *Life of Reverdy Johnson*, Baltimore, 1914
JONES: Jones, Charles H., *Life and Public Services of J. Glancy Jones*, 2 vols., Philadelphia, 1910
LAMAR: Cate, W. A., *Lucius Q. C. Lamar; Secession and Reunion*, Chapel Hill, 1935
Mayes, Edward, *Lucius Q. C. Lamar: His Life, Times and Speeches*, Nashville, 1896
LINCOLN: Donald, David, *Lincoln Reconsidered*, New York, 1956
Lincoln, Abraham, *The Collected Works of Abraham Lincoln*, ed. by Roy P. Basler, 9 vols., New Brunswick, N. J., 1933-1953
Mearns, David C. (ed.), *The Lincoln Papers*, 2 vols., New York, 1948
Nicolay, John G., and Hay, John, *Abraham Lincoln, A History*, 10 vols., New York, 1904
Potter, David, *Lincoln and His Party in the Secession Crisis*, New Haven, 1942
Randall, J. G., *Lincoln the President*, 2 vols., New York, 1945
Thomas, Benjamin P., *Abraham Lincoln*, New York, 1952
Woldman, A. A., *Lincoln and the Russians*, New York, 1952
LIVINGSTON: Hatcher, W. B., *Edward Livingston*, University, La., 1940
LOWNDES: Ravenel, Mrs. St. J., *Life and Times of William Lowndes*, New York, 1901
LYONS: Newton, Lord Thomas W. L., *Lord Lyons*, London, 1913
McDUFFIE: Green, Edwin L., *George McDuffie*, Columbia, S. C., 1936
MARCY: Spencer, Ivor D., *The Victor and the Spoils, A Life of William L. Marcy*, Providence, 1959
MEIGS: Weigley, Russell, *Quartermaster General of the Union Army, Montgomery C. Meigs*, New York, 1959
MINER: Richardson, C. F. and E. M., *Charles Miner, a Pennsylvania Pioneer*, Wilkes-Barre, Penna., 1916
PEEL: Parker, Charles S. (ed.), *Sir Robert Peel*, 3 vols., London, 1891-1899
PIERCE: Nichols, Roy F., *Franklin Pierce, Young Hickory of the Granite Hills*, 2nd ed., Philadelphia, 1958

POLK: McCormac, Eugene I., *James K. Polk, a Political Biography*, Berkeley, 1922
McCoy, Charles, *Polk and the Presidency*, Austin, Texas, 1960
Polk, James K., *Diary*, ed. by Milo M. Quaife, 4 vols., Chicago, 1910
Sellers, Charles G., *James K. Polk, Jacksonian, 1795-1843*, Princeton, N. J., 1957

POINSETT: Rippy, J. Fred, *Joel Poinsett*, Durham, N. C., 1935

RHETT: White, L. A., *Robert Barnwell Rhett, Father of Secession*, New York, 1931

RITCHIE: Ambler, C. H., *Thomas Ritchie, A Study in Virginia Politics*, Richmond, 1913

SCOTT: Elliott, Charles W., *Winfield Scott, The Soldier and the Man*, New York, 1937
Scott, Winfield, *Memoirs of Lieutenant General Scott, LLD*, 2 vols., New York, 1864
Smith, A. D. H., *Old Fuss and Feathers . . . Winfield Scott*, New York, 1937

SEWARD: Bancroft, Frederic, *Life of William H. Seward*, 2 vols., New York, 1900
Seward, Frederick W., *Seward at Washington*, New York, 1891

SICKLES: Swanberg, W. A., *Sickles the Incredible*, New York, 1956

SLIDELL: Sears, Louis M., *John Slidell*, Durham, N. C., 1925

SOULÉ: Ettinger, Amos A., *The Mission to Spain of Pierre Soulé*, New Haven, 1932

STANTON: Gorham, G. C., *Life and Public Services of Edwin M. Stanton*, 2 vols., Boston, 1899
Flower, F. A., *Edwin M. Stanton*, New York, 1905

STEPHENS: Abele, von, Rudolph, *Alexander H. Stephens*, New York, 1946
Avery, Myrta L., *Recollections of Alexander H. Stephens*, New York, 1910
Waddell, James D., *Biographical Sketch of Linton Stephens*, Atlanta, Ga., 1877

STEVENS: Current, Richard C., *Old Thad Stevens*, New York, 1942

STEVENSON: Wayland, Francis, *Andrew Stevenson, Democrat and Diplomat*, Philadelphia, 1949

SUMNER: Donald, David, *Charles Sumner and the Coming of the Civil War*, New York, 1960

TAYLOR: Dyer, Brainerd, *Zachary Taylor*, Baton Rouge, 1946
Hamilton, Holman, *Zachary Taylor*, 2 vols., Indianapolis, 1951

TOOMBS: Brewton, W. W., *Son of Thunder, an Epic of the South*, Richmond, 1936
Phillips, U. B., *Life of Robert Toombs*, New York, 1913

TRUMBULL: White, Horace, *Life of Lyman Trumbull*, Boston, 1913

TYLER: Auchampaugh, Philip G., *Robert Tyler, Southern Rights Champion, 1847-1866*, Duluth, Minn., 1934
Chitwood, Oliver P., *John Tyler, Champion of the Old South*, Philadelphia, 1939
Morgan, Robert J., *A Whig Embattled, the Presidency under John Tyler*, Lincoln, Neb., 1954
Tyler, Lyon G., *Letters and Times of the Tylers*, 3 vols., Richmond, 1884-1886

VAN BUREN: Alexander, Holmes, *The American Talleyrand, Martin Van Buren*, New York, 1936
Lynch, Dennis T., *An Epoch and a Man, Martin Van Buren and His Times*, New York, 1929
Rimini, Robert B., *Martin Van Buren and the Making of the Democratic Party*, New York, 1959
Van Buren, Martin, "Autobiography of Martin Van Buren," ed. by J. C. Fitzpatrick, Amer. Hist. Assoc. *Annual Report*, 1918, II, Washington, 1920

WALKER: Dodd, W. E., *Robert J. Walker, Imperialist*, Chicago, 1914
Shenton, James R., "The Compleat Politician, The Life of Robert John Walker," Ph.D. thesis, Columbia University, 1954
Greene, Laurence, *The Filibuster: The Career of William Walker*, Indianapolis, 1937
Scroggs, W. O., *Filibusters and Financiers, the Story of William Walker and his Associates*, New York, 1916

WEBSTER: Current, Richard, *Daniel Webster*, Boston, 1955
Fuess, Claude, *Daniel Webster*, 2 vols., Boston, 1930
Webster, Daniel, *Letters of Daniel Webster*, ed. by C. H. Van Tyne, New York, 1902
WEED: Barnes, T. W., *Life of Thurlow Weed*, 2 vols., Boston, 1884
Van Deusen, G. G., *Thurlow Weed*, Boston, 1947
Weed, Thurlow, *Autobiography of Thurlow Weed*, ed. by Harriet A. Weed, New York, 1883
WILMOT: Going, C. B., *David Wilmot, Free Soiler*, New York, 1924
WISE: Wise, Barton H., *Life of Henry A. Wise*, New York, 1899
WOOD: Pleasants, Samuel A., *Fernando Wood of New York*, New York, 1948
WRIGHT: Garraty, J. A., *Silas Wright*, New York, 1949
YANCEY: DuBose, J. W., *Life and Times of William Lowndes Yancey*, Birmingham, 1892

PRINTED REMINISCENCES, DIARIES, AND CONTEMPORARY WRITING

In the remaining part of this bibliography the following abbreviations are used:

AHR   *American Historical Review*
LCHSJ *Lancaster County Historical Society Papers (renamed after 1956 Lancaster County Historical Society Journal)*
MVHR   *Mississippi Valley Historical Review*
PMHB   *Pennsylvania Magazine of History and Biography*
TQHGM *Tyler's Quarterly Historical and Genealogical Magazine*

————, "Letters of Bancroft and Buchanan," *AHR*, V (1899), 95-102

————, "Some letters to John G. Davis, 1857-1860," *Indiana Magazine of History*, XXIV (1928), 209-213

————, "Unpublished Letters of James Buchanan," *LCHSJ*, IX (1905), 37-42; XXXII (1928), 67-72, 118-121; XXXV (1932), 59-83, 143-153, 166-172, 188-196, 222-259, 297-320; XXXVII (1933), 15-20

Adams, Henry, *The Great Secession Winter of 1860-61, and Other Essays*, ed. by George Hochfield, New York, 1958

Adams, John Quincy, *Memoirs, Comprising Parts of his Diary from 1795-1848*, ed. by C. F. Adams, 12 vols., Philadelphia, 1874-1877

Appel, Theodore, *Recollections of College Life at Marshall College, Mercersburg, Pa.*, Reading, Penna., 1886

Bates, Edward, "Diary of Edward Bates," ed. by H. K. Beale, Amer. Hist. Assoc. *Annual Report*, 1930, IV, Washington, 1932

Branch, Lawrence O'Bryan, "Letters of Lawrence O'Bryan Branch, 1856-1860," ed. by A. R. Newsome, *North Carolina Historical Review*, X (1933), 44-79

Brooks, R. P. (ed.), "The Howell Cobb Papers," *Georgia Historical Quarterly*, V (1921), #2, 29-53; #4, 43-65; VI (1922), 147-173, 233-264, 355-359

Browning, O. H., *Diary of Orville Hickman Browning, 1850-1881*, ed. by T. C. Pease and J. G. Randall, 2 vols., Springfield, Ill., 1925-1931

Bullard, F. Lauriston (ed.), *The Diary of a Public Man*, Chicago, 1945

Bungay, George W., *Off-Hand Takings or Crayon Sketches of the Noticeable Men of our Age*, New York, 1854

Chase, Henry, and Sanborn, C. W., *The North and the South, a Statistical View*, Boston, 1857

Chestnut, Mary B., *A Diary from Dixie*, ed. by Ben Ames Williams, New York, 1949

Chittenden, L. E., *Personal Reminiscences, 1840-1890*, New York, 1893

Clay-Copton, Virginia, *A Belle of the Fifties*, New York, 1905

Cox, Samuel S., *Eight Years in Congress from 1857-1865*, New York, 1865

———, *Three Decades of Federal Legislation, 1855-1885*, Providence, 1885

Day, Sherman, *Historical Collections of Pennsylvania*, Philadelphia, 1843

Doubleday, Abner, *Forts Sumter and Moultrie*, New York, 1876

Foote, Henry S., *Casket of Reminiscences*, Washington, 1874

Forster, J. Montgomery, "Recollections," in Rankin Scrapbook, Presbyterian Church, Mercersburg, Penna.

Gilpin, Joshua, "A Tour from Philadelphia in 1809," *PMHB*, L (1926), 64-78, 163-178, 380-382

Green, Duff, *Facts and Suggestions, Biographical, Historical, Financial and Political, Addressed to the People of the United States*, New York, 1866

Greeley, Horace, *Recollections*, New York, 1868

Halstead, Murat, *Three Against Lincoln, Murat Halstead Reports the Caucuses of 1860*, ed. by William B. Hesseltine, Baton Rouge, 1960

———, *Trimmers, Trucklers and Temporizers*, ed. by William B. Hesseltine and R. G. Fisher, Madison, Wis., 1961

Hamilton, James A., *Reminiscences of Men and Events at Home and Abroad*, New York, 1869

Harris, Alexander, *Biographical History of Lancaster County*, Lancaster, 1872

———, *A Review of the Political Conflict in America*, New York, 1876

Harter, Edwin P., "Recollections of the Campaign of 1856," *Indiana Magazine of History*, XVI (1920), 69-72

Hay, T. R. (ed.), "John C. Calhoun and the Presidential Campaign of 1824—Some Unpublished Calhoun Letters," *AHR*, XL (1934), 82-97

Hensel, William U., *Reminiscences of Thirty-five Years in a Country Store*, Lancaster, 1873

Hickok, Charles N., *Bedford in Ye Olden Time*, Bedford, Penna., 1907

Hunter, Andrew, "Andrew Hunter Papers, 1859-1861," *Massachusetts Historical Society Proceedings*, XLVI (1913), 243-249

Julian, G. W., *Political Recollections, 1840-1872*, Chicago, 1884

Kendall, Amos, *Autobiography*, Boston, 1872

King, Horatio, *Turning on the Light, a Dispassionate Survey of President Buchanan's Administration, from 1860 to its Close*, Philadelphia, 1895

McClure, Alexander K., *Col. Alexander McClure's Recollections of Half a Century*, Salem, Mass., 1902

———, *Old Time Notes of Pennsylvania*, 2 vols., Philadelphia, 1905

———, *Lincoln and Men of War Times*, Philadelphia, 1892

McPherson, Edward, *Political History of the U. S. of America during the Great Rebellion, from Nov. 6, 1860 to July 4, 1864*, New York, 1864

Martineau, Harriet, *A Retrospect of Western Travel*, 2 vols., London, 1838

Maury, Sarah W., *The Statesmen of America in 1846*, London, 1847

Moran, Benjamin, *The Journal of Benjamin Moran, 1857-1865*, ed. by S. A. Wallace and F. E. Gillespie, 2 vols., Chicago, 1948

Nichols, Roy F., "The Missing Diaries of George M. Dallas," *PMHB*, LXXV (1951), 295-338

———, "Mystery of the Dallas Papers," *PMHB*, LXXIII (1949), 349-393, 475-517

Parker, James A., "How James Buchanan was Made President and by Whom," *Virginia Magazine of History and Biography*, XIII (1906), 81-87

Phillips, U. B. (ed.), "Correspondence of Robert Toombs, A. H. Stephens and Howell Cobb," Amer. Hist. Assoc. *Annual Report*, 1911, II, Washington, 1913

Pollard, Edward A., *Lee and His Lieutenants*, New York, 1866

Poore, Ben Perley, *Perley's Reminiscences of Sixty Years*, 2 vols., Philadelphia, 1886

Pryor, Mrs. Roger A., *Reminiscences of Peace and War*, New York, 1905

Quincy, Josiah, *Figures of the Past*, Boston, 1926

Rainwater, Percy L. (ed.), "Letters to and from Jacob Thompson," *Journal of Southern History*, VI (1940), 95-112

Royall, Anne, *The Black Book; or a Continuation of Travels*, 3 vols., Washington, 1828-1829

————, *Mrs. Royall's Pennsylvania*, 2 vols., Washington, 1829

Sargent, Nathan, *Public Men and Events, 1817-1853*, 2 vols., Philadelphia, 1875

Schoepf, John, *Travels in the Confederation, 1783-1784*, ed. by A. J. Morrison, Philadelphia, 1911

Schurz, Carl, *Reminiscences, 1829-1869*, 3 vols., New York, 1907-1908

Sherman, John, *Recollections of Forty Years*, 2 vols., Chicago, 1895

Smith, Mrs. Samuel H., *Forty Years of Washington Society, 1800-1842*, ed. by Gaillard Hunt, New York, 1906

Sumner, Charles, *Memoirs and Letters of Charles Sumner*, ed. by Edward L. Pierce Boston, 1893

Thompson, Richard W., *Recollections of 16 Presidents, 1789-1865*, 2 vols., Indianapolis, 1894

Trescot, William H., "Narrative of William H. Trescot," ed. by C. H. Ambler, *AHR*, XIII, April, 1908

Watmough, E. C., *Scribblings and Sketches, Diplomatic, Piscatory and Oceanic, by a Fisher in Small Streams*, Philadelphia, 1844

Windle, Mary J., *Life in Washington and Life Here and There*, Philadelphia, 1859

Wise, Henry A., *Seven Decades of the Union*, Philadelphia, 1896

Wise, John S., *Recollections of Thirteen Presidents*, New York, 1906

GENERAL HISTORICAL WORKS AND MONOGRAPHS

————, *Territorial Kansas, Studies Commemorating the Centennial*, Lawrence, Kan., 1954

————, *History of Cumberland and Adams Counties, Pennsylvania*, Chicago, 1886

————, *Old Mercersburg*, New York, 1912

————, *Report of the Commission to Locate the Site of the Frontier Forts of Pennsylvania*, 2 vols., Harrisburg, 1896

Adams, E. D., *British Interests and Activities in Texas, 1838-1846*, Baltimore, 1910

Adams, James T., *America's Tragedy*, New York, 1934

Baldwin, Leland D., *Pittsburgh, the Story of a City*, Pittsburgh, 1937

Bancroft, H. H., *History of Utah, 1540-1886*, San Francisco, 1889

Baringer, William E., *A House Dividing: Lincoln as President-Elect*, Springfield, Ill., 1945

Beale, Howard K., "What Historians have said about the Causes of the Civil War," in *Theory and Practice in Historical Study*, New York, 1946

Bemis, Samuel F. (ed.), *American Secretaries of State and Their Diplomacy*, 10 vols., New York, 1927-1929

————, *Latin-American Policy of the United States, an Historical Interpretation*, New York, 1943

Billington, Ray A., *The Far Western Frontier*, New York, 1956

Bomberger, C. M. H., *Twelfth Colony Plus*, Jeannette, Penna., 1934

Boykin, Edward, *Congress and the Civil War*, New York, 1955

Burnham, W. D., *Presidential Ballots, 1836-1892*, Baltimore, 1955

Callahan, James M., *Cuba and International Relations*, Baltimore, 1899

———, *American Policy in Canadian Relations*, New York, 1937

———, *American Foreign Policy in Mexican Relations*, New York, 1932

Colman, Edna M., *Seventy-five Years of White House Gossip*, New York, 1925

Committee on Historical Research, *Forges and Furnaces in the Province of Pennsylvania*, Philadelphia, 1944

Craven, Avery, *The Repressible Conflict, 1830-1861*, Baton Rouge, 1939

———, *The Coming of the Civil War*, New York, 1942

———, *The Growth of Southern Nationalism, 1848-1861*, Baton Rouge, 1953

———, *The Civil War in the Making, 1815-1860*, Baton Rouge, 1959

Crawford, Mary C., *Romantic Days in the Early Republic*, Boston, 1912

Crenshaw, Ollinger, *The Slave States in the Presidential Election of 1860*, Baltimore, 1945

Dangerfield, George, *The Era of Good Feelings*, New York, 1952

Diffenderfer, Frank R., *History of the Farmers Bank of Lancaster*, Lancaster, 1910

Dubbs, Joseph H., *History of Franklin and Marshall College*, Lancaster, 1903

Dumond, Dwight L., *Anti-slavery Origins of the Civil War in the United States*, Ann Arbor, Mich., 1939

———, *The Secession Movement, 1860-1861*, New York, 1931

——— (ed.), *Southern Editorials on Secession*, New York, 1931

Egle, William H., *History of the County of Dauphin in the Commonwealth of Pennsylvania*, Philadelphia, 1883

Eiselen, M. R., *The Rise of Protectionism in Pennsylvania*, Philadelphia, 1921

Ellis, Franklin, *History of Lancaster County*, Philadelphia, 1883

Fish, Carl R., *The American Civil War*, New York, 1937

Fite, Emerson D., *The Presidential Campaign of 1860*, New York, 1911

Foner, Philip, *Business and Slavery: The New York Merchants and the Irrepressible Conflict*, Chapel Hill, 1941

Fuller, John D. P., *The Movement for the Acquisition of All Mexico, 1846-1848*, Baltimore, 1936

Furnas, J. C., *The Road to Harpers Ferry*, New York, 1959

Furniss, Norman F., *The Mormon Conflict, 1850-1859*, New Haven, 1960

Garrison, Curtis W., "The National Election of 1824," Ph.D. thesis, The John Hopkins University, 1928

Gates, Paul W., *50 Million Acres*, Ithaca, N. Y., 1953

Geary, M. Theophane, *A History of Third Parties in Pennsylvania, 1840-1860*, Washington, 1938

Glover, Gilbert G., *Immediate pre-Civil War Compromise Efforts*, Nashville, 1934

Graebner, Norman A., *Empire on the Pacific*, New York, 1955

Gray, Wood, *The Hidden Civil War: The Story of the Copperheads*, New York, 1942

Green, Fletcher, *Constitutional Development in the South Atlantic States, 1776-1860*, Chapel Hill, 1930

Hammond, Bray, *Banks and Politics in America from the Revolution to the Civil War*, Princeton, 1957

Hendrick, Burton J., *Lincoln's War Cabinet*, Boston, 1946

Hesseltine, William B., *Lincoln and the War Governors*, New York, 1948

Higginbotham, S. W., *Keystone of the Democratic Arch, 1800-1816*, Harrisburg, 1952

Hyman, Sidney, *The American President*, New York, 1954

Hull, Henry, *Annals of Athens, 1801-1901*, Athens, Ga., 1906

Jackson, William T., *Wagon Roads West*, Berkeley, 1952

Johannsen, Robert W., *Frontier Politics and the Sectional Conflict*, Seattle, 1955

Johnson, Gerald W., *The Secession of the Southern States*, New York, 1933

Kehl, James A., *Ill Feeling in the Era of Good Feeling*, Pittsburgh, 1956

Kirkland, E. C., *Peacemakers of 1864*, New York, 1927

Klein, H. M. J., *Lancaster County, a History*, 4 vols., New York, 1924

———, *History of Franklin and Marshall College*, Lancaster, 1952

———, *A Century of Education at Mercersburg*, Mercersburg, Penna., 1936

Klein, H. M. J., and Diller, W. F., *History of St. James Church, Lancaster, Pa.*, Lancaster, 1944

Klein, Philip S., *Pennsylvania Politics, 1817-1832; A Game without Rules*, Philadelphia, 1940

Lampert, O. P., *Presidential Politics in the United States, 1841-1844*, Durham, N. C., 1936

Leech, Margaret, *Reveille in Washington, 1860-1865*, New York, 1941

Livingood, James W., *The Philadelphia-Baltimore Trade Rivalry, 1780-1860*, Harrisburg, 1947

Logan, Mary S., *Thirty Years in Washington*, Hartford, Conn., 1901

Luthin, Reinhard H., *The First Lincoln Campaign*, Cambridge, Mass., 1944

MacDonald, Helen G., *Canadian Public Opinion on the American Civil War*, New York, 1926

Malin, James V., *John Brown and the Legend of Fifty-Six*, Philadelphia, 1942

Marbut, Frederick B., "Washington Staff Correspondents before the Civil War," Ph.D. thesis, Harvard University, 1950

Martin, Asa E., *After the White House*, State College, Penna., 1951

Masters, Donald C., *Reciprocity Treaty of 1854*, Toronto, 1937

Meneely, A. Howard, *The War Department, 1861*, New York, 1928

Minnigerode, Meade, *Presidential Years*, New York, 1928

Morgan, James H., *Dickinson College: the History of 150 Years*, Carlisle, Penna., 1933

Moore, J. W., *Picturesque Washington*, Providence, 1884

Morris, Charles (ed.), *The Makers of Philadelphia*, Philadelphia, 1894

Morris, L. R., *Incredible New York*, New York, 1951

Mueller, Henry F., *The Whig Party in Pennsylvania*, New York, 1922

Nevins, Allan, *Ordeal of the Union*, 2 vols., New York, 1947

———, *The Emergence of Lincoln*, 2 vols., New York, 1950

———, *The War for the Union*, 2 vols., New York, 1959

Nichols, Alice, *Bleeding Kansas*, New York, 1954

Nichols, Roy F., *The Democratic Machine, 1850-1854*, New York, 1923

———, *The Disruption of American Democracy*, New York, 1948

———, *The Stakes of Power, 1845-1877*, New York, 1961

Paul, James C., *Rift in the Democracy*, Philadelphia, 1951

Perkins, Dexter, *The Monroe Doctrine, 1826-1867*, Baltimore, 1933

Perkins, Howard C. (ed.), *Northern Editorials on Secession*, 2 vols., New York, 1942

Phelps, Christine, *Anglo-American Peace Movement of the Mid-Nineteenth Century*, New York, 1930

Phillips, U. B., *The Course of the South to Secession*, New York, 1939

Randall, James G., *The Civil War and Reconstruction*, New York, 1937

Rauch, Basil, *American Interest in Cuba, 1848-1855*, New York, 1948

Ray, P. Orman, *Repeal of the Missouri Compromise*, Cleveland, Ohio, 1909

Reed, G. F., *Alumni Record of Dickinson College*, Carlisle, Penna., 1905

Reeves, J. S., *American Diplomacy under Tyler and Polk*, Baltimore, 1907

Richard, J. F., *History of Franklin County, Pa.*, Chicago, 1887

Riddle, William, *The Story of Lancaster, Old and New*, Lancaster, 1910

Rhodes, J. F., *History of the United States from the Compromise of 1850*, 8 vols., New York, 1920

Rippy, J. Fred, *The United States and Mexico*, New York, 1926

Rives, G. L., *The United States and Mexico, 1821-1848*, 2 vols., New York, 1913

Roseboom, Eugene H., *A History of Presidential Elections*, New York, 1957

Scrugham, Mary, *The Peaceable Americans of 1860-1861*, New York, 1921

Settle, R. W., and M. L., *Empire on Wheels*, Stanford, Calif., 1949

Shanks, Henry T., *The Secession Movement in Virginia, 1847-1861*, Richmond, 1934

Simms, Henry H., *A Decade of Sectional Controversy, 1851-1861*, Durham, N. C., 1942

Singleton, Esther, *Story of the White House*, New York, 1907

Smith, Justin H., *The War with Mexico*, 2 vols., New York, 1919

Smith, William E., *The Francis Preston Blair Family in Politics*, 2 vols., New York, 1933

Snyder, Charles M., *The Jacksonian Heritage, 1833-1848*, Harrisburg, Penna., 1958

Sparks, Edwin E. (ed.), *Lincoln Douglas Debates of 1858*, Springfield, Ill., 1908

Spring, Leverett W., *Kansas, the Prelude to the War for the Union*, New York, 1885

Stampp, Kenneth M., *And the War Came*, Baton Rouge, 1950

———, *The Causes of the Civil War*, New York, 1959

Stanwood, Edward, *History of the Presidency*, New York, 1898

Stedman, Edmund O., *The Prince's Ball*, New York, 1860

Stephenson, Nathaniel W., *Texas and the Mexican War*, New Haven, 1921

Stuart, Graham H., *The Department of State*, New York, 1949

Thomas, Benjamin P., *Russo-American Relations, 1815-1867*, Baltimore, 1916

Tilley, John S., *Lincoln Takes Command*, Chapel Hill, 1941

Van Deusen, G. G., *The Jacksonian Era, 1828-1848*, New York, 1959

Van Vleck, G. W., *The Panic of 1857, an Analytical Study*, New York, 1943

Ward, Wilfrid, *Life and Times of Cardinal Wiseman*, 2 vols., London, 1897

Warren, Charles, *The Supreme Court in United States History*, 3 vols., Boston, 1922

Wharton, Anne H., *Social Life in the Early Republic*, Philadelphia, 1902

Weinberg, Albert K., *Manifest Destiny*, Baltimore, 1935

White, Leonard D., *The Jacksonians, a Study in Administrative History, 1829-1861*, New York, 1954

Whitton, Mary O., *First First Ladies, 1789-1865*, New York, 1948

Williams, Mary W., *Anglo-American Isthmian Diplomacy, 1815-1915*, Washington, D. C., 1916

Willson, Beckles, *America's Ambassadors to England*, London, 1928

Wise, Harvey, and Cronin, J. W., *A Bibliography of Zachary Taylor, Millard Fillmore, Franklin Pierce and James Buchanan*, Washington, 1935

HISTORICAL ARTICLES

———, "Public Dinner Tendered to James Buchanan," *LCHSJ*, XXXIV (1930), 77-81, 260-261

———, "Sidelights on an Early Political Campaign," *LCHSJ*, XVIII (1914), 90-95

Auchampaugh, Philip G., "Washington's Birthday, 1860," *TQHGM*, XXV (1943), 170-178

———, "A forgotten Journey of an Ante-Bellum President," *TQHGM*, XVII (1935), 42-48

———, "John Forney, Robert Tyler, and James Buchanan," *TQHGM*, XV (1933), 71-90

———, "John B. Floyd and James Buchanan," *TQHGM*, IV (1922), 381-388

———, "James Buchanan, Bachelor of the White House," *TQHGM*, XX (1939), 154-166, 216-234

———, "James Buchanan, the Conservatives' Choice, 1856," *The Historian* (Spring, 1945), 77-90

———, "James Buchanan, the Squire from Lancaster," *PMHB*, LV (1931), 289-300; LVI (1932), 15-33

———, "James Buchanan, the Squire in the White House," *PMHB*, LVIII (1934), 270-286

———, "James Buchanan and Some Far Western Leaders, 1860-1861," *Pacific Historical Review*, XII (1943), 169-180

———, "The Buchanan-Douglas Feud," Illinois State Historical Society *Journal*, XXV (1932), 5-48

———, "Buchanan, the Court and the Dred Scott Case," *Tennessee Historical Magazine*, XI (1926), 231-240

———, "J. Glancy Jones and the Nomination of James Buchanan," in *Topics from American History*, #1, State Teachers College, Duluth, Minn., 1932

———, "James Buchanan during the Administrations of Lincoln and Johnson," *LCHSJ*, XLIII (1939), 67-110

———, "Political Techniques—1856, or Why the *Herald* Went for Frémont," *Western Political Quarterly*, I (1948), 243-251

———, "Making Amendments in the Fifties: the Story of the New York Factions and the Buchanan Managers at Cincinnati, 1856," New York State Historical Assoc. *Quarterly*, VII (1926), 304-316

Bancroft, Frederic, "The Final Efforts at Compromise, 1860-1861," *Political Science Quarterly*, VI (1891), 401-423

Barbee, David R., "How Lincoln Rejected the Peace Overtures in 1861," *TQHGM*, XV (1933), 137-144

Baylen, Joseph O., "James Buchanan's 'Calm of Despotism,' " *PMHB*, LXVII (1953), 294-310

Beck, Herbert, "The Camerons of Donegal," *LCHSJ*, LVI (1952), 86-106

Black, Alice L., "George Washington at the Carey House," typescript, *YCHS*

Bourne, E. G., "The Proposed American Absorption of Mexico," Amer. Hist. Assoc. *Annual Report*, 1899, I, 157-169

———, "The United States and Mexico, 1847-1848," *AHR*, V (1900), 491-502

Brady, Gerard, "Buchanan's Campaign in Lancaster County," *LCHSJ*, LIII (1949), 97-134

Brown, J. Hay, "President Buchanan—Misunderstood—Wrongly Judged," *LCHSJ*, XXXII (1928), 88-92

Callahan, J. M., "The Mexican Policy of Southern Leaders under Buchanan's Administration," Amer. Hist. Assoc. *Annual Report*, 1910, 135-151

———, "The Evolution of Seward's Mexican Policy," West Virginia University *Studies in American History*, Series I (1909), nos. 4, 5, 6

Carlson, Robert E., "Pittsburgh Newspaper Reaction to James Buchanan and the Democratic Party in 1856," *Western Pennsylvania Historical Magazine*, XXXIX (1956), 71-81

Current, R. C., "Webster's Propaganda and the Ashburton Treaty," *MVHR*, XXXIV (1947), 187-200

487

Dodd, William E., "The West and the War with Mexico," Illinois State Historical Society *Transactions*, 1912, 15-23

Dowdell, George R., "John Forney, Journalist and Politician," *LCHSJ*, LV (1951), 49-66

Fehrenbacher, Don, "Origins and Purpose of Lincoln's House-Divided Speech," *MVHR*, XLVI (1960), 615-643

Finefrock, John L., "Stony Batter" and "Harriet Lane," typescript in the author's possession

Fraim, Samuel R., "Address at the Presentation of the Buchanan Memorial Placque at Lodge #43, F. and A. M., Lancaster, Pa.," Mimeo, Lancaster, 1950

Gates, Paul W., "The Struggle for Land and the Irrepressible Conflict," *Political Science Quarterly*, LXVI (1951), 248-271

Gillan, W. Rush, "James Buchanan," Kittochtinny Historical Society *Papers*, II (1901)

Gilchrist, Annie, "First on the Turnpike," Bedford *Inquirer*, Dec. 20, 1950

Golder, F. A., "The Purchase of Alaska," *AHR*, XXV (1920), 411-425

Graebner, Norman A., "James K. Polk, a Study in Federal Patronage," *MVHR*, XXXVIII (1952), 613-632

Hailperin, Herman, "Pro-Jackson Sentiment in Pennsylvania, 1820-1828," *PMHB*, L (1926), 193-240

Hamilton, Holman, "Democratic Senate Leadership and the Compromise of 1850," *MVHR*, XLI (1954), 403-418

———, "Texas Bonds and Northern Profits, a Study in Compromise, Investment and Lobby Influence," *MVHR*, XLIII (1957), 579-594

Harmon, George D., "Aspects of Slavery and Expansion, 1848-1860," Lehigh University *Publications*, III, #7 (1929), 43 pp.

———, "President James Buchanan's Betrayal of Governor Robert J. Walker," *PMHB*, LIII (1929), 51-91

———, "The Northern Clergy and the Impending Crisis, 1850-1860," *PMHB*, LXV (1941), 171-201

———, "An Indictment of the Administration of President James Buchanan and His Kansas Policy," *The Historian*, III (1940), 52-68

Heisey, M. Luther, "Postscript to the Old Buck Cannon," *LCHSJ*, LXV (1961), 106-107

Hensel, William U., "James Buchanan as a Lawyer," University of Pennsylvania *Law Review*, LX (1912), 546-573

———, "A Buchanan Myth," *LCHSJ*, X (1906), 169-172

Hodder, Frank A., "Some Aspects of the English Bill for the Admission of Kansas," Amer. Hist. Assoc. *Annual Report*, 1906, I, 201-210

Holmes, Charles N., "The First Republican-Democratic Presidential Campaign," *Journal of American History*, XIV (1920), 41-48

Hostetter, Ida L. K., "Harriet Lane," *LCHSJ*, XXXIII (1929), 97-112

Hughes, Robert M., "Floyd's Resignation from Buchanan's Cabinet," *TQHGM*, V (1923), 73-95

Johannsen, Robert W., "Stephen A. Douglas, 'Harpers Magazine' and Popular Sovereignty," *MVHR*, XLV (1959), 606-631

Jones, W. D., and Vinson, J. C., "British Preparedness and the Oregon Settlement," *Pacific Historical Review*, XXII (1953), 353-364

Klein, Frederic S., "Robert Coleman, Millionaire Ironmaster," *LCHSJ*, LXIV (1960), 17-33

Klein, Philip S., "Early Lancaster County Politics, *Pennsylvania History*, III (1936), 98-114

———, "James Buchanan and Ann Coleman," *Pennsylvania History*, XXI (1954), 1-20

———, "The Inauguration of James Buchanan," *LCHSJ*, LXI (1957), 145-161

———, "James Buchanan at Dickinson," The Boyd Lee Spahr Lectures, in *John and Mary's College*, Carlisle, Penna., 1956, 157-180

Klingberg, Frank W., "James Buchanan and the Crisis of the Union," *Journal of Southern History*, IX (1943), 455-474

Landis, D. B., "Rev. Edward Young Buchanan," *LCHSJ*, XXXII (1928), 123-132

Latané, John H., "The Diplomacy of the United States in regard to Cuba," Amer. Hist. Assoc. *Annual Report*, 1897, 219-227

Lewis, Howard T., "The Closing Month of the Buchanan Administration," *Americana*, VI (1911), 1035-1044

Luthin, Reinhard H., "The Democratic Split during Buchanan's Administration," *Pennsylvania History*, XI (1944), 13-35

———, "Pennsylvania and Lincoln," *PMHB*, LXVII (1943), 61-82

Lynch, William O., "Indiana in the Buchanan-Douglas Contest of 1856," *Indiana Magazine of History*, XXX (1934), 119-132

McMurtry, R. Gerald, "James Buchanan in Kentucky, 1813," *Filson Club Historical Quarterly*, 1934, 73-87

Martin, Thomas P., "Initiation of James Buchanan as an American Diplomat: His Mission to Russia," Washington, *Junto Selections* (1946), 48-60

———, "James Buchanan—American Diplomat," *Pennsylvanian*, III (1946), 33-34

Mendelsohn, Wallace, "Chief Justice Taney, Jacksonian Judge," University of Pittsburgh *Law Review*, XII (1951), 381-393

———, "Dred Scott's Case Reconsidered," Minnesota *Law Review*, XXXVIII (1953), 16-28

Minnigerode, Meade, "Presidential Campaigns: The Buccaneers, 1856," *Saturday Evening Post*, CC (1928), 39-40, 42, 157-158

Nash, Roderick W., "The Christiana Riot: An Evaluation of its National Significance," *LCHSJ*, LXV (1961), 66-91

Nichols, Roy F., "American Democracy and the Civil War," *Proceedings* of the American Philosophical Society, XCI (1947), 143-149

———, "The Kansas Nebraska Act—a Century of Historiography," *MVHR*, XLIII (1956), 187-212

———, "James Buchanan—Lessons in Leadership in Trying Times," The Boyd Lee Spahr Lectures, in *Bulwark of Liberty*, Carlisle, Penna., 1950

Owens, Robert L., "James Buchanan, Diplomat, International Statesman, President," *LCHSJ*, XXXII (1928), 92-97

Perkins, Howard C., "The Defense of Slavery in the Northern Press on the Eve of the Civil War," *Journal of Southern History*, IX (1943), 501-531

Ranck, James B., "The Attitude of James Buchanan towards Slavery," *PMHB*, LI (1927), 126-142

Rayback, J. G., "Martin Van Buren's Break with James K. Polk," *New York History*, XXXIV (1955), 51-62

Rawley, J. A., "Financing the Frémont Campaign," *PMHB*, LXXV (1951), 24-35

Rippy, J. Fred, "Diplomacy of the United States and Mexico Regarding the Isthmus of Tehuantepec, 1848-1860," *MVHR*, VI (1919), 503-531

Robinson, Elwyn B., "*The Pennsylvanian*, Organ of Democracy," *PMHB*, LXII (1938), 350-360

———, "The *Public Ledger*, an Independent Newspaper," *PMHB*, LXIV (1940), 43-55

Russ, William A., Jr., "Mary Kittera Snyder's Struggle for an Income," Snyder County Historical Society *Bulletin*, IV (1960), 1-27

———, "Time Lag and Political Change as Seen in the Administrations of Buchanan and Hoover," *South Atlantic Quarterly*, XLVI (1947), 335-343

Schafer, Joseph, "Who Elected Lincoln?" *AHR*, XLVII (1941), 51-64

Sears, Louis M., "Slidell and Buchanan," *AHR*, XXVII (1922), 709-730

Sellers, Charles G., "Jackson Men with Feet of Clay," *AHR*, LXII (1957), 537-551

Slick, Sewall, "William Wilkins, Pittsburgher Extraordinary," *Western Pennsylvania Historical Magazine*, XXII (1939), 217-236

Sprout, Oliver S., "James Buchanan, 'Big Wheel' of the Railroads," *LCHSJ*, LVI (1952), 21-34

Stampp, Kenneth M., "Lincoln and the Strategy of Defense in the Crisis of 1861," *Journal of Southern History*, XI (1945), 297-323

Stenberg, Richard P., "Motivation of the Wilmot Proviso," *MVHR*, XVIII (1932), 535-551

———, "Jackson, Buchanan and the Corrupt Bargain Calumny," *PMHB*, LVIII (1934), 61-85

Thorpe, Francis N., "Jeremiah S. Black," *PMHB*, L (1926), 117-133, 273-286

Van Alstyne, Richard W., "British Diplomacy and the Clayton-Bulwer Treaty, 1850-1860," *Journal of Modern History*, XI (1939), 149-183

———, "Anglo-American Relations, 1853-1857," *AHR*, XLII (1937), 491-500

———, "John F. Crampton, Conspirator or Dupe?" *AHR*, XLI (1936), 492-502

Van Horn, Lawrence, "The Old Buck Cannon," *LCHSJ*, LXIV (1960), 209-222

Webster, S., "Mr. Marcy, the Cuban Question and the Ostend Manifesto," *Political Science Quarterly*, VIII (1893), 1-32

Weisberger, B. A., "The Newspaper Reporter and the Kansas Imbroglio," *MVHR*, XXXVI (1950), 633-656

Wild, Robert, "Roger and James," *Wisconsin Magazine of History*, VIII (1924), 111-116

Wilson, H. L., "President Buchanan's Proposed Intervention in Mexico," *AHR*, V (1899), 687-701

Worner, W. F., "James Buchanan," *LCHSJ*, XXXVIII (1934), 103-144

MISCELLANEOUS

Rankin Scrapbook, parsonage of Presbyterian Church, Mercersburg, Penna., contains clippings relating to Buchanan and Lane families in Mercersburg.

John Lowry Ruth Scrapbook, York County Historical Society, contains annotated Buchanan clippings, 1840-1890.

Hiram Swarr Scrapbook, Buchanan Foundation, contains Buchanan clippings, 1840-1900

Many personal possessions and mementoes of Buchanan are at Wheatland, Lancaster County Historical Society, Franklin and Marshall College, Dickinson College, and the Smithsonian Institution.

INDEX